Lecture Notes in Artificial Intelligence 872

Subseries of Lecture Notes in Computer Science
Edited by J. G. Carbonell and J. Siekmann

Lecture Notes in Computer Science

Edited by G. Goos, J. Hartmanis and J. van Leeuwen

Setsuo Arikawa   Klaus P. Jantke (Eds.)

Algorithmic Learning Theory

4th International Workshop on
Analogical and Inductive Inference, AII '94
5th International Workshop on
Algorithmic Learning Theory, ALT '94
Reinhardsbrunn Castle, Germany
October 10-15, 1994
Proceedings

Springer-Verlag

Berlin Heidelberg New York
London Paris Tokyo
Hong Kong Barcelona
Budapest

Series Editors

Jaime G. Carbonell
School of Computer Science, Carnegie Mellon University
Schenley Park, Pittsburgh, PA 15213-3890, USA

Jörg Siekmann
University of Saarland
German Research Center for Artificial Intelligence (DFKI)
Stuhlsatzenhausweg 3, D-66123 Saarbrücken, Germany

Volume Editors

Setsuo Arikawa
Research Institute of Fundamental Information Science, Kyushu University 33
Fukuoka 812, Japan

Klaus P. Jantke
Fachbereich Informatik, Mathematik und Naturwissenschaften
Hochschule für Technik, Wirtschaft und Kultur Leipzig
Postfach 66, D-04251 Leipzig, Germany

CR Subject Classification (1991): I.2.6, I.2.3, F.4.1

ISBN 3-540-58520-6 Springer-Verlag Berlin Heidelberg New York

CIP data applied for

Typesetting: Camera ready by author
SPIN: 10479162   45/3140-543210 - Printed on acid-free paper

PREFACE

This volume contains all the papers presented at the Fourth International Workshop on Analogical and Inductive Inference (AII'94) and the Fifth International Workshop on Algorithmic Learning Theory (ALT'94) which were held October 10-11, 1994, and October 13-15, 1994, respectively, at Reinhardsbrunn Castle, Germany. This twin conference was motivated by our efforts to concentrate research work in the area called algorithmic or computational learning theory, and by the intention to extend and intensify the communication within the relevant scientific community. The series of workshops on Analogical and Inductive Inference, which was established in 1986 (cf. Lecture Notes in Computer Science 265), is the first international conference series in learning theory. Subsequently, the series COLT (founded 1988 in the USA), ALT (1990, Japan), and EURO-COLT (1993, Europe) entered the ring. Nowadays, it seems more important to integrate than to diversify the conference business. The coordinated organization of AII'94 and ALT'94 is intended to be one step in this direction. AII and ALT will be amalgamated and held jointly in the future under the single title of Algorithmic Learning Theory. The present volume of common proceedings is understood as a prelude to this amalgamation.

This volume contains the papers presented at AII'94 followed by those of ALT'94.

For AII'94, there were four invited papers by distinguished scientists: "Towards Efficient Inductive Synthesis from Input/Output Examples" by Janis Barzdins, Riga, "Deductive Plan Generation" by Wolfgang Bibel, Darmstadt, "From Specifications to Programs" by Nachum Dershowitz, Urbana-Champaign, IL, and "Average Case Analysis of Pattern Language Learning Algorithms" by Thomas Zeugmann, Fukuoka. For ALT'94 there were three such invited papers: "Towards Realistic Theories of Learning" by Naoki Abe, Tokyo, "A Unified Approach to Inductive Logic and Case-Based Reasoning" by Michael M. Richter, Kaiserslautern, and "Three Decades of Team Learning" by Carl H. Smith, College Park, MD.

There were 24 papers submitted to AII'94 and 51 to ALT'94. Of these 14 were selected for AII'94, 12 from the AII'94 submissions and two from the ALT'94 submissions. 24 papers were selected for ALT'94 from the 51 submitted. The moving of the two papers from ALT'94 submissions to AII'94 presentations was nicely facilitated by cooperation and discussion between the respective program committees. In the proceedings, the submitted papers selected for each subconference follow the invited papers for that subconference.

Among the large number of interesting papers, it seems remarkable to us that one distinguished author has been successful in getting five accepted papers into this volume: Steffen Lange, Leipzig, Germany, did exceptional research work together with several co-authors in formal language learning. Four of his papers were selected for ALT'94 and one for AII'94.

On behalf of the Steering Committee for the ALT series, the Program Committee for AII'94, and the Program Committee for ALT'94, we express our sincere gratitude to all those who made this twin conference on Algorithmic Learning Theory possible. The referees for both workshops provided a significant basis for the program committees' decisions. Erwin Keusch, as the Local Arrangements Chairman, Ingo Müller, and further members of the Algorithmic Learning Theory Group at HTWK Leipzig did an important job behind the scenes. Last but not least, Springer-Verlag provided excellent support in preparing this volume.

The workshops were supported by the German Computer Science Society (GI) and ALT'94 was held in cooperation with the Japanese Society for Artificial Intelligence (JSAI). Substantial support for AII'94 has been provided by the Volkswagen Foundation.

October 1994   Setsuo Arikawa, Fukuoka, Japan
                                      Klaus P. Jantke, Leipzig, Germany

AII '94 Conference Chairman

Rolf Wiehagen

AII '94 Program Committee

S. Arikawa	N. Dershowitz	T. Shinohara
J. Barzdins	K.P. Jantke (Chairman)	C.H. Smith
W. Bibel	Y. Kodratoff	R. Wiehagen
A.W. Biermann	S. Lange	T. Yokomori
J. Case	P. Lescanne	T. Zeugmann
R.P. Daley	C.M.I. Rattray	

ALT '94 Conference Chairman

Klaus P. Jantke

ALT '94 Program Committee

N. Abe	H. Imai	Y. Sakakibara
D. Angluin	B. Indurkhya	P.H. Schmitt
S. Arikawa (Chairman)	P.D. Laird	T. Shinohara
J. Barzdins	Y. Kodratoff	C. Smith
A.W. Biermann	A. Maruoka	E. Ukkonen
J. Case	S. Miyano	O. Watanabe
R.P. Daley	H. Motoda	R. Wiehagen
P. Flach	S. Muggleton	T. Yokomori
R. Freivalds	M. Numao	T. Zeugmann
M. Haraguchi	L. Pitt	

AII '94 and ALT '94 Local Arrangements Chairman

Erwin Keusch

Supported by
German Computer Science Society (GI)
in Cooperation with
Japanese Society for Artificial Intelligence (JSAI)
sponsored by
Volkswagen Foundation

AII '94 List of Referees

A. Albrecht	K.P. Jantke	P.H. Schmitt
K. Apsitis	B. Kalyanasundaram	B. Schulmeister
S. Arikawa	S. Kapur	A. Shinohara
J. Barzdins	E. Kinber	T. Shinohara
P. Baumgartner	H. Kleine Büning	J. Siekmann
H.R. Beick	Y. Kodratoff	C.H. Smith
W. Bibel	H.-J. Kreowski	G. Strube
A.W. Biermann	S. Lange	M.T. Suraj
I. Bratko	P. Lescanne	Y. Takada
J. Case	E. Melis	E.-Ch. Tammer
R.P. Daley	D. Mladenic	M. Thomas
D. Fensel	T. Miyahara	M. Velauthapillai
M. Franova	J. Nessel	S. Wess
R. Freivalds	U. Petermann	R. Wiehagen
U. Furbach	C.M. Rattray	T. Yokomori
J.A. Hendler	M.M. Richter	T. Zeugmann
B. Indurkhya	Y. Sakakibara	
H. Ishizaka	C. Schlieder	

IX

ALT '94 List of Referees

N. Abe
B. Alvis
A. Ambainis
D. Angluin
K. Apsitis
J. Arima
H. Arimura
A.W. Biermann
L. Blanc
A. Brazma
J. Case
R.P. Daley
P. Flach
M. Haraguchi
K. Hirata
E. Hirowatari
H. Imai
B. Indurkhya
H. Ishizaka
S. Jain
E. Kinber
J. Kivinen
S. Kobayashi

Y. Kodratoff
T. Koshiba
M. Kummer
P.D. Laird
E. Maeda
M. Matsuoka
T. Miyahara
S. Miyano
Y. Mizoguchi
C. R. Mofizur
H. Motoda
T. Motoki
S. Muggleton
Y. Mukouchi
A. Nakamura
K. Niijima
K. Ningsanond
M. Numao
P. Orponen
C.D. Page
L. Pitt
C. Rouveirol
Y. Sakai

Y. Sakakibara
A. Sakurai
S. Sakurai
P.H. Schmitt
A. Shinohara
T. Shinohara
C.H. Smith
A. Srinivasan
F. Stephan
M. Suraj
I. Tachika
J. Takeuchi
E. Takimoto
N. Tanida
E. Ukkonen
M. Velauthapillai
J. Viksna
O. Watanabe
R. Wiehagen
A. Yamamoto
T. Yokomori
Y. Yoshida
T. Zeugmann

TABLE OF CONTENTS

ANALOGICAL AND INDUCTIVE INFERENCE

INVITED TALKS

SELECTED PAPERS

ALGORITHMIC LEARNING THEORY

INVITED TALKS

SELECTED PAPERS

Towards Efficient Inductive Synthesis from Input/Output Examples

Jānis Barzdinš

Institute of Mathematics and Computer Science, University of Latvia
29 Rainis Blvd., Riga LV-1459, Latvia
E-mail: jbarzdin@mii.lu.lv

In the given paper we consider the problem whether it is possible to develop inductive algorithms efficient enough for synthesis of nontrivial formulas and algorithms in realistic time entirely from input/output examples. The basic problem which has to be dealt with in constructing efficient inductive synthesis algorithms is finding efficient implementation of Occam's Razor principle. Evidently, in the most general case it is impossible to avoid the exhaustive search. On the contrary, for the case of algebraic expressions the situation has turned out to be much better [1, 2]. We developed a method, more sophisticated then the simple sequential searching of the term space, that allowed us to construct synthesis algorithm able to infer in realistic time the formulas for the volume of frustum of the square pyramid, the solution to quadratic equation, and similar formulas entirely from i/o examples. In the given paper, first, the basic principles of this algorithm and the basic ideas for reducing the exhaustive search are analyzed. Then, the notion of the weight (complexity) of the terms, used in the algorithm, is generalized so that it can be used for describing the knowledge (or assumptions) about the target term and thus effectively to reduce the exhaustive search even further. The given algorithm is generalized also in another way, namely for synthesis of recursive expressions. This enables to synthesize, for instance, the algorithm for the greatest common divisor represented by a recursive expression.

Next the inductive synthesis of Term Rewriting Systems (TRS) is considered. We analyze the TRS synthesis algorithm of [3]. The algorithm enables to synthesize the binary addition and multiplication algorithms from i/o examples in just tens of minutes. Several generalizations and improvements of the algorithm via using of the above mentioned ideas of speeding up term synthesis are described.

In the end we report the latest computer experiments confirming the effiency of the developed synthesis methods.

References

1. J.M.Barzdins and G.Barzdins: Rapid construction of algebraic axioms from samples. Theoretical Computer Science 90 (1991), pp. 199-208
2. J.Barzdins, G.Barzdins, K.Apsitis, and U.Sarkans: Towards efficient inductive synthesis of expressions form input/output examples. Lecture Notes in Artificial Intelligence, 744 (1993), pp. 59-72.
3. G.Barzdins: Inductive synthesis of term rewriting systems. Lecture Notes in Computer Science, 502 (1991), pp. 253-285.

Deductive Plan Generation*

Wolfgang Bibel   Michael Thielscher

FG Intellektik, FB Informatik, Technische Hochschule Darmstadt
Alexanderstraße 10, D–64283 Darmstadt (Germany)
E-mail: {bibel,mit}@intellektik.informatik.th-darmstadt.de

Understanding and modeling the ability of humans to reason about actions, change, and causality is one of the key issues in Artificial Intelligence and Cognitive Science. Since logic appears to play a fundamental rôle for intelligent behavior, many deductive methods for reasoning about change were developed and thoroughly investigated. It became apparent that a straightforward use of classical logic lacks the essential property that facts describing a world state may change in the course of time. To overcome this problem, the truth value of a particular fact has to be associated with a particular state. This solution brings along the famous technical frame problem. It amounts to the difficulty of expressing that the truth values of facts not affected by some action are not changed by the execution of this action [20].

The problem of classical logic is that propositions are not treated as resources [13]. A proposition cannot be produced and consumed in the course of time. To handle this problem J. McCarthy, P. Hayes [20], and C. Green [10] introduced *frame axioms*; one for each action and each atomic fact. The obvious problem with this solution is that the number of frame axioms rapidly increases when many actions and many facts occur. R. Kowalski reduced the number of frame axioms to become linear with respect to the number of different actions [17]. Some years later, it was again J. McCarthy who proposed the use of nonmonotonic inference rules to tackle the frame problem [19]. He uses a default rule called *law of inertia* which states that a proposition does not change its value when executing an action unless the contrary is known.

Some years ago we developed a modified version of the connection method to solve the frame problem without the need of any frame axioms [2]. In the *linear* connection method proofs are restricted such that each literal is connected at most once [2, 4, 3]. Thus, connecting a literal during the inference process simulates consumption of the corresponding fact. Conversely, if the conditions of an implication are fulfilled then the conclusion can be used and, thus, the literals occurring in the conclusion are produced. This treatment of literals resembles the concept of resources.

A different approach to deductive planning which is based on equational Horn logic and also avoids frame axioms, was developed at our institute and presented in [14]. Its most significant feature is that a complete situation is represented by

---

* The second author was supported in part by ESPRIT within basic research action MEDLAR-II under grant no. 6471 and by the Deutsche Forschungsgemeinschaft (DFG) within project KONNEKTIONSBEWEISER under grant no. Bi 228/6-1.

a single term using a special binary function symbol which connects the various atomic facts (the resources) that hold in this situation.

A third deductive planning method which models the concept of resources is based on linear logic, which is a Gentzen-style proof system without weakening and contraction rules [9]. In the multiplicative fragment of the linear logic, literals and formulas cannot be copied or erased, which also provides the idea of resources [18]. In [12, 23, 11] we proved the formal equivalence of these three resource-oriented approaches [2, 18, 14] for *conjunctive* planning problems, where situations as well as the conditions and effects of actions are conjunctions of atomic facts. Moreover, in [6, 7] we revised and extended the linear connection method and the equational logic approach in order to include the treatment of disjunctions of facts. We showed that these extended approaches and a similar extension of the linear logic approach are equivalent wrt. a unique semantics of *disjunctive* planning problems where situations as well as the conditions and effects of actions are disjunctions of conjunctions of atomic facts.

Recently, we substantially extended the expressiveness of the equational logic approach by introducing the concept of specificity which allows to handle several descriptions of one and the same action, depending on the particular situation in which this action is performed [15, 16]. Specificity originates in the problem of overloading methods in object oriented frameworks but can be observed in general applications of actions and change in logic.

In order to provide a uniform semantical framework for methods to reason about actions, M. Gelfond and V. Lifschitz developed the *Action Description Language* [8] and, independently, E. Sandewall defined his *Ego-World-Semantics* [21, 22]. Both methodologies are generalizations of former work in so far as they support reasoning about the past as well as handling partial information about situations. In [25], we showed the adequacy of the equational logic approach, including the notion of specificity, wrt. the Action Description Language. Furthermore, we extended this language to express non-deterministic actions, and we established a similar adequateness result concerning our equational logic based framework. In [5], another recent extension [1] of this language was used to provide a semantics for an extension of our method that allows to express the concurrent execution of actions. Finally, in [24] we related both the Action Description Language as well as its extension concerning non-deterministic actions, to E. Sandewall's semantics. We established two formal equivalence results of slightly restricted versions of both languages wrt. two particular ontological problem classes in the latter framework. In conjunction with the relationship between our equational Horn logic approach and the Action Description Language, this result implies the adequacy of our method regarding these two classes within the hierarchy of the Ego-World-Semantics as well.

The purpose of this talk is to give an overview of our various contributions to the field of deductive planning.

References

1. C. Baral and M. Gelfond. Representing Concurrent Actions in Extended Logic Programming. In R. Bajcsy, editor, *Proceedings of the International Joint Conference on Artificial Intelligence (IJCAI)*, pages 866–871, Chambéry, August 1993. Morgan Kaufmann.

2. W. Bibel. A Deductive Solution for Plan Generation. *New Generation Computing*, 4:115–132, 1986.

3. W. Bibel. A Deductive Solution for Plan Generation. In J. W. Schmidt and C. Thanos, editors, *Foundations of Knowledge Base Management*, pages 453–473. Springer, 1989.

4. W. Bibel, L. F. del Cerro, B. Fronhöfer, and A. Herzig. Plan generation by linear proofs: on semantics. In *Proceedings of the German Workshop on Artificial Intelligence*, pages 49–62. Springer, Informatik Fachberichte 216, 1989.

5. S.-E. Bornscheuer and M. Thielscher. Representing Concurrent Actions and Solving Conflicts. In L. Drechler-Fischer and B. Nebel, editors, *Proceedings of the German Annual Conference on Artificial Intelligence (KI)*, Saarbrücken, September 1994. Springer-Verlag. (Selected Paper).

6. S. Brüning, S. Hölldobler, J. Schneeberger, U. Sigmund, and M. Thielscher. Disjunction in Resource-Oriented Deductive Planning. In D. Miller, editor, *Proceedings of the International Logic Programming Symposium (ILPS)*, page 670, Vancouver, October 1993. MIT Press. (Poster).

7. S. Brüning, S. Hölldobler, J. Schneeberger, U. Sigmund, and M. Thielscher. Disjunction in Resource-Oriented Deductive Planning. Technical Report AIDA-94-03, Intellektik, TH Darmstadt, March 1994. Available by anonymous ftp from 130.83.26.1 in /pub/AIDA/Tech-Reports/1994.

8. M. Gelfond and V. Lifschitz. Representing Action and Change by Logic Programs. *Journal of Logic Programming*, 17:301–321, 1993.

9. J.-Y. Girard. Linear Logic. *Journal of Theoretical Computer Science*, 50(1):1–102, 1987.

10. C. Green. Application of theorem proving to problem solving. In *Proceedings of the International Joint Conference on Artificial Intelligence (IJCAI)*, pages 219–239, Los Altos, CA, 1969. Morgan Kaufmann Publishers.

11. G. Große, S. Hölldobler, and J. Schneeberger. Linear Deductive Planning. *Logic and Computation*, 1994. (To appear).

12. G. Große, S. Hölldobler, J. Schneeberger, U. Sigmund, and M. Thielscher. Equational Logic Programming, Actions, and Change. In K. Apt, editor, *Proceedings of the International Joint Conference and Symposium on Logic Programming (IJC-SLP)*, pages 177–191, Washington, 1992. MIT Press.

13. S. Hölldobler. On Deductive Planning and the Frame Problem. In A. Voronkov, editor, *Proceedings of the International Conference on Logic Programming and Automated Reasoning (LPAR)*, volume 624 of *LNAI*, pages 13–29. Springer-Verlag, July 1992.

14. S. Hölldobler and J. Schneeberger. A New Deductive Approach to Planning. *New Generation Computing*, 8:225–244, 1990.

15. S. Hölldobler and M. Thielscher. Actions and Specificity. In D. Miller, editor, *Proceedings of the International Logic Programming Symposium (ILPS)*, pages 164–180, Vancouver, October 1993. MIT Press.

16. S. Hölldobler and M. Thielscher. Computing Change and Specificity with Equational Logic Programs. *Annals of Mathematics and Artificial Intelligence*, special issue on Processing of Declarative Knowledge, 1994. (To appear).

17. R. Kowalski. *Logic for Problem Solving*, volume 7 of *Artificial Intelligence Series*. Elsevier, 1979.

18. M. Masseron, C. Tollu, and J. Vauzielles. Generating Plans in Linear Logic. In *Foundations of Software Technology and Theoretical Computer Science*, volume 472 of *LNCS*, pages 63–75. Springer-Verlag, 1990.

19. J. McCarthy. Applications of circumscription to formalising common-sense knowledge. *Artificial Intelligence Journal*, 28:89–116, 1986.

20. J. McCarthy and P. J. Hayes. Some Philosophical Problems from the Standpoint of Artificial Intelligence. *Machine Intelligence*, 4:463–502, 1969.

21. E. Sandewall. Features and Fluents. Technical Report LiTH-IDA-R-92-30, Institutionen för datavetenskap, Universitetet och Tekniska högskolan i Linköping, Schweden, 1992.

22. E. Sandewall. The range of applicability of nonmonotonic logics for the inertia problem. In R. Bajcsy, editor, *Proceedings of the International Joint Conference on Artificial Intelligence (IJCAI)*, pages 738–743, Chambéry, France, August 1993. Morgan Kaufmann.

23. J. Schneeberger. *Plan Generation by Linear Deduction*. PhD thesis, FG Intellektik, TH Darmstadt, 1992.

24. M. Thielscher. An Analysis of Systematic Approaches to Reasoning about Actions and Change. In P. Jorrand, editor, *International Conference on Artificial Intelligence: Methodology, Systems, Applications (AIMSA)*, Sofia, Bulgaria, September 1994. World Scientific Publishing Co.

25. M. Thielscher. Representing Actions in Equational Logic Programming. In P. Van Hentenryck, editor, *Proceedings of the International Conference on Logic Programming (ICLP)*, pages 207–225, Santa Margherita Ligure, Italy, 1994. MIT Press.

From Specifications to Programs:
Induction in the Service of Synthesis*

Nachum Dershowitz

Department of Computer Science, University of Illinois, Urbana, IL 61801, USA

> *[Induction is] utterly vicious and incompetent.*
> — *Francis Bacon (1620)*

> *I maintain that many of our inductive inferences*
> *have all the certainty of which human knowledge is capable.*
> *Is the law of gravitation one whit less certain than*
> *the conclusion of the 47th proposition of the First Book of Euclid?*
> *...Physical generalizations are established by the Method of Difference*
> *and as actual Laws of Nature,*
> *admit, I conceive, of no doubt.*
> — *T. H. Fowler (1869)*

> *Inductive Reasoning...*
> *the glory of Science...*
> *the scandal of Philosophy.*
> — *C. D. Broad (1926)*

> *I am convinced that induction must have validity of some kind of degree,*
> *but the problem of showing how and why it is valid remains unsolved....*
> *Until it is solved, the rational man will doubt whether his food will nourish him,*
> *and whether the sun will rise tomorrow.*
> — *Bertrand Russell (1927)*

> *Induction plays no part whatever in science–*
> *that there is no inductive method and that*
> *nothing approximating to inductive inference is used.*
> *—J. O. Wisdom (1952)*

Abstract. The deductive synthesis of programs from formal specifications can be aided by various forms of induction: *Summative*, or *complete*, induction is the deductive technique of reasoning by cases and plays an important role in creating conditionals. *Recursive*, or *mathematical*, induction is a deductive technique for reasoning about an infinite number of cases; it is used in the creation of loops, and is often necessary for establishing properties of data types. *Eduction*, or analogical reasoning,

* Research supported in part by the U. S. National Science Foundation under Grants CCR-90-07195 and CCR-90-24271.

helps reduce the amount of work needed to generate a program, when similar programs already exist. *Ampliative*, or *incomplete*, induction is the process by which one generalizes from a finite number of instances; it can help the synthesizer guess what statement is needed and to verify the correctness of suggestions.

Average Case Analysis of Pattern Language Learning Algorithms

Thomas Zeugmann
Research Institute of
Fundamental Information Science
Kyushu University 33
Fukuoka 812, Japan
thomas@rifis.kyushu-u.ac.jp

Abstract

The present paper deals with the comparison of two pattern language learning algorithms with respect to their average case behavior. Pattern languages have been introduced by Angluin (1980) and are defined as follows:

Let $\Sigma = \{a, b, ..\}$ be any non–empty finite alphabet containing at least two elements. Furthermore, let $X = \{x_i \mid i \in \mathbb{N}\}$ be an infinite set of variables such that $\Sigma \cap X = \emptyset$. *Patterns* are non–empty strings from $\Sigma \cup X$, e.g., ab, ax_1ccc, $bx_1x_1cx_2x_2$ are patterns. $L(p)$, the language generated by pattern p is the set of strings which can be obtained by substituting non–null strings from Σ^* for the variables of the pattern p. Thus $aabbb$ is generable from pattern ax_1x_2b, while $aabba$ is not. *Pat* and *PAT* denote the set of all patterns and of all pattern languages over Σ, respectively. In order to deal with the learnability of pattern languages we have to specify from what information the inference algorithms are supposed to identify the target language. We consider both learning from *text* and *informant*. Intuitively, a text for L generates the language L without any information concerning the complement of L, whereas an informant of L decides L by informing the strategy whether or not any word from Σ^* belongs to L. Note that we allow a text and an informant to be non–effective.

The learning algorithms we are going to analyze learn the class of all pattern languages in the limit. The first one has been established by Angluin (1980). It mainly uses a subprocedure that finds, for any given set of positive and negative examples, a pattern that is *descriptive* for the input sample. In particular, this learning algorithm exclusively outputs *consistent* hypotheses. However, its update time is not polynomially bounded in the length of the actual input unless $\mathcal{P} = \mathcal{NP}$.

Recently, Lange and Wiehagen (1991) described a learning algorithm that might behave inconsistently. Nevertheless, its update time is polynomially bounded in the length of the actual input. On the other hand, the latter algorithm mainly exploits the fact that every pattern language is uniquely characterized by its corresponding set of all strings that have minimal length.

Hence, it is only natural to compare these algorithms with respect to their average case behavior. This might be also interesting with respect to potential applications pattern language learning algorithms have (cf. Nix (1983)). Finally, we compare the results obtained with the fact that *PAT* is not PAC-learnable unless $\mathcal{P} = \mathcal{NP}$ (cf. Schapire (1990)).

1.   References

ANGLUIN, D. (1980), Finding patterns common to a set of strings, *Journal of Computer and System Sciences* **21**, 46 – 62.

LANGE, S., AND WIEHAGEN, R. (1991), Polynomial-time inference of arbitrary pattern languages, *New Generation Computing* **8**, 361 – 370.

NIX, R.P. (1983), Editing by examples, Yale University, Dept. Computer Science, Technical Report 280.

SCHAPIRE, R.E. (1990), Pattern languages are not learnable, *in* "Proceedings 3rd Annual Workshop on Computational Learning Theory", (M.A. Fulk and J. Case, Eds.), pp. 122 – 129, Morgan Kaufmann Publishers, Inc., San Mateo.

Enumerable Classes of Total Recursive Functions:
Complexity of Inductive Inference [*]

Andris Ambainis and Juris Smotrovs

Institute of Mathematics and Computer Science, University of Latvia,
Raina bulv. 29, Riga, Latvia, e-mail: {ambainis, jsmotrov}@mii.lu.lv

Abstract. This paper includes some results on complexity of inductive inference for enumerable classes of total recursive functions, where enumeration is considered in more general meaning than usual recursive enumeration. The complexity is measured as the worst-case mindchange (error) number for the first n functions of the given class. Three generalizations are considered.

First: the numbering is computed in limit (with a fixed number of mindchanges). Then the complexity can be arbitrary fast growing recursive function. Second: a fixed number of functions are given by the enumbering function wrongly. In this case only universal strategies have large complexity function.

Third: every function given by the enumbering function can differ in a fixed number of points from the corresponding genuine function of the class. Two cases are considered: functions given by the enumbering function can be only partially defined or they must be total. In the first case there are unidentifiable classes. In the second case there are logarithmic algorithms for prediction and EX-identifying and linear algorithms for identifying of τ-indices.

1 Introduction

Inductive inference means finding out the algorithm from sample computations. The first paper in this area was [5]. This idea could be formalized in the following way. The strategy that tries to find out (to identify) the needed algorithm is a partial recursive function. In this work the function that is identified is a total recursive function. Then it is natural to consider the sample computations as the first values of the sought function.

We denote by $< x_1, x_2, \ldots, x_n >$ an effective numbering of all tuples of nonnegative integers. We denote the initial fragment $< f(0), f(1), \ldots, f(n) >$ of a total recursive function f by $f^{[n]}$, the tuple $< y_1, y_2, \ldots, y_n >$ by $y^{[n]}$.

So we come to a following definition.

Definition 1. The identifying strategy is a partial recursive function $F(f^{[n]})$, its value is the n-th hypothesis by F on f.

[*] This research was supported by Latvian Science Council Grant No. 9.599

This hypothesis is usually considered as one of the indices of function f in a fixed Goedel numbering φ.

We could consider that at some point strategy F must give a final conclusion: the function f is identical to φ_n. It is called a FIN-identification, but in this case only simple classes of functions can be identified. So we consider identification in limit or EX-identification in place of FIN-identification.

Definition 2. Strategy F identifies in limit a Goedel number of function f if $F(f^{[n]})$ is defined for all n and there are such n_0 and h that for all $n \geq n_0$: $F(f^{[n]}) = h$ and $f = \varphi_h$.

Definition 3. Strategy F EX-identifies a class U if it identifies in limit the Goedel numbers of all functions of U.

The strategy F makes a mindchange on f if for some n: $F(f^{[n]}) \neq F(f^{[n+1]})$. Though the class of all total recursive functions can not be enumerated recursively, some classes can (for example, the class of constant functions).

Definition 4. Class U is called recursively enumerable if there is such a numbering τ of the functions of this class and such a total recursive function $g(n)$ that $\tau_n = \varphi_{g(n)}$ for all n.

Usually we shall consider the pair class-numbering and denote it by (U, τ). The principal results for the identification of recursively enumerable classes can be found in [4], in it also some earlier results are compiled, [1, 2, 3] contain results important here.

The purpose of this work is to consider some special definitions of the enumerated classes and special definitions of the measuring of complexi ty of identification. The difference between the definitions of enumerable classes lies in the function g. In Sect. 2 g is a limit (in a sense similar to the limit of hypotheses in the definition of EX-identification) of total recursive function with a constant number of mindchanges allowed. In Sect. 3 ,g is recursive function, but a constant number of errors (where it is undefined or wrong) is allowed. In Sect. 4 a constant number of differences between τ_n and $\varphi_{g(n)}$ is allowed.

Now, when the numbering of class is introduced, we can consider another kind of identification (this definition is valid also for other kinds of enumeration in Sect. 2 and .

Definition 5. Strategy F identifies in limit a τ-index of f if $F(f^{[n]})$ is defined for all n and there are such n_0 and h that for all $n \geq n_0$: $F(f^{[n]}) = h$ and $f = \tau_h$.

Definition 6. Strategy F identifies τ-indices of an enumerated class (U, τ) if it identifies in limit τ-indices of all functions of U.

The notion of mindchange in this case is similar as in EX-identification. By complexity of identification of (U, τ) by strategy F we understand a function $E(n)$ that shows the maximum number of mindchanges of F on functions $\tau_0, \tau_1, \ldots, \tau_n$.

There is another interesting kind of identification that can be introduced. We could consider that strategy has figured out the algorithm for f if it can correctly predict the next value of f, given the previous values.

Definition 7. Strategy F predicts the values of f if $F(f^{[n]})$ is defined for all n and for all n but a finite number: $F(f^{[n]}) = f(n+1)$.

Definition 8. Strategy F predicts a class U if it predicts the values of all functions of U.

Strategy F makes an error on f if for some n: $F(f^{[n]}) \neq f(n+1)$. By complexity of prediction of (U, τ) by strategy F we understand a function $E(n)$ that shows the maximum number of errors of F on functions $\tau_0, \tau_1, \ldots, \tau_n$.

In [4] following results were proved for recursive numberings:

1. The complexity of EX-identifying and of predicting is at most

$$\log_2 n + \log_2 \log_2 n + \ldots + \log_2 \log_2 \ldots \log_2 n + o(\log_2 \log_2 \ldots \log_2 n)$$

   for all n, and there are classes for which it cannot be improved ([4], Theorems 2.1, 2.2, 2.4, 2.5).
2. The complexity of identifying of τ-indices is at most n for all n, and there are classes for which it cannot be improved ([4], Theorems 1.1, .2); it is at most const $\cdot n$ for infinitely many n, and there are classes for which it cannot be improved ([4], Theorems .1, .).

2   Classes That Are Enumerable in Limit

In the case of recursive enumeration strategy could use a two-dimensional table $\tau_n(x)$ of the enumerated class as a subroutine and in such a way consider, what functions have preferences before the others: it's better to make an error on a function with greater index than with a smaller, because it will have less influence on the complexity function.

Now we begin to consider in what other, more indirect way we could give the table of functions of the class to the strategy, so that it will have more information about the class than in the general case of classes of functions and less information than in the case of recursively enumerable classes.

One of the possible ideas is following: the function that gives the table could at some point change up its mind and in place of some function of class given out at present put another function, after some time it could do that again, and so on. If for a fixed function it would change its mind eternally, then it seems that it gives no information at all about the actual function of the class, so it should "stabilize" on some final hypothesis.

Definition 9. A class $U = \{ \tau_n \mid n \in \mathbb{N} \}$ is enumerable in limit if there is a total function $g(n)$ that is a limit of a total recursive function $t(k, n)$ (i.e., $(\forall n)(\exists K)(\forall k \geq K)\, t(k, n) = g(n)$) and for all n: $\tau_n = \varphi_{g(n)}$.

$t(k,n)$ is the k-th hypothesis for $g(n)$. Similarly, as for strategies, we consider mindchanges of t in computing of g.

At first we shall show that such class can be identified in all three mentioned senses.

Theorem 10. *For every class (U, τ), enumerated in limit, there are strategies F, G, H that predict, EX-identify it, identify its τ-indices, respectively.*

Proof. Strategy H uses function $t(k,n)$ that gives hypotheses for the enumbering function $g(n)$. To give its hypothesis on the initial segment $f^{[m]}$, it finds for $n = 0, 1, 2, \ldots$ such k that $k \geq m$ and $\varphi^{[m]}_{t(k,n)}$ is defined. Its hypothesis is the least such n that for the corresponding found $k := \varphi^{[m]}_{t(k,n)} = f^{[m]}$. As for all n $t(k,n)$ converges to the correct Goedel number $g(n)$ of τ_n, this hypothesis is always computed and the sequence of hypotheses converges to the least correct τ-indice of the function.

Strategy F finds for $n = 0, 1, 2, \ldots$ such k that $k \geq m$ and $\varphi^{[m+1]}_{t(k,n)}$ is defined. Its prediction is $\varphi_{t(k,n)}(m + 1)$ for the least such n that for the corresponding found k: $\varphi^{[m]}_{t(k,n)} = f^{[m]}$. As these n converge to the least correct τ-indice, all the predictions will be correct after some moment.

Strategy G uses the predictions of F. At start and every time F makes an error on $f^{[m-1]}$, strategy G gives its new hypothesis h such that $\varphi^{[m]}_h = f^{[m]}$ and $\varphi_h(x + 1) = F(\varphi^{[x]}_h)$ for $x \geq m$. On all other segments G does not change the hypothesis. As F makes only a finite number of errors for $f \in U$, there will be a hypothesis of G that will not change and will be correct. $\square$

The least difference from a recursive function we could allow for g is to allow f to make maximum one mindchange in the process of computing of every value of g. Following theorem shows that this is enough to largely increase complexity of identification of U.

Theorem 11. *For every total recursive function $r(n)$ there is a class (U, τ), enumerated in limit with one mindchange, such that every strategy identifying in limit (Goedel numbers or τ-indices) (U, τ), for all n but a finite number allows more than $r(n)$ mindchanges on one of the first $n + 1$ functions.*

Proof. We consider a Goedel numbering of strategies: $\{\, F_n \mid n \in \mathbb{N} \,\}$. We'll construct the numbering of U so that functions $\{\, \tau_{2^{n+1} \cdot k + 2^n - 1} \mid k \in \mathbb{N} \,\}$ correspond to strategy F_n. Sets of functions corresponding to the strategies are computed parallel. For every n only one time current function τ_n can be replaced by another. This is the procedure that generates the functions $\tau_0, \tau_2, \tau_4, \tau_6, \ldots$, corresponding to strategy F_0:

1. Compute $\max(r(0), r(1))$. Go to 2.
2. Define $\tau_{2k}(0), \tau_{2k}(1), \tau_{2k}(2), \ldots$. At the same time compute F_0 on the segments $< 0 >, < 0, 0 >, < 0, 0, 0 >, \ldots$. If on one of them F_0 gives a hypothesis h_0, then go to .

3. Choose x greater than the length of segment on which F_0 gave a hypothesis and such that $\tau_0(x)$ and $\tau_0(x)$ are yet undefined.
   Until this place define τ_0 and τ_2 by 0; define $\tau_0(x) =$ and $\tau_2(x) = 1$. Go to 4.
4. Continue defining τ_{2k} by 0. At the same time compute if F_0 changes hypothesis on some beginning segment of τ_0 or τ_2. If it changes (for example, on τ_2), go to 5.
5. Check if number of mindchanges on τ_2 isn't greater than $\max(r(0), r(1))$. If it is, then go to 7. If it isn't, then find such i, that τ_{2i} is yet completely undefined. Define τ_{2i} equal to τ_2 up to the place where F_0 changes hypothesis. Define for the next x: $\tau_2(x) =$ and $\tau_{2i}(x) = 1$. Go to 6.
6. Continue defining τ_{2k} by 0. At the same time compute if F_0 changes hypothesis on some beginning segment of τ_2 or τ_{2i}. If it changes, go to 5., considering the function on which F_0 changes hypothesis in place of τ_2.
7. Now we know a beginning segment on which F_0 makes $\max(r(0), r(1)) + 1$ mindchanges. Our enumerating function makes a mindchange on τ_0: the new τ_0 begins with this segment and further is defined by 0. Now we go to 1., accomplishing similarly that F_0 makes $\max(r(2), r())$ mindchanges on τ_2, $\max(r(4), r(5))$ mindchanges on τ_4 and so on or it doesn't identify at least one function among τ_{2k}.

The procedures for the functions, corresponding to other strategies, are similar. Thus strategy F_k either makes more than $r(n)$ mindchanges on one of the functions $\tau_0, \tau_1, \ldots, \tau_n$, if $n \geq 2^k - 1$, or doesn't identify a function of this class. □

Theorem 12. *For every total recursive function $r(n)$ there is a class $U = \{ \tau_n \mid n \in \mathbb{N} \}$, enumerable in limit with one mindchange, such that every strategy predicting U, for all n but a finite number allows more than $r(n)$ mindchanges on one of first $n + 1$ functions.*

Proof. It is similar to the previous. Only in place of waiting, on which segment strategy changes hypothesis, we compute what value the strategy predicts and choose the function whose value differs from the computed. □

So in this case the complexity of identification goes out of the realm of recursive functions, i. e. there are very complex classes.

3 Classes of Functions That Are Enumerated with Errors

The second possible idea is that some lines (i. e. functions) in the table given by the enumerating function wrongly.

Definition 13. A class of total recursive functions is enumerated with errors if there is a partial recursive function $g(n)$ and for some n: $g(n)$ is defined and $\tau_n = \varphi_{g(n)}$. For other n we say that g has errors at these n.

In this case enumerating function gives no information at all about the functions at which g has an error. So it's natural to let the strategy identify only the functions that are given correctly by g.

Definition 14. A strategy identifies in limit (Goedel numbers, τ-indices; predicts) a class (U, τ), enumerated with errors, if it identifies in limit (Goedel numbers, τ-indices; predicts) the class $U' = \{ \tau_n \mid n \in \mathbb{N}$ and $g(n)$ is not an error $\}$.

It's natural to limit the number of errors of g to a finite number. The algorithms for strategies in [4], Sect. 2-4 (except the one in Theorem .), were universal: they could be constructed as partial recursive function of two arguments $F(k, f^{[j]})$ where k is the Goedel number of enumerating function g (total recursive in [4]), and for right k strategy F identifies the class with good complexity bounds. The following theorem shows that for such universal strategy the complexity increases to an arbitrary partial recursive function even if we allow only one error for g.

Theorem 15. *For every universal identifying strategy $F(k, f^{[j]})$ and every total recursive function $r(n)$ there is a class (U, τ), enumerated with one error such that either F doesn't identify it in limit (Goedel numbers or τ-indices) or for every n strategy F allows more than $r(n)$ mindchanges on τ_n.*

Proof. The following procedure depends on a parameter i and defines a class with enumerating function $t(i, n)$. It uses strategy $F(i, f^{[j]})$ as a subroutine.

1. Let $n = 3$. Go to 2.
2. Suppose we've defined (U, τ) so that F makes more than $r(m)$ mindchanges on τ_m and τ_m is a total function, where $m = 1, \ldots, n-1$. We'll make F to do $r(n)+1$ mindchanges on τ_n. At the moment τ_n is maybe defined up to some point y. We leave it undefined after that point until we decide otherwise. Using functions $\tau_{n+1}, \tau_{n+2}, \ldots$ similarly as in Theorem 11 we either find an initial segment that begins with $\tau_n^{[y]}$ and on which F makes $r(m) + 1$ mindchanges, then go to ., or we have a function among $\tau_{n+1}, \tau_{n+2}, \ldots$ that is not identified by F. In the last case only one function of our class is not totally defined (τ_n), so the enumerating function of the class has only one error and F doesn't identify the class.
3. We define τ_n beginning with found segment and followed by 0; increase n by 1 and return to 2.

According to s-m-n theorem (see [8]) there is such a total recursive function $s(i)$ that $\varphi_{s(i)}(n) = t(i, n)$. According to the fixed point theorem (see [8]) there is such i' that $\varphi_{s(i')} = \varphi_{i'}$. We define $g(n) = \varphi_{i'}(n)$ and thus corresponding class is using as subroutine strategy that is working on the same class, and the above mentioned procedure guarantees that its complexity is large enough. □

Theorem 16. *For every universal predicting strategy $F(k, f^{[j]})$ and every total recursive function $r(n)$ there is a class (U, τ), enumerated with one error such that either F doesn't predict it or for every n strategy F allows more than $r(n)$ errors on τ_n.*

Proof. It is similar to the Theorem's 15 proof. Only in place of waiting, on which segment strategy changes hypothesis, we compute what value the strategy predicts and choose the function whose value differs from the computed. □

On the other side for every class there are strategies that identify (predict) it with complexity bounds according to the case of enumerable classes. Indeed, we can accomplish that by using the strategies that "guess", which are the wrong functions, ignore them and on other functions work as in corresponding theorems in [4].

4 Enumerated Classes of Functions with Errors

4.1 The Errors in Functions Can Be Undefined

At last, the following idea is considered: g could in place of giving some totally erroranous functions give functions that in general are identical to the right functions of the class, but differ from them in some places. The number of these places could be limited to some natural number N.

Definition 17. Class $U = \{ \tau_n \mid n \in \mathbb{N} \}$ is enumerated class of functions with N errors if there exists such total recursive function $g(n)$ that for all n: τ_n differs from $\varphi_{g(n)}$ for no more than N values of argument. It is allowed for function $\varphi_{g(n)}$ to be undefined on these values.

In this case we need to modify the definition of identifying of τ-indices, because otherwise they are unidentifiable even for very simple classes.

Definition 18. Strategy F identifies a τ-index of function $f \in U$ (when U is enumerated class of functions with N errors) if it stabilizes on the hypothesis h for which: f differs from $\varphi_{g(h)}$ for no more than N values of argument.

But then it turns out that this case is worst of all for the identification. Allowing only one error for every function we get that the classes cannot be identified at all. ˙

Theorem 19. *There exists such enumerated class of functions (U, τ) with 1 error that its Goedel numbers cannot be identified.*

Proof. Consider a numbering of strategies $\{ F_n \mid n \in \mathbb{N} \}$. In our class function τ_n corresponds to strategy F_n. $\varphi_{g(n)}$ is defined in following way:

1. Define $\varphi_{g(n)}(0), \varphi_{g(n)}(1), \varphi_{g(n)}(2), \ldots$ equal to 0, until F_n gives out a hypothesis h on one of the segments $< 0, 0, ..., 0 >$. Then go to 2.
2. Choose some x greater than the one on which strategy gave its last hypothesis and leave it yet undefined, for other arguments continue defining $\varphi_{g(n)}$ equal to 0. At the same time we compute if F_n changes its hypothesis on some initial segment of $\varphi_{g(n)}$, assuming that $\varphi_{g(n)}(x) =$. In this case we let

$\varphi_{g(n)}(x) =$ and go to 2. Also we compute the value of $\varphi_h(x)$. If it is computed then go to . If no one of these events happens, we let $\tau_n(x) =$ and our function $\varphi_{g(n)}$ has only one error (in this case strategy chooses a wrong hypothesis and doesn't change it).

3. Define $\varphi_{g(n)}(x)$ differently from $\varphi_{h(x)}$. After that define $\varphi_{g(n)}$ equal to 0 until $F_n(x)$ changes hypothesis. Then go to 2.

Every return to point 2 means a change of hypothesis by F_n, so, if that happens infinite number of times, then the strategy makes an infinite number of mindchanges. If the process stays forever in points 2 or , then= the strategy stabilizes on a wrong hypothesis. If the process stays forever in point 1, then strategy gives no hypothesis at all.

Thus every strategy does not identify at least one function of the class. □

Theorem 20. *There exists such enumerated class of functions (U, τ) with 1 error that it cannot be predicted.*

Proof. It is similar to the previous theorem's. Only in place of waiting for the change of hypothesis or for computing of $\varphi_h(x)$ we now wait for the prediction to be computed and after that choose the corresponding value different from the predicted. Thus strategy either does not give a prediction on some initial segment, or makes an infinite number of errors. □

Obviously, these results are valid also for the case of N errors ($N > 1$), we even don't have to change anything in the proof.

This proof is not valid (with proper small corrections) for the identifying of τ-indices, because the hypothesis h could refer now to the function τ_n, corresponding to $\varphi_{g(n)}$, and we can not so easily choose $\varphi_{q(n)}$ different from τ_n. But the result in this case is the same.

Theorem 21. *There exists such enumerated class of functions (U, τ) with N errors $(N \geq 1)$ that its τ-indices cannot be identified.*

Proof. Functions $\{\tau_{2^{n+1}\cdot k+2^n-1} \mid k \in \mathbb{N}\}$ correspond to strategy F_n and they all begin so that there is plain difference between functions corresponding to each strategy: $\tau_{2^{n+1}\cdot k+2^n-1}(x) = \varphi_{g(2^{n+1}\cdot k+2^n-1)}(x) = n$ for all k and for $x = 1, \ldots, N$. The algorithm for functions corresponding to F_0 (with even indices) follows. Algorithms for functions corresponding to other strategies are similar.

1. Let $\varphi_{g(0)}(x) = 1$ for $x = N+1, \ldots, 2N$; $\varphi_{g(0)}(2N+1)$ leave yet undefined and further define $\varphi_{g(0)}$ with 0. For $k > 0$ let $\varphi_{g(2k)}(x) = 1$ for $x = N+1, \ldots, 2N$; further define $\varphi_{g(2k)}$ with 0. Go to 2.
2. Compute one by one $F_0(< 0, \ldots, 0 >)$, $F_0(< 0, \ldots, 0, 0 >)$, and so on (the segments with at least $2N$ zeroes; the first N zeroes point to the index of the strategy; when we return to this point again, the segments with greater length than in the previous steps are used). If F_0 gives out a hypothesis h different from 0, go to .

3. We define $\varphi_{g(0)}$ equal to 0 at the point we left undefined (at start it was $2N + 1$) and if h is even then we define at some $x > 2N$: $\varphi_h(x) = 1$; at all other points define φ_h equal to 0. We repeat that for each new hypothesis not equal to 0. At the moment F_0 gives out hypothesis 0 we leave $\varphi_{g(0)}$ at some point undefined, at other points continue defining it with 0 and go to 2.

We put function $f(x) = 1$ for all x in class U. If F_0 stabilizes on hypothesis 0, we let this function to be τ_{2k} for some k such that $\varphi_{g(2k)}$ differs from f only at N points (points $x = N+1, \ldots, 2N$). F_0 does not identify f in this case because $\varphi_{g(0)}$ differs in $N + 1$ points ($x = N + 1, \ldots, 2N$ and at point where it was left undefined) from f.

If F_0 stabilizes on hypothesis different from 0, we let f to be τ_0, and it is clear from construction that F_0 stabilizes on function that is different at least in $N + 1$ points from f. If F_0 does not stabilize, we let f to be τ_0. If F_0 does not give out a hypothesis at some moment, then it's similar as if F_0 would stabilize on the last given hypothesis (on 0 if it has not given a hypothesis at all). So F_0 does not identify $f \in U$. Proof for other strategies is similar. □

4.2 The Errors in Functions Must Be Defined

We see that we can't let the enumerated class to wait on the reaction of the strategy before the class gives out a value of its function. In such a case the class is too "smart" for the strategies to identify.

So we come to the idea that the table given by the enumerating function could differ at some points from the genuine functions of the class, but it should not wait possibly eternally before giving out the values at these points, in other words, it should be defined at these points.

Definition 22. Class $U = \{\tau_n | n \in N\}$ is enumerated class of functions with N defined errors if there exists such total recursive function $g(n)$ that for all n: τ_n differs from $\varphi_{g(n)}$ for not more than N values of argument and $\varphi_{g(n)}$ is a total recursive function.

So the strategy can use a two-dimensional table, each line of which is a total recursive function and differs in at most N places from the corresponding genuine function of the class. In this case the strategies can achieve much better results. At first we shall consider the prediction.

It turns out that the strategy can achieve almost the same complexity function as in the case of the recursively enumerable functions.

Theorem 23. *For each enumerated class of functions with N defined errors and each real $\epsilon > 0$ there exists such predicting strategy F that on each of the functions $\tau_0, \ldots, \tau_n$ it makes not more than*

$$(1 + \epsilon)(\log_2 n + \log_2 \log_2 n + \ldots + \underbrace{\log_2 \ldots \log_2 n}_{(k-1) \ times} + \underbrace{\log_2 \ldots \log_2 n}_{k \ times}$$

errors for all n.

Proof. We associate with each function τ_n weight

$$w_n = \frac{c}{n \cdot (\log_2 n) \cdot (\log_2 \log_2 n) \cdot \ldots \cdot \underbrace{(\log_2 \ldots \log_2 n)}_{(k-1) \text{ times}} \cdot \underbrace{(\log_2 \ldots \log_2 n)^2}_{k \text{ times}}}$$

Here c is some constant chosen so that sum of all weights is 1. We also fix some q, $0 < q < 1$. The algorithm for prediction of $\tau_n(j+1)$ from $< \tau_n(0), \ldots, \tau_n(j) >$ is following:

Associate with each function $\varphi_{g(m)}(x)$ weight $w_m q^k$ where k is the number of differences between $\varphi_{g(m)}(x)$ and $\tau_n(x)$ with $0 \leq x \leq j$. We calculate for all y the sum of all weights associated with functions $\varphi_{g(m)}$ such that $\varphi_{g(m)}(j+1) = y$ and choose as prognosis of $\tau_n(j+1)$ the y whose sum is the largest.

As the number of functions $\varphi_{g(m)}(x)$ is infinite we cannot count these sums precisely. So, we omit all functions $\varphi_{g(m)}(x)$ for $m > M$ where M is some very large number. M is chosen so that sum of weights associated with omitted functions is very small and almost does not influence the result.

We consider this algorithm working on some function $\tau_n(x)$. There are not more than N such i that $\tau_n(i) \neq \varphi_{g(n)}(i)$. So, the weight associated with $\varphi_{g(n)}(x)$ always is at least $w_n q^N$.

Now, we consider the total sum of weights when $\tau_n(j+1)$ is predicted. We denote it by W_j. In case if our prognosis of $\tau_n(j+1)$ is incorrect it means that at least half of weights is associated with such functions $\varphi_{g(m)}(x)$ that $\varphi_{g(m)}(j+1) \neq \tau_n(j+1)$. So, when $\tau_n(j+2)$ will be predicted from $< \tau_n(0), \ldots, \tau_n(j+1) >$, these weights will be multiplied with q. Hence, we have that, if prognosis of $\tau_n(j+1)$ was incorrect, then

$$W_{j+1} \leq \frac{W_j}{2} + q \cdot \frac{W_j}{2} = \frac{1+q}{2} \cdot W_j$$

So, if algorithm makes k errors predicting $\tau_n(x)$, then after these k errors sum of weights associated with functions $\varphi_{g(m)}(x)$ is not more than $\left(\frac{1+q}{2}\right)^k$. As weight associated with $\varphi_{g(n)}(x)$ is at least $w_n q^N$, we have that

$$\left(\frac{1+q}{2}\right)^k \geq w_n q^N$$

Taking a logarithm with basis $\frac{1+q}{2}$ from both sides, we obtain

$$k \leq \log_{\frac{1+q}{2}} (w_n q^N) = (1 + \epsilon) \log_2 (\frac{1}{w_n}) + \text{const}$$

where const depends on q, but not on n, and $\epsilon_{q \to 0} \to 0$. Substituting the expression of w_n, we get the needed inequality. $\qquad \square$

As we have mentioned above, the EX-identifying strategy can achieve the same results using predicting strategy.

Theorem 24. *For each enumerated class of functions with N defined errors and each real $\epsilon > 0$ there exists such EX-identifying strategy G that on each of the functions $\tau_0, \ldots, \tau_n$ it makes no more than*

$$(1+\epsilon)(\log_2 n + \log_2 \log_2 n + \ldots + \underbrace{\log_2 \ldots \log_2 n}_{(k-1) \ times} + \underbrace{\log_2 \ldots \log_2 n}_{k \ times}$$

errors.

Proof. We use the predicting strategy F of previous theorem. G gives as its current hypothesis on segment $< y_0, \ldots, y_m >$ the Goedel number of function that uses for the computing of its values at points $x = m+1, m+2, \ldots$ strategy F that predicts one by one the succeeding values $f(m+1), f(m+2), \ldots$. If the predicting strategy has not made an error predicting $f(m+1)$, then the hypothesis given by G for the segment $f^{[m]}$ is valid also for the segment $f^{[m+1]}$, so G changes its hypothesis only if F makes an error. Hence G makes no more mindchanges than F errors. $\square$

So it seems that the lower bound for number of errors of prediction could be the same as for recursive numberings, i.e.

$$\log_2 n + \log_2 \log_2 n + \ldots + \underbrace{\log_2 \ldots \log_2 n}_{(k-1) \ times} + \underbrace{\log_2 \ldots \log_2 n}_{k \ times}$$

It turns out that there is a slight difference.

Theorem 25. *For all N there exists such class (U, τ) of functions with N defined errors that every predicting strategy makes more than $\log_2 n + (N+1) \log_2 \log_2 n$ errors on one of the first n functions for infinitely many n.*

Proof. We use the notion of Kolmogorov complexity.

Definition 26. Kolmogorov complexity of $< f(0), \ldots, f(n) >$ in numbering τ of total recursive functions $(K_\tau(f^{[n]}))$ is the logarithm of minimal i for which $< f(0), \ldots, f(n) > = < \tau_i(0), \ldots, \tau_i(n) >$ holds.

This notion was first introduced in [6]; it is much more general there.

Lemma 27. *. There exists such class (U, τ) of functions with N defined errors that for arbitrary total recursive f there are infinitely many n for which*

$$K_\tau(f^{[n]}) \leq n - (N+1)\log_2 n - a(n)$$

where $a(n)$ grows to infinity sufficiently slowly.

This lemma is an analogue of Martin-Lof theorem [7]. There are two differences:

- We consider classes of functions enumerated with N errors instead of usual recursively enumerable classes.

– We restrict f to be a total recursive function and do not consider non-recursive functions f

Proof. To prove this lemma we introduce a modification of Kolmogorov complexity.

Definition 28. Kolmogorov complexity of $< f(0), \ldots, f(n) >$ in numbering τ of total recursive functions with N errors allowed is the least such i that $f(j) \neq \tau_i(j)$ for no more than N values of j ($j = 0, 1, \ldots, n$). It is denoted as $K'_\tau(f^{[n]})$.

It can be proved that

Lemma 29. *There exists such numbering of total recursive functions ρ that for arbitrary total function f there exists infinitely many such m that*

$$K'_\rho(f^{[n]}) \leq n - (N+1)\log_2 n - a(n)$$

where $a(n)$ is a function growing to infinity sufficiently slowly.

Proof of this lemma is rather lengthy and we omit it here.

Now, we prove that Lemma 27 follows from Lemma 29.

We fix some numbering of pairs of natural numbers. We denote as $c(x, y)$ the number of pair (x, y). $l(x)$ and $r(x)$ will be such functions that $l(c(x, y)) = x$ and $r(c(x, y)) = y$.

The numbering τ of Lemma 27 can be obtained from numbering ρ of Lemma 29 if we define that $\rho_i(x) = \tau_i(x)$ with some exceptions(not more than N values of x for each i) described below.

We take some numbering $\phi_1, \phi_2, \ldots$ of all total recursive functions. (This numbering is not computable but it is not needed here.)

We denote as a_1 and b_1 such numbers that $\rho_{a_1}^{[b_1]}$ and $\phi_{l(1)}^{[b_1]}$ are different in no more than N symbols and

$$a_1 \leq b_1 - (N+1)\log_2(b_1) - a(b_1)$$

holds. Further we denote as a_{i+1} and b_{i+1} such numbers that $v_{a_{i+1}}$ and $\varphi_{l(i+1)}^{[b_{i+1}]}$ are different in no more than N symbols and

$$a_{i+1} \leq b_{i+1} - (N+1)\log_2(b_{i+1}) - a(b_{i+1}) \text{ and } a_{i+1} > a_i.$$

We define that $\tau_{a_i}(x)$ where $i \in \mathbb{N}$ is equal to $\phi_i(x)$ if $x < b_i$ and 0 otherwise. $\rho_{a_i}^{[b_i]}$ is different from $\phi_{a_i}^{[b_i]}$ in at most N values. Hence τ_{a_i} and ρ_{a_i} are different in at most N values.

□

We consider strategies that predict this class. We denote by $E_{F,\tau}(n)$ maximal number of errors made by strategy F on functions $\tau_0, \ldots, \tau_n$ and by $E_F(<$

$y_0, \ldots, y_m >)$ the number of errors made by F on the segment. Suppose there is a strategy for which

$$E_{F,\tau}(n) \leq \log_2 n + (N+1)\log_2\log_2 n$$

for almost all n. Then

$$E_{F,\tau}(n) \leq \log_2 n + (N+1)\log_2\log_2 n + c$$

for all n (c is a constant). For each segment $f^{[m]}$ we find the least n for which $f^{[m]} = \tau_n^{[m]}$. Then

$$E_F(f^{[m]}) \leq E_{F,\tau}(n) \leq \log_2 n + (N+1)\log_2\log_2 n + c =$$

$$= K_\tau(f^{[m]}) + (N+1)\log_2 K_\tau(f^{[m]}) + c$$

For f we take the function

$$f(x) = \begin{cases} 0 \text{ if } x = 0 \\ 0 \text{ if } x > 0 \text{ and } F(< f(0), \ldots, f(x-1) >) \neq 0 \\ 1 \text{ if } x > 0 \text{ and } F(< f(0), \ldots, f(x-1) >) = 0 \end{cases}$$

Evidently f is recursive (F is defined on all initial segments because functions of class U contain them all). Also, $E_F(f^{[m]}) = m$. Substituting it in the last inequality and using lemma, we get for infinitely many n

$$n \leq n - (N+1)\log_2 n - a(n) + (N+1)\log_2(n - (N+1)\log_2 n - a(n)) + c$$

Contradiction. □

As recursively enumerated class can be considered also as a class of functions with N errors, point 1) of Theorems 2.4 and 2.5 in [4] are trivially valid also for this case. That is, there is an enumerated class of functions with N defined errors such that an arbitrary predicting strategy makes more than $\log_2 n-$ errors on one of the first n functions for all n, and there is another such class that an arbitrary EX-identifying strategy makes more than $\log_2 n -$ const mindchanges for all n.

Now, similarly as in previous case, we introduce following definition vof identifying of τ-indices.

Definition 30. Strategy F identifies a τ-index of function $f \in U$ (when U is enumerated class of functions with N defined errors) if it stabilizes on the hypothesis h for which: f differs from $\varphi_{g(h)}$ for no more than N values of argument.

It turns out that the complexity of identifying of τ-indices in this case is the same as for recursive numberings.

There is a simple strategy that makes n mindchanges on first $n+1$ functions.

Theorem 31. For each enumerated class (U, τ) of functions with N defined errors there is a strategy that makes at most n mindchanges on one of the first $n+1$ functions for all n.

Proof. The strategy gives out as a hypothesis on $f^{[m]}$ the least h for which $f^{[m]}$ differs from $\varphi_{g(h)}^{[m]}$ in at most N places. Such h always exists when f is a function of class U. The sequence of hypotheses given by this strategy is non-decreasing and converges to the least correct τ-index for f, hence the number of mindchanges does not exceed this index. □

Now we shall consider the lower bounds.

Theorem 32. *There is an enumerated class (V, ρ) of functions with N defined errors such that for every strategy F identifying ρ-indices there is a constant $c > 0$ such that for all n (but a finite number) either the number of mindchanges of F on first $n + 1$ functions exceeds $\frac{n}{c}$ or F does not identify U.*

Proof. We use the class (U, τ) from the similar theorem for recursively enumerable classes in [4](Theorem .1.). We define

$$\rho_n((N+1)k+l) = \varphi_{g(n)}((N+1)k+l) = \tau_n(k), l = 0, 1, \ldots, N$$

So, if n was a τ-index of function f from class U then and only then n is a ρ-index of corresponding function f' (defined: $f'((N+1)k+l) = f(k), l = 0, 1, \ldots, N$) from class V because different functions in V differ at least in $N+1$ points. For the classes, reformatted in such a way, the definition 30 becomes equivalent to the definition 5 (for recursively enumerable classes), and the identifying of them have the same complexity.

Hence in other aspects proof is rather similar to the one in [4] and we omit it here. □

The following theorem shows that the complexity of identifying given by Theorem 31 *for all n* can't be improved.

The same construction is valid also for following theorem that is analogous to Theorem .2 in [4].

Theorem 33. *There is an enumerated class (V, ρ) of functions with N defined errors such that for every strategy F identifying ρ-indices and for infinitely many n either the number of mindchanges of F on first n functions exceeds $n - o(\sqrt{n})$ or F does not identify U.*

Proof. We use the same reformatting of the class (U, τ) from [4] (Theorem .2) as in the previous theorem to get the needed results. □

Theorem 34. *For every enumerated class (U, τ) with N defined errors and for every constant $c > 0$ there is a strategy F that identifies τ-indices of U so that for infinitely many n it makes no more than $\frac{n}{c}$ mindchanges on each of the functions $\tau_0, \ldots, \tau_n$.*

Proof. We choose an integer $k \geq c$. We'll use the idea of a team of strategies. The team in this case consists of strategies $F_1, \ldots, F_k$, that are defined below.

The strategies use the sequence $n_1, n_2, n, \ldots$, growing to infinity, such that n_i is considerably smaller than n_{i+1}, f or example, $n_{i+1} = 2^{n_i}$.

At first the strategies, given $f^{[m]}$, find the least n_i, for which there is such n that $f^{[m]}$ differs from $\tau_n^{[m]}$ in no more than N places (such n's we shall call valid for $f^{[m]}$). As far as there is such n for the found n_i, the strategies work in following way.

They give as hypotheses only indices that do not exceed n_i. At first F_1 gives as hypothesis the least valid index for $f^{[m]}$, F_2 gives the second least valid index, F - the third and so on. When m increases, some valid indices become invalid, thus some strategies have to make a mindchange. If strategy $F_l (1 \leq l \leq k)$ have to make a mindchange on the segment $f^{[m+1]}$, it finds the least valid index that is not equal to $F_1(f^{[m+1]}), \ldots, F_{l-1}(f^{[m+1]}), F_{l+1}(f^{[m]}), \ldots, F_k(f^{[m]})$ and gives it as $F_l(f^{[m+1]})$. Only if there are no more valid indices unchosen by other strategies, then F_l chooses as hypothesis some valid index already chosen by another strategy. If there is no valid index not exceeding n_i at all, then this process is repeated for n_{i+1}.

Thus, working with the functions $\tau_{n_{i-1}+1}, \ldots, \tau_{n_i}$, each of them is chosen as a hypothesis at most by one strategy, except the last k valid indices, and each strategy identifies the class. Thus there is a strategy among $F_1, \ldots, F_k$ that makes on each of these functions no more than $\frac{n_i}{k}$ mindchanges plus the ones that arise from these last k valid indices for the segments of functions corresponding to $n_1, n_2, \ldots, n_i$. By choosing k and n_1 large enough we can free ourselves from the influence of these last so that there is a strategy that makes no more than $\frac{n_i}{c}$ mindchanges on each of the functions $\tau_0, \tau_1, \ldots, \tau_{n_i}$ for all i. $\square$

5 Conclusion

We have considered four different modifications of the usual recursive numberings notion and investigated the complexity of inductive inference for them using three kinds of identification.

We see that if we allow for the classes to wait on some computations of the strategies' behaviour before giving out values, then they cannot be simply identified. Though identification with non-recursive complexity functions could be considered for the classes of sections 2 and .

The case of the classes of functions with N defined errors (section 4) is more interesting. It was quite surprising that such classes can be predicted and EX-identified with almost the same complexity as in the case of usual numberings. There are also some open problems. For example, the gap between the upper bound $(1 + \epsilon)(\log_2 n + \log_2 \log_2 n + \ldots)$ and the lower bounds for the predicting and EX-identifying maybe could be lessened.

This work shows that many modifications of the recursive numberings could be considered, and some of them give quite interesting results. I hope that it will suggest some ideas about new kinds of numberings.

6 Acknowledgement

We wish to express gratitude to prof. R.Freivalds for suggestion of an interesting theme.

References

1. J.Barzdins. Limiting synthesis of τ-indices. Theory of Algorithms and Programs, vol. 1, Latvia State University, 1974, pp. 112-116 (in Russian).
2. J.Barzdins, R.Freivalds. On the prediction of general recursive functions. Soviet Math. Dokl. 1, 1972, pp. 1224-1228.
3. J.Barzdins, R.Freivalds. Prediction and limiting synthesis of effectively enumerable classes of functions. Theory of Algorithms and Programs, vol. 1, Latvia State University, 1974, pp. 101-111 (in Russian).
4. R.Freivalds, J.Barzdins, K.Podnieks. Inductive inference of recursive functions: complexity bounds. Baltic Computer Science, Lecture Notes in Computer Science, Vol. 502, Springer Verlag, 1991, pp. 111-155.
5. E.M.Gold. Language identification in the limit. Information and Control, 10:5, 1967, pp. 447-474.
6. A.N.Kolmogorov. Three approaches to the definition of the notion "quantity of information". Problems Information Transmission 1(1965), pp.1-7.
7. P.Martin-Lof. On the notion of random sequence. Information and Control, 9(1966), pp.602-619.
8. H.Rogers, Jr. Theory of recursive functions and effective computability. McGraw-Hill, New York, 1967.

Derived Sets and Inductive Inference

Kalvis Apsītis*

Institute of Mathematics and Informatics
University of Latvia
Raina bulvaris 29
LV-1459, Riga
Latvia
apsitis@mii.lu.lv

Abstract

The paper deals with using topological concepts in studies of the Gold paradigm of inductive inference. They are — accumulation points, derived sets of order α (α — constructive ordinal) and compactness. Identifiability of a class U of total recursive functions with a bound α on the number of mindchanges implies $U^{(\alpha+1)} = \emptyset$. This allows to construct counter-examples — recursively enumerable classes of functions showing the proper inclusion between identification types: $EX_\alpha \subset EX_{\alpha+1}$.

The presence of an accumulation point in a class W determines whether or not all FIN strategies can be split into two families so that any finite team identifying W contains strategies from both families. A combinatorial idea, used to show the absence of such a splitting in the case when the derived set $W^d = \emptyset$, leads to new identification types ($FIN(2 : *)$,etc.) which may be irreducible to the team identification types (e. g. $FIN(k : m)$).

*Supported by Grant No. 93–599 from Latvian Councile of Science

1 Introduction

Most of learning paradigms in the Gold model of inductive inference allow to identify only "small" classes of total recursive functions. Besides the measure and Baire category the structure of accumulation points in a class determines whether or not the class is identifiable in some sense.

For the types EX_n (identification in the limit with no more than n mindchanges, [Gol67, CS83]) to establish proper inclusions $EX_n \subset EX_{n+1}$ classes of functions with a fixed support (see (1), Section 3) was traditionally used. This idea is extended for identification types EX_α (bound on number of mindchanges expressed by a constructive ordinal α) recently introduced in [FS93]. Moreover, for EX_α-identifiability we can use purely topological (necessary but not sufficient) criterion as described in Theorem 5. To make it also sufficient we could need to elaborate recursive analogues for the notion of derived set. Nevertheless, even classical notion of derived set of order α is informative, when describing "small" classes of functions with (recursive) measure equal to zero.

Intuitively results of Section 3 can be summarized as follows: if some function f is surrounded densely by other functions of the same class (i.e. f has common initial segment of values with them), then learning of f can need many mindchanges and the prognosis about the number of necessary mindchanges itself can be output only in the late stage of learning process.

Section 4 deals with another application of the same topological concept of accumulation points. "Splitting" properties for identification types EX and EX_n obtained previously are described in Preliminaries.

2 Preliminaries

2.1 Inductive Inference

Recursion-theoretic concepts not explained below are treated in [Rog67]. A strategy M is a (total) recursive function defined on initial lists of values of total functions: $h_0 = M(\langle \rangle)$ and $h_n = M(\langle f(0), \ldots, f(n-1) \rangle)$, $n \geq 1$. Its values are called conjectures or hypotheses. The moment when $h_n \neq h_{n+1}$ is called a mindchange.

An identification type T is a predicate from the function f and sequence $\{h_n\}$ as arguments. We say that a strategy M identifies a function f ($f \in T(M)$) iff the value of this predicate is *true*. We say that a class of total recursive functions U is identifiable in the sense T iff $\exists M \forall f \in U : f \in T(M)$. In this case we write also $U \in T$. For instance,

FIN strategy should output a correct Gödel number of the function it identifies without any mindchanges, EX_n ($n \geq 1$) perform no more than n mindchanges, but EX — any finite number of mindchanges, i. e. we require only the limit of $\{h_n\}$ to equal a correct number of f.

In Section 3 we shall use identification types requiring from a strategy to perform no more than α mindchanges where α is a constructive [Rog67] ordinal. To formalize this we introduce ordinal inductive inference machine (OIM) as described in [FS93].

At the beginning an OIM receives ordinal α. It has also a counter c for counting mindchanges.. Whenever the OIM wants to perform a mindchange (i. e. to output a conjecture excepting the very first one) it must increase c and reduce its ordinal as specified below. There are three possibilities:

1. The ordinal is 0. No modifications are done; the counter and ordinal remain the same (further mindchanges in this situation are not allowed).

2. The ordinal is a successor ordinal. The ordinal is reduced by one and the counter is incremented by one.

3. The ordinal is a limit ordinal. Then there is an effectively generated sequence of notations for larger and larger ordinals that reaches the given ordinal in the limit. Choose a member of this sequence. This choice is made deterministically by the OIM. The counter is incremented by 1.

After a finite number of such steps the counter will stabilize since there are no infinite descending sequences of constructive ordinals. We do *not* assume that an OIM always reduces its ordinal to 0. If the last conjecture made by an OIM happens to be a correct Gödel number of the function received in the input, it is identified by the given strategy in the sense EX_α. (We shall use "strategy" as a synonym for OIM as well as ordinary inductive inference machines — IIM.)

A team is a collection of strategies $M_1, \ldots, M_m$ which all work on the same function. We say that a function f is identifiable by this team in the sense $T(k : m)$ iff at least k of these m strategies identify f in the sense of identification type T. We write $U \in T(k : m)$ if a team exists identifying each function from U in the sense $T(k : m)$. As the work of m strategies can be simulated by the single one, we can speak of new, complex identification types $T(k : m)$, where k and m are arbitrary positive integers, $k < m$.

One thing which can be investigated about these team identification types is the nontrivial inclusions. For example, inclusions between $FIN(k_1 : m_1)$ and $FIN(k_2 : m_2)$ are described in [Smi82]. In Section 4 we shall be discussing a different problem though of the same origin. Namely, let a class W of total recursive functions be given which is not identifiable by a single strategy in some sense T, but it is identifiable by some team, i.e. $W \notin T, W \in T(1 : n)$. The question is: whether or not all strategies can be split into k disjoint families ($k \leq n$) so that any finite team identifying W contains strategies from at least l of these k families. (The cardinality of a team is irrelevant, it may contain much more than n strategies, where n is the minimal integer such that $W \in T(1 : n)$.) The case where identification type is EX is completely described by the following

Theorem 1 ([AFS94, Aps93]) *Let $W \notin EX(1 : n)$ for some $n \geq 1$. Then all EX strategies $M_1, M_2, \ldots$ can be split into $n + 1$ families $\mathcal{M}_1$, $\mathcal{M}_2$, $\ldots \mathcal{M}_{n+1}$ so that any finite team identifying W (if it exists at all) contains strategies from all $n + 1$ families.*

It seemed natural to switch attention to the case of limit identification with a bound on mindchanges (FIN as well as EX_n, $n \geq 1$). For the type EX_1 such a result holds:

Theorem 2 ([Aps93]) *For every $W \in EX_1(1 : m)$ (m — some positive integer) and every splitting of all strategies into two disjoint families, a finite team exists which contains strategies from one family only and identifies W.*

It can be observed that Theorem 2 contrasts Theorem 1 with $n = 1$. (Compare these two results with Lemma 3 and Lemma 4 which served in [Aps93] to prove them.) Analogues of Theorem 2 are valid for all EX_n, $n \geq 2$. For the type FIN the situation is more complicated and will be studied in Section 4.

2.2 Topology

Definition 1 ([Eng77]) *A point x in a topological space X is called an accumulation point of the set $A \subseteq X$ if every neighbourhood of x contains points from $A \setminus \{x\}$.*

Definition 2 ([Eng77]) *The set of all accumulation points of A is called the derived set of A and is denoted by A^d.*

Cantor in 1880 proposed the following generalization of this concept:

Definition 3 ([Kur66]) *For every ordinal $\alpha > 0$ the* derived set of order α *for sets $A \subset X$ are defined inductively by the formulas:*

$$A^{(1)} = A^d, \quad A^{(\alpha+1)} = (A^{(\alpha)})^d, \quad and \quad A^{(\lambda)} = \bigcap_{0 < \alpha < \lambda} A^{(\alpha)},$$

where λ is a limit ordinal.

Definition 4 ([Eng77]) *Points from $A \setminus A^d$ are called* isolated points *of the set A.*

How to define a topology in the set of functions $\mathbf{N} \to \mathbf{N}$? What can be called a neighbourhood of a recursive function?

Already French mathematician Baire [Eng77] in 1909 introduced distance between two sequences of integers by the formula

$$\rho(\{x_i\}, \{y_i\}) = \begin{cases} 1/k & \text{if } x_k \neq y_k \text{ and } x_i = y_i \text{ for } i < k \\ 0 & \text{if } x_i = y_i \text{ for all } i \end{cases}$$

Neighbourhood then consists of all those functions whose distance with the given one is less than $\epsilon > 0$. For our purpose the following equivalent (i. e. generating the same topology) notion of neighbourhood will be more convenient:

Definition 5 *For the given total recursive function f a neighbourhood is a set*

$$\{ g - \text{total recursive function} \mid g(x) = f(x) \text{ for } 0 \leq x < n \}$$

where n is an arbitrary integer.

In Section 4 we shall need the following result of compactness:

Lemma 1 (König,[KM67]) *In any infinite directed tree in which each node has only a finite number of direct successors, there is an infinite path leading from the root.*

3 Derived sets of higher order

By supp(f) we denote the support of the function f, namely,

$$\text{supp}(f) = \{x | f(x) \neq 0\}.$$

In [CS83] were considered the following classes of functions:

$$U_n = \{f \mid |\text{supp}(f)| \leq n\}. \tag{1}$$

The class U_n is identifiable by n mindchanges, but is not identifiable by $n - 1$ mindchanges, i. e. $U_n \in EX_n$ and $U_n \notin EX_{n-1}$.

This construction cannot be automatically extended to obtain counterexamples — classes of total recursive functions U_α such that $U_\alpha \in EX_\alpha$ and $U_\alpha \in EX_\xi$ (α, ξ — constructive ordinals, $\xi < \alpha$). In [FS93] a different idea — collecting nonidentifiable functions for all strategies EX_α — is used to show the proper inclusion $EX_\alpha \subset EX_{\alpha+1}$. But this leads to the classes which are not recursively enumerable any more. Our aim here is to construct recursively enumerable classes showing proper inclusions $EX_\xi \subset EX\alpha$.

To move on, let us notice that in the class U_n as defined in (1) all the functions which satisfy $|\text{supp}(f)| = n$ are isolated (neighbourhoods are introduced as in Definition 5; it is implicitly meant in all the other places of the paper). Therefore $U_n^d = U_{n-1}$ and $U_n^{(n+1)}$ — the $n + 1$-st derived set of U_n — is empty.

By $a^m b^n$ etc. we denote a string consisting of m a's and n b's. By $a_0 a_1 \ldots a_{n-1} \circ f$, where $a_0 a_1 \ldots a_{n-1}$ is a string of integers and f — total recursive function, we denote *concatenation*, i. e. the function

$$g(x) = (a_0 a_1 \ldots a_{n-1} \circ f)(x) = \begin{cases} a_x & \text{if } x < n, \\ f(x - n) & \text{if } x \geq n. \end{cases}$$

By $\sigma \circ U$ (σ — string of integers, U — class of total functions) we denote the collection of all functions in the form $\sigma \circ f$ where $f \in U$. The following lemma expresses the self-similarity for the space of all total recursive functions.

Lemma 2 *Let σ be a string of integers, U — some class of functions. Then $(\sigma \circ U)^d = \sigma \circ U^d$ and $(\sigma \circ U)^{(\alpha)} = \sigma \circ U^{(\alpha)}$.*

Theorem 3 *For any constructive ordinal $\alpha > 0$ there exists a recursive class of total recursive functions U such that $U^{(\alpha)} = \emptyset$ and $U^{(\xi)} \neq \emptyset$, $\xi < \alpha$.*

Proof. If $\alpha = 0$ we take $U = \{\lambda x.0\}$ — the class consisting of just the everywhere zero function. If α is the successor of ordinal α' then let us denote by V the recursive class of functions corresponding to α' and constructed in the previous step of induction. We define

$$U = \{\lambda x.0\} \cup \bigcup_{n=0}^{\infty} 0^n 1 \circ V. \tag{2}$$

If α is the limit, then we choose an increasing sequence of ordinals $\alpha_0, \alpha_1, \ldots$ with limit α and let $V_0, V_1, \ldots$, be the classes constructed in earlier steps for $\alpha_0, \alpha_1, \ldots$ respectively. We define

$$U = \{\lambda x.0\} \cup \bigcup_{n=0}^{\infty} 0^n 1 \circ V_n. \tag{3}$$

Now we shall check the properties needed.

As a recursive ordinal α allows to find recursively either its predecessor α' or sequence $\alpha_0, \alpha_1, \ldots$ with a limit α, recursiveness of all U can be obtained inductively.

In the case α is the successor of α' and U is found by (2) we have

$$U^{(\alpha')} = \{\lambda x.0\} \text{ and } U^{(\alpha)} = \emptyset.$$

In the case α is a limit and U is found by (3) let us consider all the elements in U. Each function from $0^n 1 \circ V_n$ is isolated from any other function from $0^m 1 \circ V_m$ $(m \neq n)$ therefore

$$(0^n 1 \circ V_n)^{(\alpha_n)} = 0^n 1 \circ V_n^{(\alpha_n)} = 0^n 1 \circ \emptyset = \emptyset.$$

So the intersection $\bigcup_{\xi < \alpha} U^{(\xi)}$ can contain at most one function — $\lambda x.0$. We obtain

$$U^{(\alpha)} = (\bigcup_{\xi < \alpha} U^{(\xi)})^d \subseteq (\{\lambda x.0\})^d = \emptyset.$$

But $U^{(\xi)} \neq \emptyset$ for any $\xi < \alpha$ — we simply find $\alpha_n > \xi$ and conclude

$$U^{(\xi)} \supseteq (0^n 1 \circ V_n)^{(\xi)} \neq \emptyset.$$

$\square$

We shall need classification of all functions in a class U.

Theorem 4 ([Kur66]) *All derived sets starting from the first one constitute nonincreasing sequence:*

$$A^{(1)} \supseteq A^{(2)} \supseteq \ldots \supseteq A^{(\alpha)} \supseteq \ldots.$$

The set A itself may be incomparable with any of its derived sets.

Definition 6 *We shall say that a point x ($x \in A$) has the* accumulation *order α iff α is the least ordinal for which $x \notin A^{(\alpha)}$. If such ordinal does not exist, we say that x has infinite accumulation order. If the set A is clear from the context, we denote this by $acc(x) = \alpha$ and $acc(x) = \infty$ respectively.*

For example, any isolated point has an accumulation order 1.

Theorem 5 *If class U of total recursive functions contains a function of accumulation order higher than α for some constructive ordinal α (i. e. $U \cap U^{(\alpha+1)} \neq \emptyset$), then U is not identifiable in the sense EX_α.*

Remark. We can easily see why $U^{(\alpha+1)}$ appears instead of $U^{(\alpha)}$ in this theorem — indexing of EX_α is based on counting mindchanges, but not conjectures themselves. Slightly modifying definition of the OIM (ordinal inference machine) we could obtain otherwise indexed hierarchy EX_α with some more "natural" identification types in it. For example, a strategy in EX_ω would decide how much mindchanges it could need at the moment when the first conjecture (and not the first mindchange!) is output. Furthermore, EX_ω would be named $EX_{\omega+1}$, etc. Such defects in notation would occur at every limit ordinal. (Analogically, the identification type FIN would then be denoted by EX_1 and not EX_0.) Certainly, we are not going to change EX_α indexing, but "difference 1" should be taken into account in this as well as in some other cases.

Proof. Suppose there exists an ordinal inductive inference machine identifying U in the sense EX_α. We fix $f_0 \in U \cap U^{(\alpha+1)}$. Clearly $acc(f_0) > \alpha$. The ordinal of the machine is equal to α. We input the initial segment of f until machine outputs its first conjecture h_0. In the neighbourhood of the function f_0 determined by the values received by the machine so far there exists a function $f_1 \in U$ with $acc(f_1) \geq \alpha$ such that $\phi_{h_0} \neq f_1$. We continue to input the values of f_1 and wait until the machine reduces its ordinal to α' and changes the conjecture to h_1. Then in the new neighbourhood of f_1 we find $f_2 \in U$ such that $acc(f_2) \geq \alpha'$ and $\phi_{h_1} \neq f_2$, etc. Either the final conjecture of the machine will be incorrect or the ordinal of if will be reduced to 0 and still we shall be able to find a function f_n cuch that $acc(f_n) \geq 0$ and $\phi_{h_{n-1}} \neq f_n$. $\square$

Corollary. For a given ordinal α class U as constructed in Theorem 3 satisfies $U \in EX_\alpha$ and $U \notin EX_\xi$, $\xi < \alpha$.

4 Splitting theorems for the type FIN

For the given class W the possibility of splitting strategies into several families so that a team identifying W must contain representatives from all the families ilustrates the variety of "thinking types" necessary to learn W. In the case of FIN the possibility of splitting strongly depends upon the presence of accumulation points in the class W.

Theorem 6 *If $W \cap W^d \neq \emptyset$ (i. e. W contains an accumulation point) all FIN strategies can be split into two (disjoint) families such that any finite team identifying W contains strategies from both families.*

Remark. W cannot be identified by a single FIN strategy (see remark to Theorem 5).

Proof. We fix $f \in U \cap U^d$. The first family — $\mathcal{M}_1$ contains all strategies which identify f. $\mathcal{M}_2$ contains all the other strategies. Each team must intersect $\mathcal{M}_1$. From the contrary, suppose that the team is subset of $\mathcal{M}_2$. Each member of the finite team outputs conjecture — Gödel number of f after receiving a finite initial segment of f. Intersection of all the corresponding neighbourhoods of f is again a neighbourhood of f. As f is an accumulation point, there is $f_1 \in U$ in this neighbourhood such that $f_1 \neq f_0$. It is not identified by any member of the team. Contradiction. $\square$

There are quite many classes $W \notin FIN$ for which the splitting of all FIN strategies in the sense of the previous Theorem is impossible.

Theorem 7 *Let $W \in FIN(k' : m)$ where $\frac{k}{m} > \frac{1}{2}$. For any splitting of all FIN strategies into two families, one of them will provide a finite team identifying W.*

Proof. Let $M_1, \ldots, M_m$ be a team identifying W in the sense $EX(k : m)$. For every $f \in W$ we determine those M_i which identify f. We express W as a union of classes of equivalence, each of them being identified by a definite set of strategies from the team:

$$W = \bigcup_{j=1}^{n} W_j, \quad n \leq \binom{m}{k} + \binom{m}{k+1} + \ldots + \binom{m}{m}.$$

Union of any two subclasses $W_{j_1} \cup W_{j_2}$ is identifiable by a single strategy from the team. Indeed, W_{j_1} and W_{j_2} are identified by more than a half of all members of the team — these 2 sets of strategies must intersect.

We consider arbitrary splitting of $\{M_1, M_2, \ldots, M_m\}$ into two finite families $\mathcal{M}_1$ and $\mathcal{M}_2$. Suppose, the team $\mathcal{M}_1$ does not identify W. Then there must be at least one subclass W_{j_0} not identified by any strategy from $\mathcal{M}_1$. Then all the strategies identifying $W_{j_0} \cup W_j$ $(j = 1, 2, \ldots, n)$ must be in $\mathcal{M}_2$. Clearly $\mathcal{M}_2$ identifies W. $\square$

Corollary. If $W \in FIN(k : m)$ where $\frac{k}{m} > \frac{1}{2}$, then all functions in W are are isolated.

It turns out that $W \cap W^d \neq \emptyset$ is not necessary for the existance of a splitting.

Theorem 8 *There exists a class $W \in FIN(1 : 2)$, $W^d = \emptyset$ an a splitting of all FIN strategies into two families such that any team identifying W contains strategies from both families.*

Proof. First we show how to split any finite set of strategies and secondly perform a step of transfinite induction.

The class W will be defined as "partly selfdescribing". Namely, among values of any $f \in W$ there are one or two even integers $2n_1$ and $2n_2$. At least one of n_1 or n_2 is a correct Gödel number of the function f. (If there was only one even number $2n_1$, then it must be the correct number of f.) Clearly $W \in FIN(1 : 2)$ and $W^d = \emptyset$.

Let a set of strategies $\{M_1, \ldots, M_m\}$ be given. We define simultaneously N functions ($N = 3^m$) with the same initial segment of values. For any strategy of the set there are three possibilities — either it does not output a conjecture at all or it outputs a partially defined conjecture or a total (everywhere defined) conjecture. Each of the 3^m functions will reflect one of these cases. The case when no strategy outputs a conjecture will be of special interest — we denote (still undefined) Gödel number of this function by n_1. Other functions receive numbers denoted by n_2 through n_N. We require that for $i = 1, \ldots, N$ $\phi_{n_i}(0)$ is the odd number encoding the set of recursive strategies $\{M_1, \ldots, M_m\}$ in some fixed way. The next value of all functions : $\phi_{n_i}(1) = 2n_1$. After this we define $\phi_{n_i} = 1$ for some time and parallely each ϕ_{n_i} (excepting ϕ_{n_1}) waits for the following event. When all the strategies which should output a conjecture (accordingly to the *a priori* information for ϕ_{n_i}) have done so, the value of ϕ_{n_i} is set equal to $2n_i$ (where all n_i as well as n_1 so far are merely parameters). After that some values of ϕ_{n_i} can be odd numbers different from 1 just to make incorrect all the conjectures which should be total (again accordingly to the *a priori* information).

Programs for all the ϕ_{n_i} depend from parameters $n_1, \ldots, n_N$ and strategies $M_1, \ldots, M_m$ via total recursive functions. We can apply the recursion Theorem in the Smullyan form and find values for the parameters $n_1, \ldots, n_N$. Exactly one function g among the functions ϕ_{n_i} had used a correct *a priori* information about the behaviour of $M_1, \ldots, M_m$ on the function $f = \phi_{n_1}$. It turns out that all M_j $(j = 1, \ldots, m)$ works incorrectly either on function g or on function f. Family $\mathcal{M}_1$ consists of all functions working incorrectly on g, and $\mathcal{M}_2$ — of all functions working incorrectly on f.

Now, the transfinite induction.

Each splitting of a finite initial fragment of sequence of recursive strategies can be represented by a node in an orientated, infinite, binary tree. Accordingly to the Lemma 1 an infinite path exists in this tree. Splitting of all *FIN* strategies can be obtained following this path. □

Formaly all functions of the class W are isolated. But never the less it seems that ϕ_{n_1} is an accumulation point of a finite set of functions ϕ_{n_i} in some sense. It would be interesting to develop some recursive analogue to the classical notions of accumulation point and derived set.

5   Some new identification types

Let us pay attention to the proof of Theorem 7. To prove the impossibility of splitting for the class W it was sufficient to express W as a union:
$$W = \bigcup_{j=1}^{n} W_j \text{ so that } W_{j_1} \cup W_{j_2} \in FIN \text{ for any } j_1, j_2 \in [1, n].$$
For the contrast we can consider types EX and EX_1 along with FIN. The following results hold:

Lemma 3 *If* $W = \bigcup_{j=1}^{n} W_j$ *and* $W_{j_1} \cup W_{j_2} \in EX$ *for any* $j_1, j_2 \in [1, n]$, *then* $W \in EX$.

Proof by the induction. The base, $n = 3$, was exposed in [AFK92].

Lemma 4 ([Aps93]) *If* $W \in EX_1(1 : m)$ *for some* m *we can represent it in the form* $W = \bigcup_{j=1}^{n} W_j$ *so that* $W_{j_1} \cup W_{j_2} \in EX_1$ *for any* $j_1, j_2 \in [1, n]$.

These are the two extremal cases. For *FIN* as we saw in the previous section the situation is much more complex. Besides the classes $W \in FIN(k : m)$ where $\frac{k}{m} > \frac{1}{2}$ there are many other for which the same idea of expressing W as $\bigcup\limits_{j=1}^{n} W_j$ can be carried out though the details are much more difficult. All these classes deserve at least a special name.

Definition 7 *We shall say that a class of total recursive functions W is identifiable in the sense $FIN(2 : *)$ if W can be expressed in the form $\bigcup\limits_{j=1}^{n} W_j$ for some integer n so that $W_{j_1} \cup W_{j_2} \in FIN$ for any $j_1, j_2 \in [1, n]$.*

Theorems 7 and 8 state $FIN(k : m) \subseteq FIN(2 : *)$ when $\frac{k}{m} > \frac{1}{2}$ and $FIN(1 : 2) \not\subseteq FIN(2 : *)$.

Theorem 9 *For a class W of total recursive functions the following two propositions are equivalent:*

1. *Every splitting of all FIN strategies into two families is such that one family provides a finite team identifying W,*

2. *$W \in FIN(2 : *)$.*

For arbitrary identification type T a generalized version of Definition 7 may be applied to obtain new types $T(k : *)$ as well as teams with growing number of members where the growth is described by some ordinal. But this requires more thorough investigation in the recursion theory rather than general topology so it is left out here.

6 Conclusion

Nonrecursive aspects of inductive inference can be described by the following model:

Game in the Banach-Mazur style. Let $A \subseteq [0, 1]$ be some bounded set of real numbers. The aim is to find a point $x \in A$ previously chosen by some external agent (we shall call it oracle). Learning subject (strategy) splits the interval $[0, 1]$ into several subintervals and asks the oracle which of them contains point x. After that the subinterval is splitted again, etc. As a result a sequence of convergent intervals

$$[0, 1] = I_0 \supset I_1 \supset I_2 \supset \ldots$$

appears. Between the queries to the oracle learning subject outputs its conjectures — which point it assumes to be fixed. The requirements to the conjecture sequence can be described by some identification type (such as EX_n), etc. The oracle may be assumed to be an active part of the game too — trying to mislead strategy.

Therefore we can formulate the following open problem: which identification types can be distinguished on the basis of this non-constructive model. As shown by Theorem 5 it can be done for hierarchy of types EX_α. On the other hand, EX and BC identification cannot be distinguished in nonrecursive terms (different Gödel numbers can correspond to the same function which is encoded by the same real number).

References

[Kur66] K. Kuratowski. Topology. Vol. 1. Academic Press New York and London, 1966.

[Gol67] E. M. Gold. Language identification in the limit. Information and control, 10:5, 1967, pp. 447–474.

[KM67] K. Kuratowski, A. Mostowski. Set Theory. North-Holland Publishing Company, 1967.

[Rog67] H. Rogers. Theory of Recursive Functions and Effective Computability. McGraw-Hill, New York, 1967.

[Eng77] R. Engelking. General Topology. Polish Scientific Publishers, Warszawa, 1977.

[Smi82] C. Smith. The power of Pluralism for Automatic Program Synthesis. *Assoc. Comput. Mach.*, **29**, 1982, pp. 1144–1165.

[CS83] J. Case, C. Smith. Comparison of identification criteria for machine inductive inference. *Theoret. Comput. Sci.*, **25**(2), 1983, pp. 193–220.

[AFK92] K. Apsītis, R. Freivalds, M. Kriķis, R. Simanovskis, J. Smotrovs. Unions of identifiable classes of total recursive functions. In K. Jantke, editor, *Analogical and Inductive Inference*, pages 99–107. Springer-Verlag, 1992. Lecture Notes in Artificial Intelligence, No. 642.

[Aps93] K. Apsītis. Topological Considerations in Composing Teams of Learning Machines. (To be published in the proceedings of International Workshop on Algorithmic Learning for Knowledge Processing (GOSLER project), November 1993, Dagstuhl Castle, Germany.)

[FS93] R. Freivalds, C. Smith. On the Role of Procrastination in Machine Learning. *Information and Computation*, **107**(2), 1993, pp. 237–271.

[AFS94] K. Apsītis, R. Freivalds, C. Smith. Choosing a Learning Team: a Topological Approach. (Manuscript accepted for the STOC conferece held in Montreal, May 23–25, 1994.)

Therapy Plan Generation as Program Synthesis*

Oksana Arnold and Klaus P. Jantke

Hochschule für Technik, Wirtschaft und Kultur Leipzig (FH)
Fachbereich Informatik, Mathematik & Naturwissenschaften
P.O.Box 66, 04251 Leipzig, Germany

Abstract. There has been developed and implemented an algorithm for the automatic synthesis of therapy plans for complex dynamic systems. This algorithm is the core of some control synthesis module which is embedded in a larger knowledge-based system for control, diagnosis and therapy. There are several applications.

The planning algorithm may be understood as an inductive program synthesis procedure. Its fundamentals are introduced and its key ideas are sketched. The dichotomy between executability and consistency is investigated.

1 Motivation and Introduction

The main intention of the present paper is to establish a new link between two areas of research: *Program Synthesis* and *Therapy Planning*. Thus, the authors wish to advance both areas of research they are active in. For program synthesis, the intended integration may result in new and exciting problems characterized by particular constraints not investigated in the classical approaches, so far. Our approach may widen the view at automatic program synthesis, in general. For therapy planning, this integration may initiate a certain shift from typical AI approaches towards theoretical computer science. This will extend the amount of methodologies and techniques available for plan generation. In [Her93], the author is pointing to the relationship between plan generation and program synthesis[2]. But this link has not been established yet, in our opinion. There may be some exception in robotics, where action plans have necessarily to be interpreted as programs. In [Wer93], this relationship is becoming almost explicit.

Initially, let us briefly exemplify the type of interaction we have in mind. In automatic program synthesis, there exists a particular concept of *consistency*

---

* The work has been partially supported by the German Federal Ministry for Research and Technology (BMFT) within the Joint Project (BMFT-Verbundprojekt) **Wiscon** on **Development of Methods for Intelligent Monitoring and Control** under contract no. 413-4001-01 IW 204 B.

[2] "Faßt man Pläne praktisch als eine Variante von Programmen auf, ist es nur konsequent, Planen mit automatischer Programmgenerierung zu identifizieren und deren Begrifflichkeit, Konzepte und Techniken zu benutzen, um z.B. auch Pläne mit nichttrivialen Kontrollkonstrukten wie Rekursion zu erzeugen."

denoting the ability of hypothetical programs to reflect the information they have been built upon. There are several well-understood formalizations of consistency in inductive learning (cf. [AS83] for an overview, [JB81] for a couple of results, [Wie92] for an up to date discussion). In therapy plan synthesis for process control, the notion of consistency needs to be refined and distinguished from executability, as we will point out in this paper. This may raise new theoretical concepts and investigations.

The paper presents and examines the basic concepts of a knowledge-based therapy planner from the viewpoint of program synthesis. The developed algorithm is implemented in LISP and running under SUN/OS on Sparc Stations (cf. [Arn92]). Thus, our paper may be considered as a report about some working program synthesis method.

1.1 Automatic Program Synthesis

For *automatic program synthesis*, [BB93] is an excellent recent reference: *The design and implementation of correct software meeting given requirements continues to be most relevant, practical, and scientifically challenging problem. There are many lines of research directed towards solving this problem. Automatic Programming is one among those. It is the study of techniques for generating executable code from information which may be fragmentary and may only indirectly specify the target behavior.*
The field ist based on the idea that ultimately we need to engage the machine itself in the process of programming machines, since only machines offer the important property needed for this task which is the ability to work without making mistakes. The "Automatic" in the name does not necessarily refer to a full automation of programming, but rather to a considerably higher degree of automation than in other lines of software production pursued by the literature. We will adopt this view in the sequel.

Among the approaches to program synthesis which are relevant to our problems, inductive program synthesis seems to be most appropriate. Generating therapy plans for process control in dynamic environments needs to be based on incomplete information, only. Processing incomplete information for coming up with complete solutions is the crux of problems attacked by inductive inference research (cf. [AS83], [KW80], [Ang92], [Wie92]), in general, and inductive program synthesis (cf. [Sum75], [BBP75], [BK76], [Sum77], [Bau79], [Sha81], [Sha83], [JK83], [BK86], [DP90], [FD93], [DR93], e.g.), in particular. The approaches referred to vary from purely recursion-theoretic to those synthesizing LISP expressions or Prolog programs ([Sum75], [Sum77], [Sha81], [Sha83] e.g.). This is the type of work we want to relate to therapy plan generation.

However, the type of control problems to be attacked below require a more explicit handling of multiple knowledge (cf. [Arn93b], [Arn94b]) than considered in most of the papers mentioned above. In this regard, approaches like [Bar79], [MW74], [MW83], and [Neu92] seem more appropriate, although the latter three are deductively oriented.

1.2 Therapy Plan Generation as Control Synthesis

Although planning is a major research area of recent artificial intelligence (cf. [BGH+93], [DW91], [Gin93], [Ham89], [Her89], [Wil88], and others), the type of planning we are faced to is substantially different from most of the approaches cited above (cf. [Arn92], [Arn94a], [Arn94b]). Therefore, we want to survey the pecularities of our approach in the next section.

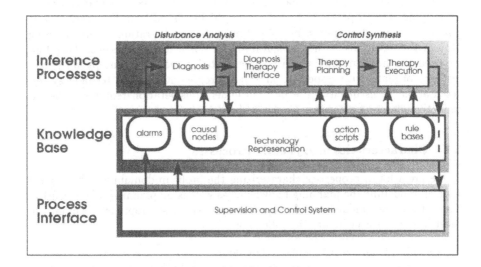

Fig. 1. System Architecture

Here, we present some investigation in therapy control and beyond. A therapy control in engineering is some ordering of control actions (a therapy plan) in order to influence the technical process in timely response. It's aim is to remove the causes of a detected disturbance, to perform a new control regime to minimize the losses of production, and to adopt the situation recognition which monitors alarm boundaries. These tasks should be done by both sending new setpoint values, control values, and alarm boundaries to a conventional supervision and control system and informing the operator about some mechanical measures (cf. [BMHC90], [BKM92], [Fri93]). Therefore, the corresponding control synthesis modules have to be embedded into comprehensive knowledge-based systems integrating process supervision, diagnosis, simulation, planning, and plan execution, among others. In dependence on the discovered fault, the current reserves of the system, and the state of the process the control synthesis should derive and execute an appropriate therapy plan (cf. [Arn93b], for further details). Thus, therapy plans are formal objects having some operational semantics in the process under consideration. They are programs.

We assume the shown architecture of a knowledge-based system. The control synthesis which consists of a planner und an execution module is triggered by disturbance analysis. The technology representation contains all information which is available about the technological equipment which is necessary for any derivation. The overall system architecture above is slightly simplified. We dropped some modules (the one for simulation, e.g.) and ignored some interactions.

2 The Problem Domain

The intention of the present chapter is to introduce the main pecularities of our underlying class of problem domains. It is distinguished from the areas investigated in most of the approaches found in the recent literature about planning. One of the essentials is that executability is not a formal concept. Therefore, we need another concept for verifying generated plans. This concept is the concistency of plans with respect to knowledge represented in the technology representation. Consequently, the domain under consideration requires rather an inductive planning algorithm than a deductive approach.

2.1 Characteristics of Dynamic Processes

There are a lot of properties charaterizing the problem domain and having impact on modelling the planning knowledge as well as on planning and execution. Thus, they are fundamental for our program synthesis approach. Among the most important aspects are the following:

I Essential Characteristics of the Domain
* Values of process parameters may be set only by indirect influence. Consequently, the effects of actions (postconditions) are not always definite.
* Sometimes, parameters which are necessary to describe the complete state of some device are not accessible.
* The success of actions depends, in general, on the availability of technological resources (preconditions), like energy, conveyance pipes and storage capacity.
* There may be some need for simultaneous actions resulting from the structure of the equipment and the running processes.

Further properties are relevant in other domains, too. In this context, they complicate the planning problem additionally.

II Further Characteristics of the Domain
* The resource dependencies on actions are not limited to those which should be fulfilled at the beginning of actions. There are resource constraints which should be met during the whole execution time of actions.
* Actions require a certain amount of time to be completed. This time has to be taken into account but may unknown in advance.
* Setpoints of process parameters may be unstable. Thus, the whole process is subject to permanent changes.
* In general, there exist alternative actions which differ in resource constraints and cost.

Consequently, the therapy control is contingent on the duration of the primary fault and the current reserves of the system. Moreover, its duration is determined by residence time of units, capacity of stores, etc. During therapy execution the conditions may change substantially, both due to unforeseeable process conditions and due to unexpected side effects of the therapy itself including interferences of individual therapy actions. Roughly speaking, there is no hope for complete information.

In order to take all pecularities of the domain into account within one approach, it is necessary to develop an appropriate language for expressing action operators.[3] Based on this language generated therapy plans should be executable to meet their goal specification, i.e. to be semantically correct like in program synthesis. But among others, the indirect setting of values exhibits that executability is determined by the process dynamics. Thus, the executability of a generated plan is not a formal concept in our domain. Correctness and completeness of any planner cannot be completely formalized with respect to the underlying process.

The ultimate goal of our present approach is a formalization of basic concepts to manifest the distinction from conventional program synthesis approaches.

2.2 A Peep at Knowledge Representation

Before developing any language for therapy planning, one should carefully examine the knowledge to be represented. *First*, the knowledge about control measures depends on the constructive performance of technological components. *Second*, technological equipments usually have a remarkable number of repeatedly occurring units. This results in similar or even identical knowledge structures for a lot of therapy actions. *Furthermore*, there is some need to express time relations between actions if they should be performed together to meet a common goal. *Finally*, therapy actions refer to process parameters within the preconditions.

These insights suggest to structure the knowledge base by modelling the technological equipment. We provide a frame-oriented language called *the technology representation*, which permits the definition of technological classes and instances (cf. [Arn92]). Action operators (in our case, action scripts) are assigned to those technological object classes[4] or instances they have relevance for. Since accessible process parameters partially describe the state of some process units, they can be defined and referred to as properties of technological classes and instances. Thus, the technology representation takes on the communication between the knowledge-based system and the upstream supervision and control

---

[3] The causes for a new approach are different. First, it seems quite impossible to use STRIPS-like action definitions. They are useless if there is no way to define precisely postconditions. Furthermore, they are only applicable in the face of interest in sequential plans. Second, we want to use as much information available about the process, disturbance states and therapy measures (i.e. manuals, experience, physical models) as possible.

[4] This allows for the generalization of therapy knowledge and for the reduction of the amount of action scripts.

computer system. For any derivation, it makes available process data about the past, the present and the future.

Further pecularities of the knowledge representation reflect the specifics of our domain.

* The persistency assumption should be droped within the process model for many process parameters on the base of unstable working points.
* A lot of process parameters are considered as fluents. Thus, their discrete representation within the knowledge base yields to intermediate states never made explicit.
* There is no reasonable way to describe the whole state space of the technological process completely.

3 Plans as Programs

Plans are built upon action scripts, which represent the basics of our language for therapy planning. Hence, we want to introduce first the syntactic structure of action scripts. Based on that, we are going to describe plans in a formal way.[5] Thus, we set the stage for formal concepts of correctness and completeness in therapy planning as well as for investigating properties like executability and consistency.

3.1 Action Scripts

Action scripts are the syntactic constituents of therapy plans. Their is not enough space here to motivate and explain action scripts in more detail. There are el-

```
(CREATE-ACTION
    :ACTION                <ActionName> ::= <SYMBOL>
    :OBJECT                <ObjectName> ::= <SYMBOL>
    :PREFERENCE            <INTEGER>
    :START-CONDITIONS      ([<Constraint>]*)
    :INTERVAL-CONDITIONS   ([<Constraint>]*)
    :PROCEDURE             (<ProcedureCall><ObjectName><ProcedureName><ProcedureArgs>) )
```

Fig. 2. Syntax of Elementary Action Scripts

ementary and compound action scripts which have a frame-like structure as depicted. These action scripts are intended to compose plans by stepwise unfolding the hierarchical structure. The action name together with the associated technological object builds the goal specification. Constraints play a crucial role in consistency investigations (see below).

---

[5] There is the urgent need for clear notions and notations. Statements like "*A plan in ILP (interval Logic Planner) is taken to be a set of assumptions about the future.*" in [Pel91] seem not only vague, but quite useless. In particular, deeper questions like the one whether or not a certain plan is always a sequentially structured object need some formal basis for consideration.

For understanding our program synthesis approach below, both the syntax presented here and the knowledge that only elementary action scripts are carrying operational semantics will do.

```
(CREATE-ACTION
  :ACTION                 <ActionName> ::= <SYMBOL>
  :OBJECT                 <ObjectName> ::= <SYMBOL>
  :PREFERENCE             <INTEGER>
  :START-CONDITIONS       ([<Constraint>]*)
  :INTERVAL-CONDITIONS    ([<Constraint>]*)
  :SUBACTIONS             ([(<SubActionName> <ObjectReference> <Intervalidentifier>)]+)
  :TIME-RELATIONS         ([(<TimeRel> <Intervalidentifier1> <Intervalidentifier2>)]*)
```

Fig. 3. Syntax of Compound Action Scripts

3.2 Building Therapy Plans from Action Scripts

From an abstract point of view, therapy plans are hierarchically structured graphs (cf. [AJ94]). Hence, therapy plan synthesis resp. program synthesis is synthesis of certain hierarchically structured graphs. There has been introduced a hierarchy of formal concepts denoted

- a hierarchically structured family of plans,
- a rooted family,
- a hierarchically structured plan,
- a plan.

They have been derived from hierarchically cellular graphs and pin graphs as in [LW88], [Wan89], and [HLW92]. The basic concept of a *hierarchically structured family of plans* corresponds to the amount of action scripts available in the knowledge base. This concept is defined as follows:

Definition 1

A *hierarchically structured family of plans* is a finite collection $\mathcal{F} = \{\mathcal{G}_1, \ldots, \mathcal{G}_k\}$ of pin graphs $\mathcal{G}_i = [V_i, E_i, P_i^{in}, P_i^{out}, C_i, sub_i]$ $(i = 1 \ldots k)$ such that for every $i \in \{1, \ldots, k\}$ we have:

1. $\mathcal{G}_i' = [V_i, E_i]$ is a finite, directed, acyclic graph with the set of vertices V_i and the set of edges E_i.
2. $P_i^{in} \cup P_i^{out}$ are called the pins of $\mathcal{G}_i$ with $P_i^{in}, P_i^{out} \subseteq V_i$ and are defined by
   (a) $P_i^{in} = \{v \mid v \in V_i \wedge \neg \exists u \in V_i \, ((u, v) \in E_i)\}$
   (b) $P_i^{out} = \{v \mid v \in V_i \wedge \neg \exists u \in V_i \, ((v, u) \in E_i)\}$
3. The vertices in $C_i \subseteq V_i$ are understood to be compound actions to be substituted lateron.
4. $sub_i : C_i \rightarrow \{1, \ldots, k\}$ is a mapping indicating which Graphs $\mathcal{G}_j$ may be substituted for the compound nodes in C_i.

Preference is implicitly specified via the indices of graphs. If two graphs are alternative substitutions, the one with the greater index has higher preference.

Definition 2

Assume any hierarchically structured family of plans $\mathcal{F} = \{\mathcal{G}_1, \ldots, \mathcal{G}_k\}$, any $\mathcal{G}_i \in \mathcal{F}$, any $c \in C_i$, and any $j \in sub_i(c)$. The *substitution of $\mathcal{G}_j$ in $\mathcal{G}_i$ at $c \in C_i$* yields another pin graph denoted by $\mathcal{G}_i[c \hookleftarrow \mathcal{G}_j] = [V, E, P^{in}, P^{out}, C, sub]$ and defined as follows.

1. $V = (V_i \setminus \{c\}) \cup V_j$ $\qquad$ (This is always assumed to be a disjoint union.[6])
2. $E = ((E_i \cup E_j) \setminus (V_i \times \{c\} \cup \{c\} \times V_i)) \cup$
   $\qquad ((\{v \mid (v, c) \in E_i\} \times P_j^{in}) \cup (P_j^{out} \times \{v \mid (c, v) \in E_i\}))$
3. $P^{in} = P_i^{in}$
4. $P^{out} = P_i^{out}$
5. $C = (C_i \setminus \{c\}) \cup C_j$
6. $sub = sub_{i/C_i \setminus \{c\}} \cup sub_j$

This definition easily generalizes graphs which do not belong to $\mathcal{F}$.

Definition 3

Assume any hierarchically structured family of plans $\mathcal{F} = \{\mathcal{G}_1, \ldots, \mathcal{G}_k\}$ and $\mathcal{G} = [V, E, P^{in}, P^{out}, C, sub]$.
For any pin graph $\mathcal{G}'$, it holds $\mathcal{G} \Rightarrow_{\mathcal{F}} \mathcal{G}'$ if and only if $\exists c \in C$ $\quad \exists j \in sub(c)$

1. $\mathcal{G}_j \in \mathcal{F}$
2. $\mathcal{G}' = \mathcal{G}[c \hookleftarrow \mathcal{G}_j]$

By $\Rightarrow_{\mathcal{F}}^{+}$ we denote the transitive closure of $\Rightarrow_{\mathcal{F}}$.

Since compound action scripts specify new goals which may be satisfied by applying further scripts, there is a substitution ordering $\preceq_{\mathcal{F}}$ for every hierarchically structured family of plans $\mathcal{F}$ on $\{\mathcal{G}_1, \ldots, \mathcal{G}_k\}$ indicating which graphs can be substituted into each other according to $\{sub_i\}_{i=1 \ldots k}$. This ordering is simply defined such that $\mathcal{G}_i \preceq_{\mathcal{F}} \mathcal{G}_j$ holds, if and only if $\exists c \in C_i \, (j \in sub_i(c))$. The transitive closure of $\preceq_{\mathcal{F}}$ is denoted by $\preceq_{\mathcal{F}}^{+}$.

Definition 4

Assume any hierarchically structured family of plans $\mathcal{F} = \{\mathcal{G}_1, \ldots, \mathcal{G}_k\}$ and any $\mathcal{G}_i \in \mathcal{F}$.

1. All normal forms of $\mathcal{G}_i$ w.r.t. $\Rightarrow_{\mathcal{F}}^{+}$ are called the (flat) *plans* specified by $\mathcal{G}_i$ via $\mathcal{F}$.
2. If any $\mathcal{G}$ is in normal form w.r.t. $\mathcal{F}$, this is denoted by $\mathcal{G} \downarrow$.
3. $\mathcal{R} = [\mathcal{F}, \mathcal{G}_i]$ is called a *rooted family*, if and only if $\forall \mathcal{G}_j \in \mathcal{F} \, (\mathcal{G}_i \neq \mathcal{G}_j \Rightarrow \mathcal{G}_i \preceq_{\mathcal{F}}^{+} \mathcal{G}_j)$.
4. Any rooted family $\mathcal{P} = [\mathcal{F}, \mathcal{G}_i]$ is called a *hierarchically structured plan*, if and only if $\mathcal{G}_i$ has a uniquely defined normal form $\mathcal{G}^{*}$ w.r.t. $\Rightarrow_{\mathcal{F}}^{+}$.
5. $\mathcal{L}(\mathcal{F}) = \{\mathcal{G} \mid \exists \mathcal{G}_i \in \mathcal{F} \, (\mathcal{G}_i \Rightarrow_{\mathcal{F}}^{+} \mathcal{G}) \wedge \mathcal{G} \downarrow \}$

These concepts are essential for a formal approach to plan synthesis, to plan execution, and to plan revision, if necessary.

---

[6] For notational convenience, the disjoint union may be constructed as follows. $\mathcal{G}_j$ is copied to some graph called $c.\mathcal{G}_j$ which results from $\mathcal{G}_j$ be renaming vertices v to $c.v$. Thus, a repeated substitution results in names of vertices like $v_m.v_{m-1}.\ldots.v_1$ which allow backtracing the ssubstitution process.

4 Therapy Plan Synthesis

In the sequel, we will put some emphasis on the use of constraints and the difficulties of constraint monitoring. These aspects are basic to understand the differences between the central concepts of *consistency* and *executability*.

4.1 Steps of Planning

The amount of action scripts which is embedded in the technology representation specifies the search space of all potentially available therapy plans. It is forming a structured family of plans $\mathcal{F}$. In the case of any disturbance, the diagnosis yields some result interpreted by the diagnosis therapy interface as some therapy control goal $\mathcal{G}_i$. $\mathcal{F}$ and $\mathcal{G}_i$ are implicitly forming the rooted family $\mathcal{R} = [\mathcal{F}', \mathcal{G}_i]$, where $\mathcal{F}'$ results from $\mathcal{F}$ by removing unnecessary action scripts. $\mathcal{R} = [\mathcal{F}', \mathcal{G}_i]$ is taken as the recent search space for planning. In order to get a consistent

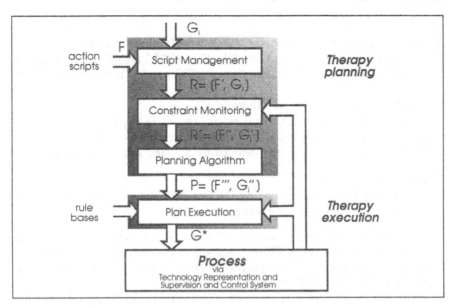

Fig. 4. Therapy Planning

plan, the resource constraints of potentially applicable action scripts should be checked. Assume that all information about the behaviour of the process in the future (especially, with respect to necessary resources like energy, conveyance pipes, and storages) as well as all exact execution times of actions would be known at planning time. With this assumption, constraint monitoring is able to remove all graphs $\mathcal{G}_i$ whose resource constraints are violated from the rooted family in one step. Furthermore, all substitution mappings referring to such graphs $\mathcal{G}_i$ should be modified, in accordance. Thus, the output of some constraint monitoring is a reduced rooted family $\mathcal{R}'$ whose normal forms are consistent.

Based on this, the pure planning algorithm constructs a hierarchically structed plan $\mathcal{P}$ having a unique normal form. $\mathcal{P}$ is derived from $\mathcal{R}'$ by paralysing all but one alternative substitutions at each compound vertex. These points are later used for backtracking, if plan revision becomes necessary. The normal form $\mathcal{G}^*$ of $\mathcal{P}$ is used as a program operating on the underlying dynamic process for therapy. Figure 4 sketches the whole therapy planning algorithm in principle.

4.2 The Main Planning Derivation

According to the insights of section 4.1, the main difficulties arise from missing precise execution time of actions at planning and from having resource dependencies on actions for which predictive information will be partially and iteratively gained by simulation, diagnosis and human's directions. This has serious impact on constraint checking and monitoring. The key formal concepts are as follows.

Definition 5

Assume any hierarchically structured family of plans $\mathcal{F} = \{\mathcal{G}_1, \ldots, \mathcal{G}_k\}$.

1. There is assumed some language $\mathcal{WFF}$ of well-formed formulae.
2. SC and IC are two mappings $SC, IC : \mathcal{F} \rightarrow 2^{\mathcal{WFF}}$ assigning to each graph $\mathcal{G}_i$ both a finite set of *start conditions* $SC(\mathcal{G}_i)$ and a finite set of *interval conditions* $IC(\mathcal{G}_i)$.
3. Constraints are inherited as follows.
   (a) $\forall i, j \in \{1, \ldots, k\} \, \forall c \in C_i \, (\, j \in sub_i(c) \Rightarrow IC_i \subseteq IC_j \,)$
   (b) $\forall i, j \in \{1, \ldots, k\} \, \forall c \in C_i \cap P_i^{in} \, (\, j \in sub_i(c) \Rightarrow SC_i \subseteq SC_j \,)$
4. $SC(\mathcal{G}_i)$ and $IC(\mathcal{G}_i)$ are briefly denoted by SC_i and IC_i, respectively.

Definition 6

Assume any formula φ containing the free variables $x_1, \ldots, x_n$. Assume t_1 and t_2 denote any points in time satisfying $t_1 \leq t_2$.

1. If x is any process parameter and v_1, v_2 are two of its possible values, the technology representation $\mathcal{TR}$ may contain some information indicating that during $[t_1, t_2]$ the value of x ranges between v_1 and v_2. This is written as $\langle x \in_{[t_1, t_2]} [v_1, v_2] \rangle \in \mathcal{TR}$, for short.
   (Note that in some cases, t_1 and t_2 or v_1 and v_2 (or even both pairs) coincide.)
2. If $v_1, \ldots, v_n$ are particular values of the corresponding variables $x_1, \ldots, x_n$, the notation $\models \varphi(v_1, \ldots, v_n)$ means that this formula is logically valid within the underlying arithmetics. $\models \neg\varphi(v_1, \ldots, v_n)$[7] is understood accordingly.
3. φ is refutable w.r.t. the technology representation during the time period $[t_1, t_2]$, if and only if there are entries $\langle x_1 \in_{[t_{11}, t_{12}]} [v_{11}, v_{12}] \rangle, \ldots, \langle x_n \in_{[t_{n1}, t_{n2}]} [v_{n1}, v_{n2}] \rangle \in \mathcal{TR}$ such that
   (a) $\forall k \in \{1, \ldots, n\} \, (\, t_{k1} \leq t_1 \leq t_2 \leq t_{k2} \,)$
   (b) $\forall k \in \{1, \ldots, n\} \, \forall v_k \in [v_{k1}, v_{k2}] \, (\, \models \neg\varphi(v_1, \ldots, v_n) \,)$
4. The refutability of φ during $[t_1, t_2]$ w.r.t. $\mathcal{TR}$ is abbreviated by $\mathcal{TR} \models_{[t_1, t_2]} \neg\varphi$.

---

[7] Naturally, we assume constraints to be decidable on given data.

Note that we have defined only some of the basic concepts. *Validity* and *satisfiability* are less important, here. For the type of constraint monitoring invoked, *refutability* is the key concept.

Definition 7

Assume any hierarchically structured family of plans $\mathcal{F} = \{\mathcal{G}_1, \ldots, \mathcal{G}_k\}$ and any elementary vertex $v \in \bigcup_{i=1,\ldots,k} (V_i \setminus C_i)$.

$to(v) \in I\!N$ denotes the time out of the procedural semantics of v.

When planning starts, there is estimated the expected time used by the planner. This is taken as a basis for estimating the expected start time t_0 of the therapy plan to be generated. One requires that constraints of action scripts must not be violated within the time interval ranging from t_0 to the latest start time of the considered action script. This time interval is called the *integral predecessor time out* $\tau(v)$.

Definition 8

Assume any pin graph $\mathcal{G} = [V, E, P^{in}, P^{out}, C, sub]$.

1. Any $v \in V$ is called *active*, if and only if it holds
   $v \in C \wedge \neg \exists u \in C \left((u, v) \in E \right)$

2. $\tau(v) = \begin{cases} \max_{(u,v) \in E}\{ \tau(u) + to(u) \} & : \exists u \in V \left((u, v) \in E \right) \\ 0 & : otherwise \end{cases}$

This is providing a sufficient basis for restricting alternative substitutions to only those being *consistent* with respect to the underlying technology representation $\mathcal{TR}$.

Definition 9

Assume any pin graph $\mathcal{G} = [V, E, P^{in}, P^{out}, C, sub]$ and any start time $t_0 \in I\!N$.

1. $sub_{t_0}^{cons}(v) = \begin{cases} \{ i \mid i \in sub(v) \wedge \\ \quad \forall \varphi \in SC_i \cup IC_i \, (\mathcal{TR} \not\models_{[t_0, t_0 + \tau(v)]} \neg\varphi) \} & : v \text{ is active} \\ sub(v) & : otherwise \end{cases}$

2. Changing every $sub(v)$ to $sub_{t_0}^{cons}(v)$ within $\mathcal{G}$ transforms the pin graph $\mathcal{G}$ into some pin graph called $\mathcal{G}_{t_0}^{cons}$.

Definition 10

Assume any hierarchically structured family of plans $\mathcal{F} = \{\mathcal{G}_1, \ldots, \mathcal{G}_k\}$. Moreover, assume any pin graph $\mathcal{G} = [V, E, P^{in}, P^{out}, C, sub]$ and any start time $t_0 \in I\!N$.

1. If $\mathcal{G} \Rightarrow_{\mathcal{F}} \mathcal{G}'$ holds by some substitution of a certain pin graph $\mathcal{G}_i$ for some compound vertex c of $\mathcal{G}$, i.e. $\mathcal{G}' = \mathcal{G}[c \hookleftarrow \mathcal{G}_i]$,
   then $\mathcal{G} \, {}_{t_0}\Rightarrow_{\mathcal{F},\mathcal{TR}} \mathcal{G}'$ holds, if and only if
   (a) c is active and
   (b) $i \in sub_{t_0}^{cons}(c)$.

2. As usual, ${}_{t_0}\Rightarrow_{\mathcal{F},\mathcal{TR}}^{+}$ denotes the transitive closure of ${}_{t_0}\Rightarrow_{\mathcal{F},\mathcal{TR}}$.

Definition 11

Assume any hierarchically structured family of plans $\mathcal{F} = \{\mathcal{G}_1, \ldots, \mathcal{G}_k\}$. TR denotes the underlying technology representation, and $t_0 \in I\!N$ is any point in time.

1. $\mathcal{NF}_{t_0 \overset{+}{\underset{\mathcal{F},TR}{\Rightarrow}}}$ denotes the set of all normal forms of graphs $\mathcal{G}_i \in \mathcal{F}$ with respect to $t_0 \overset{+}{\underset{\mathcal{F},TR}{\Rightarrow}}$, i.e. $\mathcal{NF}_{t_0 \overset{+}{\underset{\mathcal{F},TR}{\Rightarrow}}} = \{\mathcal{G} \mid \exists \mathcal{G}_i \in \mathcal{F} (\mathcal{G}_i \, _{t_0}\overset{+}{\underset{\mathcal{F},TR}{\Rightarrow}} \mathcal{G}) \wedge \mathcal{G} \downarrow_{TR} \}$.

2. $\mathcal{L}_{t_0}^{cons}(\mathcal{F}, TR) = \mathcal{L}(\mathcal{F}) \cap \mathcal{NF}_{t_0 \overset{+}{\underset{\mathcal{F},TR}{\Rightarrow}}}$

Note that the efforts to construct only consistent plans may sometimes result in empty substitution mappings, i.e. $sub_{t_0}^{cons}(v) = \emptyset$ may hold for certain compound vertices v of particular pin graphs. Thus, there may exist normal forms with respect to $_{t_0}\overset{+}{\underset{\mathcal{F},TR}{\Rightarrow}}$ which can not reasonably be interpreted as executable plans. Thus, the target language is defined less smoothly. If a particular graph $\mathcal{G}$ is in normal form w.r.t. $_{t_0}\overset{+}{\underset{\mathcal{F},TR}{\Rightarrow}}$, this is briefly indicated by $\mathcal{G}_i \downarrow_{TR}$, where the parameters t_0 and $\mathcal{F}$ are omitted, for readability. The rewrite relation $_{t_0}\overset{+}{\underset{\mathcal{F},TR}{\Rightarrow}}$ is inheriting termination from $\Rightarrow_{\mathcal{F}}$, but it may terminate earlier. This implies immediately $\mathcal{L}_{t_0}^{cons}(\mathcal{F}, TR) \subseteq \mathcal{L}(\mathcal{F})$. The language $\mathcal{L}_{t_0}^{cons}(\mathcal{F}, TR)$ is not structurally more complex than $\mathcal{L}(\mathcal{F})$. This is prooved by examining the sequential part of $\mathcal{L}_{t_0}^{cons}(\mathcal{F}, TR)$. It is *context-free*, too. The notions and proofs for that result are dropped on reasons of space.

Now, we are able to describe the plan synthesis algorithm (cf. Fig. 5 on the next page) in more detail. Due to the lack of space, we cannot provide any intensive discussion.

Note that every vertex gets it latest start time t by the integral predecessor time out. An individual elementary action script is *acceptable* w.r.t. TR, if and only if for all $\varphi \in SC \cup IC$ (see the structure of action scripts above) $TR \models_{[t_0, t]} \neg \varphi$ does not hold. A plan $\mathcal{G}^*$ is said to be *consistent* w.r.t. TR, if and only if all its vertices are acceptable w.r.t. TR. The planning process is finished, if $\mathcal{G}$ is in normal form. Backtracking is activated if some $sub_{t_0}^{cons}(v)$ returns the empty set.

Due to the overall complexity and the unforeseeable behaviour of dynamic systems, there is no formal way to prove the executabilty of plans, in general. In particular, consistency does not guarantee executability. Thus, plans generated for execution may fail such that replanning becomes necessary. To state it explicitly: *Consistency of an hierarchically structured plan does not imply executability of its normal form.* Due to the difficulties of knowledge representation, also the opposite statement is true, unfortunately: *There may be inconsistent plans that have an executable normal form.*

4.3 Planning as Inductive Inference

Note that constraint monitoring as explained above and implemented (cf. [Arn92]) is playing exactly the same role as checking consistency in inductive inference theory (cf. [AS83], [Ang92], [JB81], [Wie92], e.g.). It is operationally input: $\mathcal{G}_i, t_0, \mathcal{R} = [\mathcal{F}', \mathcal{G}_i]$

1. $\mathcal{G} := \mathcal{G}_i$
2. $\mathcal{P} := [\mathcal{F}''', \mathcal{G}_i]$ with $\mathcal{F}''' := \{\mathcal{G}_i\}$
3. while $C \neq \emptyset$ do
   3.1 $A := \{v \mid v \text{ active in } \mathcal{G}\}$
   3.2 forall $v \in A$ do
         $sub_{current}(v) := sub_{t_0}^{cons}(v)$ $*$ Def.9 for computation of $sub_{t_0}^{cons}(v)$
   3.3 while $A \neq \emptyset$ do
      3.3.1 find v with $v \in A$
      3.3.2 if $sub_{current}(v) = \emptyset$ $**$ backtracking point
         then
          i if $v = u.w$
            then   find $u.\mathcal{G}_j$ with $w \in u.V_j$
            else   return nil
          ii $\mathcal{F}''' := \mathcal{F}''' \setminus \{u.z.\mathcal{G}_k \mid \mathcal{G}_j \preceq_{\mathcal{F}'} \mathcal{G}_k \wedge z \in u.V_j\} \cup \{u.\mathcal{G}_j\}$
          iii find $\mathcal{G}$ with $\mathcal{G}_i \Rightarrow_{\mathcal{F}'''}^{+} \mathcal{G} \wedge \mathcal{G} \downarrow$
          iv $sub_{current}(u) := sub_{current}(u) \setminus \{j\}$
          v $A := A \cup \{u\} \setminus \{z \mid z \in u.V_j\}$
         else
          i find $\mathcal{G}_j$ with $j = max(sub_{current}(v))$
          ii $\mathcal{G} := \mathcal{G}[v \hookleftarrow \mathcal{G}_j]$
          iii $\mathcal{P} := [\mathcal{F}''', \mathcal{G}_i]$ with $\mathcal{F}''' := \mathcal{F}''' \cup \{v.\mathcal{G}_j\}$
4. return $\mathcal{P}$

Fig. 5. Planning Algorithm

located in the test "$sub_{current}(v) = \emptyset$". In particular, we are not dealt with proving satisfiability of constraints, but disproving unsatisfiability. This is precisely the phenomenon expressed in logical terms in [Jan84]. From the viewpoint of the unavoidable incompleteness of information about the underlying process, we are faced to a problem of inductively generating or learning plans.

The final figure is extracting the inductive inference task from our therapy plan synthesis approach. In fact, the core part of our control synthesis system is acting as an inductive inference machine (cf. [AS83], [KW80], for instance) getting fed in some information about the underlying process and generating plans resp. programs as hypotheses. Replanning is working iteratively by stepwise modification of plans within some given rooted family.

5 Results

5.1 Implementation

The sketched planning algorithm is implemented in LISP and running under SUN/OS on Sparc Stations. Technological object classes, instances, and action scripts are represented as CLOS-objects. On its top level, the planning algorithm is starting with some given goal specification $\mathcal{G}_i$. It returns a consistent hierarchically structured plan. Additionally, there has been implemented an interface (a plan tra   'n a sense) to the therapy planner which allows to display the generated hierarchically structured plan in some modes (cf. [Arn93a]). Finally, we have de facto some interpreter of plans. It is interpreting the normal form $\mathcal{G}^*$ of the generated hypothesis $\mathcal{P} = [\mathcal{F}''', \mathcal{G}_i'']$ by calling rule bases and interacting with the supervision and control system.

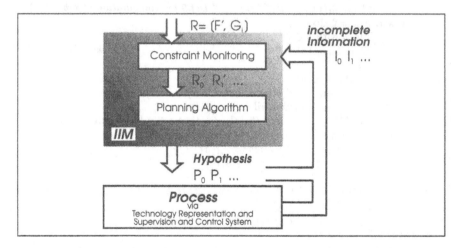

Fig. 6. Inductive Inference

5.2 Applications

Our implementation builds the therapy control synthesis component of the Wiscon system under development. There are currently three basic applications. One application is *flood prevention* for the river Werra. Another application is a *ballast tank system* for stabilizing off-shore plants. Third, there is a *chemical equipment* for the production of chemical fibres. These three application are distinguished from each other by a number of interesting pecularities. They have had a certain impact on the ideas developed above.

References

[AJ94]   Oksana Arnold and Klaus P. Jantke. Therapy plans as hierarchically structured graphs. WISCON Report 02/94, HTWK Leipzig (FH), Fachbereich IMN, April 1994.

[Ang92] Dana Angluin. Computational learning theory: Survey and selected bibliography. In *ACM Symposium on Theory of Computing, STOC'92*, pages 351–368. ACM Press, 1992.

[Arn92] Oksana Arnold. Wissensverarbeitung in dynamischen Prozeßumgebungen: Reaktive Therapieplanung in dynamischen Prozeßumgebungen. WISCON Report 10/92, Technische Hochschule Leipzig, FB Mathematik & Informatik, October 1992.

[Arn93a] Oksana Arnold. GARNET-Gadgets und LISP-Funktionen zur Gestaltung einer einheitlichen Benutzeroberfläche der WISCON-Tools. WISCON Report 02/93, HTWK Leipzig (FH), Fachbereich IMN, December 1993.

[Arn93b] Oksana Arnold. Using multiple models for therapy planning in dynamic environments. In *submitted*, 1993.

[Arn94a] Oksana Arnold. An expert system architecture to support process supervision and control. In *submitted*, 1994.

[Arn94b] Oksana Arnold. Towards structure and management of knowledge bases for controlling technological equipments. In *submitted*, 1994.

[AS83] Dana Angluin and Carl H. Smith. A survey of inductive inference: Theory and methods. *Computing Surveys*, 15:237–269, 1983.

[Bar79] David R. Barstow. An experiment in knowledge-based automatic programming. *Artificial Intelligence*, 12(1):73–119, 1979.

[Bau79] Michael A. Bauer. Programming by examples. *Artificial Intelligence*, 12(1):1–21, 1979.

[BB93] W. Bibel and A. W. Biermann. Special issue: Automatic programming - foreword of the guest editors. *Journal of Symbolic Computation*, 15(5 & 6):463–465, 1993.

[BBP75] Alan W. Biermann, Richard I. Baum, and Frederick E. Petry. Speeding up the synthesis of programs from traces. *IEEE Transactions on Computers*, 24(2):122–136, 1975.

[BGH$^+$93] Susanne Biundo, Andreas Günter, Joachim Hertzberg, Josef Schneeberger, and Wolfgang Tank. Planen und Konfigurieren. In Günther Görz, editor, *Einführung in die künstliche Intelligenz*, pages 767–828. Addison–Wesley, 1993.

[BK76] Alan W. Biermann and Ramachandran Krishnaswamy. Constructing programs from example computations. *IEEE Transactions on Software Engineering*, SE-2(3):141–153, 1976.

[BK86] Alvis Brazma and Efim B. Kinber. Generalized regular expressions - a language for synthesis of programs with branching in loops. *Theoretical Computer Science*, 46:175–195, 1986.

[BKM92] Dietrich Balzer, Volkmar Kirbach, and Volker May. Knowledge based process control. In Hartwig Steusloff and Martin Polke, editors, *Integration of Design, Implementation and Application on Measurement, Automation and Control, Intercama Congress 92*, pages 33–49, München, 1992. Oldenbourg.

[BMHC90] R. Bhatnagar, D. W. Miller, B.K. Hajek, and B. Chandasekaran. DPRL: A language for representation of operation and safety maintenance procedures of nuclear power plants. In *IEA/AIE-90*, pages 593–600. ACM, 1990.

[DP90] Nachum Dershowitz and Eli Pinchover. Inductive synthesis of equational programs. In *AAAI-90, Proceedings, Eighth National Conference on Artificial Intelligence*, pages 234–239. MIT Press, 1990.

[DR93] Nachum Dershowitz and Uday S. Reddy. Deductive and inductive synthesis of equational programs. *Journal of Symbolic Computation*, 15(5 & 6):467–494, 1993.

[DW91] T.L. Dean and M.P. Wellman. *Planning and Control*. Morgan Kaufmann, 1991.

[FD93] P. Flener and Y. Deville. Logic program synthesis from incomplete specifications. *Journal of Symbolic Computation*, 15(5 & 6):775–805, 1993.

[Fri93] Gerhard Friedrich. Model-based diagnosis and repair. *AICOM*, 6(3/4):187–206, 1993.

[Gin93] Matt Ginsberg. *Essentials of Artificial Intelligence*. Morgan Kaufmann, 1993.

[Ham89] K. Hammond. *Case Based Planning. Viewing Planning as a Memory Task*. Academic Press, 1989.

[Her89] Joachim Hertzberg. *Planen. Einführung in die Planerstellungsmethoden der Künstlichen Intelligenz*. BI Wissenschaftsverlag, 1989.

[Her93] Joachim Hertzberg. KI-Handlungsplanung – Woran wir arbeiten, und woran wir arbeiten sollten. In Otthein Herzog, Thomas Christaller, and

Dieter Schütt, editors, *Grundlagen und Anwendungen der Künstlichen Intelligenz. 17. Fachtagung für Künstliche Intelligenz (KI'93)*, pages 3–27. Springer-Verlag, 1993.

[HLW92]   Franz Höfting, Thomas Lengauer, and Egon Wanke. Processing of hierarchally defined graphs and graph families. In Burkhard Monien and Thomas Ottmann, editors, *Data Structures and Efficient Algorithms*, volume 594 of *Lecture Notes in Computer Science*, pages 44–69. Springer-Verlag, 1992.

[Jan84]   Klaus P. Jantke. The main proof-theoretic problems in inductive inference. In G. Wechsung, editor, *Frege Conference*, pages 321–330. Akademie-Verlag Berlin, 1984.

[Jan92]   Klaus P. Jantke. Case based learning in inductive inference. In *Proc. of the 5th ACM Workshop on Computational Learning Theory, COLT'92, July 27-29, 1992, Pittsburgh, PA, USA*, pages 218–223. ACM Press, 1992.

[JB81]   Klaus P. Jantke and Hans-Rainer Beick. Combining postulates of naturalness in inductive inference. *EIK*, 17(8/9):465–484, 1981.

[JK83]   Jean-Pierre Jouannaud and Yves Kodratoff. Program synthesis from examples of behavior. In Alan W. Biermann and Gérard Guiho, editors, *Computer Program Synthesis Methodologies*, pages 213–250. D. Reidel Publ. Co., 1983.

[KW80]   Reinhard Klette and Rolf Wiehagen. Research in the theory of inductive inference by GDR mathematicians - a survey. *Information Sciences*, 22:149–169, 1980.

[LW88]   Thomas Lengauer and Egon Wanke. Efficient solution of connectivity problems on hierarchically defined graphs. *SIAM Journal of Computing*, 17(6):1063–1080, 1988.

[MW74]   Zohar Manna and Richard Waldinger. Knowledge and reasoning in program synthesis. Technical Note 98, Stanford Research Institute, Menlo Park, CA, USA, November 1974.

[MW83]   Zohar Manna and Richard Waldinger. Deductive synthesis of the unification algorithm. In Alan W. Biermann and Gérard Guiho, editors, *Computer Program Synthesis Methodologies*, pages 251–307. D. Reidel Publ. Co., 1983.

[Neu92]   Gerd Neugebauer. *Pragmatische Programmsynthese*, volume 18 of *DISKI, Dissertationen zur Künstlichen Intelligenz*. infix, 1992.

[Pel91]   Richard N. Pelavin. Planning with simultaneous actions and external events. In James F. Allen, Henry A. Kautz, Richard N. Pelavin, and Josh D. Tenenberg, editors, *Reasoning about Plans*, chapter 3, pages 127–211. Morgan Kaufmann, 1991.

[Sha81]   Ehud Y. Shapiro. An algorithm that infers theories from facts. In *Proc. 7th Intern. Joint Conference on Artificial Intelligence, Vancouver, Canada*, pages 446–451, 1981.

[Sha83]   Ehud Y. Shapiro. *Algorithmic Program Debugging*. MIT Press, 1983.

[Sum75]   Philip D. Summers. *Program Construction from Examples*. PhD thesis, Yale University, Dept. Comp. Sci., 1975.

[Sum77]   Philip D. Summers. A methodology for LISP program construction from examples. *Journal of the ACM*, 24(1):161–175, 1977.

[Wan89]   Egon Wanke. Algorithms for graph problems on BNLC structured graphs. *Information and Computation*, 94(1):93–122, 1989.

[Wer93]   Gerhard Werling. *Produktorientierte automatische Planung von Prüfoperationen bei der robotergestützten Montage*, volume 46 of *DISKI, Dissertationen zur Künstlichen Intelligenz*. infix, 1993.

[Wie92]   Rolf Wiehagen. From inductive inference to algorithmic learning theory. In S. Doshita, K. Furukawa, K.P. Jantke, and T. Nishida, editors, *Proc. 3rd Workshop on Algorithmic Learning Theory, (ALT'92), October 20-22, 1992, Tokyo*, volume 743 of *Lecture Notes in Artificial Intelligence*, pages 13–24. Springer-Verlag, 1992.

[Wil88]   David E. Wilkins. *Practical Planning: Extending the Classical AI Planning Paradigm*. Morgan Kaufmann, 1988.

A Calculus for Logical Clustering

Shuo Bai

National Research Center for Intelligent Computing Systems
P. O. Box 2704, Beijing
Beijing 100080, P. R. China
Email: bai@tango.ncic.ac.cn

Abstract

A formal calculus, LC, for logical clustering is proposed in this paper. In addition to conventional first-order logic, a nonmonotonic inference rule for logical clustering is introduced, such that typical forms of induction and analogy are uniformly treated in our theory. Our result shows that the nature of induction and analogy are both "information compression", that is, the merging of indistinguishable logical symbols. Argumentation games for the implementation of LC are also discussed in this paper.

Key words: Nonmomnotonic reasoning, logical clustering, argumentation games.

1. Introduction

Induction and analogy are basic forms of human cognition. They are also important issues of AI reasoning. A lot of works have been done for a formalized theory of induction and analogy. We now try a new approach, that is, logical clustering.

Clustering is well studied in statistics and machine learning. While in those fields, clustering is based on statistical similarities. It seldom carries any logical semantics and is often inaccurate. Therefore, clustering in its traditional sense cannot be used for the formal study of induction and analogy.

By "logical clustering" we mean a process of getting a more "compact and neat" resulting theory from a given theory by merging indistinguishable logical symbols. Such a process interprets any (currently) indistinguishable pair of first-order terms, function symbols or predicate symbols as the same logical objects. We found a pretty fine proof theory based on a specific form of defaults. Some interesting results are obtained.

In Section 2, we introduce our basic system LC. The argumentation game implementation of LC is proposed in Section 3. We conclude our discussion in Section 4.

2. LC: A Calculus for Logical Clustering

2.1 Distinguishable and Indistinguishable Symbols

Let us first consider a simple example.

Suppose that $P(a), \neg P(b), Q(a)$ are known to be true. The question is: which is more believed, $Q(b)$ or $\neg Q(b)$?

Under the framework of traditional deductive logics, none of them can be justified. This is because of the incompleteness of knowledge. But by analogy, the following derivation is natural:

$$\frac{P(a) \qquad \neg P(b)}{\neg Q(b)}$$
$$Q(a)$$

The nature of the above inference is "to assume predicates P and Q to be the same if we can not prove them to be different." Or in our terms, "P and Q are 'compressed' into one cluster because they are indistinguishable."

It can be seen that indistinguishability is the core concept in logical clustering, just like the role 'similarity' plays in statistical clustering. Now let us give rigorous definitions.

Definition 2.1.1 Let α, β be two logical symbols, P be a first-order wff. Define

$$Subs(P, \alpha, \beta)$$

to be the formula obtained by substituting all the occurences of α in P by β, and all the occurences of β in P by α at the same time. $Subs(P, \alpha, \beta)$ is called the *exchange* of α and β in P.

For instance, the following equations hold:

$$Subs(F(a), a, b) = F(b),$$
$$Subs(F(a, b), a, b) = F(b, a),$$
$$Subs(F(c), a, b) = F(c).$$

Definition 2.1.2 Let Γ be any first-order theory, α, β be two logical symbols (individial terms, function symbols or predicates). If there exists a closed first-order wff P such that

$$\Gamma \vdash P,$$
$$\Gamma \vdash \neg Subs(P, \alpha, \beta).$$

then α and β are said to be *distinguishable* under Γ. Otherwise, they are said to be *indistinguishable* under Γ.

The fact that α and β are indistinguishable under Γ is denoted by

$$I(\Gamma, \alpha, \beta).$$

Correspondingly, the fact that α and β are distinguishable under Γ is denoted by

$$\neg I(\Gamma, \alpha, \beta).$$

It is not difficult to prove that I is reflexive and symmetric, but not transitive under given Γ. It is therefore not an equivalence relation. The reason of the phenomena is the incompleteness of knowledge. Our task is to find a meaningful nonmonotonic mechanism which can lead to a status with more complete knowledge and more clear classification, so that the "indistinguishability" relation becomes an equivalence relation. While the conclusions obtained during this process will capture part of the natures of induction and analogy.

2.2 Logical Clustering

Now we are going to construct a formal calculus LC for logical clustering, on the basis of conventional first-order logic. The language of LC is just the first-order language. The inference rules of LC consists of all first-order inference rules and an extra nonmonotonic rule schema for logical clustering. The rule schema is:

$$\frac{\Gamma, I(\Gamma, \alpha, \beta), \neg I(\Gamma \cup \{\neg P\}, \alpha, \beta)}{P} \qquad (LC)$$

where Γ is a set of first-order closed wffs, α, β are logical symbols, and P is a first-order closed wff. The intuitive meaning of (LC) is: "Given Γ, if α and β are indistinguishable under Γ, while introducing the negation of P into Γ will cause α and β distinguishable, then it can be nonmonotonically assumed that P holds."

In fact, our rule schema (LC) can be viewed as a family of defaults. In other words, the formulas obtained by applying (LC) can be successively added back to the original Γ to form an "extension" which is closed under deductive reasoning and logical clustering. The prerequisite for this is that the consistency of Γ will not be violated when the result of applying (LC) rule on a consistent Γ is added to Γ. This is guaranteed by the following theorem:

Theorem 2.2.1 Let Γ be a consistent set of first-order wffs. If

$$I(\Gamma, \alpha, \beta), \neg I(\Gamma \cup \{\neg P\}, \alpha, \beta)$$

then $\Gamma \cup \{P\}$ must be consistent.

Proof

Assume that $\Gamma \cup \{P\}$ is inconsistent, then $\Gamma \vdash \neg P$. Therefore, it naturally follows from $I(\Gamma, \alpha, \beta)$ that $I(\Gamma \cup \{\neg P\}, \alpha, \beta)$. This is contradictory to the known fact, namely, $\neg I(\Gamma \cup \{\neg P\}, \alpha, \beta)$.

¿From the above justification we assert that $\Gamma \cup \{P\}$ must be consistent. This completes our proof.

2.3 LC-Extensions

We now try to define the concept of an LC-extension. Given a set Γ of closed first-order wff, we want to construct a set E such that (i) E contains Γ; (ii) E is closed under deductive reasoning; and (iii) E is closed under logical clustering (i.e., the application of LC rule). Such E can be constructed by the following recursive definitions:

Definition 2.3.1 Let Γ be a consistent set of closed first-order wffs, τ be an operator on wff sets, such that for any set S of first-order wffs, $\tau(S)$ is defined as the smallest set of wffs which satisfies the following properties:

(1) $\Gamma \subseteq \tau(S)$;
(2) If $P \in \tau(S), P \vdash Q$, then $Q \in \tau(S)$;

(3) If $I(S, \alpha, \beta), \neg I(S \cup \{\neg P\}, \alpha, \beta)$. then $P \in \tau(S)$, where α, β are individual terms, function symbols or predicates.

If set E satisfies $\tau(E) = E$, that is, E is a *fixed point* of τ, then E is called an *LC-extension* of Γ.

It is obvious from Theorem 2.2.1 that if Γ is consistent, then any LC-extension E of Γ will also be consistent.

Theorem 2.3.1 Let S be a set of closed first-order wffs, a be an individual term. If $P \in S$, and there is no individual term b such that $\neg Subs(P, a, b) \in S$, then we have $\forall x Subs(P, a, x) \in \tau(S)$.

Proof

Consider the set $W = S \cup \{\neg \forall x Subs(P, a, x)\}$. Because $P \in S$, we have

$$W \vdash P.$$

While

$$W \vdash \exists x \neg Subs(P, a, x)$$
$$\vdash \neg Subs(P, a, h) \qquad h \text{ does not occur in } S$$

we obtain that $\neg I(W, a, h)$. Because h does not occur in S, we further obtain $I(S, a, h)$. By Definition 2.3.1, we have

$$\forall Subs(P, a, x) \in \tau(S).$$

Theorem 2.3.1 captures intuitive inductive reasoning process such as "If a makes P true and there is no b known to make P false, then it can be (non-monotonically) assumed that P holds for all x." In other words, a wide class of inductive reasoning can be completed by applications of LC rule schema. For example, given $\Gamma = \{a, b\}$, the following inference steps are legal:

(1)	$F(a) \vee F(b)$	(Γ)
(2)	$I(\Gamma, a, b)$	(by definition)
(3)	$\neg F(a)$	(assumption)
(4)	$F(b)$	$(1)(3)(\vee_-)$
(5)	$\neg I(\Gamma \cup \{\neg F(a)\}, a, b)$	(by definition)
(6)	$F(a)$	(LC-rule)
(7)	$\forall x F(x)$	(6)(Theorem 2.3.1)

Specifically, when S in Theorem 2.3.1 is exactly an LC-extension of Γ, we have the following property:

Corollary 2.3.1 Let E be an LC-extension of Γ. If $P \in E$, and there is no b such that

$$\neg Subs(P, a, b) \in E,$$

then

$$\forall x Subs(P, a, x) \in E.$$

That is to say, a typical form of inductive reasoning is closed over LC-extensions.

Theorem 2.3.2 Let S be a set of closed first-order wffs, α, β be individuals terms, function symbols or predicates. If $P \in S$, and $I(S, \alpha, \beta)$, then we have $Subs(P, \alpha, \beta) \in \tau(S)$.

Proof

Let $W = S \cup \{\neg Subs(P, \alpha, \beta)\}$. We have

$$W \vdash P, \qquad \text{(because } S \vdash P)$$
$$W \vdash \neg Subs(P, \alpha, \beta),$$

therefore, $\neg I(W, \alpha, \beta)$. By definition, we have $Subs(P, \alpha, \beta) \in \tau(S)$.

Theorem 2.3.2 tells us something about the relation of LC-rule application and analogical reasoning. It says that "Given P. If the up-to-date knowledge cannot tell the differences between α and β, then take them as equal." This is one of the typical forms of analogical reasoning that can be simulated by LC-rule applications. If α and β are terms, the theorem corresponds to *term analogy*; if α and β are function symbols, the theorem corresponds to *function analogy*; if α and β are predicates, the theorem corresponds to *predicate analogy*. Consider the example we discussed in Section 1. Let

$$\Gamma = \{P(a), \neg P(b), Q(a)\},$$

the following inference steps are legal:

(1)	$P(a)$	(Γ)
(2)	$\neg P(b)$	(Γ)
(3)	$Q(a)$	(Γ)
(4)	$I(\Gamma, P, Q)$	(by definition)
(5)	$\neg Q(b)$	(2)(4)(Theorem 2.3.2)

As a special case, let $S = E$ in Theorem 2.3.2, where E is an LC-extension of Γ, the following Corollary is obvious:

Corollary 2.3.2 Let E be an LC-extension of Γ. If $P \in E$, and $I(E, \alpha, \beta)$, then

$$Subs(P, \alpha, \beta) \in E.$$

That is to say, a typical form of analogical reasoning is closed over LC-extensions.

Theorem 2.3.3 Let E be an LC-extension of a given consistent set Γ of first-order wffs, then the indistinguishability relation over E is an equivalence relation.

Proof

We need only to prove the transitivity of the indistinguishability relation over E. Let α, β and γ be arbitrary logical symbols such that:

$$I(E, \alpha, \beta), I(E, \beta, \gamma).$$

Assume that $\neg I(E, \alpha, \gamma)$. By definition, there is a closed formula P such that

$$E \vdash P,$$
$$E \vdash \neg Subs(P, \alpha, \gamma).$$

We are now going to prove that this will lead to a contradiction. In fact, from $I(E, \alpha, \beta)$, we have

$$Subs(P, \alpha, \beta) \in E;$$

from $I(E, \beta, \gamma)$, we have

$$Subs(Subs(P, \alpha, \beta), \beta, \gamma) \in E;$$

again from $I(E, \alpha, \beta)$, we have

$$Subs(Subs(Subs(P, \alpha, \beta), \beta, \gamma), \alpha, \beta) \in E.$$

Notice that

$$Subs(Subs(Subs(P, \alpha, \beta), \beta, \gamma), \alpha, \beta) = Subs(P, \alpha, \gamma),$$

hence

$$E \vdash Subs(P, \alpha, \gamma).$$

This is contradictory to the consistency of E. We can therefore assert $I(E, \alpha, \gamma)$ from $I(E, \alpha, \beta)$ and $I(E, \beta, \gamma)$. This means the transitivity of the indistinguishability relation over E. Thus, it must be an equivalence relation.

Like in default logics, the multi-extension problem exits in LC system as well. Sometimes we have no reason to make choices between conflicting conclusions in different LC-extensions when no more information is given. While the conclusions "agreed" by all LC-extensions are logically significant. In the following subsection we are going to discuss the proof-theoretic properties of such conclusions.

2.4 LC-Entailments

Definition 2.4.1 Let Γ be a consistent set of closed first-order wffs. If P is in all LC-extensions of Γ, then P is said to be *accepted* under Γ. This fact is denoted by $\Gamma \vdash_{LC} P$. We also say that Γ *entails* P in LC.

Let $Acc(\Gamma) = \{P \mid \Gamma \vdash_{LC} P\}$. The foloowing theorems are true:

Theorem 2.4.1 $Acc(\Gamma)$ is deductively closed.

Proof

Obvious.

Theorem 2.4.2 $Acc(\Gamma)$ is nonmonotonic. In other words, there exists $\Gamma_1 \subset \Gamma_2$, such that $Acc(\Gamma_1) \subseteq Acc(\Gamma_2)$ does not hold.

Proof

Let $\Gamma_1 = \{F(a)\}$, $\Gamma_2 = \{F(a), \neg F(b)\}$. By Theorem 2.2.1, we have $\forall x F(x) \in Acc(\Gamma_1)$, while $\forall x F(x) \notin Acc(\Gamma_2)$.

We can thus view LC system as a special form of nonmonotonic logic. It adds a rule schema (LC) to traditional first-order logic for logical clustering, and can perform typical forms of inductive and analogical reasoning.

2.5 Merging

Now let us consider an LC-extension E of Γ. We see that indistinguishable logical symbols are divided into equivalence classes, where the symbols inside one class have exactly the same logical behaviors, so that they can refer to the same semantic entity. We are not going to talk about semantics in this paper. Instead, we will concentrate our attention to the syntactic impact of logical clustering, that is, the *merging* of logical symbols.

Denote the equivalence class containing α by $\overline{\alpha}$. Clearly, any formula can be translated into a "quotient" formula $\overline{P}$ by converting its logical symbols into their corresponding equivalence classes. For instance,

$$\overline{F(a)} = \overline{F}(\overline{a})$$
$$\overline{\forall x F(x)} = \forall x \overline{F}(x)$$

and so on. Similarly, a whole set Γ and its LC-extension E can be translated into corresponding $\overline{\Gamma}, \overline{E}$ as well. Such translations are called the *merging* of logical symbols. Take

$$\Gamma = \{P(a), \neg P(b), Q(a)\}$$

as an example. After an (LC) rule application, $\neg Q(b)$ is added. A set of clusters are then obtained:

$$\overline{P} = \overline{Q} = \{P, Q\}$$
$$\overline{a} = \{a\}$$
$$\overline{b} = \{b\}$$

It is easy to see that the merging of logical symbols leads to the simplification, or (sort of) information compression, of the original theory Γ. This is the very nature of logical clustering, and I think it must be the nature of induction and analogy as well.

3. The Argumentation Games for LC implementation

For a computational model of LC, the requirement of computability is essential. From this point of view, the LC system has two problems:

(1) The relation $I(\Gamma, \alpha, \beta)$ is defined in terms of "unprovability". While just as in default logic or autoepistemic logics, the "unprovability" relation is not effectively computable. Therefore, we often lack sufficient logical reason to decide whether $I(\Gamma, \alpha, \beta)$ holds. It is even more unrealistic to infer such conclusions by a computer.

(2) We are faced with the same sort of difficulties when dealing with $\vdash_{LC}$ relations. A proposition is acceptable under Γ if and only if it belongs to all LC-extensions of Γ. Such a definition is not operational.

The author holds that in commonsense reasoning, "nonmonotonic" implementations is at least as important as "nonmonotonic" definitions. For the difficulties we are faced with, we suggest an argumentation game approach that splits a reasoning mechanism into a "defensive" arguer MAX and "offensive" arguer MIN. In the first problem, MAX assumes that $I(\Gamma, \alpha, \beta)$, and go on reasoning; MIN tries to refute $I(\Gamma, \alpha, \beta)$ by constructing a concrete P such that $\Gamma \vdash P, \Gamma \vdash \neg subs(P, \alpha, \beta)$. If MIN succeeds, the conclusions obtained by MAX after assuming $I(\Gamma, \alpha, \beta)$ are all defeated; otherwise, the conclusions must be (practically) accepted. In our second problem, argumentation games apply as well: MAX proves P in noe LC-extension, while MIN tries to construct another LC-extension in which P does not hold. Our works have shown that such a "reasoning by argueing" approach is very effective in implementations of various kinds of nonmonotonic reasoning, with the cost of disagreement between the output at specific time point and the rigorous theoretical definitions. I don't think such a cost is worthless. In fact, such a cost is completely reasonable with respect to the resource conditions in the situation, though not quite the same with theoretical results. Remember, the theoretical nonmonotonic conclusions are defeasible themselves!

4. Conclusions

So far we have discussed the formal calculus LC for logical clustering, especially its proof theory. We see that by applying the only rule of logical clustering in LC, the mechanism of typical inductive and analogical reasoning can be carried out. Moreover, as the completion of incomplete knowledge, clustering becomes clear and unique. A complex theory is then merged into a compact and neat one. We have thus shown that logical clustering, together with some typical forms of induction and analogy, is a process of information compression in nature, logically corresponds to the merging of logical symbols and the construction of "quotient" theories.

However, as noticed by some of the careful readers of the paper, we did not touch the model-theoretic semantics of LC. This is partly because of the limit of the paper-size and also because of some technical difficulties. We will publish this part of work later.

This paper is supported by the Chinese KR&R Project No. 863-306-05-13B, National High-Tech Program for Intelligent Computing. The author thanks the help and inspirition of many scholars working in the field.

References

S. Bai, Reasoning by Argueing: A Game Theoretic Approach, in *Automated Reasoning*, IFIP Transactions A-19 (Z. Shi Ed.), Elsevier Science Publishers B. V. (NOrth-Holland) 1992, 75-82.

B. Li, Analogical Reasoning: Theory and Implementation. Ph.D. Theses, Beijing Astro. and Aeron. University. 1993.

R. Michalski and R. Stepp, Learning from Observation: Conceptual Clustering, in *Machine Learning*, Vol. 1, Springer Verlag, 1984.

R. Reiter, A Logic for Default Reasoning. *Artificial Intelligence*, **13**(1980) 81-132.

Learning with Higher Order Additional Information[*]

Ganesh Baliga[1] and John Case[2]

[1] Department of Computer Science, Rowan College of New Jersey, Glassboro, NJ 08028, USA
[2] Department of Computer and Information Sciences, University of Delaware, Newark, DE 19716, USA

1 Introduction

[Gol67] studied, among other things, algorithmic learning (in the limit) of decision procedures for languages given informants, i.e., given enumerations of the characteristic functions of the languages. [FW79] shows that learning power is increased if, in addition to the informants, the learning procedures are provided with grammars for the languages.

[CJS92, BCJS94, Vik93] study algorithmic learning (in the limit) of particular kinds of higher order programs[3]. To motivate learning *higher order* programs, [CJS92, BCJS94] show that there are cases where one can algorithmically extract (or prove) some global information about some *computable* object to be learned from suitable higher order programs for it when one cannot do so from ordinary programs. At the end of the second to last paragraph in Section 2.3 below we present an example of relevance to the present paper. In the present paper we consider two particularly natural types of higher order programs, called *lim-grammars* and *lim-decision procedures*, respectively. Intuitively, a *lim-grammar* is an algorithmic procedure for accepting a language, which procedure is allowed to change its mind about acceptance an unspecified but finite number of times. A *lim-decision procedure* is an algorithmic procedure for deciding membership in a language, which procedure is allowed to change its mind about its decisions an unspecified but finite number of times (see Section 2.3 below for rigorous definitions).

We consider herein the four cases of algorithmically learning ordinary decision procedures for recursive languages given

(1) informants for the languages,
(2) informants together with lim-grammars for the languages,
(3) informants together with lim-decision procedures for the languages, and
(4) informants together with ordinary grammars for the languages.

We show, for $1 \leq i \leq 3$, that case $i + 1$ just above yields strictly greater learning power than does case i. We also show the effects on learning power of

---

[*] Email addresses of the authors are baliga@rowan.edu and case@cis.udel.edu.
[3] Intuitively, higher order programs can be thought of as definitions of computable objects *syntactically* higher in, for example, the arithmetical hierarchy [Rog67], than definitions given by ordinary computer programs.

allowing the various ordinary and higher order programs to be slightly anomalous [BB75, CS83, CL82].

We note that in a discrete, initially finite, computable world[4] it *is* possible to have lim-decision procedures and lim-grammars as additional information, but it is *not* possible to have non-computable oracles [AB91, PGJS90, CDF+92, JS93] as additional information.

2 Preliminaries

2.1 Notation

Any unexplained recursion theoretic notation is from [Rog67]. N denotes the set of natural numbers, $\{0, 1, 2, 3, \ldots\}$. Unless otherwise specified, $e, i, j, k, m, n, p, s, w, x, y, z$, with or without decorations[5], range over N. $*$ denotes a non-member of N and is assumed to satisfy $(\forall n)[n < * < \infty]$. a, b and c with or without decorations, ranges over $N \cup \{*\}$. Let

$$n_1 \dot{-} n_2 = \begin{cases} n_1 - n_2, \text{ if } n_1 > n_2; \\ 0, \qquad\quad \text{otherwise.} \end{cases}$$

$\emptyset$ denotes the empty set. $\subseteq$ denotes subset. $\subset$ denotes proper subset. $\supseteq$ denotes superset. $\supset$ denotes proper superset. P and S, with or without decorations, range over sets. $\mathcal{P}(S)$ denotes the power set of S. $\text{card}(S)$ denotes the cardinality of S. For $n \in N$ and sets S_1 and S_2, $S_1 =^n S_2$ means that $\text{card}(\{x \mid x \in S_1 \Delta S_2\}) \leq n$; $S_1 =^* S_2$ means that $\text{card}(\{x \mid x \in S_1 \Delta S_2\})$ is finite. D_x denotes the finite set with canonical index x [Rog67]. We sometimes identify finite sets with their canonical indices. We do this when we consider functions or machines which operate on complete knowledge of a finite set (equivalently, an argument which is a canonical index of the finite set), but when we want to display the argument simply as the set itself. $\uparrow$ denotes undefined. $\max(\cdot), \min(\cdot)$ denote the maximum and minimum of a set, respectively, where $\max(\emptyset) = 0$ and $\min(\emptyset) = \uparrow$. η ranges over *partial* functions with arguments and values from N. $\eta(x)\downarrow$ denotes that $\eta(x)$ is defined; $\eta(x)\uparrow$ denotes that $\eta(x)$ is undefined. f, g and F with or without decorations range over *total* functions with arguments and values from N. $\text{domain}(\eta)$ and $\text{range}(\eta)$ denote the domain and range of the function η, respectively. $\langle i, j \rangle$ stands for an arbitrary, computable, one-to-one encoding of all pairs of natural numbers onto N [Rog67]. Similarly we can define $\langle \cdot, \ldots, \cdot \rangle$ for encoding fixed size tuples of natural numbers one-to-one onto N. φ denotes a fixed *acceptable* programming system for the partial computable functions: $N \to N$ [Rog58, Rog67, MY78]. φ_i denotes the partial computable function computed by program i in the φ-system. Φ denotes an arbitrary fixed Blum complexity measure [Blu67, HU79] for the φ-system. Church's lambda notation

---

[4] Even in a discrete, initially finite, random world with only computable probability distributions for its behavior (e.g., a discrete, initially finite, quantum mechanical world), the *expected* behavior will still be computable [dMSS56] (and constructively so [Gil72, Gil77]).

[5] Decorations are subscripts, superscripts and the like.

is explained in [Rog67]; for example, for each y, $\lambda x.xy + 1$ denotes the function that maps x to $xy + 1$. The set of all total recursive functions of one variable is denoted by $\mathcal{R}$. W_i denotes domain(φ_i). W_i is, then, the r.e. set/language ($\subseteq N$) accepted (or equivalently, generated) by the φ-program (or grammar) i. $\mathcal{E}$ denotes the set of all r.e. languages. L, with or without decorations, ranges over $\mathcal{E}$. For language L, we use χ_L to denote the characteristic function of L. MinGram(L) denotes the min($\{i \mid W_i = L\}$). $\mathcal{L}$, with or without decorations, ranges over subsets of $\mathcal{E}$. $W_i^s \stackrel{\text{def}}{=} \{x \leq s \mid \Phi_i(x) \leq s\}$. **Rec** denotes the set of all recursive languages. We sometimes consider partial computable functions with multiple arguments in the φ system. In such cases we implicitly assume that $\langle \cdot, \ldots, \cdot \rangle$ is used to code the arguments, so, for example, $\varphi_i(x, y)$ stands for $\varphi_i(\langle x, y \rangle)$. The quantifiers '$\stackrel{\infty}{\forall}$', and '$\stackrel{\infty}{\exists}$' essentially from [Blu67], mean 'for all but finitely many' and 'there exist infinitely many', respectively.

2.2 Fundamental Inference Paradigms

A *Learning Machine* (**LM**) [Gol67] is an algorithmic device which takes as its input a set of data given one element at a time, and which from time to time, as it is receiving its input, outputs programs. **LMs** have been used in the study of machine learning or inductive inference of programs for computable functions as well as algorithmic learning of grammars for languages (see, for example, [Gol67, BB75, Wie78, KW80, CS83, AS83, OSW86, CJNM94]). **M**, with or without decorations, ranges over the class of **LMs**. For the learning of a computable function f by an **LM**, **M**, the graph of f is fed to **M** in any order. Without loss of generality [BB75, CS83], we will assume that **M** is fed the graph of f in the sequence $(0, f(0)), (1, f(1)), (2, f(2)), \ldots$. For all computable functions f, $f[n]$ denotes f's finite initial segment $((0, f(0)), (1, f(1)), \ldots, (n - 1, f(n - 1)))$. Let INIT $= \{f[n] \mid f \in \mathcal{R} \wedge n \in N\}$. σ, with or without decorations, ranges over INIT. **M**(σ) is the last output of **M** by the time it receives all of σ. For the learning criteria discussed in this paper, we can and will assume, without loss of generality, that **M**(σ) is always defined. We say that **M**(f) *converges to* i (written: **M**(f)$\downarrow = i$) iff ($\stackrel{\infty}{\forall} n$)[**M**($f[n]$) = i]; **M**(f) is undefined if no such i exists. In this paper, we restrict our study to the inference of characteristic functions. In effect, this study is the study of the learning of recursive languages by machines to whom the graphs of the corresponding characteristic functions are made available. Recall, that according to our convention $a \in N \cup \{*\}$. The following definitions **Ex**^{a} and **Bc**^{a} are essentially restrictions of the general definitions of these learning criteria to the learning of $\{0, 1\}$-valued functions.

Definition 1 [Gol67, BB75, CS83]

(a) **M Ex^a-identifies** a recursive language L (written: $L \in$ **Ex^a(M)**) iff both **M**(χ_L)$\downarrow$ and $\varphi_{\mathbf{M}(\chi_L)} =^a \chi_L$.

(b) **Ex^a** = $\{\mathcal{L} \subseteq$ **Rec** $\mid (\exists \mathbf{M})[\mathcal{L} \subseteq$ **Ex^a(M)**]$\}$.

Case and Smith [CS83] introduced another infinite hierarchy of learning criteria which we describe below. "Bc" stands for *behaviorally correct*. Barzdin [Bar74] essentially introduced the notion $\mathbf{Bc}^0$.

Definition 2 [CS83]

(a) $\mathbf{M}$ $\mathbf{Bc}^a$-*identifies* a recursive language L (written: $L \in \mathbf{Bc}^a(\mathbf{M})$) iff $(\overset{\infty}{\forall} n)[\varphi_{\mathbf{M}(\chi_L[n])} =^a \chi_L]$.

(b) $\mathbf{Bc}^a = \{\mathcal{L} \subseteq \mathbf{Rec} \mid (\exists \mathbf{M})[\mathcal{L} \subseteq \mathbf{Bc}^a(\mathbf{M})]\}$.

We usually write $\mathbf{Ex}$ for $\mathbf{Ex}^0$ and $\mathbf{Bc}$ for $\mathbf{Bc}^0$. Theorem 1 just below states some of the basic hierarchy results about the $\mathbf{Ex}^a$ and $\mathbf{Bc}^a$ classes for the usual definitions of these learning criteria. However, these results hold even for our restricted versions(definitions 1 and 2) of these learning criteria. From now on, we will concern ourselves with Definitions 1 and 2 of $\mathbf{Ex}^a$ and $\mathbf{Bc}^a$ respectively.

Theorem 1. *For all n,*

(a) $\mathbf{Ex}^n \subset \mathbf{Ex}^{n+1}$,
(b) $\bigcup_n \mathbf{Ex}^n \subset \mathbf{Ex}^*$,
(c) $\mathbf{Ex}^* \subset \mathbf{Bc}$,
(d) $\mathbf{Bc}^n \subset \mathbf{Bc}^{n+1}$,
(e) $\bigcup_n \mathbf{Bc}^n \subset \mathbf{Bc}^*$,
(f) $\mathbf{Rec} \notin \mathbf{Bc}^n$ *and*
(g) $\mathbf{Rec} \in \mathbf{Bc}^*$.

Parts $(a), (b), (d), (e)$ and (f) are due to Case and Smith [CS83]. John Steel first observed that $\mathbf{Ex}^* \subseteq \mathbf{Bc}$ and the diagonalization in part (c) is due to Harrington and Case [CS83]. Part (g) is due to Harrington [CS83]. Blum and Blum [BB75] first showed that $\mathbf{Ex} \subset \mathbf{Ex}^*$. Barzdin [Bar74] first showed that $\mathbf{Ex} \subset \mathbf{Bc}$. In the next section, we will consider the inference of recursive languages in the presence of additional information about the languages.

2.3 Higher Order Programs

As noted above in Section 1, for the present paper, we need two kinds of higher order programs: *lim-decision procedures* and *lim-grammars*. First we discuss limiting programs more generally (see also [CJS92, BCJS94]).

For each i, consider the following procedure for "computing" a (partial) function φ_i^*.

On input x
    for $t = 0$ **to** ∞
    Start a new clone of φ-program i running on input (x, t)
    endfor

It should be understood that

(a) each iterate of the **for**-loop finishes since it merely *starts* a process running and

(b) in some iterates of the **for**-loop the process *started* may itself never converge.

$\varphi_i^\star(x) \stackrel{\text{def}}{=}$ the unique y (if any) output by all but finitely many of the clones of φ-program i in the **for**-loop above. Equivalently, $\varphi_i^\star(x) \stackrel{\text{def}}{=} \lim_{t\to\infty} \varphi_i(x,t)$.

We shall refer to i as *lim-program i* (in the $\varphi^\star$-system) when we are thinking of i as encoding the **for**-loop above rather than as encoding φ-program i. Intuitively, lim-program i (in the $\varphi^\star$-system) is a procedure, which on an input for which it has an output, is allowed to change its mind finitely many times about that output (or even about whether to output at all). N.B. There may be no algorithm for signaling when a lim-program has stopped changing its mind about its output.

The partial functions which are the limit of some *total* computable function are known (since Post [Sha71]) to be exactly the partial functions computable relative to an oracle for the halting problem [Sho59, Put65, Gol65, Sho71, Soa87].[6] [LMF76] studied acceptable programming systems for partial functions computable relative to oracles. The results of this paper about lim-programs also hold for programs in acceptable oracular programming systems with oracle for the halting problem attached, but we will present our lim-program results directly about systems such as $\varphi^\star$. *In any case, in the present paper, our results are about lim-programs which happen to compute recursive languages.* As is pointed out in [CJS92, BCJS94], lim-programs for *computable* objects *are* useful: it is, in some cases, possible to prove *global* properties of a *computable* object from a suitable lim-program for it when it is *not* possible to prove these properties from *any* of the ordinary (non mind-changing) programs for it. Here is an example, not from [CJS92, BCJS94], and of relevance to the present paper. We can show there is a lim-program e for deciding membership in some *infinite recursive* language L so that one *can* prove in Peano arithmetic that lim-program e decides an infinite set, *but* one can*not* prove in Peano arithmetic of any *ordinary grammar i for a finite variant of L* that W_i is infinite.

A *lim-decision procedure* is (by definition) a lim-program for a (total) zero-one valued function, i.e., for the characteristic function of some language $\subseteq N$. We let $W_i^\star \stackrel{\text{def}}{=} \text{domain}(\varphi_i^\star)$. A *lim-grammar* for a language L is (by definition) an i such that $W_i^\star = L$.

2.4 Identification With Additional Information

As mentioned in Section 1 above, [FW79] considered algorithmic learning of decision procedures for recursive languages given access to informants and arbitrary grammars for these languages. We generalize their definition in the following.

---

[6] The class of partial functions which are the limit of some *partial* computable function, i.e., $\{\varphi_i^\star \mid i \in N\}$, is a larger class than the class of partial functions computable in the halting problem.

Here and below we sometimes expand the concept (from Section 2.2 above) of *Learning Machines* **M** allowing them to have a second (program) argument.

Definition 3 [FW79]

(a) **M $G^b Ex^a$-identifies** $L \in \mathbf{Rec}$ (written: $L \in G^b Ex^a(\mathbf{M})$) $\Leftrightarrow$ $(\forall i \mid W_i =^b L)$ $[\mathbf{M}(\chi_L, i)\downarrow$ and $\varphi_{\mathbf{M}(\chi_L, i)} =^a \chi_L]$.

(b) $G^b Ex^a = \{\mathcal{L} \in \mathbf{Rec} \mid (\exists \mathbf{M})[\mathcal{L} \subseteq G^b Ex^a(\mathbf{M})]\}$.

(c) **M $G^b Bc^a$-identifies** $L \in \mathbf{Rec}$ (written: $L \in G^b Bc^a(\mathbf{M})$) $\Leftrightarrow$ $(\forall i \mid W_i =^b L)(\overset{\infty}{\forall} n)$ $[\varphi_{\mathbf{M}(\chi_L[n], i)} =^a \chi_L]$.

(d) $G^b Bc^a = \{\mathcal{L} \in \mathbf{Rec} \mid (\exists \mathbf{M})[\mathcal{L} \subseteq G^b Bc^a(\mathbf{M})]\}$.

[FW79] refers to $G^0 Ex^0$ as $\mathbf{GN}^\pi$.

Definition 4 (a) **M $\mathbf{LimD}^b Ex^a$-identifies** $L \in \mathbf{Rec}$ (written: $L \in \mathbf{LimD}^b Ex^a(\mathbf{M})$) $\Leftrightarrow$ $(\forall i \mid \varphi_i^\star =^b \chi_L)$ $[\mathbf{M}(\chi_L, i)\downarrow$ and $\varphi_{\mathbf{M}(\chi_L, i)} =^a \chi_L]$.

(b) **M $\mathbf{LimG}^b Ex^a$-identifies** $L \in \mathbf{Rec}$ (written: $L \in \mathbf{LimG}^b Ex^a(\mathbf{M})$) $\Leftrightarrow$ $(\forall i \mid W_i^\star =^b L)$ $[\mathbf{M}(\chi_L, i)\downarrow$ and $\varphi_{\mathbf{M}(\chi_L, i)} =^a \chi_L]$.

(c) $\mathbf{LimD}^b Ex^a = \{\mathcal{L} \in \mathbf{Rec} \mid (\exists \mathbf{M})[\mathcal{L} \subseteq \mathbf{LimD}^b Ex^a(\mathbf{M})]\}$.

(d) $\mathbf{LimG}^b Ex^a = \{\mathcal{L} \in \mathbf{Rec} \mid (\exists \mathbf{M})[\mathcal{L} \subseteq \mathbf{LimG}^b Ex^a(\mathbf{M})]\}$.

The learning classes $\mathbf{LimD}^b Bc^a$ and $\mathbf{LimG}^b Bc^a$ are defined analogously.

3 Results

It is clear that for all a, b, $Ex^a \subseteq \mathbf{LimG}^b Ex^a \subseteq \mathbf{LimD}^b Ex^a \subseteq G^b Ex^a$. Similar inclusions hold for Bc^a and its variants from the immediately previous section. Also, for $\mathcal{I} \in \{\mathbf{LimG}, \mathbf{LimD}, G\}$ and for all a, $\mathcal{I}^a Ex^\star \subseteq \mathcal{I}^a Bc$.

Theorem 2. *For all i, $Ex^{i+1} - G^0 Ex^i \neq \emptyset$.*

Proof. Let $\mathcal{L}_{i+1} = \{L \mid L \text{ recursive and } \varphi_{\min(\{x \mid x \in L\})} =^{i+1} \chi_L\}$. Clearly $\mathcal{L}_{i+1} \in Ex^{i+1}$. It can be proved that $\mathcal{L}_{i+1} \notin G^0 Ex^i$. We omit details. ∎

Theorem 3. $Bc - G^0 Ex^\star \neq \emptyset$.

Proof. Let $\mathcal{L} = \{L \mid L \text{ is recursive, co-infinite and } (\overset{\infty}{\forall} x \mid x \in \overline{L})[\varphi_x = \chi_L]\}$. Clearly, $\mathcal{L} \in Bc$. It can be proved that $\mathcal{L} \notin G^0 Ex^\star$. We omit details here. ∎

Theorem 4. $Bc^{i+1} - G^0 Bc^i \neq \emptyset$.

Proof. Let $\mathcal{L}_{i+1} = \{L \mid L \text{ is recursive, co-infinite and } (\overset{\infty}{\forall} x \mid x \in \overline{L})[\varphi_x =^{i+1} \chi_L]\}$. Clearly, $\mathcal{L}_{i+1} \in Bc^{i+1}$. It can be proved that $\mathcal{L}_{i+1} \notin G^0 Bc^i$. We omit details here. ∎

Theorem 5. *For all i, j, $\mathrm{Lim}\mathbf{G}^i\mathbf{Ex} - \mathbf{G}^{i+1}\mathbf{Bc}^j \neq \emptyset$.*

Proof. We actually prove a weaker result, namely, for all i, j, $\mathbf{G}^i\mathbf{Ex} - \mathbf{G}^{i+1}\mathbf{Bc}^j \neq \emptyset$. Theorem 5 can be obtained by an interesting modification of this already interesting proof. The proof and its modification each involves infinitary self-reference [Cas94] and a counting argument.

Let $\mathcal{L}_i = \{L \neq \emptyset \mid L \text{ recursive and } (\forall p \mid W_p =^i L)(\exists q \mid \varphi_q = \chi_L)[\lambda y . \varphi_{\min(\{x \mid x \in L\})}(p, y) =^* \lambda y . q]\}$. Clearly, $\mathcal{L}_i \in \mathbf{G}^i\mathbf{Ex}$. We show that for all j, $\mathcal{L}_j \notin \mathbf{G}^{i+1}\mathbf{Bc}^j$. Fix j. Suppose by way of contradiction that $\mathcal{L}_i \in \mathbf{G}^{i+1}\mathbf{Bc}^j(\mathbf{M})$. Then, by the Operator Recursion Theorem [Cas74], there exists programs e_0, e_1 and e_2 and a monotone increasing recursive function p such that $W_{e_0}, \varphi_{e_1}, \varphi_{e_2}$ and $\varphi_{p(i,j)}$, for $i, j \in N$, are defined in stages as follows. We use $W_{e_0,s}$ to denote the part of W_{e_0} enumerated before the start of stage s. $x_{k,s}$ denotes the least x such that $\varphi_{e_1}(k, x)$ is not defined before the start of stage s. For arbitrary k, $W_k^x \overset{\text{def}}{=} \{y \mid y \leq x \wedge \Phi_k(y) \leq x\}$. We use $u_{k,s}$ to denote the smallest u such that nothing is placed in domain($\varphi_{p(k,u)}$) before the start of stage s. Let $W_{e_0,0} = \{e_1\}$. Let

$$\sigma_s(x) \overset{\text{def}}{=} \begin{cases} 0, \text{ if } x \leq \max(W_{e_0,s}) \text{ and } x \notin W_{e_0,s}; \\ 1, \text{ if } x \leq \max(W_{e_0,s}) \text{ and } x \in W_{e_0,s}; \\ \uparrow, \text{ otherwise.} \end{cases}$$

Go to stage 0.

Begin stage s

1. For all $x \in$ domain(σ_s), let $\varphi_{e_2}(x) = \sigma_s(x)$. Dovetail steps 2 and 3 until (if ever) step 2 succeeds, then go to step 4.
2. Search for initial segment $\sigma \supseteq \sigma_s$ and distinct $y_0, y_1, \ldots, y_j$ such that $(\forall x \in$ domain$(\sigma))[\sigma(x) \in \{0,1\}]$ and $(\forall k \leq j)[y_k \notin$ domain$(\sigma) \wedge \varphi_{\mathbf{M}(\sigma, e_0)}(y_k)\downarrow = 0]$.
3. For $k \geq s$, dovetail the execution of substages k.
   Substage k
   3.1 Let

   $$\varphi_{p(k, u_{k,s})}(x) = \begin{cases} 1, \text{ if } x \in W_k^{x_{k,s}}; \\ 0, \text{ otherwise.} \end{cases}$$

   3.2 $x = x_{k,s}$;
   $u = u_{k,s}$;
   repeat
       if $(\exists k' < s)[W_{k'}^x - W_{k'}^{x \dot- 1} \neq \emptyset]$ **then**
           Let $m = 1 + \max(\{\max(W_{k'}^x) \mid (k' < s) \wedge (\mathrm{card}(\{y \in W_{k'}^x \mid y > \max(\mathrm{domain}(\sigma_s))\}) \leq 2i + 2)\})$.
           $u = u + 1$;
           Let

$$\varphi_{p(k,u)}(x) = \begin{cases} \sigma_s(x), & \text{if } x \in \text{domain}(\sigma_s); \\ 1, & \text{if } m \leq x \leq m+i; \\ 0, & \text{otherwise.} \end{cases}$$

    endif

    $\varphi_{e_1}(k, x) = p(k, u);$

    $x = x + 1;$

  forever

4. Enumerate, in increasing order, all the elements in the set $\{x \mid (x \in \text{domain}(\sigma) - \text{domain}(\sigma_s) \wedge \sigma(x) = 1) \vee (\exists k \leq j)[x = y_k$, where y_k was one of the $j + 1$ values found in step 1]$\}$ into W_{e_0}.

  For all $l < s$, let $\varphi_{e_1}(l, x_{l,s}) = e_2$.

  Go to stage $s + 1$

End stage s

Now consider the following cases.

Case 1: All stages terminate.

In this case, let $L = W_{e_0}$. The above construction enumerates the elements of W_{e_0} in increasing order; hence, L is recursive. First we note that in this case φ_{e_1} and φ_{e_2} are total. Also, from the construction, it is clear that $\varphi_{e_2} = \chi_L$. Note now that, for all k, $\lambda x . \varphi_{e_1}(k, x) =^* \lambda x . e_2$. Thus $L \in \mathcal{L}_i$. However, since step 2 succeeds in every stage, it is clear that **M** does not $\mathbf{G}^{i+1}\mathbf{Bc}^j$-identify L.

Case 2: Stage s starts but never finishes.

First note that in this case, W_{e_0} is finite. By the construction in substage k, it is clear that

(a) $(\forall k \geq s)(\exists u)[\varphi_{e_1}^*(k) = p(k, u)]$,

(b) $(\forall k \geq s)[\varphi_{e_1}^*(k)$ is a program which computes the characteristic function of a finite language], and,

(c) $(\forall k, k' \geq s)[\varphi_{e_1}^*(k)$ and $\varphi_{e_1}^*(k')$ compute the same function].

Let L be the language whose characteristic function is computed by $\varphi_{e_1}^*(k)$. From the substaging in step 3 of the above construction, it can be verified that $(\forall k' < s)[L \neq^i W_{k'}]$. It can be verified that $L \in \mathcal{L}_i$! But, $(\forall \sigma \subset \chi_L)[\text{card}(\{y \notin \text{domain}(\sigma) \mid \varphi_{\mathbf{M}(\sigma, e_0)}(y){\downarrow} = 0\}) \leq j]$ (otherwise step 2 would have succeeded, terminating stage s). Thus $L \notin \mathbf{G}^{i+1}\mathbf{Bc}^j(\mathbf{M})$. ∎

Theorem 6. *For all j, $\mathbf{LimD}^0\mathbf{Ex} - \mathbf{LimG}^0\mathbf{Bc}^j \neq \emptyset$.*

Proof. Let $\mathcal{L} = \{L \neq \emptyset \mid (L \text{ recursive}) \wedge (\forall i \mid \varphi_i^* = \chi_L)[\varphi_{\min(L)}^*(i){\downarrow} \wedge \varphi_{\varphi_{\min(L)}^*(i)} = \chi_L]\}$. Clearly $\mathcal{L} \in \mathbf{LimD}^0\mathbf{Ex}$. It can be proved that $\mathcal{L} \notin \mathbf{LimG}^0\mathbf{Bc}^j$. We omit the details. ∎

Theorem 7. *For all j, $\mathbf{G^*Ex} - \mathbf{LimD^0Bc}^j \neq \emptyset$.*

Proof. Let $\mathcal{L} = \{L \mid L$ is recursive, infinite and satisfies the following 2 conditions.

(a) $(\forall x, y, z)[z \in L$ and $\langle x, y \rangle \in W_z \Rightarrow y = \chi_L(x)]$ and

(b) $(\forall x)(\overset{\infty}{\exists} y \in L)[\langle x, \chi_L(x) \rangle \in W_y]$.

}

Clearly, $\mathcal{L} \in \mathbf{G^*Ex}$. Fix j. We sketch an informal proof that $\mathcal{L} \notin \mathbf{LimD^0Bc}^j$. Suppose by way of contradiction that $\mathcal{L} \in \mathbf{LimD^0Bc}^j(\mathbf{M})$. Then, by the Operator Recursion Theorem [Cas74], there exists program e and a strictly increasing recursive function p such that, $\lambda x, t.\varphi_e(x, t)$ and the sets $W_{p(i)}$ may be described in stages as follows. Since p is a strictly increasing recursive function, the predicate '$x \in \mathrm{range}(p)$?' is decidable. Let

$$\sigma_0(x) \overset{\text{def}}{=} \begin{cases} 0 & x < p(0); \\ \uparrow, & \text{otherwise.} \end{cases}$$

Go to stage 0.

Begin stage s

1. For all $x \in \mathrm{domain}(\sigma_s)$, enumerate $\langle x, \sigma_s(x) \rangle$ into $W_{p(s)}$. For all $x \in \mathrm{domain}(\sigma_s)$, let $\varphi_e^*(x) = \sigma_s(x)$. Dovetail steps 2, 3 and 4 until (if ever) step 2 succeeds, then go to step 5.

2. Let f_s be defined by

$$f_s(x) = \begin{cases} \sigma_s(x), & \text{if } x \in \mathrm{domain}(\sigma_s); \\ 1, & \text{if } x \in \mathrm{range}(p) - \mathrm{domain}(\sigma_s); \\ 0, & \text{otherwise.} \end{cases}$$

Look for σ and $j+1$ distinct values $y_0 < y_1 < \ldots < y_j$ such that $\sigma_s \subseteq \sigma \subseteq f$, $\max(\mathrm{domain}(\sigma)) \in \mathrm{range}(p)$, $y_0 > \max(\mathrm{domain}(\sigma) \cup \{p(s)\})$ and, for all $k \leq j$, $y_k \in \mathrm{range}(p)$ and $\varphi_{\mathbf{M}(\sigma, e)}(y_k)\downarrow = 1$.

3. Let $i = s + 1$.
   repeat
   $\quad$ Let $W_{p(i)} = W_{p(i-1)} \cup \{\langle p(i-1), 1 \rangle\} \cup \{\langle x, 0 \rangle \mid p(i-1) < x < p(i)\}$.
   $\quad i = i + 1$.
   forever

4. Extend φ_e at more and more inputs such that, if step 2 does not terminate, $\varphi_e^* = f_s$.

5. Let i_0 be the maximum value such that the **repeat**–loop in step 3 has defined $W_{p(i_0)}$.
   Let $y_{max} = \max(\{y_j, p(i_0+1), \max(\mathrm{domain}(\sigma))\})$. Let $s' = \min(\{s'' \mid p(s'') > y_{max}\})$.
   Let

$$\sigma_{s'}(x) = \begin{cases} \sigma(x), & \text{if } x \in \mathrm{domain}(\sigma); \\ 0, & \text{if } \max(\mathrm{domain}(\sigma)) < x < p(s'); \\ \uparrow, & \text{otherwise} \end{cases}$$

Go to stage s'.
End stage s

Now consider the following cases.
Case 1: Infinitely many stages are executed.

Let $\sigma = \bigcup_{\text{all executed stages } s} \sigma_s$. Let $L = \{x \mid \sigma(x) = 1\}$. From the construction, it is clear that L is infinite (since, for all initiated stages s, $p(s) \in L$). Also, L is recursive since it is clear from the construction that L can be enumerated in increasing order. For all x, the construction ensures that for all elements y of L such that $y > x$, $\langle x, \chi_L(x) \rangle \in W_y$. Thus $L \in \mathcal{L}$. Also, $\varphi_e^\star = \chi_L$. However, in every stage s that was initiated, step 2 succeeds. Thus, **M** does not $\mathbf{LimD^0Bc^j}$-identify L.

Case 2: Stage s starts but never finishes.

Let $L = \{x \mid f_s(x) = 1\}$. As in case 1, it can be easily seen that $L \in \mathcal{L}$. and that $\varphi_e^\star = \chi_L$. But $(\overset{\infty}{\exists} \sigma \mid \sigma_s \subset \sigma \subseteq \chi_L)[\text{card}(\{x \in \text{range}(p) - \text{domain}(\sigma) \mid \varphi_{\mathbf{M}(\sigma)}(x)\downarrow = 1\}) \leq j]$ (Otherwise, step 2 would have succeeded, terminating stage s). Thus **M** does not $\mathbf{LimD^0Bc^j}$-identify $L \in \mathcal{L}$. ∎

4 Future Work

Besides settling the comparisons open in the present paper, it is interesting to study variants of the criteria of the present paper in which the programs to be learned are grammars or higher order programs, in which informants are replaced by texts (positive information only), and/or in which the additional information involves iterating the limits, providing grammars or higher order variants of grammars for the complements of the languages to be learned, and/or (possibly partial) negative information as in [Ful85, BCJ93].

References

[AB91]   L. Adleman and M. Blum. Inductive inference and unsolvability. *Journal of Symbolic Logic*, 56(3):891–900, 1991.

[AS83]   D. Anglin and C. Smith. A survey of inductive inference: Theory and methods. *Computing Surveys*, 15:237–289, 1983.

[Bar74] J. Barzdin. Two theorems on the limiting synthesis of functions. *In Theory of Algorithms and Programs, Latvian State University, Riga*, 210:82–88, 1974.

[BB75]   L. Blum and M. Blum. Toward a mathematical theory of inductive inference. *Information and Control*, 28:125–155, 1975.

[BCJ93] G. Baliga, J. Case, and S. Jain. Language learning with some negative information. In K.W. Wagner P. Enjalbert, A. Finkel, editor, *Proceedings of the 10th Symposium on Theoretical Aspects of Computer Science*, volume 665 of *Lecture Notes in Computer Science*, pages 672–681. Springer-Verlag, Berlin, Würzburg, Germany, February 1993. Journal version to appear in *Journal of Computer and System Sciences*.

[BCJS94] G. Baliga, J. Case, S. Jain, and M. Suraj. Machine learning of higher order programs. *Journal of Symbolic Logic*, 59(2):486–500, 1994.

[Blu67] M. Blum. A machine independent theory of the complexity of recursive functions. *Journal of the ACM*, 14:322–336, 1967.

[Cas74] J. Case. Periodicity in generations of automata. *Mathematical Systems Theory*, 8:15–32, 1974.

[Cas94] J. Case. Infinitary self-reference in learning theory. *Journal of Experimental and Theoretical Artificial Intelligence*, 6:3–16, 1994.

[CDF+92] P Cholak, R. Downey, L. Fortnow, W. Gasarch, E. Kinber, M. Kummer, S. Kurtz, and T. Slaman. Degrees of inferability. In *Proceedings of the Fifth Annual Workshop on Computational Learning Theory, Pittsburgh, PA*, pages 180–192. ACM Press, July 1992.

[CJNM94] J. Case, S. Jain, and S. Ngo Manguelle. Refinements of inductive inference by Popperian and reliable machines. *Kybernetika*, 30:23–52, 1994.

[CJS92] J. Case, S. Jain, and A. Sharma. On learning limiting programs. *International Journal of Foundations of Computer Science*, 3(1):93–115, 1992.

[CL82] J. Case and C. Lynes. Machine inductive inference and language identification. In M. Nielsen and E. Schmidt, editors, *Proceedings of the 9th International Colloquium on Automata, Languages and Programming*, volume 140, pages 107–115. Springer-Verlag, Berlin, 1982.

[CS83] J. Case and C. Smith. Comparison of identification criteria for machine inductive inference. *Theoretical Computer Science*, 25:193–220, 1983.

[dMSS56] E. deLeeuw, C. Moore, C. Shannon, and N. Shapiro. Computability by probabilistic machines. *Automata Studies, Annals of Math. Studies*, 34:183–212, 1956.

[Ful85] M. Fulk. *A Study of Inductive Inference machines*. PhD thesis, SUNY at Buffalo, 1985.

[FW79] R. Freivalds and R. Wiehagen. Inductive inference with additional information. *Electronische Informationverarbeitung und Kybernetik*, 15:179–195, 1979.

[Gil72] J. Gill. *Probabilistic Turing Machines and Complexity of Computation*. PhD thesis, University of California, Berkeley, 1972.

[Gil77] J. Gill. Computational complexity of probabilistic Turing machines. *SIAM Journal on Computing*, 6:675–695, 1977.

[Gol65] E. Gold. Limiting recursion. *Journal of Symbolic Logic*, 30:28–48, 1965.

[Gol67] E. Gold. Language identification in the limit: *Information and Control*, 10:447–474, 1967.

[HU79] J. Hopcroft and J. Ullman. *Introduction to Automata Theory Languages and Computation*. Addison-Wesley Publishing Company, 1979.

[JS93] S. Jain and A. Sharma. On the non-existence of maximal inference degrees for language identification. *Information Processing Letters*, 47–2:81–88, 1993.

[KW80] R. Klette and R. Wiehagen. Research in the theory of inductive inference by GDR mathematicians – A survey. *Information Sciences*, 22:149–169, 1980.

[LMF76] N. Lynch, A. Meyer, and M. Fischer. Relativization of the theory of computational complexity. *Transactions of the American Mathematical Society*, 220:243–287, 1976.

[MY78] M. Machtey and P. Young. *An Introduction to the General Theory of Algorithms*. North Holland, New York, 1978.

[OSW86] D. Osherson, M. Stob, and S. Weinstein. *Systems that Learn, An Introduction to Learning Theory for Cognitive and Computer Scientists*. MIT Press, Cambridge, Mass., 1986.

[PGJS90] M. Pleszkoch, G. Gasarch, S. Jain, and R. Solovay. Learning via queries to an oracle, 1990. Submitted for publication.

[Put65] H. Putnam. Trial and error predicates and the solution to a problem of Mostowski. *Journal of Symbolic Logic*, 30:49–57, 1965.

[Rog58] H. Rogers. Gödel numberings of partial recursive functions. *Journal of Symbolic Logic*, 23:331–341, 1958.

[Rog67]   H. Rogers. *Theory of Recursive Functions and Effective Computability.* Mc-Graw Hill, New York, 1967. Reprinted, MIT Press, 1987.

[Sha71]   N. Shapiro. Review of "Limiting recursion" by E.M. Gold and "Trial and error predicates and the solution to a problem of Mostowski" by H. Putnam. *Journal of Symbolic Logic*, 36:342, 1971.

[Sho59]   J. Shoenfield. On degrees of unsolvability. *Annals of Mathematics*, 69:644–653, 1959.

[Sho71]   J. Shoenfield. *Degrees of Unsolvability.* North-Holland, 1971.

[Soa87]   R. Soare. *Recursively Enumerable Sets and Degrees.* Springer-Verlag, 1987.

[Vik93]   J. Viksna. Weak inductive inference. In J. Shawe-Taylor, editor, *Proceedings of the First European Workshop on Computational Learning Theory.* Oxford University Press, London, University of London, Royal Holloway, December 1993.

[Wie78]   R. Wiehagen. *Zur Theorie der Algorithmischen Erkennung.* 1978. Humboldt-Universität, Berlin.

Efficient Learning of Regular Expressions from Good Examples

Alvis Brāzma and Kārlis Čerāns

Institute of Mathematics and Computer Science, University of Latvia
29 Rainis Blvd., Riga LV-1459, Latvia
E-mail: abrazma@mii.lu.lv, karlis@mii.lu.lv

Abstract. We consider the problem of restoring regular expressions from expressive examples. We define the class of unambiguous regular expressions, the notion of the union number of an expression showing how many union operations can occur directly under any single iteration, and the notion of an expressive example. We present a polynomial time algorithm which tries to restore an unambiguous regular expression from one expressive example. We prove that if the union number of the expression is 0 or 1 and the example is long enough, then the algorithm correctly restores the original expression from one good example. The proof relies on original investigations in theory of covering symbol sequences (words) by different sets of generators. The algorithm has been implemented and we also report computer experiments which show that the proposed method is quite practical.

1 Introduction

Regular languages and regular expressions are among the most fundamental notions of computer science, which have also extensive practical applications. Regular expressions are used in the command repertoire of text editors, as in UNIX grep, and in syntax charts that define the programming languages. There is also direct relation between regular expressions and propositional calculus of programs [9]. Regular expressions are used there to describe the set of all strings corresponding to the computation of a certain program. Efficient inductive inference of regular expressions from examples would therefore help to create program synthesizers synthesizing programs from sample computations.

It is not surprising that inductive inference of regular languages has been intensively studied. In 1967 Gold [10] introduced the notion of identification in the limit and showed that in principle it is possible to identify regular languages from examples, if both positive examples and negative examples (i.e., words not belonging to the languages) are provided. Unfortunately, his algorithm was not very practical as it used exhaustive search. Moreover, in [1] Angluin showed that regular languages are not identifiable in the limit in polynomial time even in representation of deterministic finite state automata (DFA). This and a number of other negative results on efficient learning of regular languages (see [12, 16]) have encouraged researchers to look for new approaches such as introducing queries [1, 2] and learning the language only approximately [7, 18]. The most interesting approach for applications in program synthesis however seems to be restricting the class of target languages for the particular identification algorithm. In 1982 Angluin [3] considered identification of k-reversible languages in DFA representation and showed, that for any particular k the identification is possible in polynomial time from positive examples, and in almost linear time for $k = 0$. More recently, in 1992 [17] Tanida and Yokomori introduced the class of strictly regular languages and showed that they are also identifiable in polynomial time from positive examples in DFA representation. Still, until very recently almost nothing positive has been known about inference of regular languages in regular expression representation. In general the last is more difficult problem since regular expressions are more compact representation of regular languages. Moreover, for applications in program synthesis regular expressions are even more important than DFAs because of the direct relation between them and programming logic [9].

In most of the existing approaches it is assumed that the examples provided to the learner are arbitrary, while in practice a successful teacher is always carefully selecting examples suggesting the features he is trying to teach. Theoretical foundations of learning from good examples has been studied in [11] where some advantages of this approach has been shown.

Intuitively it seems, that learning from good examples should be much easier also in the case of regular languages. As noted in [15], one good example is often enough for making reasonable guesses. For instance, if we are given a word

$$abcabcabcabcabcfdededede, \qquad (1)$$

and we are told that it comes from some simple regular expression, after some consideration we would probably guess the expression:

$$(abc)^* f(de)^*. \qquad (2)$$

Or, if we are given:

$$abxyzxyzabxabxyzabxyzxyzxyzababxyzababxyzababxyzabab, \qquad (3)$$

we would probably guess:

$$(ab \cup xyz)^*. \qquad (4)$$

Such guesses are quite possible even in the cases when the expression has much greater length and *star-height* unless it possesses some complicated "counting" property or is specially tangled to trap us in some other way, which is not a typical case in practical applications. This seems suggesting that the assumption of provided examples being in some way "good", combined with the assumption of target expression belonging to some class of not too complicated expressions, is where a large potential of positive results regarding efficient learning can possibly still be found. In this paper we are exploring one such approach.

The learning of regular expressions from one good example in the case when the expression does not contain union operations has been studied in [6, 7], where an algorithm based on replacing simple "periodic" substrings by iterations is developed. For instance, given example (1), the algorithm finds periodic repetitions *abcabcabc*... and *dedede*... and replaces them by iterations $(abc)^*$ and $(de)^*$, thus obtaining the expression (2). To find the periodic repetitions the algorithm takes every substring α of length 1,2, ... in the example (and in the subsequently obtained intermediate expressions) and checks whether it is within a substring α^k, for some positive integer k. A question arises, how large should be k to imply the substitution of α^* for α^k? In making such decisions it is natural to take the length of the initial example into account: the longer the example X, the greater k should be required to make the substitution. To formalize this approach, a monotonously increasing function ϕ, such that $\phi(x) \in o(x)$, can be used and if $k \geq \phi(|X|)$, the substring α^k is replaced by the iteration, else not. It has been proved in [7] that under certain natural restrictions on the example (i.e., if the example is "good") the function *log* can be used for ϕ. There is a question, whether the same ideas can be used in learning regular expressions containing union operation, for instance containing subexpression (4). In this paper we offer one such generalization.

Note, that the idea on which our approach is based, has little similarity to identification algorithms for DFAs of Angluin [3] and Tanida, Yokomori [17], which are based on merging of equivalent states in DFA constructed to the given moment. Our idea originally comes from inductive synthesis of dot expressions [4, 5].

The paper is organized as follows. In Section 2 we describe our algorithm informally. Then, in Section 3, we give the formal definitions and the main theorems about learning. In Section 4 we present some mathematical results regarding covering strings by different sets of words. In Section 5 we use the results of section 4 to prove the theorems of Section 3. Finally, in Section 6, we touch some possible generalizations of our results.

2 Informal Description of the Learning Algorithm

Let Σ be some finite alphabet, let $\alpha_1, \ldots, \alpha_k$, be nonempty words over the alphabet Σ, and let $A = \{\alpha_1, \ldots, \alpha_k\}$. We say that a word $X \in \Sigma^*$ *can be expressed in a set of generators* A, if there exist $i_1, \ldots, i_n \in \{1, \ldots, k\}$ such that $X = \alpha_{i_1} \ldots \alpha_{i_n}$. We say that X can be *cyclically expressed* in A if there exist $Y \in \Sigma^*$ and $Z \in \Sigma^*$ such that $X = YZ$ and ZY can be expressed in A. $\alpha_1, \ldots, \alpha_k$ are called the *generators*, integer k is the *arity* of A, and $|\alpha_1| + \cdots + |\alpha_k|$ (denoted by $|A|$) the *volume*. n is called the *factor* of the word X represented in A. If, given X, there is a set of k generators in which X can be expressed, we say that X is k-*generable*. For instance, *abababab* is 1-generable and the set of generators is $\{ab\}$. *ababxyzabxyzxyzab* is 2-generable, the set of generators is $\{ab, xyz\}$, and the factor is 7. If $A = \{\alpha_1, \ldots, \alpha_k\}$, $B = \{\beta_1, \ldots, \beta_l\}$ are sets of generators, we say that B is *smaller* (*smaller or equal*) than A, if either $l < k$, or $l \leq k$ and $|B| < |A|$ ($l < k$, or $l \leq k$ and $|B| \leq |A|$, respectively). We denote it by $A < B$ ($A \leq B$, respectively).

The idea of the algorithm is, given an example X of a hypothetical expression E, to look for the smallest sets of generators which can generate some substring Y of X such that the factor of Y is at least $\log|X|$. If such set a of generators $T = \{Z_1, \ldots, Z_m\}$ is found then Y in X is replaced by $(Z_1 \cup \ldots \cup Z_m)^*$. We continue this process until a set of generators with the described property cannot be found. If the length of the obtained string at this point is smaller than $|X|/\log|X|$, we output the obtained string, otherwise we announce failure. For instance, given the example

$$abcbcdebcdeadebcdedebcabcbcbcdededebcabcdebcdedebcgggggg,$$

first we find the substring $gggggg$, which can be generated by $\{g\}$, and replace it by $(g)^*$. We obtain

$$abcbcdebcadebcdedeabcbcbcdeabcdebcde(g)^*$$

Next we find the substring $bcbcdebcde$, which can be generated by the set of generators $\{bc, de\}$, and replace it by $(bc \cup de)^*$. We find three more such substrings and after all the replacements we obtain

$$a(bc \cup de)^* a(bc \cup de)^* a(bc \cup de)^* a(bc \cup de)^*(g)^*.$$

Finally we find that the initial part of the string can be generated by $\{a(bc \cup de)^*\}$, and after the substitution we finally obtain

$$(a(bc \cup de)^*)^*(g)^*.$$

Note the incremental nature of the algorithm. Although it uses exhaustive search for finding subexpressions of the type $(E)^*$, once a subexpression has been found, it is never backtracked.

In the next section we will define the notion of good example, the class of learnable expressions and the algorithm more formally.

3   The Main Result

Since most of the ideas that we propose in this paper show already for regular expressions of star-height 1, for the sake of simplicity we will formulate the results for this class of expressions. Nevertheless, the results may be formulated also for the expressions of arbitrary star-height, and most of the proofs can be generalized stright-forwardly [8]. Let us begin with defining the class of expressions.

A *-term* is any word of the type $(\alpha_1 \cup \ldots \cup \alpha_k)^*$ where $\alpha_1, \ldots, \alpha_k$ are nonempty words over the alphabet Σ. The integer $k - 1$ is called the *union number of the *-term*. *Regular expression of star-height 1* is any word of the type

$$\beta_0 T_1 \beta_1 \ldots \beta_{m-1} T_m \beta_m,$$

where $\beta_0, \ldots, \beta_m$, are words over Σ, and $T_1, \ldots, T_m$ are *-terms. The length of expression E, denoted by $|E|$, is the length of the string of characters encoding the expression. If $T_1, \ldots, T_p$ are all the terms in the expression E, and $n_1, \ldots, n_p$ are the union numbers of $T_1, \ldots, T_k$, then $n = max\{n_1, \ldots, n_p\}$ is called the *union number of the expression*. Thus the union number of expressions without union operations is 0.

In this paper we will mostly deal with the expressions with union number 1 that satisfy some additional conditions. Essentially we want to exclude expressions of the type $(\alpha^k)^*$ for $k > 1$, and $(\alpha_{i_1} \ldots \alpha_{i_k} \cup \alpha_{i_{k+1}} \ldots \alpha_{i_l})^*$, for $k > 1$, $l - (k+1) > 1$, and $i_1, \ldots, i_l \in \{1, 2\}$ (allowing only $(\alpha_1 \cup \alpha_2)^*$). We say that the set of generators $A = \{\alpha_1, \ldots, \alpha_k\}$ is *reducible* to $B = \{\beta_1, \ldots, \beta_l\}$ if $B < A$ and every α_i in A can be expressed in B. We say that A is *cyclically reducible* to B if there exist ρ and $\gamma_1, \ldots, \gamma_k$, such that $\alpha_i = \gamma_i \rho$ or $\alpha_i = \rho \gamma_i$ and the set $\{\rho\gamma_1 \ldots \rho\gamma_k\}$ (or $\{\gamma_1\rho \ldots \gamma_k\rho\}$) is reducible to B. We call a $*$-term $T = (\alpha_1 \cup \ldots \cup \alpha_k)^*$ *cyclically reducible*, if there exist a set B such that the set $\{\alpha_1, \ldots, \alpha_k\}$ (we denote it by $\{T\}$) is cyclically reducible to B. For instance, the $*$-terms $(aa)^*$, $(aa \cup b)^*$ and $(ababcd \cup abcdcd)^*$ are cyclically reducible (to $(a)^*, (a \cup b)^*$ and $(ab \cup cd)^*$, respectively).

Let $T = (\alpha_1 \cup \ldots \cup \alpha_k)^*$ be a $*$-term. An *elementary unfolding with the factor* n $(n \in \mathbf{N})$ of T is a word

$$\alpha_{i_1} \alpha_{i_2} \ldots \alpha_{i_n},$$

where $i_1, \ldots, i_n \in \{1, \ldots, k\}$. A *total unfolding*, or *example* of expression $E = \beta_0 T_1 \beta_1 \ldots \beta_{m-1} T_m \beta_m$ is a word

$$\beta_0 \gamma_1 \beta_1 \ldots \beta_{m-1} \gamma_m \beta_m,$$

where γ_i $(1 \le i \le m)$ is an elementary unfolding of the term T_i. The respective factors $f_1, \ldots, f_n$ of the elementary unfoldings are called the *factors of the unfolding sequence*. Evidently, it is possible to define also *partial unfoldings* of the expression where some $*$-terms may remain unfolded.

Now let us turn to the question what kind of examples can be considered "good" for expressions with unions, for instance for $(ab \cup xyz)^*$? Obviously the example should contain both ab and xyz. Thus, $ababababab$ certainly is not sufficient for guessing the expression. Examples like $abababababxyzxyzxyzxyz$ or $abxyzabxyzabxyzabxyzabxyz$ are also misleading, since they look like suggesting the expressions $(ab)^*(xyz)^*$ and $(abxyz)^*$ respectively. A "good" example should evidently be free of any substring of the type $(\alpha)^k$ for "large" k, since such substrings are suggesting $(\alpha)^*$. To define the notion of good example precisely, we will interpret "large" as at least logarithmic and we define *d-complete* $(0 < d < 1)$ elementary unfolding of a $*$-term with union number 1 as follows. Let γ be elementary unfolding of $(\alpha_1 \cup \alpha_2)^*$ and let the factor of γ be n. We call the unfolding γ d-complete, if γ does not contain any substring of the type β^k for $\beta = \alpha_{i_1} \ldots \alpha_{i_p}$ $(i_j \in \{1, 2\})$ and $k \ge (\log n)^{1-d}$. We say that the example of an expression is *d-complete*, if it can be obtained by d-complete unfoldings of the terms of the expression.

Evidently, if an example is obtained from an expression by some "natural" probabilistic unfolding process (which are picking the elements α_i of $(\alpha_1 \cup \alpha_2)^*$ at random), the example will be d-complete for any $0 < d < 1$ with a large probability which is growing with the length of the example. This is one of the justifications of our definition of good examples.

Now we can formulate the first theorem.

Theorem 1 *Let α_1 and α_2 be words over Σ such that $T = (\alpha_1 \cup \alpha_2)^*$ is not cyclically reducible. Then there exist an algorithm which for any $0 < d < 1$, given a sufficiently long d-complete unfolding X of T finds α_1 and α_2 in time $O(|X|^2|T|/\log|X|)$. If a constant e such that $|T| < e$ is also provided, the run-time of the algorithm is $O(|X| \cdot e^2)$.*

Let us say that a $*$-term $T = (\alpha_1 \cup \ldots \cup \alpha_k)^*$ in an expression $E = E_1 T E_2$ has *ambiguous surroundings*, if either $E_2 = \beta E_2'$ and for some α_i ($i \in \{1, \ldots, k\}$) $\alpha_i = \beta$, or $E_1 = E_1'\beta$, and $\alpha_i = \alpha_i'\alpha_i''$ and $\beta = \alpha_i''$ (α_i' may be empty). For instance, the $*$-term $(ab)^*$ has ambiguous surroundings in expressions $(ab)^*ab$, $ab(ab)^*$ and $b(ab)^*$.

Theorem 2 *Let α_1, α_2, β_1 and β_2 be words over Σ such that $T = (\alpha_1 \cup \alpha_2)^*$ is not cyclically reducible, and the $*$-term T in $\beta_1 T \beta_2$ has not ambiguous surroundings. Then there exist an algorithm which for any $0 < d < 1$, given a sufficiently long d-complete unfolding X of $E = \beta_1 T \beta_2$, finds E in time $O(|X|^2|E|/\log|X|)$. If a constant e such that $|E| < e$ is also provided, the run-time of the algorithm is $O(|X| \cdot e^2)$.*

We call an unfolding X of an expression E *standard*, if for any two terms T_1 and T_2 of E, if T_1 is unfolded in X, but T_2 is not, then $\{T_1\} \geq \{T_2\}$. We say that a term $T = (\alpha_1 \cup \ldots \cup \alpha_k)^*$ of expression $E = E_1 T E_2$ is *ambiguous* if there exists a standard unfolding $X = E_1' T E_2'$ of E, such that T has ambiguous surroundings in X. We call an expression E *ambiguous* if it contains either a cyclically reducible or ambiguous $*$-term. We call an expression *unambiguous* if it is not ambiguous. Note that the size of unambiguous regular expressions and the respective DFAs are not polynomially bounded.

An example X of the elementary expression E is called *c-uniform* ($c \leq 1$), if it can be obtained from E by applying elementary unfoldings with the factors $f_1, \ldots, f_m$ such that $max\{f_i | 1 \leq i \leq m\}/min\{f_i | 1 \leq i \leq m\} \leq c$.

We call the example X *c-d-expressive* if it is c-uniform and d-complete.

The main result of the paper is the proof of the following theorem:

Theorem 3 *Let E be a unambiguous simple expression with the union number $u = 0$ or $u = 1$. Then for any constants $c \geq 1$ and $0 < d < 1$, there exists l, such that for any c-d-expressive example X of E of the length $|X| \geq l$, the algorithm $\mathcal{A}$ of Figure 1 on the input of X outputs the expression E in time $O(|X|^2|E|/\log|X|)$. If a constant e such that $|E| \leq e$ is additionally provided, then the run-time of the algorithm is $O(|X| \cdot e^2)$.*

Note that a similar theorem for the case of union number $u = 0$ has been proved in [7, 6]. We believe that the proof can be generalized also for the case of arbitrary u (see Section 6). Note also that algorithm $\mathcal{A}$ satisfies also Theorems 1 and 2. The idea of algorithm $\mathcal{A}$ is what we described in the previous section. The algorithm uses procedures **learn1** and **learn2**. Given a simple regular expression X and integers p and f_0, **learn$i$**(X, p, f_0, s) $(i = 1, 2)$ finds and replaces by appropriate $*$-terms all i-generable substrings with the generators volume equal to p and factor at lest f_0. The procedure **learn2** is described in Figure 2, the procedure **learn1** can be described in a similar way. If we do not know the constant e (such that the target expression $|E| \leq e$), we take $e = \lceil |X|/log|X| \rceil$.

```
algorithm A(X, e) return expression
      f₀ := ⌈log |X|⌉
      p := 1  q := 2
      while p ≤ e do
            learn1(X, p, f₀)
            p := p + 1
      end
      while q ≤ e do
            learn2(X, p, f₀)
            q := q + 1
      end
      end
      return X
end algorithm
```

Fig. 1. Algorithm $\mathcal{A}$.

The proof of Theorem 3 (the correctness of the algorithm $\mathcal{A}$) relies on combinatorial properties of sequence coverings by different sets of generators. Its main weight is carried by Theorem 4 considered in the next section.

4   Combinatorial Analysis of Sequence Coverings

Let us say that a word X can be *covered* by a generator set $G \subseteq \Sigma^+$ iff for some $Y_1, Y_2 \in \Sigma^*$ the word $Y_1 X Y_2$ can be expressed in G. X is said to be k-freely covered by $G = \{\gamma_1, \gamma_2\}$, if $Y_1 X Y_2$ is expressed in G and it does not contain substrings (i.e. repetitions) of the form δ^k for $\delta \in G^+$.

Given two generator sets $A, B \subset \Sigma^+$ of the same cardinality k we say that A and B are *cyclically equal*, and write $A \doteq B$, if there exist $\rho \in \Sigma^*$ and $\gamma_1, \ldots, \gamma_k$ such that either $A = \{\gamma_1 \rho, \ldots, \gamma_k \rho\}$ and $B = \{\rho\gamma_1, \ldots, \rho\gamma_k\}$, or vice versa: $A = \{\rho\gamma_1, \ldots, \rho\gamma_k\}$ and $B = \{\gamma_1\rho, \ldots, \gamma_k\rho\}$. A set $A \subseteq \Sigma^*$ is said to be *expressed* in $B \subset \Sigma^+$, if every $\alpha \in A$ is expressed in B. $A \subseteq \Sigma^*$ is *cyclically expressed* in B if some $C \doteq A$ is expressed in B. For A (cyclically) expressed in B, we say that A is (cyclically) *reducible* to B, if $B < A$.

```
procedure learn2(X, p, f₀,) return expression
     for p₁ = 1 to p − 1 do
         for i to |X| − p − 1 do
             X₁ := X[i..i + p₁];  X₂ := X[i + p₁ + 1..i + p]
             if X₁ and X₂ are words over Σ then do
                 find the maximal integers l₁ and l₂
                 such that X[j − l₁..j + l₂[ can be generated
                 by the set of generators {X₁, X₂}
                 let f be the factor of X[j − l₁..j + l₂[
                 if f ≥ fₘᵢₙ then do
                     replace X[j − l₁..j + l₂[ in X by
                     (X₁ ∪ X₂)*
                     j := j − l₁ + p + 4
                 end
             end
         end
     end
     return X
end procedure
```

Fig. 2. Procedure `learn2`.

Theorem 4 *Let for two sets of generators $A = \{\alpha_1, \alpha_2\}$ and $B = \{\beta_1, \beta_2\}$ (or $B = \{\beta_1\}$), such that $|A| \geq |B|$, a word $X \in \Sigma^*$ be k-freely covered by A, and covered also by B. If $|X| \geq (2k + 3)|A|^2$, then either $A \doteq B$, or A is cyclically reducible to some $C < A$.*

Proof: We show its principal outline, some details omitted here can be found in [8]. Let us call two words over the given alphabet Σ *prefix independent*, if one is not a prefix of the other.

Lemma 4.1 *Let $A = \{\alpha_1, \alpha_2\}$ and $B = \{\beta_1, \beta_2\}$ be two sets of generators. Let there be two prefix independent words U and V each expressible in both A and B. Then the set of generators $A \cup B$ is expressible in a set $C = \{\gamma_1, \gamma_2\}$ consisting of only two generators.*

Proof: A set of generators $G = \{\gamma_1, \ldots, \gamma_k\}$ is called *prefix unique* (resp. *suffix unique*), if none of the generators γ_i is a prefix (resp. suffix) of the other. It can be shown that for G being either prefix or suffix unique generator set, no word X can be expressed in G in more than one way $X = \gamma_{i_1} \gamma_{i_2} \ldots \gamma_{i_k}$, we denote $Repr(X, G) = \gamma_{i_1} \gamma_{i_2} \ldots \gamma_{i_k}$ [1], and $last(X, G) = \gamma_{i_k}$. We show also the following, later useful, result.

---

[1] $Repr(X, G)$ is read as the *representation* of X in G.

Lemma 4.2 *Let G be a prefix unique set of generators and let for $X, Y \in \Sigma^*$ both X and XY be expressible in G. Then Y is also expressible in G and $Repr(XY, G) = Repr(X, G) \cdot Repr(Y, G) \in G^*$.*

Proof: Let $Repr(XY, G) = \gamma_{i_1} \ldots \gamma_{i_k}$ and $Repr(X, G) = \gamma_{j_1} \ldots \gamma_{j_p}$. Were there some $m \leq p$ such that $\gamma_{i_m} \neq \gamma_{j_m}$, we could take the least such m. Then the shortest of γ_{i_m} and γ_{j_m} were the prefix of the longest, a contradiction. So, $\gamma_{i_m} = \gamma_{j_m}$ for all $m \leq p$, hence $X = \gamma_{i_1} \ldots \gamma_{i_p}$ and $Y = \gamma_{i_{p+1}} \ldots \gamma_{i_k}$, the result follows. $\square$

For a generator set G let us call any tuple $\langle \gamma_1, \ldots, \gamma_s \rangle$ which contains precisely all elements of G, possibly with repetitions ($\gamma_i \in G$ for $i \in \{1, \ldots, s\}$, and, if $\gamma \in G$, then $\gamma = \gamma_i$ for some $i \in \{1, \ldots, s\}$), an *extended representation* of G. If no confusion can arise, we will write $G = \langle \gamma_1, \ldots, \gamma_s \rangle$.

Lemma 4.3 *For any generator set $G = \langle \gamma_1, \ldots, \gamma_k \rangle$ there exists a corresponding prefix unique generator set $G^0 = \langle \gamma_1^0, \ldots, \gamma_k^0 \rangle$ such that*

- *G is expressible in G^0, and,*
- *$last(\gamma_i, G^0) = \gamma_i^0$ for every $i \in \{1, \ldots, k\}$.*

Proof: We start with the list $\langle \gamma_1, \ldots, \gamma_k \rangle$ and transform it in each iteration by picking in it some pair of unequal generators $\langle \mu, \delta \rangle$, which violate the prefix uniqueness due to $\delta\rho = \mu$, $\rho \in \Sigma^+$, and replacing those by $\langle \rho, \delta \rangle$. The termination of the procedure when no such pairs can be found, as well as the prefix uniqueness of the obtained set[2], are straightforward. The equalities $last(\gamma_i, G^0) = \gamma_i^0$ are proved by induction calculating the expressions for all $\gamma_i \in G$ elements in terms of the "intermediate versions" of the transformed list

$$\langle \gamma_1, \ldots, \gamma_k \rangle \rightarrow \cdots \rightarrow \langle \gamma_1^0, \ldots, \gamma_k^0 \rangle.$$

The syntactically last element for the expression of γ_i always remains in the list in the ith place[3]. More details are in [8]. $\square$

It can be shown that for the proof of Lemma 4.1 both generator sets A and B can be safely assumed to be suffix unique[4]. The main step of the proof is to reduce the generator set $A \cup B = \langle \alpha_1, \alpha_2, \beta_1, \beta_2 \rangle$ according to Lemma 4.3 to a prefix unique form

$$C = \langle \alpha_1^0, \alpha_2^0, \beta_1^0, \beta_2^0 \rangle$$

---

[2] We view all equal elements of the final list as the instances of "the same" element of the represented set.

[3] Indeed, if $\gamma_i^m = \gamma_i^m \rho$, then $\gamma_i^{m+1} = \rho$, and for all $i \neq j$ we have $\gamma_i^{m+1} = \gamma_i^m$. The expression for γ_j changes from $\ldots \gamma_i^m$ to $\ldots \gamma_i^m \rho = \ldots \gamma_i^m \gamma_j^{m+1}$. Also for $i \neq j$ the place (the location in the list) for the last element in the expression for γ_i remains unchanged.

[4] A reduction to suffix unique form, as given by Lemma 4.3 for prefix forms, is appropriate to apply, if either A or B initially is not suffix unique. The reducibility relation is transitive.

preserving $\alpha_i^0 = last(\alpha_i, C)$ and $\beta_i^0 = last(\beta_i, C)$. We show that C contains no more than two (different) elements.

First, for $Y \in \{U, V\}$ we let $i(Y)$ and $j(Y)$ be such that $\alpha_{i(Y)} = last(Y, A) \in A$ and $\beta_{j(Y)} = last(Y, B) \in B$. It can be shown that

$$\alpha_{i(Y)}^0 = last(\alpha_{i(Y)}, C) = last(Y, C) = last(\beta_{j(Y)}, C) = \beta_{j(Y)}^0 \ ^5,$$

what in case of either $i(U) \neq i(V)$, or $j(U) \neq j(V)$ completes the proof of the lemma[6].

In case when $i(U) = i(V)$ and $j(U) = j(V)$ let X_A be the longest common suffix of $Repr(U, A)$ and $Repr(V, A)$ (in the alphabet A), and X_B - the longest common suffix of $Repr(U, B)$ and $Repr(V, B)$ (in B). It can be shown (again by Lemma 4.2) that

$$Repr(U, A) = U_A^1 \cdot \alpha_i \cdot X_A \in A^*, \quad Repr(V, A) = V_A^1 \cdot \alpha_j \cdot X_A \in A^*,$$

and

$$Repr(U, B) = U_B^1 \cdot \beta_l \cdot X_B \in B^*, \quad Repr(V, B) = V_B^1 \cdot \beta_s \cdot X_B \in B^*,$$

where $i \neq j$, $l \neq s$, and the Σ^* sequences represented by X_A and X_B have different length[7]. If, for definiteness, $X_A = RX_B$, the second needed equality in C is obtained as

$$\beta_s^0 = last(\beta_s, C) = last(R, C) = last(\beta_l, C) = \beta_l^0. \ \square$$

For the proof of Theorem 4 both given generator sets A and B can safely be assumed being in *initially distinct* form: $\alpha_1[1] \neq \alpha_2[1]$ and $\beta_1[1] \neq \beta_2[1]$[8] (if B is singleton, it is also by definition initially distinct).

---

[5] Let $Y^a \in A^*$ and $Y^b \in B^*$ be such that $Repr(Y, A) = Y^a \cdot \alpha_{i(Y)}$ and $Repr(Y, B) = Y^b \cdot \beta_{j(Y)}$. C is prefix unique, Y, Y^a and Y^b are expressible in C, so by Lemma 4.2

$$Repr(Y, C) = Repr(Y^a, C) \cdot Repr(\alpha_{i(Y)}, C) = Repr(Y^b, C) \cdot Repr(\beta_{j(Y)}, C) \in C^*.$$

[6] Two different equalities $\alpha_{i(U)}^0 = \beta_{j(U)}^0$ and $\alpha_{i(V)}^0 = \beta_{j(V)}^0$ are exhibited in the list $\langle \alpha_1^0, \alpha_2^0, \beta_1^0, \beta_2^0 \rangle$ of 4 elements, so this list contains no more than 2 different elements.

[7] To have the sequences represented by X_A and X_B necessarily being of different length, one needs to make sure that U and V do not have common suffixes which are expressible both in A and B. In case if arbitrarily chosen U and V do not satisfy this property, one can find instead other words ("elementary parts" of the "original" U and V), which would have it, in addition to all other requirements put on U and V.

[8] Let for $A = \{\alpha_1, \alpha_2\}$ ρ be the longest common prefix to α_1 and α_2. If $\rho = \alpha_i$, say $\rho = \alpha_1$, then $\alpha_2 = \alpha_1 \delta$ and A is reducible to $C = \{\alpha_1, \delta\} < A$. Otherwise we let $\alpha_i = \rho \alpha_i^0$ and $A' = \{\alpha_1^0 \rho, \alpha_2^0 \rho\}$. Given that X is k-freely covered by A we get that X is $k+1$-freely covered by A' (covering of X by A' is obtained from the covering by A simply by shifting breakpoints between the A generators $|\rho|$ positions to the right). The "reduction" of B to the initially distinct B' in the case if β_1 is a prefix of β_2 may encounter the situation that B' becomes singleton.

Let the word X be covered in some way by a generator set D. Then any particular position $i \in \{1, \ldots, |X|\}$ is covered by some rth symbol of some generator $\delta_j \in D$. We define $\Delta(i, D) = \langle \delta_j, r \rangle$.

We consider the coverings of X by A and B as in the theorem. Let $\Delta(i) = \langle \Delta(i, A), \Delta(i, B) \rangle$ for any $i \in \{1, \ldots, |X|\}$. We call a position i *initial*, if $\Delta(i) = \langle \langle \alpha_u, 1 \rangle, \langle \beta_v, 1 \rangle \rangle$ for some $\alpha_u \in A, \beta_v \in B$ (intuitively, at this position of X both coverings by A and B start a new generator).

Lemma 4.4 *If for some i, j satisfying $1 \leq i < j \leq |X|$*

- *$\Delta(i) = \Delta(j)$, and*
- *there is no initial $m \in \{i, \ldots, j\}$,*

then $\Delta(m + i) = \Delta(m + j)$ for all $m \geq 0$ such that $m + j \leq |X|$. In particular, there is no initial position $u \in \{i, \ldots, |X|\}$.

Proof sketch: We show by induction on $m \geq 0$ the following assertion: for all $l \in \{0, \ldots, m\}$ both $\Delta(l + i) = \Delta(l + j)$ **and** the position $l + j$ is *not* initial. The case $m = 0$ follows directly from the conditions of the lemma.

For induction step $m \to m+1$, we first show that the position $m+1+j$ is not initial: were it initial, at $X[m + j]$ the last symbols of some generator would appear in both A- and B-coverings. By induction hypothesis, $\Delta(m+j) = \Delta(m+i)$, therefore at $X[m+i]$ both covering generators should also end, what contradicts the fact that $m + i + 1$ is not initial. The equality $\Delta(m + 1 + i) = \Delta(m + 1 + j)$ is now obtained due to initial distinctness of both A and B [9]. $\square$

In order to complete the proof of Theorem 4 let $p_1, p_2, \ldots, p_n$ be all initial positions of X (in increasing order). Whenever there are two different words U and V among $X[p_i..p_{i+1}[$ for $1 \leq i \leq n - 1$, they are prefix incomparable [10]. So, by Lemma 4.1 we get that both A and B can be expressed in some $C = \{\gamma_1, \gamma_2\}$, what means (due to initial distinctness) that either $A = B = C$, or $C < A$.

For the case when all words $X[p_i..p_{i+1}[$ are equal, it can be shown that these words are also equally expressed in A. Since the A-covering of X is k-free [11], the observation that $p_{i+1} - p_i < |A|^2$ (implied by Lemma 4.4 and the fact that there is no more than $|A|^2 - 4$ different "non-initial" values of $\Delta(i)$) gives us the estimate $p_n < (k + 2)|A|^2$. To complete the proof, notice that there should exist $j, j' \in]p_n, p_n + |A|^2]$ such that $j' > j$ and $\Delta(j') = \Delta(j)$. By Lemma 4.4 and the fact that the A-covering of X is k-free we get $|X| < (2k + 3)|A|^2$, what contradicts the given estimate of the length of X. $\square$

---

[9] $m + j + 1$ is not initial. So, at least in one covering set (A or B, say A for definiteness) a single generator covers both $X[m + j]$ and $X[m + 1 + j]$. Hence due to $\Delta(m + i, A) = \Delta(m + j, A)$ we get $\Delta(m + 1 + i, A) = \Delta(m + 1 + j, A)$. Hence we get also $X[m + 1 + j] = X[m + 1 + i]$.
  If in B a new generator starts at $X[m + 1 + j]$ (and, so, also at $X[m + 1 + i]$), we get $\Delta(m + 1 + i, B) = \Delta(m + 1 + j, B)$ by initial distinctness of B.

[10] Observe that this case is not possible, if B is singleton.

[11] We use the estimate of $k + 1$-freeness for the initially distinct form of A.

5   Proof of Correctness of Learning Algorithm

Theorem 4 implies the following result.

Lemma 5.5 *Let $\gamma \in \Sigma^*$ be i-generable word generated by some cyclically irreducible basis A. Let $\delta \in \Sigma^*$ be j-generable word generated by some basis B such that $B < A$. If $i \leq 2$, then for any integer a, and any d such that $0 < d < 1$, there exists an integer l, such that if $|A| \leq a$, $|B| \leq a$, γ is d-complete, and γ and δ intersects on a substring of length l, then $A \doteq B$.*

Proof: We consider two cases: 1) $i = 1$, and 2) $i = 2$. In the first case it follows from the condition that $B < A$ that $j = 1$. Therefore the case $i = 1$ simply follows from [14], where it is proved that if 1-generable words in basis $\{\alpha\}$ and $\{\beta\}$ have a common part of the length at least $|\alpha| + |\beta| - gcd(|\alpha|, |\beta|)$, then they can be also generated by some $\{\omega\}$ such that $|\omega| = gcd(|\alpha|, |\beta|)$. The second case follows from Theorem 4, taking into account that for any $0 < d < 1$: $l/2a^2 - 3/2 > l^{(1-d)}$ for l sufficiently large l. $\square$

Next we will show that it follows from Lemma 5.5 that in long enough c-d-expressive unfolding of unambiguous expression every 1- or 2-generable substring of sufficient factor and with the smallest possible set of generators of some bounded volume is in a sense generated by some ∗-term of the expression. Therefore, the algorithm which is based on replacing the smallest "finitely" generable substrings by appropriate ∗-terms will correctly restore the expression.

We define the *image* of the ∗-term T of expression $E = E_1 T E_2$ in an unfolding X as the substring γ such that $X = X_1 \gamma X_2$, where X_i is an unfolding of E_i $(i = 1, 2)$, and γ is an unfolding of T. Let $X \gamma Z$ be a simple expression and γ be k-generable word in a basis $\{\alpha_1, \ldots, \alpha_k\}$. We call γ *locally maximal* if neither of α_i $(1 \leq i \leq k)$ is suffix of X or prefix of Z. We call γ *locally leftmost* if neither of α_i $(1 \leq i \leq k)$ can be presented in the form $\alpha_i = \alpha_i' \alpha_i''$ such that α_i'' is a suffix of X. Let us note that if expression $E = E_1(\alpha_1 \cup \ldots \cup \alpha_k)^* E_2$ is unambiguous, then the substring $\gamma = \alpha_{i_1} \ldots \alpha_{i_l}$ in the word $E_1 \gamma E_2$ is locally maximal and leftmost. Moreover, if T is an arbitrary term (not necessarily an outermost one) with the union number u of unambiguous expression in a standard form and γ is an image of T in an unfolding X of E, then γ is a locally maximal and leftmost $u + 1$-generable substring of X.

The following simple lemma about images of ∗-terms in c-uniform unfoldings is helpful for proving Theorem 3.

Lemma 5.6 *For every simple expression E and every constant $c \geq 1$ there exist constants $l \in \mathbf{N}$, such that if γ is c-uniform unfolding of E and γ is a substring of X of length $|\gamma| \geq l$, then there exists a term T of E, such that some image of T intersects with γ on a substring of length at least $\log |X|$.*

Now combining lemmas 5.5, 5.6 and the fact that an unfolding of a term of an unambiguous expression is the locally maximal and leftmost substring we can obtain

Lemma 5.7 *For any unambiguous simple expression E in a standard form, and any constants $c \geq 1$, and $0 < d < 1$, there exists an l such that if $X = X_1 \gamma X_2$ is a c-d-expressive standard unfolding of E of length at least l, and γ is the leftmost locally maximal among i-generable ($i \in \{1, 2\}$) substrings with the smallest basis and the factor $f \geq \log l$, then the expression $X' = X_1(T)^* X_2$, where T is the basis of γ, is also a standard c-d-expressive unfolding of E.*

Let us denote by $S^i(\theta)$ the expression which is obtained from word θ by operating algorithm $\mathcal{A}$ after replacing i substrings by $*$-terms by the procedures **learn1** or **learn2**. Now, taking into account the structure of the algorithm we can easily prove by structural induction:

Lemma 5.8 *For any unambiguous simple expression E in a standard form, and any constants $c \geq 1$, $0 < d < 1$, there exists a constant l such that, if θ is c-d-expressive example of E of length at least l, then for every integer $n \geq 0$ there exists a c-d-expressive unfolding F_n of E such that $F_n = S^n(\theta)$.*

Theorem 3 follows easily from Lemma 5.8 by induction.

6 Conclusions

Although, here we are proving the correctness of the learning algorithm only for the case of star-height 1 expressions, it is quite easy to generalize the result for arbitrary star-height. In that case after "synthesizing" all $*$-terms with the union number 1 of the fixed volume the algorithm has to try again for the $*$-terms of union number 0 and greater length. Theorem 4 obviously remains the same, the proofs of the last chapter can be generalized along the lines of [7]. Unfortunately in the case of arbitrary star-height, for the final part of the proof to work, an estimate e such that $|E| \leq e$ is compulsory, although we believe that the theorem is correct even without that condition.

We have proved that a simple and natural learning method based on finding and substituting for appropriate $*$-terms long enough "finitely" generable sequences in minimal basis works for a reasonable class of regular expressions with the union number 0 or 1. Although we have presented our learning algorithm also for larger (arbitrary) union numbers, we have not yet managed to formulate any reasonable theoretical conditions on the formal notion of "good" example and the class of target expressions which would imply its correctness.

In case the union number of the expression is 3 or more, the conditions considered here (c-d-expressiveness of the example and unanbiguousness of the expression to be learned) can be shown insufficient to guarantee the correctness of our algorithm (our hypothesis is that they are sufficient for union number 2). Given the following two expressions $E_1 = (ab \cup db \cup c \cup e)^*$ and $E_2 = (a \cup bd \cup bc \cup e)^*$, it is possible to find an arbitrary long word W which both belongs to $\mathcal{L}(E_1) \cap \mathcal{L}(E_2)$ and does not contain long enough 3-generable subwords[12]. Consequently,

---

[12] Though intutively the word W will not be a typical "arbitrary" word neither in $\mathcal{L}(E_1)$, nor in $\mathcal{L}(E_2)$.

our algorithm, when run on W, will not be able to distinguish between E_1 and E_2, neither it will come up with some other, "smaller" hypothesis. We strongly believe that reasonable conditions to guarantee correctness of our algorithm also for arbitrary union numbers can be found, and consider that to be an apparent direction for the future work.

To obtain a better feeling of the practical limitations of the proposed method we are implementing the algorithm in language C and plan to carry out computer experiments. Presently, only a version of the algorithm which learn expressions with union number 0 and 1 has been implemented. The experiments show that simple regular expressions having the length up to 20 can be learned in fractions of seconds.

Another reason for computer experiments is to evaluate experimentally the necessary length of examples from which successful learning is possible. Presently we have not been able to obtain satisfactory evaluation theoretically. Still, the computer experiments show, that approximately the same length which would be sufficient for a human to guess the correct expression is sufficient also for a computer.

References

1. D.Angluin. *A note on the number of queries to identify regular languages.* Information and Computation, 51:76-87, 1981.
2. D.Angluin. *Learning regular sets from queries and counterexamples.* Information and Computation, 75(2):87-106, 1987.
3. D.Angluin. *Inference of reversible languages,* J.ACM, 29, p.741-765, 1982.
4. J.Barzdin. *Some rules of inductive inference and their use for program synthesis.* In Proc. of IFIP 1983, North Holland, 333-338, 1983.
5. A.Brazma. *Inductive synthesis of dot expressions.* Lecture Notes in Computer Science, 502, 156-212, 1991.
6. A.Brazma. *Learning a subclass of regular expressions by recognizing periodic repetitions.* Proceedings of the Fourth Scandinavian Conference on AI, IOS Press, the Netherlands, 1993, p.236-242.
7. A.Brazma. *Efficient identification of regular expressions from representative examples.* In Proceedings of Sixth Annual Workshop on Compu'.tional Learning Theory COLT'93, ACM press, 1993, p.236-242.
8. A.Brazma, K.Cerans. *Efficient Learning of Regular Expressions from Good Examples.* Technical report, LU-IMCS-TR-CS-94-1, Riga, 1994.
9. R.L.Constable. *The role of fiinite automata in the development of modern computing theory.* In Proc of The Kleene Symposium, North-Holland, 61-83, 1980.
10. E.M.Gold. *Language identification in the limit.* Inform. contr., 10:447-474, 1967.
11. R.Freivalds, E.Kinber, R.Wiehagen. *Inductive inference from good examples.* Lecture Notes in Artificial Intelligence, 397, 1-18, 1989.
12. M.Kearns, L.Valiant. *Cryptographic limitations on learning Boolean formulae and finite automata.* In Proceedings of the 1988 Workshop on Computational Learning Theory, Morgan Kaufman, 359-370, 1988.
13. E.Kinber. *Learning a class of regular expressions via restricted subset queries,* Lecture Notes in Artificial Intelligence, 642, 232-243, 1992.

14. R.C.Lyndon, M.P.Schutzenberger. *The equation $a^M = b^N c^P$ in a free group*, Michigan Math.J. 9, 289-298, 1962.
15. S.Muggleton. *Inductive Acquisition of Expert Knowledge*, Turings Institute Press, 1990.
16. L.Pitt. *Inductive Inference, DFAs, and Computational Complexity.* Lecture Notes in Artificial Intelligence, 397:18-44, Springer-Verlag, 1989
17. N.Tanida, T.Yokomori. *Polynomial-time identification of strictly regular languages in the limit.* IEICE Trans. Inf. & Syst., V E75-D, 1992, 125-132.
18. L.G.Valiant. *A theory of the learnable.* Comm. Assoc. Comp. Mach., 27(11):1134-1142, 1984.
19. R.Wiehagen. *From inductive inference to algorithmic learning.* Proc. Third Workshop on Algorithmic Learning Theory, ALT'92, Sawado, 1992, 13-24.

Identifying Nearly Minimal Gödel Numbers From Additional Information

Rūsiņš Freivalds *
Institute of Mathematics and Computer Science
University of Latvia
Raiņa bulv. 29, LV-1459 Riga, Latvia
e-mail: rusins@mii.lu.lv

Ognian Botuscharov
Department of Computer Science
University of Sofia
Sofia, Bulgaria

Rolf Wiehagen
Department of Computer Science
University of Kaiserslautern
P.O. Box 3049, D-67653 Kaiserslautern, Germany
e-mail: wiehagen@informatik.uni-kl.de

Abstract

A new identification type close to the identification of minimal Gödel numbers is considered. The type is defined by allowing as input both the graph of the target function and an arbitrary upper bound of the minimal index of the target function in a Gödel numbering of all partial recursive functions. However, the result of the inference has to be bounded by a fixed function from the given bound. Results characterizing the dependence of this identification type from the underlying Gödel numbering are obtained. In particular, it is shown that for a wide class of Gödel numberings, the class of all recursive functions can be identified even for "small" bounding functions.

*The research by the first author was supported by Latvian Science Council Grant No.93.599

1 Introduction

We consider inductive inference as introduced in the pioneering paper Gold (1965). Since then many different types of identification have been defined by various authors, cf. Freivalds (1991), for some examples. We follow the idea first used in Freivalds and Wiehagen (1979), namely we consider the inference process where the input data are not only the graph of the target function but also an arbitrary upper bound of the minimal number of the target function. The latter can be considered as additional information in terms of Freivalds and Wiehagen (1979). Intuitively, this kind of additional information can be interpreted as an upper bound on the length of a program of the target function. In a sense, the availability of such an information seems to be realistic. The usefulness of this kind of additional information was made explicit already in Freivalds (1978).

We use the following restriction, however. The result of the inference process has to be smaller or equal to the value of a fixed total recursive function from the additional information. It is obvious that if there is a strategy identifying in the limit the minimal indices for a class U of total recursive functions, then U is identifiable with additional information as well (where the fixed function is the identity function). The results below show that in general this is not so for classes U for which arbitrary indices can be identified in the limit.

The main purpose of this paper is to develop some Gödel numberings in which identification in the limit under the condition mentioned above is possible for the class of *all* general recursive functions. Note that this class is not identifyable in any Gödel numbering without this additional information, cf. Gold (1965).

Let P, R denote the sets of all partial recursive and general recursive functions of one argument. Further let L and M be sets. Then $L \subset M$ denotes the proper inclusion of L in M. For a Gödel numbering $\varphi \in P^2$ of P, cf. Rogers (1987), and $f \in P$ let $\min_\varphi f$ denote the minimal number of f in φ. If $f(x)$ is defined for all $x \leq n$ then $f[n]$ denotes a Cantor number of $(f(0), f(1), \ldots, f(n))$. We say that the sequence of natural numbers $(x_n)_{n \in N}$ converges to x ($x = \lim_n x_n$) if there exists $n_0 \in N$ such that $x_n = x$ for all $n > n_0$. Finally, let $\mathrm{id}(x) = x$ and $\mathrm{id}^2(x) = x^2$ for any $x \in N$.

The following identification types from Gold (1965), Wiehagen (1976) and Freivalds (1991) will serve as a basis for investigation.

Definition 1 *Let $U \subseteq R$ and let φ be any Gödel numbering. U is called identifiable in the limit iff there is a strategy $S \in P$ such that for any $f \in U$,*

1) $S(f[n])$ is defined for all n;

2) $a = \lim_n S(f[n])$ exists;

3) $\varphi_a = f$.

We shall write $U \in GN$.

Definition 2 *Let $U \subseteq R$ and let φ be any Gödel numbering. U is called identifiable in the limit by a consistent strategy iff there is a strategy $S \in P$ such that 1), 2) and 3) hold and further*

4) $\varphi_{S(f[n])}(x) = f(x)$ *for every n and all* $x \leq n$.

We shall write $U \in GN_{cons}$.

Note that Definition 1 and 2 do not depend from the choice of the Gödel numbering φ. In Freivalds and Wiehagen (1979) every upper bound of $min_\varphi f$ is considered as additional information. It was proved that the presence of this additional information can considerably influence the identifiability of function classes. For this purpose the following identification type was introduced.

Definition 3 *Let* $U \subseteq R$ *and let* φ *be any Gödel numbering.* $U \in GN^+$ *iff there is a strategy* $S \in P^2$ *such that for any function* $f \in U$ *and any* $b \geq min_\varphi f$,

1) $S(b, f[n])$ *is defined for all n;*

2) $a = lim_n\, S(b, f[n])$ *exists;*

3) $\varphi_a = f$.

In a similar way one can define GN^+_{cons}.

It was proved that $GN \subset pR$ where pR denotes the power set of R, cf. Gold (1965), and that $GN_{cons} \subset GN$, cf. Wiehagen (1976). The following theorem proved in Freivalds and Wiehagen (1979) leads to a characterization of GN^+ and GN^+_{cons}.

Theorem 1 $R \in GN^+_{cons}$

Consequently, $R \in GN^+$ and $GN^+_{cons} = GN^+ = pR$. Note that these results hold for arbitrary Gödel numberings. However, as it will be clear from the proof of Theorem 1, the Gödel numbers synthesized are in general greater than the given bounds on the corresponding minimal numbers. Therefore the question arises whether the additional information can provide us to construct Gödel numbers which are "small" (smaller than the additional information, possibly modulo a given recursive function). This leads to the definition of the identification type studied in the following.

Definition 4 *Let* $U \subseteq R$, φ *a Gödel numbering and* $h \in R$. $U \in GN^{+,h}_\varphi$ *iff there is a strategy* $S \in P^2$ *such that for all* $f \in U$ *and for all* $b \geq min_\varphi f$.

1) $S(b, f[n]) \leq h(b)$ *for all* $n \in N$;

2) $a = lim_n S(b, f[n])$ *exists;*

3) $\varphi_a = f$.

2   Results

Our main intention is to study the identification type $GN^{+,h}_\varphi$ in dependence on φ and h. The following theorem shows the existence of a Gödel numbering φ such that for every recursive function a φ-number of this function can be identified which is not greater than the given additional information.

Theorem 2 *There is a Gödel numbering φ such that $R \in GN_\varphi^{+,id}$.*

Proof. Let φ' be an arbitrary Gödel numbering of P and Φ' an associated complexity measure in the sense of Blum (1967). Without loss of generality we assume that φ_0' is the empty function.

We construct φ from φ' as follows:

$$\varphi_{n^2} = \varphi_n'$$

If φ proves to be a computable numbering, then φ is a Gödel numbering. Therefore, for every $n \geq 2$, we define a set $A_n = \{\varphi_{n^2-1}, \varphi_{n^2-2}, \ldots, \varphi_{(n-1)^2+1}\}$ of $2n-2$ functions such that the following conditions hold:

1. Each function from A_n is the initial fragment of a general recursive function. This fragment can be either finite, or infinite(total), or even empty. This is achieved by defining $\varphi_i(x+1)$ only after $\varphi_i(x)$ is already defined where $n^2-1 \geq i \geq (n-1)^2+1$ and $x \in N$.

2. For any two nonempty functions from

   $$A_n = \{\varphi_{n^2-1}, \varphi_{n^2-2}, \ldots, \varphi_{(n-1)^2+1}\}$$

   which have different φ-indices, there exists $x \in N$ where the two functions are defined and different.

3. If an initial fragment (finite or infinite) of a general recursive function can be found among $\varphi_0', \varphi_1', \ldots, \varphi_n'$, then it appears in A_n, too. The latter can be achieved by defining $\varphi_{n^2-1}(x+1)$ as the value $\varphi_i'(x+1)$ such that

   (a) $i \leq n$;

   (b) $\varphi_i'[x]$ is computed and $\varphi_i'[x] = \varphi_{n^2-1}[x]$;

   (c) $\Phi_i'(x+1) \leq \Phi_j'(x+1)$ for all j that satisfy conditions (3a) and (3b); if there is more than one such i, we consider the smallest.

   Further we define φ_{n^2-2} in a similar way iff among $\varphi_0', \varphi_1', \ldots, \varphi_n'$ there is an initial fragment that differs from $\varphi_{n^2-1}[x]$ (if there is no such fragment then $\varphi_{n^2-2}[x]$ is the empty function). The function φ_{n^2-3} is defined exactly in this way iff among $\varphi_0', \varphi_1', \ldots, \varphi_n'$ there is an initial fragment that differs from $\varphi_{n^2-1}[x]$ and $\varphi_{n^2-2}[x]$ etc..

Obviously, the definition of φ leads to the following property GR (GR for **general recursive**):

Property GR. If a function from A_n is general recursive, then it must coincide at least with one of the functions $\varphi_0', \varphi_1', \ldots, \varphi_n'$.

Furthermore, it follows from the definition of φ that φ is computable. Hence φ is a Gödel numbering, since the Gödel numbering φ' is reducible to φ.

For the identification in the GN^+–sense we define the strategy S as follows.

$S(b, f[x]) = $ the maximum $k \in N$ such that

- $k \leq b$,

- $k \neq n^2$ for any $n \in N$,

- there is no $y \leq x$ such that $\varphi_k(y)$ is computable within at most x steps and $\varphi_k(y) \neq f(y)$.

In order to prove that for any $f \in R$, S can identify a φ-number of f not greater than $b \geq min_\varphi f$ we distinguish two cases.

Case 1. $b = n^2$ for some n.
If $f = \varphi_{n^2} = \varphi'_n$, then, by the definition of φ, there is exactly one number of the function f among $\varphi_{n^2-1}, \varphi_{n^2-2}, \ldots, \varphi_{(n-1)^2+1}$. S stabilizes on this number.

If $f = \varphi_{l^2} = \varphi'_l$ with $l < n$, then there is again exactly one number of the function f among $\varphi_{n^2-1}, \varphi_{n^2-2}, \ldots, \varphi_{(n-1)^2+1}$ and S stabilizes on it.

If $f \neq \varphi_{l^2}$ for any $l < n$ then $f \neq \varphi_i$ for any $i \leq b$, by Property GR.

Case 2. $(n-1)^2 < b < n^2$ for some n.
The difference to Case 1 consists in that the result of the stabilization does not have to be in segment $(n-1)^2 < i \leq b$. It is possible that it lies in $(n-2)^2 < i < (n-1)^2$. But if an initial fragment is to be found in $(n-2)^2 < i < (n-1)^2$, then it can be found in $(n-1)^2 < i < n^2$, too. However, it does not have to be in $(n-1)^2 < i \leq b$. But then there must be a difference between the functions in $(n-1)^2 < i \leq b$ and those in $b < i < n^2$. Hence an infinite oscillation of the strategy S between the segments $(n-1)^2 < i \leq b$ and $(n-2)^2 < i < (n-1)^2$ is impossible. $\square$

We now consider a special class of Gödel numberings. It was introduced by A.N.Kolmogorov, cf. Kolmogorov (1965) and Schnorr (1974). Therefore a function $h \in R$ is said to be linearly bounded iff there is a constant $c \in N$ such that for any $i \in N$, $h(i) \leq c \cdot i$.

Definition 5 *The Gödel numbering φ is called optimal iff for any Gödel numbering φ', there is a linearly bounded function h such that $\varphi'_i = \varphi_{h(i)}$ for any $i \in N$.*

The optimal Gödel numberings are of particular interest. In fact, all "natural" Gödel numberings turn out to be optimal.

Theorem 3 *There is an optimal Gödel numbering φ such that $R \notin GN_\varphi^{+,id}$.*

Proof. Let φ' be an optimal Gödel numbering of P. We construct the numbering φ in the following way:

$\varphi_{3n} = \varphi'_n$ for all n; hence, if $\varphi \in P^2$ then φ will be an optimal Gödel numbering.

φ_{3n-2} and φ_{3n-1} will be defined by the following construction.

Construction M (M for mistake).

Let $S_0, S_1, S_2, \ldots$ be an effective enumeration of all strategies. We shall make every strategy complete a mistake on a particular constant function. For this purpose let us define the special pair φ_{3n-2} and φ_{3n-1}.

If $\varphi'_n(0) = \varphi_{3n}(0)$ is not defined, then φ_{3n-2} and φ_{3n-1} are defined nowhere.

If $\varphi'_n(0) = a$ then in order to compute the values of these functions, we consider the work of the strategy $S_a(3n-1, a[x])$ with $a[x]$ being the initial fragment of the constant function a and x assuming all the values of the sequence $0, 1, 2, \ldots$.

We define $\varphi_{3n-2}(0) = a$ in the first step, $\varphi_{3n-2}(1) = a$ in the second step, $\varphi_{3n-2}(2) = a$ in the third step, ...

We continue in the same way until for some x it turns out that $S_a(3n-1, a[x]) = 3n-2$. Then we stop defining the function φ_{3n-2} (assume that it was defined up to x_1) and begin to define $\varphi_{3n-2}(0) = a$ in the x_1-th step, $\varphi_{3n-2}(1) = a$ in the $x_1 + 1$-th step, $\varphi_{3n-2}(2) = a$ in the $x_1 + 2$-th step, ...

And so on until $S_a(3n-1, a[x]) = 3n-1$. At this point let φ_{3n-1} be defined up to x_2. Then $\varphi_{3n-2}(x_1 + 1) = a$ in the $x_1 + x_2$-th step, $\varphi_{3n-2}(x_1 + 2) = a$ in the $x_1 + x_2 + 1$-th step, etc. until $S_a(3n-1, a[x]) = 3n-2$.

Then we again stop defining φ_{3n-2} and continue with $\varphi_{3n-1} \ldots$. At least one of these functions receives infinitely many values, becomes the constant function a and, consequently, no stabilization of the strategy S_a on this number can take place. That means that no strategy can identify even the class of all constant functions in the $GN_\varphi^{+,id}$-sense. Actually, assume that S_a is a candidate for such a strategy. Then let n be the smallest number of a function with $\varphi'_n(0) = a$. Let us see what the strategy $S_a(3n-1, a[x])$ does. First, the upper bound $3n-1$ in the new Gödel numbering is correct for the constant function a. Second a stabilization on a number that is smaller or equal to $3n-1$ is impossible (the right number cannot be smaller than $3n-2$, since there, even at zero, the value is different from a.). $\qquad\square$

We now search for "small" functions h such that $R \in GN_\varphi^{+,h}$ for *any* optimal Gödel numbering φ. Note that the Gödel numbering from Theorem 2 where $h = id$ is not an optimal one.

Theorem 4 *For any optimal Gödel numbering φ, there is a constant c such that $R \in GN_\varphi^{+, c \cdot id^2}$.*

Proof. Let φ be any optimal Gödel numbering. Using φ construct a Gödel numbering φ' as in the proof of Theorem 2. Let S' be a strategy such that $R \in GN_{\varphi'}^{+,id}$ by S'. Let $h \in R$ and $c \in N$ be such that for any $i \in N$, $h(i) \leq c \cdot i$ and $\varphi'_i = \varphi_{h(i)}$.

The idea is to identify any $f \in R$ by S' with respect to φ' and to translate the corresponding hypotheses via h into φ. Therefore let $f \in R$ and $b \geq min_\varphi f$. Then, by the properties of φ', $f \in \{\varphi_0, \ldots, \varphi_b\} \subseteq \{\varphi'_0, \ldots, \varphi'_{b^2}\}$. Hence, $b^2 \geq min_{\varphi'} f$. Consequently, by Theorem 2, the sequence $(S'(b^2, f[n]))_{n \in N}$ converges to some $j \in N$ such that $j \leq b^2$ and $\varphi'_j = f$. Hence $\varphi_{h(j)} = f$ and $h(j) \leq c \cdot b^2$.

Now, for any $f \in R$, $n \in N$ and $b \geq min_\varphi f$, define a strategy S as follows:

$$S(b, f[n]) = h(S'(b^2, f[n])).$$

Then, obviously, $R \in GN_\varphi^{+, c \cdot id^2}$ by S. $\qquad\square$

The existence of an optimal Gödel numbering φ such that $R \in GN_\varphi^{+,c\cdot id}$ for a certain constant c is an open problem. Due to Lemma 1 below its positive solution will lead to such a statement for all optimal Gödel numberings.

Lemma 1 *Let φ and ψ be two optimal Gödel numberings. Then, for any function $h \in R$, there are constants c_1 and c_2 such that for the function $h'(b) = c_1 h(c_2 b)$ for all b, $GN_\varphi^{+,h} \subseteq GN_\psi^{+,h'}$ holds.*

Proof. Let $U \in GN_\varphi^{+,h}$ and $f \in U$. Since φ is optimal, it follows the existence of a constant c_2 such that $\{\psi_0, \ldots, \psi_b\} \subseteq \{\varphi_0, \ldots, \varphi_{c_2 b}\}$ for any b. Assume now that $b \geq min_\varphi f$. Consequently, $c_2 b \geq min_\psi f$ and the use of $c_2 b$ as an additional information leads to stabilization on a number smaller or equal to $h(c_2 b)$. A reduction to the optimal Gödel numbering ψ completes the proof with a stabilization on a number smaller or equal to $c_1 h(c_2 b)$. □

Theorem 5 *For any $c \in N$, there is an optimal Gödel numbering φ such that $R \notin GN_\varphi^{+,c\cdot id}$.*

Proof. We use the same technique as in Theorem 3. Now, however, it is $\varphi_{g(c)\cdot n} = \varphi_n'$ with g being a linearly bounded function. This condition ensures the optimality of φ.

$\varphi_{g(c)\cdot(n-1)+1}$ and $\varphi_{g(c)\cdot(n-1)+2}$ are defined with the help of Construction M, cf. Theorem 3.

$\varphi_{g(c)\cdot(n-1)+3}, \ldots, \varphi_{g(c)\cdot n-1}$ are defined as the empty function. Obviously, the class of all constant functions cannot be identified in the $GN_\varphi^{+,c\cdot id}$-sense. □

The problem mentioned above can be solved in case of general Gödel numberings with the help of the following theorem.

Theorem 6 *For any $h \in R$, there is a Gödel numbering φ such that $R \notin GN_\varphi^{+,h}$.*

Proof. Without loss of generality we consider a strictly increasing h. Let φ' be a Gödel numbering of P. We construct a sequence of natural numbers $n_1, n_2, \ldots$ as follows:

$$n_k = \begin{cases} h(2) + 1 & \text{if } k = 1 \\ h(n_{k-1} + 2) + 1 & \text{if } k > 1 \end{cases}$$

A new Gödel numbering φ can be defined in the following way:

1. $\varphi_0 = \varphi_0'$;

2. $\varphi_{n_k} = \varphi_{k-1}'$ for all k;

3. (a) φ_{n_k+1} and φ_{n_k+2} are defined as the empty function if $\varphi_n'(0)$ is not defined;

   (b) φ_{n_k+1} and φ_{n_k+2} are defined from $\varphi_k'(0)$ and $S_{\varphi_k'(0)}$ by means of Construction M, cf. Theorem 3.

4. φ_n is the empty function for all other n.

In the Gödel numbering φ the class of all constant functions cannot be identified in $GN_\varphi^{+,h}$-sense. □

Note that the Gödel numbering from Theorem 6 is not optimal.

The following corollary leads to the solution of our problem for general Gödel numberings.

Corollary 1 *There is a Gödel numbering φ such that $R \notin \bigcup_{c \in N} GN_\varphi^{+,c\cdot id}$.*

We conclude with a result which is in some sense dual to Theorem 6.

Theorem 7 *For any Gödel numbering φ, there is an $h \in R$ such that $R \in GN_\varphi^{+,h}$.*

Proof. Let φ be a Gödel numbering and Φ an associated complexity measure. For any $n \in N$, we uniformly define $n + 1$ φ-programs k_i, $0 \le i \le n$, such that for the set $A_n = \{\varphi_{k_i} | 0 \le i \le n\}$, the following conditions hold.

1. $A_n \cap R = \{\varphi_i | 0 \le i \le n\} \cap R$.

2. If two functions from A_n are both nonempty, then there must be an $x \in N$ such that the two functions are defined on x and their values differ.

3. $\varphi_{k_1}(x + 1)$ is the value of $\varphi_i(x + 1)$ with

   (a) $i \le n$,

   (b) $\varphi_i[x] = \varphi_{k_1}[x]$

   (c) $\Phi_i(x+1) \le \Phi_j(x+1)$ for all j satisfying (3a) and (3b); if there is more than one such i, we consider the smallest one);

   φ_{k_2} is nonempty iff among the $\varphi_0, \ldots, \varphi_n$, there is an initial fragment that is different from φ_{k_1}. φ_{k_3} is nonempty iff among the $\varphi_0, \ldots, \varphi_n$, there is an initial fragment that differs from φ_{k_1} and φ_{k_2} etc..

Let now $h \in R$ be defined as follows:

$$h(n) = max\{k_i | i \le n\} \text{ for any } n \in N.$$

To complete the proof we define the strategy S as follows:

$S(n, f[x]) =$ "By dovetailing search for an $i \le n$ such that $\varphi_{k_i}[x] = f[x]$. Output k_i."

Clearly, if $f \in \{\varphi_0, \ldots, \varphi_n\} \cap R$ then, by conditons (1) and (2), there is exactly one $i \le n$ such that $\varphi_{k_i} = f$. Hence $R \in GN_\varphi^{+,h}$. □

References

Blum, M. (1967), *A machine independent theory of the complexity of recursive functions*. Journal of the Association of Computing Machinery 14, 322-336

Freivalds, R. (1978), *Effective operations and functionals computable in the limit*. Zeitschrift Math. Logik und Grundlagen der Math. 24, 193-206 (in Russian)

Freivalds, R. (1991), *Inductive inference of recursive functions:qualitative theory*. Lecture Notes in Computer Science 502. 77-110

Freivald, R.V.(Freivalds, R.) and Wiehagen, R. (1979), *Inductive inference with additional information*. Journal of Information Processing and Cybernetics 15, 179-185

Gold, E.M. (1965), *Limiting recursion*. Journal of Symbolic Logic 30, 28-48

Kolmogorov, A.N. (1965), *Three approaches to the quantitative definition of information*. Problems Information Transmission 1, 1-7 (translated from Russian)

Rogers, H.Jr. (1987), *Theory of Recursive Functions and Effective Computability*. MIT Press, Cambridge, Massachussetts

Schnorr, C.P. (1974), *Optimal enumerations and optimal Gödel numberings*. Mathematical Systems Theory 8, 182-191

Wiehagen, R. (1976), *Limes-Erkennung rekursiver Funktionen durch spezielle Strategien*. Journal of Information Processing and Cybernetics 12, 93-99

Co–learnability and FIN–identifiability of enumerable classes of total recursive functions *

Rūsiņš Freivalds[†]   Dace Gobleja[‡]   Marek Karpinski[§]
Carl H.Smith[¶]

Abstract

Co-learnability is an inference process where instead of producing the final result, the strategy produces all the natural numbers
but one, and the omitted number is an encoding of the correct
result. It has been proved in [1] that co-learnability of Goedel numbers is equivalent to EX-identifiability. We consider co-learnability
of indices in recursively enumerable (r.e.) numberings. The power
of co-learnability depends on the numberings used. Every r.e. class
of total recursive functions is co-learnable in some r.e. numbering.
FIN-identifiable classes are co-learnable in all r.e. numberings, and
classes containing a function being accumulation point are not co-
learnable in some r.e. numberings. Hence it was conjectured in [1]
that only FIN-identifiable classes are co-learnable in all r.e. numberings. The conjecture is disproved in this paper using a sophisticated
construction by V.L.Selivanov.

* The research of the two first authors was supported by the grant No. 93.599 from
Latvian Science Council. The fourth author is supported, in part, by National Science
Foundation Grant 9301339.

[†] Institute of Mathematics and Computer Science, University of Latvia, Raina
bulv. 29, Riga, Latvia, e-mail: {rusins}@mii.lu.lv

[‡] Institute of Mathematics and Computer Science, University of Latvia, Raina
bulv. 29, Riga, Latvia, e-mail: {dgobleja}@mii.lu.lv

[§] Department of Computer Science, University of Bonn, 53117 Bonn, and the International Computer Science Institute, Berkeley, California. Research supported in
part by the DFG Grant KA 673/4-1, by the ESPRIT BR Grants 7097 and ECUS030,
e-mail: karpinski@cs.bonn.edu

[¶] Department of Computer Science, University of Maryland, College Park, MD,
U.S.A., e-mail: smith@cs.umd.edu

In practical problems of machine learning rather often the learning algorithm starts from a large finite set of possible formulas, refute all of them but one, and produces the remaining one as the final result of the learning process. A natural recursion-theoretical counterpart of this approach was considered in [1] and named co-learning.

We say that a strategy F co-learns τ-indices for U (where τ is a numbering for U or for a superclass of U) if for arbitrary function f in U, the strategy F outputs all natural numbers but one, and the missing one is a correct τ-index for f.

This definition reminds the well-known definition of the finite identification. We say that a partial recursive strategy G FIN-identifies τ-indices for U if for arbitrary function f in U, the strategy G outputs a natural number being a correct τ-index for f.

Since the partial recursive strategy G outputs the result after having seen only a finite initial fragment of the graph of the function f, it is obvious that the FIN-identifiability can be defined in the following way as well, and the two definitions for recursively enumerable classes U are equivalent.

A strategy H FIN-identifies U if for arbitrary function f in U, the strategy G outputs a natural number being a Goedel number of f.

We consider only recursively enumerable classes of total recursive functions in this paper. A class U of total recursive functions is called recursively enumerable if there is a total recursive function of two arguments $\tau(i, x)$ such that

$$U = \{\tau_0, \tau_1, \tau_2, \ldots\} \text{ for } \tau_i(x) = \lambda x\, \tau(i, x).$$

The abovementioned 2-argument function $\tau(i, x)$ provides a recursively enumerable numbering τ for the class U.

For every non-trivial r.e. class U there are very many r.e. numberings, and their properties can essentially differ.

We say that a numbering σ is reducible to the numbering τ of the same class U ($\sigma \leq \tau$) if there is a total recursive function h such that, for arbitrary i, the functions σ_i and $\tau_{h(i)}$ are the same.

Reducibility of the numberings are traditionally interpreted as the existence of a compiler which transforms arbitrary programs in the programming language σ into equivalent programs in the programming language τ.

We consider equivalence of numberings ($\sigma \equiv \tau$) defined as

$$(\sigma \leq \tau) \,\&\, (\tau \leq \sigma).$$

This equivalence implies a relation $\leq$ among eqivalence classes. The set of these equivalence classes with a partiar order $\leq$ is the semi-lattice $L(U)$ of the degrees of the reducibility $\leq$.

For the sequel, it is important to distinguish among the different possibilities of the cardinality of $L(U)$. It was proved in [7] that if $\text{card}(L(U)) > 1$, then $\text{card}(L(U)) = \omega$. This result was later strengthened in [6] proving that for such U the semi-lattice $L(U)$ is not a lattice.

Let φ be an arbitrary Goedel numbering of all the partial recursive functions of 1 argument (a computable numbering φ is called to be a Goedel numbering if arbitrary computable numbering ψ is reducible to φ). Several authors have considered the sets

$$\varphi^{-1}(U) = \{n \mid \varphi_n \in U\}$$

and there complexity in the Kleene-Mostowski hierarchy of sets (see [8], chapter 14 for a complete definition of the hierarchy).

A set B is in the class Π_2^0 of the Kleene-Mostowski hierarchy if there is a total recursive predicate R such that $x \in B$ if and only if $(\forall y)(\exists z)$ $(R(x, y, z)$ is true).

It was proved in [1] that the power of co-learnability of recursively enumerable classes depends very much on the numberings used.

On the one hand, for arbitrary recursively enumerable class U of total recursive functions and arbitrary recyrsively enumerable numbering τ of U, there is an equivalent numbering σ ($\sigma \equiv \tau$) such that σ-indices are co-learnable for U.

On the other hand, there are recursively enumerable classes U and their recursively enumerable numberings τ such that τ-indices are not co-learnable for U. For instance, if U contains a function f, each initial fragment of which is present in a different function $g \in U$ as well, then there is a recursively enumerable numbering τ of U such that τ-indices of U are not co-learnable.

However, if $U \in$ FIN, then U is co-learnable in all the recursively enumerable numberings of U. It was conjectured in [1] that $U \in$ FIN are the only classes with this property. Below we disprove this conjecture using a deep theorem by V.L.Selivanov.

Several authors have considered the complexity of $\varphi^{-1}(U)$. In [2], answering to a problem by A.H.Lachlan [3], V.L.Selivanov proved the following

Theorem 1 *[2] There is a recursively enumerable class A of total recursive functions that:*

1. $card(L(A)) = 1$,

2. $\varphi^{-1}(A)$ *is not in* Π^0_2.

Surprisingly, this theorem contains everything we need to solve the **Open Problem 2** from [1] and to prove

Theorem 2 *There is a recursively enumerable class A of total recursive functions such that:*

1. *A is co-learnable in all recursively enumerable numberings of* τ,

2. *A is not FIN-identifiable.*

The proof is based on the two subsequent lemmas.

Lemma 1 *If a recursively enumerable class A of total recursive functions has the property $card(L(A)) = 1$, then A is co-learnable in every recursively enumerable numbering.*

Proof. We distinguish between two cases.
Case1. The class A is finite.

In this case $A \in$ FIN and the assertion of our Lemma follows from Theorem 2 in [1].

Case 2. The class A is infinite.

In this case we use a construction proposed by Yu.L.Ershow [4]. We construct a one-to-one recursively enumerable numbering σ of A.

Let τ be an arbitrary recursively enumerable numbering of A. We define $\sigma_0(x) = \tau_0(x)$ for all x.

We consider, in parallel, the values of $\tau_i(x)$ for a growing number of various i and x'es. This way, at every particular moment we see whether the functions τ_i and τ_j (for various i, j) have already turned out to be different functions, or not yet. When we find a function τ_k different from $\sigma_0 = \tau_0$, we define $\sigma_1(x) = \tau_k(x)$ for all x.

When we find a function τ_m different from both $\sigma_0(x) = \tau_0(x)$ and $\sigma_1 = \tau_k$, we define $\sigma_2(x) = \tau_m(x)$ for all x, ... This way, we provide exactly one σ-index for every function $\tau_j \in A$. Since A is an infinite class, every number $n \in N$ is a σ-index for a function from A. Finally, there is an algoritm reducing the numbering σ to τ ($\sigma \leq \tau$), or, in other terms, σ turns out to be a recursively enumerable numbering of A.

It follows from the provisions of our Lemma that all the recursively enumerable numberings of A are reducible one to another. Hence $\tau \leq \sigma$. Recall that σ is one-to-one numbering. Hence τ has a decidable equivalece problem for the τ-indices. Hence it follows from Theorem 7 in [1] that A is co-learnable in the numbering τ. $\Box$

Lemma 2 *If a class A of total recursive functions is FIN-identifiable and φ is a Goedel number of all 1-argument partial recursive functions, then $\varphi^{-1}(A)$ is in Π_2^0.*

Proof. Let S denote the strategy FIN-identifying the class A. The property "$n \in A$" can be described in Π_2^0 form as:

$$(\forall x)(\exists k)(\exists a)(\exists t)$$

$\{\,[\,S(< \varphi_n(0), \varphi_n(1), \ldots, \varphi_n(k) >)$ converges in at most t steps of computation (Totalling the computation steps for $\varphi_n(0), \varphi_n(1), \ldots, \varphi_n(k)$ and S) and the result equals a]

$$\&$$

$[\,\varphi_a(x)$ and $\varphi_n(x)$ converge in at most t steps of computation, and the values equal $\varphi_a(x) = \varphi_n(x)]\,\}$.

The reader can easily check that the contents of the brackets is a value of a total recursive predicate of the arguments (n, x, k, a, t). $\Box$

It follows from [5] that this lemma cannot be improved. Namely, if A consists of a single total recursive function (then A is FIN-identifiable), then $\varphi^{-1}(A) \in \Pi_2^0$.

Proof of Theorem 2. Take the class A from Theorem 1. The assertion 1. follows from Lemma 1 and the assertion 2. follows from Lemma 2. $\Box$

Open Problem. Is co-learnability of a recursively enumerable class A of total recursive functions in all the recursively enumerable numberings equivalent to $\mathrm{card}(L(A)) = 1$?

Co-learnability has got already some attention because the seemingly dual types of inductive inference had turned out much more powerful than their counterparts studied earlier (co-FIN seemingly dual to FIN turns out to be equal EX, for Goedel numbers; co-learnability of recursively enumerable classes is always possible in some specific numberings of the classes, ang so on). However, the conjecture disproved in our Theorem 2 asserted that co-learnability equals FIN-identifiability in the worst case. Now when the conjecture is disproved, we have a challenging problem to understand what co-learnability really is compared with FIN-identifiability, and where else co-learnability is more powerful than FIN-identifiability.

References

[1] Freivalds R., Karpinski M., Smith C.H. *Co-learning of total recursive functions*. Accepted at COLT'94.

[2] Selivanov, V.L. *On numberings of families of total recursive functions*. Algebra i Logika, v.15, No.2 (1976), 205-226 (Russian).

[3] Lachlan, A.H. *On the indexing of classes of recursively enumerable sets*. Journal of Symbolic Logic, v.31, No.1 (1966), 10-22.

[4] Ershov, Yu.L. *Numberings of families of total recursive functions*. Sibirskij matematicheskij zhurnal, v.8, No.5 (1967), 1015-1025 (Russian).

[5] Hay, L. *Index sets of finite classes of recursively enumerable sets*. Journal of Symbolic Logic, v.34, No.1 (1969), 39-44.

[6] Marchenkov, S.S. *On computable numberings of families of total recursive functions*. Algebra i Logika, v.11, No.5 (1972), 588-607 (Russian).

[7] Khutoreckij A.B. *On the cardinality of the upper semi-lattice of the computable numberings*. Algebra i Logika, v.10, No.5 (1971), 561-569 (Russian).

[8] Rogers, H.Jr. *Theory of Recursive Functions and Effective Computability*. MIT Press, 1987.

On Case-Based Representability and Learnability of Languages*

Christoph Globig[1] and Steffen Lange[2]

[1]University of Kaiserslautern, P.O. Box 3049, D-67653 Kaiserslautern, Germany
globig@informatik.uni-kl.de
[2]HTWK Leipzig, P.O. Box 66, D-04251 Leipzig, Germany
steffen@informatik.th-leipzig.de

Abstract. Within the present paper we investigate case-based representability as well as case-based learnability of indexed families of uniformly recursive languages. Since we are mainly interested in case-based learning with respect to an arbitrary fixed similarity measure, case-based learnability of an indexed family requires its representability, first.

We show that every indexed family is case-based representable by positive and negative cases. If only positive cases are allowed the class of representable families is comparatively small. Furthermore, we present results that provide some bounds concerning the necessary size of case bases.

We study, in detail, how the choice of a case selection strategy influences the learning capabilities of a case-based learner. We define different case selection strategies and compare their learning power to one another. Furthermore, we elaborate the relations to Gold-style language learning from positive and both positive and negative examples.

1 Introduction

Case-based reasoning is currently a booming subarea of artificial intelligence. In case-based reasoning knowledge is represented by a collection of typical cases in the case base and a similarity measure, instead of using any form of rules or axioms, for example. It is widely accepted that this approach may be considered as an reasonable model of how human experts structure their knowledge. Within case-based reasoning, case-based learning as understood in [1] seems to be of particular interest.

There are three possibilities to improve the knowledge representation in a case-based learning system (cf. [5]). The system can

- store new cases in the case base or remove cases from the case base,
- change the measure of similarity,
- or change both the case base and the similarity measure.

* This work has been supported by the DEUTSCHE FORSCHUNGSGEMEINSCHAFT (DFG) within the project IND-CBL.

In [7] a formalization of case-based learning in an Inductive Inference manner has been introduced. As it turns out case-based learning algorithms are of remarkable power, if effective classifiers should be learned, for instance. This power mainly results from one source, namely the ability of the case-based learner to change the underlying similarity measure within the learning task arbitrarily. Thereby, all knowledge will be more or less directly encoded within the similarity measure, no matter which cases have been stored in the case base. In order to overcome such undesirable encoding tricks we investigate case-based learning under the assumption that the underlying similarity measure cannot be changed during the whole learning task.

On a first glance, this approach seems to be too restrictive. Nevertheless, the results in [8] witness that also under this assumption interesting classes of formal languages are case-based learnable. Since we are mainly interested in investigating the problem of how the choice of a case selection strategy influences the learning capabilities of case-based learners, the above assumption seems to be particularly tailored.

In the sequel we confine ourselves to learning of indexed families of formal languages. Because of the underlying assumption that a case-based learner is not allowed to change its measure of similarity, case-based learnability of an indexed family requires its representability, first. In Section 3 we show that every indexed family is case-based representable by positive and negative cases. If positive cases are allowed, only, the class of representable families is comparatively small. Furthermore, the minimal size of case bases is discussed.

If we have a fixed measure of similarity the learning capability of a case-based learning system depends on the strategy used to select the cases for the case base, only. Section 4 discusses the influence of the following properties a case selection strategy may or may not have:

Access to case history: Is the case selection strategy allowed to store any case that is already presented or has the strategy access to the last one, only?

Deleting cases from the case base: Is the case selection strategy allowed to delete cases from the case base or does the case base grow monotonically?

The different case selection strategies define different types of case-based learning. We elaborate relations between these types of case-based learning and relate them to Gold-style language learning from positive and both positive and negative examples.

2 Preliminaries

The definitions of this section are adapted from the Inductive Inference literature (cf. [2]). Our target objects are (formal) languages over a finite alphabet A. By A^+ we denote the set of all non-empty strings over the alphabet A. Any subset L of A^+ is called a language. We set $\overline{L} = A^+ \setminus L$.

By $\mathbb{N} = \{1, 2, \ldots\}$ we denote the set of all natural numbers. Let $c : \mathbb{N} \times \mathbb{N} \to \mathbb{N}$ denote *Cantor's pairing function*. We use $\mathbb{Q}_{[0,1]}$ to denote the set of all rational numbers between 0 and 1. We write $B \subseteq_{fin} C$, if B is a finite subset of C. Furthermore, by $card(B)$ we denote the cardinality of set B.

There are two basic ways to present information about a language to a learner. We can present positive data only or positive and negative data. These presentations are called *text* and *informant*, respectively. A *text* for a language L is an infinite sequence $t = (s_1, b_1), (s_2, b_2), \ldots$ $((s_j, b_j) \in A^+ \times \{+\})$ such that $\{s_j \mid j \in \mathbb{N}\} = L$. $t[k]$ is the initial sequence $(s_1, b_1), (s_2, b_2), \ldots, (s_k, b_k)$ of t. We set $t^+[k] = \{s_j \mid j \leq k\}$. Let $text(L)$ denote the set of all texts of L. An *informant* for a language L is an infinite sequence $i = (s_1, b_1), (s_2, b_2), \ldots$ $((s_j, b_j) \in A^+ \times \{+, -\})$ such that $\{s_j \mid j \in \mathbb{N}, b_j = +\} = L$ and $\{s_j \mid j \in \mathbb{N}, b_j = -\} = A^+ \backslash L$. $i[k]$ is the initial sequence $(s_1, b_1), (s_2, b_2), \ldots, (s_k, b_k)$ of i. Furthermore, we set $i^+[k] = \{s_j \mid j \leq k, b_j = +\}$ and $i^-[k] = \{s_j \mid j \leq k, b_j = -\}$. By $informant(L)$ we denote the set of all informants of L. Without loss of generality we assume that $t[k]$ $(i[k])$ is a natural number that represents the initial segment of the text (resp. informant).

We restrict ourselves to investigate the learnability of indexed families of recursive languages over A (cf. [2]). A sequence $\mathcal{L} = L_1, L_2, \ldots$ is said to be an *indexed family* if all L_j are non-empty and there is a recursive function f such that for all indices j and all strings $w \in A^+$ holds

$$f(j, w) = \begin{cases} 1 & \text{if } w \in L_j \\ 0 & \text{otherwise} \end{cases}$$

So given an indexed family $\mathcal{L}$ the membership problem is uniformly decidable for all languages in $\mathcal{L}$ by a single function.

IF denotes the set of all indexed families.

The following definition is adapted from [2]. We use $f(x) \downarrow$ to denote that a function f is defined on input x.

Definition 1. Let $\mathcal{L} \in$ **IF**.
Then we say $\mathcal{L}$ is *learnable from text* (resp. *learnable from informant*) iff
$\exists M \in \mathbf{P} \; \forall L \in \mathcal{L} \; \forall t \in text(L)$ (resp. $\forall i \in informant(L)$)

(1) $\forall n \in \mathbb{N} \; M(t[n]) \downarrow$ (*resp.* $\forall n \in \mathbb{N} \; M(i[n]) \downarrow$),
(2) $\lim_{n \to \infty} M(t[n]) = a$ exists (*resp.* $\lim_{n \to \infty} M(i[n]) = a$ exists),
(3) $L_a = L$.

LIM.TXT (**LIM.INF**) is the set of all indexed families that are learnable from text (informant).

P denotes the set of the unary computable functions.

3   Case-Based Representability

This section summarizes the results obtained about case-based representability. First we have to define the language that is described by a set of cases and a similarity measure.[2] $\sigma : A^+ \times A^+ \to \mathbb{Q}_{[0,1]}$ is called a measure of similarity. Σ denotes the set of all totally defined and computable similarity measures. Let $\Sigma_{\{0,1\}} \subseteq \Sigma$ be the subset of all similarity measures that have the range $\{0, 1\}$.

We use the so called standard semantics L_{st} (cf. [8]).

Definition 2. Let $CB \subseteq_{fin} A^+ \times \{+, -\}$ and $\sigma \in \Sigma$ a similarity measure. Furthermore, let $CB^+ := \{s \mid (s, +) \in CB\}$, $CB^- := \{s \mid (s, -) \in CB\}$. Then we say CB and σ describe the language $L_{st}(CB, \sigma) = L_{st}(CB^+, CB^-, \sigma) := \{w \in A^+ \mid \exists c \in CB^+ \ (\sigma(c, w) > 0 \wedge \forall c' \in CB^- \sigma(c, w) > \sigma(c', w))\}$.

Definition 3. Let $\mathcal{L} \in \mathbf{IF}$ and $\sigma \in \Sigma$.
Then, $\mathcal{L} \in \mathbf{REPR}^+(\sigma)$ iff for every $L \in \mathcal{L}$ there is a $CB^+ \subseteq_{fin} L$ such that $L_{st}(CB^+, \emptyset, \sigma) = L$. Moreover, $\mathcal{L} \in \mathbf{REPR}^\pm(\sigma)$ iff for every $L \in \mathcal{L}$ there are $CB^+ \subseteq_{fin} L$ and $CB^- \subseteq_{fin} \overline{L}$ such that $L_{st}(CB^+, CB^-, \sigma) = L$.
Let $\mathbf{REPR}^+ := \bigcup_{\sigma \in \Sigma} \mathbf{REPR}^+(\sigma)$ and $\mathbf{REPR}^\pm := \bigcup_{\sigma \in \Sigma} \mathbf{REPR}^\pm(\sigma)$.

So $\mathcal{L} \in \mathbf{REPR}^+$ ($\mathcal{L} \in \mathbf{REPR}^\pm$) means that there is a σ such that $\mathcal{L} \in \mathbf{REPR}^+(\sigma)$ ($\mathcal{L} \in \mathbf{REPR}^\pm(\sigma)$).

If we allow only positive cases to be stored in the case base, we have the following lemma, which follows directly from Definition 2.

Lemma 4. *For any similarity measure $\sigma \in \Sigma$, there exists a measure $\sigma' \in \Sigma_{\{0,1\}}$ such that $\mathbf{REPR}^+(\sigma) = \mathbf{REPR}^+(\sigma')$.*

Applying the results of [8] we obtain:

Theorem 5. $\mathbf{REPR}^+ \subsetneq \mathbf{IF}$

In [8] it is proved that the family of pattern languages are not representable with positive cases.

On the other hand, it is possible to represent every indexed family if positive and negative cases can be stored within the case base.

Next, we introduce the concept of representative cases for languages. Let $L \subseteq A^+$, $w \in L$, and $\sigma \in \Sigma$. w is said to be a *representative case for L w.r.t. σ* provided that $\sigma(w, v) > 0$ iff $v \in L$. The notion of representative cases will be used subsequently in order to simplify some of the proofs.

---

[2] These definitions are adapted from [7].

Theorem 6. REPR$^{\pm}$ = IF

Proof. Let $\mathcal{L} = L_1, L_2, \ldots$ be an indexed family. Instead of $\mathcal{L}$ we use another enumeration $\tilde{\mathcal{L}}$ which includes the range of $\mathcal{L}$. We set $\tilde{\mathcal{L}} := \tilde{L}_1, \tilde{L}_2, \ldots$ such that for all $j \in \mathbb{N}$, $\tilde{L}_{2j} = L_j$ and $\tilde{L}_{2j-1} = A^+$. Furthermore, let $w_1, w_2, \ldots$ be the lexicographical enumeration of the strings over A^+.

We define the following total recursive function $r : \mathbb{N} \to \mathbb{N}$. Initially, we set $r(1) = 1$. We proceed inductively. Let $i > 1$. We set $r(i) = j$, if j is the least index satisfying $w_i \in \tilde{L}_j$ and $r(k) \neq j$, for all $k < i$.

Since for all $j \in \mathbb{N}$ $\tilde{L}_{2j-1} = A^+$, r is indeed total recursive. If $r(i) = j$, then w_i is a representative case for $\tilde{L}_j$. Moreover, we can easily conclude:

Claim 1: For every $j \in \mathbb{N}$, if $\tilde{L}_j$ is infinite, then there is a $k \in \mathbb{N}$ such that $r(k) = j$.

Now, we use r to define the desired similarity measure σ. Let $k, j \in \mathbb{N}$.

$$\sigma(w_k, w_j) = \begin{cases} 1 & \text{if } w_k = w_j \\ 1 - \frac{1}{k+1} & \text{if } r(k) = l, \ w_j \in \tilde{L}_l \setminus \{w_k\} \\ 0 & \text{otherwise} \end{cases}$$

Claim 2: $\mathcal{L} \in \mathbf{REPR}^{\pm}(\sigma)$.

Let $j \in \mathbb{N}$. First, suppose L_j to be infinite. By Claim 1 there is an $i \in \mathbb{N}$ such that $r(i) = 2j$. Note that $\tilde{L}_{2j} = L_j$. Moreover, $w_i \in \tilde{L}_{2j}$ by construction. Since w_i is a representative case for $\tilde{L}_{2j}$, we obtain $L_{st}(\{w_i\}, \emptyset, \sigma) = \tilde{L}_{2j} = L_j$.

It remains to handle the case that L_j is finite. Now, let $z \in \mathbb{N}$ such that w_z is the maximal element in L_j. By Claim 1 there are infinitely many representative cases for A^+. Hence, there is a $k > z$ such that $r(k) = 2m - 1$ for some $m \in \mathbb{N}$. By the choice of k, $w_k \notin L_j = \tilde{L}_{2j}$. Furthermore, for all $w \in \tilde{L}_{2j}$ and all $v \in A^+ \setminus \{w\}$, it holds $\sigma(w_k, v) > \sigma(w, v)$. Thus, $L_{st}(\tilde{L}_{2j}, \{w_k\}, \sigma) = \tilde{L}_{2j} = L_j$.

Hence, the theorem is proved. $\qquad\square$

As we have seen, every $\mathcal{L} \in \mathbf{REPR}^+$ can be represented by a measure from $\Sigma_{\{0,1\}}$. Recently, Billhardt (cf. [4]) has shown that this results remains valid, if case bases containing both positive and negative cases are admissible. The underlying idea is quite similar to that used in the definition of the representatives in the last proof.

Lemma 7. *For every indexed family $\mathcal{L} \in \mathbf{REPR}^{\pm}$, there exists a $\sigma \in \Sigma_{\{0,1\}}$ such that $\mathcal{L} \in \mathbf{REPR}^{\pm}(\sigma)$.*

Notice that Billhardt's as well as our proof mainly exploit the fact that a case base used in order to represent a language has not necessarily to be computable itself. If we assume that the finiteness of L_j is decidable for all $j \in \mathbb{N}$, then the case bases are computable.

Furthermore, from a practical point of view it seems to be rather natural to choose the corresponding case bases as small as possible. Applying the construction underlying the proof of Theorem 6, at least some finite languages will be represented by putting all their elements into the corresponding case base. As we will see, we can do better.

Theorem 8. *Let $\mathcal{L} \in$ IF. Then there exists a $\sigma \in \Sigma$ such that for every $L \in \mathcal{L}$, there are $CB^+ \subseteq L$ and $CB^- \subseteq \overline{L}$ with $card(CB^+) = 1$ and $card(CB^-) \leq 1$ such that $L_{st}(CB^+, CB^-, \sigma) = L$.*

Proof. We use a slightly modified version of the concept of representatives introduced in the proof of Theorem 6. Let $\mathcal{L} = L_1, L_2, \ldots$ be an indexed family.

In order to obtain the desired result the following similarity measure is used. Again, let $(w_i)_{i \in \mathbb{N}}$ be the lexicographical enumeration of the strings over A^+. Let $j, k \in \mathbb{N}$ and $v \in A^+$.

Case 1: $w_{c(j,k)} \in L_j$.

Then we set:

$$\sigma(w_{c(j,k)}, v) = \begin{cases} 1 & \text{if } w_{c(j,k)} = v \\ 1 - \frac{1}{c(j,k)+2} & v \in L_j \setminus \{w_{c(j,k)}\} \\ \frac{1}{c(j,k)+2} & v \in \overline{L_j} \end{cases}$$

Case 2: $w_{c(j,k)} \notin L_j$.

Now we set:

$$\sigma(w_{c(j,k)}, v) = \begin{cases} 1 & \text{if } w_{c(j,k)} = v \\ 1 - \frac{1}{c(j,k)+2} & v \in \overline{L_j} \setminus \{w_{c(j,k)}\} \\ \frac{1}{c(j,k)+2} & v \in L_j \end{cases}$$

By definition, σ belongs to Σ. Moreover, for every $j, k \in \mathbb{N}$, the string $w_{c(j,k)}$ serves as a representative case for either L_j or $\overline{L_j}$. Now, let $j \in \mathbb{N}$. In order to show that every $L_j \in \mathcal{L}$ can be represented with respect to σ, we distinguish the following cases.

- Case 1: $L_j = A^+$.

  We simply choose $CB^+ = \{w_1\}$ and $CB^- = \emptyset$. By definition, $\sigma(w_1, v) > 0$ for all $v \in A^+$. Thus, $L_{st}(CB^+, CB^-, \sigma) = A^+$.

- Case 2: $L_j \neq A^+$.

  We proceed as follows. Choose any two strings $w_z, w_{\hat{z}}$ satisfying $w_z \in L_j$ and $w_{\hat{z}} \notin L_j$, respectively. Consider the string $w_{c(j,z+\hat{z})}$.

  - Subcase 2.1: $w_{c(j,z+\hat{z})} \in L_j$.

    By definition $w_{c(j,z+\hat{z})}$ is a representative case for L_j. Therefore, set $CB^+ = \{w_{c(j,z+\hat{z})}\}$ and $CB^- = \{w_{\hat{z}}\}$. By definition of σ we have for all $v \in L_j$, $\sigma(w_{c(j,z+\hat{z})}, v) > \sigma(w_{\hat{z}}, v)$ because $c(j, z+\hat{z}) > \hat{z}$ (cf. Case 1 in the definition of σ). On the other hand, applying the same argument yields $\sigma(w_{c(j,z+\hat{z})}, v) < \sigma(w_{\hat{z}}, v)$ for all $v \in \overline{L_j}$. Therefore, $L_{st}(CB^+, CB^-, \sigma) = L_j$.

- Subcase 2.2: $w_{c(j,z+\hat{\imath})} \notin L_j$.
  In contrast to Subcase 2.1, now $w_{c(j,z+\hat{\imath})}$ serves as a representative case for $\overline{L_j}$. Consequently, let $CB^+ = \{w_z\}$ and $CB^- = \{w_{c(j,z+\hat{\imath})}\}$. Finally, $L_{st}(CB^+, CB^-, \sigma) = L_j$ can be shown in a similar manner as above. We omit the details.

By construction we have $card(CB^+) = 1$ and $card(CB^-) \leq 1$ in each of the discussed cases. This finishes the proof. $\qquad\qquad\square$

Again, the corresponding case bases are not computable. Nevertheless, if we can assume that "$L_j =: A^+$" is decidable for all $j \in \mathbb{N}$, the case bases themselves are computable as well.

4 Case-Based Learnability

Based on the representability results of the last section we now study case-based learnability of indexed families.

Definition 9. An indexed family $\mathcal{L}$ is said to be *case-based learnable from text* by the case selection strategy $S : \mathbb{N} \to A^+ \times \{+\}$ iff
$\exists \sigma \in \Sigma \; \forall L \in \mathcal{L} \; \forall t \in text(L)$

  (1) $\forall n \in \mathbb{N} \; CB_n = S(t[n]) \downarrow$, and $S(t[n]) \subseteq t^+[n] \times \{+\}$,

  (2) $CB = \lim_{n \to \infty} CB_n$ exists,

  (3) $L_{st}(CB, \sigma) = L$.

Definition 10. An indexed family $\mathcal{L}$ is said to be *case-based learnable from informant* by the case selection strategy $S : \mathbb{N} \to A^+ \times \{+, -\}$ iff
$\exists \sigma \in \Sigma \; \forall L \in \mathcal{L} \; \forall i \in informant(L)$

  (1) $\forall n \in \mathbb{N} \; CB_n = S(i[n]) \downarrow$, and $S(i[n]) \subseteq (i^+[n] \times \{+\}) \cup (i^-[n] \times \{-\})$,

  (2) $CB = \lim_{n \to \infty} CB_n$ exists,

  (3) $L_{st}(CB, \sigma) = L$.

By our underlying assumption the learner is not allowed to change the measure of similarity during the learning process. Therefore, its learning capability depends on the case selection strategy, only.

Let us first informally describe possible dimensions that characterize our case selection strategies.

Access to case history: Is the case selection strategy allowed to store any case that is already presented or has the strategy access to the last one, only?

Deleting cases from the case base: Is the case selection strategy allowed to delete cases from the case base or does the case base grow monotonically?

With respect to these dimensions we can define types of case selection strategies. Let CB_k be the case base constructed when a learner has seen an initial sequence of length k.

Definition 11. Let S be a case selection strategy. Then S is said to be of type[3] **MO-LC**, **MO-RA**, **DE-LC**, and **DE-RA**, respectively, iff the corresponding condition holds for all $k \in \mathbb{N}$ ($CB_0 := \emptyset$).

MO-LC	$CB_{k-1} \subseteq CB_k \subseteq CB_{k-1} \cup \{(s_k, b_k)\}$
MO-RA	$CB_{k-1} \subseteq CB_k \subseteq \{(s_1, b_1), \dots, (s_k, b_k)\}$
DE-LC	$CB_k \subseteq CB_{k-1} \cup \{(s_k, b_k)\}$
DE-RA	$CB_k \subseteq \{(s_1, b_1), \dots, (s_k, b_k)\}$

We use these abbreviations as prefixes to **CBL.TXT** and **CBL.INF**. For example, $\mathcal{L} \in$ **DE-RA-CBL.TXT** means that there is a case selection strategy $S \in$ **DE-RA** such that $\mathcal{L}$ can be learned by S in the sense of Definition 9.

Strategies of type **MO-RA** and **DE-RA**, respectively, may store multiple cases in a single learning step. If we demand that strategies of both types store at most a single case in every learning step their learning capabilities will not change.

Because many existing systems simply collect all presented cases, we model this approach, too. A case selection strategy S is said to be of type[4] **CA**, if $CB_k = \{(s_j, b_j) \mid j \leq k\}$ for all $k \in \mathbb{N}$.

It is possible that a **CA-CBL.TXT**-strategy leads to a case base of infinite size, for instance, if the language that is described by a text is infinite. So we have to define what it means that such a strategy learns successfully.

Definition 12. Let $\mathcal{L}$ be an indexed family. We say $\mathcal{L} \in$ **CA-CBL.TXT** iff $\exists \sigma \in \Sigma \ \forall L \in \mathcal{L} \ \forall t \in text(L)$

$$(1) \ \forall n \in \mathbb{N} \ CB_n = t^+[n] \times \{+\},$$

$$(2) \ \exists j \in \mathbb{N} \ L_{st}(CB_k, \sigma) = L \text{ for all } k > j.$$

CA-CBL.INF is defined analogously.

We say $\mathcal{L} \in$ **CA-CBL.TXT** if for all texts of L, $(L_{st}(CB_n, \sigma))_{n \in \mathbb{N}}$ converges *semantically*. This is somehow comparable to the notion of convergence underlying the identification type **BC** in Inductive Inference of recursive functions [3]. All other case-based learning types demand that the sequence $(CB_n)_{n \in \mathbb{N}}$ itself has to converge.

4.1 Learning from Text

In this section we study case-based language learning from positive cases. The first theorem shows that representability and learnability are incomparable. # denotes set incomparability.

Theorem 13. **LIM.TXT** # **REPR**[+]

---

[3] *MO* stands for "monotonically", *DE* for "delete", *RA* for "random access" and *LC* for "last case"

[4] *CA* stands for "collect all"

To prove that there are representable classes that cannot be learned from text look at the indexed family $\mathcal{L}$ with $L_1 := \{a\}^+$ and for $j > 1$, $L_j := \{a^k \mid 1 \leq k \leq j\}$. $\mathcal{L}$ is representable but is not learnable from text. On the other hand the family of all pattern languages is learnable but not representable (cf. [8]).

Theorem 14. LIM.TXT $\cap$ REPR$^+$ = DE-RA-CBL.TXT

Proof. For "$\subseteq$" let $\mathcal{L} = L_1, L_2, \ldots$ be any indexed family with $\mathcal{L} \in$ **LIM.TXT** $\cap$ **REPR$^+$**. In order to show $\mathcal{L} \in$ **DE-RA-CBL.TXT**, we try to simulate a learning strategy M which **LIM.TXT**-identifies $\mathcal{L}$. To do so, we have to interleave two limiting processes

Let $\sigma \in \Sigma$ such that $\mathcal{L} \in$ **REPR$^+$**(σ). Moreover, assume any effective enumeration $(F_k)_{k \in \mathbb{N}}$ of all finite subsets of A^+. Since $\sigma \in \Sigma$ and membership is uniformly decidable in $\mathcal{L}$, we may conclude:

Claim: There exists a total recursive function $f : \mathbb{N} \times \mathbb{N} \to \mathbb{N}$ such that for all $j \in \mathbb{N}$:

(1) $\forall x \; f(j, x) \downarrow$,
(2) $\lim_{x \to \infty} = a$ exists,
(3) $F_a \subseteq L_j$ and $L_{st}(F_a, \emptyset, \sigma) = L_j$.

Thus, on input j f may be used to compute in the limit a finite case base for L_j.

On the other hand, assume any $M \in \mathbf{P}$ which **LIM.TXT**-identifies $\mathcal{L}$. Now let $L \in \mathcal{L}$, $t = (s_1, +), (s_2, +), \ldots$ be any text for L, and $x \in \mathbb{N}$. The desired case-based learner S will be defined as follows:

  – Compute $j_x = M(t[x])$.
  – Compute $z_x = f(j_x, x)$.
  – If $F_{z_x} \subseteq t^+[x]$, then set $CB_x^+ = F_{z_x}$. Otherwise, set $CB_x^+ = \{s_1\}$.

Finally, taking into consideration that M infers L on text t it follows by the claim above that S converges to a correct case base for L. By definition S is indeed a case selection strategy of type **DE-RA**. $\square$

Theorem 15.
(1) **MO-LC-CBL.TXT $\subsetneq$ DE-LC-CBL.TXT**
(2) **DE-LC-CBL.TXT $\subsetneq$ DE-RA-CBL.TXT**
(3) **DE-RA-CBL.TXT $\subsetneq$ LIM.TXT**

Proof. We only prove Assertion (1). The remaining part can be handled in a similar manner.

By definition **MO-LC-CBL.TXT $\subseteq$ DE-LC-CBL.TXT**. Let $L_1 = \{a\}^+$, $L_2 = \{a, b\}$ and for all $j > 2$, $L_j = \{a^{j-1}\}$. We show that $\mathcal{L} = (L_j)_{j \in \mathbb{N}}$ witnesses the desired separation.

Claim 1: $\mathcal{L} \notin$ **MO-LC-CBL.TXT**

Suppose the converse, i.e., $\mathcal{L} \in$ **MO-LC-CBL.TXT**. Let σ denote the underlying similarity measure. Obviously, for every $k > 1$, the string a^k has to serve as a representative case for the singleton language $\{a^k\} \in \mathcal{L}$. Furthermore, $L_1 = \{a\}^+$ has to be representable w.r.t. σ, too. Consequently, the string a has to be the only representative case for L_1 w.r.t. σ. Now, suppose S is a **MO-LC-CBL.TXT**–strategy for $\mathcal{L}$. Assume that, initially, $(a, +)$ is presented in a text for L_1 and L_2, respectively. Now, it is easy to verify that S, when putting $(a, +)$ into the case base, definitely fails to learn L_2 because S is not allowed to delete $(a, +)$ subsequently. On the other hand, if $(a, +)$ will not be included in the case base, S fails to learn L_1 on its text $t = (a, +), (a^2, +), \ldots$ because $\sigma(a^k\ a) = 0$ for all $k > 2$. Thus, S is fooled, a contradiction.

Claim 2: $\mathcal{L} \in$ **DE-LC-CBL.TXT**.

Recall that a **DE-LC-CBL.TXT**–strategy S is allowed to delete cases from its actual case base. Obviously, S can be easily defined provided that the underlying similarity measure σ fulfills the following requirements:

- a is representative for L_1 w.r.t. σ,
- b is representative for L_2 w.r.t. σ,
- for all $k > 1$, a^k is representative for L_{k+1} w.r.t. σ.

We omit the details. □

Theorem 16.
(1) **CA-CBL.TXT $\subsetneqq$ MO-LC-CBL.TXT**
(2) **MO-LC-CBL.TXT $\subsetneqq$ MO-RA-CBL.TXT**
(3) **MO-RA-CBL.TXT $\subsetneqq$ DE-RA-CBL.TXT**

Proof. Again we present only the proof of the first Assertion. First, we show **CA-CBL.TXT $\subseteq$ MO-LC-CBL.TXT**. As we will see, this is the most interesting part of the proof. Let $\mathcal{L}$ be an indexed family of languages over the alphabet A that is learnable by a **CA-CBL.TXT**–strategy using σ. In order to show $\mathcal{L} \in$ **MO-LC-CBL.TXT** we define a different similarity measure $\tilde{\sigma}$. This will be done in two steps.

Without loss of generality we assume $\sigma \in \Sigma_{\{0,1\}}$. Moreover, assume for all $w \in A^+$, $\sigma(w, w) = 1$. Furthermore, let $w_1, w_2, \ldots$ be an effective enumeration of all strings in A^+.

- Step 1: For all $j, k \in \mathbb{N}$, we set $\hat{\sigma}(w_j, w_k) = \sigma(w_j, w_k)$, if $j \leq k$. Otherwise, set $\hat{\sigma}(w_j, w_k) = 0$. It is easy to verify that $\mathcal{L}$ is learnable by a **CA-CBL.TXT**–strategy S using $\hat{\sigma}$.
- Step 2: The definition of $\tilde{\sigma}$ is based on $\hat{\sigma}$. Let $j, k \in \mathbb{N}$. Then we set $\tilde{\sigma}(w_j, w_k) = 1$, if there are indices $j_1 < j_2 < \ldots < j_n$ such that $j_1 = j$, $j_n = k$ as well as $\hat{\sigma}(w_{j_m}, w_{j_{m+1}}) = 1$ for all $m \leq n - 1$. Otherwise, set $\tilde{\sigma}(w_j, w_k) = \hat{\sigma}(w_j, w_k)$.
  Now, we may conclude:
  - Observation A: Let $j \in \mathbb{N}$, and $B \subseteq L_j$. Then $L_{st}(B, \emptyset, \hat{\sigma}) \subseteq L_{st}(B, \emptyset, \tilde{\sigma}) \subseteq L_j$.
    To see this, assume any $v \in L_{st}(B, \emptyset, \tilde{\sigma})$ which does not belong to L_j. By definition there has to be a $w \in B$ such that $\tilde{\sigma}(w, v) = 1$. Hence,

there are strings $w = s_1, ..., s_n = v$ such that $1 = \hat{\sigma}(s_1, s_2) = \cdots = \hat{\sigma}(s_{n-1}, v)$. Since $\mathcal{L} \in$ **CA-CBL.TXT** by S w.r.t. $\hat{\sigma}$, $w \in L_j$ together with $\hat{\sigma}(w, s_2) = 1$ directly implies $s_2 \in L_j$. By iterating this argument we obtain $s_n = v \in L_j$. This contradicts our assumption that $v \notin L_j$.

- Observation B: Let $j \in \mathbb{N}$, $B \subseteq L_j$, and $w \in A^+$. Then, $w \in L_{st}(B, \emptyset, \tilde{\sigma})$ implies $L_{st}(B, \emptyset, \tilde{\sigma}) = L_{st}(B \cup \{w\}, \emptyset, \tilde{\sigma})$.

This observation can be proved in a similar manner.

Now, we are ready to define a strategy T witnessing $\mathcal{L} \in$ **MO-LC-CBL** w.r.t. $\tilde{\sigma}$. Let $L \in \mathcal{L}$ and let $t = (s_1, +), (s_2, +), \ldots$ be any text for L. Initially, set $CB_1 = (s_1, +)$. Let $k \in \mathbb{N}$.

- If $s_{k+1} \notin L_{st}(CB_k, \tilde{\sigma})$, then set $CB_{k+1} = CB_k \cup \{(s_{k+1}, +)\}$
- Otherwise, set $CB_{k+1} = CB_k$

Since S learns L from t by simply collecting all cases, there is an $x \in \mathbb{N}$ such that $L_{st}(t^+[x], \emptyset, \hat{\sigma}) = L_j$. By Observations A and B it follows $L_j = L_{st}(t^+[x], \emptyset, \hat{\sigma}) \subseteq L_{st}(t^+[x], \emptyset, \tilde{\sigma}) = L_{st}(CB_x, \tilde{\sigma}) \subseteq L_j$. Consequently, $L_{st}(CB_x, \tilde{\sigma}) = L_j$. By the definition of T we have $CB_x = CB_{x+r}$ for all $r \in \mathbb{N}$. Thus, T works as required.

Finally, we show **MO-LC-CBL.TXT** \ **CA-CBL.TXT** $\neq \emptyset$.

Let $L := \{a^{3k} \mid k \in \mathbb{N}\}$, and for $k \in \mathbb{N}$, $L_k := \{a^{3k}, a^{3k+1}\}$. Let $\mathcal{L}$ be an enumeration of L and all L_k. As we will see, $\mathcal{L}$ witnesses the separation.

Claim 1: $\mathcal{L} \notin$ **CA-CBL.TXT**

Suppose there is a $k \in \mathbb{N}$ such that $\sigma(a^{3k}, w) > 0$ for infinitely many $w \in A^+$. Then L_k cannot be learned by a **CA-CBL.TXT**-strategy for the following reason. If the text $t = (a^{3k}, +), (a^{3k+1}, +), (a^{3k+1}, +), \ldots$ is presented, then $card(L_{st}(t^+[j], \emptyset, \sigma)) = \infty$ for all $j \in \mathbb{N}$. But the language described by the text t is finite.

Suppose there is no $k \in \mathbb{N}$ such that $\sigma(a^{3k}, w) > 0$ for infinitely many $w \in A^+$. Then L is not representable by finitely many cases. Therefore, $\mathcal{L} \notin$ **CA-CBL.TXT** is proved.

Claim 2: $\mathcal{L} \in$ **MO-LC-CBL.TXT**

We need a similarity measure that fulfills the following requirements. Each a^{3k} is a representative for L and each a^{3k+1} is a representative for L_k. Such a measure exists, because the set of representatives for the languages are pairwise disjoint. The corresponding **MO-LC-CBL.TXT**-strategy waits for a a^{3k+1} and the second a^{3k}, respectively, and stores it in the case base. $\square$

Theorem 17. MO-RA-CBL.TXT # DE-LC-CBL.TXT

Proof. **MO-RA-CBL.TXT** \ **DE-LC-CBL.TXT** $\neq \emptyset$: Let $L_1 := \{a\}^+$ and $L_j := \{a, a^j\}$ for all $j \geq 2$. Let $\mathcal{L} = (L_j)_{j \in \mathbb{N}}$. Using similar ideas as in the proof of Theorem 15 one can show that $\mathcal{L} \in$ **MO-RA-CBL.TXT** \ **DE-LC-CBL.TXT**.

DE-LC-CBL.TXT \ **MO-RA-CBL.TXT** $\neq \emptyset$: Let $\mathcal{L}$ be an enumeration of $L_1 = \{a\}^+$, $L_k = (L_1 \cup \{b^k\}) \setminus \{a^k\}$ for $k > 1$, $\hat{L}_k = \{a^k\}$ for $k > 1$. Then $\mathcal{L} \in$ **DE-LC-CBL.TXT** \ **MO-RA-CBL.TXT**. $\square$

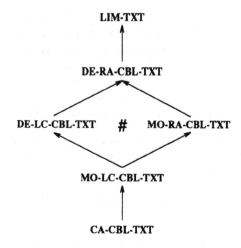

Fig. 1. Relationship between the learning types

These theorems show that both random access to the already presented cases and the ability to delete cases from the actual case base increase the learning power of a case-based learning system. But neither subsumes the other.

Figure 1 illustrates the relationships between all types of case-based learning from text. A path from type T_1 to type T_2 indicates that T_1 is a proper subset of T_2.

4.2 Learning from Informant

Learning from informant is more powerful than learning from text. It is known that every indexed family is learnable from informant. The main result of this section is that every indexed family is case-based learnable with an appropriate fixed measure.

Theorem 18. IF = LIM.INF = DE-RA-CBL.INF

Proof. **IF = LIM.INF** follows from [6]. **LIM.INF = DE-RA-CBL.INF** can be shown using the same idea as in the proof of Theorem 14. □

If we consider case-based learning from informant the relations between the case-based learning types change. If the case selection strategy is either allowed to store any case from the informant or to drop cases from the case base, every indexed family is learnable.

Theorem 19.
(1) **MO-RA-CBL.INF = IF**
(2) **DE-LC-CBL.INF = IF**

Proof. It suffices to show **IF** $\subseteq$ **MO-RA-CBL.INF** as well as **IF** $\subseteq$ **DE-LC-CBL.INF**. The main idea is to define the target case selection strategies w.r.t. the similarity measure σ introduced in the proof of Theorem 8. We omit the details. $\qquad\square$

From the last theorem we can easy conclude that the learning capability will not increase if we combine both free access to the case history and the ability to delete cases from the case base.

Corollary 20. DE-RA-CBL.INF = IF

Theorem 21. MO-LC-CBL.INF $\subsetneq$ IF

Proof. Let $A = \{a\}$ be an alphabet. $\mathcal{L}$ is an indexed family that contains A^+, all finite languages and $A^+ \setminus \{a^k\}$ for all $k \in \mathbb{N}$. Then $\mathcal{L} \notin$ **MO-LC-CBL.INF**.

Suppose to the contrary that there is a strategy S and a similarity measure σ such that $\mathcal{L} \in$ **MO-LC-CBL.INF** by S w.r.t. σ. Because S learns A^+ there has to be an informant i for A^+ and an $x \in \mathbb{N}$ such that for all $w \in A^+$, $S(i[x]) = S(i[x], (w,+)) = CB_x \subseteq i^+[x] \times \{+\}$ and $L_{st}(CB_x, \sigma) = A^+$. Let $L = i^+[x]$.

Now, taking into account that S has to learn L, in particular, when fed any informant $\hat{i}$ that has $i[x]$ as prefix, we can conclude: There are distinct $w, v \in \overline{L}$ such that for all $u \in CB_x^+$, $\sigma(u,v) \leq \sigma(w,v)$. Otherwise, S would fail to learn L when fed $\hat{i}$ because for all $y > x$, $CB_x \subseteq S(\hat{i}[y])$ and, therefore, $v \in L_{st}(S(\hat{i}[y]), \sigma)$, but $v \in \overline{L}$

Now, choose $w, v \in \overline{L}$ such that for all $u \in CB^+$, $\sigma(u,w) \leq \sigma(v,w)$. Finally, consider S when fed the initial segment $i[x], (w,+), (v,-)$. We distinguish two cases.

- Let $S(i[x], (w,+), (v,-)) = CB_x$. Then S fails to learn $\hat{L} = \{a\}^+ \setminus \{v\}$ on each of its informants that have the prefix $i[x], (w,+), (v,-)$ and contain the case $(v,-)$ exactly once.
- Now, let $S(i[x], (w,+), (v,-)) = CB_x \cup \{(v,-)\}$. Obviously, this implies that S fails to learn $\hat{L} = L \cup \{w\}$ on every extension of $i[x], (w,+), (v,-)$ which yields an informant for $\hat{L}$ containing the case $(w,+)$ exactly once.

Hence, in each of the above cases S can be easily fooled, a contradiction. $\qquad\square$

Theorem 22. CA-CBL.INF $\setminus$ MO-LC-CBL.INF $\neq \emptyset$

Proof. Let $\mathcal{L}$ be the family of all finite and co-finite languages. We show that there exists a $\sigma \in \Sigma$ such that $\mathcal{L} \in$ **CA-CBL.INF** w.r.t. σ. Let $m, n \in \mathbb{N}$.

$$\sigma(a^m, a^n) = \begin{cases} 1 & \text{if } m = n \\ 1 - \frac{1}{m} & m < n \\ 0 & \text{otherwise} \end{cases}$$

By definition for all $m \in \mathbb{N}$, it holds $L_{st}(\{a^m\}, \emptyset, \sigma) = \{a^n \mid n \geq m\}$ as well as $L_{st}(\emptyset, \{a^m\}, \sigma) = \emptyset$. Furthermore, assume any sets $B, C \subseteq \{a\}^+$ such that $B \cap C = \emptyset$ and $B \cup C = \{a^n \mid n < m\}$. Then, $L_{st}(\{a^m\} \cup B, C, \sigma) = B \cup \{a^n \mid n \geq m\}$ as well as $L_{st}(B, \{a^m\} \cup C, \sigma) = B$. Finally, taking both properties of σ into consideration it is easy to verify that the family of all finite and co-finite languages is learnable by a case-selection strategy which simply collects all cases.

It remains to prove that $\mathcal{L}$ is not in **MO-LC-CBL.INF**. This follows directly from Theorem 21 where we have already shown that a proper subfamily of $\mathcal{L}$ does not belong to **MO-LC-CBL.INF**. This completes the proof. □

While the learning power of **CA-CBL.TXT** is very limited **CA-CBL.INF** contains remarkably rich indexed families like that used in the proof above.

5 Conclusion

Within the present paper we studied different types of case-based learning of indexed families from positive data and both positive and negative data. Following the approach in [8], we considered case-based learning with respect to an arbitrary fixed similarity measure. Thereby, we focused our attention on the problem of how the underlying case selection strategies influence the capabilities of case-based learners. In order to answer this question a couple of new results concerning case-based representability of indexed families have been achieved. As it turns out, the choice of the case selection strategy is of particular importance, if case-based learning from text is investigated. If both positive and negative data are provided, even quite simple case selection strategies are sufficient in order to exhaust the full power of case-based learning.

From our point of view, further investigations concerning case-based learning of indexed families should be oriented in the following way. On the one hand, it seems to be rather natural to give up the assumption that a case-based learner is allowed to use the whole history of the learning task in order to determine its next hypothesis. This may lead to the notion *iteratively working* case-based learning strategies (cf. [7]). On the other hand, when formalizing case-based learning one has to take into consideration that in existing systems a case-based learner has the freedom to change the underlying similarity measure during the learning task, too.

References

1. David W. Aha. Case-Based Learning Algorithms. In Ray Bareiss, editor, *Proc. CBR91*, pages 147 – 158. Morgan Kaufmann Publishers, 1991.
2. D. Angluin. Inductive inference of formal languages from positive data. *Information and Control*, 45:117–135, 1980.
3. D. Angluin and C. H. Smith. Inductive Inference: Theory and Methods. *Computing Surveys*, 15(3):237–269, 1983.
4. H. Billhardt. On case-based representability of classes of formal languages. Diploma thesis, HTWK Leipzig, June 1994.

5. Christoph Globig and Stefan Wess. Symbolic Learning and Nearest-Neighbor Classification. In P. Bock, W. Lenski, and M. M. Richter, editors, *Information Systems and Data Analysis*, Studies in Classification, Data Analysis, and Knowledge Organization, pages 17–27. Springer Verlag, 1994.
6. E. Mark Gold. Language identification in the limit. *Information and Control*, 10:447–474, 1967.
7. Klaus P. Jantke. Case-Based Learning in Inductive Inference. In *Proceedings of the 5th ACM Workshop on Computational Learning Theory (COLT'92)*, pages 218–223. ACM-Press, 1992.
8. K.P. Jantke and Steffen Lange. Case-based representation and learning of pattern languages. In *Proceedings of the 4th International Workshop on Algorithmic learning Theory (ALT'93)*, volume 744 of *LNAI*, pages 87–100. Springer-Verlag, 1993.

Rule-Generating Abduction
for Recursive Prolog

Kouichi Hirata

Research Institute of Fundamental Information Science
Kyushu University 33, Fukuoka 812, Japan
hirata@rifis.kyushu-u.ac.jp

Abstract. The rule-generating abduction is a kind of abduction which generates a rule and proposes a hypothesis from *a surprising fact*. In general, there may exist infinitely many rules and hypotheses to explain such a surprising fact. Hence, we need to put some restriction on the class of rules. In rule-generating abduction, only one surprising fact is given. Hence, we also need to generalize the concept of a surprising fact. When we deal with such generalizations, we must avoid overgeneralization. It should be determined whether or not a generalization is overgeneral by an intended model. However, it is hard to give in advance such an intended model in our rule-generating abduction. Hence, in this paper we introduce a syntactical formulation of generalization, in which it can be determined whether or not a generalization is overgeneral by the forms of atoms and substitutions. On the other hand, by the restriction of rules, it suffices to consider only two types of terms, constants and lists, and two types of substitutions with these two terms. By using the above generalizations and substitutions, we design an algorithm for rule-generating abduction, which generates rules and proposes hypotheses in polynomial time with respect to the length of a surprising fact. The number of rules and hypotheses is at most the number of common terms in a surprising fact. Furthermore, we show that a common term in some argument of a surprising fact also appears in the same argument of the proposed hypothesis by this algorithm.

1 Introduction

C. S. Peirce, who was a philosopher, scientist and logician, asserted that a scientific research consists of three stages, *abduction*, *deduction*, and *induction* [Pei65, Ino92, Yon82]. According to him, abduction is an inference which begins with an observation of *a surprising fact*, and proposes a hypothesis to explain why the fact arises. The main role of abduction is to propose a hypothesis. Thus, abduction is *a method of scientific discovery*. An inference schema by abduction is described by the following three steps [Pei65, Ino92, Yon82]:

1. A surprising fact C is observed.
2. If A were true, then C would be a matter of course.
3. Hence, there is reason to suspect that A is true.

In general, the above inference schema is depicted by a syllogism:

$$\frac{C \quad A \to C}{A}.$$

In computer science, especially in computational logic and logic programming, many researchers have extensively studied the abduction from various viewpoints. Plotkin [Plo71] has studied abduction together with inductive generalization. It is considered that Shapiro's model inference system [Sha81] and inductive logic programming [Lin89a, Lin89b, Mug92a, Mug92b] are the extensions of Plotkin. These are also related to machine learning and knowledge acquisition. On the other hand, Pople [Ino92, Kun87] has given one direction for the researches of abduction. It is considered that Poole's Theorist [Poo88, Ino92, Kun87], Kunifuji's hypothesis-based reasoning [Kun87], and abductive logic programming [Dun91, EK89, KM90] are the extensions of Pople. These are also related to knowledge representation.

In order to systematically understand these various researches of abduction, we have classified abduction into five types by an interpretation of syllogism [Hir93]; *rule-selecting abduction*, *rule-finding abduction*, *rule-generating abduction*, *theory-selecting abduction*, and *theory-generating abduction*. By this classification, the above researches are placed in the following positions [Hir93]: Abductive logic programming [Dun91, EK89, KM90] is a sort of rule-selecting abduction. The constructive operators such as V and W operators [Mug92b] in inductive logic programming are a sort of rule-generating abduction. Poole's Theorist [Poo88] and hypothesis-based reasoning [Kun87] are a sort of theory-selecting abduction. Shapiro's model inference system [Sha81] and inductive logic programming [Lin89a, Lin89b, Mug92a, Mug92b] are a sort of theory-generating abduction.

In this paper, we investigate the *rule-generating abduction*, which generates a rule and proposes a hypothesis from a surprising fact. In rule-generating abduction, only one surprising fact is given. Hence, we need to generalize the concept of a surprising fact.

A *generalization* is an important tool for inductive logic programming and program synthesis. Plotkin has introduced and developed the *least generalization* and the *relative least generalization* [Plo70, Plo71]. Arimura *et al.* have developed Plotkin's least generalization as the *minimal multiple generalization* [ASO91]. Note that all of them are researches on the generalization of at least two atoms. Thus, the following problem arises; Is the generalization of one atom worth or worthless? Hirowatari and Arikawa [HA94] have introduced the *partially isomorphic generalization* and answered this problem affirmatively in the framework of analogical reasoning.

When we deal with generalizations, we must avoid overgeneralization. It should be determined whether or not a generalization is overgeneral by an intended model. However, it is hard to give in advance such an intended model in our rule-generating abduction. Hence, in this paper we introduce a syntactical formulation of generalization, in which it can be determined whether or not a generalization is overgeneral by the forms of atoms and substitutions. In this formulation, a common ground term is replaced by a common variable, because an atom represents a relation which holds between its arguments.

This paper is organized as follows: In general, there may exist infinitely many rules and hypotheses to explain a surprising fact in rule-generating abduction. Hence, we need to put some restriction on the class of logic programs. In Section 2, we introduce the syntactical characterization of the rule $p(t_1, \cdots, t_n) \leftarrow p(s_1, \cdots, s_n)$. Throughout this paper, we deal with these classes.

In Section 3, we formulate a *safe generalization*, in which it can be determined whether or not a generalization is overgeneral by the forms of atoms and substitutions, instead of an intended model. On the other hand, by the restriction of logic programs, it suffices to consider only two types of terms, constants and lists, and two types of substitutions with these two terms, *constant substitutions* and *list substitutions*. A constant substitution θ_c consists of the bindings $x := c$, where c is a constant symbol, while a list substitution θ_l consists of the bindings $x := l$, where l is a list. For these substitutions, we give a condition that the generalization is safe with respect to the composition $\theta_c \theta_l$ of θ_c and θ_l.

In Section 4, by using the above generalizations and substitutions, we design an algorithm for rule-generating abduction, which generates rules and proposes hypotheses in polynomial time with respect to the length of a surprising fact. The number of rules and hypotheses is at most the number of common terms in a surprising fact. Furthermore, we show that a common term in some argument of a surprising fact also appears in the same argument of the proposed hypothesis by this algorithm.

In Section 5, we discuss the several examples for this algorithm.

2 Preliminary

Throughout this paper, we deal with the following class of programs:

$$P = \{p(t_1, \cdots, t_n) \leftarrow p(s_1, \cdots, s_n)\}.$$

Hirata [Hir93] has introduced a class such that, for a given definite program P in the class and a ground atom α, all the derivations of $P \cup \{\leftarrow \alpha\}$ are finite. In this section, we reform the definitions [Hir93] for the above rule. In this paper, we assume that readers are familiar with the notions of logic programming and definite clause [Llo87]. We also assume that any term in $\mathcal{L}$ is either a constant or a list, where $\mathcal{L}$ is a first-order language with an n-ary predicate symbol p, a list constructor $[\_|\_]$, and finitely many constant symbols $[\ ], a_1, \cdots, a_n$.

For a term t, $|t|$ denotes the length of t, that is, the number of all occurrences of symbols in t. In particular, for a list l, the length $|l|$ of l is defined as follows: $|l| = 1$, if l is an empty list $[\ ]$. Otherwise $|l| = n + 1$, if t is a list $[a|list]$ and $|list| = n$.

In order to discuss the termination of derivations, we introduce some classes in the following way:

Definition 1. (Hirata [Hir93], Yamamoto [Yam92]) Let C be a clause $p(t_1, \cdots, t_n) \leftarrow p(s_1, \cdots, s_n)$.

1. C is *head-reducing* if there exists an i such that $|t_i\theta| > |s_i\theta|$ for any ground substitution θ.
2. C is *weakly reducing* if $|t_i\theta| \geq |s_i\theta|$ for any ground substitution θ and for any i.
3. C is *weakly head-reducing* if it is head-reducing and weakly reducing.

In other words, a clause $p(t_1,\cdots,t_n) \leftarrow p(s_1,\cdots,s_n)$ is weakly head-reducing if $|t_i\theta| \geq |s_i\theta|$ for any i, and $|t_k\theta| > |s_k\theta|$ for at least one argument k and for any ground substitution θ.

There are many Prolog programs for list processing such that any argument of the head is either x or $[w|x]$. Then, we restrict the form of clause as follows: A clause $p(t_1,\cdots,t_n) \leftarrow p(s_1,\cdots,s_n)$ is *2-reducing*, if t_i is either x_i or $[w_i|x_i]$ for any i, and it is head-reducing. A clause $p(t_1,\cdots,t_n) \leftarrow p(s_1,\cdots,s_n)$ is *weakly 2-reducing* if it is weakly reducing and 2-reducing.

Example 1. The following Prolog programs in Sterling and Shapiro [SS86] are weakly 2-reducing.

```
list([W|X]):- list(X)
member(X,[W|Y]):- member(X,Y)
prefix([W|X],[W|Y]):- prefix(X,Y)
suffix(X,[W|Y]):- suffix(X,Y)
append([W|X],Y,[W|Z]):- append(X,Y,Z)
concat(X,[W|Y],[W|Z]):- concat(X,Y,Z)
```

Note that the clauses of member and suffix are the same forms. The first argument of member is a constant, while that of suffix is a list.

Then, the following theorem holds.

Theorem 2. (Hirata [Hir93], Yamamoto [Yam92]) *Let α be a ground atom with a predicate p and C be a clause $p(t_1,\cdots,t_n) \leftarrow p(s_1,\cdots,s_n)$.*

1. *If C is head-reducing, in particular 2-reducing, then the derivation of $\{p(t_1,\cdots,t_n) \leftarrow p(s_1,\cdots,s_n)\} \cup \{\leftarrow \alpha\}$ is finite.*
2. *If C is weakly head-reducing, in particular weakly 2-reducing, then the derivation of $\{p(t_1,\cdots,t_n) \leftarrow p(s_1,\cdots,s_n)\} \cup \{\leftarrow \alpha\}$ is finite, and all nodes of derivation are ground goals.*

3 Safe Generalization

It is an important point to avoid overgeneralization when we deal with generalization. In general, it is determined whether or not a generalization β of α is overgeneral is determined by an intended model. Let $\beta\theta = \alpha$ and M be an intended model. Then, β is an overgeneralization of α if there exists a ground atom γ such that $\forall\beta \vdash \gamma$ and $M \not\models \gamma$ for an intended model M. However, the decision problem of whether or not there exists such a γ is undecidable. On the other hand, in rule-generating abduction, only one surprising fact is given, and it is hard to give in advance an intended model. To overcome these difficulties, we introduce a syntactical formulation of generalization.

Let θ be a ground substitution, that is, $\theta = \cup_{i=1}^{n}\{x_i := t_i\}$, where any t_i is a ground term. Let α be a ground atom and β be an atom such that $\beta\theta = \alpha$. Note that, throughout this paper, if $\beta\theta = \alpha$ then a variable x_i appears in β and $t_i \neq [\ ]$. A substitution θ is *well-defined* if, for any t_i, there exists no term t_j such that t_j is a subterm of t_i. In general, β is called an *overgeneralization* of α if θ is not well-defined.

Example 2. Let α be a ground atom $p([a, b], [b])$. Let

$$\beta_1 = p([a, x], [b]), \ \beta_2 = p([a|x], [b]), \ \beta_3 = p([x|y], y),$$
$$\beta_4 = p([a|x], [y]), \ \beta_5 = p([a|x], y).$$

For any β_i, there exist the following substitutions θ_i such that $\beta_i\theta_i = \alpha$:

$$\theta_1 = \{x := b\}, \ \theta_2 = \{x := [b]\}, \ \theta_3 = \{x := a, y := [b]\},$$
$$\theta_4 = \{x := [b], y := b\}, \ \theta_5 = \{x := [b], y := [b]\}.$$

Then, θ_1, θ_2, and θ_3 are well-defined, while θ_3 and θ_4 are not.

Let α be a ground atom and β be an atom such that $\beta\theta = \alpha$. If a substitution $\theta = \cup_{i=1}^{n}\{x_i := t_i\}$ is well-defined, then we can define the reversal $\theta^{-1} = \cup_{i=1}^{n}\{t_i := x_i\}$. Note that, if θ is well-defined, then, for any t_i and x_i, there exists no term t_j such that t_j is a subterm of t_i and no variables x_i such that $x_i = x_j (j \neq i)$. However, even if θ is well-defined, β is not always $\alpha\theta^{-1}$.

Example 3. For β_1 and β_2 in Example 2,

$$\alpha\theta_1^{-1} = p([a, b], [b])\{b := x\} = p([a, x], [x]) \neq \beta_1,$$
$$\alpha\theta_2^{-1} = p([a, b], [b])\{[b] := x\} = p([a|x], x) \neq \beta_2.$$

On the other hand, $\alpha\theta_3^{-1} = p([a, b], [b])\{a := x, [b] := y\} = p([x|y], y) = \beta_3$.

For the reversal θ^{-1}, the following lemma holds.

Lemma 3. *Let α be a ground atom and β be an atom such that $\beta\theta = \alpha$. Suppose that a substitution $\theta = \cup_{i=1}^{n}\{x_i := t_i\}$ is well-defined. Then, $\beta = \alpha\theta^{-1}$ if and only if no t_i appears in β.*

Proof. Suppose $\beta = \alpha\theta^{-1}$. By the definition of θ^{-1}, $\alpha\theta^{-1}$ is an atom which replaces all t_i in α with variable x_i. Then, no t_i appears in $\alpha\theta^{-1} = \beta$.

For simplicity, suppose that $\theta = \{x := t\}$. If t appears once in α, that is $\alpha = p(\cdots t \cdots)$, then $\alpha\theta^{-1} = p(\cdots t \cdots)\{t := x\} = p(\cdots x \cdots)$. Since α is ground, $\alpha\theta^{-1} = \beta$.

If t appears at least twice in α, that is $\alpha = p(\cdots t \cdots t \cdots)$, then β is $p(\cdots x \cdots y \cdots)$. If $x \neq y$, then, by $\beta\theta = \alpha$, θ is $\{x := t, y := t\}$. Since θ is not well-defined, it is contradiction. Then, $x = y$, $\theta = \{x := t\}$, and $\beta = p(\cdots x \cdots x \cdots)$. Hence, $\beta = \alpha\theta^{-1}$. $\qquad\square$

A ground term $t(\neq [\,])$ is a *common term* in α if t appears at least twice in α except an empty list $[\,]$. In particular, if a common term is a ground list, it is called a *common list*.

Definition 4. Let α be a ground atom, θ be a substitution $\cup_{i=1}^{n}\{x_i := t_i\}$, and β be an atom such that $\beta\theta = \alpha$. An atom β is a *safe generalization* of α if (β, θ) satisfies the following *safeness conditions*:

1. θ is well-defined,
2. $\beta = \alpha\theta^{-1}$, and
3. if there exist common terms in α, then there exists a ground term $t_j \in \cup_{i=1}^{n}\{t_i\}$ such that t_j is a common term in α.

The safeness condition 1 means that β is not overgeneral on α. The safeness condition 2 and 3 mean that a generalization of β is not overgeneral on α. Hence, if a given ground atom is generalized *safely*, then we can avoid overgeneralization. Furthermore, each of safe generalizations is corresponding to the relation which is represented by a given ground atom.

Let α be a ground atom and β be an atom such that $\beta\theta = \alpha$. Let t be some common term in α. If θ is well-defined and θ^{-1} is the form $\{t := x\}$, then β is safe on α.

Example 4. Let α be a ground atom $p([a, b], [b])$ and β be an atom such that $\beta\theta = \alpha$. Then, the common terms in α are $[b]$ and b.

1. Let β_1 be an atom $p(x, y)$ and θ_1 be a substitution $\theta_1 = \{x := [a, b], y := [b]\}$. By the safeness condition 1, β_1 is not safe on α.
2. Let β_2 be an atom $p([x, b], [y])$ and θ_2 be a substitution $\{x := a, y := b\}$. By the safeness condition 2, β_2 is not safe on α.
3. Let β_3 be an atom $p(x, [b])$ and θ_3 be a substitution $\{x := [a, b]\}$. By the safeness condition 3, β_3 is not safe on α.

For the above α, atoms $p([a|x], x), p([a, x], [x]), p([y, x], [x])$, and $p([y|x], x)$ are safe on α.

In general, an atom represents a relation which holds between its arguments. Thus, the syntactical generalization of one atom should obtained by replacing a common term by a common variable. The above safe generalization is an example of such generalizations. On the other hand, it suffices to consider only two types of terms, constants and lists. Then, we also define the following two types of substitution.

Let θ be a substitution $\cup_{i=1}^{n}\{x_i := t_i\}$. Then, θ is a *constant substitution* (*resp.* a *list substitution*) if every t_i is a constant symbol (*resp.* a ground list) without an empty list $[\,]$. In particular, a constant substitution is related to *partially isomorphic generalizations* which have been introduced by Hirowatari and Arikawa [HA94].

Let α be an atom. A term t is a *replaceable term* of α if t is a constant symbol. For a replaceable term t of α, let $\alpha[t]$ be an atom obtained by replacing each t

in α by a new variable Z which does not appear in α. Then, we write $\alpha \to \beta$ when $\alpha[t]$ is a variant of β. We define $\to^*$ as the reflexive and transitive closure of $\to$.

Definition 5. (Hirowatari and Arikawa [HA94]) Let α and β be atoms. Then, β is a *partially isomorphic generalization* of α if $\alpha \to^* \beta$.

For a set of atoms S, let $[S]$ denote the equivalence class of all atoms in S. In particular, for any $\alpha \in S$ and $\beta \in S$, α is a variant of β.

Theorem 6. (Hirowatari and Arikawa [HA94]) *Let α be an atom and S be the set of all partially isomorphic generalizations of α. Then, $[S]$ is a lattice whose partial order is $\to^*$, meet operator is the greatest instantiation, and join operator is the least generalization.*

Note that, though a replaceable term includes an empty list $[\ ]$, the definition of a replaceable term is independent of the proof of Theorem 6. Let RT be the set of all replaceable terms of α and $T \subseteq RT$. Then, we can re-formulate a partially isomorphic generalization by using T instead of RT, and the above Theorem 6 also holds for a set T of replaceable terms. Let α be a ground atom, θ_c be a constant substitution, and β be an atom such that $\beta\theta_c = \alpha$. Thus, we assume that β *is a partially isomorphic generalization of α, whose replaceable terms are all constant symbols in α except an empty list $[\ ]$.*

In the next section, we apply rule-generating abduction to a list substitution θ_l and a constant substitution θ_c in the following way: Let α be a ground atom, i.e., a surprising fact. First, by using a list substitution, we obtain an atom β such that $\beta\theta_l = \alpha$ and β is safe on α. Secondly, by using a constant substitution, we obtain an atom γ such that $\gamma\theta_c = \beta$ and γ is safe on β. By the above assumption, γ is also a partially isomorphic generalization of β.

Unfortunately, $\theta_c\theta_l$ is not always well-defined, and γ is not always safe on α. For example, let α be a ground atom $p([a, b, c], [b, c], [a, b, c])$. Then, there exist the following atoms β_i such that $\beta_i\theta_i = \alpha$ and θ_i is a well-defined list substitution:

$$\begin{aligned}
\beta_1 &= p([a, b|x], [b|x], [a, b|x]) & \theta_1 &= \{x := [c]\}, \\
\beta_2 &= p([a|y], y, [a|y]) & \theta_2 &= \{y := [b, c]\}, \\
\beta_3 &= p(z, [b, c], z) & \theta_3 &= \{z := [a, b, c]\}.
\end{aligned}$$

There exists no atom γ and substitutions $\sigma(\neq \varepsilon)$ such that $\gamma\sigma = \beta_3$ and $\theta_3\sigma$ is well-defined. Note that there does not exist the greatest list generalization of α.

Let α be a ground atom. Let β and γ be atoms such that $\beta\theta_l = \alpha$ and $\gamma\theta_c = \beta$. Suppose that both (β, θ_l) and (γ, θ_c) satisfy the safeness conditions. Then, the following two theorems hold.

Theorem 7. *If $\theta_c\theta_l$ is well-defined, then γ is a safe generalization of α.*

Proof. Suppose that $\theta_c\theta_l$ is well-defined. Then, $(\gamma, \theta_c\theta_l)$ satisfies the safeness condition 1.

Since both (β, θ_l) and (γ, θ_c) satisfy the safeness conditions, $(\gamma, \theta_c\theta_l)$ satisfies the safeness condition 3.

By supposition, $\beta = \alpha\theta_l^{-1}$ and $\gamma = \beta\theta_c^{-1}$. The list substitution θ_l replaces the common lists in α by variables. The constant substitution θ_c replaces the same constant symbols in β by the same variables and other constant symbols by other variables. Hence, the composition $\theta_c\theta_l$ replaces the common lists in α by variables, the same constant symbols in α except common terms by the same variables, and other constant symbols by other variables. By Lemma 3 and well-definedness of $\theta_c\theta_l$, $(\gamma, \theta_c\theta_l)$ satisfies the safeness condition 2. $\square$

Theorem 8. *Suppose that any constant which appears in common lists in α does not appear in α except them. If $\beta = \alpha\theta_l^{-1}$ and $\gamma = \beta\theta_c^{-1}$, then $\theta_c\theta_l$ is well-defined. Hence, γ is a safe generalization of α.*

Proof. Suppose that $\theta_l = \cup_{i=1}^n \{x_i := l_i\}$, where l_i is a common list in α. For any j-th argument's term t_j of α, if t_j includes l_i, then $t_j = [a_1^j, a_2^j, \cdots, a_{n_j}^j, |l_i|]$, and no constants $a_1^j, a_2^j, \cdots, a_{n_j}^j$ appear in l_i. Then, θ_c does not include the binding $x := c$ such that c appears in l_i. Hence, $\theta_c\theta_l$ is well-defined. By Theorem 7, $(\gamma, \theta_c\theta_l)$ satisfies the safeness conditions. Then, for γ such that $\gamma\theta_c\theta_l = \alpha$, γ is a safe generalization of α. $\square$

4   Rule-Generating Abduction

The *rule-generating abduction* is a process which generates a rule and proposes a hypothesis from a surprising fact. An inference schema by rule-generating abduction is described by the following three steps:

1. A ground atom C is given.
2. A rule $C' \leftarrow A'$ is generated, where $C'\theta = C$ and $A'\theta = A$.
3. A hypothesis A is proposed.

In Section 2, we have discussed the head-reducing clause of which all the derivations are finite. Suppose that the rule $p(s_1', \cdots, s_n') \leftarrow p(t_1', \cdots, t_n')$ is head-reducing. Then, for a given ground atom $p(t_1, \cdots, t_n)$, the head-reducing rule

$$p(t_1', \cdots, t_n') \leftarrow p(s_1', \cdots, s_n')$$

is generated and the hypothesis $p(s_1, \cdots, s_n)$ is proposed by rule-generating abduction, where $p(t_1', \cdots, t_n')\theta = p(t_1, \cdots, t_n)$ and $p(s_1', \cdots, s_n')\theta = p(s_1, \cdots, s_n)$. An inference schema is depicted by the following syllogism:

$$\frac{p(t_1, \cdots, t_n) \quad p(t_1', \cdots, t_n') \leftarrow p(s_1', \cdots, s_n')}{p(s_1, \cdots, s_n)}.$$

Unfortunately, the number of head-reducing rules is at most

$$(m-1)^n \sum_{i=1}^n \frac{n!}{i!},$$

where $m = \max_{1 \leq i \leq n} |t_i|$ for a ground atom $p(t_1, \cdots, t_n)$.

In usual, there exists no variable which appears only once in the body of the rule $p(t_1', \cdots, t_n') \leftarrow p(s_1', \cdots, s_n')$. Then, the number of weakly head-reducing rules is at most m^n, where $m = \max_{1 \leq i \leq n} |t_i|$ for a ground atom $p(t_1, \cdots, t_n)$.

Furthermore, suppose that a given program is 2-reducing or weakly 2-reducing. Then, for a ground atom with n-ary predicate symbol, the number of 2-reducing rules is at most

$$\sum_{i=1}^{n} \frac{n!}{i!},$$

while the number of weakly 2-reducing rules is at most 2^n.

On the other hand, by using safe generalizations in Section 3, we design an algorithm to generate weakly 2-reducing rules as follows: Suppose that a ground atom α is given. First, by generalizing α with a list substitution θ_l, we obtain an atom β such that $\beta\theta_l = \alpha$ and β is safe on α. We call such β a *list generalization* of α. Secondly, by generalizing β with a constant substitution θ_c, we obtain an atom γ such that $\gamma\theta_c = \beta$ and γ is safe on β. We call such γ a *constant generalization* of β. Note that γ is also assumed the *partially isomorphic generalization* of β. For this algorithm, the number of rules is at most the number of generalizations. Then, we investigate the number of generalizations.

Let α be a ground atom $p(t_1, \cdots, t_n)$. For all common lists in α, we can classify them by the *sublist relation*. For example, let α be a ground atom $p([a, b, c, d], [c, d], [b, c], [c], [b, c, d])$ and t_i be the i-th argument's term of α. Then, t_2, t_4, and t_5 are common lists in α. By the sublist relation, we classify them into $\{t_2, t_5\}$ and $\{t_4\}$. Let l be the number of such classes. Then, the number of the maximal generalizations is at most

$$\left(\frac{(\sqrt{2})^n}{l} \right)^l.$$

Even if $l = 1$, the number of the maximal list generalizations of α is at most $(\sqrt{2})^n$. We discuss more detail in Appendix at the end of this paper.

The number of the maximal list generalizations increases exponentially with respect to n. Thus, in the following algorithm *PROPOSE*, we restrict the reversal of list generalizations to the form $\{t := x\}$, where t is both a common term in α and some argument's term of α. Obviously, the generalization $\alpha\{x := t\}$ is safe on α. The number of weakly 2-reducing rules generated by the algorithm *PROPOSE* is at most n.

An important basis on the algorithm *PROPOSE* is that, *if the i-th argument's term is some common list in α, then the i-th argument's term of the head of the generated rule is a variable; otherwise, it is a list.* Furthermore, by the algorithm *PROPOSE*, the rules in Example 1 are constructed from one ground atom.

In *PROPOSE*, $rs\_abd(fact, head \leftarrow body, hyp)$, which is rule-selecting abduction, is a procedure to propose a hypothesis hyp such that $(head)\sigma = fact$ and $(body)\sigma = hyp$ for some substitution σ.

Algorithm *PROPOSE*

    input $\alpha = p(t_1, \cdots, t_n)$: fact, i.e., ground atom

    output *head* $\leftarrow$ *body* : rule

        δ : hypothesis

        $L := \{\beta \mid \beta = \alpha\{t_i := v_i\}, t_i$: common list in $\alpha\} \cup \{\alpha\}$;

                                        /* β : safe on α */

    while $L \neq \phi$ **do**

        select $\beta \in L$;

        $\gamma = p(s_1, \cdots, s_n)$: the greatest constant generalization of β;

        for $i = 1$ **to** n

            if $s_i = [\,]$ **then**   /* base step */

                output $\gamma \leftarrow$ *true* : rule

                output *true* : hypothesis

                halt;

            else if s_i: a variable **then**   /* induction step */

                $head\_arg_i := x_i$;   /* x_i is a new variable */

            else   /* $s_i = [w_1^i, \cdots]$ */

                $head\_arg_i := [w_1^i | x_i]$;   /* x_i is a new variable */

            end

        end

        $head := p(head\_arg_1, \cdots, head\_arg_n)$;

                              /* $head\_arg_i = [w_1^i | x_i]$ or x_i */

        $body := p(x_1, \cdots, x_n)$;

        output *head* $\leftarrow$ *body* : rule

        $rs\_abd(\alpha, head \leftarrow body, \delta)$;

        output δ : hypothesis

        $L := L - \{\beta\}$

    end

Then, the following two theorems hold.

Theorem 9. *Let α be a ground atom $p(t_1, \cdots, t_n)$ and $k = |t_1| + \cdots + |t_n|$. Then, the algorithm PROPOSE computes the rules and hypotheses in $O(k^3)$ time.*

Proof. For any t_i, it can be determined whether or not t_i is a sublist of t_j in $O(|t_i|)$. Then, for any i, it can be determined whether or not t_i is a sublist of any $t_j (j \neq i)$ in $O((n-1)|t_i|)$. Hence, the set L in the algorithm *PROPOSE* can be constructed in $O((n-1)k)$.

For the selected β in L, the greatest constant generalization of β is also a partially isomorphic generalization of β. By Hirowatari and Arikawa [HA94], a partially isomorphic generalization γ of β can be computed in $O(k^2)$. Since the procedures in the for-loop can be computed in $O(n)$, the for-loop terminates in $O(n^2)$. Then, the procedures in while-loop can be computed in $O(k^2 + n^2)$. Since the number of elements in L is at most n, the while-loop terminates in $O(k^2 n + n^3)$. Hence, the algorithm *PROPOSE* terminates in $O((n-1)k + k^2 n + n^3)$.

Since $n \leq k$, the algorithm *PROPOSE* computes rules and hypotheses in $O(k^3)$ time. $\qquad\qquad\Box$

Theorem 10. *Let α be a ground atom $p(t_1, \cdots, t_n)$. If there exists a common list l in α and l appears in t_i, then l also appears in the i-th argument of the proposed hypothesis δ by the algorithm PROPOSE.*

Proof. Let l be a common list in α. If some argument's term t_i of α is l, then each of the i-th argument's terms of the head and of the body is a variable x_i by the algorithm *PROPOSE*. Then, the i-th argument's term of δ is also l.

If l appears in some argument's term t_i of α, then $t_i = [a_1^i, a_2^i, \cdots, a_{n_i}^i | l]$. By the algorithm *PROPOSE*, the i-th argument's term of the head is a list $[y_1^i | x_i]$, where y_1^i is a variable corresponding to a_1^i, while one of the body is a variable x_i. Then, for the hypothesis δ, the i-th argument's term of δ is $[a_2^i, \cdots, a_{n_i}^i | l]$.

Hence, a common list also appears in the same argument of the proposed hypothesis δ by the algorithm *PROPOSE*. $\qquad\qquad\square$

Hence, if a given ground atom satisfies the relation on common lists, then the proposed hypothesis by the algorithm *PROPOSE* also satisfies it.

5 Examples

In this section, we discuss the several examples for the algorithm *PROPOSE*.

Example 5. Let α be a ground atom $p([a, b], [c, d], [a, b, c, d])$. The list $[c, d]$ is both a common list in α and the second argument's term of α. By the construction of L, $\beta = p([a, b], v_2, [a, b | v_2]) \in L$ is a *safe* list generalization of α, and $\gamma = p([x, y], v_2, [x, y | v_2])$ is the greatest constant generalization of β. The first argument's term of γ is a list which begins with x, the second argument's term is a variable v_2, and the third argument's term is also a list which begins with x. By the for-loop in *PROPOSE*, we obtain the head $p([x | x_1], x_2, [x | x_3])$ and the body $p(x_1, x_2, x_3)$. Hence, *PROPOSE* generates the rule

$$p([x | x_1], x_2, [x | x_3]) \leftarrow p(x_1, x_2, x_3)$$

and proposes the hypothesis $p([b], [c, d], [b, c, d])$. Note that the predicate p means append in Example 1.

Since L includes α, let $\beta = \alpha$. Then, $\gamma = p([x, y], [z, w], [x, y, z, w])$. The first argument's term of γ is a list which begins with x, the second argument's term is a list which begins with z, and the third argument's term is also a list which begins with x. By the for-loop in *PROPOSE*, we obtain the head $p([x | x_1], [z | x_2], [x | x_3])$ and the body $p(x_1, x_2, x_3)$. Hence, *PROPOSE* generates the rule

$$p([x | x_1], [z | x_2], [x | x_3]) \leftarrow p(x_1, x_2, x_3)$$

and proposes the hypothesis $p([b], [d], [b, c, d])$.

Furthermore, each of the rules and hypotheses by *PROPOSE* satisfies the following syllogism respectively:

$$\frac{p([a, b], [c, d], [a, b, c, d]) \quad p([x | x_1], x_2, [x | x_3]) \leftarrow p(x_1, x_2, x_3)}{p([b], [c, d], [b, c, d])},$$

$$\frac{p([a,b],[c,d],[a,b,c,d]) \quad p([x|x_1],[z|x_2],[x|x_3]) \leftarrow p(x_1,x_2,x_3)}{p([b],[d],[b,c,d])}.$$

Example 6. Let α be a ground atom $p(a,[a,b])$. Since there exists no common list in α, $\beta = p(a,[a,b])$ and $\gamma = p(x,[x,y])$. The first argument's term of γ is a variable x, and the second argument's term is a list which begins with x. By the for-loop in *PROPOSE*, we obtain the head $p(x_1,[x|x_2])$ and the body $p(x_1,x_2)$. Hence, *PROPOSE* generates the rule

$$p(x_1,[x|x_2]) \leftarrow p(x_1,x_2)$$

and proposes the hypothesis $p(a,[b])$. Note that the predicate p means **member** in Example 1.

Let α be a ground atom $p([a],[a,b])$. Since there exists no common list in α, $\beta = p([a],[a,b])$ and $\gamma = p([x],[x,y])$. The first argument's term of γ is a list which begins with x, and the second argument's term is also a list which begins with x. By the for-loop in *PROPOSE*, we obtain the head $p([x|x_1],[x|x_2])$ and the body $p(x_1,x_2)$. Hence, *PROPOSE* generates the rule

$$p([x|x_1],[x|x_2]) \leftarrow p(x_1,x_2)$$

and proposes the hypothesis $p([\ ],[b])$. Note that the predicate p means **prefix** in Example 1.

Let α be a ground atom $p([b],[a,b])$. The list $[b]$ is both a common list in α and the first argument's term of α. Then, $\beta = p(v_1,[a|v_1])$ and $\gamma = p(v_1,[x|v_1])$. The first argument's term of γ is a variable v_1, and the second argument's term is a list which begins with x. By the for-loop in *PROPOSE*, we obtain the head $p(x_1,[x|x_2])$ and the body $p(x_1,x_2)$. Hence, *PROPOSE* generates the rule

$$p(x_1,[x|x_2]) \leftarrow p(x_1,x_2)$$

and proposes the hypothesis $p([b],[b])$. Note that the predicate p means **suffix** in Example 1. On the other hand, since L includes $\alpha = p([a,b],[b])$, let $\beta = \alpha$. Then, $\gamma = p([x],[y,x])$. The first argument's term of γ is a list which begins with x, and the second argument's term is a list which begins with y. By the for-loop in *PROPOSE*, we obtain the head $p([x|x_1],[y|x_2])$ and the body $p(x_1,x_2)$. Hence, *PROPOSE* generates the rule

$$p([x|x_1],[y|x_2]) \leftarrow p(x_1,x_2)$$

and proposes the hypothesis $p([\ ],[b])$.

If $\alpha = p([a,b],[c,d],[a,b,c,d])$, then *PROPOSE* generates the rule

$$p([x|x_1],x_2,[x|x_3]) \leftarrow p(x_1,x_2,x_3)$$

and proposes the hypothesis $p([b],[c,d],[b,c,d])$. On the other hand, if $\alpha = p([a,b],[a,b,c,d],[c,d])$, then *PROPOSE* also generates the rule

$$p([x|x_1],[x|x_2],x_3) \leftarrow p(x_1,x_2,x_3)$$

and proposes the hypothesis $p([b], [b, c, d], [c, d])$. Hence, the algorithm *PRO-POSE* is independent of the order of argument. Furthermore, as member and suffix in Example 6, the algorithm *PROPOSE* is also independent of the types of argument. In other words, *PROPOSE* needs no types of argument.

We have implemented the algorithm *PROPOSE* by Prolog. The predicate propose returns the generated rule as the third argument. It also returns the hypothesis proposed by the generated rule as the second argument.

```
: ?- propose(p([a,b],[c,d],[a,b,c,d]),X,Y).
X = p([b],[d],[b,c,d]),
Y = p([_2046|_2602],[_1378|_2600],[_2046|_2598]):-p(_2602,_2600,_2598) ;
X = p([b],[c,d],[b,c,d]),
Y = p([_1578|_2070],_2058,[_1578|_2066]):-p(_2070,_2058,_2066) ;
no
: ?- propose(p(a,[a,b]),X,Y).
X = p(a,[b]),
Y = p(_1334,[_972|_1340]):-p(_1334,_1340) ;
no
: ?- propose(p([a],[a,b]),X,Y).
X = p([],[b]),
Y = p([_1016|_1418],[_1016|_1416]):-p(_1418,_1416) ;
no
: ?- propose(p([b],[a,b]),X,Y).
X = p([],[b]),
Y = p([_1158|_1560],[_904|_1558]):-p(_1560,_1558) ;
X = p([b],[b]),
Y = p(_1220,[_872|_1226]):-p(_1220,_1226) ;
no
: ?- propose(p([a,b,c],[b,c],[a,b,c]),X,Y).
X = p([b,c],[c],[b,c]),
Y = p([_2066|_2622],[_1738|_2620],[_2066|_2618]):-p(_2622,_2620,_2618) ;
X = p([b,c],[b,c],[b,c]),
Y = p([_1638|_2102],_2090,[_1638|_2098]):-p(_2102,_2090,_2098) ;
X = p([a,b,c],[c],[a,b,c]),
Y = p(_2360,[_1670|_2368],_2356):-p(_2360,_2368,_2356) ;
no
```

Note that, in the last example, $\beta_1 = p([a|v_2], v_2, [a|v_2])$ and $\beta_2 = p(v_1, [b, c], v_1)$ are the safe generalizations of $p([a, b, c], [b, c], [a, b, c])$. Hence, there are three hypotheses and rules for a ground atom $p([a, b, c], [b, c], [a, b, c])$.

On the other hand, for a ground atom $p([a, b, c], [d, e], [a, b, c])$, the predicate propose returns the following two rules and hypotheses:

```
: ?- propose(p([a,b,c],[d,e],[a,b,c]),X,Y).
X = p([b,c],[e],[b,c]),
Y = p([_2510|_3066],[_1490|_3064],[_2510|_3062]):-p(_3066,_3064,_3062) ;
X = p([a,b,c],[e],[a,b,c]),
Y = p(_2056,[_1366|_2064],_2052):-p(_2056,_2064,_2052) ;
no
```

6 Conclusion

In this paper, we have formulated an overgeneralization and a safe generalization, and given the algorithm *PROPOSE* to construct weakly 2-reducing rules. We have shown that the algorithm *PROPOSE* can generate rules and propose hypotheses in polynomial time with respect to the length of a surprising fact. Also we have shown that a common term in some argument of a surprising fact appears in the same argument of the proposed hypothesis by *PROPOSE*.

Abduction is an inference to propose hypotheses to be used before deduction and induction. We have left as a future work to combine abduction and inductive logic programming. Ling [Lin89a, Lin89b] has introduced the constructive inductive logic programming. There may exist a relationship between such works and this paper.

Furthermore, as to the inductive logic programming, we have left the problem of predicate invention. The number of rules and hypotheses becomes exponentially large. Hence, we need to introduce some heuristics such as on a distinction between a necessary and useful intermediate term, the number of local variables, invented predicate symbols and rules, and so on.

Acknowledgment

The author would like to thank Setsuo Arikawa and Eiju Hirowatari for many precious discussions about partially isomorphic generalizations. He also thanks the reviewers for valuable comments.

References

[ASO91]   Arimura, H., Shinohara, T., Otsuki, S.: A polynomial time algorithm for finite unions of tree pattern languages. In Proceedings of the 2nd Workshop on Algorithmic Learning Theory (1991) 105–114.

[Dun91]   Dung, P. M.: Negation as hypothesis: an abductive foundation for logic programming. In Proceedings of the 8th International Conference on Logic Programming (1991) 3–17.

[EK89]   Eshghi, K., Kowalski, R. A.: Abduction compared with negation by failure. In Proceedings of the 6th International Conference on Logic Programming (1989) 234–254.

[Hir93]   Hirata, K.: A classification of abduction: abduction of logic programming. Machine Intelligence 14 (to appear).

[HA94]   Hirowatari, E., Arikawa, S.: Partially isomorphic generalization and analogical reasoning. In Proceedings of European Conference on Machine Learning (1994), Lecture Notes in Artificial Intelligence 784 (1994) 363–366.

[Ino92]   Inoue, K.: Principles of abduction. Journal of Japanese Society for Artificial Intelligence 7 (1992) 48–59 (in Japanese).

[KM90]   Kakas, A. C., Mancarella, P.: Generalized stable models: a semantics for abduction. In Proceedings of the 9th European Conference on Artificial Intelligence (1990) 385–391.

[Kun87] Kunifuji, S.: Hypothesis-based reasoning. Journal of Japanese Society for Artificial Intelligence **2** (1987) 22–87 (in Japanese).

[Lin89a] Ling, X.: Learning and invention of Horn clause theories - a constructive method. Methodologies for Intelligent Systems **4** (1989) 323–331.

[Lin89b] Ling, X.: Inventing theoretical terms in inductive learning of functions - search and constructive methods. Methodologies for Intelligent Systems **4** (1989) 332–341.

[Llo87] Lloyd, J. W.: Foundations of logic programming (second, extended edition). Springer-Verlag (1987).

[Mug92a] Muggleton, S. (ed.): Inductive logic programming. Academic Press (1992).

[Mug92b] Muggleton, S.: Machine invention of first-order predicates by inverting resolution. In Proceedings of the 5th International Conference on Machine Learning (1988) 339-352; In [Mug92a].

[Pei65] Peirce, C. S.: Collected papers of Charles Sanders Peirce (1839-1914). Hartshone, C. S., Weiss, P.(eds.), The Belknap Press (1965).

[Plo70] Plotkin, G. D.: A note on inductive generalization. Machine Intelligence **5** (1970) 153–163.

[Plo71] Plotkin, G. D.: A further note on inductive generalization. Machine Intelligence **6** (1971) 101–124.

[Poo88] Poole, D.: A logical framework for default reasoning. Artificial Intelligence **36** (1988) 27–47.

[Sha81] Shapiro, E. Y.: Inductive inference of theories from facts. Research Report **192**, Yale University (1981).

[SS86] Sterling, L., Shapiro, E.: The art of Prolog. The MIT Press (1986).

[Yam92] Yamamoto, A.: Procedural semantics and negative information of elementary formal system. Journal of Logic Programming **13** (1992) 89–97.

[Yon82] Yonemori, Y.: Peirce's semiotics. Keisou Syobou (1982) (in Japanese).

Appendix

In Section 4, we investigate the number of the maximal list generalizations. In this appendix, we explain how to solve the upper bound of this number.

Let α be a ground atom $p(t_1, \cdots, t_n)$ and K_n be the number of the maximal list generalizations of α. In Section 4, we introduce the classification by the sublist relation. Suppose that l is the number of such classes. If $l = 1$, then we can find the upper bound of K_n in the following way.

For simplicity, suppose that the common lists in α are $t_1, t_2, \cdots, t_{n-1}$, and $|t_1| > |t_2| > \cdots > |t_{n-1}|$. We denote the generalization $\alpha\{t_{j_1} := x_{j_1}, \cdots, t_{j_f} := x_{j_f}\}$ by $\beta_{(j_1,\cdots,j_f)}$. Note that t_{j_i+1} is not a common list in $\beta_{(j_i)}$. Furthermore, for $\beta_{(j_i,j_i+a,j_i+a+b)}$ $(a, b = 2 \text{ or } 3)$, there exist substitutions θ_{j_i+a+b}, θ_{j_i+a}, and θ_{j_i} such that

$$\beta_{(j_i,j_i+a)} = \beta_{(j_i,j_i+a,j_i+a+b)}\theta_{j_i+a+b},$$
$$\beta_{(j_i,j_i+a+b)} = \beta_{(j_i,j_i+a,j_i+a+b)}\theta_{j_i+a},$$
$$\beta_{(j_i+a,j_i+a+b)} = \beta_{(j_i,j_i+a,j_i+a+b)}\theta_{j_i}.$$

Hence, $\beta_{(j_i,j_i+a)}$, $\beta_{(j_i,j_i+a+b)}$, and $\beta_{(j_i+a,j_i+a+b)}$ are not maximal list generalizations.

By using the index of β, K_n is equal to the number of the sequences $(j_1, \cdots, j_f)$ which satisfy the following conditions:

1. $j_1 = 1$ or 2,
2. $j_f = n - 1$ or n, and
3. the adjacent number of j_i is either $j_i + 2$ or $j_i + 3$.

For example, let $n = 8$. Then, the following seven sequences

$$(1,3,5,7),(1,3,6),(1,4,6),(1,4,7),(2,4,6),(2,4,7),(2,5,8)$$

satisfy the above conditions. For the sequence $(j_1, \cdots, j_f)$ which satisfies the above conditions, the number of sequences such that $j_1 = 1$ is greater that $j_1 = 2$. Let A_n be the set of the sequences $(j_1, \cdots, j_f)$ which satisfy the above conditions and $j_1 = 1$. Then, $K_n \leq 2|A_n|$. Furthermore, for $n \geq 6$, we can construct the set A_n in the following way:

1. if $(j_1, \cdots, j_f) \in A_{n-2}$, then $(j_1, \cdots, j_f, n) \in A_n$, and
2. if $(j'_1, \cdots, j'_f) \in A_{n-3}$, then $(j'_1, \cdots, j'_f, n - 1) \in A_n$.

Hence, $|A_n|$ satisfies the following equations:

$$|A_3| = 1, \ |A_4| = 1, \ |A_5| = 2, \ |A_n| = |A_{n-2}| + |A_{n-3}| \ (n \geq 6).$$

By the mathematical induction, we obtain the following formula:

$$\left(\sqrt[3]{2}\right)^{n-2} \leq |A_n| \leq \left(\sqrt{2}\right)^{n-2} \ (n \geq 6).$$

Hence, the number K_n of the maximal generalizations is characterized by the following formula:

$$K_n \leq 2\left(\sqrt{2}\right)^{n-2} = \left(\sqrt{2}\right)^n.$$

Note that this formula holds for any $n \geq 1$.

Let l be the number of classes by the sublist relation and C_j be such class for $1 \leq j \leq l$. For any C_j, the number of the sequences which satisfy the above conditions is at most $\left(\sqrt{2}\right)^{|C_j|}$. Then, the number K_n of the maximal generalizations is at most $\left(\sqrt{2}\right)^{|C_1|} \times \cdots \times \left(\sqrt{2}\right)^{|C_l|}$. Hence, K_n is also characterized by the following formula:

$$K_n \leq \left(\frac{(\sqrt{2})^n}{l}\right)^l.$$

Fuzzy Analogy Based Reasoning and Classification of Fuzzy Analogies

Toshiharu IWATANI, Shun'ichi TANO, Atsushi INOUE, Wataru OKAMOTO

Laboratory for International Fuzzy Engineering Research (LIFE)
Siber Hegner Building, 89-1 Yamashita-cho Naka-ku Yokohama-shi 231 JAPAN
e-mail iwatani@fuzzy.or.jp

Abstract: Conventional research on analogical reasoning (AR, for short) theory has not yet addressed the management of fuzzy matching between two different predicates, though human beings essentially utilize fuzzy matching when they infer analogically. On the other hand, fuzzy logic has been successfully applied to deductive and inductive reasoning to make them more flexible. Although the goal of both fuzzy logic and AR is to achieve more flexible human-like reasoning, there have been few applications of fuzzy logic to analogical reasoning. In this paper, fuzzy-analogy based reasoning (F-ABR), an extension of ABR, is proposed. In ABR, an analogy represents clear partial agreements between two knowledge areas, each of which is described as a set of predicates. In F-ABR, a knowledge area is a set of fuzzy predicates and a fuzzy analogy means fuzzy partial agreements between two knowledge areas. Using fuzzy logic, F-ABR can infer in a way that is more flexible and human-like than conventional ABR. This paper discusses three topics: first, a fuzzy matching method between two fuzzy predicate symbols is described. A fuzzy analogy contains a set of pairs composed of a predicate symbol and a similarity degree, and three methods for calculating the similarity degree are also described. Second, methods for classifying and ordering fuzzy analogies, based mainly on similarity degrees, are introduced. These methods are necessary when selecting a single fuzzy analogy to use in the reasoning process. Finally, the features of each type of fuzzy analogy are analyzed in order to show that many kinds of flexible reasoning can be achieved by selecting a fuzzy analogy.

1. Introduction

Analogical reasoning (AR)[1], one of the most important inference methods, along with deductive reasoning and inductive reasoning, has been studied since the days of Aristotle. In the future, we expect AR to play an important role in both machine learning and flexible reasoning research. If we concisely explain AR in the context of machine learning, it consists of two processes. The first process detects any agreement between two different systems. (The term 'system' means a set of facts and is taken to mean one knowledge area in this paper). The second process projects facts from one system to the other, considering the agreements that are detected in the first process. The system from which the projected facts are selected is called the source system while the other is called the target system. For example, there is a fact "The sun is much bigger than the earth." in the source system and a fact "A nucleus is much bigger than an electron." in the target system. A human can project the fact "The earth rotates around the sun." from the source system into the target system and conclude that "An electron rotates around a nucleus." considering the two original facts as a ground. This is a typical example of AR. Many conventional studies of AR have invented models and algorithms that can achieve such reasoning processes.

It is natural that people also derive a similar conclusion, even if the given fact in the target system is "A nucleus is 10^5 times bigger than an electron". They can easily find an agreement that is fuzzy rather than crisp between 'much bigger' and '10^5 times bigger' though they, of course, know the difference between these two phrases. Conventional AR models are not suitable to achieve or analyze such a reasoning process because they do not treat fuzzy matching between two predicates. Fuzzy logic [2] has been successfully applied to deductive reasoning and inductive reasoning to make them more flexible and useful. However, there have been few applications of fuzzy logic to AR though both theories are important concepts for achieving flexible inference.

In this paper, we propose F-ABR, an extension of ABR [3] using fuzzy logic, which is one of the inference systems used in the FLINS [4]-[6] (Fuzzy LINgual System) currently under development at LIFE (Laboratory for International Fuzzy Engineering Research). ABR is one of the most important theoretical results of conventional AR research. The basic opinion of this paper is that it is essential to combine fuzzy logic and AR to facilitate and analyze flexible and human-like reasoning.

The organization of this paper is as follows: first, conventional ABR is introduced to show the necessity of extension using fuzzy logic, which is covered in Section 2. Second, a method to derive three kinds of similarity degrees between two fuzzy predicates as well as a definition of fuzzy analogies are proposed in Section 3. Classifying and ordering methods, which are necessary to select one analogy when using F-ABR, are discussed in Section 4, while features of each type of analogy are analyzed in Section 5. Finally, a brief conclusion is given in Section 6.

2. Conventional ABR and its Problems

2.1 Formalization of ABR and Definition of Analogies

Though there are many kinds of ABR problem formalization, we will use the concise one shown in **Problem 1** throughout this paper to quickly explain the concept and make the problem clear.

Problem 1. When an action V1 is applied to the source system S1, the result is as shown in Fig. 1(a). Show the result if V1 is applied to the target system T1, provided that each of S1, T1, and V1 are sets of facts as described in formula (1):

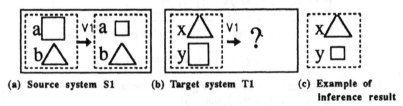

(a) Source system S1   (b) Target system T1   (c) Example of inference result

Fig. 1 Example Problem 1

$$S1= \{big\_square(a), triangle(b), above(a, b)\} \tag{1.a}$$
$$T1= \{triangle(x), big\_square(y), above(x,y)\} \tag{1.b}$$
$$V1= \{shrink(a)\} \tag{1.c}$$

We can find clear agreements between the facts: These correspondences are, "big_square X1" and "triangle X2" if X1 is 'a' in S1 and 'y' in T1, and X2 is 'b' in S1 and 'x' in T1. A clear partial identity, that is, a set of crisp agreements between facts under the pairing of constant symbols, is called an analogy. The definition of an analogy is given below.

Definition 1. Analogy
Let S1 and T1 be finite sets of ground predicates with no common constant between the two sets. Let θ s and θ t be substitutions of a constant for a variable and θ be a pair

$< \theta$ s, θ t>. For a variable X, the pair $<$X θ s, X θ t> is denoted by X θ . For a set W of predicates whose argument(s) is/are variable(s), the set $\{$P θ :P$\in$W$\}$ is denoted by W θ . Here, Var(W) represents the set of all variables in W. We call the pair A = (W, θ) an analogy if Conditions 1.1 and 1.2 are satisfied.

Condition 1.1 W $\theta \subseteq$S1$\times$T1 and W θ is a one-to-one relation of ground predicates.
Condition 1.2 Var(W) θ is a one-to-one relation of constants.

Example 1. A=(W, θ) is an analogy between S1 and T1 where
  W=$\{$big_square(X1), triangle(X2)$\}$ and
  θ =$<\theta$ s, θ t>, θ s =$\{$X1$\leftarrow$a, X2$\leftarrow$b$\}$ and θ t =$\{$X1$\leftarrow$y, X2$\leftarrow$x$\}$.

In Example 1, '$\leftarrow$' means a substitution. If we select the analogy A=(W, θ) in the reasoning process, the constant 'a' in the source system corresponds to 'y'(= a θ s^{-1} θ t, where θ s^{-1} means a set of substitutions $\{$a$\leftarrow$X1,b$\leftarrow$X2$\}$) in the target system. Therefore, shrink(a) is modified into shrink(y) in the target system. Hence, the inference result is as shown in Fig. 1(c).

2.2 The Problem of Conventional Analogy

Let us consider Problem 2 to highlight the problem of conventional ABR.

Problem 2. When an action V2 is applied to the source system S2, the result is as shown in Fig. 2(a). Show the result if V2 is applied to the target system T2 provided that each of S2, T2, and V2 are sets of facts as described in formula (2):

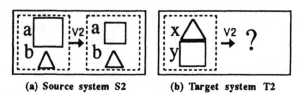

(a) Source system S2   (b) Target system T2

Fig. 2 Example Problem 2

S2= $\{$very_big_square(a), small_triangle(b), above(a, b)$\}$ (2.a)
T2= $\{$triangle(x), big_square(y), on(x,y)$\}$ (2.b)
V2= $\{$shrink(a)$\}$ (2.c)

Since there is no clear agreement between the facts in S2 and T2, it is impossible to detect any analogy and start the ABR process as long as we adopt the conventional definition of analogy. However, it is easy for humans to find fuzzy agreements between very_big_square(a) and big_square(y), and between small_triangle(b) and triangle(x) by using fuzzy matching. We should extend the definition of an analogy to achieve human-like flexible AR. A fuzzy partial identity that is a set of fuzzy agreements of facts under the pairing of constant symbols is considered to be a fuzzy analogy. To express the fuzzified agreement, a similarity degree si $\in$ [0,1] is associated with each predicate wi $\in$ W in the conventional analogy. We call a predicate with a similarity degree [wi, si] a PSD. An example of a fuzzy analogy between S2 and T2 is shown below to illustrate the basic concepts while the formal definition will be given in Section 3.

Example 2. FA =(WF, θ) is a fuzzy analogy between S2 and T2 where,

WF={[big_square(X1), 0.6], [triangle(X2), 0.75]} and
θ =< θ s, θ t>, θ s={X1←a, X2←b} and θ t={X1←y, X2←x}.

In this example, FA means that there are two predicates in each system S2 and T2. One predicate must have a similarity degree higher than 0.6 to big_square( ) and the other predicate must have a similarity degree higher than 0.75 to triangle( ) under the pairing of constants in each system {<a,y>, <b,x>}. Since it is difficult to define a reasonable method for calculating the similarity degree between two conventional predicate symbols, we assume that each system is a set of ground fuzzy predicates whose truth values range from 0.0 to 1.0. Further, it is assumed that μ_p represents the truth value function (TVF) of the fuzzy predicate symbol P. Strictly speaking, it is sometimes natural for $\mu_p(x)$ to be defined not in terms of x but in terms of some attribute values of x. For example, the TVF of predicate tall( ), that is $\mu_{tall}( )$, should be defined in terms of the height of x. However, the notation $\mu_{tall}(x)$ is used for convenience.

3. Definition of a Fuzzy Analogy

Similarity degrees between two fuzzy predicate symbols P and Q are calculated in terms of μ_p and μ_Q. There is only one method to determine whether or not μ_p equals μ_Q. However, there are many theories on ways to define the similarity degree between two given functions. We will introduce three kinds of similarity degrees in this section, the possibility degree, the necessity degree, and the compatibility degree, which we will use to develop several kinds of more flexible AR.

3.1 Possibility Degrees and Necessity Degrees[7]

First, let us introduce the concept of a possibility measure and a necessity measure, which forms the background of possibility degrees and necessity degrees. Let U denote the universe of discourse and ϕ denote the empty set. A function g( ) that satisfies formulas (3.a) and (3.b) is called a fuzzy measure in U.

$$g(\phi) = 0, g(U) = 1.0 \tag{3.a}$$
$$A \subseteq B \rightarrow g(A) \leq g(B) \tag{3.b}$$

Moreover, a measure Π( ), which satisfies formula (4.a), is called a possibility measure. A measure N( ), which satisfies formula (4.b), is called a necessity measure.

$$\Pi(A \cap B) = \max \{ \Pi(A), \Pi(B)\} \tag{4.a}$$
$$N(A \cap B) = \min \{N(A), N(B)\} \tag{4.b}$$

Let $\pi(x)$ $(0 \leq \pi(x) \leq 1)$ denote a possibility measure function, expressing the possibility of each element $x \in U$ and let $\mu_A(x)$ be a membership function of a fuzzy set A. Here, $\Pi(A)$ and N(A) can be determined by formulas (5.a) and (5.b), respectively.

$$\Pi(A) = \sup_x (\pi(x) \wedge \mu_A(x)) \tag{5.a}$$

$$N(A) = \inf_x ((1 - \pi(x)) \vee \mu_A(x)) \tag{5.b}$$

Let $\Pi(Q|P)$ denote the possibility degree of Q with respect to P and $N(Q|P)$ denote the necessity degree of Q with respect to P. The term $\Pi(Q|P)$ is defined as the possibility measure when the membership function $\mu_A(x)$ in formula (5.a) is replaced by $\mu_Q(x)$ and the possibility measure function $\pi(x)$ is replaced by $\mu_P(x)$. Furthermore, $N(Q|P)$ is the necessity measure under the same conditions. Therefore, formulas (6.a) and (6.b) show the definitions of $\Pi(Q|P)$ and $N(Q|P)$, respectively.

$$\Pi(Q|P) = \sup_x (\mu_P(x) \wedge \mu_Q(x)) \tag{6.a}$$

$$N(Q|P) = \inf_x ((1 - \mu_P(x)) \vee \mu_Q(x)) \tag{6.b}$$

3.2 Compatibility Degree

Let $\tau_{Q|P}(\mu)$ denote the compatibility of Q with respect to P. The compatibility is a function whose domain and codomain belong to the closed interval [0, 1]. Formula (7) shows the definition of $\tau_{Q|P}(\mu)$.

$$\tau_{Q|P}(\mu) = \sup_{\mu_P(x)=\mu} \mu_Q(x) \tag{7}$$

Let $L(Q|P)$ denote the compatibility degree of Q with respect to P. We define $L(Q|P)$ as the mean value of the compatibility function $\tau_{Q|P}(\mu)$. Formula (8) shows the definition of $L(Q|P)$.

$$L(Q|P) = \frac{\int_0^1 \tau_{Q|P}(\mu) \cdot \mu \, d\mu}{\int_0^1 \tau_{Q|P}(\mu) \, d\mu} \tag{8}$$

3.3 Features of each Similarity Degree

According to formula (5), the value of $\Pi(Q|P)$, which is always equal to $\Pi(P|Q)$, is larger than $N(Q|P)$ for any Q and P. Moreover, $\Pi(Q|P)$ is often nearly equal to 1, even if μ_Q is not particularly similar to μ_P. For example, $\Pi(Q|P)$ equals 1.0 while $N(Q|P)$ equals 0.0 in the case shown in Fig. 3(a).

Qualitatively speaking, when $Q(x) \rightarrow P(x)$ (in this case, '$\rightarrow$' means implication) is true for almost any x, $N(P|Q)$ and $L(Q|P)$ are close to 1.0 (Fig. 3(b)). The typical difference between $N(P|Q)$ and $L(Q|P)$ is shown in Fig. 3(c). When the shape of μ_P is slightly shifted from the shape of μ_Q, $N(P|Q)$ is almost equal to 0, while $L(Q|P)$ is medium (= 0.5−0.6).

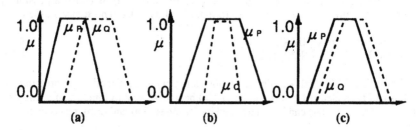

Fig. 3 Example of TVFs 1

3.4 Definition of a Fuzzy Analogy

Usually a fuzzy analogy contains more than one PSD. If several kinds of similarity degrees are contained, for example, one similarity degree is calculated as a possibility degree while another is a compatibility degree, it is difficult to analyze the meaning of the fuzzy analogy. Moreover, it is also difficult to define an ordering method of fuzzy analogies in such a case. Therefore, we assume that every similarity degree in a fuzzy analogy is determined by one of three methods and so there are three kinds of analogies for one W(= a set of fuzzy predicate symbols); one is the possibility fuzzy analogy, another is the necessity fuzzy analogy, and the last is the compatibility fuzzy analogy. The word 'similarity degree', throughout the definition of fuzzy analogy here, can be interpreted arbitrarily as any kind of similarity degree.

For the convenience of the reader, some notations are introduced in advance before showing the definition of fuzzy analogy. First, a subset of a PSD set is defined as follows:

Definition 2. Subset of a PSD Set
Let WF1 and WF2 be a set of PSDs. For any [Q1(a), s1] ∈ WF1, there exists [Q1(a), s2] ∈ WF2 such that s1 ≦ s2. In this case, WF1 is a subset of WF2, that is, WF1 ⊆ WF2.

Furthermore, when the fuzzy predicate symbol P( ) has a similarity degree to the fuzzy predicate symbol Q( ) higher than si, we describe this relation using a new symbol '--->' (e.g. P( ) ---> [Q( ), si]). Using these notations, the definition of the transformability from a set of predicates to a set of PSDs is given below.

Definition 3. Transformability
Let W denote a set of predicates and WF denote a set of PSDs. For any [Q(a), s] ∈ WF, there exists R(a) ∈ W such that R(a)--->[Q(a), s]. We say that W is transformable to WF, and write W ⇒ WF.

Now, a fuzzy analogy is defined as follows;

Definition 4. Fuzzy Analogy
Assume that all notations used in **Definition 1** are available and that both S and T are sets of ground fuzzy predicates. Further, let WF={[wi, si]} be a set of PSDs where si denotes a positive similarity degree and W ={wi} denotes the set of predicates in WF. We call a pair FA = (WF, θ) a fuzzy analogy when Conditions 4.1 and 4.2 below are satisfied.

Condition 4.1 S⇒WF θ s, T⇒WF θ t and W θ is a one-to-one relation of ground predicates.
Condition 4.2 Var(W) θ is a one-to-one relation of constants.

4. Methods for Classifying and Ordering Fuzzy Analogies

4.1 A Classifying Method for Fuzzy Analogies

Figure 4 shows the difference between ABR and F-ABR. In conventional ABR, it is assumed that action V is caused by W θ s =S'⊆S and so W θ t =T'⊆T causes V θ s^{-1} θ t, which is an inference result in the target system. Therefore the set of predicates (=W) in a conventional analogy is strictly constrained; any wi θ s must belong to the source system and any wi θ t must belong to the target system (Fig. 4(a)).

In contrast, the constraint on the set of predicates {wi} in fuzzy analogy is very weak (Fig. 4(b)); even a predicate that does not exist either in S or T can be an element of {wi}. So, the variety of fuzzy analogies is very wide and F-ABR can achieve many types of AR. This is an important advantages of F-ABR over conventional ABR which will be explained in detail in section 5. On the other hand, the variety of fuzzy analogies makes it difficult to define any reasonable ordering method common to all of them. They must be divided into several groups that share the same features. In the rest of this sub-section, two special groups of fuzzy analogies and a concept of non-redundancy of a fuzzy analogy are defined before an ordering criteria of fuzzy analogies is introduced in sub-section 4.2.

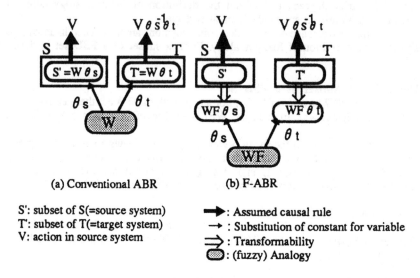

(a) Conventional ABR   (b) F-ABR

S': subset of S(=source system)   ➡: Assumed causal rule
T': subset of T(=target system)   →: Substitution of constant for variable
V: action in source system   ⇒: Transformability
                                      ◉: (fuzzy) Analogy

Fig. 4 The difference between ABR and F-ABR

Definition 5. Source-oriented Fuzzy Analogies and Target-oriented Fuzzy Analogies

Let FA=(WF, θ) be a fuzzy analogy and W be a set of predicates in WF. Any fuzzy analogy that satisfies Condition 5.1 is called a source-oriented fuzzy analogy (SFA), while one that satisfies Condition 5.2 is called a target-oriented fuzzy analogy (TFA).

Condition 5.1 $W\theta s \subseteq S1$
Condition 5.2 $W\theta t \subseteq T1$

Figure 5 shows the relations between the normal fuzzy analogy, SFA, TFA, and the conventional analogy. A fuzzy analogy that does not belong to TFA nor SFA is called a non-restricted fuzzy analogy here in after.

Fuzzy Analogy

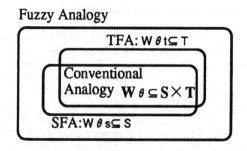

Fig. 5 Relations among groups of analogies

Because an AR algorithm is usually discussed after both a source system and a target system have been already given exactly (see **Problem 1**), there are few research on the methods of selecting the best source system to solve a given problem. However, in a natural situation there are many candidates for a source system when we solve a problem using the AR method. In such cases, we must select one system by comparing each TFA, which shows how one candidate system is similar to the given target system. On the contrary, SFA is useful in selecting a target system. (How to compare the fuzzy analogies between different knowledge areas is another important problem; however, it is beyond the scope of this paper).

The weakness of constraints on wi causes redundancy in fuzzy analogies. For example, if one fuzzy analogy contains both [tall(R), 0.8] and [very_tall(R), 0.6], it seems to be redundant and complicated to define a dominance relation among fuzzy analogies. So, it is necessary to introduce non-redundancy of the fuzzy analogies. Before defining it, a simple concept to classify fuzzy predicate symbols is introduced. Let Z denote the set of all the predicate symbols defined in the given problem. Any predicate symbol P can be uniquely classified according to a set of variables on which TVF of P (= μ p) is defined. Therefore, it can be assumed that Z is divided into subsets of predicate symbols, PS1, PS2, ..., PSn such that PSi $\subseteq$ Z for $^\forall$i, Z=PS1 $\cup$ PS2 $\cup$ ... $\cup$ PSn and PSi $\cap$ PSj = ϕ for i $\neq$ j (Fig. 6).

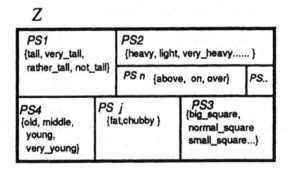

Fig. 6 Classification of fuzzy predicate symbols

Then, the definition of a non-redundant fuzzy analogy is given as follows:

Definition 6. Non-redundant Fuzzy Analogy
Let FA=(WF, θ) be a fuzzy analogy, where WF={[wi, si]} is a set of PSDs and W ={wi} is a set of predicates. FA is non-redundant if there is no predicate wj $\in$ W for $^\forall$i (i $\neq$ j) such that wi and wj belong to the same subset PSk and Var(wi) = Var(wj).

For the rest of this paper, the term 'fuzzy analogy' means 'non-redundant fuzzy analogy' unless otherwise mentioned.

4.2 An Ordering Method for Fuzzy Analogies

Here, we show the definition of a dominance relation between fuzzy analogies and the local maximum fuzzy analogy.

Definition 7 Dominance of a Fuzzy Analogy
Let FA1=(WF1, θ 1) and FA2=(WF2, θ 2) be fuzzy analogies. If for $^\forall$[wi, si] $\in$ WF1,

there exists [wj, sj] ∈ WF2 such that wi and wj belong to the same subset PS ⊆ Z and si ≤ sj, then FA2 is dominant over FA1.

Definition 8 The Local Maximum Analogy

Let FA=(WF, θ) be a fuzzy analogy between a source system S and target system T. When there is no fuzzy analogy between S and T that dominates FA, FA is a local maximum analogy.

It is a natural restriction that the fuzzy analogy used in F-ABR should be a local maximum in SFA or in TFA or in non-redundant fuzzy analogies. The choice depends on the given problem.

5. Analysis of F-ABR Features

In section 3, we showed that fuzzy analogies can be divided into three types, possibility fuzzy analogies, necessity fuzzy analogies, and compatibility fuzzy analogies according to the method of deciding the similarity degree. In section 4, SFA, TFA, and non-restricted (and non-redundant) fuzzy analogies were introduced depending on the restriction on wi. Altogether, we can find nine types of fuzzy analogies. In this section, the features of each F-ABR that is caused by each type of fuzzy analogy are analyzed.

Several TVFs of fuzzy predicates are introduced in formula (9) in order to analyze F-ABR. Figure. 7 shows the shape of these functions.

young(x): $\mu_{young}(a(X)) =$

$$
\begin{array}{llll}
& = & (a(x) -10) / 10 & :10 < a(x) \leq 20 & (9.a)\\
& = & 1.0 & :20 < a(x) \leq 35 \\
& = & (45 -a(x)) /10 & :35 < a(x) \leq 45 \\
& = & 0.0 & :else
\end{array}
$$

middle(x): $\mu_{middle}(a(X)) =$
=middle aged

$$
\begin{array}{llll}
& = & (a(x) -30) / 5 & :30 < a(x) \leq 35 & (9.b)\\
& = & 1.0 & :35 < a(x) \leq 55 \\
& = & (60 -a(x)) / 5 & :55 < a(x) \leq 60 \\
& = & 0.0 & :else
\end{array}
$$

old(x): $\mu_{old}(a(X))$

$$
\begin{array}{llll}
& = & (a(x) -45) / 5 & :45 < a(x) \leq 50 & (9.c)\\
& = & 1.0 & :50 < a(x) \\
& = & 0.0 & :else
\end{array}
$$

very_young(x) $\mu_{very\_young}(a(X)) =$

$$
\begin{array}{llll}
& & (a(x) -5) / 10 & :5 < a(x) \leq 15 & (9.d)\\
& = & 1.0 & :15 < a(x) \leq 30 \\
& = & (40 -a(x)) / 10 & :30 < a(x) \leq 40 \\
& = & 0.0 & :else
\end{array}
$$

about_50(x): $\mu_{about\_50}(a(X)) =$
=about 50 years old

$$
\begin{array}{llll}
& & (a(x) - 47) / 3 & :47 < a(x) \leq 50 & (9.e)\\
& = & (53 - a(x)) / 3 & :50 < a(x) \leq 53 \\
& = & 0.0 & :else
\end{array}
$$

about_60(x): $\mu_{about\_60}(a(X)) =$
=about 60 years old

$$
\begin{array}{llll}
& & (a(x) - 57) / 3 & :57 < a(x) \leq 60 & (9.f)\\
& = & (63 - a(x)) / 3 & :60 < a(x) \leq 63 \\
& = & 0.0 & :else
\end{array}
$$

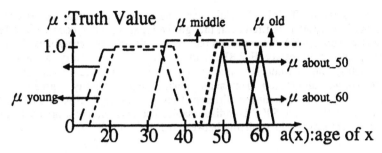

Fig.7 Example of TVFs 2

5.1 Possibility Fuzzy-Analogy Based Reasoning

Figure 8 shows the three types of possibility F-ABR. (In Fig. 8-10, the striped area means {wi} in fuzzy analogy.) For instance, Fig. 8(a) shows possibility F-ABR with SFA when the given source system S is {young(a)}, the target system T is {middle(x)}, and the action V in source system is {wise(a)}. The inferred result is {wise(x)} and the set of predicates {wi} contained in SFA is {young( )}. In this inference procedure, first the rule "young( ) → wise( )" is assumed. Further, the rule is fired even though the input is middle(x) assuming that some 'middle-aged' men are possibly young. Figure. 8(b) shows possibility F-ABR with TFA. In this case, the rule "young( ) → wise( )" is also assumed and it is fired even though the input is middle(x) assuming that some young men are possibly middle-aged. Figure. 8(c) shows possibility F-ABR with non-restricted fuzzy analogy when S is {young(a)} and T is {old(x)}. There is no common area between predicate old( ) and young( ). However non-restricted fuzzy analogy whose {wi} is {middle( )} can be detected with similarity degree 1.0. Although such reasoning has little validity, humans sometimes follows this process to get some clue to solve given problem if any other type of reasoning cannot be carried out.

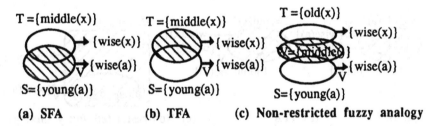

(a) SFA   (b) TFA   (c) Non-restricted fuzzy analogy

Fig. 8 Examples of Possibility Fuzzy-Analogy Based Reasoning

5.2 Necessity Fuzzy-Analogy Based Reasoning

According to formula (5.a) in section 3, formula (10) is derived.

$$N(Q|P) = \min_{x}.\{Q(x) \to P(x)\} \qquad \to : \text{Implication by Kleene} \qquad (10)$$

Qualitatively speaking, when "$Q(x) \to P(x)$" is true for almost every x, N(P|Q) is close to 1.0. Figure.9(b) shows necessity F-ABR with a TFA when S={old(a)} and T={about_60(x)}. This type of reasoning, which is similar to deductive reasoning, has high validity. On the other hand, Fig. 9(a) shows necessity F-ABR with an SFA when

S={about_60(a)} and T={old(x)}. This reasoning in this case is that the assumed rule "about_60( ) → wise( )" is fired even though the input is 'old( )' because it is further assumed that about_60( ), the condition part of the rule, can be generalized. Moreover, Fig. 9(c) shows necessity F-ABR with a non-restricted fuzzy analogy when S={middle(a)} and T={old(x)}. Although both N(old|middle) and N(middle|old) are equal to 0.0, we can detect a fuzzy analogy with a high necessity degree when {wi} ={about_50( )}. This reasoning is different from possibility F-ABR in that the fuzzy predicate symbol 'about_50( )' is indispensable. The existence of a predicate symbol 'about_50( )' emphasizes the similarity between old( ) and middle( ).

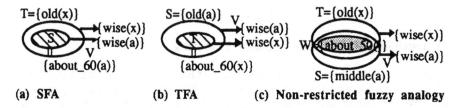

(a) SFA   (b) TFA   (c) Non-restricted fuzzy analogy

Fig. 9 Examples of Necessity Fuzzy-Analogy Based Reasoning

5.3 Compatibility Fuzzy-Analogy Based Reasoning

In the case of compatibility F-ABR, the similarity degree is close to 1.0 when "Q(x) → P(x)" is true for almost every x. Therefore, compatibility F-ABR with an SFA means a reasoning similar to deductive reasoning (Fig. 10(a)). Figure. 10(b) describes that compatibility F-ABR with a TFA introduces a generalization of the rule's condition part. This correspondence is in a reverse order to the necessity F-ABR. Fig. 10(c) shows compatibility F-ABR with a non-restricted fuzzy analogy. This type of reasoning fires the rule "about_60( ) → wise( )" considering that both predicates 'about_60( )' and 'about_50( )' can be generalized with the upper concept 'old( )'.

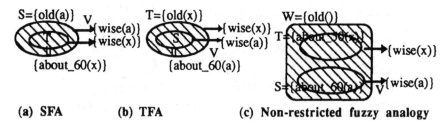

(a) SFA   (b) TFA   (c) Non-restricted fuzzy analogy

Fig. 10 Examples of Compatibility Fuzzy-Analogy Based Reasoning

6. Conclusion

F-ABR, the extension of ABR using fuzzy logic, was introduced. First, a fuzzy analogy representing a set of fuzzy agreements between a source system and a target system was defined after the introduction of three kinds of similarity degrees. Second, classifying and ordering methods for fuzzy analogies were defined. Finally, the features of each type of F-ABR were analyzed.

It was shown that F-ABR can achieve several types of analogical reasoning in a way that is more flexible and human-like than conventional ABR. We can select the reasoning type by changing the fuzzy analogy used in the reasoning process.

More detailed analysis of fuzzy analogies as well as fuzzification of the modifying method for selected facts from a source system remain as subjects for future work.

References:

[1]P. H. Winston:"Learning and Reasoning by Analogy", Comm. ACM, Vol. 13, No. 12, pp. 689-703 (1980).

[2]L. A. Zadeh: Fuzzy Sets and Applications: Selected Papers by L. A. Zadeh (ed. R. R. Yager), John Wiley & Sons (1988).

[3]M. Haraguchi: "Towards a Mathematical Theory of Analogy", Bull. of Inform. Cybernetics, Vol. 21, pp. 29-56 (1985).

[4]S. Tano, W. Okamoto, and T. Iwatani: "New Design Concepts for the FLINS-Fuzzy Lingual System: Text-Based and Fuzzy-centered Architectures", Proc. of Int'l Symposium on Methodologies for Intelligent Systems, pp. 284-294 (1993).

[5]T. Iwatani, S. Tano, and W. Okamoto:"F-CBR in Natural Language Communication System", Proc. of ANZIIS-93, pp. 619-623 (1993).

[6]W. Okamoto, S. Tano, and T. Iwatani: "Estimation of Fuzzy Quantifiers in FLINS", Proc. of 1'st Asian Fuzzy Systems Symposium, pp. 1020-1028 (1993).

[7]D.Dubois and H.Prade: Possibility Theory, Plenum Publishing Corp. (1988).

Explanation-Based Reuse of Prolog Programs*

Yasuyuki Koga, Eiju Hirowatari ** and Setsuo Arikawa

Research Institute of Fundamental Information Science,
Kyushu University 33, Fukuoka 812, Japan
e-mail: {koga, eiju, arikawa}@rifis.kyushu-u.ac.jp

Abstract. This paper presents a method of extracting subprograms from background knowledge. Most studies on learning logic programs so far developed are mainly concerned with pure Prolog, so that we can not deal with programs with system predicates such as the cut symbol, *true*, *false*, and so on. Explanation-based generalization system builds an explanation and learns a concept definition as its generalization, provided an input program. However, it assumes the input program be pure Prolog program. This paper proposes explanation-based reuse (EBR, for short), which is an extension of the explanation-based generalization and a method of program reuse. In EBR, we can deal with some system predicates. In extracting subprograms, we need to extract correct subprograms based on not only an explanation but also the whole background knowledge for a goal concept. This paper also shows that such extracted subprograms by EBR are correct.

1 Introduction

In learning Prolog programs, background knowledge is frequently given before an input is given. It is not efficient to deal with the whole background knowledge in order to solve specific problems. In general, if a problem is solved by the whole Prolog program, then so is by its smaller subprogram. Hence, this paper investigates how to extract such subprograms. Then, we can regard extracting a subprogram from a Prolog program as a kind of machine learning from background knowledge.

As to such machine learning from background knowledge, the explanation-based generalization (EBG, for short) has been studied by many researchers from various viewpoints [1, 2, 4, 5, 6, 8, 10, 11, 13, 14]. EBG enables a learner to reformulate, operationalize or deduce what the learner already knows implicitly [3, 9]. EBG takes as inputs a domain theory, a training example, a goal concept and an operationality criterion. EBG has two stages, explanation and generalization. In the explanation stage, EBG constructs an explanation in terms of the domain theory that proves how the training example satisfies the goal concept. In the generalization stage, EBG determines a set of operationally sufficient conditions for the goal concept under which the explanation holds, and returns it as an

---

* This work is partly supported by Grants-in-Aid for JSPS fellows and Scientific Research on Priority Areas from the Ministry of Education, Science and Culture, Japan.
** JSPS Fellowship for Japanese Junior Scientists.

output. Thus, EBG can be regarded as a method of learning from a pure Prolog program which consists of a domain theory and a training example.

This paper introduces a method of extracting a subprogram from a given Prolog program and a given goal concept The subprogram is the collection of all rules in an explanation of EBG for a goal concept. Hence, our problem is how to extract a correct subprogram for a goal concept from a Prolog program. In general, a Prolog program contains the cut symbol !. However, the cut makes it impossible for the EBG method to correctly control the pruning, because EBG assumes an input program to be a pure Prolog program. Hence, This paper proposes explanation-based reuse (EBR, for short), based on the original EBG. EBR enables the learner to extract a correct subprogram for a goal concept from a background Prolog program.

We deal with Prolog programs which contain the system predicates such as !, $true$, $fail$ and so on. Furthermore, by means of EBR, we can extract a correct subprogram for the given goal concept not only from an explanation but also from the whole background knowledge.

The remainder of this paper is organized as follows. In Section 2, we define a computation for Prolog programs with the cut symbol in a mathematical way. In Section 3, we prepare some concepts on EBG which deals with pure Prolog programs. In Section 4, we discuss how to extract a correct subprogram of a standard Prolog program for a goal concept. Then, we propose EBR and show some properties of EBR. In Section 5, we realize our EBR system as a Prolog program.

2 Formulation of Prolog Computation

In this section, we define some notions on first order logic and logic programming, and formulate computations in Prolog systems in a mathematical way. See [7, 12] for detailed definitions on first order logic, logic programming and Prolog programs.

An atomic formula is called an *atom* and an atom without variables is called a *ground atom*. In this paper, we regard some system predicates, for example !, $true$, $fail$ and so on, as atoms. A predicate symbol of a 0-ary system predicate is identified with the system predicate itself. A *program clause* is a clause of the form

$$A \leftarrow B_1, \ldots, B_n \ (n \geq 0),$$

where $A, B_1, \cdots, B_n$ are atoms. A is called the *head* and $B_1, \ldots, B_n$ is called the *body* of the clause. A program clause with the body is called a *rule*. A program clause without the head is called a *goal*. Then, by $|B_1, \ldots, B_n|_!$ we denote the number of occurrences of the cut symbol ! in the body $B_1, \ldots, B_n$.

A program is a finite set of program clauses in the textual order, that is, in the order of the clauses as they are in the program. A program P_1 is a subprogram of a program P_2, denoted by $P_1 \subseteq P_2$, if P_1 is a subset of P_2 and the program clauses in P_1 are listed in the textual order of P_2.

In Prolog systems, we can usually reduce the search spaces by the cut. Then, we modify SLD-trees for programs and goals, and define the search trees and the pruned branches by the cut as follows:

Definition 1. Let P be a program and $\leftarrow G$ be a goal. Then, a *search tree* for $P \cup \{\leftarrow G\}$ is a tree satisfying the following conditions:

(a) Each node of the tree is a goal.
(b) The root node is $\leftarrow G$.
(c) Let $\leftarrow A_1, \ldots, A_k (k \geq 1)$ be a node in the tree. Suppose that the clauses

$$B_1 \leftarrow C_1^1, \ldots, C_1^{m_1},$$

$$\vdots$$

$$B_n \leftarrow C_n^1, \ldots, C_n^{m_n},$$

are input clauses in the textual order of P, where B_i and A_1 are unifiable with a most general unifier θ_i for each i $(1 \leq i \leq n)$. Then, the node has children

$$\leftarrow (C_1^1, \ldots, C_1^{m_1}, A_2, \ldots, A_k)\theta_1,$$

$$\vdots$$

$$\leftarrow (C_n^1, \ldots, C_n^{m_n}, A_2, \ldots, A_k)\theta_n,$$

in this order.
(d) Each node with the empty clause has no children.
(e) Let $\leftarrow A_1, \ldots, A_k (k \geq 1)$ be a node in the tree. If A_1 is a system predicate and a goal $\leftarrow A_1$ can be evaluated with a substitution θ, then the node has a child

$$\leftarrow (A_2, \ldots, A_k)\theta.$$

Let P be a program, $\leftarrow G$ be a goal, and T be a search tree for $P \cup \{\leftarrow G\}$. In order to simulate the cut effect, we assign a sequence of natural numbers to each goal in a search tree for $P \cup \{\leftarrow G\}$ in the following way:

(a) Assign a sequence (0) to the root goal of T.
(b) If a sequence $(n_1, \ldots, n_m)$ $(m \geq 1)$ is assigned to a goal $\leftarrow A_1, \ldots, A_k$ $(k \geq 1)$ in T, then assign a sequence $(n_1, \ldots, n_m, s)$ to a resolvent $\leftarrow (C_1, \ldots, C_l, A_2, \ldots, A_k)\theta$, where $B \leftarrow C_1, \ldots, C_l$ is an input clause such that A_1 and B are unifiable with a most general unifier θ, and $|C_1, \ldots, C_l|_! = s$.
(c) If a sequence $(n_1, \ldots, n_m)$ $(m \geq 1)$ is assigned to a goal $\leftarrow A_1, \ldots, A_k$ $(k \geq 1)$ in T and A_1 is the cut, then assign a sequence $(n_1, \ldots, n_i - 1, \ldots, n_m)$ to a resolvent $\leftarrow A_2, \ldots, A_k$, where n_i is the rightmost positive number in $(n_1, \ldots, n_m)$.

Let us call the goal which caused the clause containing a cut to be activated a *parent goal* of the cut. That is, the selected atom in the parent matches with the head of the clause whose body contains the cut. When "selected", the cut simply "succeeds" immediately. However, if backtracking later returns to the cut, the system discontinues the searching in the subtree which has the parent goal at the root. The cut thus causes the remainder of that subtree to be pruned from the search tree.

A path from the root node to a leaf in the tree is called a *branch*. Then we propose the search tree with the sequence of natural number assigned to each goal for the cut effect.

Lemma 2. *Let P be a program, $\leftarrow G$ be a goal, and T be a search tree for $P \cup \{\leftarrow G\}$. Suppose that a sequence $(n_1, \ldots, n_m)$ is assigned to a goal $\leftarrow A_1, \ldots, A_k$ ($k \geq 1$) in the branch of T, where n_i is the rightmost positive number in $(n_1, \ldots, n_m)$. If A_1 is a cut, then the parent goal of the cut is the goal in this branch to which $(n_1, \ldots, n_{i-1})$ is assigned.*

Let $\leftarrow G_0$ be a goal whose leftmost atom is a cut. Suppose that $\leftarrow G_0$ occurs in a branch B. By Lemma 2, there exists the parent goal $\leftarrow G_0'$ of the cut in B. Then, for all branches between $\leftarrow G_0$ and $\leftarrow G_0'$, the branches which occur in the right side of B are pruned. In general, the Prolog systems do not realize such execution. The pruned branches are called *senseless branches*. Except for senseless branches, a branch is a *success branch* if its leaf is an empty clause. Furthermore, a branch is a *fail branch* if its leaf is a non-empty clause, and a branch is an *infinite branch* if it has not a leaf. By the above definitions, the *computation* for $P \cup \{\leftarrow G\}$ is a process that searches for success branches by the depth-first search to the search tree for $P \cup \{\leftarrow G\}$. The computation for $P \cup \{\leftarrow G\}$ *succeeds* when the success branches is found in the computation $P \cup \{\leftarrow G\}$.

When the the search tree for $P \cup \{\leftarrow G\}$ has success branches and no infinite branches, G is called a *query* for P. A substitution given by the computation for $P \cup \{\leftarrow G\}$ is called an *answer* for G and P. By $(P, G) \vdash_{PC} G\theta$, we denote that the computation for $P \cup \{\leftarrow G\}$ succeeds and the substitution θ is an answer for G and P.

3 Explanation-Based Generalization

First we recall some concepts on EBG according to [5]. In EBG which deals with programs, it is assumed that an input program is a pure Prolog program, that is, a finite set of definite clauses listed in the textual order.

A *domain theory* is a finite set of program clauses, denoted by D. A *training example* is a non-empty finite set of ground atoms, denoted by T. Both D and T are sets of program clauses. In this paper, a set $D \cup T$, denoted by P, is called a *program*. A *goal concept* is an atom G of the target for learning. Let Π_P be the set of all predicate symbols in P. Then, an *operationality criterion* is a subset O of Π_P. Let $\Pi(O)$ be the set of all atoms that have predicate symbols in O. In this paper, we identify an operationality criterion O with $\Pi(O)$. A triplet (P, G, O) is called an *input*, denoted by I, of EBG.

Definition 3. An *explanation tree* for an input $I = (P, G, O)$ is a finite tree satisfying the following conditions:

(a) each node of the tree is an element of M_P, where M_P is the least Herbrand model of P.
(b) the root node is an instance of G.
(c) if a node α in the tree has children $\beta_1, \cdots, \beta_n$ $(n \geq 1)$ in this order, then $\alpha \leftarrow \beta_1, \cdots, \beta_n$ is a ground instance of a rule in P, that is, we get child nodes by applying rule in P to a parent node.
(d) each node in an element of $\Pi(O)$ has no children.

We assign a number to each rule in the explanation tree in the following way:

(1) Assign a number to each node that is not an element of $\Pi(O)$ in depth-first order starting from 1.
(2) Let α be a node which has children $\beta_1, \ldots, \beta_n$ $(n \geq 1)$ in this order, and to which number j assigned. Then, assign the number j to a rule in P, denoted by C_j, which is a generalization of $\alpha \leftarrow \beta_1, \ldots, \beta_n$.

We use the rules with numbers in the following generalized derivation.

Definition 4. A *generalized derivation* for $I = (P, G, O)$ is an SLD-derivation via CR which consists of a finite sequence $\leftarrow G_0(=\leftarrow G), \leftarrow G_1, \ldots, \leftarrow G_n$ of goals, a sequence $C'_1, \ldots, C'_n$ of variants of rules in P, and a sequence $\theta_1, \ldots, \theta_n$ of most general unifiers, where CR is a computation rule to select the leftmost atom not included in $\Pi(O)$.

For the rules $C_1, \ldots, C_n$ in the explanation tree, each C'_i $(1 \leq i \leq n)$ is a suitable variant of C_i in the sense that C'_i does not have any variables which already appear in the derivation up to G_{i-1}.

A generalized derivation depends on an explanation tree. An *explanation* is a construction of an explanation tree, and a *generalization* is a regression to a goal concept through the explanation tree using a generalized derivation.

Definition 5. *EBG* is a procedure that derives a *general definition R of G* from its input $I = (P, G, O)$ by an explanation and a generalization, and it is denoted by

$$I \xrightarrow{EBG} R,$$

where

$$R = \begin{cases} G & \text{if } n = 0, \\ G\theta_1 \cdots \theta_n \leftarrow G_n & \text{otherwise}, \end{cases}$$

and $(\leftarrow G_n)$ is the goal and $(\theta_1, \ldots, \theta_n)$ is the sequence of most general unifiers in the generalized derivation of depth n.

Usually, an atom α in P is identified with a rule $\alpha \leftarrow true$ by regarding the system predicate *true* as an atom. Thus, in Theorem 6, we assume that an program contains the true symbol and an operationality criterion is $\{true\}$.

Theorem 6. *Let $I = (P, G, O)$ be an input such that the search tree for $P \cup \{\leftarrow G\}$ has no infinite branch. Let P' be a subprogram of P for G which consists of all input clauses in the explanation for I. Then, for any substitution θ,*

$$(P', G) \vdash_{PC} G\theta \text{ iff } (P, G) \vdash_{PC} G\theta.$$

Proof. ($\Rightarrow$) Suppose $(P', G) \vdash_{PC} G\theta$ for a substitution θ. For any subprogram P'' of P, each answer for G and P'' is an answer for G and P, because the search tree for $P \cup \{\leftarrow G\}$ has no infinite branch. Then, we can compute all answers for G and P' by using P instead of P'. Hence, $(P, G) \vdash_{PC} G\theta$.

($\Leftarrow$) Suppose $(P, G) \vdash_{PC} G\theta$ for a substitution θ. Then, we can compute all answers for G and P, because the search tree for $P \cup \{\leftarrow G\}$ has no infinite branch. Thus, we can construct the explanation tree for I. Then, P' includes enough clauses in P to compute all answers for G and P. Hence, $(P', G) \vdash_{PC} G\theta$.
□

Suppose that $I = (P, G, O)$ is an input and P' is the subprogram of P satisfying the condition in Theorem 6. Since P is identified with a pure Prolog, P' is the least subprogram of P to compute all answers for G and P. Hence, we should construct such a program P' obtained from the explanation for I, and use P' instead of P in order to compute an answer for G and P.

4 Explanation-Based Reuse

In this section, we investigate the method of extracting subprograms. In EBG, it is assumed that an input program is a pure Prolog program. However, this assumption is not adequate for knowledge acquisition from the standard Prolog programs. In this section, we regard an input program as a standard Prolog program which may contain the cut symbol and some other system predicates.

For a program P and a goal concept G, when we construct a subprogram P' of P we require that the answer for G and P' should be identical to the answer for G and P. From now on, we assume that G is a query for P.

Definition 7. Let P be a program, G be a goal concept, and P' be a subprogram of P. Then, P' is an *extracted program* of P for G if, for any substitution θ,

$$(P', G) \vdash_{PC} G\theta \iff (P, G) \vdash_{PC} G\theta.$$

An input is a triplet $I = (P, G, O)$ similar to EBG, where O is the set of all predicate symbol of system predicates. Then, we can construct a subprogram of P, which consists of all input clauses in the explanation for I.

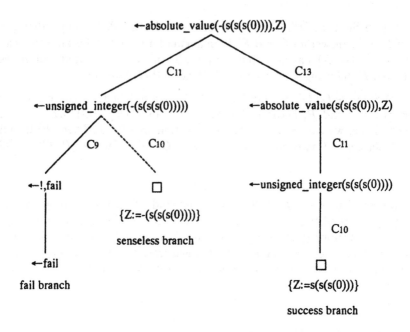

Fig. 1. Search tree for $P \cup \{\leftarrow G\}$ in Example 1.

Example 1. Let P be the following program:

$$P = \left\{ \begin{array}{l} C_1 : number\_value(0,0,\_) :\!- \,!. \\ C_2 : number\_value(X,Y,Z) :\!- i\_number(X),!, \\ \qquad absolute\_value(X,Y), sign(X,Z). \\ C_3 : i\_number(+(X)) :\!- i\_number(X). \\ C_4 : i\_number(-(X)) :\!- i\_number(X). \\ C_5 : i\_number(X) :\!- n\_number(X). \\ C_6 : n\_number(0). \\ C_7 : n\_number(s(X)) :\!- n\_number(X). \\ C_8 : unsigned\_integer(+(X)) :\!- !, fail. \\ C_9 : unsigned\_integer(-(X)) :\!- !, fail. \\ C_{10} : unsigned\_integer(X). \\ C_{11} : absolute\_value(X,X) :\!- unsigned\_integer(X). \\ C_{12} : absolute\_value(+(X),Y) :\!- absolute\_value(X,Y). \\ C_{13} : absolute\_value(-(X),Y) :\!- absolute\_value(X,Y). \\ C_{14} : sign(X,+) :\!- unsigned\_integer(X),!. \\ C_{15} : sign(+(X),Y) :\!- sign(X,Y). \\ C_{16} : sign(-(X),Y) :\!- sign(X,Z), change(Y,Z). \\ C_{17} : change(+,-). \\ C_{18} : change(-,+). \end{array} \right\},$$

and $G = absolute\_value(-(s(s(s(0)))), Z)$ be a goal concept. Fig. 1 illustrates the search tree for $P \cup \{\leftarrow G\}$.

Then, the following program is obtained from the explanation for I.

$$P_0 = \left\{ \begin{array}{l} C_{10} : unsigned\_integer(X). \\ C_{11} : absolute\_value(X,X) :- unsigned\_integer(X). \\ C_{13} : absolute\_value(-(X),Y) :- absolute\_value(X,Y). \end{array} \right\}.$$

Fig. 2 illustrates the search tree for $P_0 \cup \{\leftarrow G\}$. This program is not an extracted program of P for G, because

$$(P_0, G) \vdash_{PC} absolute\_value(-(s(s(s(0)))), -(s(s(s(0))))),$$

but

$$(P, G) \not\vdash_{PC} absolute\_value(-(s(s(s(0)))), -(s(s(s(0))))).$$

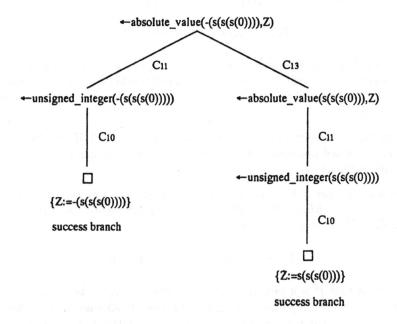

Fig. 2. Search tree for $P_0 \cup \{\leftarrow G\}$ in Example 1.

The above example means that we can not extract subprograms correctly only by the explanation, if an input program contains the cut symbol. Thus, we should pay attention to not only explanations, i.e., success branches, but also fail branches in order to obtain extracted programs of a program for a goal concept. Then, we propose explanation-based reuse as a method of constructing subprograms.

Definition 8. Let P be a program and G be a goal concept. Then, *explanation-based reuse of P satisfying G* (EBR of P satisfying G, for short) is a method of constructing subprograms, which is the collection of all input clauses in all success branches and fail branches in a search tree for $P \cup \{\leftarrow G\}$.

Example 2. Let P be the program and G be the goal concept in Example 1. Then, the following program is obtained by EBR of P satisfying G.

$$P_G = \begin{cases} C_9 : unsigned\_integer(-(X)) :- !, fail. \\ C_{10} : unsigned\_integer(X). \\ C_{11} : absolute\_value(X, X) :- unsigned\_integer(X). \\ C_{13} : absolute\_value(-(X), Y) :- absolute\_value(X, Y). \end{cases}.$$

This subprogram is the extracted program of P for G.

Theorem 9. *Let P be a program, G be a goal concept, and P_G be the subprogram obtained by EBR of P satisfying G. Then, for any substitution θ,*

$$(P_G, G) \vdash_{PC} G\theta \text{ iff } (P, G) \vdash_{PC} G\theta.$$

Proof. Let T and T_G be search trees for $P \cup \{\leftarrow G\}$ and $P_G \cup \{\leftarrow G\}$, respectively. By EBR of P satisfying G, P_G consists of all program clauses needed to construct T. Thus, T is identical to T_G. Hence, for any substitution θ, $(P_G, G) \vdash_{PC} G\theta$ iff $(P, G) \vdash_{PC} G\theta$. □

This theorem asserts that the subprogram obtained by EBR of P satisfying G is an extracted program of P for G. By Theorem 9, we can easily prove the following corollary:

Corollary 10. *Let P be a program, G be a goal concept, and P_G be the subprogram obtained by EBR of P satisfying G. For any subprogram P_0 of P such that $P_G \subseteq P_0 \subseteq P$ and any substitution θ,*

$$(P_0, G) \vdash_{PC} G\theta \text{ iff } (P_G, G) \vdash_{PC} G\theta.$$

Suppose that P is a program and G is a goal concept. Then, EBR returns the least extracted subprogram of P for G to compute all answers for G and P.

Just as we have done for one goal concept, we can naturally give the definition for many goal concepts.

Definition 11. Let P be a program, $G_1, \ldots, G_n$ be goal concepts, and P_{G_i} be the subprogram obtained by EBR of P satisfying G_i. Then, a subprogram $P_{\{G_1, \ldots, G_n\}}$ obtained by EBR of P satisfying $G_1, \ldots, G_n$ is the union of subprograms $P_{G_1}, \ldots, P_{G_n}$, where the program clauses in $P_{\{G_1, \ldots, G_n\}}$ are listed in the textual order of P. It is defined by $P_{\{G_1, \ldots, G_n\}} = \cup_i P_{G_i}$.

The following theorem asserts that we can obtain an extracted program of a program for goal concepts $G_1, \ldots, G_n$.

Theorem 12. *Let P be a program, $G_1 \ldots G_n$ be goal concepts, and $P_{\{G_1,\ldots,G_n\}}$ be a subprogram obtained by EBR of P satisfying $G_1, \ldots, G_n$. Then, for any substitution θ,*

$$(P_{\{G_1,\ldots,G_n\}}, G_i) \vdash_{PC} G_i\theta \text{ iff } (P, G_i) \vdash_{PC} G_i\theta \ (1 \leq i \leq n).$$

Proof. Let P_{G_i} be the subprogram obtained by EBR of P satisfying G_i. Then, $P_{G_i} \subseteq P_{\{G_1,\ldots,G_n\}} \subseteq P$. By Theorem 9 and Corollary 10, for any substitution θ, $(P_{\{G_1,\ldots,G_n\}}, G_i) \vdash_{PC} G_i\theta$ iff $(P, G_i) \vdash_{PC} G_i\theta$. □

If a goal concept is a query, then the subprogram obtained by EBR of P satisfying G is the extracted program of P for G by Theorem 9. In general, a goal concept is not always a query. Hence, for a goal concept which is not a query, we extend EBR as follows: By presenting a sequence of queries g for P which are instances of G to the system one by one, we can eventually obtain a subprogram P_G such that the answer for g and P_G is identical to the answer for g and P. This method is called an *extended EBR* of P satisfying G. An extended EBR of P satisfying G identifies such a subprogram P_G in the limit by presenting a sequence of queries.

5 Prolog Implementation

The EBR system we have introduced takes as an input a Prolog program P and a goal concept G, and returns an extracted program by EBR of P satisfying G. As we have discussed in Section 4, the EBR system has the following three stages:

(a) Assign a number to each clause in P in the textual order starting from 1.
(b) Collect the numbers which are assigned to input clauses in all success and fail branches in the search tree for $P \cup \{\leftarrow G\}$.
(c) Extract a subprogram of P in the textual order, in which all clauses are assigned numbers in the set determined in the stage (b).

In the stage (a), the system replaces the i-th clause $A \leftarrow B_1, \ldots B_n \ (n \geq 0)$ from the top of a input Prolog program with a clause

$$A \leftarrow counter(i), B_1, \ldots B_n$$

for each i, where *counter* is a predicate symbol which does not appear in the input program. Then, the system stores it in a Prolog database and uses it as background knowledge in the stage (b).

The stage (b) is a main part of the EBR system. To see the stage (b) more concretely, we show the main Prolog program.

```
/*Explanation-Based Reuse from Prolog Program*/

ebr(Goal,List) :- assert(count([])),Goal,fail.
ebr(Goal,List) :- !,count(X),uniq(X,List).

counter(X) :- count(L),Y=[X|L],retract(count(L)),assert(count(Y)).
```

The predicate ebr takes as its first argument a goal concept and returns as its second argument the set of all numbers assigned to clauses in a program extracted by the EBR system.

Consider Example 1 again. For the input Prolog program P, in the stage (a), we transform P to the following program.

```
number_value(0,0,_):-counter(1),!.
number_value(X,Y,Z):-counter(2),i_number(X),!,
                        absolute_value(X,Y),sign(X,Z).
i_number(+(X)):-counter(3),i_number(X).
i_number(-(X)):-counter(4),i_number(X).
i_number(X):-counter(5),n_number(X).
n_number(0):-counter(6).
n_number(s(X)):-counter(7),n_number(X).
unsigned_integer(+(X)):-counter(8),!,fail.
unsigned_integer(-(X)):-counter(9),!,fail.
unsigned_integer(X):-counter(10).
absolute_value(X,X):-counter(11),unsigned_integer(X).
absolute_value(+(X),Y):-counter(12),absolute_value(X,Y).
absolute_value(-(X),Y):-counter(13),absolute_value(X,Y).
sign(X,+):-counter(14),unsigned_integer(X),!.
sign(+(X),Y):-counter(15),sign(X,Y).
sign(-(X),Y):-counter(16),sign(X,Z),change(Y,Z).
change(+,-):-counter(17).
change(-,+):-counter(18).
```

Let $G = \mathtt{absolute\_value}(-(s(s(s(0)))), Z)$ be a goal concept. The question to the EBR system is

```
?- ebr(absolute_value(-(s(s(s(0)))),Z),List).
```

The answers from the EBR system is

```
Z = Z,
List = [9,10,11,13]
```

Then, the answer from the total system is

```
unsigned_integer(-(X)):-!,fail.
unsigned_integer(X).
absolute_value(X,X):-unsigned_integer(X).
absolute_value(-(X),Y):-absolute_value(X,Y).
```

References

1. Ali, K. M.: Augmenting domain theory for explanation-based generalization. In Proceedings of the Sixth International Workshop on Machine Learning (1989) 40–42

2. Boström, H.: Improving example-guided unfolding. In Proceedings of European Conference on Machine Learning (1993) 124–135

3. Ellman, T.: Explanation-based learning: A survey of programs and perspectives. ACM Computing Surveys **21** (1989) 163–221

4. Etzioni, O.: Acquiring search-control knowledge via static analysis. Artificial Intelligence **62** (1993) 255–301

5. Hirowatari, E., Arikawa, S.: Incorporating explanation-based generalization with analogical reasoning. Bulletin of Informatics and Cybernetics **26** (1994) 13–33

6. Kedar-Cabelli, S.T., McCarty, L.T.: Explanation-based generalization as resolution theorem proving. In Proceedings of the Fourth International Workshop on Machine Learning (1987) 383–389

7. Lloyd, J. W.: Foundation of logic programming (second edition). Springer-Verlag (1987)

8. Mahadevan, S., Mitchell, T.M., Mostow, J., Steinberg, L., Tadepalli, P.V.: An apprentice-based approach to knowledge acquisition. Artificial Intelligence **64** (1993) 1–52

9. Mitchell, T.M., Keller, R. M., Kedar-Cabelli, S. T.: Explanation-based generalization: a unifying view. Machine Learning **1** (1986) 47–80

10. Numao, M., Maruoka, T., Shimura, M.: Speed-up learning by extracting partial structures of explanations. Journal of Japanese Society for Artificial Intelligence (in Japanese) **7** (1992) 1018–1026

11. Puget, J.-F.: Explicit representation of concept negation. Machine Learning **14** (1994) 233–247

12. Sterling, L., Shapiro, E.: The art of Prolog. The MIT Press (1986).

13. van Harmelen, F., Bundy, A.: Explanation-based generalization = partial evaluation. Artificial Intelligence **36** (1988) 401–412

14. Yamada, S.: Computing the utility of EBL in a logic programming environment. Journal of Japanese Society for Artificial Intelligence (in Japanese) **7** (1992) 309–319

Constructive Induction
for
Recursive Programs

Chowdhury Rahman Mofizur and Masayuki Numao

Department of Computer Science, Tokyo Institute of Technology
Tokyo 152, JAPAN
Email: {rahman, numao} @ cs.titech.ac.jp

Abstract. This paper presents an algorithm for inducing recursive first order Horn clause programs from examples without background knowledge. This algorithm invents new predicates and their definitions exhaustively until the instances of a new predicate become the same as examples except for the name of the predicate. Our system CIRP switches into constructive induction mode using a new heuristic taking advantage of the goal directed usefulness of incomplete clauses and of the fact that it is supplied with no background knowledge. It enables CIRP to avoid exhaustive search and to overcome some difficulties associated with employing encoding length principle as a switching element for constructive induction. This paper also describes a method for deciding the argument set for a new predicate by employing the structure of the arguments of the original predicate and reports the scope, limitation and remedy of limitation of this method.

1 Introduction

Due to the lack of expressive power in feature-value languages, there has been increase interest in systems which induce a first-order Horn clause logic program from examples. Some of these systems perform constructive induction if initial vocabulary is not sufficient enough to finitely axiomatize the example set. There are systems like CIGOL [6], LFP2 [14], ITOU [11], RINCON [16], which introduces new predicate as a reformulation of the already existing theory in order to make the theory more compact and concise. On the other hand, systems like SIERES [15] and CHAMP [3] are self-switching systems using heuristic to infer the situation that the given vocabulary is insufficient to build a complete and consistent theory. Also some other systems like CIA [10], FOCL [13] define a new predicate as a combination of known predicate literals to overcome the search myopia problem.

This paper presents an algorithm for inducing recursive first order Horn clause programs from examples without background knowledge. This algorithm invents new predicates and their definitions exhaustively until the instances of a new predicate become the same as examples except for the name of the predicate. Some known system adopts top-down specialization of the most general clauses until either the specialized clause covers no negative examples or the search space violates the encoding length principle. In the later case the system calls its predicate invention component and discovers new vocabulary to finitely axiomatize the example set. The process thus requires a huge search space before fixing that the given vocabulary is insufficient and new predicate is necessary. In some cases the adoption of encoding length principle as a guide for stopping further specialization and switching into the constructive induction mode prevents learning the desirable theory. Our system CIRP switches into constructive induction mode using a new heuristic taking advantage of the goal directed usefulness of clauses and of the fact that it is supplied with no background knowledge. It enables CIRP to avoid exhaustive search and to overcome the difficulties associated with employing encoding length principle as a switching element for constructive induction. The suitability of using goal directed usefulness of a clause over the information gain measure [9] for predicate invention has been illustrated in this paper. As a matter of fact the incompleteness of the information gain measure as the true desirability of a clause for the target theory has been well established. This paper describes a method for deciding the argument set for the new predicate by employing the argument structure of the original predicate and reports the scope, limitation and remedy of the limitation of this method. Also this paper focuses the order dependencies of the DBC algorithm [3] to result in a true argument set for the new predicate.

In section 2 we will present CIRP algorithm and mention the difficulties associated with a system which uses encoding length bias for switching into predicate invention mode. Also the superiority of likelihood measure of a clause over information gain measure for predicate invention in recursive programs has been illustrated in this section. The following section will illustrate the method employed for deciding the argument set for the new predicate along with the constraints of applicability. A possible ramification of the constraints has also been enlightened at the end of section 3. Section 4 will focus some of the results obtained through an early experiment and section 5 will be devoted to summarization.

2 Overview of CIRP

CIRP uses Merit heuristic [2] as a measure of desirability of a clause which contributes to its self switching ability to constructive induction. A logic program transforms the initial state of the input variables of a clause to the goal state of the output variables through intermediate states. The antecedents of a clause represent these intermediate states. The appropriate selection of antecedent which is closer to the goal state at each step of induction will eventually converge to the desired theory. It is evident that two incomplete clauses having the same information gain [9] may have different desirability because of their different distance from the target clause. The Merit heuristic represents the combination of discrimination (Information gain measure) ability and goal directed usefulness (Likelihood measure) of a clause.

2.1 Merit Heuristic

The Merit heuristic uses the following heuristic function:

$$\Gamma(\text{Clause}) = \frac{\sum_{i=1}^{m} \sum_{j=1}^{n} \sum_{k,l} \gamma(VIn_{i,k}, VOut_{j,l})}{\sum_{i=1}^{m} \sum_{j=1}^{n} \sum_{k,l} \sigma(VIn_{i,k}, VOut_{j,l})}$$

where m is the number of input and intermediate variables in the clause, and n is that of output variables. A variable in a non-determinate literal has multiple values, all of which is enumerated by $\sum_{k,l}$. $\gamma(v_1, v_2)$ and $\sigma(v_1, v_2)$ define closeness between v_1 and v_2 as follows:

- Closeness between two atoms:
  $\gamma(atom1, atom2) = 1$ if $atom1 = atom2$; 0 otherwise
  and $\sigma(atom1, atom2) = 1$.
- Closeness between two lists:

$$\gamma(list1, list2) = \frac{\max(\text{length of matched sublists})}{\max(\text{length of } list1, \text{length of } list2)}$$

and $\sigma(list1, list2) = 1$.
- $\gamma(v_1, v_2) = \sigma(v_1, v_2) = 0$ if v_1 and v_2 have different types.

The combination of Γ and Gain heuristic used by FOIL constitutes the Merit of a clause:

$$\text{Merit}(C) = \text{Gain}(C) + \text{likelihood}(C)$$
$$\text{likelihood}(C) = T^+(C) * \Gamma(C)$$
$$\text{Gain}(C) = T^+(C) * (I(T(0)) - I(T(C)))$$
$$I(T(0)) = -\log_2 \left(\frac{T^+(0)}{T^+(0) + T^-(0)} \right)$$
$$I(T(C)) = -\log_2 \left(\frac{T^+(C)}{T^+(C) + T^-(C)} \right)$$

where C is the current clause and $T^+(0), T^-(0), T^+(C)$ and $T^-(C)$ are the number of given positive examples, negative examples, positive examples that satisfy C and negative examples that satisfy C, respectively.

2.2 CIRP Algorithm

CIRP learns from the following input:

- A set of positive and negative examples in the form of ground facts.
- Mode declarations declaring data types and input/output modes of variables in a literal.

Example 1. The literal `pred(X,Y,Z)` may be assigned the mode declaration `pred(+x,+[x],-[x])` where + and - indicate that the arguments are input and output, respectively. The term `x` and `[x]` indicate that their types are atomic and a list of atoms, respectively.

CIRP employs beam search using the refinement operators in MIS[12] to specialize a clause by: (i) instantiating a head variable to a function, (ii) unifying variables, and (iii) adding a background predicate to the body. In our case the background knowledge is the desired predicate itself. CIRP randomly selects a seed example and begins to specialize the most general term MGT of this seed example.

The algorithm always tracks the best clause in the beam. If the best clause is complete and consistent, it is either a ground clause for the recursive definition or some pure recursive clauses. If such a clause is found, the positive examples covered by it are removed and the procedure continues with the rest of the positive examples. The algorithm terminates when all the positive examples are exhausted. If the Merit of the current best recursive clause is greater than or equal to that of the last one and it is also greater than the best clause of the following round of refinement, the system takes this as the legitimate incomplete clause for constructive induction and switches into the predicate invention mode stopping further refinements. This heuristic of detecting peak value for the Merit applies because of the presence of no background knowledge and of smooth specialization of the clauses in the refinement graph. It is important to note that the likelihood measure of a clause plays an important role (Merit = Gain + Likelihood) to achieve this heuristic and information gain alone cannot help in this situation as will be illustrated soon.

Let us illustrate the heuristic to find out the definition for the reverse program. If the selected seed example is an instance of the ground clause, i.e., `reverse([],[])`, CIRP begins with the most general term of the seed example, `reverse(X,Y)` and finds the complete and consistent clause `reverse([],[])` after a small number of refinements. Let us assume that the next seed example selected randomly is `rev([1,2,3],[3,2,1])`. CIRP begins refining the MGT `reverse(X,Y)`, and obtains the following specialized clauses in the course of first refinement:

Current clauses in beam # 1	Merit	Likelihood	Gain
2 ... (rev([X|Y],Z):-true)	3.2	5.0	1.3
3 ... (rev(X,[Y|Z]):-true)	3.2	5.0	1.3

The second round of refinement generates the following beam, which includes a clause having Merit greater than the previous best. This clause with Merit 4.4 will be taken as an appropriate incomplete clause for predicate invention if and only if the next round of refinement produces clauses having Merit less than 4.4.

Current clauses in beam # 2	Merit	Likelihood	Gain
4 ... (rev([X,Y|Z],U):-true)	2.5	4.0	1.5
5 ... (rev([X|Y],[Z|U]):-true)	3.2	3.8	2.7
6 ... (rev([X|Y],Z):-rev(Y,V))	4.4	7.5	1.3

7 ... (rev(X,[Y,Z|U]):-true)   2.5   4.0   1.0

The best clause in the 3rd beam having Merit less than 4.4 ensures that the best one from the 2nd beam is indeed the candidate for predicate invention. If there were some clause in 3rd beam having merit value higher than 4.4, we would have to refine further to find the local peak.

Current clauses in beam # 3	Merit	Likelihood	Gain
8 ... (rev([X,Y|Z],[U|V]):-true)	1.1	0.0	2.2
9 ... (rev([X|Y],[Z,U|V]):-true)	1.1	0.0	2.2
10 ... (rev([X|Y],[Z|U]):-rev(Y,W))	3.9	5.0	2.7
11 ... (rev([X,Y,Z|U],V):-true),	0.3	0.0	0.5
12 ... (rev(X,[Y,Z,U|V]):-true)	0.3	0.0	0.5

Thus, CIRP selects the best clause from a beam as the appropriate clause for predicate invention if its merit value is higher than the merit value of both the more generalized and more specialized clauses.

From the illustration it is evident that the information gain of a clause is of little help to conclude anything important and is rather misleading. Clause #2 from the first beam and clause #6 from the second beam has similar gain value, but variable V in the later clause, representing the reversed output of the tail of the input list, being very close to goal state has higher Merit. Since the system has no background knowledge available, the various recursive clauses in the specialization phase only differ in possible variable instantiations of the arguments. Among these specializations, the incomplete clause which is more close to the goal state naturally should have more desirability. The information gain measure cannot predict the goal directed usefulness of a clause. This is one of the reasons that gain heuristic fails to discover some non-discriminant literal in a clause which is not important from the view of 'discriminating power, but useful for achieving the goal state. To eliminate this incompleteness, FOIL has borrowed the idea of determinant terms from GOLEM[7] in order to widen its scope of learning. Since a recursive incomplete clause represents the true output of some subset of the input, the combination of closeness (likelihood) and discriminating (information gain) measure of an incomplete clause has successfully enabled CIRP to select the appropriate clause for predicate invention. CIRP stops specializing the clauses after it detects a peak value for the Merit and switches into the predicate invention mode.

After fixing the incomplete clause, CIRP uses procedure described in section 3 to determine the possible argument variables for the new predicate. CIRP adds the new predicate to the over general recursive clause and its instantiation for the positive and negative examples of the clause are used as the positive and negative examples for the new predicate in the subsequent induction process. CIRP terminates predicate invention when one of the following happens: (i) the number of bits encoding the theory exceeds the bits needed to encode the positive examples and (ii) the instances of a new predicate are the same as examples except for the name of the predicate.

Procedure CIRP
Input: A set of positive and negative examples
Output: A set of complete and consistent clauses
begin
   while there are some positive examples uncovered **do begin**
      Randomly choose a seed example E from positive examples
      Creat the most general term of E, call it MGT
      Q := {MGT}; R := {}; FLAG := false
       while all elements of Q cover any -ve example **do begin**
         PreviousBest := bestclause(Q) according to Merit
           for each element of Q **do**
              Compute the refinements of the element that cover E by using
              the refinements operators, and add them to R
           endfor
         if R := {} **then** add the positive examples as a ground atoms and break
         Q := the best N clauses in R according to Merit
         CurrentBest := bestclause(Q)
         if merit(CurrentBest) $\geq$ merit(PreviousBest) and exist(recursive predicate)
           FLAG := true
         else if merit(CurrentBest) < merit(PreviousBest) and FLAG = true
           Take PreviousBest as incomplete clause for predicate invention
           Decide the argument set for the new predicate
           Assert positive and -ve examples for the new predicate
           Call CIRP for finding the definition of the new predicate
           Remove the positive examples covered by the recursive clause
           break
         endif
       endwhile
   endwhile
end

Fig. 1. CIRP Algorithm

2.3 Demerits of Exhaustive Search

By observing the local peak of Merit, CIRP switches into the constructive induction mode. We will mention one system CHAMP[3] which exhaustively searches the hypothesis space until either a complete and consistent clause is found or the encoding length principle is violated. The encoding length principle says that for a sensible clause the number of bits representing the clause must not be higher than that is needed for encoding the positive examples covered by the clause. But this exhaustive search often diverges from the desired theory and leads to undesirable complete and consistent unit clauses. Let us illustrate it with an example for the learning task of reversing a list. For convenience, let us consider the previous seed example rev([1,2,3],[3,2,1]). If the exhaustive search finds the clause rev([X,Y,Z],[Z,Y,X]) before it violates the encoding length principle, CHAMP recognizes this as a correct clause because it covers all positive examples consisting of three element lists and it does not cover any negative examples. In other words, CHAMP may end up with the exact variabilization of the seed examples producing no meaningful program. Specially this phenomenon occurs when the system has no background knowledge and it tries to find the recursive definition of the desired predicate. One of the solutions to this problem is to dynamically adjust the beam width so that the search procedure may be able to shrink the search space sufficiently to avoid the occurrence of such problematic complete clauses. Again too much shrinking may cause discarding some search space containing the desired clause. CIRP on the other hand has eliminated this problem and its positive impact is that it reduces the total search space in a significant amount as is evident from the experimental results.

3 Argument Set for New Predicate

The discriminating variables in the incomplete clause will form the minimal argument set for the new predicate. DBC algorithm employed in CHAMP has successfully collected the minimal set of variables from an incomplete clause to form the argument set for the new predicate. In [3] it has been proved that the discriminating variables from an incomplete clause constitute the meaningful minimal argument set for the new predicate. DBC checks each variable in the incomplete clause in turn to see whether it discriminates positive examples from the negatives. If the variable satisfies this criteria, it is included in the argument set for the new predicate, otherwise the next one from the incomplete clause is chosen for consideration.

CIRP focuses the possibility of determining the argument set for the new predicate from the argument structure of the original predicate. Since CIRP is using no background knowledge, it can only learn recursively definable concepts. A recursively definable concept may induce new recursively definable subconcepts and this process may go on recursively as the demand needs. *The crucial point is that these concepts must use some form of recursive data structures as arguments, otherwise these concepts cannot be learned without background knowledge. Only and only the recursively defined argument set allows these concepts to be learnable without using any background knowledge.* The use of recursive data structures by these concepts have encouraged to adopt a new procedure in determining the argument set for the new predicate. We argue that the structure of recursive arguments in an incomplete recursive clause often provide hints about the discriminancy of the variables in the incomplete clause. In this section we will mention a procedure to decide the argument set for the new predicate which is suited to recursive functional logic programs [1] using recursive data structure as its arguments. A functional predicate can be defined as follows:

- The predicate has some input arguments.
- The rest of the arguments act as output.
- For every given sequence of input values, there is one and only one sequence of output values that makes the predicate true.

Let in some incomplete recursive clause some input recursive structure X (e.g. a list) is decomposed into variables X1 and X2 such that X1 (e.g. an atom) is a basic constituent element of the structure X, X2 being of the same type as X. Here basic constituent element means the separable unit of a recursive structure of depth zero. For example, for the recursive list structure {[[a,b],c,d,[e,f]]}, [a,b], c, d or [e,f] is the basic constituent element. Note that a, b, e or f is not the basic constituent elements because they are separable units of depth greater than zero. From now on variables like X1 and X2 will be termed as *instantiated variables* and specifically variable like X1 will be termed as *basic_constituent element* of the original recursive structure X. Any variable which is not decomposed will be termed as *uninstantiated variable*.

The input to the procedure collectVars of Fig. 2 is the set VarSet which consists of variables and their types in the incomplete clause and the output of the procedure is OutVarSet which comprises the argument set for the new predicate. The collectVars procedure first form the set InVarSet consisting of the input variables from the VarSet and MarkedVarSet which comprises all uninstantiated input variables qualifying the following criteria:

If for every distinct value of the output variable, there is only and only one value for an uninstantiated input variable, the output variable is a representative for that input variable, making it non-discriminating. Such uninstantiated input variables are collected in the set named MarkedVarSet.

After creating the aforesaid variable sets, the procedure checks each variable in the VarSet in turn in the first while loop of Fig. 2 to see whether it can be included in the OutVarSet. The conditions of inclusion is as follows:

- Any instantiated input variable and of the type of basic_constituent.
- Any uninstantiated input variable which is not a member of the Marked-VarSet.
- Any intermediate variable in the right hand side of the incomplete clause.
- The output variable if it is absent from the right hand side of the clause and the intermediate variable set is non-null.

After collecting the variables for the new predicate in the first while loop, the second while loop checks to see if there exist any input variable which is absent from both the right hand side of the clause and from the OutVarSet. Such a variable is also included in the OutVarSet to form the argument set for the new predicate. The second while loop is important when the recursive antecedent is preceded by some non-discriminating literal which is the desired new predicate. It should be noted that the above mentioned procedure is sufficient enough to satisfy the needs of CIRP algorithm. In addition it can be applied to any incomplete clause derived from an arbitrary system if the incomplete clause uses recursive data structure for its arguments.

Let us apply the collectVars procedure to some incomplete clauses produced by an arbitrary system. The first example is an incomplete clause for the quick-sort program:

Procedure collectVars
Input : VarSet, OutVarSet
VarSet = {Variables and their types in incomplete clause}
OutVarSet = {}
Output : OutVarSet which constitutes the variable set for the new predicate
begin
InVarSet = {∀ X | X ∈ member(VarSet) ⋀ inputVar(X) }
MarkedVarSet = {∀ X | X ∈ member(InVarSet) ⋀ non-Discriminant(X)}
while nonempty(VarSet)
X = member(VarSet)
VarSet = VarSet − X
if instantiated(X) ⋀ basic_constituent(X) ⋀ inputVar(X)
   OutVarSet = OutVarSet ⋃ X
else if uninstantiated(X) ⋀ inputVar(X) ⋀ notMember(MarkedVarSet)
   OutVarSet = OutVarSet ⋃ X
else if intermediate(X)
   OutVarSet = OutVarSet ⋃ X
else if output(X) ⋀ notNull(IntermediateVarSet) ⋀ notMember(R.H.S of the clause)
   OutVarSet = OutVarSet ⋃ X
endif
endwhile
while nonempty(InVarSet)
X = member(InVarSet)
InVarSet = InVarSet − X
if X = notMember(R.H.S of the clause) ⋀ notMember(OutVarSet)
   OutVarSet = OutVarSet ⋃ X
endif
endwhile
end

Fig. 2. collectVars Procedure

```
sort([],[]).
sort([X|Xs],Ys):- sort(Ls,L1), sort(Gs,G1),
                   components(X,G1,G2), append(L1,G2,Ys).
```

The input variable X is a basic constituent element of the instantiated input
structure, that is why it will be one of the arguments for the new predicate.
Since the output variable Ys is present in the right hand side of the clause,
only the intermediate variable set {Ls,Gs} will combine with X to form the
OutVarSet in the first while loop. Since input variable Xs is absent from both
the right hand side of the incomplete clause and from the OutVarSet, it will be
also be included in OutVarSet to form the argument set for the new predicate
partition in the second while loop. It is to be noted that the second while loop
has been used to collect the remaining argument for the non-discriminating new

predicate partition which was not covered by the first while loop of Fig. 2. The completed clause will be as follows:

```
sort([],[]).
sort([X|Xs],Ys):- partition(X,Xs,Ls,Gs),
                   sort(Ls,L1), sort(Gs,G1),
                   components(X,G1,G2), append(L1,G2,Ys).
```

Let us consider another example from merging two sorted lists:

```
merge(Xs,[],Xs).
merge([],Xs,Xs).
merge([X|Xs],[Y|Ys],[X|Zs]):- merge(Xs,[Y|Ys],Zs).
merge([X|Xs],[Y|Ys],[X,Y|Zs]):- merge(Xs,Ys,Zs).
merge([X|Xs],[Y|Ys],[Y|Zs]):- merge([X|Xs],Ys,Zs).
```

The only variables fulfilling the conditions of inclusion in the new predicate are X and Y, since input variables X and Y are both instantiated and basic constituent element of the instantiated recursive structure. Other variables cannot fulfill the conditions of inclusion as stated by the procedure and are ignored. Therefore, the argument set for the new predicates lessThan, equalTo and greaterThan is {X,Y} and completes the clauses as follows:

```
merge([X|Xs],[Y|Ys],[X|Zs]):- lessThan(X,Y),
                               merge(Xs,[Y|Ys],Zs).
merge([X|Xs],[Y|Ys],[X,Y|Zs]):- equalTo(X,Y),
                                 merge(Xs,Ys,Zs).
merge([X|Xs],[Y|Ys],[Y|Zs]):- greaterThan(X,Y),
                               merge([X|Xs],Ys,Zs).
```

We now like to precede one more example from tree domain:

```
substitute(X,Y,void,void).

substitute(X,Y,tree(X,Left,Right),tree(Y,Left1,Right1)):-
    substitute(X,Y,Left,Left1), substitute(X,Y,Right,Right1).

substitute(X,Y,tree(Z,Left,Right),tree(Z,Left1,Right1)):-
    substitute(X,Y,Left,Left1), substitute(X,Y,Right,Right1).
```

This is a logic program for replacing all occurrences of an element X in a binary tree by the element Y. Here tree(X,Left,Right) denotes the root, the left and right subtree, respectively. The first argument is the element to be replaced, the second argument is the replacing element, the third argument is the input tree and the last one is the desired output tree. In this example, the first and second clauses are complete recursive clauses, we need only to find a new predicate for the third incomplete clause. The analysis of the given examples shows that for each distinct output tree, there is only and only one value for the replacing element Y. In other words the presence of the output argument destroys the discriminating capability of the uninstantiated input argument, Y. After analyzing the example set, the collectVars procedure will include variable Y in the MarkedVarSet. The first while loop, out of uninstantiated input variables X and Y, will only include X as an argument for the new predicate as Y is a member of the MarkedVarSet. Therefore X along with the basic constituent element Z of the recursive input structure will form the argument set for the new predicate not-equal(X,Z). The completed clause will be as follows:

```
substitute(X,Y,void,void).

substitute(X,Y,tree(X,Left,Right),tree(Y,Left1,Right1)):-
    substitute(X,Y,Left,Left1), substitute(X,Y,Right,Right1).

substitute(X,Y,tree(Z,Left,Right),tree(Z,Left1,Right1)):-
    not-equal(X,Z),
    substitute(X,Y,Left,Left1), substitute(X,Y,Right,Right1).
```

The analysis of the following general incomplete clause shows that DBC algorithm employed in CHAMP depends on the sequence of checking the discriminating ability of variables in order to result in a true argument set for the new predicate:

Let us consider the incomplete recursive clause P([X1|X2],Xs):- P(X2,Y) with the mode declaration P(+[x],-[x]). This type of recursive clause introduces a non-discriminating literal on the right hand side. Initially all the variables in the tuples {X1,X2,Xs} are discriminating. After the introduction of a non-discriminating literal on the right hand side with a new variable, the number of positive, negative and total examples covered by the clause remains the same, only the size of each tuple has been increased by the new variable Y. Since each X2 produces Y using the predicate for which the definition is sought for, each Y is representing the corresponding X2. That is why, the presence of Y makes X2 non-discriminating. Thus, the discriminating variables constitute the set (X1,Xs,Y). The DBC algorithm will also produce the same variable set if the variables are checked for discriminancy in the order X1, X2, Xs and Y. But if the order is changed so that Y is considered before X2, then it will come out with the set X1, X2, Xs the same as that of input arguments.

One of the principle requirements for the DBC algorithm is that the tuples should reflect the discriminating ability of individual variables. This requirement demands a complete example set for the new predicate. Since the tuples are generated from the projected set [4], it may happen that DBC fails to determine the discriminancy of the variables because of the incompleteness of the example set. But the collectVars procedure for deciding the argument set does not depend at all on the completeness of the tuple set. This procedure has been applied initially to list type data structure though it is possible to apply it in similar recursive structures (e.g. tree) as has been shown before.

The restriction for the applicability of collectVars procedure can be described as follows:

– The instantiated basic constituent element must not make a relation with the rest of the instantiated recursive structure while the later takes part in recursion.

Let us illustrate an example where our procedure is not applicable:

```
no_doubles([],[]).
no_doubles([X|Xs],Ys):- no_doubles(Xs,Ys),
                        member(X,Xs).
no_doubles([X|Xs],[X|Ys]):- no_doubles(Xs,Ys),
                            not_member(X,Xs).
```

This is a logic program for removing duplicate elements from a list. Here we cannot predict the argument set for the member and not_member predicate because the instantiated basic constituent element X makes a relation with the rest of the structure Xs while Xs is taking part in recursion. But this type of problem is not much common in practice and does not reduce the applicability of collectVars procedure in a large extent.

In order to circumvent the problem related with the above example, we can change our learning sequence. We will first learn all the incomplete clauses until all the positive examples are exhausted. Then we will compare the right hand side of each recursive clause before trying to find the argument set for each incomplete clause. If some pair is found equal, then and only then we will explicitly check the instantiated recursive structure for discriminancy. For example, in the above example, since the right hand side of two clauses are equal, we have to check explicitly the discriminating ability of the instantiated recursive structure Xs.

Another important point about the collectVars procedure is that the analysis of the examples is carried out only once for the first level of learning to collect the non-discriminating input variables caused by the output variables. That is, the collectVars procedure builds the MarkedVarSet only once for the first level of learning. If CIRP needs to invent recursive subconcepts, the generation of discriminating arguments for this subconcept produced by the collectVars procedure avoids the need to further check whether any input variable is non-discriminating caused by the output variable of that subconcept.

4   Results and Comparison with other Systems

In this section, we will first compare our system with CHAMP because in many respects these two systems bear close resemblance. The initial motivation for the development of CIRP is to invent some heuristic which is able to switch into constructive induction mode in an efficient way and to suppress the outcome of undesirable clauses due to exhaustive search. The second objective is to determine the argument set for a new predicate in a way which is more data independent than the previous systems. The initial experiments with CIRP shows a considerable savings in search space as compared to CHAMP. The training set for our experiments contains all instances for lists of length three or less, using up to three distinct atoms. As an example of predicate invention, the example set for union program was given as input and the system found the definition for member, not_member and not_equal predicate in addition to the correct clauses for union (predicates beginning with $ sign indicates invented predicates) as follows:

```
union([],X,X).
union([X|Y],V,Z):- union(Y,V,Z),$member(X,V).
union([X|Y],V,[X|Z]):- union(Y,V,Z), $not_member(X,V).
$member(X,[X|Y]).
$member(X,[Y|Z]):- $member(X,Z).
$not_member(X,[]).
$not_member(X,[Y|Z]):- $not_member(X,Z), $not_equal(X,Y).
$not_equal(2,1). $not_equal(2,0). $not_equal(1,0).
$not_equal(1,2). $not_equal(0,2). $not_equal(0,1).
```

The fourth column in Table 1 shows the total number of nodes in the refinement graph visited by each algorithm. For each of the new invented predicates shown in the Table 1, CIRP has successfully determined the argument set for the invented predicates using the collectVars procedure. In our experiments we have not provided the system with any kind of irreflexive order as used in FOIL to avoid infinite recursion. Since CIRP finds recursive clauses which are either pure recursive or left recursive in nature, the mode declaration provided as input is sufficient to avoid undesirable infinite recursion.

Table 1. Experimental Results

Problem	Training Set	New predicates invented	Nodes Visited	Time used in ms
Sort	16 +ve Exs 240 -ve Exs	insert greaterThan	41(CIRP) 84 (CHAMP)	10070(CIRP) 20790(CHAMP)
Reverse	16 +ve Exs 240 -ve Exs	concat	14(CIRP) 14(CHAMP)	4129(CIRP) 4889(CHAMP)
Insert	12 +ve Exs 180 -ve Exs	greaterThan	29(CIRP) 42(CHAMP)	5460(CIRP) 7480(CHAMP)
Union	100 +ve Exs 3300 -ve Exs	member not_member not_equal	41(CIRP) 140(CHAMP)	209429(CIRP) 787160(CHAMP)

Next we will compare CIRP with another system CILP[4] which also induces recursive programs and invents new predicates when there is no background knowledge available. CILP has used Inverse Implication as its basic tool which allows it to learn from examples more than one resolution step apart from each other. CILP is limited to the subclass of all recursive logic programs satisfying the following syntactic formats:

(i) p(...).
     p(...):- p(...).

(ii) q(...).
     q(...):- q(...), newp(...).
     newp(...).
     newp(...):- newp(...).

where newp is a new predicate defined as a purely recursive clause. CILP first attempts to induce a definition in format (i) and if it fails, it attempts to find a definition in format (ii) and invents a new predicate in a purely recursive format. Thus, regularities in the expected syntax allows it to find a new predicate in a restrictive format and it has no explicit switching element like that employed in CIRP to infer the necessity of constructive induction. The major restriction is that when it induces definition in format (ii), it employs sub-unification between only the input arguments of the examples, assuming the presence of a new variable in the right hand side of the left recursive clause, representing the partial result of recursion. This restriction will not allow CILP to learn programs like union which has no new variable in the right hand side of the left recursive clause to represent partial result of recursion. Though the adoption of Inverse Implication has allowed CILP to learn recursive programs from a few examples which are more than one resolution step apart from each other, the aforesaid restrictions have limited its scope compared to CIRP.

CIRP has learned many useful logic programs of considerable depth as has been verified in our experimental results. The present implementation of CIRP is employing collectVars procedure to infer the argument set for the new predicate which is insensitive to the completeness of example set. With the help of this insensitiveness, we believe, like CILP, CIRP will be able to learn from a small number of examples which are more than one resolution step apart from each other. Our future research will involve some more experimentation in this direction.

5 Discussion

CIRP is an attempt to build an efficient system for learning recursive concepts from examples without any background predicate. The system is able to learn recursive concepts and subconepts up to an appreciable level. The system has used the combination of goal directed usefulness and discriminating ability of a clause to form a new heuristic which enabled it to switch into constructive induction mode efficiently. In doing this it has overcome the demerits of exhaustive search to switch into predicate invention mode. Since recursive concepts learnable without background knowledge must use some form of recursive data structure for their arguments, a new method has been employed to find the argument set for the new predicate using the argument structures. Though this procedure is sufficient enough to satisfy the needs of CIRP, it has been shown through examples that it can be applied to any incomplete clause from any arbitrary system satisfying the criteria of applicability. The limitation of this procedure and possible remedy of it has been enlightened. The system has been compared with CHAMP and CILP to show its relative strength and generality. Comparison with other systems were not possible because of the absence of comparable systems which use similar ideology.

References

1. F. Bergadano and D. Gunetti. An interactive system to learn functional logic programs. In *Procedings of the 13th IJCAI*, 1993.
2. B. Kijsirikul, M. Numao, and M. Shimura. Efficient learning of logic programs with non-determinate, non-discriminating literals. In *8th Intl. Workshop on Machine Learning*, 1991.
3. B. Kijsirikul, M. Numao, and M. Shimura. Discrimination-based constructive induction. In *AAAI*, 1992.
4. S. Lapointe, C. Ling, and S. Matwin. Constructive inductive logic programming. In *International Joint Conference on Artificial Intelligence*, 1993.
5. S. Lapointe and S. Matwin. Sub-unification: A tool for efficient induction of recursive programs. In *9th Intl. Workshop on Machine Learning*, 1992.
6. S. Muggleton and W. Buntine. Machine invention of first-order predicates by inverting resolution. In *5th Intl. Workshop on Machine Learning*, 1988.
7. S. Muggleton and C. Feng. Efficient induction of logic programs. In *Procedings of the 1st International workshop on Algorithmic Learning Theory*, 1990.
8. J. R. Quinlan. Induction of decision trees. *Machine Learning*, 1(1), 1986.
9. J. R. Quinlan. Learning logical definitions from relations. *Machine Learning*, 5:239–266, 1990.
10. L. De Raedt and M. Bruynooghe. Interactive concept-learning and constructive induction by analogy. *Machine Learning*, 8(2):107–150, 1992.
11. C. Rouveirol. *Extensions of Inversion of Resolution Applied to Theory Completion*. Inductive Logic Programming, Academic Press, 1992.
12. Ehud Shapiro. *Algorithmic Program Debugging*. MIT Press, 1982.
13. G. Silverstein and M. J. Pazzani. Relational cliches: Constraining constructive induction during relational learning. In *Procedings of Machine Learning Workshop*, 1991.
14. R. Wirth. Learning by failure to prove. In *Proceedings of EWSL*, 1988.
15. R. Wirth and P. O'Rorke. *Constraints for Predicate Invention*. Inductive Logic Programming, Academic Press, 1992.
16. J. Wogulis and P. Langley. Improving efficiency by learning intermediate concepts. In *Proceedings of the 11th IJCAI*, 1989.

TRAINING DIGRAPHS

Hsieh-Chang Tu and Carl H. Smith
Department of Computer Science
University of Maryland
College Park, MD 20742

Abstract

A formal definition of what it means for a machine to learn a collection
of concepts in an order determined by a finite acyclic digraph of recursive
functions is presented. We show that given a labelled graph $G = (V, E)$
representing the learning structure, there are sets S such that in order
to learn a program corresponding to some node i, a machine must have
precisely learned programs corresponding to all the predecessor nodes.

1 Introduction

Intuitively, the more a machine knows the more it can learn. Learning by
induction becomes interesting to computer scientists because of artificial intelligence considerations [2, 8]. Situations where learning algorithms were given
a sequence of learning tasks were previously investigated [1]. It was discovered
that there are finite sets of concepts such that each concept in the set can be
learned, but only if the concepts are presented to the learning algorithm in the
proper order. That is to say, there is an ordering of the concepts such that the
learning algorithm can learn the first concept in the usual manor. Furthermore,
if the learning algorithm is given the successful results of learning some initial
segment of the concepts, with respect to the distinguished ordering, then the
next concept in the sequence can also be learned. Moreover, learning is not
possible, by an algorithm, if the concepts in the set are presented in a different
order.

The previously studied situation represented a simple, straight line, prerequisite structure. That is, the first concept in the sequence must be learned before
the second one can be attempted. Likewise, learning the third concept can succeed only after the second concept has been mastered. In this paper we consider
more complicated prerequisite structures. Considered herein is the learning of
finite sets of concepts with prerequisite structures represented by directed acyclic
graphs. As in other studies in inductive inference, we use recursive functions to
model concepts.

An *inductive inference machine* (IIM) [1] is an algorithmic device that takes as input the graph of a recursive function and produces programs as output. These programs are assumed to come from some acceptable programming system [10, 11] so that we have *enumeration* and *s-m-n* theorems. Consequently, every program (or partial recursive function) has a natural number as its name, i.e., program i is said to compute the (partial recursive) function ϕ_i.

We say that an IIM M *identifies* f iff when M is fed longer and longer initial segments of f it outputs programs which, past some point, are all i, where $\phi_i = f$. In other words, there is some sufficiently large N such that, given any initial segment of f longer than N, M will output some number i, which names the function ϕ_i, having the same behavior as function f.

We are interested in the idea of "learning how to learn". One possible model of showing machines can learn how to learn is one of inferring *sequences* of functions. Two slightly different scenarios were discussed in [1]. A rigorous comparsion of the two scenarios reveals some interesting results [1].

We will review the idea of *training sequences* in the next section. Here we have a "trainer" which gives an IIM M some programs as a preamble to the graph of some function f. The output of this IIM M will be the function f, showing that it can infer this function by its graph and preamble programs.

A further extension to training sequences is *training digraphs*. That is, the learning order is no longer specified by a sequence but a more complicated acyclic digraphs. A formal definition will be given in the following. We will show that given a labelled graph $G = (V, E)$ representing the learning structure, there are sets S such that in order to learn a program corresponding to some node i, a machine must have precisely learned programs corresponding to *all* the predecessor nodes.

2 Review: Training Sequences

In this section we review some formal definitions that will be used later. Most of our definitions can be found in [1, 3]. Assume that $\phi_0, \phi_1, \phi_2, ...$ is a fixed acceptable programming system of all (and only all) partial recursive functions. Let ω denote the set of all natural numbers [11]. We will assume the universe discussed is *always* on ω, so, e.g., sometimes we will use $(\forall x)$ instead of $(\forall x \in \omega)$. If f is a partial recursive function and $e \in \omega$ is such that $\phi_e = f$, then e is called a *program* for f. For each natural number n, let ω^n be the Cartesian product of n times of ω, e.g., $\omega^3 = \omega \times \omega \times \omega$. Let $\langle \cdot, \cdot, ..., \cdot \rangle$ be a recursive bijection from $\bigcup_{i=0}^{\infty} \omega^i$ to ω. For any n-ary partial recursive function $f : \omega^n \to \omega$, we write $f(x_1, ..., x_n)$ rather than $f(\langle x_1, ..., x_n \rangle)$ [6, p.3]. For convenience, we will use c_i to denote the constant i function, i.e., $\lambda x[i]$. Thus $\phi_{p_i} = c_i$ means the program p_i computes c_i, i.e., $\phi_{p_i}(x) = i$ for all $x \in \omega$. The symbol '$\subset$' will be used for 'proper subset of', for example, $x \subset y$ means $x \subseteq y$ and $x \neq y$.

If S is a nonempty finite set $\{x_1, x_2, ..., x_n\}$ where $x_1 < x_2 < ... < x_n \in \omega$, then the integer $x = \sum_{i=1}^{n} 2^{x_i}$ is called the *canonical index* of S. If $S = \emptyset$, the canonical index assigned to S is 0 [10]. Let D_x be the finite set whose canonical index is x. It is easy to see that every finite set has a unique canonical index, and every integer is the canonical index of some finite set. The symbol $(\cdot, \cdot)$ will be used for ordered pairs of sets. As usual, $|S|$ stands for the cardinality of the set S.

Definition 1 *An IIM (inductive inference machine) M is some partial recursive function in our acceptable programming system. Let f be a recursive function. M converges on input f to program i (written: $M(f) \downarrow= i$) iff almost all (i.e., all but finitely many) elements of the sequence $M(\langle f(0)\rangle)$, $M(\langle f(0), f(1)\rangle)$, $M(\langle f(0), f(1), f(2)\rangle), ...,$ are equal to i.*

Definition 2 *A set S of recursive functions is learnable (or inferrible or EX-identifiable) if there exists an IIM M such that for any $f \in S$, $M(f) \downarrow= e$ for some e such that $\phi_e = f$. Let EX be the set of all subsets of recursive functions that are learnable.*

Note that in the above we have assumed that each inference machine is viewing the input function in the natural, domain increasing order. It has been proved that the order can have dramatic effects on the complexity of performing the inference but not on what can and cannot be inferred [5].

Some examples of learnable sets are: (1) any finite subset of recursive functions, (2) the set $\{c_i : c_i = \lambda x[i]\}$, (3) the set $\bigcup_{n=0}^{\infty}\{f : f(x) = nx\}$. There also exists sets that are not learnable, e.g., the set of all recursive functions [7].

Training sequences [1] is a study about, in some sense, how machines can be taught how to learn finite *sequences* of functions. Suppose that the n-tuple $\langle f_1, f_2, ...f_n\rangle$ is such a sequence of recursive functions and M is an IIM. We say that M can infer $\langle f_1, f_2, ...f_n\rangle$ (written: $\langle f_1, f_2, ...f_n\rangle \in S^n EX(M)$) iff (1) M can identify f_1 from the graph of f_1 with no additional information, and (2) for $1 \leq i < n$, M can identify f_{i+1} from the graph of f_{i+1} if it is also provided with a sequence of programs e_1, e_2,...,e_i, where e_j's $(1 \leq j \leq i)$ are programs for f_j (i.e., $\phi_{e_1} = f_1,...,\phi_{e_i} = f_i$).

Definition 3 *For any IIM M, $M(\langle e_1, ..., e_m\rangle; f) \downarrow= e$ means that the sequence of outputs produced by M when given programs $e_1, ..., e_m$ and the graph of f converges to program e. That is, almost all the elements of the sequence $M(n, \langle f(0)\rangle)$, $M(n, \langle f(0), f(1)\rangle)$, $M(n, \langle f(0), f(1), f(2)\rangle), ...,$ are equal to e, where $n = \langle e_1, ..., e_m\rangle$.*

Definition 4 *Let $n \geq 1$ be any natural number. For $1 \leq i \leq n$, let J_i be any subset of $\{1, 2, ..., i-1\}$, (J_1 will always be $\emptyset$). Let $J = \langle J_1, ..., J_n\rangle$. A set S of n-tuples of recursive functions is J-learnable (or J-inferrible, or J-$S^n EX$-identifiable) if there exists an IIM M such that for all $\langle f_1, ..., f_n\rangle \in S$, for all $\langle e_1, ...e_n\rangle$ such that e_j is a program for f_j $(1 \leq j \leq n)$, for all i with $J_i = \{b_i^1, b_i^2, ..., b_i^m\}$ $(1 \leq i \leq n, b_i^p < b_i^q$ for $1 \leq p < q \leq m)$, (Note that m may vary with i), $M(\langle e_{b_i^1}, e_{b_i^2}, ...e_{b_i^m}\rangle; f_i) \downarrow= e$, where e is a program for f_i. M*

is called a sequence IIM *(SIIM) for S. We will reference* $\langle e_{b_i^1}, e_{b_i^2}, ... e_{b_i^m} \rangle$ *as* preambled *programs (to learn function f_i).*

Notice in the above definition, we insist that the preamble of programs $\langle e_{b_i^1}, e_{b_i^2}, ... e_{b_i^m} \rangle$ is ordered by $b_i^1, b_i^2, ..., b_i^m$ such that $b_i^1 < b_i^2 < ... < b_i^m$. A quick oberservation is that for any J-learnable set S, the set $\{f_1 : \langle f_1, ..., f_n \rangle \in S\}$ must be inferrible. In particular, a set S is inferrible iff $\{\langle f \rangle : f \in S\}$ is $\langle \emptyset \rangle$-learnable.

Let $S^n REC$ be the set consisting of all sets of n-tuples of recursive functions. Let $S^n EX \subseteq S^n REC$ be a set such that each member $S \in S^n EX$ is J-learnable with $J = \langle J_1, ..., J_n \rangle$ and $J_i = \{1, 2, ..., i-1\}$ $(1 \leq i \leq n)$. That is, $S^n EX$ is the set consists of members which are sequences such that any function in the sequence can be learned if *all* the previous ones have already been learned. Notice that we may change the above conditions $J_i = \{1, 2, ..., i-1\}$ to $J_i \subseteq \{1, 2, ..., i-1\}$ since, if S is J-learnable for some $J = \langle J_1, ..., J_n \rangle$ then S is also J'-learnable for any $J' = \langle J_1', ..., J_n' \rangle$ such that $(\forall 1 \leq i \leq n)(J_i \subseteq J_i')$.

We are interested in the case where inferring the ith function of a sequence requires knowing *all* the previous ones. This motivates the following two definitions about *redundancies* of sets.

Definition 5 *A set $S \in S^n REC$ is* redundant *if there is an SIIM that can infer all f_n with a preamble of fewer than $n-1$ programs for $f_1, f_2, ..., f_{n-1}$. Every J-learnable set S is either redundant or nonredundant.*

Definition 6 *A set $S \in S^n REC$ is* strictly redundant *if it is J-learnable for some $J = \langle J_1, ..., J_n \rangle$ and there exists an i, $1 < i \leq n$, such that J_i is a proper subset of $\{1, ..., i-1\}$.*

Intuitively, a set S of n-tuples of recursive functions ($S \in S^n REC$) being nonredundant means that we need all the previous functions to learn the *last* one. On the other hand, strictly nonredundancy is a slightly stronger notion. S being strictly nonredundant means that in order to learn any function (not only the last one) in the sequence, we need all functions in front of it. The sets in which we are really interested are the strictly nonredundant ones. However, it is proved that the existence of certain nonredundant sets implies the existence of a strictly nonredundant set [1].

Some examples of redundant sets are: (1) the set $S \in S^2 EX$ where $S = \{ \langle f, g \rangle : f \in S_1, g \in S_2, S_1, S_2 \in EX \}$. (2) the set $S = \{ \langle f, g, h \rangle : f(0)$ is a program for f, $\langle g, h \rangle \in R \}$ where R is redundant. A more complicated redundant set which is in $S^3 EX$ is given in [1]. Note that for any S inferrible, the set $\{\langle f \rangle : f \in S\} \in S^1 EX$ is nonredundant. Any set $S \in S^2 EX$ being nonredundant is also strictly nonredundant.

Definition 7 *Suppose f is a recursive function and $n \in \omega$. For $j < n$, the jth n-ply of f is the recursive function $\lambda x[f(n \cdot x + j)]$.*

n-Plies of recursive functions are useful in our technical proofs. Notice that any recursive function can be constructed from its n-plies. For the special case $n = 2$, we will refer to the even and odd plies of a given function. The following two theorems tells us the existence of certain nonredundant sets. Notice that Theorem 2 is a generalization of Theorem 1. Both proofs are given by [1].

Theorem 1 $S = \{(c_i, \phi_i) : \phi_i$ *is a recursive function*$\}$ *is a nonredundant member of* S^2EX.

Theorem 2 *For all* $n \in \omega$, S_{n+1} *is a nonredundant member of* $S^n EX$, *where*

$$S_{n+1} = \{ \langle f_0, f_1, ..., f_n \rangle : f_n \text{ is any recursive function and for each } i < n,$$
$$f_i \text{ is the constant } j_i \text{ function where } \phi_{j_i} \text{ is the}$$
$$i^{th} \text{ } n\text{-ply of } f_n \}.$$

3 Training Digraphs

In this section we want to extend our ideas further, from sequences of recursive functions to acyclic digraphs. The basic idea is to consider more complicated prerequisite knowledge structures. For example, we may want to say functions f_1, f_2 and f_3 are necessary to learn f_4, but f_1 is enough to learn f_3. We will represent this kind of learning dependencies by *directed graphs*. The definitions of graphs (digraphs) can be found in some standard textbooks such as [9]

Definition 8 *A directed graph (digraph)* G *is an ordered pair* $G = (V, E)$ *where* V *is a set of* vertices (nodes) *and* $E \subseteq V \times V$ *is a set of* edges. $G = (V, E)$ *is said to be* finite *if* $|V| \in \omega$. $G = (V, E)$ *is called* acyclic *if there is no path* $e_1, ..., e_m \in E$ $(m \in \omega)$ *such that* $e_1 = (v, \cdot)$ *and* $e_m = (\cdot, v)$. *A finite, acyclic digraph* $G = (V, E) \neq \emptyset$ *with* $|V| = n$ *is called* concise *if* $V = \{1, ..., n\}$.

Throughout this paper, we will use 'concise graph G' instead of 'finite, acyclic, concise digraph G' if it won't cause confusion. Two concise graphs $G_1 = (V_1, E_1)$, $G_2 = (V_2, E_2)$ are *isomorphic* iff there is some 1-1, onto function $h : V_1 \rightarrow V_2$ *(isomorphism function)* such that for all $n_1, n_2 \in V_1$, $(n_1, n_2) \in E_1$ iff $(h(n_1), h(n_2)) \in E_2$. Given any concise graph G, let $P_j(G)$, predecessor nodes of node j, be the set consisting of all nodes i such that there is a path from node i to node j. Let $P'_j(G) = P_j(G) \cup \{j\}$. For notational convenience, we will use P_j, P'_j rather than $P_j(G)$, $P'_j(G)$, respectively, if they won't cause confusion.

Example 1 (concise graphs): Figure 1 gives five concise graphs. We will reference these graphs by $G_1^*, ..., G_5^*$, respectively, in the following examples. Notice that the graphs G_3^* and G_4^* are isomorphic. For graph G_5^*, $P_4 = \emptyset$, $P_2 = P_3 = \{4\}$, $P_1 = \{2,3,4\}$, $P_5 = \{1,2,3,4\}$, and thus $P'_4 = \{4\}$, $P'_2 = \{2,4\}$, $P'_3 = \{3,4\}$, $P'_1 = \{1,2,3,4\}$, $P'_5 = \{1,2,3,4,5\}$. □

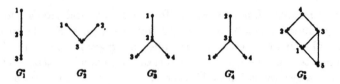

Figure 1: Some concise graphs

We may encode a concise graph G into some natural number and decode it (i.e., realize the graph structure) recursively. This is done by coding $G = (V, E)$ into $G' = \langle n, x \rangle$ where $|V| = n$ and x is the canonical index of the set $D_x = \{\langle n_1, n_2 \rangle : (n_1, n_2) \in E\}$. The number G' is called the *concise coding* of G.

Definition 9 *Given a concise graph G, let G' be the concise coding of G. For any IIM M, $M(G, \langle e_1, ..., e_m \rangle; f) \downarrow = e$ means that the sequence of outputs produced by M when given the concise graph G, programs $e_1, ..., e_m$, and the graph of f converges to program e. That is, almost all elements of the sequence $M(n, \langle f(0) \rangle)$, $M(n, \langle f(0), f(1) \rangle)$, $M(n, \langle f(0), f(1), f(2) \rangle)$, ..., are equal to e, where $n = \langle G', \langle e_1, ..., e_m \rangle \rangle$.*

Definition 10 *Let $G = (V, E)$ be a concise graph with $|V| = n$. Let $J = \langle J_1, ..., J_n \rangle$ where J_i is any subset of P_i $(1 \le i \le n)$. A set S of n-tuples of recursive functions is called (G, J)-learnable if there exists an IIM M such that for all $(f_1, ..., f_n) \in S$, for all e_j being a program for f_j $(1 \le j \le n)$, for all i $(1 \le i \le n)$ with $J_i = \{b_i^1, b_i^2, ..., b_i^m\}$ $(1 \le i \le n$, $b_i^p < b_i^q$ for $1 \le p < q \le m)$, (Note that m may vary with i), $M(G, \langle e_{b_i^1}, e_{b_i^2}, ... e_{b_i^m} \rangle; f_i) \downarrow = e$ where e is a program for f_i. S is called G-learnable if S is (G, J)-learnable for some J.*

Note that given concise graph G, we can recursively construct, for any $i \in V$ with $|P_i'| = m$, a bijection function $h_i : P_i' \to \{1, ..., m\}$ such that h_i is monotonic increasing on the domain P_i and $h_i(i) = m$. For example, in graph G_5^*, $h_1 = \{(1, 4), (2, 1), (3, 2), (4, 3)\}$, $h_2 = \{(2, 2), (4, 1)\}$, $h_3 = \{(3, 2), (4, 1)\}$, $h_4 = \{(4, 1)\}$, and $h_5 = \{(1, 1), (2, 2), (3, 3), (4, 4), (5, 5)\}$. Intuitively, function h_i gives us some way to reference the predecessor nodes of node i, which will be important in the technical arguments that follow.

Proposition 1 *Given two concise graphs $G_1 = (V_1, E_1)$, $G_2 = (V_2, E_2)$ with $|V_1| = |V_2|$ but not isomorphic, there may exist a set which is both G_1 and G_2 learnable.*

Proof: Let $S = \{\langle c_i, c_i, \phi_i \rangle :$ and ϕ_i is any recursive function $\}$. Notice that $c_i = \lambda x[i]$ can be any (recursive) constant i function. Then S is both G_1^*-learnable and G_2^*- learnable. In particular, S is both (G_1^*, J)-learnable and (G_2^*, J)-learnable for $J = \langle J_1, J_2, J_3 \rangle$ with $J_1 = J_2 = \emptyset$, $J_3 = \{2\}$. To see this, it suffices to show that there is some M such that (G^* can be either G_1^* or G_2^*) for all $\langle c_i, c_i, \phi_i \rangle \in S$,

$$
\begin{cases}
M(G^*, \langle\rangle; c_i) \downarrow = e & \text{where } \phi_e = c_i \\
M(G^*, \langle e_2 \rangle; \phi_i) \downarrow = e & \text{where } \phi_e = \phi_i,\ e_2 = \lambda x[i] \text{ and } \phi_i \text{ recursive}
\end{cases}
\tag{1}
$$

Let $S' = \{\langle c_i, \phi_i \rangle : \phi_i \text{ recursive}\}$. By Theorem 1, $S' \in S^2EX$, thus can be learned by some IIM M'. To output correct e's in Equation (1), M first checks if there is some input preamble programs. If no, just output some e such that $\phi_e = \lambda x[i] = c_i$, where i is found from the range of the input function. Otherwise, output the result e of $M'(\langle e_2 \rangle; \phi_i)$. This e must satisfy $\phi_e = \phi_i$ since e_2 is an index for c_i. $\qquad\square$

Proposition 2 *Given two concise graph $G_1 = (V_1, E_1)$, $G_2 = (V_2, E_2)$ with $|V_1| = |V_2|$ but not isomorphic, there may exist a set which is G_1 but not G_2 learnable.*

Proof: Let $S = \{\langle c_i, \phi_i, \phi_i \rangle : \phi_i \text{ is any recursive function}\}$. Then S is G_1^*-learnable (see Figure 1) but not G_2^*-learnable.

(1). Let $J = \langle J_1, J_2, J_3 \rangle$ where $J_1 = \{\emptyset\}$, $J_2 = \{1\}$, $J_3 = \{1\}$. From Theorem 1, the set $S' = \{\langle c_i, \phi_i \rangle : \phi_i \text{ recursive}\}$ is an element of S^2EX, so there is some IIM M' such that for all $\langle g, f \rangle \in S'$, $M'(\langle e' \rangle; f) \downarrow = e$ where $\phi_{e'} = g$ and $\phi_e = f$. Let M be the program acting as follows: $M(G, \langle\rangle; f)$ outputs some program e such that $(\forall x)\phi_e(x) = f(0)$ (M knows the value $f(0)$ from the graph of f), and $M(G, \langle e' \rangle; f)$ produces the same result as $M'(\langle e' \rangle; f)$. It follows that S is (G_1^*, J)-learnable by M, and therefore S is (G_1^*, J)-learnable.

(2). Suppose S were G_2^*-learnable by some IIM M. Let $G_2^* = (V, E)$. By definition S is (G_2^*, J)-learnable for some $J = \langle J_1, J_2, J_3 \rangle$ where $J_i \subseteq P_i$ for all $i \in V$. Notice that $P_2 = \emptyset$, thus J_2 must be empty. That is, for all $\langle \cdot, f, \cdot \rangle \in S$, $M(G_2^*, \langle\rangle; f) \downarrow = e$ where e is a program for f. Let M' be a IIM which contains the concise coding of G_2^* as its built-in data. Then it can simulate $M(G_2^*, \langle\rangle; f)$ to produce $M'(\langle\rangle; f)$. It follows that the set $\{f : f \text{ recursive}\}$ would be learnable by M', which is a contradiction. $\qquad\square$

Intuitively, concise graphs which are isomorphic imply they have the same learning structures. That is, once we know how to learn a set whose learning order is represented by the concise graph G_1, we know how to infer the sets whose learning orders are represented by any G_2 which is isomorphic to G_1. This idea is formally stated in the following proposition.

Proposition 3 *Let G_1 and G_2 be two isomorphic concise graphs. Then S_1 is G_1-learnable iff there is some S_2 which is G_2-learnable.*

Proof: Let $|G_1| = n$ and $h(x)$ be the isomorphic function from G_1 to G_2. Let $S \in S^n REC$. Then S is G_1-learnable iff $\{ \langle f_1', ..., f_n' \rangle : \langle f_1, ..., f_n \rangle \in S, f_i' = f_{h(i)}$ for all $i \in V_1 \}$ is G_2-learnable. $\qquad \square$

The following definition is motivated by the analogy of strictly nonredundancy sets in training sequences.

Definition 11 *Let G be a concise graph. A set S of n-tuples of recursive functions is called G-strictly redundant iff it is G-learnable and, if S is (G, J)-learnable for $J = \langle J_1, ..., J_n \rangle$ $(J_i \subseteq P_i$ for all $1 \leq i \leq n)$ then there exists an i such that $J_i \subset P_i$ (J_i is a proper subset of P_i). A G-learnable set is G-strictly nonredundant if it is not G-strictly redundant.*

Suppose G is a *chain* (e.g., Figure 1(G_1^*)) with $|V| = n$. Then a set $S \in S^n REC$ is G-learnable iff S is J-learnable for some J iff $S \in S^n EX$. Furthermore, $S \in S^n REC$ is G-strictly redundant iff S is strictly redundant. So strictly redundancy in training sequences is a special case of G-redundancy, for G a chain.

Example 2 (G-strictly redundant set): The set $S = \{ \langle c_i, c_i, \phi_i \rangle$: ϕ_i recursive $\}$ in example 2 is G_1^*-strictly redundant since it is (G_1^*, J)-learnable with $J = \langle \emptyset, \emptyset, \{2\} \rangle$ and $\{2\}$ is a proper subset of $P_3 = \{1, 2\}$. $\qquad \square$

Theorem 3 *Let G_2^* be the concise graph shown in Figure 1. There is a G_2^*-strictly nonredundant set.*

Proof: Given G_2^* (see Figure 1), a concise graph with $|V_2^*| = 3$. Let $S_1 = \{ \langle c_i \rangle :$ c_i is the constant i function $\}$, $S_3 = \{ \langle f_0, f_1, f_2 \rangle :$ f_2 any recursive function, f_0, f_1 are the constant c and d functions such that ϕ_c, ϕ_d are the even and odd plies of $f_2 \}$. Then $S_1 \in S^1 EX$, $S_3 \in S^3 EX$ and both are non-redundant by Theorem 2. Let M_1, M_3 to be the machines that can infer S_1 and S_3. Let $S = R_1 \cup R_2 \cup R_3$ where

$R_1 =$
$\quad \{ \langle f_1, f_2, f_3 \rangle : (\forall x)(f_1(x) = \langle 1, g(x) \rangle \wedge f_2(x) = f_3(x) = 0),$ *where* $\langle g \rangle \in S_1 \}$
$R_2 =$
$\quad \{ \langle f_1, f_2, f_3 \rangle : (\forall x)(f_2(x) = \langle 2, g(x) \rangle \wedge f_1(x) = f_3(x) = 0),$ *where* $\langle g \rangle \in S_1 \}$
$R_3 =$
$\quad \{ \langle f_1, f_2, f_3 \rangle : (\forall i \in \{1, 2, 3\})(\forall x)(f_i(x) = \langle 3, g_i(x) \rangle)),$ *where* $\langle g_1, g_2; g_3 \rangle \in S_3 \}$

We will show that S is G_2^*-strictly nonredundant:
(1). S is $(G_2^*, \langle \emptyset, \emptyset, \{1, 2\} \rangle)$-learnable. For example, suppose we want to show node 3 is learnable from its predecessors. That is, we want to show $M(G_2^*, \langle e_1, e_2 \rangle; f_3)$ ($\phi_{e_1} = f_1$, $\phi_{e_2} = f_2$ and $\langle f_1, f_2, f_3 \rangle \in S$) converges to e_3

such that $\phi_{e_3} = f_3$. To see this, we (machine M) first computes $f_3(0)$ to see if it's zero. If it is, $\langle f_1, f_2, f_3 \rangle \in R_1 \cup R_2$ and f_3 must be a constant zero function, so we output any number e such that $\phi_e = \lambda x[0]$. If not, it must be of the form $\langle 3, \cdot \rangle$. Extract the number 3 from the first argument (which means we are considering concise node 3). From the graph G_2^* we see node 1 and 2 are predecessors of node 3. So we know e_1, e_2 must be programs for node 1 and 2 respectively. Thus we know that $(\forall x)(\phi_{e_1}(x) = f_1(x) = \langle 3, g_1(x) \rangle)$, $(\forall x)(\phi_{e_2}(x) = f_2(x) = \langle 3, g_2(x) \rangle)$ for some $\langle g_1, g_2, g_3 \rangle \in S_3$. It follows that we are able to compute, recursively, e_1', e_2' such that $\phi_{e_1'} = g_1$ and $\phi_{e_2'} = g_2$. Now we feed e_1', e_2', and the graph of g_3 (obtained from the graph of f_3) into M_3, which will return e_3' such that $\phi_{e_3'} = g_3$. Finally we recursively find e such that $(\forall x)(\phi_e(x) = \langle 3, \phi_{e'}(x) \rangle$. Output e. This e must be a program for f_3.

(2). S is not $(G_2^*, \langle \emptyset, \emptyset, J_3 \rangle)$-learnable for any $J_3 \subset \{1,2\}$. Suppose not and, without loss of generality, assume $J_3 = \{1\}$. So for all $\langle f_1, f_2, f_3 \rangle \in S$, $M(G_2^*, \langle e_1' \rangle; f_3) \downarrow = e'$ where $\phi_{e_1'} = f_1$ and $\phi_{e'} = f_3$. We will construct an IIM M' such that, for all $\langle g_1, g_2, g_3 \rangle \in S_3$, for all e_1 a program for g_1, $M'(\langle e_1 \rangle; g_3)$ converges to e where $\phi_e = g_3$. This will contradict to the nonredundancy of S_3, since the program for g_2 is unused for learning g_3.

In first step, we compute the index e_1' from e_1 (recursively find e_1 such that $(\forall x)[\phi_{e_1'}(x) = \langle 3, \phi_{e_1}(x) \rangle]$). Next we compute the graph of f_3 from the graph of g_3 by $f_3(x) = \langle 3, g_3(x) \rangle$. It follows that for all $\langle g_1, g_2, g_3 \rangle \in S_3$, $M(G_2^*, \langle e_1' \rangle; f_3)$ converges to some e' which is a program for f_3. M' then computes e such that $(\forall x)(\phi_{e'}(x) = \langle 3, \phi_e(x) \rangle)$ (therefore $(\forall x)[\phi_e(x) = g_3(x)]$) and outputs it as the final result. □

To generalize the idea shown in the above result, we introduce the following lemma.

Lemma 1 *Given any concise graph G with $|V| = n \geq 1$. If there exists sets S_i $(1 \leq i \leq n)$ of non-redundant i-tuples of recursive functions, then there exists a set S of n-tuples of recursive functions which is G-strictly nonredundant.*

Proof: For every $i \in V$, let h_i be the recursive bijection function from P_i' to $\{1, ..., |P_i'|\}$ such that h_i is monotonic increasing on P_i and $h_i(i) = |P_i'|$. Let

$$S = \bigcup_{i=1}^{n} \{ \langle f_1, ..., f_n \rangle : \quad \exists \langle g_1, ..., g_m \rangle \in S_m, \quad \text{where } m = |P_i'|,$$
$$f_j(x) = \langle i, g_{h_i(j)} \rangle \quad \text{if } j \in P_i'$$
$$f_j(x) = 0 \quad \text{otherwise} \}$$

We must show that S is G-learnable and, if S is (G, J)-learnable with $J = \langle J_1, ..., J_n \rangle$ then $J_i = P_i$ for all $i \in V$. Let $M_1, ..., M_n$ be machines that learn $S_1, ..., S_n$.

(1). S is (G, J)-learnable with $J = \langle P_1, ..., P_n \rangle$. It suffices to construct an IIM M such that for all $\langle f_1, ...f_n \rangle \in S$, for all e_j programs of f_j $(j \in V)$, for all i with $J_i = P_i = \{b_i^1, b_i^2, ..., b_i^m\}$, $M(G, \langle e_{b_i^1}, e_{b_i^2}, ...e_{b_i^m} \rangle; f_i) \downarrow = e$ where e is a program for f_i.

To infer f_i, M first computes $f_i(0)$.(note M knows the graph of f_i). If $f_i(0) = 0$, then f_i must be a constant zero function, so M just outputs some e such that $\phi_e = c_0$. Otherwise, M gets i from the output of $f_i(0) = \langle i, \cdot \rangle$, computes $m = |P_i'|$ and the function $h_i : P_i' \rightarrow \{1, 2, ..., m\}$. Note that every e_k $(k \in P_i')$ in the preamble is just a program for f_k, where $f_k(x) = \langle i, g_{h_i(k)}(x) \rangle$ for all $x \in \omega$. So, from e_k we can compute e_k', a program for $g_{h_i(k)}$. But M_i can infer $g_{h_i(m)} = g_m$ once given all programs $g_{h_i(k)}$, $k \in P_i$ (note we will need the monotonicity property of h_i on domain P_i to have this conclusion). Say the output is program e' (so $\phi_{e'} = g_m$). Now M recursively finds a program e such that $\phi_e(x) = \langle i, \phi_{e'}(x) \rangle$ for all $x \in \omega$. Output e as the final result.

(2). Suppose by way of contradiction that S is (G, J)-learnable by M with some $J = \langle J_1, ..., J_n \rangle$, some $k \in V$ such that $J_k \subset P_k$. Let $|P_k'| = m$, $|J_k| = t$ with $J_k = \{b_1, ..., b_t\} \subset P_k$ $(b_i < b_j$ for $i < j)$, and $h_k : P_k' \rightarrow \{1, ..., m\}$. Let b_i' denote $h_k(b_i)$ and let $J^* = h(J_k)$. Then $J^* = \{b_1', ..., b_t'\} \subset \{1, ..., m\}$

From (G, J)-learnability we know that for all $\langle f_1, ..., f_n \rangle \in S$, for all e_j' being program indices for f_j $(1 \leq j \leq n)$,

$$M(G, \langle e_{b_1}', ..., e_{b_t}' \rangle; f_m) \downarrow = e' \qquad (2)$$

where $\phi_{e'} = f_m$. We will show that M can be modified to some M' which can infer $g_{h_k(k)} = g_m$ from the indices of $g_{h_k(j)}$ for $j \in J_k$ (i.e., indices of g_j where $j \in J^*$), and the graph of g_k. This contradicts the nonredundancy of S_m. Note the machine M' can have the graph G and the node label k (so that it can compute h_k) as its built-in data.

M' works as follows: from the given preamble $\langle e_{b_1'}, ..., e_{b_t'} \rangle$ $(e_j$ is a program for g_j for $1 \leq j < m$, $\langle g_1, ..., g_m \rangle \in S_m)$, it computes indices e_{b_j}', $1 \leq j \leq t$ such that e_{b_j}' is a program for the function $f_j(x) = \lambda x[\langle m, g_j(x) \rangle]$. Take G, $\langle e_{b_1}', ..., e_{b_t}' \rangle$, and the graph of $f_m(x) = \langle m, g_m(x) \rangle$ as inputs to the machine M. It will produce some e' such that $\phi_{e'} = f_m$ (Equation (2)). Using e' to compute a program index e so that $(\forall x)(\phi_{e'}(x) = \langle m, \phi_e(x) \rangle)$. Output e as the final result. Clearly this e satisfies $\phi_e = g_m$. $\square$

Theorem 4 *For any concise graph G, there exists a G-strictly nonredundant set.*

Proof: Given any concise graph G with $|V| = n \geq 1$ (from the definition of concise graph we know $G \neq \emptyset$ and thus $|V| \geq 1$). From Theorem 2, there are sets S_i $(1 \leq i \leq n)$ which are nonredundant i-tuples of recursive functions. Applying the above Lemma we obtain a set S which is G-strictly nonredundant. $\square$

4 Conclusions

We have shown that, in some sense, machines can be taught how to learn how to learn. Given a concise graph G representing the learning order, we have shown that there are sets which cannot be inferred without learning all the preambles. In other words, there are sets that must be learned in the order given by G.

Some problems are still open. If G_1 is a subgraph of G_2, how much effort do we need to learn G_2 from G_1? What is the relationship between the strictly nonredundant sets of G_1 and G_2? Can we extend the definitions further to cover cyclic digraphs? The latest question will become trivial if there is no 'head' (e.g., a circle) in the graph, but can we say more about that?

Parallel learning is an interesting topic to inductive inferences. It has been shown that parallel learning is strictly more powerful than sequence learning [1]. Can this result be generalized to training digraphs?

References

[1] D. Angluin, W.I. Gasarch, C.H. Smith, *Training Sequences*, Theoretical Computer Science **66** (1989) pp. 255-272.

[2] D. Angluin, C.H. Smith, *Inductive inference: theory and methods*, Computing Survey **15** (1983) pp.237-269.

[3] J. Case and C. Smith, *Comparison of identification criteria for machine inductive inference*, Theoretical Computer Science **25** (1983) pp. 193-220.

[4] N.J. Cutland, *Computability: An introduction to recursive function theory*, Cambridge University Press (1980).

[5] R.P. Daley and C.H. Smith, *On the complexity of inductive inference*, Information and Control **69** (1986) pp. 12-40.

[6] M.D. Davis, E.J. Weyuker, *Computability, Complexity, and Languages*, Academic Press (1983).

[7] E.M. Gold, *Language identification in the limit*, Information and Control **10** (1967) pp. 447-474.

[8] D.B. Lenat, E.A. Feigenbaum *On the thresholds of knowledge*, Artificial Intelligence **47** (1991) pp.185-250.

[9] C.H. Papadimitriou, K. Steiglitz *Combinatorial Optimization: Algorithms and Complexity*, Prentice Hall (1982).

[10] H. Rogers, Jr., *Theory of Recursive Functions and Effective Computability*, The MIT Press (1988).

[11] Robert I. Soare, *Recursively Enumerable Sets and Degrees*, Springer-Verlag (1980).

Towards Realistic Theories of Learning

Naoki Abe*

Theory NEC Laboratory, RWCP†

c/o C&C Research Laboratories, NEC Corporation

4-1-1 Miyazaki, Miyamae-ku

Kawasaki 216, Japan

Abstract

In computational learning theory continuous efforts are made to formulate models of machine learning that are more realistic than previously available models. Two of the most popular models that have been recently proposed, Valiant's PAC learning model and Angluin's query learning model, can be thought of as refinements of preceding models such as Gold's classic pradigm of identification in the limit, in which the question of *how fast* the learning can take place is emphasized. A considerable amount of results have been obtained within these two frameworks, resolving the learnability questions of many important classes of functions and languages. These two particular learning models are by no means comprehensive, and many important aspects of learning are not directly addressed in these models. Aiming towards more *realistic* theories of learning, many new models and extensions of existing learning models that attempt to formalize such aspects have been developed recently. In this paper, we will review some of these new extensions and models in computational learning theory, concentrating in particular on those proposed and studied by researchers at Theory NEC Laboratory RWCP, and their colleagues at other institutions.

1 Introduction

Research in computational learning theory consists of two phases: (i) formal modeling of a real world learning scenario as a 'learning model' and (ii) mathematical characterization of learnability (or more generally learning complexity) of various target classes in the formalized model. In their comprehensive textbook on learning theory [OSW86], Osherson, Stob and Weinstein define a learning model to be a formal specification of the following five elements: (i) (restrictions on) the learner, (ii) the target objects to be learned, (iii) the environment via which the information concerning the target object is presented to the learner, (iv) (restrictions on) the hypotheses that are used by the learner,

---

*The author's e-mail address is abe@sbl.cl.nec.co.jp.

†Real World Computing Partnership

and (v) a criterion of success. More recently, Sloan [Slo89] has added the following two items to this list: (vi) how can they be learned ? (vii) how fast can they be learned ? It can be argued that these last two items can be taken care of by the items (i) and (v) – by restricting the learner to be *fast* learners or learning algorithms with a certain property. Although this is true, the fact still remains that recently proposed learning models tend to emphasize these last two questions much more than their predecessors.

This is but an instance of continuing efforts by researchers in this field to formulate models of machine learning in a more realistic way than in previously available models. Two of the most popular models that have been recently proposed, Valiant's PAC learning model and Angluin's query learning model, can be thought of as refinements of preceding models such as Gold's classic pradigm of identification in the limit, in which the question of *how* and *how fast* the learning can take place is emphasized. Considerable progress has been made towards resolving the learnability questions of important classes of functions and languages within these frameworks. Learning is such a diverse phenomenon, however, that these two particular learning models are by no means comprehensive, and many important aspects of learning are not directly addressed in them. New models and extensions of existing learning models are called for, that formalize these other aspects. In formulating a learning model, the above list of five elements of a learning model provide a useful guideline. We must also ask, however, what conditions they must satisfy for the resulting model to be a *realistic* learning model ? The two additional items due to Sloan are perhaps a first step towards answering this question.

In our effort towards realistic learning models, we will first examine the conditions that must be satisfied by a learner situated in a realistic environment. First of all, no learning agent can escape the requirements for existing in the physical world, i.e. it is subject to all the real world constraints of *space, time* and *uncertainty*. Although all learners exist in the same real world, each learner holds a unique relationship to the world, namely it interacts with the world to obtain information via a certain *protocol*. (This is essentially the same as the *environment* in the list of five elements of a learning model.) Finally, though existing in a physical world, a learner must also be an agent having a certain *purpose*. Thus, these five aspects can be considered to constitute the dimensions of realistic learning models: 1. Space, 2, Time, 3. Uncertainty, 4. Protocol and 5. Purpose. We repeat that the first three are dimensions of the real world in which the learner is situated, the fourth determines the relationship between the learner and the real world, and the fifth distinguishes the learner as an agent in the real world.

Each of these five dimensions can manifest itself in several ways in a learning model, as listed in Table 1. We note that the (a) columns represent aspects that are already present in (generalized versions of) Valiant's PAC learning model.

The most obvious spacial constraint on a learner is via the *space complexity* of a learning algorithm (1(a)). Another way in which space restriction comes into play is via a retriction on the number of learners in a model of *parallel*

1. Space	(a) Space Complexity	(b) Parallel Learning
2. Time	(a) Time Complexity	(b) Incremental Learning
3. Uncertainty	(a) Performance Evaluation	(b) Probabilistic Targets
4. Protocol	(a) Labeled Examples	(b) Function Value Query
5. Purpose	(a) Minimize Loss	(b) Maximize Function Value

Figure 1: Dimensions of Realistic Learning Models

learning in which a multiple number of learners are learning in parallel, each based on a sample independently drawn (1(b)). The former issue was considered by Vitter and Lin [VL92] in their model of learning in parallel. The issue addressed in this model was the parallel complexity of learning algorithms, and in this sense it is an application of ordinary complexity theory. The latter issue, on the other hand, attempts to capture a situation that is unique to learning. Such a model of parallel learning was originally proposed and studied by Kearns and Seung [KS93], and has been extended to the distribution-free scenario by Nakamura, Abe and Takeuchi [NAT94]. We will discuss this latter model called the 'population learning model' briefly in Section 6.

Time complexity of a learning algorithm is an important requirement of a realistic learner, which most of the recent learning models deal with directly (2(a)). Another way time comes into play is the fact that learning in a realistic environment is *incremental* in nature, that is examples are received one by one, and learning takes place after receiving each example (2(b)). The goal of a learner in this situation is not necessarily to achieve the highest possible accuracy at the end of a learning session, but instead (usually) to maximize the cumulative benefits obtained throuout the learning session.

Uncertainty present in the generation of learning examples is modeled in the PAC learning model by a fixed but unknown distribution over the domain, and the *performance* of a learning algorithm is evaluated probabilistically, with respect to such a distribution (3(a)). The target functions themselves, however, are assumed to be 'deterministic' in the original PAC learning model, although there are some extensions of this model that consider samples affected by noise. A more general treatment of this issue is obtained by assuming that the target functions themselves are *probabilistic*, not deterministic (3(b)). These are the probabilistic extensions of the PAC learning model, proposed independently by Kearns and Schapire [KS94], Yamanishi [Yam92], Laird [Lai88] and Abe and Warmuth [AW92]. We will discuss these models and some of the results within them in Section 2. We will also review an application of probabilistic PAC learning to a concrete problem in genetic information processing due to Abe and Mamitsuka [AM94] in Section 3. We believe that it demonstrates the effectiveness of this approach to handling noise present in realistic learning scenarios.

The two most popular learning models mentioned earlier, the PAC-learning model and the query learning model, provide two of the most typical *protocols* for learning: via labeled examples obtained passively, or via labeled examples obtained by querying the membership of the points of the learner's choice in the target concept. There are realistic situations in which a learner can get more information than just the labels of the chosen points. Depending on the nature of this information, this situation can be modeled as querying the values of a certain function associated with the target concept (4(a)). In an extension of Angluin's model of learning boolean functions (formulas in DNF in particular), the learner is provided the number of satisfied terms as a response to its query, rather than the value of the target function, which is their logical sum. In Section 5, we will discuss this model considered by Nakamura and Abe [NA94] and results they obtained, which indicate the differnece in powers of various information sources.

In most learning models, the goal of a learner is to identify, approxiamtely or exactly, the target concept about which it receives information from the environment. For example, in the PAC learning model, the learner's goal is to find a hypothesis which is as good an approximation of the target concept as possible. Here the accuracy of a hypothesis is measued in terms of its expected error probability, and this can be generalized as the average loss, as formulated by Haussler [Hau92]. Here a *loss function* is a function of the form $L : Y \times Y \rightarrow \mathbf{R}$, where Y is the range of the target function. The PAC learning model can be obtained in this generalized formulation by setting the loss function to be $L(y_1, y_2) = |y_1 - y_2|$, where y_1 is the predicted label and y_2 is the actual label. In some cases, however, the purpose of the learner can be modeled more directly as maximizing the output of the target function itself. In a new model called 'the on-line learning model of rational choice,' Abe and Takeuchi [AT93] formulate the goal of a learner to be the maximization of the total sum of the outputs of the target (probabilistic) function, throuout a learning session. This model is an *incremental* learning model, in which the purpose of the learner is modeled by letting the target function values represent its profits. We will discuss this model in Section 4.

2 Probabilistic PAC Learning Models

We will first review the definition of the PAC learning model in its original form. In this model, a learning algorithm is presented an infinite stream of *labeled* examples for some concept (a 0,1-function mapping examples of the domain into 0 or 1 depending on whether it is a positive or a negative example) randomly drawn from an unknown but fixed distribution over the domain. the algorithm is to output a hypothesis, a concept representation, after each initial segment of the example stream, or *sample*. We say that a class of concept representations R is *PAC-learnable in terms of* another representation class H with sample complexity $f(\frac{1}{\epsilon}, \frac{1}{\delta}, n, s)$, if there is a learning algorithm which, for any underlying distribution, any degrees of accuracy and confidence $\epsilon, \delta > 0$ and any target concept representable by some r in R, whenever it is given an input sample of size exceeding $f(\frac{1}{\epsilon}, \frac{1}{\delta}, n(r), size(r))$, where $n(r)$ denotes (an upper bound on) the length of the examples in the concept represented by r and $size(r)$ the length of r as representation, outputs a representation in H which is ϵ-accurate, with probability at least $1 - \delta$. Here a hypothesis is said to be ϵ-accurate if the probability that it would wrongly predict the *next* example drawn from the same distribution is at most ϵ. A class R is *polynomially PAC-learnable* in terms of H if there exists a polynomial time learning algorithm which PAC-learns R in terms of H with a polynomial sample complexity.

Since Valiant's proposal of the PAC learning model, a number of variations on this model have been proposed to deal with the issue of noise. In a typical real world pattern classification task, a distribution is associated with each class and as in general the distributions for different classes overlap with one another, the resulting classification function is not deterministic. It is therefore more natural to consider that the target object to be learned is a distribution (when learning an individual class) or a conditional distribution (when learning a classification function). This view, which had been commonly accepted in the pattern recognition literature, was formalized and incorporated into the framework of PAC learning model in Kearns and Schapire's model of probabilistic concept learning [KS94], Yamanishi's model of stochastic rule learning [Yam92], and Laird's [Lai88] as well as Abe and Warmuth's models of distribution learning [AW92]. Here, *stochastic rules* over domain X and range Y are conditional probabilities over Y given elements of X. That is, a stochastic rule p defines a probability distribution $p(\cdot|x)$ over Y for each $x \in X$, and a conditional probability $p(y|x)$ for each $x \in X$ and $y \in Y$. *Probabilistic concepts* (p-concepts) are stochastic rules with $Y = \{0, 1\}$, over a discrete domain $X_n = \Sigma^n$ or $X_n = \Sigma^{\leq n} = \cup_{0 \leq i \leq n} \Sigma^i$ for some n. *Distributions* are also assumed to be over a discrete domain X, in particular, $X = \Sigma^n$ for some alphabet Σ.

In a probabilistic PAC learning model, we assume that there is an unknown (conditional) probability distribution over some domain (and a range), and the goal of a learning algorithm is to approximate this distribution with a member of some prescribed hypothesis class, based on a finite sample which is independently and randomly generated according to that distribution. The hypotheses used by the learning algorithm are some efficiently computable representations for distributions, such as probabilistic automata[1] (c.f. [Paz71, AW92]) for non-conditional distributions, and probabilistic decision lists (c.f. [Yam92, KS94]) for conditional distributions. The size of a representation is usually the length of its binary encoding. In general, we let R_s denote the subclass of a representation class R with size at most s.

We now review the notion of *polynomial PAC-learnability* for non-conditional distributions. We say that a class R of representations of probability distributions is PAC (Probably Approximately Correctly) learnable, if there exists a polynomial time learning algorithm which takes as input a finite sample generated from an arbitrary distribution representable by a member r of R over domain Σ^n and an upper bound s on the size of the target distribution (i.e. $r \in R_s$)

---

[1] There are at least two different formulations of 'probabilistic automata' known in the literature: Probabilistic automata as 'acceptors' and as 'generators.' (In a probabilistic automaton as generator, the transition probabilities sum to one for *each state*, whereas in a probabilistic automaton as acceptor, they sum to one for *each state-letter pair*.) The probabilistic automata considered here are generators, and they are closely related to hidden Markov models (c.f. [LRS83]) used extensively as models of speech generation for the purpose of speech recognition.

such that whenever the sample size m exceeds $poly(1/\epsilon, 1/\delta, n, s)$, its output is only ϵ away (with respect to some notion of distance between distributions) from the target distribution with probability at least $1 - \delta$, where $poly$ is some fixed polynomial. As the 'distance' measure between distributions, we could use any of the distance measures known in the literature, but probably the most natural choice is the Kullback-Leibler divergence (or KL-divergence for short). The KL-divergence of distribution q from p is defined as $d(p, q) = E_p(\log \frac{p}{q})$, where $E_p(f)$ denotes, in general, the expectation of random variable f according to distribution p. Note that KL-divergence is asymmetric and therefore is not a metric. Normally, the first argument (p in $d(p, q)$) is thought to be the true distribution, and the second a hypothesis. The number of examples required by the algorithm, expressed as a function of $1/\epsilon, 1/\delta, n, s$, is called the *sample complexity* of the algorithm, and the amount of computation required by the algorithm, the *computational complexity* of the algorithm. By 'the sample complexity of a representation class,' we mean the sample complexity of the best learning strategy for that class, disregarding the computational complexity of the strategy.

In an alternative formulation called the *robust* PAC-learning model, the target distribution need not be representable by a member of R. In this case, the learning algorithm is given an upper bound s on the size of a hypothesis it can use, and it is to output a *near optimal* (within ϵ) hypothesis from R_s with high probability. This is in fact the way the notion of learnability for non-conditional distributions was originally defined by Abe and Warmuth [AW92].

As soon as we adopt the view that the target object to be learned is a probabilistic information source, then the learning problem becomes essentially one of statistical estimation. We can then take advantage of known strategies for statistical estimation, such as the maximum likelihood estimator. Note that KL-divergence, which we are trying to minimize, can be written as $d(p, q) = E_p(-\log q(x)) - E_p(-\log p(x))$. In other words, $d(p, q)$ is the difference between the 'average log-loss'[2] of the hypothesis $E_p(-\log q(x))$, and that of the target distribution $E_p(-\log p(x))$. Thus, the average log-loss $E_p(-\log q(x))$ measures the 'badness' of a hypothesis q with respect to KL-divergence. A natural learning strategy, therefore, is one that outputs a hypothesis q minimizing the *empirical log loss*[3] observed in the sample S, that is, $\sum_{w \in S} -\log q(w)$. A simple algebraic manipulation shows that this strategy is in fact nothing but the well-known *maximum likelihood estimator* (MLE), namely the strategy that outputs a hypothesis which maximizes the probability of generating the input sample, $\prod_{w \in S} q(w)$.

In the probabilistic PAC learning model for probability distributions using probabilistic automata as hypotheses, Abe and Warmuth [AW92] obtained the

---

[2] In coding theoretic terms, the quantity $E_p(-\log q(x))$ is also known as the average code length according to the ideal coding scheme for distribution q. $d(p, q)$ is therefore the difference between the average code length according to the ideal coding scheme for distribution q, and that for the true distribution p.

[3] This is an instance of the general learning strategy that minimizes the 'empirical loss,' which is treated in detail in Haussler's decision theoretic generalization of the PAC learning model [Hau92].

following characterization of learnability: A (hypothesis) class of probabilistic automata (with an explicit upper bound on the number of states) is *robustly* polynomially PAC learnable if and only if the 'maximum likelihood model' (MLM) problem[4] for the same class is polynomially approximable. A more precise statement of this result is found in the following theorem.

Theorem 1 (Abe and Warmuth) *For an arbitrary class C of probabilistic automata, the following statements are equivalent. Below, we let s denote the maximum size of any probabilistic automaton in the hypothesis class, m the sample size, and n the length of each example.*

1. *There exists a polynomial robust PAC-learning algorithm for C.*

2. *The maximum likilihood model problem for C is approximable within a factor $1 + \epsilon$ in random time polynomial in $\frac{1}{\epsilon}, s, n$ and m.*

The above result was shown essentially as a corollary of the following sample complexity upper bound.

Theorem 2 (Abe and Warmuth) *An arbitrary class of probabilistic automata C is robustly PAC-learnable with sample complexity $O((\frac{n}{\epsilon})^2 sa \cdot \log^3 \frac{nsa}{\epsilon} \cdot \log \frac{1}{\delta} \cdot \log^2 \log \frac{1}{\delta})$, where s denotes the number of states allowed in the hypothesis, n the length of each example, and a the alphabet size.*

The technique used in obtaining this result is based on bounds on the rate of *uniform convergence* of the empirical estimates to the true means for the set of log-loss functions associated with the hypothesis class. Various dimension-based approaches for deriving bounds on the sample complexity of uniform convergence using such notions as the combinatorial dimension were developed by Pollard [Pol84] and Haussler [Hau92], and applied by Kearns and Schapire [KS94] to obtain sample complexity bounds for learning probabilistic concepts. The dimension-based method, however, is not applicable here because the combinatorial dimension of the class of log loss functions associated with probabilistic automata of a fixed number of states is infinite.[5] Abe and Warmuth managed to derive a polynomial upper bound for this class, nonetheless, using a direct approximation method in place of the dimension-based approach. There is another factor which prohibits the application of Kearns and Schapire's method: Their result is for bounded loss functions (the quadratic loss having bounded range $[0, 1]$), whereas the class of log loss functions is *unbounded*. Abe and Warmuth

---

[4]The maximum likelihood model problem for a class of representations for probability distributions is the problem of finding a member of that class which maximises the probability of having generated the input sample.

[5]Note that in the original PAC learning model, the VC-dimension of the target concept class gives both upper and lower bounds on the sample complexity of learning that class, and thus almost completely characterise the sample complexity of learning. The combinatorial dimension of loss functions associated with a given hypothesis class, on the other hand, *does not yield a lower bound* on the sample complexity of learning that class, thus making it possible to establish a polynomial lower bound even when the combinatorial dimension is infinite.

resolved this problem by using as hypothesis classes the subclass of probabilistic automata whose probability parameters are bounded away from zero by $\Omega(\frac{1}{m})$.

Abe and Warmuth [AW92] also showed that the maximum likelihood model problem for the hypothesis class of *two state* probabilistic automata is not even weakly approximable in polynomial time (unless **RP = NP**) even when the input sample is restricted to consist of a single string, as stated in the following theorem.

Theorem 3 (Abe and Warmuth) *For any $\alpha > 0$, the single string MLM problem for the class of 2-state probabilistic automata is not approximable within $2^{|w|^{1-\alpha}}$ in time polynomial in the alphabet size a and $|w|$, where w is the input string, unless* **RP = NP**.

It follows from this theorem that the same class is not *robustly* PAC learnable in polynomial time under the same assumption (unless **RP = NP**). It is perhaps surprising, and certainly dissappointing, that the class of probabilistic automata cannot be robustly learned in polynomial time even for a constant number of states.

3   Application of Probabilistic PAC Learning

Through the development of the probabilistic PAC learning models and results obtained within them such as those reviewed in Section 2, two things have become clear: (i) The canonical learning strategies adopted from theories of statistical estimation, such as the maximum likelihood estimator, are desirable from the point of view of sample complexity. (ii) The computational complexity of realizing such strategies is often intractable, even for a reasonably restricted hypothesis class. These facts suggest that in practical applications, a sensible strategy is to employ these criteria as guidelines of what measure should be maximized (minimized) among the given hypothesis class, and then use some form of an optimization algorithm for the actual maximization (minimization), even though there is no theoretical guarantee that it finds the global optimum. Such an approach has been used by a number of authors in various application domains. One domain in which such a statistical approach appears to be especially effective is the field of genetic information processing, due in part to the fact that the genome data available via public databases is neither noise-free, nor complete. For example, a GA-type optimization algorithm using MDL as the criterion of fitness was used by Yamanishi and Konagaya to perform motif extraction and proved effective [YK91].

The probabilistic automata, for which the computational intractability of the approximate maximum likelihood model problem was shown (as reviewed in Section 2), is in fact a very important representation class that is used often in practical applications. They are very closely related to the Hidden Markov Models (HMM), which are used as models of speech generation for the purpose of speech recognition. In practice, a local optimization algorithm for the maximum likelihood parameter settings of HMM called 'the Baum-Welch algorithm' is used extensively in speech recognition applications, and is reported to work quite well. Abe and Mamitsuka [AM94] have recently extended this algorithm for a certain class of stochastic tree grammars (which properly extends Hidden Markov models), called the stochastic Ranked Node Rewriting Grammars, or stochastic RNRG for shor, and have applied it to a problem of extreme importance in genetic information processing – the protein secondary structure prediction problem.

Protein secondary structures are relatively small and regular groups of protein structures exhibiting certain notable characteristics, which function as intermediate building blocks for the overall protein structure, and can be classified into three types: α-helix, β-sheet, and others. The problem of determining which regions in a given amino acid sequence correspond to each of the three categories is the classical secondary structure prediction problem and it has been attempted by many researchers using various techniques [RS93].

Among the three types of secondary structures, they concentrate on the problem of predicting the β-sheet regions in a given amino acid sequence. Their method receives as input amino acid sequences known to contain β-sheet regions, and train the probability parameters of a stochastic RNRG so that the likelihood (generation probability) assigned on the input sample is maximized. Some of the rules in the grammar are intended *apriori* for generating β-sheet regions and others for non-β-sheets. After training, the method is given a sequence of amino acids with *unknown* secondary structure, and predicts according to which regions are generated by the β-sheet rules, in the *most likely* parse for the input sequence.

The problem of predicting β-sheet regions has been considered more difficult as compared to that of α-helix regions, because of the property of β-sheets that their structures typically range over several discontinuous sections in an amino acid sequence, whereas the structures of α-helix are continuous and more regular. It is precisely because of this that Abe and Mamitsuka employed the aforementioned stochastic Ranked Node Rewriting Grammars (SRNRGs), whose expressive powers exceed not only that of Hidden Markov Models (HMMs), but also stochastic context free grammars (SCFGs).[6] Context free grammars are not powerful enough to capture the kind of long-distance dependencies exhibited by the amino acid sequences of β-sheet regions, which contain the 'anti-parallel' dependency (of the type 'abccba'), and 'parallel' dependency (of the type 'abcabc') and various combinations of them. SRNRG is one of the rare families of grammatical systems that have both enough expressive power to cope with all of these dependencies and at the same time enjoy efficient parsability and learnability.

The Ranked Node Rewriting Grammar, or RNRG for short, is a system that generates trees by rewriting a node in a tree structure by an incomplete tree structure.[7] The sequences of terminal symbols at the leaves of the trees

---

[6] HMMs and SCFGs have recently been used in genetic information processing, see for example [BHK+93, SBU+94].

[7] The Ranked Node Rewriting Grammars were briefly introduced in the context of computationally efficient learnability of grammars by Abe [Abe88]. The discovery of RNRG was inspired by the pioneering work of Joshi et al. (see for example [VSJ85]) on a tree grammatical system for natural language called 'Tree Adjoining Grammars' (or TAG for short). RNRG generalises TAG into a hierarchy of families of grammars with increasing expressive powers.

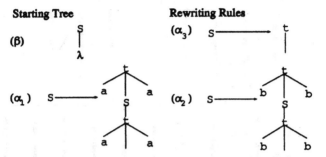

Figure 2: RNRG(1) grammar G_1 generating $\{ww^R ww^R | w \in \{a, b\}\}$

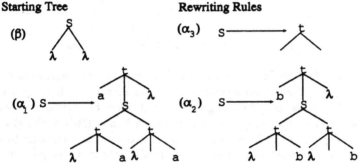

Figure 3: RNRG(2) grammar G_2 generating $\{www | w \in \{a, b\}^*\}$

generated by a grammar form its string language. When a node is rewritten by an incomplete tree structure, the incomplete tree structure must have exactly the same number of empty nodes as the 'rank' of that node, i.e. the number of its children (thus the name 'ranked node rewriting'). By placing an upper bound, say k, on the rank of a node that can be rewritten, we obtain a family of grammars, $RNRG(k)$, each of which has varying expressive power and efficiency of processing. The string languages of $RNRG(0)$, denoted $RNRL(0)$, equal the context free languages (CFL), those of $RNRG(1)$ equal the tree adjoining languages (TAL), and for any $k \geq 2$, $RNRL(k)$ properly contains $RNRL(k-1)$.

Let us now see some examples of RNRG grammars. The language $L_1 = \{ww^R ww^R | w \in \{a, b\}^*\}$ is generated by the RNRG(1) grammar G_1 shown[8] in Figure 2. Note that L_1 is a tree adjoining language, but not the '3 copy' language, $L_2 = \{www \mid w \in \{a, b\}^*\}$. This language can be generated by the RNRG(2) grammar G_2 shown in Figure 3.

Given the definition of RNRG, the *stochastic* RNRG is defined analogously to the way stochastic CFG is defined from CFG. That is, associated with each rewriting rule in a stochastic RNRG is its *rule application probability*, which is constrained so that for each non-terminal, the sum total of rule application

---
[8]Note that 'λ' indicates the empty string, and an edge leading to no letter leads to an empty node.

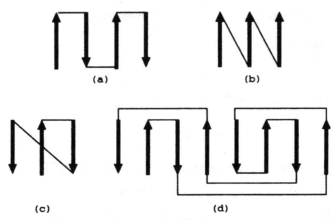

Figure 4: Some typical β-sheet structures

probabilities of all the rewriting rules for that non-terminal equals unity.

Some typical β-sheet structures are given in Figure 4. The arrows indicate the β-sheet strands, and the line going through them the amino acid sequence. The β-sheet structure is retained by hydrogen bonds (H-bonds) between the corresponding amino acids in neighboring strands, so it is reasonable to suspect that there are correlations between the amino acids in those positions. The structure exhibited in Figure 4 (a) is known as the 'anti-parallel' β-sheet, as the dependency follows the pattern *abc..cba..abc...cba*, where the use of a same letter indicates that those positions are connected by H-bonds and believed to be correlated. In contrast, the structure exhibited in Figure 4 (b) is known as the 'parallel' β-sheet, since the dependency here is more of the pattern in *abc..abc...* Both of these types of dependency can be captured by RNRG, in particular by G_1 in Figure 2 and G_2 in Figure 3, respectively.

The learning algorithm used by Abe and Mamitsuka is an extension of the 'Inside-Outside' algorithm for the stochastic context free grammars, and is also related to the extension of the Inside-Outside algorithm recently developed for the stochastic tree adjoining grammars by Schabes [Sch92]. These are all iterative algorithms guarateed to find a local optimal for the maximum likelihood settings of the rule application probabilities. The most serious difficulty with this method is the extensive computation required by the learning algorithm. In order to reduce the computational requirement, they have restricted the form of grammars to a certain subclass of RNRG, and designed a simpler and faster learning algorithm for the subclass. This subclass is obtained by placing the restriction that the right hand side of any rewriting rule contains exactly one occurrence of a non-terminal, except for lexical non-terminals. This significantly simplifies the learning algorithm as the computation of each entry in the parsing table becomes much simpler.

They performed some preliminary experiments using this method using data obtained from HSSP (Homology-derived Secondary Structures of Proteins Ver

1.0 [SS91]). The results obtained indicate that this method is able to capture and generalize the type of long-distance dependencies that characterize β-sheets, and actually predict the location of β-sheets in a new sequence. In their experiments, Abe and Mamitsuka trained a stochastic RNRG with training data consisting effectively of *bracketed* sequences (i.e. the location of the β-sheets are marked) for a particular type of protein called 'Trypsinogen inhibitor' (1tgsi), and the acquired grammar was able to predict *exactly* the location of β-sheet regions in an amino acid sequence of another protein called 'Serine protease inhibitor' (3sgbi). Their method was also able to predict the *structure* of the β-sheet correctly, namely the locations of the hydrogen bonds. It is to be emphasized that, since the sequences for the two proteins are less than 25 per cent homologous, the prediction of the β-sheet regions of one given the other is not possible by alignment alone.

The success of these methods, including Abe and Mamitsuka's method for predicting β-sheet regions among others, seems to demonstrate the effectiveness of the general probabistic PAC learning approach in which noise and uncertainty are formalized in terms of 'probabilistic information sources.'

4 On-line Learning Model of Rational Choice

In most learning models, the goal of a learner is to identify, either exactly or approximately, the target function, making use of information it obtains via the environment about that function. In realistic situations, a pragmatist would argue, the purpose of a learning agent is not in the identification of a function itself but in the utility of that knowledge. As an example, consider the following scenario. A *gourmet* bachelor is trying to eat well at restaurants in a new neighborhood, say Chinatown, he just moved into. Every night he carefully chooses a restaurant by its appearance, and eats his dinner there. He starts noticing that there is a certain correlation between how the restaurant looks and how much satisfaction he gets out of his meal. He also starts to notice about a trade-off: The more he learns about such a regularity, the better he gets at choosing the right restaurant, but in order to learn more about such a regularity, he must take risks. He is a *gourmet*, so of course he tries out a large number of different restaurants, and after a few weeks settles on a few restaurants that are his favourite. A more conservative person might have settled with the first agreeable restaurant and have eaten there from then on night after night, and always got a reasonably good meal. He might later discover, however, that the restaurant next door served a superb hot and sour soup which he would have discovered if only had he tried it once ! Supposing that he is staying in Chinatown indefinitely, what strategy ought he employ, if he is to maximize the total gastronomical pleasure he gets during his stay ?

Abe and Takeuchi [AT93] modeled situations like the above by a learning model which they called 'on-line learning model of rational choice.' In this model, the environment of the learning agent is modeled by a possibly probabilistic function which maps the agent's actions (or possibly the past history of the agent's actions) to the benefits that agents obtain through those actions. The learner's goal is not to learn the environment *per se*, but to choose its actions so as to maximize the benefits obtained by them in a given number of trials, while learning about that environment through those very actions. They then ask, for a given class of (probabilistic) rules which might possibly represent the environment, what strategy maximizes the total benefits it obtains in a given number of trials, for the worst-case enviroment belonging to that class.

Within this general model, Abe and Takeuchi considered the following specific on-line, one-sided model of tennis play, in which the only actions that a player can take are a 'pass' (passing shot) and a 'lob,' and the goal of the player is to win as many points as possible. For simplicity, it is assumed that with each shot the player either wins a point or loses a point. The opponent is modeled by two probabilistic functions which determine the probability that a lob (and a pass, respectively) played by the player will win a point, as a function of the proportion of lobs in the past trials. These probabilistic functions are called *rate probabilistic functions*. In particular, it is assumed that these are linear (probabilistic) functions $f_L(r) = a_1 r + b_1$ and $f_P(r) = a_2 r + b_2$, satisfying $a_1 < 0$, $a_2 > 0$, $0 \leq f_L(r), f_P(r) \leq 1$, and for some $r_m \in [0, 1]$, $f_L(r_m) = f_P(r_m)$, where r denotes the proportion of lobs in the past trials. (See Figure 5.(a)) The form of these functions is assumed to be known to the player, but *not* the specific coefficients. In the default version of the model (called the 'unknown-t model') it is assumed that the player is not told in advance how many trials there will be in total, but they also consider a variant (called the 'known-t model') in which the player knows how many trials he or she is to play in advance. Within this model, it is asked how many trials out of t trials in total the best player can expect to win. Specifically, the performance of a playing strategy is quantified by measuring the expected *regret* of the player where the regret is defined to be how many less trials it expects to win as compared to the *ideal* player, as a function of the total number t of trials, which is unknown to the player *a priori*. Here the ideal player is one that knows the rate probabilistic functions exactly, and uses an optimal playing strategy for those specific functions. The expected regret of a class of lob-pass problems is defined to be the expected regret of the best player for that class.

The particular way of modeling the environment in terms of two linear probabilistic functions was first formulated by Herrnstein in the context of behavioral psychology [Her90]. Simple though it may seem, this model is applicable in a wide range of phenomena in nature, such as animals' choice in feeding, and consumers' choice in economic consumptions.

Within this model, Abe and Takeuchi obtain a variety of results. As it appears to be difficult to obtain good upper bounds for the general case, they give several upper bounds for restrictions and assumptions of varying degrees. The most important restriction is that the rate probabilistic functions have 'matching shoulders,' that is, $f_L(0) = f_P(1)$ or equivalently $b_1 = a_2 + b_2$ holds. (See Figure 5.(b)) A lob-pass problem with the matching shoulders condition (abbreviated the MS condition) satisfies the especially desirable property that the 'matching point' (i.e. r_m at which $f_L(r_m) = f_P(r_m)$) equals the 'optimal stationary rate' (i.e. r^* at which $r^* = \arg\max_{r \in [0,1]} r f_L(r) + (1 - r) f_P(r)$). The MS

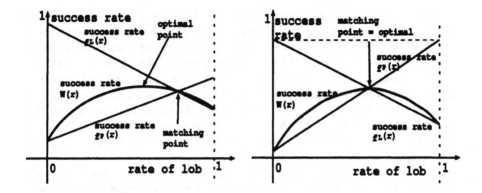

Figure 5: (a) A Lob-Pass problem (b) A Lob-Pass problem with matching shoulders

condition is assumed for *all* cases they consider, while other additional restrictions are optional. These optional conditions are: (i) the sum of (the absolute values of) the slopes is known ($a_2 - a_1 = a$ for some a); (ii) the sum of (the absolute values of) the slopes is bounded below by some constant ($a_2 - a_1 \geq a$); (iii) the optimal rate r^*, at which $w(r)$ is maximized, is bounded away from zero and one ($0 < r_1 \leq r^* \leq r_2 < 1$, abbreviated BO); (iv) $f_L(0)$ is known ($b_1 = b$). Depending on which ones of these additional restrictions are assumed, different upper bounds on the expected regret are obtained, as stated in the theorem below.

Theorem 4 (Abe and Takeuchi) *In the 'unknown-t' model, each of the following holds. Below, LINEAR(⟨conditions⟩) denotes the class of lob-pass problems with linear rate probabilistic functions satisfying ⟨conditions⟩. R(C) in general denotes the expected regret of a class C of lob-pass problems.*

1. $R(LINEAR(a_2 - a_1 = a, b_1 = b, MS)) = O(\log t)$.

2. $R(LINEAR(a_2 - a_1 = a, BO, MS)) = O(\log t)$.

3. $R(LINEAR(a_2 - a_1 = a, MS)) = O(t^{\frac{1}{3}})$.

4. $R(LINEAR(a_2 - a_1 \geq a, BO, MS)) = O(t^{\frac{1}{2}})$.

5. $R(LINEAR(a_2 - a_1 \geq a, MS)) = O(t^{\frac{2}{3}})$.

6. $R(LINEAR(BO, MS)) = O(t^{\frac{2}{3}})$.

7. $R(LINEAR(MS)) = O(t^{\frac{4}{5}})$.

The algorithm exhibited to prove the last four of these bounds is an incremental, hill-climbing type algorithm that optimizes the lob rate, and is designed to overcome the trade-off between winning and learning of the rate probabilistic functions. At any point in its execution, the algorithm can be thought of as being *at* its current rate (of lobs to the total number of trials) and it *travels* to different rates by playing lobs or passes appropriately. At each iteration it tries to estimate the optimal lob rate by moving within an interval around its current rate, which is large enough to get information but is small enough that traveling there does not cause too many losses. We can show, in each case, that the expected position, that is the current lob rate, approaches the optimal rate at an appropriate rate and the expected regret incurred in the process is also appropriately bounded.

Part of the difficulty in obtaining good bounds for the general case is the fact that the total number of trials t is not given to the player in advance. When the total number of trials t is given to the player in advance, better upper bounds with less restrictions can be obtained, also assuming the matching shoulder condition. First, given that the sum of the slopes $a_2 - a_1$ is bounded from below by some constant, an upper bound of order $O(\sqrt{t})$ can be obtained. In the general case with no restriction on the sum of the slopes, an upper bound of order $O(t^{\frac{2}{3}+\epsilon})$ can be obtained for any $\epsilon > 0$. Upper bounds for the case with an unknown t for all other cases clearly hold for this case.

Theorem 5 (Abe and Takeuchi) *In the 'known-t' model, each of the following holds.*

1. *$R(LINEAR(a_2 - a_1 \geq a, MS)) = O(t^{\frac{1}{2}})$.*

2. *For every $\epsilon > 0$, $R(LINEAR(MS)) = O(t^{\frac{2}{3}+\epsilon})$.*

They also establish a lower bound on the expected regret by making use of Rissanen's lower bound on the expected total log-loss of any learning strategy for probabilistic functions [Ris86]. The lower bound they obtain is $\Omega(\log t)$, which matches the first two upper bounds mentioned earlier.

Theorem 6 (Abe and Takeuchi) *In the 'unknown-t' model, any player has an expected regret lower bounded by $\Omega(\log t)$ on $LINEAR(a_2 - a_2 = 1, MS)$.*

Subsequent to the work of Abe and Takeuchi, Prof. Amari of University of Tokyo designed a novel on-line learning strategy for matching-shoulders lob-pass problems using the technique of 'stochastic approximation.' It can be shown, under conditions (ii) and (iii), that the expected regret of his strategy is upper bounded by $O(\log t)$, and hence this strategy is optimal within a constant factor under these conditions. Note that conditions (ii) and (iii) are weaker than the conditions Abe and Takeuchi assumed to obtain an upper bound of the same order. We are currently in the process of preparing a joint journal paper containing these results.

5   Exact Learning via Function Value Queries

The problem of learning boolean functions expressible as formulas in DNF (disjunctive normal form), via passive examples only or via membership queries, is one of the most important problems in computational learning theory, with a wide range of potentail applications. Several negative results have been reported, however, which seem to indicate that learning DNF is hard in both PAC learning model and the query learning model with membership and equivalence queries [AK91]. This raises the question of whether this class becomes learnable if more informative queries are allowed in place of the membership quries. The results obtained by Nakamura and Abe [NA94] on learning linear combinations of monotone terms from function value queries are suggestive of such possibilities.

Consider the following scenario. A young bachelor moves to a new city, say uptown New York. He goes out to a party every night dressed in a certain way and tries to make as many friends as possible. He wants to learn what is 'in' in New York City, so every night he dresses differently and observes how many new friends he manages to make. Suppose for now that each friend he manages make liked something about his clothes, such as the combination of a loud bow tie with pink glasses, and suppose for simplicity that each one has a unique taste. Then, how many friends he makes each night tells him how many of these trendy combinations of properties his clothes satisfied that night. After visiting enough parties, he learns that the secret to success in this city can be summarized in the following formula, $f =$ loud-bow-tie·pink-glasses+black-jacket·black-shoes. And the more terms are satified, the better he does !

The above example is of course unrealistic, but it is suggestive of a realistic possibility – that in some real world scenarios, more information may be available than just the binary value of whether something is good or bad. Depending on the nature of that information, a lot richer classes of functions might become learnable. Recall that a DNF formula is the disjunction of a number of terms, which in turn, are conjunctions of literals. A term is monotone, if none of the literals in it is negated. It may be reasonable to suppose in some situation, that in addition to whether a given assignment satisfies the target DNF formula, the number of terms satisfied by the assignment is available to the learner. This corresponds exactly to the above example of the trendy clothes in New York city. It may be more reasonable to suppose that different combinations of attributes count towards being trendy in varying degrees. For example, the degree of trendiness in New York city might be expressible as the formula, $g = 5$ loud-bow-tie·pink-glasses+ 2 black-jacket·black-shoes, where each term is accompanied by a coefficient that is intended to capture its importance. In this case, the value of the function g might be measured by the amount of 'sympathy' he receives from an average person he meets. It is also possible that some combinations are very untrendy, which might result in a trendy function including negative coefficients like $h = 5$ loud-bow-tie·pink-glasses $+2$ black-jacket·black-shoes -3 loud-bow-tie·black-jacket.

The learning problem illustrated above is exactly the learning problem considered by Nakamura and Abe, i.e. the problem of learning linear combinations of monotone terms via *function value queries*, namely queries that ask for the value of the target function at an assignment of the learner's choice. Within this model, they obtain a number of positive learnability results for this and related classes of functions. If all coefficients are restricted to be nonnegative, then the linear combinations of monotone terms can be learned exactly by an efficient learning algorithm, using a number of function value queries bounded above by $(n - \lfloor \log s \rfloor + 1)s$, where n is the number of variables and s is the number of terms (with nonzero coefficients) in the target function.

Theorem 1 (Nakamura and Abe) *The class of linear combinations of monotone terms with nonnegative coefficients can be learned exactly, using at most $(n - \lfloor \log s \rfloor + 1)s$ function value queries in time $O(ns^2)$, where s is the number of terms with nonzero coefficients in the target function.*

They also obtain a lower bound of order $\Omega(\frac{ns}{\log s})$ on the number of queries needed to learn this class, so their algorithm is optimal within a logarithmic factor. The technique used to obtain the above results can actually be extended to handle the non-monotone case in some restricted sense: A similar algorithm can efficiently learn the *unate* (i.e. each variable can appear either negated or non-negated but not both) linear combinations of terms, with the addition of *equivalence queries*. The learning algorithm makes at most $s + 1$ equivalence queries and $(n + 1)s$ function value queries, and runs in time $O(ns^2)$, where s is the number of terms in the target function.

In the general case, namely for the class of linear combinations of monotone terms with coefficients varying over the reals, the resulting class is expressively complete in the sense that an arbitrary real-valued function over the boolean domain can be represented by a formula in this class. In this case, the same upper and lower bounds on the number of required queries as those known to hold for learning multivariate polynomials over GF(2) hold: It is upper bounded by $O(n^{\lfloor \log k \rfloor + 1})$ and is lower bounded also by $\Omega(n^{\lfloor \log k \rfloor + 1})$.

Theorem 2 (Nakamura and Abe) *Let k-term-$\mathcal{F}$ denote the class of linear combinations with real coefficients with at most k terms.*

1. *There exists an algorithm that exactly learns k-term-$\mathcal{F}$, making $O(n^{\lfloor \log k \rfloor + 1})$ function value queries and running in time $O(kn^{\lfloor \log k \rfloor + 2})$.*

2. *Any exact learning algorithm for k-term-$\mathcal{F}$ must make at least $\Omega(n^{\lfloor \log k \rfloor + 1})$ function value queries, in the worst case.*

These bounds are obtained by generalizing Roth and Benedek's technique for analyzing the learning problem for multivariate polynomials over GF(2). All the results for the 'general case' are actually shown to hold for coefficients belonging to an arbitrary field.

Together with previously known results due to various authors on the complexity of learning monotone DNF and multivariate polynomials over GF(2), these results imply that the summation ('+') is significantly more valuable than the logical OR ('∨') or the exclusive OR ('⊕'), as a source of additional information for identifying a set of monotone terms. For example, for identifying a set of k monotone terms, the required numbers of queries for the three operators progress roughly as $O(n^k)$ for '∨,' $O(n^{\log k})$ for '⊕,' and $O(nk)$ for '+'. Note that the number of queries polynomial in both n and k is only for '+'.

6 Efficient Distribution-free Population Learning

Suppose that a market analyst is stationed in Tokyo, and is expected to find out about the trend in dancing music. Being a successful career woman, she is too busy to visit all the clubs herself, but she has a number of willing men working for her, so she can give them orders to visit various clubs to learn about what constitutes trendy dancing music in Tokyo clubs. She is free to send these agents to different places, but since they are not so smart, she has to give them exact orders as to how to induce the trend from information they collect. So each agent is using the same learning strategy. These agents go off for a week and learn the trend rule, say expressed as a DNF. For example, a good rule of thumb f might be 'f = funky·with·trumpet·rap + mellow·with·sax·female·vocal.' At the end of the week, they each report to her the rule they computed based on the learning strategy they were taught by her, and report it to her. She carefully examines all the reported DNF rules and makes her final DNF for the true trend rule, based on some strategy.

The following questions naturally arise as a test of the effectiveness of her overall strategy. Can she learn more quickly using these agents than doing it all by herself? In other words, can she learn more from say 10 agents each learning from 10 different clubs than if she goes to 10 different clubs herself? Supposing that each agent can visit only one club, can she still learn faster if she can increase the number of agents? What if she has only one agent but the agent can visit as many places as possible? Is there one common strategy that works well in all cases mentioned above ? Suppose next that since she proves to be successful in Tokyo, they send her to Kobe and tell her to do the same. Again she can use agents, but this time, she is more lazy and decides not to make her own DNF based on the agents' DNF. Rather, each time she is consulted on whether a new song will sell well in Kobe, she asks the same question to all of the agents, and makes her decision by majority vote. The natural question is 'will she do as well in Kobe as she did in Tokyo?'

Learning scenarios such as above were first formalized as a model of learning from a population of hypotheses ('population learning') in the pioneering work of Kearns and Seung [KS93]. In their initial investigation, they considered the scenario in which the market analyst knows the nature of the information each agent obtains, namely she knows the distribution of the examples they receive. Extending this model, Nakamura, Abe and Takeuchi [NAT94] considered a variant in which the learner is required to perform well without the knowledge of the underlying distribution, as well as be computationally efficient. They then investigated conditions on learnability of simpler and more specific concept classes under these stronger requirements.

In the population learning model, the learner (called the 'population learner') receives as input hypotheses from a large population of agents and produces as output its final hypothesis. Each agent is assumed to independently obtain labeled sample for the target concept drawn according to some fixed but unknown distribution over the domain, and output a hypothesis. A polynomial time population learner is said to 'PAC learn' a concept class, if its hypothesis is probably approximately correct whenever the population size exceeds a certain (polynomial) bound even if the sample size for each agent is fixed at some constant. In their extended model, it is also required that the agent algorithm itself is a PAC-learning algorithm, and that for some appropriate choices of sample and population sizes, the population learner can be used to speed up the best sequential PAC-learning algorithm for the same class.

Within this model, they obtain a number of learnability results. First they exhibit some general population learning strategies, and establish sufficient conditions on concept classes and agent algorithms for these strategies to be PAC learners. They then exhibit various concept classes to be learnable using each of these strategies, and prove bounds on the sample as well as population sizes required to do so. These strategies include the 'min-max hypothesis finder,' and various voting schemes including the 'majority vote.' When coupled with appropriate agent algorithms, these strategies can be shown to PAC learn a variety of simple concept classes such as the 'high-low game,'[9] conjunctions, axis-parallel rectangles and others, with reasonable population sizes.

A population learner can be said to achieve *ideal parallelization*, if the population size required is the sample complexity of the agent divided by the sample size of each agent. This can be done, for example, when the concept class is such that for every finite subset of the domain, a unique concept containing the set exists and can be found efficiently (by a 'closure algorithm'), and there exists an efficient algorithm to find the minimum hypothesis containing all input hypotheses (a 'minimum super-concept finder'). Such a concept class is learnable from positive examples only, with the closure algorithm as the agent algorithm, and the minimum superset finder as the population learner. For example, the class of conjunctions is learnable by this strategy with population size $\frac{1}{m\epsilon}(\log \frac{1}{\delta} + n \ln 3)$. Note that by setting $m = \sqrt{\frac{1}{\epsilon}(\log \frac{1}{\delta} + n \ln 3)}$, a speed-up in overall computation time (with respect to ϵ and δ) from $\Omega(\frac{1}{\epsilon} \log \frac{1}{\delta})$ in the ordinary PAC-learning model to $O(\sqrt{\frac{1}{\epsilon} \log \frac{1}{\delta}})$ can be achieved, provided that the computation time is linear in the sample size and the population size.

A population learner is a voting scheme if its hypothesis can be expressed as a threshold function of the input hypotheses, including the majority vote, OR-gate and AND-gate. For example, using the OR-gate as the population learner, the class of axis-parallel rectangles of an arbitrary dimension n can be learned with population size of $O((\frac{2n}{m\epsilon})^{2n} \log \frac{1}{\delta})$. By setting $N = m = (\frac{2n}{\epsilon})^{2n/2n+1}(\log \frac{1}{\delta})^{1/2}$, a speed-up from $\Omega(\frac{2n}{\epsilon} \log \frac{1}{\delta})$ in the sequential PAC-learning model to $O((\frac{2n}{\epsilon})^{2n/2n+1} (\log \frac{1}{\delta})^{1/2})$ is achieved.

If the population learner is restricted to be a voting scheme, what results is effectively a model of 'population prediction,' in which the learner is to *predict* the value of the target concept at an arbitrarily drawn point, as a threshold function of the predictions made by its agents on the same point. This model corresponds to the earlier scenario of the market analyst in Kobe. Nakamura,

---

[9]The 'high-low game' is the following concept class considered by Kearns and Seung, $\{[0, b] | b \in [0, 1]\}$.

Abe and Takeuchi show that the population learning model is strictly more powerful than the population prediction model, in the sense that there exists a concept class that can be PAC learned in the former model but not in the latter, as stated below.

Theorem 3 (Nakamura, Abe and Takeuchi) *There exists a concept class $C \subseteq 2^{\{0,1\}^n}$ such that C is population PAC learnable, but C is not population PAC predictable.*

This is proved using the class of parity functions. The population learning of parity functions (more precisely their complements) is possible by a minimum super-concept finder with the agents employing the closure algorithm. For the non-predictability of the parity functions in the population prediction model, they first establish that any class that is population predictable by any voting scheme, can be predicted by majority vote. They then show that there is no agent algorithm, in combination with majority vote, that can predict this class, by making use of a super constant lower bound on the sample complexity for weak learning of the same class, due to Goldman, Kearns and Schapire [GKS90].

They also consider a variant of this model in which the samples are affected by classification noise of a (known) constant rate η. In this setting, they exhibit an efficient population learning system for conjunctions requiring population size $2(2n)^2((1 - e^{-\frac{1}{2n}m})\epsilon^2(1 - 2\eta)^2)^{-1}\ln\frac{1}{\delta}$. Note that this gives a polynomial upper bound even when the sample size m is constant, although it does not provide any speed-up.

7 Conclusions

We have reviewed some new models and extensions in computational learning theory which have recently been proposed to reflect aspects of real world learning scenarios which have not been satisfactorily treated in existing learning models. The models discussed in this paper represents just a small fraction of the models already existing in the literature, let alone those potentially interesting models that are yet to be studied. Some combinations of the aspects of a learning model discussed here may result in an interesting learning model. A natural example is the combibation of the model of 'learning via function value query' with the 'on-line learning model of rational choice,' which gives a model in which the goal of the learner is the on-line maximization of the cumulative outputs of the target linear combination of monotone terms via function value queries. There are numerous other possible combinations, some of which may be more interesting than others. Finally, it should be noted that too much emphasis should not be placed on the proposal of new models. Resolving important open problems within already existing learning models, as well as the investigation of relatinships between these competing learning models, are certainly components of research in computational learning theory of prime importance.

References

[Abe88]   N. Abe. Feasible learnability of formal grammars and the theory of natural language acquisition. In *Proceedings of COLING-88*, August 1988.

[AK91]   D. Angluin and M. Kharitonov. When won't membership queries help? In *Proc. of the 23rd Symposium on Theory of Computing*, pages 444–454. ACM Press, New York, NY, 1991.

[AM94]   N. Abe and H. Mamitsuka. A new method for predicting protein secondary structures based on stochastic tree grammars. In *Proceedings of the Eleventh International Conference on Machine Learning*, 1994.

[AT93]   N. Abe and J. Takeuchi. The 'lob-pass' problem and an on-line learning model of rational choice. In *Proceedings of the Sixth Annual ACM Workshop on Computational Learning Theory*. Morgan Kaufmann, San Mateo, California, August 1993.

[AW92]   N. Abe and M. K. Warmuth. On the computational complexity of approximating probability distributions by probabilistic automata. *Machine Learning*, 9(2/3), 1992. A special issue for COLT'90.

[BHK+93]   M. Brown, R. Hughey, A. Krogh, I. S. Mian, K. Sjolander, and D. Haussler. Using dirichlet mixture priors to derive hidden markov models for protein families. In *Proceedings of the First International Conference on Intelligent Systems for Molecular Biology*, pages 47–55, 1993.

[GKS90]   S. Goldman, M. Kearns, and R. Schapire. On the sample complexity of weak learning. In *Proceedings of the 1990 Workshop on Computational Learning Theory*. Morgan Kaufmann, San Mateo, California, August 1990.

[Hau92]   D. Haussler. Decision theoretic generalizations of the PAC model for neural net and other learning applications. *Information and Computation*, 100(1), September 1992.

[Her90]   R. Herrnstein. Rational choice theory. *American Psychologist*, 45(3):356–367, 1990.

[KS93]   M. Kearns and S. Seung. Learning from a population of hypotheses. In *Proceedings of the Sixth Annual ACM Workshop on Computational Learning Theory*. Morgan Kaufmann, San Mateo, California, August 1993.

[KS94]   M. Kearns and R. Schapire. Efficient distribution-free learning of probabilistic concepts. *Journal of Computer and System Sciences*, 48(3), June 1994. A special issue on 31st IEEE Conference on Foundations of Computer Science.

[Lai88]   P. D. Laird. Efficient unsupervised learning. In *Proceedings of the 1988 Workshop on Computational Learning Theory*. Morgan Kaufmann, San Mateo, California, August 1988.

[LRS83]   S. E. Levinson, L. R. Rabiner, and M. M. Sondhi. An introduction to the application of the theory of probabilistic functions of a markov process to automatic speech recognition. *The Bell System Technical Journal*, 62(4), April 1983.

[NA94]   A. Nakamura and N. Abe. Exact learning of linear combinations of monotone terms from function value queries. In *Proceedings of the Fourth International Workshop on Algorithmic Learning Theory*. Springer-Verlag, October 1994.

[NAT94]   A. Nakamura, N. Abe, and J. Takeuchi. Efficient distribution-free population learning of simple concepts. In *Proceedings of the Fifth International Workshop on Algorithmic Learning Theory*. Springer-Verlag, October 1994.

[OSW86]   D. Osherson, M. Stob, and S. Weinstein. *Systems that Learn: An Introduction for Cognitive and Computer Scientists*. MIT Press, 1986.

[Paz71]   A. Paz. *Introduction to Probabilistic Automata*. Academic Press, 1971.

[Pol84]   D. Pollard. *Convergence of Stochastic Processes*. Springer-Verlag, 1984.

[Ris86]   J. Rissanen. Stochastic complexity and modeling. *The Annals of Statistics*, 14(3):1080 – 1100, 1986.

[RS93]   B. Rost and C. Sander. Prediction of protein secondary structure at better than 70 % accuracy. *J. Mol. Biol.*, 232:584–599, 1993.

[SBU$^+$94] Y. Sakakibara, M. Brown, R. C. Underwood, I. S. Mian, and D. Haussler. Stochastic context-free grammars for modeling RNA. In *Proceedings of the 27th Hawaii International Conference on System Sciences*, volume V, pages 284–293, 1994.

[Sch92]   Y. Schabes. Stochastic lexicalized tree adjoining grammars. In *Proceedings of COLING-92*, pages 426–432, 1992.

[Slo89]   R. H. Sloan. *Computational Learning Theory: New Models and Algorithms*. PhD thesis, MIT, 1989. Issued as MIT/LCS/TR-448.

[SS91]   C. Sander and R. Schneider. Database of homology-derived structures and the structural meaning of sequence alignment. *Proteins: Struct. Funct. Genet.*, 9:56–68, 1991.

[VL92]   J. Vitter and J. Lin. Learning in parallel. *Inform. Comput.*, pages 179–202, 1992.

[VSJ85]   K. Vijay-Shanker and A. K. Joshi. Some computational properties of tree adjoining grammars. In *23rd Meeting of A.C.L.*, 1985.

[Yam92]   K. Yamanishi. A learning criterion for stochastic rules. *Machine Learning*, 9(2/3), 1992. A special issue for COLT'90.

[YK91]   K. Yamanishi and A. Konagaya. Learning stochastic motifs from genetic sequences. In *The Eighth International Workshop on Machine Learning*, 1991.

A Unified Approach to Inductive Logic and Case-Based Reasoning

Michael M. Richter
Universität Kaiserslautern
FB Informatik
PF 3049
67653 Kaiserslautern

Extended Abstract

We will present a general formal approach which for different learning paradigms will extract the major common elements and at the same time will make the essential differences visible. Our focus here is on case-based reasoning (cbr) and on inductive inference. From the application side we distinguish between

- diagnosis and classification: "Learning what is the case"

and

- design: "Learning what should be the case".

The most elementary methods (and algorithms) in this context are the nearest neigbor method and the version space algorithm. So we will first discuss their relation on an algorithmic level. In particular, we will see in how far both approaches can be translated into each other.

Concerning semantic questions the semantics of a similarity measure sim is not yet handled convincingly in the literature. We will point out that the semantics of sim in classification is completely different from the semantics in design. In classification sim is connected with evidence or probability, e.g. $sem(sim(a,b)) = prob(Class\ a = Class\ b\ |\ given\ an\ observation)$ (or an estimate of this probability).

In design not only sim plays a role but in addition a solution transformation T. Here the notion of truth is replaced by the concepts of correctness and optimality of a design. A first approach is

$$sem(sim, T) = (\alpha, \beta)$$

where α measures the degree of correctness and β measures its optimality.

In cbr as well as in inductive inference a certain number of hypotheses is generated, e.g. the version space. Its ordering structure is generalized and modified in order to cover design problems as well.

We have two interpretations of the version space:

Classification: Candidates for the description of the classes after the presentation of some classified objects.

Design: Candidates for the derived design after the incorporation of constraints.

Three Decades of Team Learning

Carl H. Smith*
Department of Computer Science
University of Maryland
College Park, MD 20742 USA
smith@cs.umd.edu

1 Introduction

The philosophers of science were the first group to apply formal methods to the process of discovery [Bur58, Car52, Res70]. They developed models of the scientific method that entailed ·alternating phases of data acquisition and hypothesis formation. The linguists used amazingly similar models to study language acquisition [Gol67]. Unifying, computationally based formal models of learning were presented in [TB73] and [BB75], stimulating much research in the field now called inductive inference.

The original intentions of the philosophers was to be able to discuss the process of scientific discovery. A common trend in contemporary science is for *teams* of scientists to focus on a single project. Computer scientists are very familiar with the technique of dispatching hordes of processors to solve some problem. Essentially, every parallel processor is a team of more or less independent machines. It is not surprising then that researchers in inductive inference considered formal learning by teams of learning machines. This paper is an attempt to survey the highlights of what has become a major theme in the study of inductive inference. The organization of the paper is roughly chronological, with a preamble containing the technical definitions.

2 Various Definitions of Learning

When discussing learning, the first point that needs to be determined is what precisely are we supposed to be learning. The philosophers were interested in the work of scientists such as the physicists who perform experiments in an attempt to discover the nature of the universe. The linguists were concerned with learning languages. The basis of the study of inductive inference is that both these situations can be encoded into the paradigm of learning recursive functions. The idea is that any description of an experiment is just a string of

*Supported in part by NSF Grant 9301339 and ONR Grant N000149310773.

symbols, as is any sentence from a natural language. Using suitable encoding techniques of the type pioneered by K. Gödel [G65], it is possible to encode any such string of symbols as single natural number. Likewise, the result of the experiment is another string of symbols. The encodings enable us to represent any phenomenon to be learned as a mapping from encodings of descriptions of experiments to encodings of descriptions of results. Consequently, inductive inference is concerned with the learning of recursive functions, without mention of the underlying codings. The natural numbers will be denoted by $\mathbb{N}$ and the class of all recursive functions will be denoted by $\mathcal{R}$. Languages are essentially $\{0, 1\}$ valued functions. The results that we discuss concern the learning of arbitrary recursive functions. The results are similar, but not identical, if the domain of discourse is restricted to languages [OSW86a].

The algorithms that we will call *inductive inference machines* (or IIMs for short) take as input the graph of a function, an ordered pair at a time. They produce as output a sequence of programs intended to compute the function providing the input. Sometimes it is obvious when learning has been completed. For example, when people learn how to add two numbers, all that is needed to know is a table of digit sums and carries. Once the table has been ascertained, the learning is complete. In other cases, such as learning a natural language, the learning is *never* complete as new words are constantly being introduced as a result of technology. In other cases it is not at all clear when the learning has been completed. Consider the case of learning how to drive a car. Almost everyone driving a car believes that they know how to drive. However, with amazing frequency we observe drivers who clearly have more to learn. Among even the most experienced drivers, very few have even heard about such esoteric driving procedures such as the heel-toe maneuver or the four wheel drift. Since it is sometimes impossible to tell when the learning has been completed we must consider the limiting behavior of the sequence of programs produced by the IIM. If the sequence converges, e.g. there is either a last program or past some point all the programs are syntactically identical, and the final program is correct, e.g. it computes the function serving as input, then we say the the IIM has learned the input function. Some form of learning must have taken place, since the correct answer was produced after observing only a finite portion of the graph of the input function.

Every learning algorithm will learn some (possibly empty) set of recursive functions. In general, the set of functions learnable by a given IIM forms an undecidable set. For M an IIM, we denote the set of recursive functions that M can learn as $EX(M)$. The "ex" stands for "explain" since if M learns some function, then it has found an "explanation" for the phenomenon it represents. The collection of all sets of recursive functions that are learnable by some learning algorithm is denoted by EX.

As an example, consider the learning of the functions of finite support. These are the functions that take the value 0 on all but a finite number of arguments. Below is the definition of a learning algorithm that can learn any function of finite support.

Start by initializing a table T of ordered pairs to contain no entries. Output a program for the everywhere zero function and then repeat the following step forever:

> Input the pair (x, y). If $y \neq 0$ then add (x, y) to the table T and output a new program p. Program p has a copy of T built into it. When p receives an input x it first consults the table T looking for a pair (x, y) for some y. If such a pair is found, then p outputs y, otherwise p outputs 0.

We will now argue that the above algorithm has the promised behavior. If the function serving as input really is a function of finite support, then there will only be finitely many input pairs (x, y) for which $y \neq 0$. Hence, the above algorithm will only output finitely many programs, e.g. it converges. At the point when the last such program is output, all the pairs (x, y) for which $y \neq 0$ will be in the table. Hence, when the final program is produced, it will have a complete list of all the points where it should not return 0. Clearly, the program will compute the input function. This ends the example.

In this paper we discuss several variations on the above definition of EX. Rather than discuss them as the arise, we put all the definitions here in a single section. All of the variations modify the criteria of successful inference. The modifications are intended to resemble some aspect of human learning. The goal of the studies was to compare what is learnable with respect to both definitions, to find out which results in inherently more powerful learning. In this way, the dominant characteristics of learning systems emerge. Many of these comparisons will be mentioned and interpreted below. In our formulations of these results, $\subseteq$ will denote subset and $\subset$ will denote proper subset. The empty set will be denoted by $\emptyset$.

For example, rather than have the final program be absolutely correct, we may consider the result close enough if it is correct an all but a few arguments. If the learning algorithm converges on some function to a program that computes the given function everywhere *except* on $a \in \mathbb{N}$ anomalous points, then we say the the IIM EX^a learns the functions. Notice that there are two types of anomalies. It may be that program p fails to compute some function f on argument x because program p, on input x, converges to some value other than $f(x)$. Alternatively, program p, on input x, may not converge. The collection of all sets of recursive functions that are learnable in this fashion is denoted by EX^a. In some cases we may not be able to set a fixed a priori bound on the number of anomalies but nonetheless guarantee that their number is finite. In this case we will say that the IIM has $EX^\star$ learned the input function. $EX^\star$ denotes the collection of all sets of recursive functions that are learnable in this fashion. In numerical inequalities, $\star$ will be considered larger than any member of $\mathbb{N}$. Notice that as an immediate consequence of our definitions, $EX^0 \subseteq EX^1 \subseteq \ldots \subseteq EX^\star$. What was previously called EX should now be referred to as EX^0. To reduce notation, we will assume that an omitted superscript represents a zero so that we may continue to call EX^0 simply EX. The definition of $EX^\star$ is due to [BB75] while the other cases are from [CS83]. Also considered has been learning with respect to infinitely many errors distributed throughout the domain [Roy86, SV90].

Another popular modification to the basic definition is to restrict the learning algorithms so that they may only change their conjecture in the sequence of programs they produce as output only $b \in \mathbb{N}$ times. The resulting class is called EX_b. The learning in the limit case that we defined initially admits an arbitrary finite number of mind changes. As with anomalies, $\star$ will stand for an arbitrary finite number. Consequently, what we were calling EX should now be called $EX_\star$. However, we will again adhere to simplified notation and make the convention that an omitted subscript represents a $\star$ so that we may continue to call $EX_\star^0$ simply EX. As a consequence of the definition, $EX_0 \subseteq EX_1 \subseteq \ldots \subseteq EX_\star$. The definition of EX_0 is due to [FW79] while the other (non $\star$) cases are from [CS83].

The drive to find more and more powerful learning algorithms led researchers to consider probabilistic learning algorithms. Essentially, this means giving an IIM a fair coin to toss. The criterion of successful learning now become relative to a given probability. Notationally, we denote the collection of all sets of recursive functions that are learnable with probability p by $EX \langle p \rangle$. Keeping with our desire to use the simplest possible notation we will continue to write EX for $EX_\star^0 \langle 1 \rangle$. For the definition of probabilistic inductive inference see [Fre75, Pit89].

Other attempts to make learning algorithms more powerful has been to give IIMs more information to work with. For example, allowing the IIMs to ask questions can boost learning potential [GS91]. Teams of learning machines that asked questions was discussed in [GKP+94]. Similarly, one can give the IIM an algorithm to decide membership in some other set [AB91]. The set containing the extra information is called an *oracle* [Rog67, Soa87]. Notationally, we will write $EX[A]$ to denote the class of sets that are EX learnable with respect to oracle A. Oracles can be combined with all the previous modifications of EX. We will continue to write EX for $EX_\star^0[\emptyset] \langle 1 \rangle$. The definition of inference with respect to an oracle is from [GP89].

Another variation on the theme of EX learning deserves mention. Consider using the result of some learning machine. Since we may not know if the machine has converged, we will continually use the most recent conjecture for our calculations. From this perspective, it does not matter if the IIM converges at all. What really counts is that after some point, all the conjectures produced by the IIM are correct. If an IIM, on input from the graph of a function f, produces a sequence of programs as output such that almost all of them compute f, then we will say that the IIM has BC learned f. The "bc" stands for "behaviorally correct." Each IIM will BC learn some set of recursive functions. As usual, BC denotes the collection of sets of recursive functions such that each one is BC learned by some IIM. The notion of BC inference can be combined with anomalies, probability and oracles, but not mind changes. Another name then for BC is $BC^0[\emptyset] \langle 1 \rangle$. The first definition of BC appears in [Bar74].

Finally, we get to the notation involving teams of learning machines, the main topic of this paper. Consider a team of n learning algorithms. For $m \leq n$, we will say that the team $[m, n]EX$ *learns a set of recursive functions*, if for any function in the set, *at least* m of the machines EX learn the function. Notice that for different members of the set of recursive functions to be learned, there may be a different size m subset of the team that actually learns the given member. As usual, we will continue to call $[1, 1]EX^0_*\langle 1 \rangle$ simply EX. An immediate consequence of the definition is that if $m \geq m'$ and $n \leq n'$ then $[m, n]EX \subseteq [m', n']EX$. Of course, teams of learning machines can be defined with respect to all the other types of inference discussed above. The $m = 1$ case of the definition is from [Smi82] while the more general definition is from [OSW86b].

3 Prehistory

In this section we will discuss the results that are part of the team learning story but appeared prior to the formal definition, hence the title of this section. The first results that we will discuss concern attempts to learn all the recursive functions with a single learning algorithm. If this task could be accomplished, then the story of team learning would be very short. The first attempt was by Putnam [Put75]. He was the first to point out that there may be some difficulty with the mechanization of science.

Theorem 1 *[Put75] No learning algorithm that only outputs total functions can learn all the recursive functions.*

Putnam was actually trying to prove the more general result is stated as Theorem 2. In a sense, these results are the first results in team learning. They show that no team of size 1 can learn all the recursive functions.

Theorem 2 *[Gol67] No learning algorithm can learn all the recursive functions. In symbols, $\mathcal{R} \notin EX$.*

We will present a proof of this result, for the non experts, because it illustrates the basic proof techniques used in the area. The character of the following proof is shared by many of the unpresented proofs of the results that we will discuss below.

Proof: Suppose by way of contradiction that M is an IIM that can learn all the recursive functions. To reach a contradiction we must find a recursive function that M can not learn. to do so, we construct a recursive function f in effective stages of finite extension. We start by giving M the sequence of inputs $(0,0)$, $(1,0)$, $(2,0)$, ... and simultaneously define $f(0) = 0$, $f(1) = 0$, $f(2) = 0$, ... until M produces its first program. If M never produces any program at all, then we end up defining f to be the everywhere 0 function. Clearly, in this case we have found a recursive function that M cannot learn. Suppose however that M does produce a conjecture. Then we may suppose at any point in the construction that f has been defined on some initial segment of its eventual domain and that M's conjecture on that segment is defined.

Let σ denote the finite initial segment defined so far and let p be the last program produced by M when it is given σ, and no more, as input. Let x be the least number not in the domain of σ. Simultaneously perform the two searches below:

1. Look for a τ extending σ such that M's last output when given τ as input is different from p. If such a τ is found before the search in part 2 completes, then define $f(x) = \tau(x)$ for all points in the domain of τ for which f has not yet been defined. Reset the values of σ, p and x and start the parallel search again.

2. Run program p on input x and wait for it to converge. If it does converge, say to y, then define $f(x) = y + 1$. Reset the values of σ, p and x and start the parallel search again.

To complete the proof, we must consider the two cases below. The recursive function that is found that M cannot learn depends on which of the two mutually disjoint case below hold. It can not be effectively determined which of the two cases holds.

Case 1. f is always defined on a new argument and the values of σ, p and x are always reset by (1) or (2) above. Then the above construction will define f on all arguments. Hence, f is a recursive function. If M on input from f outputs a final program, one of the conditions for learning, then the extensions to f must, past some point, always be made by (2) above. Suppose the final program is p. But then f will be made to output a value different from the one produced by p on infinitely many arguments. Hence, M converges to a program that fails to compute f, e.g. M can not EX learn f.

Case 2. Not case 1. Then f is defined to be a function with finite domain. Let g be a recursive function that agrees with f where ever f is defined and takes the value 0 elsewhere. Consider giving g to M as input. Then M must output a final program as otherwise (1) would have found an extension to f. Also, this final program must not be defined on very many arguments as otherwise (2) would have found an extension to f. Since neither extension was found, M on input from g converges to a program that computes a finite function. Hence, M can not EX learn g. This completes the proof.

As mentioned earlier, much of the work in inductive inference has been to set-theoretically compare the various variants on EX defined above and elsewhere. The goal is to understand how the basic parameters of learning interact with one another. For example, one might expect that it should be the case that by allowing a learning algorithm to see some more data and make another conjecture, a more accurate answer will result. Unfortunately, this is not the case.

Theorem 3 *[CS83] For all a, b, c, d in $(\mathbb{N} \cup \{\star\})$, $EX^a_b \subseteq EX^c_d$ iff $a \leq c$ and $b \leq d$.*

Even though Theorem 3 is not explicitly about teams it is important to know this result in order to properly interpret the results below that investigate the trade offs between team size, anomalies and mind changes. A similar result holds for behaviorally correct inference.

Theorem 4 *[CS83] For all* $a \in \mathbb{N}$, $BC^a \subset BC^{a+1}$.

Now we can start with the results that explicitly mention teams, at least in our formulations. Theorem 5 was initially stated as a closure result. To show that the collection of learnable sets (EX) is not closed under union one must give an example of a team of two learning algorithms that can learn some set not in EX. Hence, the non union theorem below was the first result that indicated the advantage of teams for learning. In our notation, we have the following.

Theorem 5 *[Bar74, BB75]* $[1, 2]EX - EX \neq \emptyset$.

To prove this theorem, one must give two sets of recursive functions and then show that each is learnable while their union is not. The functions of finite support from our initial example serve as one of the two sets. The second is the so called *self describing functions*. There are several different formulations of the self describing functions. The essential feature is that the range of any self describing function f contains an easy to find encoding of a description of a program to compute f. Such functions are easily constructed using various recursion theorem [Kle38, Smi94]. Various types of self describing functions are ubiquitous in the study of inductive inference. A slightly more careful analysis of the proof of Theorem 2 shows that in Case 2, the function g is a function of finite support. The remainder of the proof of the Theorem 5 is to concoct a variation of the proof of Theorem 2 so that the f that is used in Case 1 turns out to be a self describing function.

4 The First Thread

Attempts to generalize Theorem 5 led to a series of interesting results. These are the subject of this section. Other threads of the team learning story will be elaborated on in subsequent sections. We start with the following team hierarchy result.

Theorem 6 *[Smi82] For any* $n \in \mathbb{N}$, $[1, n]EX \subset [1, n + 1]EX$.

This result yields the intuitively obvious conclusion that the larger the team size, the greater the chances of having one of the team members succeed. Similar hierarchies exist for team inference with anomalies and mind change bounds, These enhancements will be included in the generalizations of Theorem 6 presented below.

The proof of Theorem 6 gives an example set that can be learned by a team of $n + 1$ machines and then gives an iterated version of the proof of Theorem 2 to construct a member of the example set that cannot be learned by an arbitrarily chosen team of n IIMs. Since the team of size n is chosen arbitrarily, it may be that they operate independently, in close cooperation or in any one of the myriad of possibilities in between. It is perhaps curious that the team of $n+1$ machines that can learn the example set cooperates only in the very beginning. The team divides the input into $n+1$ disjoint pieces and each team member chooses one of the pieces. Then, each of the team members executes the precisely the same algorithm on their piece of the data.

An easy observation relates team learning to probabilistic learning. Suppose that some team of n learning algorithms can learn some set S of recursive functions. A single, probabilistic learning strategy to learn S is to randomly pick a number i between 1 and n and then simulate the ith team member. Clearly, this new strategy will succeed with probability $1/n$. What was startling is that some version of the converse also holds.

To relate probabilistic learning to team learning we must have some way to convert real numbers in the interval $[0,1]$ representing probabilities into positive integers representing team size. This is accomplished using the notion of *intervals*. For p a real number in the interval $[0,1]$, define

$$IN(p) = \frac{1}{\left\lfloor \frac{1}{p} \right\rfloor}.$$

It works out that $IN(p) = 1/n$ for n the unique natural number such that

$$\frac{1}{n+1} < p \leq \frac{1}{n}.$$

The following result, the converse of Theorem 6, indicates that team learning is a discrete analogue of probabilistic learning.

Theorem 7 *[Pit89] For all $0 < p \leq 1$, $EX \langle p \rangle = [1, 1/IN(p)]EX$.*

Theorems 6 and 7 are easily combined to yield a hierarchy based on probability. This indicates that the more uncertainty you are willing to entertain about finally learning something, the more likely it is that you will learn it. Furthermore, the hierarchy is not continuous over the interval $[0,1]$, but rather it is discrete, with steps defined by the function IN. A formalization of the combinations of Theorems 6 and 7 is given next.

Theorem 8 *[PS88] For $m \leq n$,*

$$[m, n]EX = [1, \lfloor n/m \rfloor]EX = EX \langle IN(m/n) \rangle.$$

Theorem 8 clearly indicates that m out of n teams behave as indicated by the ratio of m to n. Each of Theorems 6, 7 and 8 also hold with "EX" replaced with "EX^a" for any $a \in \mathbb{N} \cup \{\star\}$ and also with "EX" replaced with "BC." This indicates that team composition dominates error tolerance as a factor influencing learning. We conclude this section with the characterizations of the trade offs between team size, probability and anomalies. It is noteworthy that again the dominant factor in assessing the learning power of a team is the ratio of the number of machines that must be correct relative to the total team size.

Theorem 9 *[PS88] For all $a, a' \in \mathbb{N}$, for all positive $m, m', n, n' \in \mathbb{N}$ with $m \leq n$ and $m' \leq n'$, for all positive $p, p' \leq 1$,*

$$[m, n]EX^a \langle p \rangle \subseteq [m', n']EX^{a'} \langle p' \rangle \iff$$
$$IN\left(\frac{m}{n} \cdot IN(p)\right) \geq IN\left(\frac{m'}{n'} \cdot IN(p')\right)\left(1 + \left\lfloor \frac{a}{a'+1} \right\rfloor\right).$$

A corollary of Theorem 9 appeared [Smi82]. Actually, Theorem 10 was used to prove Theorem 9. An analogue of the corollary was obtained for BC style inference. We conclude this section with the statement of both results which display trade offs between anomalies and team size. Essentially, the larger of two teams will be the one with more learning potential, provided that the difference in the team size is at least a factor as large as the ratio of the error bounds.

Theorem 10 *[Smi82] For all positive m and n in $\mathbb{N}$ and all a and b in n, $[1, m]EX^a \subseteq [1, n]EX^b$ iff either $m \leq n$ and $a \leq b$ or*

$$n \geq m\left(1 + \left\lfloor \frac{a}{(b+1)} \right\rfloor\right).$$

Theorem 11 *[Dal89] For all positive m and n in $\mathbb{N}$ and all a and b in n, $[1, m]BC^a \subseteq [1, n]BC^b$ iff either $m \leq n$ and $a \leq b$ or*

$$n \geq m\left\lceil \frac{(a+1)}{(b+1)} \right\rceil.$$

5 Considering Mind Changes

Theorem 9 would seem to have answered all the questions concerning team size. However, in light of Theorem 3, there are still many unanswered questions concerning how team size interacts with restrictions on the number of mind changes allowed. A fascinating and mysterious story unfolded when this avenue was pursued. The following result extends Theorem 3 to partially cover the teams case.

Theorem 12 *[FSV89] For all n, a, b, c and $d \in \mathbb{N}$ with n positive and $c \geq a$ $[1, n]EX^a_b \subseteq EX^c_d$ iff*

$$d \geq \left\lfloor \frac{a(n-1)}{(c-a+1)} \right\rfloor (b+1) + 2nb + \left\lfloor \frac{a}{(c-a+1)} \right\rfloor b + 2(n-1).$$

A complete trade off formula remains a difficult open problem. Progress has been made which indicates why the problem is so difficult. The effort to solve the problem has focused on special cases. First, the effect of anomalies was removed. Notice that the ratio of team sizes remains a dominant term.

Theorem 13 *[KV94] For all m, n, a and $b \in \mathbb{N}$ with $m > n > 1$, $[1,m]EX_a \subseteq$*
$[1,n]EX_b$ *iff*

$$b \geq \left\lceil \frac{2(a+1)m}{n} \right\rceil - (a+2).$$

To make further progress, the effect of mind changes was eliminated. The remaining results in this section focus on the case of no mind changes at all. These so called *one shot* learners form an important subclass of learning algorithms. They represent the class of practical learning algorithms that analyze a training set and then produce the correct answer on the first try. The first result not only shows that the hierarchy of larger and larger inferrible classes based on a diminishing probability of success exists, but that it has *discrete* boundaries of the same type as Theorem 7.

Theorem 14 *[Fre75] If*
$$\frac{n+1}{2n+1} < p \leq \frac{n}{2n-1}$$

Then
$$EX_0 \langle p \rangle = EX_0 \left\langle \frac{n}{2n-1} \right\rangle.$$

The next results shows that again there is a precise correspondence between probability and teams for learning. Again, the ratio of the successful members to the total team size is a dominant factor.

Theorem 15 *[DPVW91] If*

$$\frac{n+1}{2n+1} < \frac{m_1}{m_2} \leq \frac{n}{2n-1}$$

then
$$[m_1, m_2]EX_0 = EX_0 \left\langle \frac{n}{2n-1} \right\rangle.$$

Theorems 14 and 15 easily combine to give the following.

Corollary 16 *Of both m_1/m_2 and p are in the real interval*

$$\left(\frac{n+1}{2n+1}, \frac{n}{2n-1} \right]$$

Then $[m_1, m_2]EX_0 = EX \langle p \rangle$.

Given all the results above showing the dominance of the ratio of successful IIMs to total team size, the research community was very surprised by the following result. It shows that there is something very subtle and strange about the relationships between various team compositions and EX_0 type learning. It also explains why a completion of the trade off picture hinted at by Theorem 12 is a very difficult problem.

Theorem 17 *[Vel89]* $[2,4]EX_0 - [1,2]EX_0 \neq \emptyset$.

One of the first questions that came to mind as a result of Theorem 17 was how many different team classes are there for ratios of 1/2 of successful machines to total team size. The answer turns out to be 2.

Theorem 18 *[JS90a]* $[2,4]EX_0 = [4,8]EX_0 = [6,12]EX_0 \cdots$ *and* $[1,2]EX_0 = [3,6]EX_0 = [5,10]EX_0 \cdots$.

The above results completely explain the relationships between team composition and probabilities for all probabilities greater than 1/2. Current research concerns what happens for probabilities at most 1/2. The following two results indicate that even this very restricted problem is quite difficult.

Theorem 19 *[DKV92]* If $24/49 < p \leq 1/2$ then $[2,4]EX_0 = EX_0 \langle p \rangle$.

Theorem 20 *[DKV92]* Let $p_1 = 24/49$, $p_2 = 20/41$, $p_3 = 18/37$, $p_4 = 17/35$. For $1 \leq n < 4$, if $p_{n+1} < p \leq p_n$ then $EX_0 \langle p \rangle = EX_0 \langle p_n \rangle$.

The sequence p_1, p_2, p_3, p_4 of Theorem 20 is most curious. The sequence of numerators 24, 29, 18, 17 is a decreasing sequence of natural numbers and the sequence of denominators is a decreasing sequence of positive natural numbers. How many probability classes exist for probabilities smaller than p_4 remains a tantalizing and difficult open problem.

6   Learning with Oracles

In this section we examine what happens if we allow our IIM's access to an oracle. Some oracles help significantly and others not so much. If A is such that $\mathcal{R} \in EX[A]$ then we say A is *omniscient* with respect to EX. If A is such that $EX[A] = EX$ then we say that A is *trivial* with respect to EX. Of course, the notions if omniscient and trivial are also valid with respect to other classes as well.

Some A's are omniscient for EX and some A's are omniscient for $[m,n]EX$. The question arises as to whether a weaker oracle might suffice for the more powerful class, i.e., for $[m,n]EX$. The answer is no. The following theorem appears in [FJG+94] but a portion appeared earlier in [AB91].

Theorem 21 *For all m, n and a, the following are equivalent.*

1. $\mathcal{R} \in EX[A]$.

2. $\mathcal{R} \in [m, n]EX[A]$.

3. $\mathcal{R} \in [m, n]EX^a[A]$.

4. $\mathcal{R} \in [m, n]EX^*[A]$.

5. A is high (i.e., $\emptyset'' \leq_T A'$).

For the case of BC much less is known. There are low sets A (e.g., $A' \leq_T K$) such that $\mathcal{R} \in BC[A]$. This makes a characterization of the omniscient oracles for BC unlikely. A plausible conjecture is that for all m, n and a $\mathcal{R} \in BC[A]$ iff $REC \in [m, n]BC$ iff $\mathcal{R} \in [m, n]BC^a$.

If mind changes are bounded then a very different picture emerges: no matter how strong A is one cannot obtain all of $\mathcal{R}$. Formally, it was shown that for all numbers m, n and a, and for all sets A, $\mathcal{R} \notin [m, n]EX_a^*$, see [FJG+94].

Some oracles are trivial for EX and others are trivial for $[m, n]EX$. The question arises as to whether stronger oracles are needed to make weaker classes non-trivial. The answer is no.

The following theorem appears in [FJG+94] but portions appeared in [SS91]. A shorter proof of that part can be found in [KS93].

Theorem 22 *For any m, n and a the following are equivalent.*

1. $EX[A] = EX$.

2. $BC[A] = BC$.

3. $[m, n]EX[A] = [m, n]EX$.

4. $[m, n]EX^a[A] = [m, n]EX^a$.

5. $[m, n]EX^*[A] = [m, n]EX^*$.

6. $[m, n]BC[A] = [m, n]BC$.

7. $A \leq_T K$ and there exists 1-generic G such that $A \equiv_T G$.

It is an open problem to classify the set of all oracles A for which the equality $[m, n]BC^a[A] = [m, n]BC^a$ holds. A plausible conjecture is that this is the same oracles as in the above list. The picture is different if the number of mind changes allowed is bounded. The following are equivalent.

Theorem 23 *[FJG+94] For any m, n, a and b, the following are equivalent.*

1. $EX_a[A] = EX_a$

2. $[m, n]EX_a[A] = [m, n]EX_a$

3. $[m, n]EX_a^b[A] = [m, n]EX_a^b$

4. $[m,n]EX^\star_a[A] = [m,n]EX^\star_a$

5. A is recursive.

One way to measure how strong a separation is is to see what strength oracle is needed to break it. For example it is consider the inclusion $EX \subset BC$. We know that for some oracle A we have $BC \subseteq EX[A]$ since there are oracles A such that $\mathcal{R} \in EX[A]$. But it turns out that these are the *only* oracles such that $\mathcal{R} \in EX[A]$ (see [KS93]). Hence this is a strong inclusion. The following results specify exactly which oracles break the inclusions having to do with teams of EX_0 machines.

Theorem 24 *[KS94] For all m, n, m', n' with $\frac{m'}{n'} > \frac{1}{2}$ one of the following conditions holds:*

1. $[m,n]EX_0 \subseteq [m',n']EX_0$.

2. $(\forall A)[[m,n]EX_0 \not\subseteq [m',n']EX_0[A]]$.

3. $(\forall A)[[m,n]EX_0 \subseteq [m',n']EX_0[A] \Leftrightarrow K \leq_T A]$.

Theorem 25 *[KS94] For any oracle A, $[2,4]EX_0 \subseteq [1,2]EX_0[A] \Leftrightarrow K \leq_T A$.*

For the next result we need a little notation. Let PA denote the class of all degrees containing a complete and consistent extension of Peano Arithmetic. Let DNR_2 be the class of all $\{0,1\}$ valued functions that differ from the ith computable function, in some standard list, on argument i. It is known that PA coincides with the degrees of functions in DNR_2.

Theorem 26 *[KS94] For all $A, [24,49]EX_0 \subseteq [2,4]EX_0[A] \Leftrightarrow dg_T(A) \in PA$.*

7 How to Choose a Team

All of the results above point to the benefit of applying teams to a learning situation. The results clearly indicate that adding more members to the team can enable the learning of new functions. The results, however, do not suggest how to go about selecting a learning team. While this endeavor may sound like it belongs in the realm of psychology, it turns out that there are some interesting things that can be formally proved. To do so, we must consider the class of all learning algorithms. This is in sharp contrast to all the results mentioned above where the focus was on the sets of recursive functions to be learned. The idea of reversing the perspective on the learning process was initiated in [FS93]. We begin with a theorem.

Theorem 27 *[tFS94] Suppose S is any set that cannot be learned by any single learning algorithm ($S \notin EX$). Then there is a partition of all learning algorithms into two groups, $\mathcal{M}_1$ and $\mathcal{M}_2$ such that*

1. $\mathcal{M}_1 \cap \mathcal{M}_2 = \emptyset$,

2. $\mathcal{M}_1 \cup \mathcal{M}_2$ *is all of the learning algorithms, and*

3. S cannot be learned by any finite team of machines drawn only from $\mathcal{M}_i$, *for* $i \in \{1, 2\}$.

Applying Theorem 6 (the $n = 1$ case), let S be a set that is in $[1, 2]EX$, but is not in EX. The partitioning given Theorem 27 guarantees that the two learning algorithms that together as a team can learn S must lie on opposite sides of the boundary. Perhaps this is only a peculiar property of the particular partition, and that perturbing the problem slightly would give a different results. It turns out however, as indicated by the following result, that similar learning algorithms will always lie on the same side of the partition.

Theorem 28 *[tFS94] Suppose* M_1 *and* M_2 *are IIMs such that* $(EX(M_1) \cup EX(M_2)) \notin EX$. *Let* $\mathcal{M}_1$ *and* $\mathcal{M}_2$ *be a partitioning of all the IIMs according to Theorem 27. Suppose without loss of generality that* $M_1 \in \mathcal{M}_1$ *and* $M_2 \in \mathcal{M}_2$. *Choose* $M_3 \in \mathcal{M}_2$. *If* $EX(M_3) \cap EX(M_1)$ *is infinite, then so is* $EX(M_1) - EX(M_3)$.

Intuitively, Theorem 28 says that if some learning algorithm is close to learning what some algorithm on the other side of the boundary can learn (infinite overlap) then it fails to learn infinitely many recursive functions that the algorithm on the other side of the partition can. Mathematically, we vary the number of partitions in Theorem 27. For every $n > 1$, there is a set S that is learnable by a team of n machines and a separation of all the learning algorithms into n partitions such that there is no finite team of learning algorithms, chosen from any $n - 1$ of the partitions, that can learn S. Hence, in order to learn S we must choose team members from at least n different types. These results yield the following intuition: when choosing a learning team it is best to choose individuals with different proclivities and strengths for learning.

8 Conclusions and Directions for Future Research

The results in team learning show that there is a great advantage to teamwork in learning. There is also an intimate relationship between team learning and probabilistic learning. This relationship breaks down when considering the important, practical class of one shot learners. Other results indicate that the strength of teams for learning comes not from shear size, but from diversity of approach.

There are still many interesting open problems that were not mentioned previously in this paper. Although there has been considerable amount of attention paid to the learning of languages there are very few papers on the subject of teams for language learning [JS90b, JS93, JS94].

Another interesting trend in the study of inductive inference has been to consider inductive inference machines that are somehow *monotone* in their operation, i.e. the successive conjectures of the machine are quantitatively better than the previous ones [LZ93]. Combining the notions of teams and monotone learning is a natural area for future research.

9 Acknowledgements

As with any scientific project, the preparation of this paper was a team effort. Bill Gasarch, Sanjay Jain, Mahendran Velauthapillai and Thomas Zeugmann provided considerable assistance with reminding me of results, tracking down references and proofreading. Financial support was provided by the National Science Foundation and the Office of Naval Research.

References

[AB91] L. Adleman and M. Blum. Inductive inference and unsolvability. *Journal of Symbolic Logic*, 56(3):891–900, September 1991.

[Bar74] J. Barzdins. Two theorems on the limiting synthesis of functions. In Barzdins, editor, *Theory of Algorithms and Programs*, volume 1, pages 82–88. Latvian State University, Riga, U.S.S.R., 1974.

[BB75] L. Blum and M. Blum. Toward a mathematical theory of inductive inference. *Information and Control*, 28:125–155, 1975.

[Bur58] A. W. Burks. *Collected Papers of Charles Sanders Peirce*, volume 7. Harvard University Press, Cambridge, Mass., 1958.

[Car52] R. Carnap. *The Continuum of Inductive Methods*. The University of Chicago Press, Chicago, Illinois, 1952.

[CS83] J. Case and C. Smith. Comparison of identification criteria for machine inductive inference. *Theoretical Computer Science*, 25(2):193–220, 1983.

[Dal83] R. Daley. On the error correcting power of pluralism in bc-type inductive inference. *Theoretical Computer Science*, 24(1):95–104, 1983.

[DKV92] R. Daley, B. Kalyanasundaram, and M. Velauthapillai. Breaking the probability 1/2 barrier in fin-type learning. In L. Valiant and M. Warmuth, editors, *Proceedings of the Fifth Annual Workshop on Computational Learning Theory*, pages 203–217. ACM Press, 1992.

[DPVW91] R. Daley, L. Pitt, M. Velauthapillai, and T. Will. Relations between probabilistic and team one-shot learners. In M. Warmuth and L. Valiant, editors, *Proceedings of the 1991 Workshop on Computational Learning Theory*, pages 228–239, Palo Alto, CA., 1991. Morgan Kaufmann Publishers.

[FJG+94] Lance Fortnow, Sanjay Jain, William Gasarch, Efim Kinber, Martin Kummer, Stuart Kurtz, Mark Pleszkoch, Theodore Slaman, Frank Stephan, and Robert Solovay. Extremes in the degrees of inferability. *Annals of pure and applied logic*, 66:21–276, 1994.

[Fre75] R. V. Freivalds. Functions computable in the limit by probabilistic machines. *Lecture Notes in Computer Science*, 28:77–87, 1975.

[FS93] R. Freivalds and C. Smith. On the duality between mechanistic learners and what it is they learn. In *Lecture Notes in Artificial Intelligence Vol. 744*, pages 137–149. Springer-Verlag, 1993.

[FSV89] R. Freivalds, C. Smith, and M. Velauthapillai. Trade-offs amongst parameters effecting the inductive inferribility of classes of recursive functions. *Information and Computation*, 82(3):323–349, 1989.

[FW79] R. V. Freivalds and R. Wiehagen. Inductive inference with additional information. *Elektronische Informationsverabeitung und Kybernetik*, 15(4):179–184, 1979.

[Gö5] K. Gödel. On undecidable propositions of formal mathematical systems. In M. Davis, editor, *The Undecidable*, pages 39–73. Raven Press, Hewlett, N.Y., 1965.

[GKP+94] W. Gasarch, E. Kinber, M. Pleszkoch, C. Smith, and T. Zeugmann. Learning via queries with teams and anomalies. *Fundamenta Informaticae*, 1994. to appear.

[Gol67] E. M. Gold. Language identification in the limit. *Information and Control*, 10:447–474, 1967.

[GP89] W. Gasarch and M. Pleszkoch. Learning via queries to an oracle. In *Second Annual Workshop on Computational Learning Theory*, pages 214–229. Morgan Kaufmann, 1989.

[GS91] W. Gasarch and C. Smith. Learning via queries. *Journal of the ACM*, pages 649–674, 1991.

[JS90a] S. Jain and A. Sharma. Finite learning by a team. In M. Fulk and J. Case, editors, *Proceedings of the Third Annual Workshop on Computational Learning Theory*, pages 163–177, Palo Alto, CA., 1990. Morgan Kaufmann Publishers.

[JS90b]   S. Jain and A. Sharma. Language learning by a "team". In M. Paterson, editor, *Automata, Languages and Programming*, 17th *International Colloquium*, pages 153–166. Springer Verlag, Lecture Notes in Computer Science No. 443, 1990.

[JS93]   S. Jain and A. Sharma. Probability is more powerful than team for language identification. In *Proceedings of the Workshop on Computational Learning Theory*, pages 192–198. ACM, 1993.

[JS94]   S. Jain and A. Sharma. On aggregating teams of learning machines. *Theoretical Computer Science*, 1994. To appear.

[Kle38]   S. Kleene. On notation for ordinal numbers. *Journal of Symbolic Logic*, 3:150–155, 1938.

[KS93]   M. Kummer and F. Stephan. Structure in the degrees of inferability. In *Sixth Annual Workshop on Computational Learning Theory*. ACM, 1993.

[KS94]   Martin Kummer and Frank Stephan. On the strength of non-inclusion. In *Seventh Annual Conference on Computational Learning Theory*, 1994.

[KV94]   B. Kalyanasundaram and M. Velauthapillai. Simulating teams with many conjectures. 1994.

[LZ93]   S. Lange and T. Zeugmann. Language learning in dependence on the space of hypotheses. In *Proceedings of the Workshop on Computational Learning Theory*, pages 127–136. ACM, 1993.

[OSW86a]   D. Osherson, M. Stob, and S. Weinstein. *Systems that Learn*. MIT Press, Cambridge, Mass., 1986.

[OSW86b]   D. N. Osherson, M. Stob, and S. Weinstein. Aggregating inductive expertise. *Information and Control*, 70:69–95, 1986.

[Pit89]   L. Pitt. Probabilistic inductive inference. *Journal of the ACM*, 36(2):383–433, 1989.

[PS88]   L. Pitt and C. Smith. Probability and plurality for aggregations of learning machines. *Information and Computation*, 77:77–92, 1988.

[Put75]   H. Putnam. Probability and confirmation. In *Mathematics, Matter and Method*, volume 1. Cambridge University Press, 1975.

[Res70]   N. Rescher. *Scientific Explanation*. The Free Press, New York, 1970.

[Rog67]   H. Rogers, Jr. *Theory of Recursive Functions and Effective Computability*. McGraw Hill, New York, 1967.

[Roy86]   J. S. Royer. Inductive inference of approximations. *Information and Control*, 70(2/3):156–178, 1986.

[Smi82]   C. H. Smith. The power of pluralism for automatic program synthesis. *Journal of the ACM*, 29(4):1144–1165, 1982.

[Smi94]   C. Smith. *A Recursive Introduction to the Theory of Computation*. Springer-Verlag, 1994. To appear.

[Soa87]   R. I. Soare. *Recursively Enumerable Sets and Degrees*. Springer Verlag, New York, 1987.

[SS91]   T. Slaman and R. Solovay. When oracles do not help. In *Fourth Annual Workshop on Computational Learning Theory*, pages 379–383. Morgan Kaufmann, 1991.

[SV90]   C. H. Smith and M. Velauthapillai. On the inference of approximate explanations. *Theoretical Computer Science*, 77:249–266, 1990.

[TB73]   B. Trakhtenbrot and J. A. Barzdins. *Finite Automata: Behavior and Synthesis:* North Holland, 1973.

[tFS94]   K. Apsītis, R. Freivalds, and C. Smith. Choosing a learning team: A topological approach. In *Proceedings of the 26th Symposium on the Theory of Computing*, pages 283–289. ACM, 1994.

[Vel89]   M. Velauthapillai. Inductive inference with a bounded number of mind changes. In R. Rivest, D. Haussler, and M. Warmuth, editors, *Proceedings of the 1989 Workshop on Computational Learning Theory*, pages 200–213, Palo Alto, CA., 1989. Morgan Kaufmann.

On-line Learning with Malicious Noise and the Closure Algorithm

Peter Auer
Nicolò Cesa-Bianchi

IGI, Graz University of Technology
Klosterwiesgasse 32/2
A–8010 Graz (Austria)
{pauer,cesabian}@igi.tu-graz.ac.at

Abstract. We investigate a variant of the on-line learning model for classes of $\{0,1\}$-valued functions (concepts) in which the labels of a certain amount of the input instances are corrupted by adversarial noise. We propose an extension of a general learning strategy, known as "Closure Algorithm", to this noise model, and show a worst-case mistake bound of $m + (d + 1)K$ for learning an arbitrary intersection-closed concept class $\mathcal{C}$, where K is the number of noisy labels, d is a combinatorial parameter measuring $\mathcal{C}$'s complexity, and m is the worst-case mistake bound of the Closure Algorithm for learning $\mathcal{C}$ in the noise-free model. For several concept classes our extended Closure Algorithm is efficient and can tolerate a noise rate equal to the information-theoretic upper bound. We also show how to efficiently turn any algorithm for the on-line noise model into a learning algorithm for the PAC model with malicious noise.

1 Introduction

In the on-line learning model introduced in [1, 15] a learner has to identify a target chosen from a given class of concepts (i.e. subsets of a fixed set X) by seeing a sequence of labeled instances (i.e. elements of $X \times \{0, 1\}$). Each instance is labeled according to whether it belongs or not to the target and the learner must exhibit some hypothesized target concept before seeing the next labeled instance. To evaluate a learner we look at the worst-case number of times (over all choices of targets and instance sequences) the current hypothesis misclassified the next instance.

In this paper we investigate an extension of the above framework to take in account the presence of adversarial noise. Namely, an adversary is allowed to choose the labels of a certain amount of the instances in the sequence presented to the learner. The learner's goal is to minimize the worst-case number of mistakes made over all noisy sequences. This approach can be compared to the ideas and results contained in [3, 6, 18] where general (nonefficient) "conversion strategies" to make an on-line learning algorithm robust to adversarial noise were proposed.

We consider a very general on-line strategy known as "Closure Algorithm" [8, 10, 11, 20] for learning intersection-closed concept classes in the noise-free model. We extend this strategy to our noisy learning setting and show a worst-case mistake bound of $m + (d + 1)K$ for learning an arbitrary intersection-closed concept class C, where K is the number of noisy labels, d is a combinatorial parameter measuring C's complexity (for a particular implementation of our algorithm this combinatorial parameter is bounded from above by the VC dimension of C), and m is the worst-case mistake bound of the Closure Algorithm for learning C in the noise-free model.

For several concept classes our extension is efficient and in some cases it can tolerate a noise rate equal to the information-theoretic upper bound for that class. Using the results of [7, 11] we show that the classes of monotone monomials, k-CNF functions, parity functions, integer lattices, and k-ring-sum expansions can be efficiently learned on-line with adversarial noise. We also propose a general technique for showing upper bounds on the noise rate tolerated by any on-line learner disregarding computational constraints. This technique is applied to the classes of subspaces of a linear space, halfspaces in $\{0, 1\}^n$, and to most of the classes mentioned above.

Finally, we show how any on-line algorithm for learning a concept class C using hypotheses chosen from $\mathcal{H}$ and with noise rate r can be efficiently turned into an algorithm for learning C by $\mathcal{H}$ in the malicious PAC model [14] with any accuracy ϵ and noise rate $\frac{r\epsilon}{4(r+1)+r\epsilon} - \alpha$ for any $\alpha > 0$. For parameterized hypothesis classes $\mathcal{H}_n$ such that $\ln |\mathcal{H}_n|$ is polynomial in n we show via a different analysis an improved noise tolerance of $\frac{r\epsilon}{1+r\epsilon} - \alpha$ for any $\alpha > 0$.

2 Notation, terminology, and basic facts

Fix an arbitrary set X (the *instance domain*). A *concept class* over X is any collection of subsets of X. If C is a subset of X we will use the same symbol C also to denote the characteristic function of the subset. For any concept class C let $\overline{C}$ the class of the complements $\overline{C}$ for all $C \in C$. Following Littlestone [15] we define the on-line learning process by a sequence of trials. On each trial the learner outputs a current hypothesis $H \in \mathcal{H}$ from some fixed concept class $\mathcal{H}$ (the *hypothesis class*). Afterwards, the next labeled instance $(x, C(x))$ is revealed, where $x \in X$ and C is some fixed target concept from the *target class* C. The boolean label $C(x)$ is 1 if and only if x belongs to C. The learner makes a mistake on the trial if $H(x) \neq C(x)$, in this case we say that the instance x

is a *counterexample* to hypothesis H. The counterexample x is *positive* if $C(x) = 1$ and *negative* otherwise. A "learner" in this model is thus defined by a mapping from finite sequences (possibly of zero length) of labeled instances to hypotheses $H \in \mathcal{H}$. In general, the mapping defining a learner needs not to be computable. When computable mappings are considered, we will use the term learning algorithm instead of learner.

Let $\mathcal{H}$ be the hypothesis class of learner A. We write $\text{MB}(A, C, \mathcal{H})$ to denote the worst-case number of mistakes made by A over all choices of the target $C \in \mathcal{C}$ and over all trial sequences labeled by C. Finally, let $\text{MB}(\mathcal{C}, \mathcal{H})$ denote the minimum of $\text{MB}(A, C, \mathcal{H})$ over all learners A using hypothesis class $\mathcal{H}$. If $\mathcal{H} \equiv \mathcal{C}$, then we use the abbreviations $\text{MB}(A, \mathcal{C})$ and $\text{MB}(\mathcal{C})$.

A closely related on-line learning model was independently introduced by Angluin [1]. In this setting the learner receives *on each trial* a counterexample $x \in X$ to the current hypothesis H such that $H(x) \neq C(x)$. The learning process ends as soon as the learner's hypothesis H satisfies $H \equiv C$.

For any on-line learner A using hypothesis class $\mathcal{H}$, $\text{EQ}(A, C, \mathcal{H})$ is defined by the maximal length of a sequence of counterexamples received by A when the target is chosen from $\mathcal{C}$. Accordingly, $\text{EQ}(\mathcal{C}, \mathcal{H})$ is the minimum of $\text{EQ}(A, C, \mathcal{H})$ over all learners A.

The following result (proven in [17]) relates Littlestone's MB model to Angluin's EQ model.

We say that a learner is conservative if it changes its hypothesis only when a mistake occurs.

Fact 1. *Any on-line learner A in the MB model is an on-line learner in the EQ model. Vice versa, any on-line learner A' in the EQ model is a conservative learner in the MB model. Moreover $\text{EQ}(A, C, \mathcal{H}) \leq \text{MB}(A, C, \mathcal{H})$ and $\text{MB}(A', C, \mathcal{H}') = \text{EQ}(A', C, \mathcal{H}')$ for all target classes $\mathcal{C}$.*

We now consider the following extensions of the above definitions taking into account the presence of adversarial noise in the learning process.

Again assume $\mathcal{H}$ is the hypothesis class of learner A. For any nonnegative integer K, let $\text{MB}(A, C, \mathcal{H}, K)$ be the worst-case number of mistakes made by A over all sequences $(x_1, \ell_1), (x_2, \ell_2), \ldots$ of labeled instances such that there is some $C \in \mathcal{C}$ for which $C(x_t) \neq \ell_t$ holds for at most K indices t in the sequence. (In this model the learner makes a mistake if it predicts the next label incorrectly, i.e. if $H(x_t) \neq \ell_t$.) The quantity $\text{MB}(\mathcal{C}, \mathcal{H}, K)$ is defined analogously to $\text{MB}(\mathcal{C}, \mathcal{H})$ before.

For any $0 \leq r < 1$ define $\text{EQ}(A, C, \mathcal{H}, r)$ as the maximal length of a sequence of counterexamples received by A such that there is some $C \in \mathcal{C}$

for which $C(x_t) \neq \ell_t$ holds for at most a fraction r of the counterexamples in the sequence. The quantity $EQ(C, \mathcal{H}, r)$ is defined as before. (The quantities $EQ(A, C, \mathcal{H}, r)$ and $EQ(C, \mathcal{H}, r)$ were introduced in [2].)

The next result extends Fact 1 by showing the relationships between the EQ model and the MB model in presence of adversarial noise.

Fact 2. *Let A be an on-line learner with hypothesis class $\mathcal{H}$.*

1. *If $MB(A, C, \mathcal{H}, K) \leq M + RK$ for some $M, R > 0$ then for all $r < 1/R$ and $m \geq m_0 = \frac{M}{1-rR}$, $MB(A, C, \mathcal{H}, rm) \leq m$. Furthermore $EQ(A, C, \mathcal{H}, r) \leq m_0$.*
2. *If $EQ(A, C, \mathcal{H}, r) = m_0$ then there is an on-line learner A' with $MB(A', C, \mathcal{H}, K) \leq m_0 + RK$ where $R = \frac{1 + 1/m_0}{r}$.*

Proof. For proving part 1 we have $MB(A, C, \mathcal{H}, rm) \leq M + Rrm = (1 - rR)m_0 + Rrm \leq m$. Now assume that $EQ(A, C, \mathcal{H}, r) > m_0$. Then there is a sequence of counterexamples to the hypotheses of A of length $m > m_0$ such that at most rm of the counterexamples are noisy, contradicting $MB(A, C, \mathcal{H}, rm) \leq M + Rrm = (1 - Rr)m_0 + Rrm < m$.

For proving part 2 let A' be the learner which runs A as subroutine until A makes $m_0 + 1$ mistakes. Then A' restarts A and runs A until it again makes $m_0 + 1$ mistakes. This continues for the whole sequence of trials. Observe that among the $m_0 + 1$ mistakes of one run of A there are at least $\lfloor rm_0 + 1 \rfloor$ noisy trials since $EQ(A, C, \mathcal{H}, r) = m_0$. Hence there are at most $K/\lfloor rm_0 + 1 \rfloor + 1$ runs of A where the last run makes at most m_0 mistakes, thus giving

$$MB(A, C, \mathcal{H}, K) \leq \frac{K}{\lfloor rm_0 + 1 \rfloor}(m_0 + 1) + m_0 \leq \frac{K}{rm_0}(m_0 + 1) + m_0$$

and concluding the proof. □

Part 1 of Fact 2 will be used (along with Theorem 6) to show applications of our extended Closure Algorithm to specific concept classes in the PAC model with malicious noise.

We close the section with some further definitions and notation. We use N to denote the nonnegative integers and Z to denote the integers. If S is an arbitrary set, P a distribution over S, and R a random variable over S, then the expectation of R with respect to P is denoted by $E_{s \sim P}[R(s)]$. Finally, for all $n, k \in N$ let $\binom{n}{\leq k} = \sum_{i=0}^{k} \binom{n}{i}$.

3   An extension of the Closure Algorithm

We begin by showing that whenever a target class is noise-free on-line learnable (i.e. on-line learnable with noise rate 0), then there exists a general (nonefficient) strategy such that C is on-line learnable with noise rate bound $1/2$.

Theorem 3. *Fix a target class* C. *Let* A *be any algorithm such that* $EQ(A, C, \mathcal{H}, 0) = q$ *for some hypothesis class* $\mathcal{H}$ *and for some positive integer* q. *Then for any* $0 \leq r < 1/2$ *there is an algorithm* CV *that yields*

$$EQ(CV, C, 2^X, r) \leq 2.14 \frac{q}{1 - H(r)} \log_2 \frac{q}{1 - H(r)},$$

where H *is the binary entropy function* $H(x) = -x \log_2(x) - (1 - x) \log_2(1 - x)$ *for all* $0 \leq x \leq 1$.

Proof. By using the conversion strategy CV from [6] and standard Chernoff bounds. $\square$

The following result is derived directly from Theorem 3 and the fact $EQ(C, 2^X) \leq \log_2 |C|$ (see [15]).

Corollary 4. *If* $|C| < \infty$ *then* $EQ(C, 2^X, r) < \infty$ *for all* $0 \leq r < 1/2$.

We now move on to the description of the Closure Algorithm and its extension to the noisy on-line learning model. Some preliminary definitions are needed.

The *closure* operator $\mathrm{Cl}_C : 2^X \rightarrow 2^X$ is defined by the formula

$$\mathrm{Cl}_C(S) = \bigcap_{\{C \in C : S \subseteq C\}} C.$$

(If $\{C \in C : S \subseteq C\} = \emptyset$ then $\mathrm{Cl}_C(S) = X$.)

Notice that, if C is the class of all subspaces of a linear space X, then the closure operator $\mathrm{Cl}_C(S)$ returns the subspace spanned by $S \subseteq X$.

A concept class C on domain X is *intersection-closed* if for all finite $S \subseteq X$, $\mathrm{Cl}_C(S) \in C$. In other words the intersection-closedness property holds whenever the intersection of all concepts in C containing an arbitrary subset of the domain belongs to C as well.

Examples of intersection-closed concept classes include: axis-parallel n-dimensional rectangles, k-CNF boolean functions, subspaces of a linear space, integer lattices. However, notice that any concept class can be made intersection-closed by adding the set of all intersections of concepts in the class.

Algorithm CA.
  – Initialize the state variable $S_0 := \emptyset$.
  – For $t = 0, 1, \ldots$
    1. Let $H_t = \mathrm{Cl}(S_t)$ be the current hypothesis.
    2. Read next labeled instance (x_{t+1}, ℓ_{t+1}).
    3. If $H_t(x_{t+1}) = 0$ and $\ell_{t+1} = 1$ then $S_{t+1} := S_t \cup \{x_{t+1}\}$.
       Else $S_{t+1} := S_t$.

The Closure Algorithm CA (sketched above) simply hypothesizes the closure of the set of all counterexamples received up to the current trial. Due to the intersection-closedness property of the target class, the algorithm's hypotheses always are the smallest concepts consistent with all previously seen (positive) counterexamples, and thus in the noise-free case the Closure Algorithm will only receive positive counterexamples. For instance let C be all subspaces of a d-dimensional linear space X. We then immediately have $\mathrm{MB}(\mathrm{CA}, C) = d$, since the Closure Algorithm will receive only linearly independent counterexamples.

We now introduce a class of operators Bas_C mapping subsets of X to subsets of X. A mapping $\mathrm{Bas}_C : 2^X \rightarrow 2^X$ is a *basis operator* with respect to a concept class C if for all $S \subseteq X$ it holds that $\mathrm{Bas}_C(S) \subseteq S$ and $\mathrm{Cl}_C(\mathrm{Bas}_C(S)) = \mathrm{Cl}_C(S)$. (This definition of basis operator is analogous to that of *spanning set* for a set S as given in [8].) A trivial basis operator is the identity mapping. In the case C is the class of all subspaces of a linear space, a very natural basis operator maps each $S \subseteq X$ to a maximal subset $S' \subseteq S$ of linearly independent vectors.

We say that a basis operator Bas_C^* is *minimal* if for all basis operators Bas_C for C and for all $S \subseteq X$ it holds that $|\mathrm{Bas}_C^*(S)| \leq |\mathrm{Bas}_C(S)|$. Minimal basis operators enjoy the following property.

Lemma 5 [4, 19]. *For all intersection-closed concept classes C on a set X, if Bas_C is minimal then for all $S \subseteq X$, $|\mathrm{Bas}_C(S)|$ is at most the VC-dimension of C.*

Whenever clear from the context the subscript C will be dropped from Cl_C and Bas_C.

Algorithm XCA.

- Initialize the state variable $S_0 := \emptyset$.
- For $t = 0, 1, \ldots$
    1. Let $H_t := \mathrm{Cl}(\mathrm{Bas}(S_t))$ be the current hypothesis.
    2. Read next labeled instance (x_{t+1}, ℓ_{t+1}).
    3. If $H_t(x_{t+1}) = 0$ and $\ell_{t+1} = 1$ then $S_{t+1} := S_t \cup \{x_{t+1}\}$.
       If $H_t(x_{t+1}) = 1$ and $\ell_{t+1} = 0$ then $S_{t+1} := S_t \setminus \mathrm{Bas}(S_t)$.
       Else $S_{t+1} := S_t$.

The Extended Closure Algorithm XCA (sketched above) is designed to cope with noisy counterexamples. On each trial XCA chooses as current hypothesis the closure of the basis for the current set of positive counterexamples. When a (possibly noisy) positive counterexample x is received, the algorithm behaves like in the noiseless case adding x to the current set of positive counterexamples and recomputing the basis. However, if x was noisy, then a negative counterexample might be received in a later trial, since the new H will be too big containing at least the noisy x. Whenever that happens, that is XCA receives a negative counterexample, H is shrunk by removing from the current set S of positive counterexamples its basis (thus possibly all of S).

We are now ready to prove the main result of this section.

Theorem 6. *Let C be a concept class and $\mathcal{H}$ be an intersection-closed concept class such that $C \subseteq \mathcal{H}$. Then for any basis operator Bas, and for any $K \geq 0$,*

$$MB(XCA, C, \mathcal{H}, K) \leq MB(CA, C, \mathcal{H}) + (d+1)K \qquad (1)$$

where $d = \max\{|Bas(S)| : S \subseteq X, |S| \leq MB(CA, \mathcal{H})\}$. Moreover, if Bas is minimal, then d is at most the VC-dimension of $\mathcal{H}$.

In the proof of the theorem we will assume without loss of generality that algorithm XCA does not receive supporting examples such that $\ell_{t+1} = H_t(x_{t+1})$. We will use the following lemma bounding the number of counterexamples kept in the state variable.

Lemma 7. *After any sequence of counterexamples $x_1, \ldots, x_q$ the state variable S_q of algorithm XCA satisfies $|S_q| \leq MB(CA, \mathcal{H})$.*

Proof. Let $\emptyset = T_0, T_1, \ldots, T_m$ be a sequence of subsets of X such that for all $i \geq 1$

$$T_i = T_{i-1} \cup \{x_i\} \quad \text{for some } x_i \in X \setminus \text{Cl}(T_{i-1}). \tag{2}$$

Obviously $|T_i| = i$ and $m \leq \text{MB}(\text{CA}, \mathcal{H})$.

We prove the lemma by induction on q, showing that for any sequence of counterexamples $x_1, \ldots, x_q$ there is a sequence $\emptyset = T_0, T_1, \ldots, T_{m_q} \subseteq X$ with property (2) such that T_{m_q} equals the current content of the state variable S_q of algorithm XCA. The case $q = 0$ is trivial.

Assume that there exists a sequence $\emptyset = T_0, T_1, \ldots, T_{m_{q-1}}$ with property (2) and $T_{m_{q-1}} = S_{q-1}$. If x_q is a positive counterexample then $x_q \notin \text{Cl}(S_{q-1})$, $S_q = S_{q-1} \cup \{x_q\}$, and $T_0, T_1, \ldots, T_{m_{q-1}} = S_{q-1}, T_{m_q} = S_q$ satisfies (2). If x_q is a negative counterexample then $S_q = S_{q-1} \setminus \text{Bas}(S_{q-1})$. Define $T_i' = T_i \setminus \text{Bas}(S_{q-1})$ for $i = 0, 1, \ldots, m_{q-1}$. If $x_i \in \text{Bas}(S_{q-1})$ then $T_i' = T_{i-1}'$, if $x_i \notin \text{Bas}(S_{q-1})$ then $T_i' = T_{i-1}' \cup \{x_i\}$ and $x_i \notin \text{Cl}(T_{i-1}')$ since $\text{Cl}(T_{i-1}') \subseteq \text{Cl}(T_{i-1})$. Hence after removing duplicates from $T_0', T_1', \ldots, T_{m_{q-1}}'$ we have a sequence satisfying (2), which completes the proof of the lemma. $\square$

Proof of Theorem 6. We first introduce some notation. Let C_T be the target concept, $q \geq 0$, $x_1, \ldots, x_q$ a sequence of counterexamples and $H_0, H_1, \ldots, H_q$ the sequence of hypotheses. Let

$$\#_+^{(c)}(q) = |\{1 \leq i \leq q : x_i \in C_T \setminus H_{i-1}\}|,$$
$$\#_+^{(n)}(q) = |\{1 \leq i \leq q : x_i \notin C_T \cup H_{i-1}\}|,$$
$$\#_-^{(c)}(q) = |\{1 \leq i \leq q : x_i \in H_{i-1} \setminus C_T\}|,$$
$$\#_-^{(n)}(q) = |\{1 \leq i \leq q : x_i \in C_T \cap H_{i-1}\}|,$$

respectively denote the number of correct positive, noisy positive, correct negative, and noisy negative counterexamples. Furthermore let $s^{(c)}(q) = |S_q \cap C_T|$ and $s^{(n)}(q) = |S_q \setminus C_T|$ be, respectively, the number of correct and noisy elements in the state variable. We investigate the effect of counterexamples on the above quantities.

If x_q is a correct positive counterexample then $s^{(c)}(q) = s^{(c)}(q-1) + 1$ and $s^{(n)}(q) = s^{(n)}(q-1)$. If x_q is a noisy positive counterexample then $s^{(c)}(q) = s^{(c)}(q-1)$ and $s^{(n)}(q) = s^{(n)}(q-1) + 1$. If x_q is a correct negative counterexample then, since $H_{q-1} = \text{Cl}(\text{Bas}(S_{q-1}))$, at least one element of $\text{Bas}(S_{q-1})$ is noisy. Therefore $s^{(c)}(q) \geq s^{(c)}(q-1) - (d-1)$ and $s^{(n)}(q) \leq s^{(n)}(q-1) - 1$. If x_q is a noisy negative counterexample then $s^{(c)}(q) \geq s^{(c)}(q-1) - d$ and $s^{(n)}(q) \leq s^{(n)}(q-1)$.

Summing over a maximal sequence of counterexamples $x_1, \ldots, x_Q$ we get

$$s^{(c)}(Q) \geq \#_+^{(c)}(Q) - (d-1)\#_-^{(c)}(Q) - d\#_-^{(n)}(Q),$$
$$s^{(n)}(Q) \leq \#_+^{(n)}(Q) - \#_-^{(c)}(Q).$$

Since $s^{(n)}(Q) \geq 0$ and by Lemma 7 $s^{(c)}(Q) \leq \mathrm{MB}(\mathrm{CA}, \mathcal{H})$ we get

$$Q = \#_+^{(c)}(Q) + \#_+^{(n)}(Q) + \#_-^{(c)}(Q) + \#_-^{(n)}(Q)$$
$$\leq \mathrm{MB}(\mathrm{CA}, \mathcal{H}) + \#_+^{(n)}(Q) + d\#_-^{(c)}(Q) + (d+1)\#_-^{(n)}(Q)$$
$$\leq \mathrm{MB}(\mathrm{CA}, \mathcal{H}) + (d+1)\#_+^{(n)}(Q) + (d+1)\#_-^{(n)}(Q)$$
$$\leq \mathrm{MB}(\mathrm{CA}, \mathcal{H}) + (d+1)K,$$

where K is the number of noisy counterexamples. This proves (1). An application of Lemma 5 concludes the proof. □

4 A general upper bound on the noise rate

In this section we introduce a general technique to prove upper bounds on the noise rate tolerable by any on-line learner (therefore disregarding computational issues.)

Theorem 8. *Let $\mathcal{C}, \mathcal{H}$ be (possibly identical) concept classes on domain X. Let $S = \{(x_1, \ell_1), \ldots, (x_s, \ell_s)\}$ be a subset of $X \times \{0, 1\}$ and, for all $1 \leq i \leq s$, let S_i be S where (x_i, ℓ_i) has been replaced by $(x_i, 1 - \ell_i)$. If the following hold*
1. *$x_i \neq x_j$ for $1 \leq i < j \leq s$,*
2. *no $H \in \mathcal{H}$ is consistent with S,*
3. *for all $1 \leq i \leq s$, S_i is consistent with some $C \in \mathcal{C}$,*
then $EQ(\mathcal{C}, \mathcal{H}, 1/s) = \infty$ and $EQ(\overline{\mathcal{C}}, \overline{\mathcal{H}}, 1/s) = \infty$. Furthermore, $MB(\mathcal{C}, \mathcal{H}, K)) \geq (s-1) + sK$ and $MB(\overline{\mathcal{C}}, \overline{\mathcal{H}}, K) \geq (s-1) + sK$ for all $K \geq 0$.

Proof. Let A be an on-line learner for $\mathcal{C}$ using hypotheses from $\mathcal{H}$. For all $q \geq 0$, let $H_q \in \mathcal{H}$ be A's hypothesis after the adversary has returned q counterexamples. By definition of S, some $(x_j, \ell_j) \in S$ can be found such that $H_q(x_j) \neq \ell_j$. The adversary then returns the counterexample x_j.

We now show that after any number of counterexamples q there is a target $C \in \mathcal{C}$ such that at most q/s counterexamples disagrees with C. Fix a $q \geq 0$. By the pigeonhole principle, after q counterexamples there is some $1 \leq j \leq s$ such that the adversary returned the counterexample x_j

at most q/s times. Let C_j be any concept in C consistent with S_j. Notice that, by definition of S, C_j is consistent with all counterexamples x_i such that $i \neq j$. Thus C_j will disagree with at most q/s counterexamples.

By flipping the labels of S one can apply the same argument to the concept classes $\overline{C}, \overline{\mathcal{H}}$.

The bound for the MB model is derived similarly. $\qquad\square$

5 Applications

In this section we give some applications of Theorems 6 and 8. The first one is a simple upper bound on the tolerable noise rate when learning subspaces of an arbitrary linear space.

Corollary 9. *Let V be the class of all subspaces of a d-dimensional linear space V. Then $EQ(V, 1/(d+1)) = \infty$ and $MB(V, K) \geq d + (d+1)K$ for all $K \geq 0$.*

Proof. We fix d linearly independent vectors $v_1, \ldots, v_d$ in V and set $u = \sum_{i=1}^{d} v_i$. It is then easy to see that the set $\{(v_1, 1), \ldots, (v_d, 1), (u, 0)\}$ fulfills the conditions of Theorem 8. $\qquad\square$

Let $0 = (0, \ldots, 0)$, $1 = (1, \ldots, 1)$, and $e_1, \ldots, e_n$ the unit vectors of $\{0, 1\}^n$, where n is made clear from the context.

Let MON_n be the concept class of all the boolean functions that can be expressed as monotone monomials (that is monomials containing only unnegated variables) over n boolean variables. Let $k\text{-CNF}_n$ be the concept class of all boolean functions over $\{0, 1\}^n$ that can be expressed in conjunctive normal form using clauses with at most k literals (k-clauses.) Notice that both classes are intersection-closed. An easy result is the following.

Corollary 10. *For any $K \geq 0$ the class MON_n is on-line learnable in time polynomial in n and K. Furthermore*

$$MB(\mathrm{MON}_n, K) = MB(XCA, \mathrm{MON}_n, K) = n + (n+1)K.$$

Proof. Notice that the closure of a set S of positive counterexamples is the longest monomial M satisfying all counterexamples. Thus all hypotheses in MON_n are representable with $O(n)$ bits and their values are computable in linear time. Also, each positive counterexample added to S shortens M by dropping at least one variable. Thus $EQ(CA, \text{MON}_n) \leq n$. Consider now the Extended Closure Algorithm using MON_n as hypothesis class and the identity basis operator for the class MON_n. By Theorem 6 we immediately conclude $MB(XCA, \text{MON}_n, K) \leq n + (n+1)K$. To prove the lower bound on $MB(\text{MON}_n, K)$ let S be the set $\{(\overline{e}_1, 1), \ldots, (\overline{e}_n, 1), (1, 0)\}$. Clearly, all the instances are distinct and no monotone monomial is consistent with S (the empty monomial has constant value 1 on all of $\{0, 1\}^n$.) Moreover, we can easily find a monotone monomial consistent with the set S' obtained by flipping the label of any single instance in S. An application Theorem 8 then concludes the proof. $\square$

Corollary 10 allows us to state a second result whose proof is deferred to the full paper.

Corollary 11. Let $N = \sum_{i=0}^{k} \binom{n}{i} 2^i$. Then for any $K \geq 0$ the class $k\text{-CNF}_n$ is on-line learnable in time polynomial in N and K. Furthermore $MB(k\text{-CNF}_n, K) \leq N + (N+1)K$.

For all $n \geq 1$ let PARITY_n be the class of parity functions over all subsets of $\{x_1, \ldots, x_n\}$. The following observation legitimates the use of the Extended Closure Algorithm to learn PARITY_n.

Lemma 12 [7]. Each $C \in \text{PARITY}_n$ is a linear subspace of $\{0, 1\}^n$ with respect to the addition modulo 2 and the usual scalar product over $\{0, 1\}$.

Let SUB_n be the class of all linear subspaces $\{0, 1\}^n$ with respect to the operations defined in the statement of Lemma 12.

Corollary 13. For all $K \geq 0$ the class PARITY_n is on-line learnable by the Extended Closure Algorithm in time polynomial in n and K. Furthermore $MB(\text{PARITY}_n, \text{SUB}_n, K) = MB(XCA, \text{PARITY}_n, \text{SUB}_n, K) = n + (n+1)K$.

Proof. By Lemma 12 we have $\text{PARITY}_n \subseteq \text{SUB}_n$. We run the Extended Closure Algorithm using the identity basis operator Bas_I for SUB_n. Since SUB_n is the class of all linear subspaces of an n-dimensional linear space we immediately have $EQ(CA, \text{SUB}_n) \leq n$ and therefore $|\text{Bas}_I(S)| = |S| \leq n$ for all sets S of positive counterexamples. By Theorem 6 this implies

$MB(XCA, \text{PARITY}_n, \text{SUB}_n, K) \leq n + (n+1)K$. Finally, all hypotheses $H \in \text{SUB}_n$ can be represented using $O(n^2)$ bits and computing the value of any H (i.e. testing for linear independence a set of at most n boolean vectors over $\{0, 1\}^n$) takes time polynomial in n (see e.g. [21].) Thus XCA spends polynomial time (in n) on each trial.

The lower bound on $MB(\text{PARITY}_n, \text{SUB}_n, K)$ can be established analogously to Corollary 9 if the v_i are chosen as the unit vectors. □

Notice that $\overline{\text{PARITY}}_n$ is the concept class $\{C_I : I \subseteq \{1, \dots, n\}\}$ where $C_I(x) = \bigoplus_{i \in I} x_i$ for all $x \in \{0, 1\}^n$ and $\bigoplus$ denotes addition modulo 2. A generalization of $\overline{\text{PARITY}}_n$ is the class of *ring-sum expansions* over n variables whose learnability in the PAC model was studied in [7]. A ring-sum expansion is a boolean function $C_{\mathcal{M}}(x) = \bigoplus_{M \in \mathcal{M}} M(x)$ for an arbitrary $\mathcal{M} \subseteq \text{MON}_n$. A well-known fact states that any boolean function can be represented as a ring-sum expansion. By insisting that at most k variables (for $k \leq n$) appear in each monomial one obtains the class of k-ring-sum expansions (k-RSE).

Corollary 14. Let $N = \binom{n}{\leq k}$. Then for all $K \geq 0$ the class k-RSE_n of k-ring-sum expansions over $\{0, 1\}^n$ is on-line learnable in time polynomial in N and K. Furthermore $MB(k\text{-RSE}_n, \mathcal{H}_{k,n}, K) \leq N + (N+1)K$ where $\mathcal{H}_{k,n}$ contains k-RSE_n, is evaluatable in polynomial time, and its complement $\overline{\mathcal{H}}_{k,n}$ is intersection-closed.

Another application of Theorem 6 yields the learnability of *integer lattices* in the presence of noise. An integer lattice $\mathcal{L}^k$ is a subset of Z^k closed with respect to the operations of addition and multiplication by an integer. Let $\mathcal{L}^k(n)$ be the restriction of $\mathcal{L}^k$ on $\{-n, \dots, -1, 0, 1, \dots, n\}^k$. Notice that $\mathcal{L}^k(n)$ is intersection-closed.

In [11] it is shown that $\mathcal{L}^k(n)$ is noise-free on-line learnable by the Closure Algorithm in time polynomial in $\log n$ and k. We can show the following.

Corollary 15. Let $g = \lfloor k \log_2 n + k(\log_2 k)/2 \rfloor + k$. Then

1. for all $K \geq 0$ the class $\mathcal{L}^k(n)$ is on-line learnable in time polynomial in g and K with $MB(XCA, \mathcal{L}^k(n), K) \leq g + (g+1)K$;

2. $EQ(XCA, \mathcal{L}^k(n), r) = \infty$ for $r \geq (1 + o(1)) \frac{\log \log n}{k \log n}$ where $o(1) \to 0$ as $n \to \infty$.

Proof. To prove part 1 we apply the Extended Closure Algorithm with the identity basis operator. Checking for membership in the closure of a set S of counterexamples is computable in polynomial time (see e.g.

[21].) The bound of the number of mistakes is then obtained by applying Theorem 6 to the bound $MB(CA, \mathcal{L}^k(n)) \leq g$ proven in [11].

To prove part 2 let $p_1, \ldots, p_m \in \mathbb{Z}$ be distinct primes with $\prod_{i=1}^m p_i \leq 2n$. Denote by $e_1, \ldots, e_k$ the unit vectors of $\mathbb{Z}^k$. For $1 \leq \kappa \leq k$, $1 \leq i \leq m$, let $x_{\kappa i} = \left(\prod_{j \neq i} p_j \right) e_\kappa$, and $x_0 = (1, \ldots, 1)$.

No $C \in \mathcal{L}^k(n)$ is consistent with $S = \{(x_0, 0), (x_{1,1}, 1), \ldots, (x_{k,m}, 1)\}$. Furthermore the set $\{(x_0, 1), (x_{1,1}, 1), \ldots, (x_{k,m}, 1)\}$ is consistent with $\{-n, \ldots, -1, 0, 1, \ldots, n\}^k \in \mathcal{L}^k(n)$.

Now assume that $(x_{\kappa,i}, 1)$ is replaced by $(x_{\kappa,i}, 0)$ giving $S_{\kappa,i}$. Then $S_{\kappa,i}$ is consistent with $Cl(\{e_1, \ldots, e_{\kappa-1}, p_i e_\kappa, e_{\kappa+1}, \ldots, e_k\})$. Using [11, Equation (1), p. 245] for all $\epsilon > 0$ there exists n_ϵ such that for all $n \geq n_\epsilon$ we can choose $m > \frac{(1+\epsilon)\log n}{\log \log n}$ primes satisfying $\prod_{i=1}^m p_i \leq 2n$ and thus proving the result. $\qquad \square$

We conclude the section by proving an upper bound on the noise rate tolerable by any on-line learner for the class HALFSPACES$_n$ of all linearly separable boolean functions over $\{0, 1\}^n$.

Corollary 16. For all $n > 1$, $EQ(\text{HALFSPACES}_n, 1/(n+2)) = \infty$ and $MB(\text{HALFSPACES}_n, K) \geq n + 1 + (n+2)K$ for all $K \geq 0$.

Proof. Let S be the set $\{(0,0), (e_1, 1), \ldots, (e_n, 1), (1, 0)\}$. Clearly, no halfspace is consistent with S. It is also easy to see that by flipping the label of either $(0, \ldots, 0)$ or $(1, \ldots, 1)$ we can find consistent halfspaces. Finally, choose $1 \leq i \leq n$ and let S_i be S with $(e_i, 0)$ in place of $(e_i, 1)$. Consider the halfspace $\{(v_1, \ldots, v_n) : \sum_{i=1}^n w_i v_i \geq 1\}$ where $w_j = 1$ for $j \neq i$ and $w_i = 1 - n$. It is easy to see that this halfspace is consistent with S_i. Thus Theorem 8 can be applied and the result immediately follows. $\square$

Remark. In the above applications we did not use the full generality of algorithm XCA because we only used the identity mapping as basis operator. Nevertheless the analysis of XCA is not much easier in this case, and in fact there are concept classes were other basis operators can be used, e.g. the class of axis-parallel rectangles (see [2]).

6 From on-line to PAC learning in the presence of noise

In this section we show how any learning algorithm for our on-line noise model can be used to learn in the PAC model with malicious noise.

In the standard PAC model introduced by Valiant [22] the learner has access to an oracle returning on each query some labeled instance $(x, C(x))$ where C is some fixed concept belonging to a given target class $\mathcal{C}$ and x is randomly drawn from a fixed distribution D over the domain X. Both C and D are unknown to the learner and each random draw of x is independent on the outcomes of the other draws.

In the malicious variant of the PAC model introduced by Kearns and Li [14] (the reader is referred to that paper for motivations) on each query the oracle is allowed to flip a coin with fixed bias η for heads. If the outcome is heads, the oracle returns some labeled instance (x, ℓ) adversarially chosen from $X \times \{0, 1\}$. If the outcome is tails, the oracle behaves exactly like in the standard model returning the correctly labeled instance $(x, C(x))$ where $x \sim D$.

In both the standard and the malicious PAC model the learner's goal on all inputs $\epsilon, \delta > 0$ is to output some hypothesis $H \in \mathcal{H}$ (where $\mathcal{H}$ is the learner's fixed hypothesis class) by querying the oracle at most m times for some $m = m(\epsilon, \delta)$ in the standard model and for some $m = m(\epsilon, \delta, \eta)$ in the malicious model. For all targets $C \in \mathcal{C}$ and distributions D, the hypothesis H of the learner must satisfy $E_{x \sim D}[H(x) \neq C(x)] \leq \epsilon$ with probability at least $1 - \delta$ with respect to the oracle's randomization.

Let B_η be a Bernoulli random variable taking value 1 with probability η. Then, for each $C \in \mathcal{C}$ the oracle for the malicious model can be described using a function Or_C taking two sequences $(x_1, \ldots, x_t) \in X^t$ and $(b_1, \ldots, b_t) \in \{0, 1\}^t$, for any $t \geq 1$, as arguments. The function Or_C returns a labeled instance $(x', \ell') \in X \times \{0, 1\}$ where $(x', \ell') = (x_t, C(x_t))$ if $b_t = 0$ and (x', ℓ') is arbitrary if $b_t = 1$.

We say that an algorithm A *learns* $\mathcal{C}$ by $\mathcal{H}$ with malicious noise η if A uses $\mathcal{H}$ as hypothesis class and for all $\epsilon, \delta > 0$,

$$E_{x \sim D}[A[x, b, \text{Or}_C](x) \neq C(x)] \leq \epsilon$$

holds with probability at least $1 - \delta$ over $(x, b) \sim D^m \times B_\eta^m$ for some $m = m(\epsilon, \delta, \eta)$ and for all distributions D, targets $C \in \mathcal{C}$, and oracles Or_C. Here $A[x, b, \text{Or}_C] \in \mathcal{H}$ is the hypothesis output by A when the input is the sequence $\langle \text{Or}_C, x, b \rangle = \langle (x'_t, \ell'_t) \rangle_t$ of the oracle's responses to A's queries.

The following simple fact is used to prove the results of this section.

Fact 17. *Choose* $0 \leq \eta < 1$, *two concepts* C, H, *an oracle* Or_C, *and a pair* $(x, b) \in X \times \{0, 1\}$. *Then*

$$(1 - \eta) E_{x \sim D}[H(x) \neq C(x)] \leq E_{(x,b) \sim D \times B_\eta}[H(x') \neq \ell']$$
$$\leq \eta + (1 - \eta) E_{x \sim D}[H(x) \neq C(x)],$$

where $(x', \ell') = Or_C(x, b)$.

We will also make use of the Höffding bounds [13] on the tails of a binomial distribution as stated below.

Lemma 18 (Höffding bounds). *For all distributions* P *over a set* X, *for all families* $\mathcal{F}$ *of* $\{0,1\}$-*valued random variables* F *on* $X^+ = \bigcup_{i \geq 1} X^i$ *which are measurable with respect to* P^+, *and for all* $\alpha > 0$. *If for all* $F \in \mathcal{F}$, $P\{x : F(x_1, \ldots, x_i; x) = 1\} \leq \mu$ *for all* $i \geq 0$ *and all* $(x_1, \ldots, x_i) \in X^i$, *then*

$$P^m \left\{ x \in X^m : \sup_{F \in \mathcal{F}} \sum_{i=1}^{m} F(x^i) \geq (\mu + \alpha)m \right\} \leq |\mathcal{F}| \exp\left[-\frac{m\alpha^2}{2} \right].$$

The following is a conversion of an on-line algorithm A to a PAC learning algorithm A_{pac}.

Algorithm A_{pac}.
Input: N samples of size m_1 each and one labeled sample of size m_2.
1. Let $\mathcal{H}_0$ be the empty set.
2. For $i = 1, \ldots, N$:
   - Initialize algorithm A.
   - Run A on the ith sample of size m_1 and put all hypotheses generated during the run in $\mathcal{H}_0$.
3. Output the hypothesis in $\mathcal{H}_0$ with minimal error on the sample of size m_2.

We are now ready to present the main result of this section (proof deferred to the full paper) showing that the algorithm A_{pac} (sketched above) can learn in the PAC model with malicious noise. In the analysis of A_{pac} a trade-off exists between the tolerable noise rate and the sample complexity. We worked towards obtaining a high noise rate while keeping the sample size polynomial.

Theorem 19. *Let A be an on-line learning algorithm such that for some positive integer m_0 and for all $m \geq m_0$ $MB(A, C, \mathcal{H}, rm) \leq m$ holds. Then for all $\alpha > 0$ the algorithm A_{pac} using A as a subroutine learns C using hypothesis class $\mathcal{H}$ in the PAC model with a malicious error rate of $\frac{r\epsilon}{4(r+1)+r\epsilon} - \alpha$, where ϵ is the required accuracy. A_{pac} uses a sample of total size*

$$m = O\left[\frac{1}{\alpha^2\epsilon^2}\left(\ln\frac{1}{\delta} + \ln\left(\frac{1}{\epsilon} + \frac{1}{\alpha^2}\ln\frac{1}{\delta}\right)\right) + \frac{1}{\alpha^2}\left(\ln\frac{1}{\delta}\right)^2\right]$$

and runs in time polynomial in m and the running time of A.

In the case $\mathcal{H}$ has finite cardinality, we can get a better noise tolerance with a simpler analysis as shown by the next result.

Algorithm A_{fin}.
Input: A labeled sample $(x_1, \ell_1), \ldots, (x_m, \ell_m)$.
1. Initialize algorithm A.
2. Remove from the sample a counterexample (x_i, ℓ_i) to A's current hypothesis and present it to A until all examples have been removed from the sample or no further counterexamples can be found.
3. Output A's current hypothesis $H \in \mathcal{H}$.

Theorem 20. *Let A be an on-line learning algorithm such that for some positive integer m_0 and for all $m \geq m_0$ $MB(A, C, \mathcal{H}, rm) \leq m$ holds. Then for all $\alpha > 0$ the algorithm A_{fin} using A as a subroutine learns C using hypothesis class $\mathcal{H}$ in the PAC model with a malicious error rate of $\frac{r\epsilon}{1+r\epsilon} - \alpha$, where ϵ is the required accuracy. A_{pac} uses a sample of size*

$$m = \max\left\{\frac{4m_0}{\epsilon}, \frac{8}{\alpha^2\epsilon^2}\left(\ln(|\mathcal{H}| + 1) + \ln\frac{1}{\delta}\right)\right\}$$

and runs in time polynomial in m and the running time of A.

Proof. Choose $\epsilon, \delta, \alpha > 0$, a malicious error rate $\eta = \eta_b - \alpha$ where $\eta_b = \frac{r\epsilon}{1+r\epsilon}$, a distribution D over X, and a malicious oracle Or_C. Let A be an on-line learning algorithm. Let $K/r \geq m_0$ and choose $(x, b) \in X^m \times \{0,1\}^m$ for $m \geq K/r$. Run A_{fin} on the sample $\langle Or_C, x, b\rangle$. If $\#1(b) \leq K$, then A can receive at most K/r counterexamples. Thus, the hypothesis $H^* \in \mathcal{H}$ output by A_{fin} will be correct on the remaining sample of size at least $m - K/r$. Denoting by $\hat{er}(H^*)$ the average error of H^* on $\langle Or_C, x, b\rangle$, we then have $\hat{er}(H^*) \leq \frac{K}{rm}$.
Now draw $(x, b) \sim D^m \times B_\eta^m$ (where $m \geq 4m_0/\epsilon$) and let $K = (\eta_b - \alpha/2)m$. Since $\alpha \leq \eta_b$ $K/r \geq m_0$. Consider the following events:

1. $\#1(b) \leq K$,
2. for all $H \in \mathcal{H}$, if $E_{(x,b)\sim D \times B_\eta}[H(x_t) \neq \ell_t] > \frac{K}{rm} + \alpha/2$ for all $1 \leq t \leq m$ where $(x_t, \ell_t) = \mathrm{Or}_C(x^{t-1}x, b^{t-1}b)$, then $\hat{\mathrm{er}}(H) > \frac{K}{rm}$.

By Höffding bounds the probability that event 1 does not hold is at most $\exp(-\alpha^2 m/8)$. Also, the probability that event 2 does not hold for some $H \in \mathcal{H}$ is at most $|\mathcal{H}|\exp(-\alpha^2 m/8)$. For $m \geq \frac{8}{\alpha^2 \epsilon^2}\left(\ln(|\mathcal{H}|+1) + \ln\frac{1}{\delta}\right)$ the probability that any of the two events does not hold is at most δ. Given that both event 1 and 2 hold, we have $E_{(x,b)\in D \times B_\eta}[H^*(x_t) \neq \ell_t] \leq (\eta_b - \alpha/2)/r + \alpha/2 = \eta_b/r \leq (1-\eta_b)\epsilon$ for any $1 \leq t \leq m$. By Fact 17, first inequality, and the above we conclude $E_{x\sim D}[H^*(x) \neq C(x)] \leq \epsilon$ with probability at least $1 - \delta$ for $m \geq \max\left\{\frac{4m_0}{\epsilon}, \frac{8}{\alpha^2 \epsilon^2}\left(\ln(|\mathcal{H}|+1) + \ln\frac{1}{\delta}\right)\right\}$. $\square$

By applying the results of Section 3 we can then prove the following.

Theorem 21. *The class* PARITY$_n$ *of parity functions over* $\{0,1\}^n$ *is learnable in the PAC model with any malicious noise rate* $\eta < \frac{\epsilon}{n+1+\epsilon}$ *in time polynomial in* $\frac{1}{\delta}$ *and* $\left(\frac{\epsilon}{n+1+\epsilon} - \eta\right)^{-1}$.

The proof of Theorem 21 is immediate from Theorem 20, Corollary 13, and the fact $|\text{PARITY}_n| = 2^n$. Results analogous to Theorem 21 can be obtained for the concept classes MON$_n$, k-CNF$_n$, k-RSE$_n$, and $\mathcal{L}^k(n)$. It should be also noted that there exist techniques to efficiently turn any learning algorithms for the noise-free PAC model into algorithms tolerating a certain rate of malicious noise. In [14, Theorem 11, p. 824] it is shown that any PAC learning algorithm using sample size m can be efficiently turned into an algorithm tolerating a malicious noise rate of $\frac{\ln m}{m}$. Moreover, using [9, Corollary 8, p. 10] and a result from [5], it can be shown how to efficiently use any PAC learning algorithm with finite hypothesis space of VC-dimension d to learn in presence of a malicious noise rate arbitrarily close to $\frac{\epsilon}{7d+1+\epsilon}$.

7 Conclusions and open problems

In this paper we have introduced a new on-line algorithm (a simple variant of the popular "Closure Algorithm") for learning intersection-closed concept classes while tolerating a bounded fraction of adversarial noise. In several natural cases the running time of our algorithm has been shown to be polynomial in the problem's parameters. To our knowledge, this is the first example of a quite general and efficient on-line strategy for learning in presence of noise.

We are currently investigating the extension of our results to the noisy learning of nested differences of intersection-closed concept classes (see [10].) An open problem is whether the sample size bounds for converting an on-line algorithm to a malicious PAC learning algorithm can be substantially improved without being dependent on the size of the hypothesis class as in Theorem 20.

Acknowledgments

Nicolò Cesa-Bianchi is also with DSI, Università di Milano (Italy). Email cesabian0dsi.unimi.it. His work was partially supported by the "Progetto finalizzato sistemi informatici e calcolo parallelo" of CNR under grant 91.00884.69.115.09672 and by EU through the NeuroCOLT project.

References

1. D. Angluin. Queries and concept learning. *Machine Learning*, 2:319–342, 1988.
2. P. Auer. On-line learning of rectangles in noisy environments. In *Proceedings of the 6th Annual ACM Workshop on Computational Learning Theory*, pages 253–261. ACM Press, 1993.
3. P. Auer and P.M Long. Simulating access to hidden information while learning. In *Proceedings of the 26th ACM Symposium on the Theory of Computation*, pages 263–272. ACM Press, 1994.
4. S. Boucheron. Learnability from positive examples in the Valiant framework. Manuscript, 1988.
5. N. Cesa-Bianchi. Models of learning with noise. Manuscript, 1994.
6. N. Cesa-Bianchi, Y. Freund, D.P. Helmbold, and M.K. Warmuth. On-line prediction and conversion strategies. In *Proceedings of the First Euro-COLT Workshop*. The Institute of Mathematics and its Applications, 1994. To appear.
7. P. Fischer and H.U. Simon. On learning ring-sum-expansions. *SIAM Journal on Computing*, 21:181–192, 1992.
8. D. Haussler, N. Littlestone, and M.K. Warmuth. Predicting $\{0,1\}$ functions on randomly drawn points. Technical Report UCSC-CRL-90-54, University of California at Santa Cruz, 1990. An extended abstract appeared in: *Proceedings of the 29th Annual Symposium on the Foundations of Computer Science*.

9. D.P. Helmbold and P.M Long. Tracking drifting concepts by minimizing disagreements. Technical Report UCSC-CRL-91-26, University of California at Santa Cruz, 1991.

10. D.P. Helmbold, R. Sloan, and M.K. Warmuth. Learning nested differences of intersection-closed concept classes. *Machine Learning*, 5(2):165–196, 1990.

11. D.P. Helmbold, R. Sloan, and M.K. Warmuth. Learning integer lattices. *SIAM Journal on Computing*, 21(2):240–266, 1992.

12. D.P. Helmbold and M.K. Warmuth. On weak learning. Technical Report UCSC-CRL-92-54, University of California at Santa Cruz, 1992.

13. W. Hoeffding. Probability inequalities for sums of bounded random variables. *Journal of the American Statistical Association*, 58:13–30, 1963.

14. M.J. Kearns and M. Li. Learning in the presence of malicious errors. *SIAM Journal on Computing*, 22(4):807–837, 1993. A preliminary version appeared in: *Proceedings of the 20th ACM Symposium on the Theory of Computation*.

15. N. Littlestone. Learning quickly when irrelevant attributes abound: a new linear-threshold algorithm. *Machine Learning*, 2(4):285–318, 1988.

16. N. Littlestone. From on-line to batch learning. In *Proceedings of the 2nd Annual Workshop on Computational Learning Theory*, pages 269–284. Morgan Kaufmann, 1989.

17. N. Littlestone. *Mistake Bounds and Logarithmic Linear-threshold Learning Algorithms*. PhD thesis, University of California at Santa Cruz, 1989.

18. N. Littlestone and M.K. Warmuth. The weighted majority algorithm. Technical Report UCSC-CRL-91-28, University of California at Santa Cruz, 1991. An extended abstract appeared in: *Proceedings of the 30th Annual Symposium on the Foundations of Computer Science*.

19. B.K. Natarajan. On learning boolean functions. In *Proceedings of the 19th ACM Symposium on the Theory of Computation*, pages 296–304. ACM Press, 1987.

20. B.K. Natarajan. *Machine Learning: A Theoretical Approach*. Morgan Kaufmann, 1991.

21. A. Schrijver. *Theory of Linear and Integer Programming*. John Wiley and sons, 1986.

22. L. Valiant. A theory of the learnable. *Communications of the ACM*, 27(11):1134–1142, 1984.

Learnability with Restricted Focus of Attention guarantees Noise-Tolerance

Shai Ben-David and Eli Dichterman

Department of Computer Science
Technion - Israel Institue of Technology
Haifa 32000, Israel

Abstract. We consider the question of learning in the presence of classification noise. More specifically, we address the issue of identifying conditions that, once a learning algorithm meets them, it can be transformed into a noise-tolerant algorithm.
While the question of whether every PAC learning algorithm can be made noise-tolerant is still open, the bottom line of this work, loosely stated, is that *any* restriction on the amount of data an algorithm is allowed to retrieve from its input samples, suffices to render the existence of a noise-tolerant variant that is efficient whenever the original algorithm is. The result is obtained by proving that such a restricted learning is equivalent to learning from statistical queries, and by applying Kearns transformation from statistical learning into noise-tolerant learning.

1 Introduction

A learner, trying to learn a target concept from randomly drawn examples, may be confronted with the problem of classification noise, i.e., some of the instances he observes may be misclassified. A common paradigm for this problem, in both theoretical and experimental research, is the classification noise model, in which the true classification of each instance may be inverted with some probability (fixed and independent of the instances) [Lai87, AL88, Slo88]. The task of providing methods by which efficient learning algorithms can be efficiently strengthened to noise-tolerant ones is one of the most important in computational learning theory. As this task seems to be a very difficult one, one naturally seeks partial solutions.

A natural approach, in dealing with such a question, is to consider weaker models of learning, i.e., restrictions on the power of the learner in the learning setting, such that learnability by such weaker learners can be shown to entail learnability in the presence of noise.

A significant step in this direction was taken by Kearns, who presented a new model for learning - the Statistical Queries (SQ) model [Kea93]. In this model the learning algorithm is restricted to using only statistics of space of classified examples, rather than having the flexibility of being sensitive to properties of individual examples. It is proved in [Kea93] that any learning algorithm obeying such a restriction can be transformed into a noise-tolerant one (the transformation preserves the efficiency of the learning algorithm). Kearns demonstrates the usefulness of the SQ model by showing that many of the known efficient learning algorithms can be naturally adapted to meet the restrictions that the SQ framework imposes upon the learner.

At the same time that Kearns proposed his SQ model, the authors of this paper have independently proposed a different weakened variation of common learning models; the framework of Learning with Restricted Focus of Attention (RFA), introduced in [BDD93], models learning scenarios in which the learner may access only partial information derived from the randomly drawn classified examples. Technically speaking, the RFA setting allows the learner to use examples only via queries that he makes. These queries are functions from classified examples into some arbitrary range. Rather than seeing the example itself, the learner receives only the value of a his query function on the labeled example. By restricting the range of these functions we can guarantee that the information accessible to the learner is only partial.

The motivation behind introducing the RFA framework was to reflect real life situations in which the process of extracting information from a given example is costly, forcing the learner to settle for only a fraction of the potential data of any example. The formalism we have chosen is a very general way of imposing such a restriction; the learner may choose his query functions adaptively along the learning process, and, in its most lenient version, the only restriction imposed on these functions is an upper bound on the size of their range (this guarantees that some information remains inaccessible to the learner). We refer the reader to [BDD93] for further elaboration and motivating examples.

The main result of this work is the discovery that the two models mentioned above – learning with restricted focus of attention, and learning from statistical queries – have equivalent learning power. Applying Kearns' result, we can therefore conclude that any algorithm which learns by restricting its attention (i.e., any algorithm that uses only part of the information of any given example) can be made noise-tolerant, without giving away its efficiency.

A possible reservation about the SQ model may be that its restriction is 'not natural'; the idea of a teacher answering statistical queries does not seem to reflect a realistic learning situation. One way of viewing our results is that they provide a strong justification to the SQ model, namely, they state that *any* significant restriction imposed on the information accessible to the learner is equivalent to forcing him to acquire his knowledge via statistical queries.

Since the RFA condition is defined in the context of learning from random examples, and holds whenever an algorithm does not make full use of the information content of the examples, it is naturally applicable to many well-known algorithms. Often, a slight change (or even none) is needed to make a given PAC algorithm satisfies the RFA condition. Another way to view this work is, therefore, as providing a new and intuitive tool for the development of noise-tolerant algorithms.

A notable aspect of our transformation of an RFA algorithm into a noise-tolerant one, is that it preserves the RFA restriction. I.e., when applied to an algorithm that views the examples via a certain set of query functions, its resulting noise-tolerant version can also settle for the same set of functions to collect its data. This implies that robustness against noise can be achieved for many learning problems in which the learner is inherently restricted (see [KS90, BC92, KSS92] for hidden-variables problems, and [BDD93] for other types of restrictions).

The paper is organized as follows. In Section 2 we formally define the three learning models used in this work – the RFA model (which we also call *learning from projections*), its classification-noise extension, and the Statistical Query (SQ) model. In Section 3 we prove that, under rather lenient and easily verifiable conditions, efficient learning from projections is equivalent to efficient learning from statistical queries. In Section 4 we apply Kearns' reduction to obtain our main result, namely, that efficient RFA learning algorithms can be transformed into efficient noise-tolerant learning algorithms; furthermore, the resulting noise-tolerant algorithms are RFA algorithms (i.e. they obey the same restrictions). In both Section 3 and Section 4 we provide some examples of learning algorithms complying with the RFA restriction, thus being transformable into efficient noise-tolerant algorithms.

2 Learning Models

2.1 Learning from Projections

In [BDD93] a framework for generalizing learning models is presented – the Learning with Restricted Focus of Attention paradigm. This framework is intended to capture two basic features of many realistic learning problems. The first feature is the distinction between the data supplied to the learner by the environment, e.g. labeled examples, and the data actually collected by him, his observations. In many cases the observations used as input by the learner constitute only a small fraction of a large body of data that presents in the examples. (As an example consider a researcher investigating the social life of bees. While each bee in his sample population may be considered 'an example', it is clear that the researcher's observations can cover only a tiny fraction of the information presents in each of these examples). The second feature that the RFA framework is meant to model is the flexibility available to the learner, in some scenarios, to dynamically choose how to extract observations from each incoming learning example (i.e., he may change his focus of attention while the instances are randomly drawn).

For concreteness, let us concentrate on the RFA generalization of the Valiant PAC model.

Let $\mathcal{F}$ be a class of $\{0, 1\}$-valued functions (concepts) over an instance space X. We assume that there is a fixed but arbitrary and unknown target distribution D over X, according to which random examples are generated (let $x \in D$ denote randomly drawing an instance $x \in X$ from the distribution D).

On top of these familiar PAC components we add a pair $\langle \mathcal{O}, W \rangle$; $\mathcal{O}$ is a set called the *observation space*, and W is a set of functions $w : X \times \{0, 1\} \to \mathcal{O}$, which we call *projectors*. In trying to learn a *target function* $f \in \mathcal{F}$, the learner is given access to an oracle $EX_{f,D}(\cdot)$, which gets as input a projector $w \in W$, draws a random instance $x \in D$, and returns the projection $w(x, f(x))$. The data-collection mechanism just described is the new element that distinguishes the RFA model from the familiar PAC learning scene.

The definitions of successful learning and of efficient algorithms, listed in the remainder of this subsection, are exactly like in the PAC model and are mentioned only for the sake of completeness of the representation.

After the learning phase the learner chooses a hypothesis $h : X \to \{0, 1\}$ from the *hypothesis class* $\mathcal{H}$. The error of any h with respect to f and D is measured by $error(h) \triangleq \Pr_{x \in D}[h(x) \neq f(x)]$, and a hypothesis h is called ϵ-good if $error(h) \leq \epsilon$.

Usually there is a natural complexity parameter n associated with the domain X, implying parameterization of the other components of the learning problem ($\mathcal{F}, \mathcal{H}, \mathcal{O}$ and W). For instance, n can be the number of boolean variables or the number of real dimensions in the Euclidean space. Another complexity parameter is the smallest representation length of the target function f, denoted by $size(f)$.

Definition 1 (learning from projections). $\mathcal{F}$ is efficiently learnable *via* W (and using $\mathcal{H}$), if there is an algorithm A, such that for every $f \in \mathcal{F}$, any distribution D, and every $0 < \epsilon, \delta \leq 1$, given inputs ϵ, δ, n and $size(f)$, and given access to the oracle $EX_{f,D}(\cdot)$, A halts in time $poly(\epsilon^{-1}, \delta^{-1}, n, size(f))$, and with probability of at least $1 - \delta$ outputs an ϵ-good hypothesis $h \in \mathcal{H}$.

As our main results apply to efficiently computable projectors, we restrict the projector class W to be efficiently computable ; that is, $w(x, f(x))$ can be computed in time $poly(\epsilon^{-1}, \delta^{-1}, n, size(f))$, for every $w \in W$ and every $x \in X$.

2.2 Noise-Tolerant Learning

In many learning situations the correct classification of some of the examples may be randomly corrupted. A common paradigm for this problem, in both theoretical and experimental research, is the *classification-noise* model. The classification-noise model replaces the (deterministic) classification of the examples supplied to the learner, by a random i.i.d. variable that has some fixed probability η of assuming the inverse of the true classification value, and with probability $(1 - \eta)$ assumes the correct classification value [KL88, Lai87, Slo88, AL88].

To incorporate this variant into the RFA learning scheme, we fix a *noise rate* $0 \leq \eta < 1/2$ and replace the oracle $EX_{f,D}(\cdot)$ with an oracle $EX_{f,D}^{\eta}(\cdot)$. This oracle gets a projector $w \in W$, draws $x \in D$, and returns $w(x, f(x))$ with probability $1 - \eta$, and $w(x, 1 - f(x))$ with probability η (note that this model assume a noisy source of classified examples, while the projecting mechanism is noise-free).

As before, an efficient learning algorithm has to find an ϵ-good hypothesis with high probability, but now we let its running time be also polynomial in $(\frac{1}{2} - \eta)^{-1}$. For sake of simplicity we assume that the noise rate η is known to the learner. It is shown in [Lai87, Kea93] how to handle unknown noise rate.

2.3 Statistical Learning

As mentioned in the introduction above, the Statistical Queries model of learning was introduced by Kearns [Kea93]. In this model, rather than having an access to randomly drawn examples, the learner interacts with a statistical oracle in the following way: the learner may ask the oracle a statistical query, which consists of a function $w : X \times \{0,1\} \to \{0,1\}$, and an accuracy parameter α. The oracle returns an estimation of $\Pr_{x \in D}[w(x, f(x)) = 1]$ up to an additive factor of α (D is the underlying distribution over X and f is the target function).

An efficient learner may only query for efficiently computable functions, i.e. functions which are computable in time $poly(\epsilon^{-1}, \delta^{-1}, n, size(f))$, and the accuracy parameter may not be smaller than an inverse of a polynomial (in $\epsilon^{-1}, \delta^{-1}, n$ and $size(f)$).

Since the statistical oracle always gives a good estimation, the model defined in [Kea93] does not include the confidence parameter δ (that does exist in the PAC model). We discuss randomized learning algorithms and, therefore, choose to keep the confidence parameter, allowing for a probability of failure of the learning algorithm. Indeed, in transforming a learning algorithm into a noise-tolerant one, we first transform it into a *randomized* statistical algorithm.

The statistical model is weaker than Valiant's model. That is, any statistical algorithm can be simulated by a learning algorithm in Valiant's model (using random samples to estimate statistics). The converse, however, is not true ; the class of parity functions is efficiently learnable in Valiant's model, but is not efficiently learnable from statistical queries.

The usefulness of the statistical model is mainly due to the following theorem:

Theorem 2 (Kearns 93). *If $\mathcal{F}$ is efficiently learnable from statistical queries then $\mathcal{F}$ is efficiently learnable in the presence of classification noise.*

The theorem was proved by Kearns for deterministic statistical algorithm, but can be adapted to hold for randomized statistical algorithms as well. In addition, the theorem holds also in the framework of fixed distributions (see [BI88] for a discussion on learnability under a fixed and known distribution).

Another extension of the statistical model is to give the learner an access to an oracle which supplies unclassified instances drawn from the underlying target distribution D. Since the instances themselves are not corrupted, both the statistical algorithm and its noise-tolerant transform can use this extra oracle in exactly the same way, so Theorem 2 holds in this extended model as well. Notice that this extra oracle can be used by the learning algorithm to compute a fine estimation of an unknown target distribution. In many cases, it is the use of this oracle that enhance a statistical algorithm with the quality of being distribution-free.

3 RFA learning vs. SQ Learning

In this section we show that under certain conditions learning with restricted focus of attention is equivalent to learning from statistical queries. It is proved in [Kea93] that efficient statistical learning implies efficient PAC learning (in the Valiant noise-free model). This implication is based on the possibility of answering any statistical query (w, α) by drawing a sufficiently large sample. Observing that such a sample can be drawn via w (letting the observation space be $\mathcal{O} = \{0, 1\}$ we may regard any query as a projector), and that the statistical learning algorithm may be randomized as well, we get the following:

Proposition 3. *If $\mathcal{F}$ is efficiently learnable using a statistical query class W, then $\mathcal{F}$ is efficiently learnable via (projector class) W.*

Proof sketch. Let A be a (randomized) statistical algorithm, which asks $m = m(\epsilon, \delta/2, n, size(f))$ statistical queries from the class W, and produces with probability of at least $1 - \frac{\delta}{2}$ an ϵ-good hypothesis. A learning algorithm B which learns via the projector class W can simulate the statistical oracle by taking a sufficiently large sample for each query. Given a query (w, α), B draws a sample of size $O(\frac{1}{\alpha^2} \log \frac{2m}{\delta})$ via the projector w, and computes the fraction $\hat{p}_w$ of the positive observations. Having a sample of that size, it can be verified using Chernoff bounds that, with probability of at least $1 - \frac{\delta}{2m}$, the estimation $\hat{p}_w$ is close to the true probability $p_w = \Pr[w = 1]$ within an additive factor of α. Thus, with probability of at least $1 - \frac{\delta}{2}$, all the estimations of the simulating algorithm B are sufficiently accurate, and B produces with probability of at least $1 - \delta$ an ϵ-good hypothesis. $\qquad\qquad\square$

Next we show that under certain condition the converse implication is also true ; namely, that learning from projections implies statistical learning. To formalize this implication we first review some basic notions from the theory of randomized computation. In the sequel we assume that X is finite (and depends on the complexity parameter n), and for every $S \subseteq X$ we denote by $D[S]$ the probability $\Pr_{x \in D}(S)$

Definition 4 (statistical distance). We define a metric on the class of distributions over a domain X. Let D, D' be two distributions on X. The *statistical distance* between D and D' is defined by

$$\Delta_s(D, D') \triangleq \frac{1}{2} \sum_{x \in X} |D[\{x\}] - D'[\{x\}]|$$

It is easy to verify that the statistical distance is indeed a metric (i.e., it is symmetric, it satisfies the triangle inequality, and $\Delta_s(D, D) = 0$ for every distribution D).

Proposition 5. *Let $\underline{D} = \langle D_i \rangle_{i=1}^m$ and $\underline{D}' = \langle D_i' \rangle_{i=1}^m$ be two m-fold product distribution over X^m. Then*

$$\Delta_s(\underline{D}, \underline{D}') \leq \Sigma_{i=1}^m \Delta_s(D_i, D_i')$$

Proof. Define $H_i \triangleq \langle D_1, \ldots, D_i, D_{i+1}', \ldots, D_m' \rangle$, for every $0 \leq i \leq m$. Since $H_0 = \underline{D}'$ and $H_m = \underline{D}$, it is sufficient (using iteratively the triangle inequality) to observe that $\Delta_s(H_{i-1}, H_i) = \Delta_s(D_i, D_i')$ for every $1 \leq i \leq n$. $\qquad\qquad\square$

The following definitions of efficiently computable distribution and efficiently samplable distribution originate from [BDCGL92].

Definition 6 (efficiently computable distribution). Let D be a distribution over X (with complexity parameter n). D is *efficiently computable* if there exists an efficient (polynomial in n) deterministic algorithm, which on input x produces $D[\{u \in X : u \leq x\}]$ (where '$<$' may be any order on X).

Definition 7 (efficiently samplable distribution). Let D be a distribution over X (with complexity parameter n). D is *efficiently samplable* if there exists an efficient (polynomial in n) probabilistic algorithm which produces $x \in X$ with probability $D[\{x\}]$.

Theorem 8 ([BDCGL92]). *Every efficiently computable distribution is also efficiently samplable.*

Definition 9 (observable projector class). A class W of projectors $w : X \times \{0,1\} \to \mathcal{O}$ is observable if $|\mathcal{O}| = poly(n)$.

Definition 10 (induced projector class). Let $\mathcal{O}$ be any observation space and let W be a projector class over an observation space $\mathcal{O}$. Define, for every projector $w \in W$ and every observation $z \in \mathcal{O}$, a projector

$$w_z(x,y) \triangleq \begin{cases} 0 & w(x,y) \neq z \\ 1 & w(x,y) = z \end{cases}$$

(Notice that w_z is efficiently computable whenever w is). Let $W_\mathcal{O}$ denote the projector class $\{w_z : w \in W , z \in \mathcal{O}\}$. We call $W_\mathcal{O}$ the projector class induced by W on $\mathcal{O}$.

We are now ready to prove that essentially any algorithm which learns from projections can be transformed into a statistical learning algorithm.

Theorem 11. *If $\mathcal{F}$ is efficiently learnable via an observable projector class W, then $\mathcal{F}$ is efficiently learnable using the statistical query class $W_\mathcal{O}$.*

Proof. Let A be a learning algorithm for the class $\mathcal{F}$, which uses the projector class W. We construct a statistical algorithm B which uses statistics in order to provide A with observations derived from a distribution D' which is statistically close to the target distribution D.

Assume that A uses $m = m(\epsilon, \delta/2, n, size(f))$ observations, via the projectors $w_1, \ldots, w_m$, and let $|\mathcal{O}| = l = poly(n)$. For each projector $w \in \{w_1, \ldots, w_m\}$, B has to supply A with an observation $w(x, f(x))$, where $(x, f(x))$ is a randomly drawn classified example. To generate such an observation B makes a sequence of queries ; for each $z \in \mathcal{O}$, B presents the query $(w_z, \frac{\delta}{2ml})$ (since w is efficiently computable so is w_z, and $\frac{2ml}{\delta}$ is polynomial in $\epsilon^{-1}, \delta^{-1}$, n, and $size(f)$). Upon receiving the estimations from the statistical oracle, B has a set of l probabilities, constituting a distribution P' over the observation space $\mathcal{O}$. Since $l = poly(n)$, the distribution P' is efficiently computable, and by Theorem 8, it is also efficiently samplable; i.e., B can efficiently draw a random observation $z \in \mathcal{O}$ from the distribution P'. Let P denote the true distribution induced on $\mathcal{O}$ by the target distribution D, by the target function f, and by the projector w. Then $\Delta_s(P, P') \leq l \cdot \frac{\delta}{2ml} = \frac{\delta}{2m}$.

The target distribution D, the target function f, and the sequence of projectors $\langle w_i \rangle_{i=1}^m$, induce an m-fold product distribution $\underline{P}$ on $\mathcal{O}^m$. Fix any valid statistical oracle, i.e., an oracle which gives estimations which are accurate up to an additive factor of $\frac{\delta}{2ml}$. Such an oracle induces a product distribution $\underline{P}'$ on $\mathcal{O}$, which by Proposition 5 satisfies $\Delta_s(\underline{P}, \underline{P}') \leq \frac{\delta}{2}$.

The probability that A fails to find an ϵ-good hypothesis, when fed with $m = m(\epsilon, \delta/2, n, \text{size}(f))$ observations drawn by $\underline{P}$, is bounded by $\delta/2$. Since the statistical distance between $\underline{P}$ and $\underline{P}'$ is bounded by $\delta/2$, it follows that the failure probability of A, when fed with observations drawn from $\underline{P}'$, is bounded by δ. Thus, B is guaranteed to succeed with probability of at least $1 - \delta$. □

Example 1. Consider the class of k-DNF formulas, for which an efficient learning algorithm appears in [Val84]. Let $\mathcal{O} = \{0,1\}^{k+1}$, and define, for any set s of k variables, a projector w_s which maps any classified example into an observation consisting of $k + 1$ bits ; the first k bits are the values of the variables which are in the set s (the projection of the instance on the set s), and the $(k + 1)'th$ bit is the classification bit. In [BDD93] a variant of Valiant's algorithm is shown to efficiently learns $\mathcal{F}$ via the projector class $W = \{w_s : s \subset \{1, \ldots, n\}, |s| = k\}$. The algorithm observes a sample via the projector $w_s \in W$, and for each of the terms corresponding to the set s, verifies its existence in the target function; it excludes from its hypothesis (initially consists of all possible terms) each term negatively observed. Since $|\mathcal{O}| = 2^{k+1}$ (k is fixed and independent of n), we can apply Theorem 11, deriving an efficient statistical learning algorithm for k-DNF. In Section 4 we show that this implies the existence of an efficient noise-tolerant algorithm for k-DNF via W.

Definition 12 (insensitive projector classes). We say that a projector $w : X \times \{0,1\} \rightarrow \mathcal{O}$ is *insensitive* if $w(x, 0) = w(x, 1)$ for every $x \in X$. A projector class W is called insensitive if each $w \in W$ is insensitive.

Corollary 13. If $\mathcal{F}$ is efficiently learnable via $W \cup W'$, where W is observable and W' is insensitive, then $\mathcal{F}$ is efficiently learnable in the (extended) model for learning from statistical queries (using the query class $W_\mathcal{O}$).

Proof. Recall that the statistical model can be extended to include an oracle which supplies unclassified instances from the (unknown) underlying distribution. The simulating algorithm may use this oracle to supply the learning algorithm with insensitive observations. □

Example 2. Let $\mathcal{F}$ be the class of axis-aligned rectangles in $\mathbb{R}^n$, and let $W = \{w_I^i : I = [a, b] \subset \mathbb{R}, 1 \leq i \leq n\}$, where $w_I^i(x_1, \ldots, x_n, y)$ is $(1, y)$ if $x_i \in I$ and $(0, y)$ otherwise. That is, for each axis x_i, and for each interval I on that axis, there is a projector w_I^i which indicates whether an instance is drawn in the cylinder defined by I, and whether it is positive or negative.

A slight variation on the algorithms presented in [BDD93, Kea93] yields a learning algorithm for $\mathcal{F}$ via W, provided that the underlying distribution is known. The learning algorithm partitions each axis x_i into $\frac{n}{\epsilon}$ intervals, such that, for each interval I there is a probability of roughly $\frac{\epsilon}{n}$ of drawing an instance whose x_i's coordinate falls in I. Then, for each axis x_i and each interval I of x_i's partition, the algorithm observes a sufficiently large sample via w_I^i, and finds the edge intervals of the projection of the target rectangle on x_i (e.g., the smaller edge point of x_i is the smaller edge point of the first interval in x_1 for which a positive observation was received).

By Theorem 11 there is an efficient statistical algorithm for learning $\mathcal{F}$, implying an efficient noise-tolerant algorithm for learning $\mathcal{F}$ via W.

Armed with a proper class of insensitive projectors, this algorithm can be made distribution-free. Specifically, let $W' = \{w_i : 1 \le i \le n\}$, where w_i maps the example $(x_1, \ldots, x_n, y)$ into x_i (notice that this projector class still imposes a significant restriction on observability). The learning algorithm can use W' to compute the axis partitions needed to find the projections of the target rectangle (see [BDD93, Kea93] for the details).

The transformation scheme presented in Theorem 11 and Corollary 13 can be also applied to non-efficient learning algorithms; any non-trivial time bound on the running time of the RFA learning algorithm implies a corresponding non-trivial time-bound on the running time of the statistical algorithm.

Example 3. In [LMN89] a learning algorithm for the class of AC^0 boolean circuits is demonstrated, with respect to the uniform distribution (a generalization for product distributions appears in [FJS91]). The learning algorithm is not efficient ; its running time is $O(n^{2k} + \log \frac{n}{\delta})$, where $k = O(\log^d \frac{n}{\epsilon})$ and d is the depth of the target circuit.

The algorithm learns the target function by estimating the coefficients of its Fourier representation with respect to the basis $B = \{\chi_S : S \subset \{1, \ldots, n\}\}$, where $\chi_S(x_1, \ldots, x_n) = \sum_{i \in S} x_i \bmod 2$. It is shown in [LMN89] that it is sufficient to estimate the coefficients corresponding to the subset $\{\chi_S \in B : |S| = k\}$. The algorithm can be easily adapted to learn via the projector class $W \triangleq \{w_S : S \subset \{1, \ldots, n\}, |S| = k\}$, where $w_S(x_1, \ldots, x_n, y) = (\chi_S(x_1, \ldots, x_n), y)$ (the running time is multiplied by a factor of $|W| = O(n^k)$; see [BDD93] for the details). As the observation space of this algorithm is of size 4, there is a statistical learning algorithm which runs in time $O(n^{poly(\log n)})$, implying a noise-tolerant version with the same time bound.

We conclude this section by noting that the restriction made on the projector class in Theorem 11 and its consequences can be somewhat relaxed. We shall only define the notion of a *weakly observable projector class* and postpone to the full paper the proof that Theorem 11 (as well as all of its subsequent implications) remain valid when the observability condition they require is replaced by weak observability.

Definition 14. A class W of projectors $w : X \times \{0, 1\} \to \mathcal{O}$ is *weakly observable* with respect to a class $\mathcal{F}$ of functions $f : X \to \{0, 1\}$), if there is an algorithm A, such that for every distribution D over X and every $f \in \mathcal{F}$, given $w \in W$ and $0 < \epsilon, \delta \leq 1$, and using observations via W, A halts in time $poly(\epsilon^{-1}, \delta^{-1}, n, size(f))$, and outputs a partition Z of the observation space $\mathcal{O}$, and a corresponding set of probabilities P, such that $|Z| = |P| = poly(\epsilon^{-1}, \delta^{-1}, n, size(f))$, and, with probability of at least $1 - \delta$, P constitutes a distribution on Z which is statistically ϵ-close to the distribution induced by D, f and w on Z.

Example 4. First notice that instead of learning via the observable class of projectors in Example 2, the learning algorithm may use the weakly observable class $\{w_i : 1 \leq i \leq n\}$, where $w_i(x_1, \dots, x_n, y) = (x_i, y)$. As an example for the limitation of this notion, consider the problem of learning the class of parity functions under the uniform distribution. There exists an efficient learning algorithm for this class via the identity projector $w(x_1, \dots, x_n, y) = (x_1, \dots, x_n, y)$ (by solving a system of n linear equations modulo 2). Since this class is not efficiently learnable from statistical queries ([Kea93]) (even with respect to the uniform distribution), the class $\{w\}$ is not weakly observable. I.e., given ϵ (say $\frac{1}{4}$), no algorithm can efficiently find a polynomial-sized partition of the observation space $\{0, 1\}^{n+1}$, and a corresponding set of probabilities, constituting a distribution which is statistically ϵ-close to the distribution induced on the partition by the unknown parity function (and the uniform distribution).

4 From RFA Learning to Noise-Tolerance

In [Kea93] Kearns shows how to simulate statistical queries using noisy examples (Theorem 2 above). Adapting his result to randomized learning algorithms, and using Theorem 11 we get the following result.

Corollary 15. If $\mathcal{F}$ is efficiently learnable via an observable projector class W, then $\mathcal{F}$ is efficiently learnable in the presence of classification noise (with no restriction on observability).

Thus, all the learning algorithms mentioned in the examples of Section 3, complying with the observability constrains, can be transformed into noise-tolerant ones. Actually, we can show that the resulting noise-tolerant algorithm obtained by the transformation is still an RFA algorithm. This feature may be of great importance in scenarios in which observability is inherently restricted, or in cases where each observed bit incurs some cost on the learner. In such cases it is desired to obtain a learning algorithm which is noise-tolerant, but still obey certain observability restrictions.

Definition 16 (sensitive projector class). A projector $w : X \times \{0, 1\} \to \mathcal{O}$ is *sensitive* if for every $x \in X$ and every $y \in \{0, 1\}$, the value y can be efficiently computed from $w(x, y)$. The class W is sensitive if each $w \in W$ is sensitive.

Theorem 17. *If $\mathcal{F}$ is efficiently learnable via $W \cup W'$, where W is observable and sensitive and W' is insensitive, then $\mathcal{F}$ is efficiently learnable via $W \cup W'$ in the presence of classification noise.*

Proof. First notice that the noise has no effect on the use of insensitive projectors. By Theorem 11 it is sufficient to prove that if $\mathcal{F}$ is efficiently learnable from statistical queries $W_{\mathcal{O}}$, then it is efficiently learnable via W in the presence of classification noise.

Basically, the same simulation of [Kea93] is valid here, where for each query (w_z, α), $w_z \in W_{\mathcal{O}}$, the simulating algorithm takes a large noisy sample, and estimate $p_{w_z} = \Pr[w_z = 1]$, using estimations of probabilities obtained from the noisy examples. The reason for ensuring that W is sensitive is that, in estimating p_{w_z}, one of the probabilities needed to be estimated is the probability of drawing an instance x for which $w_z(x, y) = w_z(x, 1 - y)$; this cannot be done unless w_z is sensitive. $\qquad\square$

Learning is usually done via a sensitive projector class W. In such cases, we get that the noise-tolerant algorithm obtained by Theorem 17 uses the same projectors as the original algorithm. Furthermore, any projector class W can be made sensitive, simply by projecting, in addition to $w(x, y)$, the classification bit y. That is, we may replace each $w \in W$ with the projector $\tilde{w} = (w(x, y), y)$, thus obtaining a sensitive projector class $\{\tilde{w} : w \in W\}$, where the size of observation space is multiplied by a factor of 2. Thus, the restriction on the sensitivity of the projector class in Theorem 17 is very lenient. That is, in any case, the restrictions obeyed by the original learning algorithm are also obeyed by the resulting noise-tolerant transform.

Example 5. Theorem 17 can be applied to all the algorithms mentioned in Section 3.

k-DNF Formulas: The learning algorithm mentioned in Example 1 learns k-DNF formulas via an observable and sensitive projector class W. Thus, we can apply Theorem 17 to obtain an efficient noise-tolerant learning algorithm for k-DNF via W (compare with the algorithm presented in [AL88]).

Axis-aligned Rectangles: In Example 2 we demonstrated that the class of axis-aligned rectangles in $\mathbb{R}^n$ is efficiently learnable via a projector class $W \cup W'$, where W is observable and sensitive and W' is insensitive. Applying Theorem 17 we obtain an efficient noise-tolerant algorithm which learns that class via $W \cup W'$.

AC^0 Boolean Circuits: The algorithm mentioned in Example 3 learns the class of AC^0 boolean circuits (under the uniform distribution) via an observable and sensitive projector class W. Applying Theorem 17 we obtain a noise-tolerant algorithm which learns AC^0 circuits (in time $O(n^{poly(\log n)})$) via W.

Example 6. Let $\mathcal{G}$ be a class of functions $g : \mathbb{R} \rightarrow \mathbb{R}$ with finite number of extrema, and let $\mathcal{F}$ be halve-spaces in $\mathbb{R}^2$ defined by $f(x, y) = 1$ iff $y < g(x)$, for some function $g \in \mathcal{G}$. It is shown in [BDD93] how to learn $\mathcal{F}$ via $W \cup W'$, where W and W' are the same projector classes used to learn axis-aligned rectangles (see Example 2). Applying Theorem 17 we obtain an efficient noise-tolerant algorithm for learning $\mathcal{F}$ via $W \cup W'$.

Remark. Finally, we remark that the noise-tolerant algorithms obtained by the above transformations are randomized (even when the original ones are deterministic). Since a learning algorithm is allowed, by definition, to fail with some low probability (over the sample space), it seems natural to let it use random bits, and allow for some failure probability over these random bits. Furthermore, it turns out that there exists a general derandomization scheme, transforming the type of randomized algorithms we consider into deterministic algorithms, while preserving efficiency and noise-tolerance (details in the full paper).

Acknowledgment

We thank the anonymous referees for helpful comments.

References

[AL88]   Dana Angluin and Philip Laird. Learning from noisy examples. *Machine Learning*, 2(4):343–370, 1988.

[BC92]   Avrim Blum and Prasad Chalasani. Learning switching concepts. In *5th COLT*, pages 231–242, 1992.

[BDCGL92] Shai Ben-David, Benny Chor, Oded Goldreich, and Michael Luby. On the theory of average case complexity. *Journal of Computer and System Sciences*, 44(2):193–219, 1992.

[BDD93]   Shai Ben-David and Eli Dichterman. Learning with restricted focus of attention. In *6th COLT*, pages 287–296, 1993.

[BI88]   Gyora M. Benedek and Alon Itai. Learnability by fixed distributions. In *1st COLT*, pages 80–90, August 1988.

[FJS91]   Merrick L. Furst, Jeffrey C. Jackson, and Sean W. Smith. Improved learning of AC^0 functions. In *4th COLT*, pages 317–325, August 1991.

[Kea93]   Michael J. Kearns. Efficient noise-tolrant learning from statistical queries. In *25th STOC*, pages 392–401, May 1993.

[KL88]   Michael J. Kearns and Ming Li. Learning in the presence of malicious errors. In *20th STOC*, pages 267–280, May 1988.

[KS90]   Michael J. Kearns and Robert E. Schapire. Efficient distribution-free learning of probabilistic concepts. In *31st FOCS*, pages 382–391, 1990.

[KSS92]   Michael J. Kearns, Robert E. Schapire, and Linda M. Sellie. Towards efficient agnostic learning. In *5th COLT*, pages 341–352, 1992.

[Lai87]   Philip D. Laird. Learning from good and bad data. Technical Report YALEU/DCS/TR-551, Yale University, 1987. Ph.d. Dissertation.

[LMN89]   Nathan Linial, Yishai Mansour, and Noam Nisan. Constant depth circuits, fourier transform, and learnability. In *30th FOCS*, pages 574–579, 1989.

[Slo88]   Robert H. Sloan. Types of noise in data for concept learning. In *1st COLT*, pages 91–96, 1988.

[Val84]   L. G. Valiant. A theory of the learnable. *CACM*, 27(11):1134–1142, 1984.

Efficient Algorithm for Learning Simple Regular Expressions from Noisy Examples

Alvis Brāzma

Institute of Mathematics and Computer Science, University of Latvia
29 Rainis Blvd., Riga LV-1459, Latvia
E-mail: abrazma@mii.lu.lv

Abstract. We present an efficient algorithm for finding approximate repetitions in a given sequence of characters. First, we define a class of simple regular expressions which are of star-height one and do not contain union operations, and a stochastic mutation process of a given length over a string of characters. Then, assuming that a given string of characters is obtained corrupted by the defined mutation process from some long enough word generated by a simple regular expression, we try to restore the expression. We prove that to within some reasonable accuracy it is always possible if the length of the mutation process is bounded comparing to the length of the example. We provide an algorithm by which the expression can be restored in linear time in the length of the example and no worse than quadratic in the length of the expression. We discuss some extensions of the method and possible applications to bioinformatics.

1 Introduction

There has been collected and stored into databases a large amount of information about the known DNA and protein sequences. The utilization of these databases requires methods of automatic extraction of information. One of the essential tools is searching for a given pattern, or patterns which are close to the given. A separate problem is discovering useful patterns themselves by analyzing the database. A whole new scientific domain named molecular bioinformatics has recently appeared for dealing with the analysis of the biosequential information. It has been frequently acknowledged that machine learning theory would play there an essential role [11, 12].

An important property of (particularly, *eukaryotic*) genes is that 'a very large proportion [of them] is composed of DNA segments that are repeated either precisely or in variant form more than once. Copy numbers vary from two to millions. (...) Fifty percent or more of these genomes are frequently composed of reiterations, and there may in fact be very few truly unique DNA segments' [13] (pp.624-625). Periodicities are also one of the most important factor for classification of protein structure [7]. More general kind of repetitions, for instance repeated random order concatenation of two or more different substrings, can be described by regular expressions. Identification of such regular parts in a genom may tell about genom structure, properties, regulation mechanisms, and evolution.

Recently, there have been developed a number of efficient algorithms for learning regular languages [1, 4, 15], but these algorithms work only in case of perfect examples and cannot be used in presence of noise. Therefore, their applicability to problems of bioinformatics is very restricted as there are no exact rules in biology. Algorithms which are intended for applications in this field have to be able to deal with noise.

Theoretical foundations of learning in presence of noise has been studied in [2, 8, 14]. Kearns and Li [8] studied learning in presence of the so called *malicious errors*, i.e., learning from examples which are misclassified as positive and nega-tive in the worst possible way with error rate not exceeding some given constant. Angluin and Laird [2] studied "less malicious" random errors. In [16] Yamanashi studied the learning of the so called stochastic motives from noisy examples by using minimal description length principle, and in [11] a genetic algorithm based on this idea has been developed for learning stochastic substrings present in a set of sequences.

Very little has been known about efficient learning of regular languages in presence of noise. In this paper we are trying to deal with this problem, particu-larly we are interested in efficient learning of iterations in presence of noise. For instance, given a sequence:

$$\ldots\texttt{CCTGCTACGAATATAATATAAGATAATATAATATATATAATATAATATCGTTGATC}\ldots,$$

we want to obtain the expression

$$\ldots\texttt{CCTGCTACG(AATAT)}^{*}\texttt{CGTTGATC}\ldots$$

even though it does not describe the sequence precisely. We have developed an efficient algorithm which can realistically deal with large amount of information, and which run on the data would output reasonable hypothesis about which parts of the data are possibly constructed by iterating some smaller fragments.

The essence of our approach is, assuming that the data is produced by "un-folding" some simple regular expression and subsequently corrupting the unfold-ing by applying point mutations, to try to restore the original expression. We prove that, if the mutation "density" is less than a certain constant (depending on the expression), the expression can be approximately restored in linear time in the length of the data times square of the length of the expression.

The method is based on learning by pattern matching described in [4, 5], and on quick finding of the least cost path in the so called edit graph, similar to one used in [10, 17]. We prove the correctness of the algorithm and evaluate its complexity.

Although, in this paper we prove correctness of the algorithm for the case of point mutations and the class of simple regular expressions, it is easy to general-ize the algorithm also for the case of gap mutations, if gaps can be assumed not to exceed some bounded length, and for more complicated expressions. We have implemented the more general algorithms in the language C++ and performed computer experiments showing that the algorithms work also in cases which so far have not been studied theoretically. The more general cases are discussed in the last section of the paper along with other possible extensions.

The paper is organized as follows. First, in Section 2 we formulate the main results of the paper. Then, in Section 3 we present the algorithm finding the regularities in noisy data, and in Section 4 we sketch the proof of the correctness of the algorithm. Finally, in Section 5 we discuss some implications of the results and the generalizations.

2 The Main Result

We begin with defining the class of simple regular expressions, examples, and mutation process.

Let Σ be a finite alphabet such that characters $(,),*$ do not belong to Σ. Let $|\gamma|$ denote the length of the word γ. Let $\alpha_i \in \Sigma^*$ ($i = 0, \ldots, n$), $\beta_i \in \Sigma^+$ ($i = 1, \ldots, n$), and let β_i be such that for no $\beta_i' \in \Sigma^+$, and $k > 1$: $\beta_i = \beta_i'^k$ (where $\beta_i'^k$ denotes the word obtained by concatenating β_i' to itself k times). Then any word E of the type

$$E = \alpha_0(\beta_1)^*\alpha_1 \ldots \alpha_{n-1}(\beta_n)^*\alpha_n$$

($n \geq 0$) is called a *simple regular expression*. Any word

$$\gamma = \alpha_0\beta_1^{m_1}\alpha_1 \ldots \alpha_{n-1}\beta_n^{m_n}\alpha_n,$$

is called an *example of the expression E*. Example γ is called *l-expanded* (l_1-l_2-bounded) if for a positive integer l (resp., integers l_1 and l_2) and for all $1 \leq i \leq n$: $l \leq m_i$ (resp., $l_1 \leq m_i \leq l_2$).

Next let us describe a stochastic mutation process by which examples can be "corrupted". Let γ be a word over alphabet Σ, and d be a positive integer. Let $p_D, p_I,$ and p_S be nonnegative numbers, called *probabilities of deletion, insertion* and *substitution* respectively, such that $p_D + p_I + p_S = 1$. *Point mutation process of length d over γ with the given probability distributions* consists of the following four repeatedly applied steps.

1. An event called *deletion, insertion,* or *substitution* is randomly chosen with the respective probabilities p_D, p_I, and p_S (i.e., a three sided "coin" with probabilities p_D, p_I, and p_S of coming with the respective side "up" is tossed);

2. If *insertion* or *substitution* has been chosen in the previous step, an arbitrary character $\sigma_i \in \Sigma$ is randomly chosen with an equal probability (i.e., the probability of choosing any particular character from Σ is the same);

3. An arbitrary integer $j \in \{0, \ldots, |\gamma| - 1\}$, if the choice in step 1 has been *deletion* or *substitution*, or $j \in \{0, \ldots, |\gamma|\}$, if the choice has been *insertion*, is chosen with an equal probability;

4. Depending on choices in the first three steps, either j-th character is deleted from γ, or replaced by the character σ_i chosen in step 2 or the character σ_i chosen in step 2, is inserted immediately before j-th character of γ (or at the end of γ if $j = |\gamma|$).

The four steps are repeated d times each time being applied to the result of the previous mutations and taking into account the possibly changing length of γ. It γ' is obtained from γ in the described way, we say that γ' *is obtained from γ in point mutation process of length d.*

The process can easily be redefined for case of nonuniform distributions of the probabilities.

Let β and β' be two words over alphabet Σ. We say that β and β' are *cyclically equal,* if there exists such β_1 and β_2 that $\beta = \beta_1\beta_2$ and $\beta' = \beta_2\beta_1$. Let $\Theta = \{\beta_1, \ldots, \beta_n\}$, and $\Theta' = \{\beta'_1, \ldots, \beta'_m\}$. We say that the sets Θ and Θ' are *cyclically equivalent,* if for any $\beta_i \in \Theta$ there exists $\beta'_j \in \Theta'$ cyclically equal to β_i, and vice versa, for any $\beta'_i \in \Theta'$ there exists $\beta_j \in \Theta$ cyclically equal to β'_i.

The following theorem can be proved.

Theorem 1. *There exists an algorithm $\mathcal{A}_1$ such that for any $\epsilon > 0$, any $r > 1$, and any simple regular expression $E = \alpha_0(\beta_1)^*\alpha_1 \ldots (\beta_n)^*\alpha_n$, there exists a positive constant l, such that if γ is at least l-expanded example of E and γ' is a obtained from γ in a mutation process of length $d \le d_0 = |\gamma|/r \cdot max\{|\beta_i| : 1 \le i \le n\}$, then, given γ', l and d' such that $d \le d' \le d_0$, the algorithm will return a set of words Θ cyclically equivalent to $\{\beta_1, \ldots, \beta_n\}$, with the probability at least $1 - \epsilon$. The run-time of the algorithm is $O(|\gamma'||E|^2)$ in the worst case.*

If we can assume, that in obtaining the example γ, all the iterations are unfolded more or less the same number of times, the algorithm do not need to know l. More precisely:

Theorem 2. *There exists an algorithm $\mathcal{A}_2$ such that for any $\epsilon > 0$, $r > 1$, and $c \ge 1$, and any simple regular expression $E = \alpha_0(\beta_1)^*\alpha_1 \ldots (\beta_n)^*\alpha_n$, there exists a positive constant l, such that if γ is l-cl-bounded example of E and γ' is a obtained from γ in a mutation process of length $d \le d_0 = |\gamma|/r \cdot max\{|\beta_i| : 1 \le i \le n\}$, then, given γ' and d' such that $d \le d' \le d_0$, the algorithm will return set of words Θ cyclically equivalent to $\{\beta_1, \ldots, \beta_n\}$, with the probability at least $1 - \epsilon$. The run-time of the algorithm is $O(|\gamma'||E|^2)$ in the worst case.*

Under a simple additional restriction on the expression we can also find the approximate parts of the mutated example γ' which comes from the respective iterations $(\beta_i)^*$.

Let us call a simple regular expression $E = \alpha_0(\beta_1)^*\alpha_1 \ldots \alpha_{n-1}(\beta_n)^*\alpha_n$ *non-confusing,* if β_i is not cyclically equal to β_{i+1} for any $i = 1, \ldots, n - 1$.

Theorem 3. *There exists an algorithm $\mathcal{A}_3$ such that for any $\epsilon > 0$, any $r > 1$ (and $c \ge 0$), and any simple nonconfusing regular expression $E = \alpha_0(\beta_1)^*\alpha_1 \ldots (\beta_n)^*\alpha_n$, there exists a positive constant l, such that if γ is at least l-expanded* example (l-cl-bounded example) of E and γ' is a obtained from $\gamma = \alpha_0 \beta_1^{m_1} \alpha_1 \ldots$ $\alpha_{n-1} \beta_n^{m_n} \alpha_n$ in a mutation process of length $d \leq d_0 = |\gamma|/r \cdot max\{|\beta_i| : 1 \leq i \leq n\}$, then, given γ', l and d' (resp., given γ' and d') such that $d \leq d' \leq d_0$, the algorithm will return integers $p_1, \ldots, p_n$, such that $p_j - a \leq |\beta_j^{m_j}| \leq p_j + a$, where $a = O(|E| \cdot \log_{|E||\Sigma|} \epsilon + |E|)$, with the probability at least $1 - \epsilon$. The run-time of the algorithm is $O(|\gamma'||E|^2)$ in the worst case.

We define *edit distance* between two strings α and β, $edit\_distance(\alpha, \beta)$, as the smallest number of the so called *editing transformations*: insertion, deletion or substitution of one character for another, required to change the first string into the second. We call two simple regular expressions $E = \alpha_0 (\beta_1)^* \alpha_1 \ldots$ $(\beta_n)^* \alpha_n$, and $E = \alpha_0'(\beta_1')^* \alpha_1' \ldots (\beta_m')^* \alpha_m'$, *a-equivalent* ($a \geq 0$), if 1) $n = m$, 2) for every $i = 1, \ldots, n$, β_i is cyclically equal to β_i', and 3) for $i = 0, \ldots, n$, $edit\_distance(\alpha_i, \alpha_i') \leq a$.

Combining Theorems 1, 2, and 3, we can obtain

Theorem 4. *There exists an algorithm $\mathcal{A}_4$ such that for any $\epsilon > 0$, any $r > 1$ (and $c \geq 0$), and any simple nonconfusing regular expression $E = \alpha_0 (\beta_1)^* \alpha_1 \ldots$ $(\beta_n)^* \alpha_n$, there exists a positive constant l, such that if γ is at least l-expanded example (l-cl-bounded example) of E, and γ' is a obtained from γ in a mutation process of length $d \leq d_0 = |\gamma|/r \cdot max\{|\beta_i| : 1 \leq i \leq n\}$, then, given γ', l and d' (resp., given γ and d') such that $d \leq d' \leq d_0$, the algorithm will return a simple regular expression E', such that E' is a-equivalent to E, where $a = O(|E| \cdot \log_{|E||\Sigma|} \epsilon + |E|)$ with the probability at least $1 - \epsilon$. The run-time of the algorithm is $O(|\gamma'||E|^2)$ in the worst case.*

The value of a in the theorem can be reduced if we assume the additional condition that edit distances between α_i and all strings β_i' cyclically equal to β_i or β_{i+1} exceeds a certain given constant.

Our algorithms $\mathcal{A}_1, \ldots, \mathcal{A}_4$ can be generalized so that the condition $d < |\gamma|/r \cdot max\{|\beta_i| : 1 \leq i \leq n\}$ is not essential, but the run-time of the generalized algorithm is no longer linear in the length of the example. It is interesting to see whether a linear time algorithm can be found also for larger d, and what is the computational complexity of the problem depending on d. We also do not know whether it is possible to dispense with the knowledge of the length of the mutation process d' without substantially increasing the run-time.

Although, here we are formulating the results for the case of mutation process with uniform distribution of probabilities in γ and Σ, the result is valid also for more general distributions, which is important for practical applications.

In the next section we will describe the learning algorithm, and in the section 4 we will prove Theorem 1.

3   Algorithm

Let us denote by $\alpha[p..q[$ the substring of α beginning in p-th and ending in $(q-1)$-th character. In [4, 5] there is described an algorithm learning regular expression from perfect examples based on the procedure which, given a word α, and integers i and j, finds the largest n and the respective k such that $\alpha[j..j+k[=(\alpha[j..j+i[)^n$, and if n is "large enough", replaces $\alpha[j..j+k[$ by $(\alpha[j..j+i[)^*$ in α. Note that the mentioned algorithm in fact is based on pattern matching: find the largest n such that $\alpha[j..j+k[$ can be matched by $(\alpha[j..j+i[)^n$ for some k. To generalize the algorithm for imperfect examples we use "imperfect matching", or in fact calculating the edit distance, instead of matching. The basic procedure becomes the following: given α, j and i, and some constant $0 < c \leq 1$, find the largest n, such that $edit\_distance((\alpha[j..j+i[)^n, \alpha[j..j+k[) \leq ck$ for some k. Again, if n is "large enough" then $(\alpha[j..j+i[)^*$ is assumed to be the "source". For instance, let $c = 1/6$ and we are given example

$$\alpha = abcdedededdedfdeghi.$$

First, we check all the substrings of α of length 1, and for all $0 \leq j \leq |\alpha| - 1$ we find the maximal integer n, and respective k, such that $edit\_distance((\alpha[j..j])^n, \alpha[j..j+k[) \leq c \cdot k$. We do not find any larger than 1. Then we start checking substrings of length 2. For $j = 3$, $\alpha[3..4] = ed$, and we find that $edit\_distance((de)^7, dedededdedfde) = 2$, and since $2 \leq |dedededdedfde|/6$, $(de)^*$ is assumed to be the source of $\alpha[3..15]$ (assuming that 7 is "large enough").

To describe the learning algorithm more precisely let us first describe a procedure $max\_reg\_r(\alpha, i, p, c)$ which, given a string α, integers i and p, and c, such that $0 < c \leq 1$, finds the largest integer n, such that for some k the edit distance between $\alpha[i..i+k[$ and $(\alpha[i..i+p[)^n$ does not exceed $c \cdot k$. The procedure returns the n and k' such that for the particular n $edit\_distance((\alpha[i..i+p[)^n, \alpha[i..k'[))$ is the minimal for all k. Note that we cannot afford to search for the largest n simply by consecutively checking all $n = 1, 2, \ldots$, if we are to achieve the time complexity given in the theorems. The fact what makes an efficient implementation of the procedure possible is that k and n can be found very quickly by using a modification of the algorithms finding the edit distance between a string and a regular expression [10, 17]. To describe the respective algorithm we need a few more notions.

The edit distance $edit\_distance(\pi, \alpha)$ between a word α and a regular expression π is the smallest edit distance between the word α and some word which can be described by the expression π. We will represent finite state machines [3] by *transitional diagrams* which are directed, labeled graphs with one distinguished node called *starting state* and a set of distinguished nodes called *accepting states*. The edges of the graph are labeled with letters of the alphabet Σ. The machine is said to *accept* a word $a_1 \ldots a_m$ iff some path beginning at the starting state and following edges labeled $a_1, \ldots, a_m$ ends at an accepting state. An example of a finite state machine accepting the language $(abc)^*$ is given in Figure 1.

We will use a *regular expression edit graph* defined in [10, 17]. Let $\alpha = a_1 \ldots a_m$ be a string and π be a regular expression. The edit graph $G_{\alpha,\pi}$ is a directed, weighted graph which is defined as follows. Let P be a diagram of finite state machine recognizing a regular expression π, let V be the set of vertices of P and E be the set of edges. The nodes of $G_{\alpha,\pi}$ are the pairs (i, s), where $s \in V$ and

$0 \le i \le |\alpha|$. Informally, the graph contains $m + 1$ copies of P, where (i, s) is in the "column i". The following edges and only these edges are in $G_{\alpha, \pi}$.

1. $(i - 1, s) \rightarrow (i, s)$ is in $G_{\alpha, \pi}$ for every $s \in V$, and $1 \le i \le m$. The weight of these edges is 1.
2. If $t \rightarrow s$ is in E, then $(i, t) \rightarrow (i, s)$ is an edge in $G_{\alpha, \pi}$ for all $0 \le i \le m$. The weight of these edges is 1.
3. If $t \rightarrow s$ in E, then $(i - 1, t) \rightarrow (i, s)$ is an edge of $G_{\alpha, \pi}$ for all $1 \le i \le m$. The weight of the edge is 0, if a_i coincides with the label of the edge $t \rightarrow s$ in E, and 1, otherwise.

It evident that $G_{\alpha, \pi}$ has a size $O(|\alpha||\pi|)$. In Figure 2 there is the diagram of the graph $G_{abcabeacefgh, (abc)^*}$.

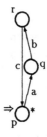

Fig. 1. *The transitional diagram of finite state machine recognizing regular expression* $(abc)^*$. *The starting state is marked by* $\Rightarrow$, *accepting state is marked by* $*$.

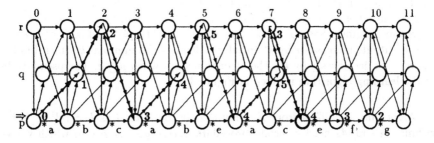

Fig. 2. *Edit graph* $G_{abcabeacefg, (abc)^*}$. *The node of the raw* $v \in \{p, q, r\}$ *and column* $i \in \{0, \dots, 11\}$ *corresponds to* (v, i). *The weight of the thick edges equals* 0, *the weight of the thin edges equals* 1. *The least weight path is shown by the arrowed line. The bold integers along the path show the value of regularity at the node. The last maximum regularity accepting node is achieved at the node marked by a thick circle.*

It can be proved that $G_{\alpha, \pi}$ is designed so that paths' weight between the node $(0, s_0)$ and nodes (k, s), where s is an accepting node in P, is $edit\_distance(\pi, \alpha[0..k[)$. If $\pi = (\pi')^*$ we can find the maximal n such that $edit\_distance((\pi')^n,$

$\alpha[0..k[) \leq c \cdot k$ for some k, by finding the minimal weight path in $G_{\alpha,\pi}$ and counting the number of accepting nodes along the path. Finding the minimal weight path can be done by a "single sweep" of the edit graph like in [17]. An efficient way to find k' is to assign another cost function *regularity* to every node which is increasing along "successful" edges by 1, and decreasing along "unsuccessful" ones by 1 or 2, depending whether the edge is leading to the next column, or stays in the same, as in Figure 2, and taking the node with the largest regularity along the path with the cost smaller or equal to $c \cdot k$. The run-time of the algorithm is $O(k \cdot edit\_distance(\pi, \alpha[0..k[)$.

Thus the procedure max_reg_r can be implemented as follows. First we construct the graph $G_{\alpha[i..|\alpha|[,(\alpha[i..i+p[)^*}$, and then search for the least weight path from the starting node while the weight of the nodes along the path does not exceed $c \cdot k$. In fact to obtain the run-time given in the theorems the edit graph has to be built not at once, but gradually with the running of the graph search algorithm only one step ahead of the rightmost vertex considered by the algorithm so far. That is, we initialize the edit graph G gradually by columns, one column farther to the right as the furthest advanced path at the moment with weight less of equal to $c \cdot k$. The run-time of max_reg_r is $O(p \cdot k)$. When no such path exists any further we stop.

Now, using the described procedure max_reg_r the learning algorithm $\mathcal{A}_1$ itself works as follows. Given an example γ, and constants d and l, the algorithm runs procedure $max\_reg\_r(\gamma, i, p, c)$ for all i: $0 \leq i \leq |\gamma| - p$, $p = 1, 2, \ldots$, and $c = d/|\gamma|$. The algorithm uses integer q showing how much of the example γ is not yet found to be "produced" by any iteration of the expression is set to $|\gamma|$ at the beginning. If the procedures find that there exists a substring $\gamma[i..i+k[$ the edit distance between which and $(\gamma[i..i+p[)^n$ is less than $c \cdot n$, and $n \geq l/2$ the algorithm assumes that $\gamma[i..i+k[$ comes form $(\gamma[i..i+p[)^*$ and adds $\gamma[i..i+p[$ to the output, increases i by k' (recall, k' denotes the minimal k which fits for the n), and decreases q by k'. The algorithm stops when $p \geq q$. The pseudocode of the learning algorithm is given in Figure 3.

Algorithm $\mathcal{A}_2$ differs from $\mathcal{A}_1$ only that it computes l as $l = |\gamma|^{1/2}$. Algorithms $\mathcal{A}_3$ and $\mathcal{A}_4$ need a second procedure $max\_reg\_l(\gamma, i, p, c, b)$ which works like max_reg_r, except that it looks leftwards and finds the largest n_2 such that $edit\_distance((\gamma[i..i + p[)^{n_2}, \gamma[i - k_2..i + p[) \leq c \cdot k_2 + b$, where $b = edit\_distance((\gamma[i..i+p[)^n, \gamma[i..i+k'[)$, and uses n and n_2 for finding the substrings of γ produced by iterations. More precisely, given an example γ, and a constant c, the algorithm runs procedures $max\_reg\_r(\gamma, i, p, c)$ returning n_1 and k_1, and $max\_reg\_l(\gamma, i, p, c, b)$, for $b = edit\_distance((\alpha[i..i + p[)^{n_1}, \alpha[i..i + k_1[)$, returning n_2 and k_2, for all i: $0 \leq i \leq |\gamma| - p$ and $p = 1, 2, \ldots$. If the procedures find that there exists a substring $\gamma[i - k_2..i + k_1[$ the edit distance between which and $(\gamma[i..i+p[)^{n_1+n_2}$ is less than $r \cdot (n_1 + n_2)$, and $n_1 + n_2 \geq |\gamma|^{1/2}$, the algorithm assumes that $\gamma[i - k_2..i + k_1[$ comes form $(\gamma[i..i+p[)^*$.

```
algorithm 𝒜₁(γ, d, l) return set
    output := Λ
    q := l;  p := 1
    c = d/|γ|
    while p < q do
        i := 0
        while i ≤ |X| − p do
            (k', n) := max_reg_l(γ, i, p, c)
            if n > l/2 then do
                add γ[i..i + p[ to output
                q := q − k';  i := i + k'
                end
            else i := i + 1
        end
        p := p + 1
    end
    return output
end algorithm
```

Fig. 3. algorithm $\mathcal{A}_1$

4 Sketch of Proof

A complete proof of the correctness of the algorithms are rather long and technical, therefore let us only sketch the basic ideas. The proof that procedures *max_reg_r* and *max_reg_l* satisfy their specifications is very similar to [17], therefore here we concentrate on the "learning part" of the algorithm. Let us call a string δ over an alphabet Σ *periodic with the period* $p \in \mathbf{N}$ if there exists a string α and an integer f such that $\delta = \alpha^f$ and $|\alpha| = p$. α is called the *body* of the periodic string γ. The basic idea of the proof is to show that while looking for substrings which on the average do not differ from some periodic string more than one edit transformation on any second period a wrong periodic substring cannot be accepted and the right one cannot be missed. The difficult part is to prove that a wrong substring cannot be accepted. The basic idea behind the proof of this fact is based on the following lemma.

Lemma 5. *Let γ and δ be periodic strings over some alphabet Σ with the bodies α and β respectively. Then, if α and β are not cyclically equal, then*

$$edit\_distance(\delta, \gamma) \geq \frac{max\{|\gamma|, |\delta|\}}{max(|\alpha|, |\beta|)}.$$

The proof of the lemma easily follows from the fact, that if two periodic strings with the periods p and q intersect on a substring of length $p + q$, then their bodies are cyclically equal (the last assertion follows directly from [9]). Thus, every substring of γ of length $p + q$, which is less than $2max\{p, q\}$, should contain at least one different place in both strings, which implies the lemma.

Next we can prove

Lemma 6. *Let $\gamma = \alpha^n$ be a periodic string over Σ with the minimal period $p = |\alpha|$. Let γ' be obtained from γ in a mutation process of length $d = n/r$, for some $r > 1$, let $\gamma' = \gamma_1 \gamma'' \gamma_2$, where $|\gamma''| \geq (|\gamma'|)^{1/2}$, and let there exist a string β and integer m, such that $|\beta| \leq |\alpha|$ and $edit\_distance(\beta^m, \gamma'') \leq m$. Then for every $\epsilon > 0$ and every $r > 1$ there exist n_0 such that, if $n \geq n_0$, then β is cyclically equal to α with the probability at least $1 - \epsilon$.*

Let us assume for simplicity that $\Sigma = \{a, b\}$ (the case of larger alphabet can be proved similarly). First, let us consider the case when $\alpha = a$. The the only β which is not equal to α and for which $|\beta| \leq |\alpha|$ is $\beta = b$. Therefore what we should prove in this case is that for sufficiently large n after less than n mutations there will not exist a substring of length at least $n^{1/2}$ containing more b's than a's. This follows easily from the law of large numbers since the average number of b's introduced into the string in a mutation process of length n/r does not exceed $n/2r$. Therefore, the probability that in some long enough substring the average number of b's will exceed $n/2$ is arbitrary small.

Now let us consider the case when $|\alpha| \geq 2$. According to lemma 5, for any β which is not cyclically equal to α and for which $|\beta| \leq |\alpha|$, in alignment of α^n with β^m, there has to be (roughly) at least one difference in each substring α. Therefore if γ'' is obtained from α^n in a mutation process and is such that $edit\_distance(\gamma'', \beta^m) \leq m$, then there should be at least one mutation on every second substring α, i.e., altogether there should be at least $n/2$ mutations in the part of the string which is mutated to γ''. The probability that any particular position will mutate is $1/r|\alpha| \leq 1/2r$, since $|\alpha| \geq 2$. Therefore, the probability that any substring of length $l \cdot |\alpha|$ will have at least $l/2$ mutations is arbitrary small for sufficiently large l according to the law of large numbers. To complete the proof of Lemma 6, it remains to notice, that that there are only finitely many different β's such that $|\beta| \leq p$, for any fixed p.

Now let us consider algorithm $\mathcal{A}_1$. It checks every substring $\alpha = \gamma[i..i + p[$ of the given example γ, and finds whether some long enough substring $\gamma' = \gamma[i..i + k[$ and α^n for some n and k are "closer" than n in the sense of edit distance. Lemma 6 says, that it is possible only if γ' has been obtained from α^n (or α'^n, where α' is cyclically equal to α). If $n > l/2$ for l from Theorem 1, and if, according to the conditions of Theorem 1, l is large enough, the source of α^n should be α^* since the length of α^n exceeds any constant part of the expression E. Therefore the algorithm $\mathcal{A}_1$ cannot output a wrong substring with any required probability. On the other hand the algorithm will not miss the right substring since the length d of the mutation process is less than one mutation on every α on the average, so the probability that the edit distance between γ' and α^n will exceed n is arbitrary small for large enough n.

The proof of the correctness of $\mathcal{A}_2$ additionally uses the fact that for and constant c, cn becomes larger than $n^{1/2}$ for sufficiently large n (a more detailed proof is given in [5]). The correctness of $\mathcal{A}_3$ and $\mathcal{A}_4$ is based on the fact, that the probability to "spoil" k substrings α in a row is $O(\log k)$.

5 Extensions and Computer Experiments

So far we have shown that, if a string containing parts composed from many consecutively repeated segments has been corrupted by some mutation process with no more than one mutation on each copy of the segment on average, then it is possible to find the original "building blocks" and the way the string has been built, in linear time in the length of the string times square of the total length of the building blocks. The algorithm can be easily modified so that it works also for more corrupted data, but in this case the run-time of the algorithm substantially increases. The generalization is achieved by iteratively applying the algorithm assuming different mutation levels d starting with very low (say 0), and then gradually increasing it in each iteration. More efficient is to use divide and conquer strategy. It may be interesting to find computational complexity of the problem of restoring the regular expression for different noise levels.

There are at least two more possible extensions of the offered approach which seems to us promising. The first is to generalize the edit graph used in the algorithm to the gap penalty model of [10], so that the algorithm can also be used for discovering the repetitions which are interrupted by longer substrings. If the length of the interruptions does not exceed the length of the building blocks, than it can be proved that the algorithm works. The gap mutation model is actually the model which is most interesting for bioinformatical applications. Unfortunately, if the gaps are long, the algorithm becomes too slow.

An other interesting extension of the algorithm is discovering more complicated patterns, like mixed iterations of two are more substrings. This in fact means looking for regular expressions of the type $\alpha_0(\beta_1 \cup \beta_1')^* \alpha_1 \ldots (\beta_n \cup \beta_n')^* \alpha_n$, the learning of which in case of perfect examples is studied in [6]. Seems that the proofs given in [6] can be generalized also for noisy examples. Such algorithm, for instance, could help in finding primitive protein domains by analyzing known protein sequences.

The algorithms for gap mutations and the expressions of the above mentioned type have been implemented in C++, and first computer experiments show that they are very efficient. The fact that the algorithms are linear time in the length of the given data, enables to use them on very long strings, for instance on sequences of known DNA and protein molecules. We have recently started computer experiment of applying the algorithms to the sequences from available databases of biosequential information. We have already found a number of regularities, although we do not know yet, if they have any biological significance.

References

1. D.Angluin. *Inference of reversible languages.* Journal of the ACM, 29(3):741-765, 1982.

2. D.Angluin, P.Laird. *Learning from noisy examples.* Machine Learning, V2, 1988, 343-370

3. A.Aho."Pattern Matching in Strings." In Formal Language Theory, R. Book (Ed.), New York: Academic Press.

4. A.Brazma. *Learning a subclass of regular expressions by recognizing periodic repetitions.* Proceedings of the Fourth Scandinavian Conference on AI, IOS Press, 137-146, 1993.

5. A.Brazma. *Efficient identification of regular expressions from representative examples.* In Proceedings of Sixth ACM Conference on Computational Learning Theory: COLT'93, ACM Press, 1993, 236-242.

6. A.Brazma, K.Cerans. *Efficient Learning of Regular Expressions from Good Examples.* Technical Report, LU-IMSC-TR-CS-94-1, University of Latvia, Riga, 1994 (also to appear in proceedings of AII'94).

7. C.DeLisi, *Computers in molecular biology: current applications and emerging trends.* Science, V.240, April 1988, 47-51

8. M.Kearns, M.Li., *Learning in the presence of malicious errors.* In Proc. of the 20-th Annual Symposium on Theory of Computing, Chicago, Illinois, May 1988.

9. R.C.Lyndon, M.P.Schutzenberg. *The equation $a^M = b^N c^P$ in a free group.* Michigan Math. J. V9, 289-298, 1962.

10. E.Myers, W.Miller. *Approximate matching of regular expression.* Bulletin of Mathematical Biology, V.51, N.1, 5-37, 1989.

11. A.Konagaya. *A Stochastic Approach to Genetic Information.* In Proc. of the 3-rd Workshop on Algorithmic Learning Theory ALT'92, JSAI, 25-36, 1992.

12. S.Miyano. *Learning Theory Toward Genome Informatics.* In Proc. of the 4-th Workshop on Algorithmic Learning Theory ALT'93, Lect.Notes in Artific. Int., Springer, 19-36, 1993.

13. M.Singer and P.Berg. *Genes and Genomes.* University Science Books, Mill Valey, California, 1991.

14. R.Sloan. *Types of noise in data for concept learning.* In Proc. of 1988 Workshop on Computational Learning Theory, Morgan Kaufman, 1988, 91-96.

15. N.Tanida, T.Yokomori. *Polynomial-time identification of strictly regular languages in the limit.* IEICE Trans. Inf. & Syst., V E75-D, 1992, 125-132.

16. K. Yamanishi. *A learning criterion for stochastic rules.* In Proc. of the 3-rd Workshop on Computational Learning Theory, Rochester, NY: Morgan Kaufman, 1990, 67-81.

17. R.A.Wagner, J.I.Seiferas. *Correcting counter-automaton-recognizable languages.* SIAM J. Computing. V7, 1978, 357-375.

A Note on Learning DNF Formulas Using Equivalence and Incomplete Membership Queries

Zhixiang Chen*

Department of Computer Science

Boston University

Boston, MA 02215

Abstract. In this note, we prove with derandomization techniques that a subclass of DNF formulas with nonconstant number of terms is polynomial time learnable using equivalence and incomplete membership queries. Although many concept classes are known to be polynomial time learnable using equivalence and membership queries, so far only two concept classes are known to be polynomial time learnable (see, [AS] and [GM]) when incomplete membership queries are used.

1 Introduction

Angluin and Slonim [AS] introduced an error-tolerant learning model using equivalence and incomplete membership queries, in which the answers to a random subset of the learner's membership queries may not be obtained. They proved that, with high probability, one can learn the class of monotone DNF formulas in polynomial time, provided that the fraction of unobtained answers is bounded by some constant p with $0 < p < 1$. Goldman and Mathias [GM] show that the class of DNF formulas with constant number of terms is also polynomial time learnable in this model. It seems, however, very difficult to apply this model to many other concept classes that are known to be polynomial time learnable using equivalence and complete membership queries (see, for example, concept classes listed in [AS]). Another interesting problem suggested in [GM] is whether some classes of DNF formulas with nonconstant number of terms are polynomial time learnable in this model.

We consider a subclass $C_n(j, k)$ of DNF formulas consisting of at most n variables such that, for any formula $F \in C_n(j, k)$, F has at most k terms, each term T of F has at most j literals, and T has at least one variable which doesn't occur in

---

*Department of Computer Science, Boston University, Boston, MA 02215. Email: zchen@cs.bu.edu. The author was supported by by NSF grant CCR91-9103055 and by a Boston University Presidential Graduate Fellowship.

any other terms of F. By a simple counting argument, the class $C_n(j, k)$ contains $O(n^{jk} 2^j)$ many DNF formulas. When j and k are nonconstant, there are no obvious ways to learn $C_n(j, k)$ using only equivalence queries in polynomial time. When $k = O(\log n)$, Blum and Rudich's work [BR] implies that $C_n(j, k)$ is polynomial time learnable using equivalence and membership queries. On the other hand, it seems that DNF formulas with $O(\log n)$ relevant variables are hard to predict (see, for example, the remarks in [BCJ]), in other words, those formulas seems hard to learn using only equivalence queries. We will restrict $C_n(j, k)$ to the case in which $j = k = O(\log n)$. We prove with derandomization techniques developed in [NN] that, for any $0 < \delta < 1$, the class $C_n(O(\log n), O(\log n))$ is learnable with probability at least $1 - \delta$, using equivalence and incomplete membership queries, while the time complexity of the learning algorithm is bounded by a polynomial in n and $\log(1/\delta)$.

2 Definitions

Let $n \geq 1$ be an integer. Let V_n be the set of n variables $x_1, \ldots, x_n$. We consider DNF formulas that consists of variables in V_n. Our example space is $X_n = \{0, 1\}^n$. A literal is a variable or a negation of a variable. For any example $\alpha \in X_n$, let $\alpha[i]$ denote the i-th bit value of α, i.e., the value of the variable x_i in α. In general, for any literal l, $\alpha[l]$ denotes the value of l in α. A term is a conjunction of literals, we may also view a term as a set of literals. Throughout this paper, we consider only those terms that do not contain a literal l and its negation $\bar{l}$. A k-term DNF formula is a disjunction of at most k terms. An example α satisfies a term T (we denote $T(\alpha) = 1$) if and only if α satisfies every literals in T. An empty term is considered to be identically true. An example α is a positive example of a DNF formula F (we write $F(\alpha) = 1$) if it satisfies at least one term in F and a negative example if otherwise (we write $F(\alpha) = 0$). For a term T, let $vars(T)$ denote the set $\{x \in V_n \mid x \in T \text{ or } \bar{x} \in T\}$.

In the standard on-line learning model with equivalence and membership queries, the learner is required to infer an unknown target formula F that is chosen from the concept class by the teacher. The learner may either propose a hypothesis H to an equivalence oracle EQ, or propose an example α to a membership oracle MQ. $EQ(H)$ returns "yes" if H is logically equivalent to the target formula F, or returns a counterexample if otherwise. $MQ(\alpha)$ returns the value of the target formula F on the example α. We say an example α is a positive counterexample if $F(\alpha) = 1$ but $H(\alpha) = 0$, we say α is a negative counterexample if $F(\alpha) = 0$ but $H(\alpha) = 1$. A learning algorithm achieves exact identification of the concept class (with high probability) if it can infer a formula that is logically equivalent to the target formula on all inputs (with probability at least $1 - \delta$, where $0 < \delta < 1$, and the probability is taken over all truth assignments to the formula). An algorithm is a polynomial time algorithm if it runs in time polynomial in n (and $\log(1/\delta)$).

The on-line learning model with incomplete membership queries introduced in [AS] is a modification of the standard on-line learning model from equivalence and membership queries in such a way that the complete membership oracle MQ is replaced with an incomplete membership oracle IMQ. An IMQ is identical to an MQ except that it answers "I don't know" to some subset of the membership queries. The oracle determines this subset by answering "I don't know" independently with probability $0 < p < 1$ the first time a membership query is made for each example. This missing information is persistent in the sense that all repetitions of a query result in the answer given the first time the query was asked.

3 Technical Lemmas

As in [AS] and [GM], we define a partial relation $\leq$ over the sample space X_n. For any $v, w \in X_n, v \leq w$ if and only if each bit in v is less than or equal to the corresponding bit in w. We know that $< X_n, \leq >$ is a partially ordered set. The maximum element is 1^n and the minimum element is 0^n. The descendants (resp., ancestors) of an example v are all examples $w \in X_n$ such that $w \leq v$ (resp., $w \geq v$). For an integer $d > 0$, the d-descendants of v are all of descendants w of v that can be obtained from v by replacing at most d $1's$ with $0's$. The d-ancestors are defined analogously.

Let $F = T_1 + \cdots + T_k$ be a k-term DNF formulas, let A and B be two sets of literals. We say that (A, B) is a separator for a term T_i in F if, $vars(A) \cup vars(B) = V_n$, $vars(A) \cap vars(B) = \phi$, $T_i \subseteq A$, and $T_j \cap B \neq \phi$ for any $j \in \{1, \ldots, k\} - \{i\}$.

Let T be a term in a DNF formula F, let (A, B) be a separator for the term T. We define $max(T, A, B)$ as the example obtained by turning on all literals in T, turning off all literals in B, and setting all positions i to 1 when $x_i \in vars(A) - vars(T)$. Similarly, we define $min(T, A, B)$ as the example obtained by turning on all literals in T, turning off all literals in B, and setting all positions i to 0 when $x_i \in vars(A) - vars(T)$.

For any examples $x, y \in X_n$, for any set L of literals, let $combine(x, y, L)$ denote the conjunction of all literals in L that are true in both x and y.

Lemma 3.1. Let $F = T_1 + \cdots + T_k$ be a k-term DNF formulas. Assume that (A, B) is a separator for a term T_i in F. Then $combine(max(T_i, A, B), min(T_i, A, B), A) = T_i$.

Proof. Since (A, B) is a separator for T_i, $T_i \subseteq A$. For any literal $l \in T_i = T_i \cap A$, l is true in $max(T_i, A, B)$ and $min(T_i, A, B)$. This implies that

$$T_i \subseteq combine(max(T_i, A, B), min(T_i, A, B), A).$$

On the other hand, any literal

$$l \in combine(max(T_i, A, B), min(T_i, A, B), A)$$

is true in T_i, so

$$combine(max(T_i, A, B), min(T_i, A, B), A) \subseteq T_i.$$

□

Suppose that one knows that (A, B) is a separator for an unknown term T, then in order to learn T, by Lemma 3.1, one only needs to find $max(T, A, B)$ and $min(T, A, B)$.

For any example $w \in X_n$, for any set L of literals, let $w(L)$ denote the example obtained by turning every literal in L off in w. The following algorithm $CSFMax$ is the constrained version of Goldman and Mathias' *Search-For-Max* algorithm [GM], where $CSFMax$ stands for *Constrained-Search-For-Max*.

Algorithm CSFMax($v, d, maxset, B$):
    Set $maxset = maxset \cup \{v\}$.
    Let $Q = \{w(B) \mid w \in X_n \text{ and } w(B) \text{ is a d-ancestors of } v\}$.
    For each $a \in Q$ in breadth-first order,
            if $IMQ(a) =$ "I don't know" ,
                then set $maxset = maxset \cup \{a\}$;
            else if $IMQ(a) =$ "yes",
                Recursively call $CSFMax(a, d, maxset, B)$.
End of Algorithm.

For a DNF formulas $F = T_1 + \cdots + T_k$, for a term T_i in F, $1 \leq i \leq k$, assume that $D_i = (A_i, B_i)$ is a separator for T_i. We define, for any example α, $ancestor(\alpha, D_i) = \{v(B_i) \mid v \in X_n \text{ and } v(B_i) \geq \alpha\}$, $descendant(\alpha, D_i) = \{v(B_i) \mid v \in X_n \text{ and } v(B_i) \leq \alpha\}$. We also define $sat(T_i, D_i) = \{v(B_i) \mid v \in X_n \text{ and } T_i(v(B_i)) = 1\}$. The following lemma is a generalization of Lemma 3 in [AS].

Lemma 3.2. Let v be a positive example for a term T_i in a DNF formula $F = T_1 + \cdots + T_k$, $1 \leq i \leq k$. Let $D_i = (A_i, B_i)$ be a separator for T_i. Let $CSFMax$ be called with parameters $v, d, maxset$ and B_i, where $d \geq \lceil f(p) \rceil$, and

$$f(p) = \log(2 + \frac{1 + \log(1/(1 - p))}{\log(1/p)}) - 1.$$

Assume that no example in $ancestor(v, D_i) \cap sat(T_i, D_i)$ has yet been queried to the incomplete oracle, then $max(T_i, A_i, B_i) \in maxset$ with probability at least $1/2$.

Proof. The proof is similar to Lemma 3 in [AS]. For any example $w \in sat(T_i, D_i)$, for any positive integer m, let $PA(w, m)$ denote the number of all proper m-ancestors of w that are in $ancestor(w, D_i) \cap sat(T_i, D_i)$.

Claim 1. For any example $\alpha \in sat(T_i, D_i)$, assume that $max(T_i, A_i, B_i)$ is not one of the m-ancestors of α, then $PA(\alpha, m) \geq 2^{m+1} - 2$.

Proof of Claim 1. Since $max(T_i, A_i, B_i)$ is not one of the m-ancestors of α, $|A_i - T_i| \geq m + 1$, and there are at least $m + 1$ positions q in α with $x_q \in vars(A_i - T_i)$ such that the values of α in those positions are 0. Now, setting any $1 \leq r \leq m$ of those positions to 1 results in a proper m-ancestor of α in $ancestor(\alpha, D_i) \cap sat(T_i, D_i)$. The total number of such m-ancestors is

$$\sum_{r=1}^{m} \binom{m+1}{r} = 2^{m+1} - 2.$$

This implies that $PA(\alpha, m) \geq 2^{m+1} - 2$. $\square$

Claim 2. For any examples $\alpha, \beta \in sat(T_i, D_i)$ with $\alpha < \beta$, $PA(\beta, m) < PA(\alpha, m)$ for any positive integer m.

Proof of Claim 2. Let r_α be the number of all positions i in α with $x_i \in vars(A_i - T_i)$ such that the values of α in those positions are 0. Similarly, let r_β be the number of all positions i in β with $x_i \in vars(A_i - T_i)$ such that the value of β in those positions are 0. Since $\alpha < \beta$, $r_\beta < r_\alpha$. Note that,

$$PA(\alpha, m) = \sum_{q=1}^{m} \binom{r_\alpha}{j}, \quad PA(\beta, m) = \sum_{q=1}^{m} \binom{r_\beta}{q}.$$

Hence, $PA(\beta, m) < PA(\alpha, m)$. □

We now ready to prove Lemma 3.2. Let $PA(v, d) = r$. We will prove the following statement: the probability that the algorithm $CSFMax$ fails to find $max(T_i, A_i, B_i)$ in $maxset$ is bounded by

$$p^{2^{d+1}-2} + p^{2^{d+1}-1} + \cdots + p^{r-1} + p^r$$

Note that the above formulas is strictly bounded by $p^{2^{d+1}-2}/(1-p)$, and by choosing $d \geq \lceil f(p) \rceil$, it is bounded by $1/2$. Therefore, by the above statement, with probability at least $1/2$, the algorithm $SCFMax$ will find $max(T_i, A_i, B_i)$ in $maxset$.

We now prove the above statement by induction on $PA(v, d)$. By Claim 1, if $PA(v, d) < 2^{d+1} - 2$, then $max(T_i, A_i, B_i) \in maxset$. We now consider the case that $PA(v, d) = 2^{d+1} - 2$. Suppose that $max(T_i, A_i, B_i) \notin maxset$. Then, the algorithm $CSFmax$ must not be called recursively, since otherwise by Claim 1 and Claim 2, $max(T_i, A_i, B_i) \in maxset$. Thus, the algorithm $CSFMax$ will make queries for all those $2^{d+1} - 2$ d-ancestors of v in $ancestor(v, D_i) \cap sat(T_i, D_i)$, and the answers received by the learner for the queries will all be "I don't know". By the assumption that those examples have not been queried before, thus the probability that all those queries result in "I don't know" is $p^{2^{d+1}-2}$.

Suppose that Lemma 3.2 holds for any example v with $2^{d+1}-2 \leq PA(v, d) \leq r-1$, we now prove that it holds also for $PA(v, d) = r$. There are only two possible executions of the algorithm $CSFMax$, one is that it make no recursive call, the other is that it make a recursive call. In the first case, it will make queries for all those $PA(v, d) = r$ d-ancestors in $ancestor(v, D_i) \cap sat(T_i, D_i)$, and the answers received by the learner for all those queries are "I don't know". Since by the assumption that all those examples have not been queried before, the probability that all those queries result in "I don't know" is p^r.

In the case that the algorithm $CSFMax$ makes a recursive call, say, $CSFMax$ makes a recursive call for an example w, then $v < w$, and $w \in ancestor(v, D_i) \cap sat(T_i, D_i)$. Note that the search is done in breadth-first order, and by the assumption of the lemma no example in $ancestor(w, D_i) \cap sat(T_i, D_i)$ has been queried before. By Claim 2, $PA(w, d) < PA(v, d)$. So, $PA(w, d) \leq r - 1$. If $PA(w, d) < 2^{d+1} - 2$, then by Claim 1, the algorithm $CSFMax$ must find $max(T_i, A_i, B_i)$ in $maxset$ at the recursive call. When $PA(w, d) \geq 2^{d+1} - 2$, suppose that the algorithm $CSFMax$ fails to find $max(T_i, A_i, B_i)$ in $maxset$ at the recursive call. By the induction hypothesis, the probability of such failure is bounded by

$$p^{2^{d+1}-2} + p^{2^{d+1}-1} + \cdots + p^{r-1}$$

Hence, the probability that the algorithm $CSFMax$ fails to find $max(T_i, A_i, B_i)$ in $maxset$ for the input example v is bounded by

$$p^{2^{d+1}-2} + p^{2^{d+1}-1} + \cdots + p^{r-1} + p^r$$

Thus the proof of Lemma 3.2 is verified. $\square$

Remark 3.3. There is a dual version of the algorithm $CSFMax$ that constructs the candidate set minset for $min(T_i, A_i, B_i)$, given an example v satisfies T_i. We denote the algorithm by $CSFMin$, where $CSFMin$ stands for "*Constrained-Search-For-Min*". A dual version of Lemma 3.2 holds for the algorithm $CSFMin$.

Remark 3.4. We observe that, the essence of the assumption in Lemma 3.2 that no example in $ancestor(v, D_i) \cap sat(T_i, D_i)$ has yet been queried to the incomplete oracle is to allow the algorithm to flip a fair coin, when it makes a membership query for an example in $ancestor(v, D_i) \cap sat(T_i, D_i)$. Each flip of the coin results in "heads" with probability p. When a flip results in a "heads", the teacher gives an answer "I don't know". A very technical subtlety in applying Lemma 3.2 is that one designs a global algorithm that works at stages. At each stage for a given example v, the global algorithm runs several copies of the algorithm $SCFMax$ (or $SCFMin$). In this kind of design format, we can weaken the assumption for each copy of the algorithm $SCFMax$ (or $SCFMin$) so that no example in $ancestor(v, D_i) \cap sat(T_i, D_i)$ has yet been queried to the incomplete oracle before the current stage. With this assumption for the global algorithm, the probability of the global algorithm finding $max(T_i, A_i, B_i)$ (or $min(T_i, A_i, B_i)$) at the current stage is at least $1/2$.

4 Constructing Separators for Terms in a Formula

In Lemma 3.2, with a separator for a term T_i in a DNF formula F, one can allow the algorithm $CSFMax$ to search for examples that satisfy only the term T_i. Thus, when one obtains a maximal (or minimal) example, then one knows that it must be a maximal (or minimal) example for the term T_i. It seems in general very difficult to find separators for all terms in a DNF formula. We now consider how to use the derandomization technique (see, [NN]) to construct separators for all terms in a DNF formula.

For a DNF formula $F = T_1 + \cdots + T_k$, we say $D = \{D_1, \ldots, D_k\}$ with $D_i = (A_i, B_i)$ is a separator for the formula F if D_i is a separator for the term T_i for $1 \leq i \leq k$.

Lemma 4.1. There is a separator for every DNF formula $F \in C_n(j, k)$.

Proof. Given $F \in C_n(j, k)$, let $F = T_1 + \cdots + T_k$. For any $i \in \{1, \ldots, k\}$, one can choose a literal $l_i \in T_i$ such that

$$vars(\{l_i\}) \subseteq vars(T_i) - \cup_{q \neq i} vars(T_q).$$

Let

$$A_i = T_i, \quad B_i = \cup_{q \neq i} \{l_q\} \cup (V_n - (vars(T_i) \cup \cup_{q \neq i} vars(\{l_q\}))).$$

Then $T_i \subseteq A_i$, $l_q \in T_q \cap B_i$, $q \neq i$, $vars(A_i) \cap vars(B_i) = \phi$, $vars(A_i) \cup vars(B_i) = V_n$. Let $D_i = (A_i, B_i)$, $D = \{D_1, \ldots, D_k\}$. D is a separator for F. $\square$

Let Q be a subset of the example space X_n. We say that Q is (n, q)-universal if for any subset of q variables in V_n the induced examples to those q variables contains all possible 2^q configurations. Naor and Naor [NN] gave a derandomization technique that can be used to construct a (n, q)-universal set $\Omega(n, q)$ of examples of size $2^{O(q)} \log n$ in time $O(2^{O(q)} \log n)$. For $q = O(\log n)$, the construction is of polynomial time. We now show how to construct from $\Omega(n, q)$ a set of possible separators for formulas in $C_n(j, k)$.

Lemma 4.2. One can construct a set S_n of possible separators for all formulas in $C_n(j, k)$ such that, 1) $\mid S_n \mid = 2^{O(j+k)} \log^2 n$; 2) for each $F \in C_n(j, k)$, there is a separator $D \subseteq S_n$ for F; 3) the construction can be done in time $O(2^{O(j+k)} \log^2 n)$ (thus, when j and k are $O(\log n)$, the construction is of polynomial time).

Proof. We first construct a $(n, (j+k))$-universal set $\Omega(n, (j+k))$ with Naor and Naor's derandomization technique. We now construct S_n from $\Omega(n, (j + k))$ as follows.

For any example $v \in X_n$, for any literal x, let $v|_x$ denote the literal x if the value of x in v is 1 or $\bar{x}$ if otherwise. For any $a, b \in \Omega(n, (j + k))$, let

$$A_{ab} = \{a|_x \mid the \ values \ of \ x \ in \ a \ and \ b \ are \ the \ same\},$$

$$B_{ab} = \{a|_x \mid the \ values \ of \ x \ in \ a \ and \ b \ are \ different\}.$$

Let $S_n = \{(A_{ab}, B_{ab}) \mid a, b \in \Omega(n, (j + k))\}$. Since $\mid \Omega(n, (j + k)) \mid = 2^{O(j+k)} \log n$, $\mid S_n \mid = 2^{O(j+k)} \log^2 n$. Because the construction of $\Omega(n, (j + k))$ can be done in time $O(2^{O(j+k)} \log n)$, so the construction of S_n can be done in time $O(2^{O(j+k)} \log^2 n)$.

Let $F = T_1 + \cdots + T_k \in C_n(j, k)$. By Lemma 4.1, there is a separator for F. Moreover, let $A_i = T_i$, $B_i = \cup_{q \neq i} \{l_q\} \cup (V_n - (vars(T_i) \cup \cup_{q \neq i} vars(\{l_q\})))$. Then by the proof of Lemma 4.1, $D = \{(A_i, B_i) \mid i = 1, \ldots, k\}$ is a separator for F and $l_q \in T_q \cap B_i$ for $q \neq i$.

Fix i, $1 \leq i \leq k$. Let $A_i = T_i = l_i r_1 \cdots r_m$, $1 \leq m \leq j - 1$. Since $\Omega(n, (j + k))$ is $(n, (j + k))$-universal, there exist examples $a_i, b_i \in \Omega(n, (j + k))$ such that

$$a_i|_{l_q} = l_q, \quad q \in \{1, \ldots, k\}; \quad a_i|_{r_q} = r_q, \quad q \in \{1, \ldots, m\}; \quad b_i|_{l_i} = l_i;$$

$$b_i|_{l_q} = \bar{l}_q, \quad q \neq i, q \in \{1, \ldots, k\}; \quad b_i|_{r_q} = r_q, q \in \{1, \ldots, m\}.$$

Thus, $A_i = T_i \subseteq A_{a_i b_i}$, and $\{l_q \mid q \neq i \ and \ q \in \{1, \ldots, k\}\} \subseteq B_{a_i b_i}$. Note also that

$$vars(A_{a_i b_i}) \cap vars(B_{a_i b_i}) = \phi, \quad vars(A_{a_i b_i}) \cup vars(B_{a_i b_i}) = V_n.$$

Hence, $\{(A_{a_i b_i}, B_{a_i b_i}) \mid i = 1, \ldots, k\} \subseteq S_n$ is a separator for F. $\square$

5 The Learning Algorithm and Its Analysis

We now design and analyze the algorithm for learning DNF formulas in $C_n(j, k)$. If $D = \{(A_i, B_i) \mid i = 1, \ldots, k\}$ is a separator for a DNF formula $F = T_1 + \cdots + T_k \in$

$C_n(j, k)$, then for any $v \in X_n$, by the definition of a separator, $T_j(v(B_i)) = 0$ for any $j \in \{1, \ldots, k\} - \{i\}$. Thus, if $F(v(B_i)) = 1$, then it must be the case that $T_i(v[B_i]) = 1$. So, constraining the search using B_i guarantees that the search never finds a maximal (or minimal) example for a term other than T_i. Since $T_i \subseteq A_i$, one can use $combine(x, y, A_i)$ to build candidate terms for T_i. We now use $CSFMax(\cdots)$ $(CSFMin(\cdots))$ to denote the *maxset* after the execution of the algorithm $CSFMax(\cdots)$ $(CSFmin(\cdots))$. We describe the algorithm LORO that runs in stages as follows.

Algorithm LORO(j, k, n, d):

Stage 0. Construct with derandomization technique the set S_n of possible separators for all formulas in $C_n(j, k)$. Set $E_0 = H_0 = \phi$.

Stage $r \geq 1$. Ask an equivalence query for the hypothesis H_{r-1} to EQ. If $EQ(H_{r-1}) = $ "yes", then stop and return H_{r-1}. Otherwise one receives a counterexample e_{r-1}. If $H_{r-1}(e_{r-1}) = 1$ then set H_r to be the formula obtained by removing from H_{r-1} all terms T with $T(e_{r-1}) = 1$. Otherwise, use IMQ to find $I = \{(A, B) \in S_n \mid IMQ(e_{r-1}(B)) = $ "yes" or "I don't know"$\}$. For each $(A, B) \in I$, set

$$E_r = E_{r-1} \cup CSFMax(e_{r-1}, d, maxset, B) \cup CSFMin(e_{r-1}, d, maxset, B).$$

One Defines

$$H_r = H_{r-1} \vee (\bigvee \{combine(x, y, A) \mid x, y \in E_r \ and (A, B) \in S_n\}).$$

End of Algorithm.

We say that the algorithm *LORO* makes progress at stage $r \geq 1$ for the input DNF formula F, if there exist a term T_i in F and a separator $D_i = (A_i, B_i)$ for T_i such that $max(T_i, A_i, B_i) \in E_r$ or $min(T_i, A_i, B_i) \in E_r$.

Lemma 5.1. Given $0 < p < 1$, let $d = \lceil f(p) \rceil$ as in Lemma 3.2. Assume that at stage $r \geq 1$, the learner receives a positive counterexample e_{r-1}. Then, with probability at least $1/2$, the algorithm *LORO* makes progress.

Proof. Assume that $T_i(e_{r-1}) = 1$. By Lemma 4.2, there is a separator $D_i = (A_i, B_i)$ for T_i. By Lemma 3.2, we only need to show that either no example in $ancestor(e_{r-1}, D_i) \cap sat(T_i, D_i)$ or no example in $descendant(e_{r-1}, D_i) \cap sat(T_i, D_i)$ has been queried before stage r. Suppose by contradiction that this is not true. Let $u \in ancestor(e_{r-1}, D_i) \cap sat(T_i, D_i)$, $v \in descendant(e_{r-1}, D_i) \cap sat(T_i, D_i)$, u and v have been queried before stage r. Then, u and v have already been in E_{r-1}. Hence, at stage $r - 1$, we have the term $T_i^* = combine(u, v, A_i)$ in the hypothesis H_{r-1}. This implies that $T_i^*(e_{r-1}) = 1$, so $H_{r-1}(e_{r-1}) = 1$, contradicting that e_{r-1} is a positive counterexample. $\square$

Theorem 5.2. Given $0 < p < 1$, let $d = \lceil f(p) \rceil$ as in Lemma 3.2. For any $0 < \delta < 1$, for any DNF formula $F \in C_n(j, k)$, the algorithm *LORO* can learn F with probability at least $1 - \delta$ in time polynomial in n, 2^{j+k}, and $\log(1/\delta)$.

Proof. Note that the algorithm *LORO* uses an equivalence oracle EQ, *LORO* stops if and only if $EQ(H_r) = $ "yes" for some hypothesis H_r. Thus, one only needs to prove that the algorithm $LORO$ stops with probability at least $1 - \delta$ in time polynomial in $n, 2^{j+k}$ and $\log(1/\delta)$. We also note that once a term in the target formula F has been added into the hypothesis H_r at some stage r, then at any later stage $s \geq r$, the term cannot be removed from the hypothesis H_s by a negative counterexample e_s, since e_s will turn the term to 0. We now analyze how many positive counterexample the algorithm LORO needs in order to add all terms in the target formula F to the hypothesis.

By Lemma 5.1, when the algorithm receives a positive counterexample at a stage r, it will make progress with probability at least $1/2$. Since F contains k terms, in order to add all terms in F into the hypothesis, the algorithm $LORO$ is required to make progress $2k$ times. Thus, the expected number of positive counterexamples required by the algorithm $LORO$ is $4k$. For any $0 < \delta < 1$, by Chernoff bounds, after receiving $16k \log(1/\delta)$ positive counterexamples, the algorithm $LORO$ will add all terms in F into the hypothesis with probability at least $1 - \delta$.

Assume that at stage $r \geq 1$ the algorithm $LORO$ receives a positive counterexample e_{r-1}, then $LORO$ will run one copy of each of the algorithms $CSFMax$ and $CSFMin$ for every element in S_n. By Lemma 4.2, $|S_n| = 2^{O(j+k)} \log^2 n$, and each calling of the algorithms $CSFMax$ and $CSFMin$ will produce $O(n^{d+1})$ many elements into the set E_r. Hence, at stage r, at most $O(2^{O(j+k)} n^{d+1} \log^2 n)$ many elements will be added to E_r. With the above analysis, with probability at least $1 - \delta$, the algorithm learns F after receiving $16k \log(1/\delta)$ positive counterexamples and thus it adds

$$sum = \sum_{q=1}^{16k\log(1/\delta)} O(q 2^{O(j+k)} n^{d+1} \log^2 n)^2 |S_n| = O(k^3 2^{O(j+k)} n^{2(d+1)} \log^3(1/\delta) \log^6 n)$$

many terms into the hypothesis. Each negative counterexample will remove at least one term from the hypothesis. Thus the algorithm $LORO$ requires at most sum negative counterexamples.

At a stage when the algorithm $LORO$ receives a negative counterexample, it needs to scan the current hypothesis to remove unnecessary terms, so the time spent for a negative counterexample is $O(sum)$. When the algorithm receives a positive counterexample, it runs $O(|S_n|)$ copies of the algorithms $CSFMax$ and $CSFMin$. Each copy of those algorithms runs in time $O(n^{d+1})$, so the time spent for each positive counterexample is bounded by $O(|S_n| n^{d+1})$. By Lemma 4.2, S_n can be constructed in time $O(2^{O(j+k)} \log^2 n)$. Therefore, the time complexity of the algorithm is bounded by a polynomial in $n, 2^{j+k}$, and $\log(1/\delta)$. $\square$

6 Open Problems

We don't know whether the class $C_n(n, O(\log n))$ and in general the class of DNF formulas with $O(\log n)$ terms are polynomial time learnable when incomplete membership queries are used.

Acknowledgments. The author thanks his advisor Steve Homer for his encouragement and helpful discussions and, especially his careful reading of the draft of this note. Thanks to Rajogopalan for valuable discussions on this topic. The author also thanks two anonymous referees of ALT'94 Program Committee for their valuable comments.

References

[AS] D. Angluin, D. Slonim, "Learning monotone DNF formula with an incomplete membership oracle", *Proc of the 4th Annual Workshop on Computational Learning Theory*, pages 139-146. Morgan Kaufmann Publishers, Inc.,San Mateo, CA, 1991.

[BR] A. Blum, S. Rudich, "Fast learning of k-term DNF formulas with queries", *Proc of the 24th Annual ACM Symposium on Theory of Computing*, May 1992, pages 382-389.

[BCJ] A. Blum, P. Chalasani, J. Jackson, "On learning embedded symmetric concepts" *Proc of the Sixth Annual ACM Conference on Computational Learning Theory*, pages 337-346.

[GM] S. Goldman, H. Mathias, "Learning k-term DNF formulas with an incomplete membership oracle", *Proc of the 5th Annual Workshop on Computational Learning Theory*, pages 72-77, Morgan Kaufmann Publishers, Inc.,San Mateo, CA, 1992.

[NN] J. Naor, M. Naor, "Small-bias probability space: efficient constructions and applications", *Proc of the 22th Annual ACM Symposium on Theory of Computing*, May 1992, pages 213-223.

Identifying Regular Languages over Partially-Commutative Monoids

Claudio Ferretti – Giancarlo Mauri
{ferretti,mauri}@imiucca.csi.unimi.it

Dipartimento di Scienze dell'Informazione
via Comelico 39, 20135 Milano
Università di Milano - ITALY

Abstract. We define a new technique useful in identifying a subclass of regular languages defined on a free partially commutative monoid (regular trace languages), using equivalence and membership queries. Our algorithm extends an algorithm defined by Dana Angluin in 1987 to learn DFA's. The words of a trace language can be seen as equivalence classes of strings. We show how to extract, from a given equivalence class, a string of an unknown underlying regular language. These strings can drive the original learning algorithm which identify a regular string language that defines also the target trace language. In this way the algorithm applies also to classes of unrecognizable regular trace languages and, as a corollary, to a class of unrecognizable string languages. We also discuss bounds on the number of examples needed to identify the target language and on the time required to process them.

1 Introduction

The problem of learning languages from examples has been studied by many authors, starting from the classical work by Gold [Gol67]. In recent years, Dana Angluin gave many results about learnability of regular languages, especially in [Ang87], where an efficient algorithm to learn deterministic finite automata by membership and equivalence queries with counterexamples was given. We call this algorithm DFAL, and we will show how to use it to learn languages not represented by automata. Other results on the learnability of regular languages are reviewed in [Pit89].

Recently, researches on formal models for concurrent processes underlined the importance of trace languages [Maz85], defined as subsets of a free partially commutative monoid (f.p.c.m.), and a theory of trace languages has been developed [BMS89, AR86], parallel to that of classical languages on free non-commutative monoids (string languages).

While this formalism becomes widely used to model concurrency, it turns out that it could be interesting to have a method to learn the corresponding trace languages. Consider to have a concurrent environment, and to accept the constraints needed to model it by traces, a learning system could experiment on it to automatically get its formal description. But the problem of finding a learning system for trace languages is especially interesting from a theoretical point of view, as it involves some specific techniques and it has been seldom studied.

A fundamental difference between trace languages and string languages is that regular trace languages are in general not recognized by a finite state automaton on the f.p.c.m., i.e. Kleene's theorem cannot be generalized to trace languages. As known results about the identification of regular languages are based on automata, they cannot be directly used on regular trace languages.

In this work we try to explore a method to identify regular trace languages on a class of f.p.c. monoids. In Section 2 we introduce the definition of regular trace languages and some useful notations. In Section 3 we describe a method to extract a regular language from a regular trace language and we state our main results. In Section 4 we discuss some relations with other recent works and some open problems.

2 Definitions and Notations

In the following Σ denotes a finite alphabet, of cardinality k, and Σ^* the free monoid generated by Σ. The empty word is denoted by ϵ. A *concurrence relation* θ is a subset of $\Sigma \times \Sigma$ and $\equiv_\theta$ denotes the congruence relation of Σ^* generated by the set $C_\theta = \{(ab, ba) \mid (a, b) \in \theta\}$. The quotient $M(\Sigma, \theta) = \Sigma^* / \equiv_\theta$ is the *free partially commutative monoid* associated with the concurrence relation θ.

An element of $M(\Sigma, \theta) = \Sigma^* / \equiv_\theta$ is a *trace*, and can be seen as a set of strings. Given a string s, $[s]_\theta$ is the trace containing s; given a string language L, $[L]_\theta$ is the set of traces containing at least a string from L.

Any subset of $T \subseteq M(\Sigma, \theta)$ will be said to be a *trace language* on $M(\Sigma, \theta)$. As in the sequential case, the class RTL_θ of *regular* trace languages on $M(\Sigma, \theta)$ can be defined as the least class containing finite trace languages and closed with respect to set-theoretic union, concatenation and $(\cdot)^*$ closure of languages, being the concatenation of two traces the equivalence class of the concatenations of their strings. We know that these languages can always be defined by regular expressions on finite sets. Moreover, it can be shown that a trace language T is regular if and only if there is a regular string language L such that $T = [L]_\theta$ [BMS89].

We will consider only the case in which θ is a transitive relation. As a consequence, the maximal cliques of the graph associated to the concurrence relation induce a partition on Σ. Two letters will be in the same element of this partition if and only if they are nodes of the same maximal clique in the graph associated to θ, i.e., if and only if they commute in C_θ. For instance, consider $\Sigma = \{a, b, c, x, y\}$ and

$$\theta = \{(a, b), (a, c), (b, c), (x, y)\}$$

The corresponding graph on Σ is:

and the cliques $\{a, b, c\}$ and $\{x, y\}$.

Then we can define in an unique way the alphabet as a partition: $\Sigma = \bigcup_{i=1}^{n} c_i$, where n is the number of maximal cliques in the graph of θ. The term *clique* is from now on extended to the elements c_i of the partition on Σ, when not explicitly referred to the graph of θ.

Given the above described conditions, we can prove a useful result, where letters from Σ are grouped as the variables in a usual algebraic monomial:

Theorem 1. *Each trace t in $M(\Sigma, \theta)$, with transitive θ, can be uniquely represented as a sequence of monomials $t_1 \ldots t_m$, where each monomial contains letters of a unique clique, and any two adjacent monomials are from different cliques.*

Proof. Any string of the trace t can be divided in substrings by grouping consecutive letters from the same clique. Any other string in t will have these groups of letters in the same order, even if internally permuted, as in C_θ they commute among themselves and with no other letter from the contiguous sequences. Given a group, any permutation in it will be possible, and will create a string in the same trace t. So we only count the occurrences of each letter in each group and give this number as degree to the letter itself, finally constituting a factor of one monomial for each group.

Given a monomial t_i, $|t_i|_{a_j}$ denotes the degree of a_j in t_i, and $MCD(|t_i|_\Sigma)$ denotes the Maximum Common Divisor of the degrees of the letters appearing in t_i.

Our results apply to the restricted class of regular trace languages of the following definition:

Definition 2. Consider the trace languages defined by a transitive θ and by regular expressions where, when an operation of the expression joins two different traces, the trailing letters of the first don't commute in θ with the leading letters of the second. We call them *isolating* regular expressions and *isolating* regular trace languages.

This means that in such a regular expression the joining of different traces never mix letters, while this is still allowed when concatenating one or more copies of the same trace. Briefly, no different words are concatenated on letters of the same clique. This is the subclass of RTL_θ we are going to study, as it offers a way to extract strings with interesting properties from each trace. In this way we mainly allow any concatenation between traces when they don't mix joining letters, and when they mix letters between two copies of the same trace. It includes both recognizable and unrecognizable regular trace languages. Given $\Sigma = \{a, b, x\}$ and $\theta = \{(a, b)\}$, isolating languages are: $[ax \cdot \{axb\}^\star]_\theta$, $[\{ab\}^\star]_\theta$.

3 Choosing a String

The learning algorithm we will use doesn't work directly on traces. It receives one string from the equivalence class of strings constituting a given trace, chosen as specified in the following definition:

Definition 3. Given the monoid $M(\Sigma, \theta)$, with θ transitive, we can choose from any trace t, represented by the sequence of monomials $t_1 \ldots t_m$, the string $os(t) = s_1 \ldots s_m$ made in the following way: for each t_i write the string $s_i = a_1^{p_1} a_2^{p_2} \ldots a_1^{p_1} a_2^{p_2} \ldots$, where a_i is a letter and $p_j = |t_i|_{a_j}/MCD(|t_i|_\Sigma)$. We call these strings *ordered* strings.

E.g., given that (a, b) is in θ, the trace $[aaabbbbbb]_\theta$ can be represented by the monomial $a^3 b^6$, and the corresponding ordered string is *abbabbabb*.

The first key property of this rule is that the ordered string of a trace, obtained concatenating an unbounded number of times the same unknown trace, is the concatenation of the ordered strings of the repeated trace.

Lemma 4. *If the trace t is represented by a single monomial, and $os(t)$ is the ordered string of t, then $os(t \cdot t) = os(t) \cdot os(t)$.*

Proof. The single monomial representing $t \cdot t$ will have each letter with twice the degree it has in t. Therefore also the MCD is doubled, and the exponents p_i in the resulting ordered string will be the same. Then this string will be the concatenation of two copies of the ordered string of t.

When the concatenated trace is more complex we can state a weaker property: from any trace generated by the closure of a regular language, the ordered string we choose belongs to a slightly bigger regular language generating the same traces.

Lemma 5. *If θ is transitive, $s = s_1 s_2 s_3$ is a string on Σ, with strings s_1 and s_3 containing letters from the same clique, and s_2 an ordered string with trailing and leading letters from cliques different from that of s_1 and s_3:*

$$[\{L \cup \{s_1 s_2 s_3\}\}^\star]_\theta = [\{L \cup \{s_1 s_2 \{s' s_2\}^\star s_3\}\}^\star]_\theta,$$

where s' is the ordered string of $[s_3 s_1]_\theta$.

Proof. Clearly, $[s']_\theta = [s_3 s_1]_\theta$, and the inner closure adds strings to the language between square brackets, but doesn't add new traces to the trace language. Any trace $[\ldots s_1 s_2 s_3 s_1 s_2 s_3 \ldots]_\theta$, generated by the first language, will contain also the string $\ldots s_1 s_2 s' s_2 s_3 \ldots$, which belong to the second language and that is its ordered string.

Given any regular expression for T we can find an equivalent, w.r.t. θ, regular expression on Σ^* made of ordered strings. This means that the ordered strings of traces of T belong to a regular trace language L such that $[L]_\theta = T$.

Theorem 6. *Given an isolating regular trace language T over a transitive concurrence relation θ, there exists a regular language L on Σ^* such that $[L]_\theta = T$ and any ordered string extracted from a $t \in M(\Sigma, \theta)$ belongs to L if and only if t belongs to T.*

Proof. Consider the regular expression that defines T as being built from finite trace languages, applying to them many subsequent union, concatenation, and closure operations. We will build a regular expression on Σ^*, that defines a language L which satisfies our statement, by induction on the structure of the regular expression for T, using the properties stated for ordered strings over regular operations.

Any finite trace language T' is clearly equal to $[L']_\theta$, where L' is the finite language made of the ordered words of each trace in T'. Moreover, they also immediately define the regular expression of L'.

Now consider to have proved the theorem on two trace languages T' and T'', having found regular languages L' and L'' satisfying our statement, and their regular expressions. A trace language $T = T' \cup T''$ is easily verified to be equal to $[L' \cup L'']_\theta$, and the regular expression is defined consequently.

For a trace language $T = T' \cdot T''$ we consider three situations. Being T isolating, the traces of T' and T'' in their regular expressions can:

- either join on letters of different cliques, and in this case the concatenation of the respective ordered strings will do for us, as no letter would flow in the concatenated string,
- or be the same trace $t = t_1 \ldots t_m$, but with t_1 and t_m monomials on the same clique; then their concatenation will be represented by the sequence of monomials $t' = t_1 \ldots t_{m-1} t' t_2 \ldots t_m$. Then we can simply take the concatenation of the two original expressions, and use the union of it and of the set containing only the ordered string of the new trace represented by t',
- or be the same trace $t = t_1$, and by Lemma 4 we can keep only the concatenation of the original expressions.

When $T = T'^*$, being it a union of concatenations, we could have the same three cases of concatenations, and we could make the same considerations, but being this time an unbounded operation, we have to act differently in the second situation. In this case, each string in the regular expression defining L' of the form $s_1 s_2 s_3$ can be substituted, by Lemma 5, by the expression $s_1 s_2 (s' s_2)^* s_3$. In this way we obtain an expression defining a regular language R such that $[R^*]_\theta = [L'^*]_\theta = T$.

4 Identifying Isolating Languages

We will learn an isolating target language T using a Minimally Adequate Teacher (MAT) working on T and a corresponding algorithm DFAL working on Σ^*

[Ang87] to identify a regular language L such that $[L]_\theta = T$.

DFAL identifies an automaton, and in this way it represents L and then also the regular trace language$[L]_\theta$. An important fact is that some of the regular trace languages, also in the subclass of isolating regular trace languages, have no finite automaton recognizing them, as it is for $[\{ab\}^\star]_\theta$ (otherwise one could obtain by regular operations $\{a^n b^n \mid n \geq 0\}$, which is not regular).

Given any regular expression for T, by Theorem 6 we know that there exists an equivalent, w.r.t. θ, regular expression made of ordered strings. This means that the ordered strings of traces of T belong to a regular language L such that $[L]_\theta = T$. This same L is the real target of DFAL.

Using algorithm DFAL there may be three different interactions with the MAT:

- a membership query: DFAL gives a string s and we can translate it to the representation of $[s]_\theta$, giving this to the MAT,
- an equivalence query with a positive counterexample: we give to DFAL the oredered string of the counterexample trace, as it belongs to the target L, by Theorem 6, and no string in the trace is recognized by the current hypothesis language L' unless $[L']_\theta = T$,
- an equivalence query with a negative counterexample: we can give counterexample trace that is recognized by the current hypothesis (this action may take time). This is true because no string in the counterexample belongs to the target regular language, while at least one string of it belongs to the hypothesis. Our problem in this situation is that we are not guaranteed that this string, recognized by the hypothesis, is the ordered string of the counterexample trace. But the time required to find this string in a trace $[s]_\theta$, with s of length m, is exponential in m, since there is in general a number exponential in m of strings in the trace.

The fourth interaction, the equivalence query with no counterexample, require no processing, as it states the successful identification of the target language.

The time needed by DFAL to identify a canonical DFA with n states, after having received counterexamples of length at most m, has been shown to be polynomial in n and in m [Ang87].

Given the regular expression for a trace language T, consider n the number of states of the minimal DFA recognizing a regular string language L such that $[L]_\theta = T$. Our operations enlarge the corresponding regular expression as shown in Theorem 6, to build the regular expression of the language we are going to learn with our protocol. The operations that enlarge the regular expression can only add permutations of strings from the original expression, that is accepting paths in the automaton, and star closures, that is loops in the automaton. But this additions cannot require more than a polynomial, in n, number of new states in the automaton recognizing the new regular language.

The number of states of the resulting canonical DFA will then be polynomial in n, and we will have to learn it to identify T. Then, together with the observation on the time required to process a negative counterexample, we can state the following

Theorem 7. *Isolating regular trace languages with transitive concurrence relation, and generated by a regular language recognized by a DFA of n states, can be exactly identified in polynomial time in n and in the length of positive counterexamples, but in general in exponential time in the length of negative counterexamples.*

As a corollary to results on trace languages, we can use this method to learn string languages that are the union of the traces of a regular trace language. When the trace language is not recognizable, the union of its traces cannot be recognizable. Otherwise I could work on the automaton for the latter language to write an automaton for the former. But for our method of processing informations flowing between the MAT and DFLA, to have as target a trace language or the union of its traces makes no difference.

4.1 Problems with non-Isolating Languages

We are now asking whether this technique applies only to isolating languages. Consider to have $\theta = \{(a, b), (b, a)\}$ and the regular trace language $[b]_\theta \cdot [ab]_\theta^*$. This is not an isolating language.

The traces belonging to this language are represented by the monomials $a^n b^{n+1}$, and is easy to see that the Maximum Common Divisor of the two exponents is always 1, and then $os([a^n b^{n+1}]_\theta) = a^n b^{n+1}$. This means that the ordered string of such traces will never be of the form $b(ab)^*$, and the set of the ordered strings of positive traces won't build a regular language able to drive DFAL.

We *conjecture* that without restricting ourselves to a subclass of regular trace languages any extraction rule will have similar troubles in collecting strings from a regular trace language to a regular string language.

5 Discussion and Open Problems

We extend the applications of the DFAL algorithm [Ang87] to regular trace languages. Observe that other extensions have been considered in literature. [BR87] apply it to a subclass of context-free languages, [Sak90] to bottom-up tree automata.

The idea of learning regular expressions instead of automata, which would be useful in our context, is studied for expressions without union by [Bra93].

Our technique extends from the hidden trace language to the interaction with the DFAL algorithm. An interesting open problem is to refine directly the algorithm, to make use of the information we have about the structure of the extracted regular language, defined only by ordered strings. In this way we could give clear bounds on the efficiency of the learning system on this class of regular trace languages, trying to reduce the exponential dependence on the length m of negative counterexamples.

References

[AR86]   IJ. Aalbersberg, G. Rozenberg. Theory of traces. *Theoretical Computer Science*, 60:1–83, 1986.

[Ang87] D. Angluin. Learning regular sets from queries and counterexamples. *Information and Computation*, 75:87–106, 1987.

[BR87]   P. Berman, R. Roos. Learning one-counter languages in polynomial time. In *Proceedings of the Symposium on Foundations of Computer Science*, 61–67, 1987.

[BMS89] A. Bertoni, G. Mauri, N. Sabadini. Membership problems for regular and context-free trace languages. *Information and Computation*, 82:135–150, 1989.

[Bra93] A. Brazma. Efficient identification of regular expressions from representative examples. In *Proceedings of the Computational Learning Theory Conference*, 236–242, 1993.

[Gol67] E.M. Gold. Language identification in the limit. *Inform. Contr.*, 10:447–474, 1967.

[Maz85] A. Mazurkiewicz. Semantics of concurrent systems: A modular fixed point trace approach. *Lecture Notes in Comp. Sci.*, vol. 188, 353–375, Springer-Verlag, 1985.

[Pit89] L. Pitt. Inductive inference, DFAs, and computational complexity. In *Proceedings of the Analogical and Inductive Inference Workshop*, 18–, 1989.

[Sak90] Y. Sakakibara. Inductive inference of logic programs based on algebraic semantics. *New Generation Computing*, 7:365–, 1990.

Classification Using Information

William I. Gasarch[†]
Department of Computer Science and
Institute for Advanced Computer Studies
The University of Maryland
College Park, MD 20742
gasarch@cs.umd.edu

Mark G. Pleszkoch
IBM Corporation
Gaithersburg, MD 20879
markp@vnet.ibm.com

Mahendran Velauthapillai
Department of Computer Science
Georgetown University
Washington, D.C. 20057
mahe@cs.georgetown.edu

Abstract

Smith and Wiehagen [9] introduced a model of classification that is similar to the Gold model of learning [2]. The classifier is told that a recursive function f is either in $\mathcal{A}$ or $\mathcal{B}$. After seeing initial segments of f the classifier has to (in the limit) determine which of the sets f is in. In this model the classifier is limited in *both* computing power and access to information. In particular the learner is limited to Turing computability and initial segments of the function to be classified. When a function cannot be classified with respect to some desired property, it may be for either computational or information-theoretic reasons.

We would like to separate the computational limitations from the information-theoretic ones. To this end we study a model of learning originally due to Kelly [6] that has *no* computational limits; however, the objects that we will be concerned with are rather complex. Fix a set $\mathcal{A} \subseteq \{0,1\}^\omega$ We will examine if a classifier (without computational limits) can classify a string $x \in \{0,1\}^\omega$ with respect to $\mathcal{A}$.

We will be varying the amount of information the learner can access. To increase the models ability to access information, we will give it the ability to ask more powerful questions. To decrease the models ability to access information, we will bound the number of mindchanges it may make.

I. Introduction

Smith and Wiehagen [9] introduced a model of classification that is similar to the Gold model of learning [2]. The classifier is told that a recursive function f is either in $\mathcal{A}$ or $\mathcal{B}$. After seeing initial segments of f the classifier has to (in the limit) determine which of the sets f is in. In this model the learner is limited in *both* computing power and access to information. In particular the learner is limited to Turing computability and initial segments of the function to be classified.

[†] Supported by NSF grants CCR 9020079 and CCR-9401842

When a function cannot be classified it may be for either computational or information-theoretic reasons. For ease of presentation we will give examples from learning (as opposed to classification) where these two parameters are relevant. The set of all recursive function (REC) cannot be learned in the EX model; however, this is because EX lacks the needed computing power. Additional computing power helps: if an oracle for the halting problem is allowed then REC can be EX-learned (by enumeration). The set of functions that are almost always zero (FS for finite support) cannot be learned by EX_0; however, this is because EX_0 has to make a guess before having enough information. More computing power would not help: for all oracles X, $FS \notin EX_0^X$ (same proof as $FS \notin EX_0$).

We would like to separate the computational limitations from the information-theoretic ones. To this end we study a model of learning originally due to Kelly [6] that has *no* computational limits; however, the objects that we will be concerned with are rather complex. Fix a set $\mathcal{A} \subseteq \{0,1\}^\omega$ We will examine if a classifier (without computational limits) can classify a string $x \in \{0,1\}^\omega$ with respect to $\mathcal{A}$.

We will be varying the amount of information the learner can access. To increase the models ability to access information, we will give it the ability to ask more powerful questions. To decrease the models ability to access information, we will bound the number of mindchanges it may make.

II. Definitions and Notations

In this section we formalize our notions. Throughout this section $\mathcal{A}$ denotes a subset of N^ω and $\overline{\mathcal{A}}$ denotes its complement. All these definitions make sense for $\mathcal{A} \subseteq \{0,1\}^\omega$ as well.

A *classification function* (denoted c.f.) is a function F from N^* to $\{YES, NO, DK\}$ (DK stands for DON"T KNOW). Our intention is that F is fed initial segments of some f and eventually decides if it is in $\mathcal{A}$ or not. Let f be a function from N to N. *F classifies f with respect to $\mathcal{A}$* if (1) when F is given initial segments of f as input, the resultant sequence of answers converges (after some point there are no more mind changes) (2) if $f \in \mathcal{A}$ then the sequence converges to YES, and (3) if $f \notin \mathcal{A}$ then the sequence converges to NO.

F classifies $\mathcal{A}$ if, for every function f, F classifies f with respect to $\mathcal{A}$. The class DE is the collection of all sets $\mathcal{A}$ such that there exists a c.f. (DE stands for DEcsion) F that classifies $\mathcal{A}$. We denote this by saying "$\mathcal{A} \in DE$ via F." Formally F is a function; however, we will often describe it as a process that continually receives values of f (in order) and outputs conjectures. Such a description can clearly be restated in terms of F being a function.

The class DE_c is the collection of all sets in DE that have classification functions that change there mind about each f at most c times. The initial change from DK to either YES or NO is not counted as a mind change.

A *query inference machine* (QIM), defined by Gasarch and Smith [4] is an algorithmic device that asks a teacher questions about some unknown function, and while doing so, outputs programs. For more details and technical results about QIM's see [3,4,5].

We want to define an analog of that notion in our context. The c.f. F will no longer be seeing initial segments of the function. Instead it will be asking questions about the function. The questions are formulated in some query language L. The nature of the language and the questions will be given after the formal definition.

A *query classification function* (denoted q.c.f.) is a function F, which takes as input a string of bits $\bar{b}$ (the empty string is allowed), corresponding to the answers to previous queries about f, and outputs an ordered pair whose first component is one of $\{YES, NO, DK\}$ and whose second component is a question ψ in the language L. Our intention is that F is conjecturing whether f is in $\mathcal{A}$ or not and also generating the next question to ask about f. The definition of when F *classifies f with respect to $\mathcal{A}$* is straightforward but tedious (it is analogous to the definition in [4]). Formally F is a function; however, we will often describe it as a process that continually asks questions about f, receives answers, and outputs conjectures. Such a description can clearly be restated in terms of F being a function. We will also allow F to ask for the value of f at a place (e.g. 17) though formally if would actually have to ask '$f(17) = 0$?', '$f(17) = 1$?', $\ldots$', until a YES is given.

Every language L allows the use of $\wedge$, $\neg$, $=$, symbols for each natural numbers, variables that range over N, and a single unary function symbol f which represents the function being classified. (If we are classifying a set of 0-1 valued functions then we will have a single unary set symbol X representing the set being classified.) Inclusion of these symbols in every language will be implicit. The *base* language contains only these symbols. If L has auxiliary symbols, then L is denoted just by these symbols. For example, the language that has auxiliary symbols for plus and less than is denoted by $[+, <]$. The language that has auxiliary symbols for plus and times is denoted by $[+, \times]$. The language with auxiliary symbols for successor and less than is denoted by $[S, <]$, where S indicates the symbol for the successor operation. The symbol "$\star$" will be used to denote an arbitrary set of auxiliary symbols. This set can really be anything: it may be empty but it may contain symbols for nonrecursive operations.

By convention, all questions are assumed to be sentences in prenex normal form (quantifiers followed by a quantifier-free formula, called the matrix of the formula) and questions containing quantifiers are assumed to begin with an existential quantifier. This convention entails no loss of generality.

Let L be a language. The class $QDE[L]$ is the collection of all sets $\mathcal{A}$ such that there exists a q.c.f. F that classifies $\mathcal{A}$ and only asks queries that use the symbols in L. We denote this by saying "$\mathcal{A} \in QDE[L]$ via F." The class $QDE_c[L]$ is the collection of all sets in $QDE[L]$ that have classification functions that change there mind about each f at most c times. The initial change from DK to either YES or NO is not counted as a mind change.

All the query languages that we will consider allow the use of quantifiers. Restricting the applications of quantifiers is a technique that we will use to regulate the expressive power of a language. Of concern to us is the alternations between blocks of existential and universal quantifiers. Suppose that $f \in QDE[L](F)$ for some F and L. If F only asks quantifier-free questions, then we will say that $f \in Q_0DE[L](F)$. If F only asks questions with existential quantifiers, then we will say that $f \in Q_1DE[L](F)$ In general, if F's questions begin with an existential quantifier and involve $a > 0$ alternations between blocks of universal and existential quantifiers, then we say that $f \in Q_{a+1}DE[L](F)$. The classes $Q_aDE[L]$ and $Q_aDE_c[L]$ are defined analogously. By convention, if a QDE restricted to c mind changes actually achieves that bound, then it will ask no further questions.

III. Decisions with Queries

III.1 *Existential queries but no mind changes.*

We show that $Q_1 DE_0[\star]$ is not very powerful.

THEOREM 1. $Q_1 DE_0[\star] \subseteq DE$.

Proof: Let F be any q.c.f. that shows some $\mathcal{A} \in Q_1 DE_0[\star]$. We can construct a DE function F' such that F' simulates F. Since F is allowed only $\exists$ questions we first answer NO to a query until later evidence is found otherwise. The number of questions asked by the q.c.f. is finite since it is allowed only one guess. Hence F' can answer those questions by waiting and seeing the inputs from the function.   ⊠

Theorem 1 can easily be extended to the following.

COROLLARY 2. $a \in N$, $Q_{a+1} DE_0[\star] \subseteq Q_a DE[\star]$

We now show that Theorem 1 is optimal in terms of (1) mindchanges for DE, (2) mindchanges for QDE, and (3) quantifiers for QDE (some special cases).

THEOREM 3. $(\forall n \geq 0)[Q_1 DE_0[\star] - DE_n \neq \emptyset]$.

Proof: The set used in the proof of this theorem consists of all possible step functions which tail off with an even number that is $\leq 2n$. Formally

$$\mathcal{A} = \bigcup_{i=0}^{n} \{0^* 1^* 2^* \cdots (2i-1)^* (2i)^\omega\}$$

We show $\mathcal{A} \in Q_1 DE_0[\star]$. Let F be the q.c.f. that operates as follows.

0) Set $i = n$.
1) F asks $(\exists x)\,[f(x) = 2i]$. If the answer is yes goto step (3), if the answer is no goto step (2).
2) If ($i = 0$) then F outputs NO, else set $i = i - 1$ and goto step (1).
3) F waits until it sees $2i$ and x_0 such that $f(x_0) = 2i$. It also makes sure that the initial segment of the function it has seen so far is from one of the functions in $\mathcal{A}$. If it is not the case F outputs NO, else F asks $(\forall x)\,[(\bigwedge_{i=0}^{x_0} x \neq i) \rightarrow f(x) = 2i]$. If the answer is no then F outputs NO else outputs YES.

We will show that $\mathcal{A} \notin DE_n$. Assume, by way of contradiction, that $\mathcal{A} \in DE_n$ via F. We construct a function f that leads to contradiction.

0) Let $t = 0$, $\sigma = \emptyset$.
1) (t is even and $t \leq 2n$) Extend σ with more and more values of t until F produces a YES. Set $t = t + 1$.
2) (t is odd) Extend σ with more and more values of t until F produces NO. Set $t = t + 1$. If $t \leq 2n$ then goto step (1), else exit the construction.

The construction produces a finite initial segment that forces F to change its mind $2n$ times. Let f be any extension of that segment. Since F changes its mind $2n$ times while classifying f, and it was supposed to only change its mind n times, we have a contradiction. ⊠

THEOREM 4. $Q_1 DE_1[*] - DE \neq \emptyset$.

Proof: Let $\mathcal{A} = \{f \mid (\overset{\infty}{\forall} x)[f(x) = 0]\}$.

We will exhibit a q.c.f. F such that $\mathcal{A} \in Q_1 DE_1[*]$ via F. Given any f, F execute the following steps. Let i be a variable.

0) Set $i = 0$ and $A = \emptyset$.

1) F asks $(\exists x)[x \notin A \wedge f(x) \neq 0]$. If the answer is no then F outputs YES forever more. If the answer is yes then (1) by observing f find an a such that $a \notin A$ and $f(a) \neq 0$, (2) let A be $A \cup \{a\}$, (3) output NO, and (4) repeat this step.

It is easy to see that this q.c.f. will classify $\mathcal{A}$.

We show $\mathcal{A} \notin DE$. Assume, by way of contradiction, that $\mathcal{A} \in DE$ via F. We will construct an f that leads to a contradiction.

0) Let $\sigma = \emptyset$.

1) Extend σ with more and more values of zeros until F produces a YES. Goto step 2.

2) Extend σ with more and more values of 1 until F produces a NO. Goto step 1.

Let f be the limit of the σ's. Clearly F does not converge while trying to classify f. Hence F does not classify $\mathcal{A}$. ⊠

We would like to proof that Theorem 1 is optimal in terms of number of quantifiers. We do not have this for general languages but we do have it for any language that contains $<$. It is an open question to obtain this result for the empty language.

THEOREM 5. $Q_2 DE_0[<] - DE \neq \emptyset$.

Proof: Let $\mathcal{A} = \{f \mid (\overset{\infty}{\forall} x)[f(x) = 0]\}$ We show $\mathcal{A} \in Q_2 DE_0[<] - DE$

$\mathcal{A} \in Q_2 DE_0[<]$ via a F: The q.c.f. F operates as follows. Given any f F asks $(\exists y)(\forall x)[x > y \rightarrow f(x) = 0]$. If the answer is Yes then F conjectures YES, else NO. Clearly F classifies $\mathcal{A}$.

$\mathcal{A} \notin DE$ by the proof of Theorem 4.

⊠

III.2 *Existential queries and $n \geq 1$ mindchanges.*

THEOREM 6. Let $n \geq 1$. a) $DE_n \subset Q_1 DE_n[*]$. b) $DE \subset Q_1 DE[*]$.

Proof: The inclusions are obvious. The inclusions are proper by Theorem 4. ⊠

We show that Theorem 6 is optimal. We need some of the machinery from [3].

DEFINITION 7. A finite function is a cycle if it is of the form

$$\{(a+i, a+i+1) | 0 \leq i < k\} \cup \{(a+k, a)\},$$

where $a, k \in N$ and $k \geq 1$. The cycle above has *starting point* a and *length* k. It is denoted by $C(a, k)$.

LEMMA 8. Let $\Theta(f)$ be an existential query. Let σ be a finite initial segment such that $\sigma(0) = 0$. Assume that, for all functions h such that h extends σ and $h - \sigma$ is cycle free then $\Theta(h)$ is false. Then there exists $k \geq 1$ with the following property: if g extends σ and the only cycles in $(g - \sigma)$ are of length $\geq k$, then $\Theta(g)$ is false.

Proof: Similar to Lemma 14 of [3].　　　　　　　　　　　　　　　　　　　　　　⊠

THEOREM 9. $(\forall n > 0)$ $DE_n - Q_1 DE_{n-1}[*] \neq \emptyset$.

Proof: We prove this theorem for n even. The proof for n odd is similar.

Let $\mathcal{A} = \{f | f \text{ has } 1 \text{ or } 3 \text{ or } \cdots \text{ or } n - 1 \text{ cycles }\}$

We construct a c.f F such that $\mathcal{A} \in DE_n$ via F. Given any f, F executes the following steps.

0) Let $i = 0$. (i will keep track of the number of cycles seen.)

1) (We have seen $i < n$ cycles and i is even.) While looking at the function output NO. Look for an $i + 1$st cycle in f. If such is observed then set $i = i + 1$ and goto step 2.

2) (We have seen $i < n$ cycles and i is odd.) While looking at the function output YES. Look for an $i + 1$st cycle in f. If such is observed then (a) let $i = i + 1$, and (b) if $i < n$ then goto step (1), else output NO forever more.

It is easy to see that the function F classifies $\mathcal{A}$

We show that $\mathcal{A} \notin Q_1 DE_{n-1}[*]$. Assume, by way of contradiction, that $\mathcal{A} \in Q_1 DE_{n-1}[*]$ via F. We will construct an f that causes a contradiction.

0) Let $\sigma = \emptyset$, let $i = 0$. (i will count the number of cycles in f.) Let Θ be the statement $(\exists x)[f(x) = x + 1 \wedge f(x + 1) = x]$. (The only important property of Θ is no finite cycle free extension of σ can make it true. Θ and σ will have this property throughout the construction.)

1) ($i \leq n$) Let q be the current query produced by F. If a cycle free finite extension for σ exists such that q is true, then extend σ using that extension and answer the query q as true. If not then answer q as false and set $\Theta = \Theta \wedge q$. (The queries we answered yes will remain true no matter how σ is extended. The queries we answered no form Θ which can be made into an existential question. No finite cycle free extension can makes Θ true.) If i is even then repeat this step until F produces a YES. If i is odd then repeat this step until F produces a NO. (This must happen since F classifies $\mathcal{A}$.) Goto step (2).

2) By Lemma 8 there exists an extension of σ that has a new cycle and is consistent with the answers to all the queries. Extend σ using this extension and set $i = i + 1$. If $i \leq n$ then goto step (1) else exit.

At the end of the construction we have a finite initial segment σ. Let $f = \sigma 0^\omega$. If F tries to classify f then n mindchanges will be encountered. This contradicts the nature of F.　　　　　　⊠

III.3 *Unbounded quantification*

We have seen that mindchanges impose a restriction and queries enhance with power. The question arises as to whether the restriction of queries can overcome the limitation of mindchanges. The next theorem shows that mindchanges can be so severe a restriction that even unbounded queries do not help.

THEOREM 10. $DE_1 - Q.DE_0[\star] \neq \emptyset$

Proof: Let the language have symbols $S_1, S_2, \ldots$. Let s_i be the Turing degree of S_i. Let B be a set of Turing degree $\bigoplus_{i=1}^{\infty} s_i$. Let $A = B'$. Finally, let $\mathcal{A} = \{A\}$. (That is, $\mathcal{A}$ is the singleton set that contains one 0-1 valued function which is the characteristic function of A.) We show $\mathcal{A} \in DE_1 - Q.DE_0[\star]$.

$\mathcal{A} \in DE_1$: Initially the classifier guesses YES. If ever the function being observed differs from A guess NO forever more.

$\mathcal{A} \notin Q.DE_0[\star]$. Assume, by way of contradiction, that $\mathcal{A} \in Q.DE_0[\star]$ via F. Since $\mathcal{A}$ contains just 0-1 valued functions we can assume the queries have a set symbol X instead of a function symbol. Simulate F by answering questions as though A is the set being classified. After a finite number of questions F will produce a YES. Let $q(X)$ be the conjunction of all queries asked about A that were true and the negations of those that were false. Note that if C is any set such that $q(C)$ is true then F will classify $C \in \mathcal{A}$, so $C = A$.

We claim

$$(\forall x)[x \in A \rightarrow (q(X) \vdash x \in X)];$$
$$(\forall x)[x \notin A \rightarrow (q(X) \vdash x \notin X)];$$

We proof the first one, the second is similar. Assume, by way of contradiction, that there is an x_0 such that $[x_0 \in A \wedge q(X) \not\vdash x_0 \in X]$. Then $\Gamma = \{q(X), x_0 \notin X\}$ is a consistent set of sentences. By the completeness theorem Γ has a model. This model is a set C such that $q(C)$ is true but $x_0 \notin C$. Since $x_0 \notin C$ we know $C \neq A$; but since $q(C)$ is true F will classify $C \in \mathcal{A}$ so $C = A$. This is a contradiction.

We can use these two facts to obtain a reduction $A \leq_T B$: on input x enumerate all proofs that can use $q(X)$ as an axiom (you need the set B to be able to use $q(X)$ intelligently) until either $x \in X$ or $x \notin X$ is derived. One of the two must be derived since either $x \in A$ or $x \notin A$. Whichever one is derived is true for A. Since $A = B'$ we have $B' \leq_T B$ which is a contradiction. $\boxtimes$

It is an open question to extend Theorem 10

Conjecture $DE_n - Q.DE_{n-1}[\star] \neq \emptyset$.

We can obtain the conjecture in the special case of $L = [S, <]$.

DEFINITION 11. A string is *dull* if it is of the form $\sigma(\tau)^{|\sigma|}$ where $3 \leq |\tau| \leq |\sigma|$.

THEOREM 12. $DE_{n+1} - QDE_n[S, <] \neq \emptyset$.

Proof: We prove this for n odd. The proof for n even is similar.

Let $\mathcal{A} = \{A \in \{0,1\}^{\omega} \mid A$ has either 1 or 3 or ... or n dull prefixes$\}$. We show $\mathcal{A} \in DE_{n+1} - QDE_n[S, <]$.

$\mathcal{A} \in DE_{n+1}$: Initially conjecture NO. If an ith dull prefix is seen where i is odd and $i \leq n$ then say YES. If an ith dull prefix is seen where i is even or $i \geq n+1$ then say NO.

$\mathcal{A} \notin QDE_n[S, <]$: Assume, by way of contradiction, that $\mathcal{A} \in QDE_n[S, <]$ via F. We construct a set A that F does not classify correctly.

CONSTRUCTION

1) Set A to a set that has no dull prefixes. Set MC and ND to 0. (MC is the number of mindchanges seen so far; ND is the number of dull prefixes seen so far.)

2) (MC and ND are even and $\leq n+1$.) Simulate F. Answer questions about it as if the set is A. Stop when the conjecture is NO. (This must happen.) If $ND = n+1$ then stop. Else set MC to $MC+1$.

3) Let N be the ω-automata that accepts all languages that satisfy the query answers supplied in the simulation. Note that N accepts A. Therefore we can find $\sigma, \tau \in \{0,1\}^*$, $\gamma \in \{0,1\}^{\omega}$, and $i < |\sigma|$ such that $A = \sigma(\tau)^i \gamma$, $\sigma(\tau)^{i+1} \not\preceq A$, and N accepts $\sigma(\tau)^j \gamma$ for any $j \geq i$. Note that the set $\sigma(\tau)^{|\sigma|} \gamma$ has *exactly* one more dull prefix then A. Set A to $\sigma(\tau)^{|\sigma|} \gamma$ and ND to $ND+1$. Note that the answers supplied by the simulation are also correct for the new A.

4) (MC and ND are odd and $\leq n$.) Simulate F. Answer questions about it as if the set is A. Stop when the conjecture is YES. (This must happen.) Set MC to $MC+1$ and goto step

5) Identical to step 3 except that when its over we goto step 2.

END OF CONSTRUCTION

The set A we obtain at the end forces F to change its mind $n+1$ times, which is a contradiction.

⊠

IV. Classification with Mind Changes and Anomalies

In this section we establish exactly when $DE_a^b \subseteq DE_c^d$. We will show that only the obvious inclusions hold except for the case of $d = *$.

DEFINITION 13. Let $\mathcal{A}$ be any set, $|\mathcal{A}|$ will denote the cardinality of $\mathcal{A}$.

DEFINITION 14. Let f and g be functions. If $|\{x|g(x) \neq f(x)\}| \leq a$, then we say that g is an a *variant of* f. If $|\{x|g(x) \neq f(x)\}|$ is finite then we say g is a *finite variant of* f.

DEFINITION 15. Let $\mathcal{A}$ be a set of functions, F a classification function, $a \in N$ and f be any function. We say $f \in DE^a(F)$ if the following hold.

$$(f \in \mathcal{A} \text{ and no } a\text{-variant of } g \text{ is in } \overline{\mathcal{A}}) \rightarrow F(f) \downarrow = YES.$$

$$(f \in \overline{\mathcal{A}} \text{ and no } a\text{-variant of } g \text{ is in } \mathcal{A}) \rightarrow F(f) \downarrow = NO.$$

Note that for functions that are in $\mathcal{A}$ ($\overline{\mathcal{A}}$) but have a-variants in $\overline{\mathcal{A}}$ ($\mathcal{A}$) there are no constraints on what F will do.

DEFINITION 16. Let $\mathcal{A}$ be a set of functions, F a classification function and f be any function. We say $f \in DE^*(F)$ if the following hold.

$$(f \in \mathcal{A} \wedge \text{ no finite variant of } g \text{ is in } \overline{\mathcal{A}}) \rightarrow F(f) \downarrow = YES.$$

$$(f \in \overline{\mathcal{A}} \wedge \text{ no finite variant of } g \text{ is in } \mathcal{A}) \rightarrow F(f) \downarrow = NO.$$

Note that for functions that are in $\mathcal{A}$ ($\overline{\mathcal{A}}$) but have finite variants in $\overline{\mathcal{A}}$ ($\mathcal{A}$) there are no constraints on what F will do.

THEOREM 17. $(\forall a > 0)$ and $(\forall n \geq 0)$ $DE_a - DE^n_{a-1} \neq \emptyset$

Proof: Let $a > 0$ and $n \geq 0$ be given.

Case 1. a Even, let $b = a/2$.

Let $\mathcal{A} = \{f \mid \text{range } f \text{ has exactly } 2(n+1) \text{ 1's or } 4(n+1) \text{ 1's or } \cdots \text{ or } 2b(n+1) \text{ 1's } \}.$

We show $\mathcal{A} \in DE_a$. Let F be a classification function such that given any f it initially conjectures NO, then waits until it sees $2(n+1)$ ones and then says YES. If F sees a one, it changes its conjecture to NO. Waits for a total of $4(n+1)$ ones and changes its conjecture to YES. It can repeat this process until it sees $2b(n+1)$ ones and says YES. Up to now M has made $2b = a$ conjectures. If F sees an additional one it will say NO. Clearly F has made at most $a+1$ conjectures and F is correct. Since $2b = a$, $\mathcal{A} \subseteq DE_a(F)$.

We show $\mathcal{A} \notin DE^n_{a-1}$. Assume, by way of contraction, that $\mathcal{A} \in DE^n_{a-1}$ via F. We will construct an f that causes a contradiction.

0) Let $\sigma = \emptyset$.

1) (The number of 1's seen so far is an even multiple of $n+1$.) Extend σ with $(n+1)$ ones and then with more and more zeros until F produces NO. (This must happen since the resulting function is in $\overline{\mathcal{A}}$ and no n-variant is in $\mathcal{A}$.) Goto step (2).

2) (The number of 1's seen so far is an odd multiple of $n+1$.) Extend σ with $(n+1)$ ones. Then extend σ with zeros, until F changes its produces YES. (This must happen since the resulting function is in $\mathcal{A}$ and no n-variant is in $\overline{\mathcal{A}}$.) Goto step (1).

Clearly, F has to make $2b+1$ conjectures to be correct on a function with $(2b+1)(n+1)$ ones, or it has converged to a wrong conjecture. Hence $\mathcal{A} \notin DE^n_{a-1}$ for the case a even.

Case 2. a odd, let $b = (a+1)/2$.

Let $\mathcal{A} = \{f \mid \text{range } f \text{ has exactly } 2(n+1) \text{ 1's or } 4(n+1) \text{ 1's } \cdots \text{ or } \geq 2b(n+1) \text{ 1's } \}.$

The rest of the proof is similar to the proof in case (1). ⊠

THEOREM 18. $(\forall n \geq 0)$ $DE^{n+1}_0 - DE^n_* \neq \emptyset$

Proof: Let

$$\mathcal{A} = \{f \mid \text{number of 1's in the range of } f \text{ is a multiple of } 2(n+1) \text{ or is infinite}\}.$$

Let f be any function. If f has an infinite number of 1's then $f \in \mathcal{A}$. If f has a finite number of 1's then that number is at most $n+1$ away from a multiple of $2(n+1)$. Hence f is an $n+1$-variant of some function in $\mathcal{A}$. This is true for *any* f. Hence the c.f. that always answers YES shows that $\mathcal{A} \in DE_0^{n+1}$.

We show that $\mathcal{A} \notin DE_*^n$. Assume, by way of contradiction, that $\mathcal{A} \in DE_*^n$ via F. We will construct an f that leads to a contradiction.

0) Let $\sigma = \emptyset$,

1) (the number of 1's seen so far is an even multiple of $n+1$) Extend σ with more and more zeros until F says YES. (This must happen since the resulting function is in $\mathcal{A}$ and no n-variant of it is in $\overline{\mathcal{A}}$.) Add $n+1$ 1's and goto to step (2).

2) (the number of 1's seen so far is an odd multiple of $n+1$) Extend σ with more and more zeros until F says NO. (This must happen since the resulting function is in $\overline{\mathcal{A}}$ and no n-variant of it is in $\mathcal{A}$.)

Let f be the limit of the σ's. Clearly F does not converge on f. This contradicts the nature of F. ☒

The last two theorems seem to indicate that one cannot compensate for less mindchanges with more errors or vice versa. The next theorem, perhaps surprisingly, states that for the case of $*$ errors you can compensate.

THEOREM 19. $DE_1 \subset DE_0^*$

Proof: By Theorem 18 $DE_0^* - DE_1 \neq \emptyset$. Now we will show the inclusion. Let $\mathcal{A} \in DE_1$ via F. Now we will construct an F' such that $\mathcal{A} \in DE_0^*$ via F'

Let f be any function, now F on some initial segment σ of f will conjecture G (either YES or NO). Now F' asks if there is a τ such that $F(\sigma\tau) = NOT(G)$. Recall that F' has no computational limitations and that this question does not depend on information about f, so it can be determined. If no mind change is found the F' output F's initial conjecture G, else output $NOT(G)$.

We now show that F' is a DE_0^* classifier for $\mathcal{A}$. Clearly F' uses 0 mindchanges. If F' outputs G then no extension of σ, including the extension that really is f, forced a mindchange. Therefore G is the correct answer. Assume F' output $NOT(G)$. Let h be the function that has initial segment $\sigma\tau$ and is then f thereafter (formally $\sigma\tau f(|\sigma\tau|)f(|\sigma\tau|+1)\cdots$). Upon seeing $\sigma\tau$ F makes one mindchange and classifies h as $NOT(G)$ forevermore. Hence the status of h with respect to $\mathcal{A}$ is $NOT(G)$. Since f is a finite variant of h classifying f as $NOT(G)$ is correct for DE_0^* classification.

☒

THEOREM 20. $(\forall a, b, n, m \in N)$ $DE_n^a \subseteq DE_m^b$ if and only if $(a \leq b)$ and $(n \leq m)$.

Proof: $\Rightarrow$ Let $a, b, n, m \in N$ be given. Suppose $DE_n^a \subseteq DE_m^b$ and $a > b$. Then by Theorem 18 $DE_n^a - DE_m^b \neq \emptyset$. Hence $a \leq b$. suppose $DE_n^a \subseteq DE_m^b$ and $n > m$. Then by Theorem 17 $DE_n^a - DE_m^b \neq \emptyset$. Hence $n \leq m$.

$\Leftarrow$ Let $a, b, n, m \in N$ be given. if $(a \leq b)$ and $(n \leq m)$ the result is obvious. ☒

Note that Theorem 20 will not hold if $b = *$ since it will contradict Theorem 19

V. Decisions with Teams

Team inference was introduced by Smith [7]. Next we define team classification similar to team inference defined by Smith.

DEFINITION 21. For $n, m \in N$ such that $n \leq m$, $a \in N$ and for any f, $[n,m]DE_a$ denotes a team of m classifiers out of which at least n of them correctly classify f after at most a mind changes.

THEOREM 22. Let $\mathcal{A}$ be any set of functions then $\mathcal{A} \in [1,2]DE_0$.

Proof: Let F_1 and F_2, be two classification functions which do the following: on input from any function f, F_1 will always conjecture YES and F_2 will always conjecture NO. ☒

THEOREM 23. $(\forall n > 0) \ [n+1, 2n+1]DE_0 = DE_0$

Proof: Let $\mathcal{A} \in [n+1, 2n+1]DE_0$, this implies that there exists classifications functions $F_1, F_2, \cdots, F_{2n+1}$ such that on any f $n+1$ of these classifiers can correctly classify f with respect to $\mathcal{A}$. We will construct a classification function F such that $\mathcal{A} \subseteq DE_0(F)$. F simulates the the team by waiting for at least $n+1$ of the team members to agree (either YES or NO). Then F outputs that answer. This implies that $[n+1, 2n+1]DE_0 \subseteq DE_0$. Clearly $DE_0 \subseteq [n+1, 2n+1]DE_0$. ☒

References

1) L. Fortnow, S. Jain, W. Gasarch, E. Kinber, M. Kummer, S. Kurtz, M. Pleszkoch, T. Slaman, F. Stephan and R. Solovay, *Extremes in the Degrees of Inferability*, Annals of pure and applied logic, vol 66, 1994, 231-276.

2) E. M. Gold, *Learning Identification in the Limit*, Information and Control, vol 10, 1967, pp. 447-474.

3) William Gasarch, Mark Pleszkoch and Robert Solovay, *Learning via Queries to* $[+, <]^n$, Journal of Symbolic Logic; vol 57, March 1992,pp. 53-81.

4) William Gasarch and Carl H. Smith, *Learning via Queries*, Journal of the Association for Computing Machinery, vol 39, July 1992, pp. 649-675.

5) William Gasarch, Efim Kinber, Mark Pleszkoch, Carl Smith, and Thomas Zeugmann, *Learning via Queries with Teams and Anomalies*, Fundamenta Informaticae (to appear).

6) Kelly, Kevin T., 1994, *The Logic of Reliable Inquiry* Oxford: Oxford University Press, forthcoming.

7) C. H. Smith, *The Power of Pluralism for Automatic Program Synthesis*, Journal of the Association for Computing Machinery, vol 29, 1982, pp. 1144-1165.

8) L. G. Valiant, *A theory of Learnable*, Communications of the ACM, vol 27, 1987, pp.1134-1142.

9) R. Wiehagen and C.H. Smith, *Classification versus Generalization*, in Proceedings 5th Annual ACM Workshop on Computational Learning Theory, Pittsburgh (1992), pp. 224-230, ACM Press, New York.

10) R. Wiehagen, C.H. Smith and T. Zeugmann *Classifying Recursive Predicates and Languages*, Gossler Report 21/93, December 93.

Learning from Examples with Typed Equational Programming

Akira ISHINO and Akihiro YAMAMOTO

Department of Electrical Engineering
Hokkaido University
North 13, West 8, Sapporo, Japan

akira@huee.hokudai.ac.jp, yamamoto@huee.hokudai.ac.jp

Abstract. In this paper we present a constructive method of learning from examples using typed equational programming. The main contribution is a concept of type maintenance which appears to be theoretically and practically useful. Type maintenance is based on polymorphic types and is not applicable to a type system without polymorphism. Because equational programming possesses good properties of both functional programming and logic programming, we will refine results in inductive inference of logic programs and that of functions. Our learning method is based on the type maintenance, the generalization given by Plotkin and Arimura et al. and the technique finding recursion given by Summers.

1 Introduction

In this paper we present a constructive method of inductive inference using typed equational programming. Equational programming is a programming paradigm using sets of equations as programs. It has attracted much attention of many researchers since it was proposed in 1970's [14]. Recently it is adopted in some practical programming languages, e.g. ML [11, 12] and Haskell [5]. In these languages a static and polymorphic type system, Hindley-Milner type system [10], is used in order to associate the value of each term with a type and to ensure application of functions safe. The main contribution we obtained by using the polymorphic type system is a concept of type maintenance. Moreover, equational programming possesses good properties of both functional programming and logic programming as was shown in [4]. We will not simply combine results in inductive inference of logic programs and that of functions, but refine them from the view point of comparing the programming paradigms.

Type maintenance is to transform an equation into a more general one when the type of the target function is given. For example consider the case that our machine is learning a projection function *first*, which returns the first component of a pair. It would be given examples, e.g. $first(1, 2) = 1$. Then, if it finds that the type of *first* is $(\alpha, \beta) \to \alpha$ where α and β are two type variables, it regards '1' and '2' as no more than identifiers because each arguments of *first* can posses an arbitrary type. We can therefore replaces these with new variables, and obtain an equation $first(x, y) = y$. Type maintenance, and moreover, has another advantage that it reduces a set of examples, this make a learning method efficient.

Some researchers have already tried to construct learning theories using equational programming or typed logic programming. For example, Togashi and Noguchi [19] gave a method to learn non-typed equations. It assumes an oracle like MIS [16]. Our learning method is different from it because we use typed equations and give a data-driven method. Our method is based on the generalization of Plotkin [15] and Arimura et al. [1], and on the technique finding recursion given in Summers' method [17, 18]. Page Jr. and Frish [6] gave a theory of inductive logic programming using typed logic programming. The type in the theory is written as a first order theory, which, however, cannot treat polymorphic type. Our type maintenance is based on polymorphic types and is not applicable to a type system without polymorphism. Moreover, we adopt not logic programming but equational programming, some refinement of searching hypothesis is obtained.

The paper is organized as follows. In Section 2 we define notions of equations and types. We regard a non-overlapping set of equations as programs. We also define well-typed equations and programs. Our expression language of learning is the class of well-typed programs. In Section 3 we define the notion of *type maintenance* and present a type maintenance algorithm $\mathcal{M}$ which takes an equation and a type and then outputs a *maintenance* of an equation. In Section 4 we define and justify a generalization relation for well-typed equations. Then, we give the definition of the least generalization of well-typed equations and present an algorithm $\mathcal{LG}$ which computes it if it exists or fails otherwise. We also give a formal definition of k-mmg. For pattern programs, which are simple programs, we present an algorithm k-$\mathcal{MMG}$ to compute k-mmg's. Because we assume several conditions to equations as programs, there is a set of equations which has no k-mmg's for fixed $k \geq 1$. Thus to find proper k-mmg's k-$\mathcal{MMG}$ is repeatedly applied to the set of given examples, from $k = 1$ up to the number of examples. In Section 5 we give our learning method for recursive programs. The method computes k-mmg's from examples repeatedly with increasing k and infers a class of recursive programs by applying the k-mmg's to Summers' method.

2   Preliminaries

A set of symbols Σ consists of three classes, *variables*, *constructors*, and *functions*. We will use $x, x_1, y, \ldots$ for variables, $a, a_1, b, \ldots$ for constructors, and $f, f_1, g, \ldots$ for functions. Every constructor and function is assumed to have its arity.

Definition.
A *pattern* is defined inductively as follows:

1. A variable is a pattern.
2. If a is an n-ary constructor and $p_1, \ldots, p_n$ are patterns, then $a(p_1, \ldots, p_n)$ is a pattern.

A *term* is defined inductively as follows:

1. A pattern is a term
2. If f is an n-ary function and $t_1, \ldots, t_n$ are terms, then $f(t_1, \ldots, t_n)$ is a term.

Let t, s be two terms. We say t is *more general than* s and write $s \leqslant t$ if $t = s\sigma$ for some substitution σ. The set of variables contained in a term t is denoted by $\mathcal{V}(t)$.

Definition. We denote sequences of integers by $I, J, \ldots$. The set of *occurrence* $\mathcal{O}(t)$ in the term t, and a term t/I is defined inductively as follows:

1. When t is a variable, then $\mathcal{O}(t) = \{\langle\rangle\}$ and $t/\langle\rangle = t$.
2. When t has the form $f(t_1, \ldots, t_m)$ (f is a constructor or function), then $\mathcal{O}(t) = \{\langle\rangle\} \cup \{\langle i, j_1, \ldots, j_l\rangle \mid i \leq m, \langle j_1, \ldots, j_l\rangle \in \mathcal{O}(t_i)\}$, and $t/\langle\rangle = t$, $t/\langle i, j_1, \ldots, j_l\rangle = t_i/\langle j_1, \ldots, j_l\rangle$.

Definition. An *equation* is an expression of the form $s = t$ where s and t are terms. Equations are denoted by $F, F_1, G, \ldots$. It is *collapse* if s is a variable.

In the paper we will not treat any collapse equation. Thus from now on an equation is assumed to be non-collapse.

Definition. An equation is *of a function* f if it is of the form

$$f(p_1, \ldots, p_n) = t$$

where n is the arity of f. f is called its *initial symbol*. The equation is called a *functional rule* (or a *rule*, for short) of f if each p_i is a pattern and $\mathcal{V}(t) \subseteq \mathcal{V}(p_1) \cup \cdots \cup \mathcal{V}(p_n)$. It is called *a ground pattern rule* if $p_1, \ldots, p_n, t$ are all ground patterns.

Definition. A *program* is a finite set P of functional rules. It is *non-overlapping* if there is no pair of distinct rules in P whose left-hand-sides are unifiable.

We assume that a program should be non-overlapping.

Definition. The *definition* of a function f in a program P is the set of all functional rules whose initial symbol is f.

Definition. For a program P and a function f with arity n, we define

$$\mathcal{F}(P, f) = \left\{ (t_1, t_2, \ldots, t_n, s) \,\middle|\, \begin{array}{l} (t_1, t_2, \ldots, t_n, s) \text{ are all ground patterns and} \\ P \vdash f(t_1, t_2, \ldots, t_n) = s \end{array} \right\}$$

where $P \vdash F$ means F is provable from P in equational logic.

Now we give definitions on types. A set of symbols Ψ consists of two classes, *basic types* and *type variables*. We will use $\iota, \iota_0, \ldots$ for basic types, $\alpha, \alpha_1, \beta, \ldots$ for type variables, and $\tau, \tau_1, \mu, \ldots$ for arbitrary types. Every basic type is assumed to have its arity.

Definition. A *type* is defined inductively as follows:

1. A 0-ary basic type is a type.
2. A type variable is a type.
3. If ι is an n-ary basic type and $\tau_1,\ldots,\tau_n$ are types, then $\iota(\tau_1,\ldots,\tau_n)$ is a type.
4. If $\tau_1,\ldots,\tau_n$ and μ are types, then $(\tau_1,\ldots,\tau_n) \to \mu$ is a type.

The set of all types is denoted by $\mathcal{T}$. Let μ, τ be two types. We say μ is *more general than* τ and write $\tau \leqslant \mu$ if $\tau = \mu\sigma$ for some substitution σ.

Definition. A *type context* Γ is a mapping from Σ to $\mathcal{T}$ such that for every constructor or function a with arity n, $\Gamma(a) = (\tau_1,\tau_2,\ldots,\tau_n) \to \mu$.

Definition. Let Γ be a type context. We define a relation $\Gamma \vdash t : \tau$ for a term t and type τ inductively as follows:

1. For every variable x, $\Gamma \vdash x : \Gamma(x)$.
2. For every 0-ary constructor a, $\Gamma \vdash a : \tau$ where $\tau \leqslant \Gamma(a)$.
3. If f is an n-ary constructor or function, $(\tau_1,\ldots,\tau_n) \to \mu \leqslant \Gamma(f)$, $\Gamma \vdash t_1 : \tau_1$, ..., and $\Gamma \vdash t_n : \tau_n$, then $\Gamma \vdash f(t_1,\ldots,t_n) : \mu$.

A term t is *well-typed* and *possesses* τ *under* Γ if $\Gamma \vdash t : \tau$.

Definition. Let $\Gamma(f) = (\tau_1,\ldots,\tau_n) \to \mu$. A functional rule $f(t_1,\ldots,t_n) = s$ is *well-typed* under Γ if $\Gamma \vdash t_1 : \tau_1$, ..., $\Gamma \vdash t_n : \tau_n$, and $\Gamma \vdash s : \mu$. It is *well-typed* if there exists Γ under which it is well-typed.

Definition. A program P is *well-typed* under Γ if for all functional rules in P are well-typed under Γ. A program P is *well-typed* if there exists Γ under which P is well-typed.

3 Type Maintenance

In this section we explain the main contribution of our work, type maintenance. At first we illustrate what is type maintenance by means of a simple example.

Example 1. Let *append* be a function symbol which concatenates a pair of lists. For instance,

$$append([0,1],[2,3]) = [0,1,2,3] \; , \tag{1}$$

where $0,1,\ldots$ represent $zero, suc(zero),\ldots$ respectively and also $[0,1]$ represent $cons(zero, cons(suc(zero), nil))$.

The equation (1) possesses a type $(List(int), List(int)) \to List(int)$. However, *append* can be applied to other types of two lists. In general, *append* possesses a type

$$(List(\alpha), List(\alpha)) \to List(\alpha) \; ,$$

where α is a type variable. So *append* can possess types

$$(List(bool), List(bool)) \to List(bool) \ ,$$
$$(List(List(int)), List(List(int))) \to List(List(int))$$

and so on. Indeed, there exist expressions which possess the type which mentioned above:

$$append([true, false], [false, true]) = [true, false, false, true] \ , \qquad (2)$$
$$append([[0], [1]], [[2], [3]]) = [[0], [1], [2], [3]] \ . \qquad (3)$$

From the equations it become clear that terms $0, 1, 2, 3$ in the equation (1) is no more than identifier. The terms can be replaced with new variables x_0, x_1, x_2, x_3 respectively, and we obtain an equation

$$append([x_0, x_1], [x_2, x_3]) = [x_0, x_1, x_2, x_3] \ . \qquad (4)$$

We call the equation (4) a maintenance of (1). Type maintenance is to get a maintenance of an equation by the type of the target function. In passing, note that the equation (4) is a least generalization of the set of (1), (2) and (3).

Type maintenance is extension of generalization in the sence of Plotkin[15] from the following reason. In Lassez et.al[7] it is shown that a term t is more general than s iff every ground instance of s is a ground instance of t. The result means that a term t can be interpreted as the set of all ground instance of t. We can consider that generalization is to replace a set of constructor terms with its super set. A type has the two interpretations. It is interpreted as a set of values and as a set of ground constructor terms. Then a well-typed term can be interpreted as a set of ground constructor terms. Then we can regard our type maintenance as replacement of a set of constructor term with its super set which a type represents.

Now we define type maintenance as follows.

Definition. Let t be a term, τ be a type, and Γ is a type context. A term s is a *maintenance of t relative to τ and Γ* iff the following three hold:

1. $t \leqslant s$.
2. $\Gamma \vdash s : \tau$.
3. For any term r s.t. $\Gamma \vdash r : \tau$, $t \leqslant r$ implies $s \leqslant r$.

Definition. Let F, G be equations and Γ be a type context. Then G is a *maintenance of F relative to Γ* if the following three hold:

1. $F \leqslant G$.
2. G is well-typed under Γ.
3. For any rule H of f well-typed under Γ, $F \leqslant H$ implies $G \leqslant H$.

The algorithm $\mathcal{M}$ illustrated below specifies the type maintenance for a functional rule. It uses a data structure *environment* defined as follows.

Definition. An *environment* is a set of tuples (s, τ, x) where s is a term s, τ is a type and x is a variable. It is *consistent* if for every symbol x there is at most one tuple of the form (s, τ, x).

For a consistent environment E we define a set $\mathcal{V}(E)$ of variables and a substitution θ_E as

$$\mathcal{V}(E) = \{x \mid (s, \tau, x) \in E\},$$
$$\theta_E = \{x \leftarrow s \,;\, (s, \tau, x) \in E\}.$$

Moreover, for a type context Γ, we define a type context Γ_E as

$$\Gamma_E(x) = \begin{cases} \tau & \text{if } (s, \tau, x) \in E \,, \\ \Gamma(x) & \text{otherwise} \,. \end{cases}$$

$\mathcal{M}$ takes a pair of a functional rule $f(p_1, \ldots, p_n) = u$ and a type context Γ as input. It outputs a maintenance of the rule by calling a subroutine $\mathcal{TM}$.

Algorithm $\mathcal{M}(F, \Gamma)$

Input: a rule F of of the form $f(p_1, \ldots, p_n)$
a type context Γ.
Output: an equation.
Procedure:

```
1      E←φ;
2      for each tᵢ do
3         (sᵢ,E)←𝒯ℳ(tᵢ,τᵢ,E,Γ)
4      end ;
5      (v,E)←𝒯ℳ(u,μ,E,Γ);
6      output f(s₁,...,sₙ) = v.
```

The subroutine $\mathcal{TM}$ takes as input a term t, a type τ, a type context Γ, and an environment E. It returns a pair of a term and an environment. $\mathcal{TM}$ calls itself recursively, and traverses the term t, from its root to its leaves, inferring the type of each subterm from Γ and the judgment $\Gamma \vdash t : \tau$. If $\mathcal{TM}$ detects a subterm s whose type must be a type variable α, $\mathcal{TM}$ replaces s with a variable. The variable is x if a tuple (s, α, x) is in E, otherwise, it is a new variable y. In the latter case $\mathcal{TM}$ adds a tuple (s, α, y) to E.

Theorem 1. *Let F be a ground rule of n-ary function f and Γ be a type context. The algorithm $\mathcal{M}$ returns a maintenance of F relative to Γ if it exists.*

To prove the theorem we prepare two lemmas.

Lemma 2. *Let p be a ground pattern, τ be a type and E be a consistent environment. If the output of $\mathcal{TM}(t, \tau, E)$ is (s, E'), then E' is consistent, $t\theta_E = s\theta_{E'-E}\theta_E$ and $\Gamma'_E \vdash s : \tau$.*

Algorithm $\mathcal{TM}(t, \tau, E, \Gamma)$

Input: a term t, a type τ, a type context Γ and a set E.

Output: a term s and E'.

Procedure:

1   **if** τ is a type variable **then**
2   **if** $(t, \tau, x) \in E$ for some x **then**
3   **output** (x, E)
4   **else**
5           $E \leftarrow E \cup \{(t, \tau, x)\}$ where x is a new variable;
6   **output** (x, E)
7   **else**   ▷ τ is not a variable
8   let $\tau_1, \ldots, \tau_n, \mu$ be types s.t. $\Gamma(f) = (\tau_1, \ldots, \tau_n) \to \mu$
          and θ be a substitution s.t. $\mu\theta = \tau$;
9   **for each** t_i **do**   ▷ t is of the form $f(t_1, \ldots, t_n)$ $(n \geq 0)$
10           $(s_i, E) \leftarrow \mathcal{TM}(t_i, \tau_i\theta, E)$
11   **end** ;
12   **output** $(f(s_1, \ldots, s_n), E)$.

Proof. At first we consider the case τ is a type variable. If $(t, \tau, x) \in E$ for some variable x, then $s = x$, $\theta_{E'-E}$ is an identity, and $\Gamma_E \vdash x : \tau$. If there is no x s.t. $(t, \tau, x) \in E$, s is a new variable x and $\theta_{E'-E} = \{x \leftarrow t\}$ and $\Gamma_{E'} \vdash x : \tau$. Thus the results hold in the case.

Next we consider the case τ is not a type variable. Assume that t is of the form $f(t_1, \ldots, t_n)$ and $\Gamma_E(f) = (\tau_1, \ldots, \tau_n) \to \mu$. If τ is not an instance of μ, then $\mathcal{TM}$ must halt. So there is a substitution θ s.t. $\mu\theta = \tau$. Here as an induction hypothesis we can assume that the results hold for $(t_i, \tau_i\theta, E_i)$ $(i = 1, \ldots n)$ where $E_1 = E$ and E_{i+1} is in the output of $\mathcal{TM}(t_i, \tau_i\theta, E_i)$. Then $E' = E_{n+1}$ and thus the results hold because the variables introduced into E_i, to makes E_i, are all new and E_i are all consistent.

Lemma 3. *Let p be a ground pattern and Γ be a type context, and (q, E) is the output of $\mathcal{TM}(q, \tau, \Gamma, \phi)$. If a pattern r satisfies $r \leqslant p$ and $\Gamma \vdash r : \tau$ then $q \leqslant r$.*

Proof. Assume that $q \not\leqslant r$. Then at least one of the following two causes:

- There is an occurrence I such that q/I is a variable, but r/I is not.
- There are two distinct occurrences I and J s.t. r/I and r/J are the same variable but q/I and q/J are different variables.

In the first case the type of r/I must not be a type variable, but q/J must be a type variable. Since no substitutions are executed to type variables in τ, the case does not cause. Next we consider the second case. Since r/I and r/J are the same, they must possess the same type and be substituted the same term for. However, q/I and q/J are different variables. So they have different types or are substituted different terms for when we get p from q. Again no substitutions are executed to type variables in τ, we get a contradiction.

Theorem 1 is proved with the lemmas in an analogous way to them.

4 Generalization for Well-Typed Functional Rules

4.1 Generalization relation for Well-typed Functional Rules

We introduce a generalization relation on well-typed functional rules.

Definition. Let F and G be functional rules well-typed under Γ. If $F = G\sigma$ for some substitution σ then G is more general than F and we write $F \leqslant_\Gamma G$.

Example 2. Let *and* be a function, *true* be a constant. Then it holds that

$$and(true, true) = true \ \leqslant_\Gamma \ and(true, x) = x \ .$$

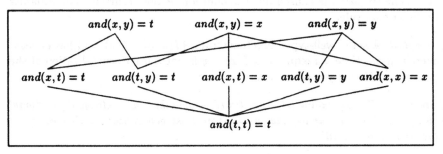

Fig. 1. Graph of a generalization relation

Our definition of a generalization relation is justified by the following theorem.

Theorem 4. *Let F be a functional rules well-typed under Γ, and G be a functional rule s.t. $F \leqslant G$. Then there is a type context Γ' s.t. $F \leqslant_{\Gamma'} G$.*

Proof. Since $F \leqslant G$, there exists a substitution θ such that $G\theta = F$. Let $\theta = \{x_1 \leftarrow t_1, \ldots, x_n \leftarrow t_n\}$ and $\Gamma \vdash t_i : \tau_i$ for each $i = 1, \ldots, n$. Without loss of generality we can assume $\{x_1, \ldots, x_n\} \cap \mathcal{V}(F) = \phi$. Then we get the type context Γ' by defining

$$\Gamma'(e) = \begin{cases} \tau_i & \text{if } e = x_1, \ldots, x_n, \\ \Gamma(e) & \text{otherwise .} \end{cases}$$

From the theorem above, we can omit the subscript Γ of $F \leqslant_\Gamma G$ if F is well-typed. The following theorem shows that our generalization relation for functional rules is natural.

Theorem 5. *Let P be a well-typed program under Γ and $F \in P$ be a functional rule for f. Then for any G s.t. $F \leqslant_\Gamma G$, $\mathcal{F}(P, f) \subseteq \mathcal{F}((P - \{F\}) \cup \{G\}, f)$.*

Proof. The conclusion is proved by the induction on the application of inference rules of equality theory. $\square$

4.2 Least Generalization of Well-typed Functional Rules

Definition. If S is a set of well-typed functional rules of a function f, then a well-typed functional rule G is a *least generalization* of S if:

1. For every F in S, $F \leqslant G$.
2. If for every F in S, $F \leqslant G'$, then $G \leqslant G'$.

In the definition of the least generalization by Plotkin [15], every non-empty, a finite set of words has a least generalization if and only if any two words in the set are compatible. Two words are compatible if their initial symbols are the same. We are now treating functional rules, we define that two rules are compatible if they are for the same function. Even if any two functional rules in a set are compatible, there is a case that no least generalization of the set exists. The situation is caused by the condition of the occurrences of variables in a functional rule.

Example 3. A set of well-typed functional rules $\{f(a) = a, f(b) = c\}$ has no least generalization. Here, an expression $f(x) = y$ is not a least generalization of the set, because $f(x) = y$ is not a functional rule.

Lemma 6. *The algorithm $\mathscr{LG}$ illustrated below takes two well-typed functional rules F_1 and F_2 as inputs and yields their least generalization if it exists or otherwise reports 'fail'.*

Proof. The algorithm $\mathscr{LG}$ is improved version of the least generalization algorithm of Plotkin [15]. Since the difference of our algorithm from Plotkin's is introduced to avoid wasteful computations. So it is easy that Algorithm $\mathscr{LG}$ halts and that reports a least generalization G_1 of $\{F_1, F_2\}$. If it reports 'fail' then there is no generalization. $\square$

Example 4. Let F_1 be *and*$(true, true) = T$ and F_2 be *and*$(true, false) = false$. Both are well-typed. We will use the algorithm to find a least generalization of $\{F_1, F_2\}$. Initially, the algorithm

puts G_1 as *and*$(true, true) = true$,   puts G_2 as *and*$(true, false) = false$.

We take an occurrence $I = \langle 1, 2 \rangle$ and x as the new variable. Then after executing line 8 and 9,

$$G_1 \text{ and } G_2 \text{ are } and(true, x) = x, \text{ and}$$
$$\sigma_1 = \{x \leftarrow true\}, \qquad \sigma_2 = \{x \leftarrow false\}.$$

The algorithm halts with the output *and*$(true, x) = x$, and by Lemma 6 we get

$$and(true, x) = x$$

as the least generalization of $\{F_1, F_2\}$.

Algorithm $\mathscr{LG}(F_1, F_2)$

Input: a pair of functional rules F_1 and F_2.

Output: a least generalization G.

Procedure:

1     $G_i \leftarrow F_i; \sigma_i \leftarrow \varepsilon; (i = 1, 2)$ $\triangleright \varepsilon$ is an empty substitution.

2     $O \leftarrow \{O \in \mathcal{O}(G_1) \cap \mathcal{O}(G_2) | O = \langle 1, \ldots \rangle\}$;

3   while $O \neq \phi$ do

4   take an occurrence I in O;

5        $t_i \leftarrow G_i / I; (i = 1, 2)$;

6   if terms t_1, t_2 are the form $f_1(\ldots), f_2(\ldots)$ respectively and
           $f_1 \neq f_2$, or one of them is a variable then

7   Choose a variable x distinct from any in G_1 and G_2;

8   Whenever t_1 and t_2 occur in the same occurrence in G_1 and G_2,
            replace each by x;

9           $\sigma_i \leftarrow \{x := t_i\}\sigma_i \quad (i = 1, 2)$;

10       $O \leftarrow O - \{\langle i_1, \ldots, i_m, \ldots, i_n \rangle \in O \mid I = \langle i_1, \ldots, i_m \rangle, m \leq n\}$;

11   else $O \leftarrow O - I$;

12   end

13   if $G_1 = G_2$ then output G_1 else report 'fail';

Theorem 7. *Let S be a set of functional rules of a function f. It is decidable whether S has a least generalization or not.*

Proof. Let $\{F_1, \ldots, F_n\}$ be a finite definition of f. If $n = 1$, then the theorem is trivial. For $n > 1$, it is easy to see that if a least generalization of the set is exist then it is the result of $\mathscr{LG}(F_1, \ldots, \mathscr{LG}(F_{n-1}, F_n) \ldots)$, otherwise some $\mathscr{LG}(F_i, \mathscr{LG}(\ldots))$ reposts 'fail'. $\square$

4.3   Minimal Multiple Generalization

At first we formally define the k-multiple generalization of well-typed functional rules in an analogous way to Arimura et al. [1].

Notation. For a class $\mathcal{C}$ of sets of functional rules $\mathcal{C}^k$ denotes the class

$$\{S \in P \,;\ \text{the cardinality of } S \text{ is less than or equal to } k\}.$$

Definition. Let $\mathcal{C}$ be a class of well-typed programs, and $k \geq 1$ be an integer. A program $T \in \mathcal{C}^k$ is a *k-minimal multiple generalization (k-mmg)* in $\mathcal{C}$ of a program S if, for any well-typed program P which is a superset of S and for any $U \in \mathcal{C}^k$, $\mathcal{F}(P, f) \subseteq \mathcal{F}((P - S) \cup T, f)$ and $\mathcal{F}((P - S) \cup U, f) \subset \mathcal{F}((P - S) \cup T, f)$ implies $\mathcal{F}(P, f) \not\subseteq \mathcal{F}((P - S) \cup U)$.

We consider a class where there is an algorithm to compute k-*mmg* of S.

Definition. A *pattern program* is a program that consists of functional rules whose right hand side is is a pattern.

We denote the class of pattern programs by $\mathcal{PP}$, and a class of pattern programs which is consist of at most k rules by $\mathcal{PP}^k$. The class $\mathcal{PP}$ and $\mathcal{PP}^k$ is based on the class of logic programs that consists of only unit clauses $\mathcal{UCP}$ and $\mathcal{UCP}^k$ which was introduced in [1]. We get an algorithm for k-mmg's of a set of well-typed functional rules by slightly modifying the algorithm in [1].

Algorithm $\mathcal{L.MMG}(k, S)$

Input: a positive integer k and a set of functional rules S.
Output: a k-Minimal Multiple Generalizations $G_1, \ldots, G_k$.
Procedure:

1   **for each splits** $\{S_1, \ldots, S_n\}$ of S
     s.t. $S_1, \ldots, S_n$ are non-empty and mutually disjoint subsets. **do**
2   Let G_i be a least generalization of S_i;
3   **if** all G_i are not an empty set and a set of functional rules $\{G_1, \ldots, G_k\}$
         is non-overlapping
4   **then output** $\{G_1, \ldots, G_k\}$ **and halt;**
5   **end**
6   There is no k-mmg, thus the algorithm **reports 'fail'.**

Example 5. We will use the algorithm to find a 2-mmg of

$$S = \left\{ \begin{array}{l} and(true, true) = true, \\ and(true, false) = false, \\ and(false, true) = false, \\ and(false, false) = false \end{array} \right\}.$$

To find 2-mmg of S, we split S into

$$S_1 = \{ and(true, true) = true, and(true, false) = false \},$$

$$S_2 = \{ and(false, true) = false, and(false, false) = false \}.$$

Then, we get a set of functional rules

$$G = \left\{ \begin{array}{l} and(true, x) = x, \\ and(false, x) = false \end{array} \right\}.$$

Here, G is a non-overlapping set of functional rules. The algorithm then halts with G as 2-mmg of S.

5 Inference of Functions

In this section, we present an inductive inference algorithm. The algorithm generates a well-typed program, which satisfies a set of examples represented by ground pattern rules. It works as follows: At first, it infers a type of the target function from a set of examples. Once a type is inferred, there are three main tasks. The first task is to reduce examples by the type maintenance algorithm. The second is to find k-mmg's. The third is synthesis of recursive programs from k-mmg's.

5.1 Finding a Type for Examples

We overcome the problem of finding a type for examples, by presenting a simple algorithm $\mathscr{T}$. $\mathscr{T}$ is based on the well-typing algorithm of Milner [10] and the least generalization algorithm of Plotkin [15].

Algorithm $\mathscr{T}$

Input: a finite set of examples $\{e_1, \ldots, e_n\}$.
Output: a type τ.
Procedure:

1   for each example e_i do
2   By using the well-typing algorithm, find a type context Γ and a type
         τ_i with one type variable s.t. $\Gamma \vdash e_i : \tau_i$
3   end ;
4   Let τ be a least generalization of $\{\tau_1, \ldots, \tau_n\}$;
5   output τ.

Example 6. We use the algorithm $\mathscr{T}$ to find a type of the set of examples

$$E = \left\{ \begin{array}{l} last([[]]) = [], \\ last([1, 2]) = 2, \\ last([true, false]) = false, \\ last([true, false, true]) = true, \\ last([1, 2, 2]) = 2 \end{array} \right\} . \tag{5}$$

For a examples $last([[]]) = []$, the well-typing algorithm yields a type $List(\alpha) \to \beta$. However there is the constraint that all type variables must be the same, then the type is

$$List(\alpha) \to \alpha .$$

In a similar way, we get well-typing's of the rest of the examples as

$$List(int) \to int,$$
$$List(bool) \to bool .$$

Hence a type of the set of examples E is $List(\alpha) \to \alpha$, which is a least generalization of the three types.

5.2 Reducing Examples with a Type

Once a type is obtained, it should be reflected in the set of examples. Type maintenance is used for the requirement. After type maintenance we do not need to be concerned with any types. Type maintenance has another advantage to efficiency on inductive inference, that is, $\mathscr{M}$ transforms some examples to equations which are variants.

Example 7. We use the type maintenance algorithm $\mathscr{M}$ for examples E in Example 6 with a type $List(\alpha) \to \alpha$. We get the set of equations as follows:

$$E' = \left\{ \begin{array}{l} last([x]) = x, \\ last([x, y]) = y, \\ last([x, y, x]) = x, \\ last([x, y, y]) = y \end{array} \right\}. \tag{6}$$

Note that both $last([1, 2]) = 2$ and $last([true, false]) = false$ are reduced to $last([x, y]) = y$.

5.3 Finding Minimal Multiple Generalizations

A 1-*mmg* is equivalent to a least generalization. Generally, a 1-*mmg* of a pattern program in the class $\mathcal{PP}^k$ does not exist. But k-*mmg* of any pattern program in the class $\mathcal{PP}^k$ exists, because any pattern program in the class $\mathcal{PP}^k$ is k-*mmg*. From this property, we will gradually compute n-*mmg* from 1-*mmg* up to k-*mmg* of a pattern program in the class $\mathcal{PP}^k$ by The algorithm $\mathscr{MMG}(S)$.

Algorithm $\mathscr{MMG}(S)$

Input: a set of functional rules S.
Output: a Minimal Multiple Generalizations $G_1, \ldots, G_n$.
Procedure:

1   **for** each $i = 1, \ldots, k$ **do**
2         $\{G_1, \ldots, G_i\} \leftarrow \mathscr{k.MMG}(i, S)$;
3   **if** $\mathscr{k.MMG}(i, S)$ succeeds **then** output $\{G_1, \ldots, G_i\}$ and **halt**;
4   **end**

Example 8. We will use the algorithm to find a *mmg* of the set of functional rules E' in Example 7.

First, we try to find a 1-*mmg* of E', however, there is no 1-*mmg*. In a similar way, there is no 2-*mmg*'s. Next we try to find 3-*mmg*'s of E'. Now, we split E' into

$$\begin{array}{l} S_1 = \{last([x]) = x\}, \\ S_2 = \{last([x, y]) = y\}, \\ S_3 = \left\{ \begin{array}{l} last([x, y, x]) = x, \\ last([x, y, y]) = y \end{array} \right\}. \end{array}$$

Then,

$$G = \left\{ \begin{array}{c} last([x]) = x, \\ last([x,y]) = y, \\ last([x,y,z]) = z \end{array} \right\}.$$

Here, G is a non-overlapping program. The algorithm then halts with G as a 3-mmg of S.

Inference algorithm for $\mathcal{PP}$

Input: a sequence of an input and output pair of f and a type context Γ.
Output: a sequence of programs in $\mathcal{PP}$.
Procedure:
```
1      P_H ← φ; S ← φ;
2      repeat
3          read the next input and output pair e = (p₁ⁱ,...,pₙⁱ,pᵒ);
4          S ← S ∪ {f(p₁ⁱ,...,pₙⁱ) = pᵒ};
5          if pᵒ ∉ F(P_H, f(p₁ⁱ,...,pₙⁱ)) then
6              Γ(f) ← T(S);
7              P_H ← MMG(M(S,Γ));
8          output P_H;
9      forever
       end .
```

5.4 Synthesis of Recursive Programs from k-mmg's

The class of recursive programs have the power to define functions which are defined on infinite domain, e.g. integer, list, tree, ... Indeed the class of pattern programs $\mathcal{PP}$ does not represent recursive programs, but we illustrate that k-mmg of well-typed equations is useful to infer a recursive program. In Example 8, we get a 3-mmg $G = \{G_1, G_2, G_3\}$. This 3-mmg is correspond to *program fragments* in the method of Summers [17, 18]; each generalization is regarded as a transformation from inputs to a output and as a recursive step on computation where G_1 is a base step, and G_2, G_3 are induction steps. We will apply the method of Summers to equations as programs.

Definition. A *context* is a special pattern which includes a special symbol $\square$. For a context C and a pattern p, $C[p]$ is a pattern which replaces a symbol $\square$ by p.

Example 9. Let C be a context $cons(x, \square)$. Then $C[cons(y, nil)]$ is a pattern $cons(x, cons(y, nil))$.

Definition. Let p be a pattern. A variable x in p is *labeled* if x is of the form x_I and x is p/I. A pattern p is *labeled* if for all variables $x \in \mathcal{V}(p)$ are labeled.

Example 10. $cons(x_{\langle 1 \rangle}, cons(x_{\langle 2,1 \rangle}, nil))$ is a labeled pattern.

Definition. Let p be a labeled pattern and I be a sequence of integers. A labeled pattern p^I is a pattern which replaces each variable x_J with $x_{I.J}$.

Example 11. Let p be a labeled pattern $cons(x_{\langle 1 \rangle}, cons(x_{\langle 2,1 \rangle}, nil))$. Then $p^{\langle 2,1 \rangle}$ is a pattern $cons(x_{\langle 2,1,1 \rangle}, cons(x_{\langle 2,1,2,1 \rangle}, nil))$.

Proposition 8. ([17, 18]) *If a series of equations*

$$f(p_1) = q_1, \ldots, f(p_n) = q_n$$

holds a property that

$$p_2 \equiv C[p_1^I], \ldots, p_n \equiv C[p_{n-1}^I] \quad and,$$
$$q_2 \equiv D[q_1^I], \ldots, q_n \equiv D[q_{n-1}^I]$$

for some contexts C and D, and a sequence of integers I, then we can get an equivalent series of recursive equations

$$f(p_1) = q_1, \qquad f(C[y]) = D[y] \ .$$

Example 12. For Example 8, the result is as follows:

$$\left\{ \begin{array}{l} last(cons(x, nil)) = x, \\ last(cons(x, z)) = last(z) \end{array} \right\} .$$

6 Concluding Remarks

We have presented a constructive method of learning from examples using typed equational programming. We have given a concept of type maintenance, and shown that it is theoretically and practically useful. We have given the type maintenance algorithm, and have shown that this algorithm is correct. Another important result of this paper is generalization procedures for well-typed functional rules.

Though we have left the computational complexity of our algorithms out of consideration. We conjecture that the complexity of type maintenance algorithm $\mathcal{M}$ is almost same as that of the least generalization algorithm of Plotkin [15]. The algorithms $\mathcal{t\text{-}MMG}$ and $\mathcal{MMG}$ are quite expensive. However, using the property "there is a case that no least generalization exists", we hope to make these algorithms more efficient. We are now analyzing these complexity and implementation of our method.

Acknowledgments

We are indebted to the referees for their valuable comments on an earlier version of this paper, which pointed out some inaccuracies. Our thanks also go to Prof. Yuzuru Tanaka for helpful discussions and supports.

References

1. H. Arimura, H. Ishizaka, T. Shinohara, and S. Otsuki. *A Generalization of the Least Generalization.* Machine Intelligence 13. December 1992.
2. A. W. Biermann. The inference of regular lisp programs from examples. *IEEE Transaction on System, Man and Cybernetics,* 8(8):585–600, 1978.
3. A. W. Biermann. A production rule mechanism for generating lisp code. *IEEE Transaction on System, Man and Cybernetics,* 5(9):260–276, 1979.
4. S. Hölldobler. *Foundations of Equational Logic Programming.* Lecture Notes in Artifical Intelligence 353. Springer-Verlag, 1989.
5. P. Hudak, S. P. Jones, and P. Wadler (editors). Report on the programming language haskell, a non-strict purely functional language (version 1.2). *ACM SIG-PLAN Notices,* 21(12):37–79, December 1986.
6. C. D. Page Jr. and A. M. Frisch. *Generalization and Learnability: A Study of Constrained Atoms,* chapter 2, pages 29–61. Inductive Logic Programming. Academic Press Inc., 1992.
7. J-L. Lassez, M.J. Maher, and K. Marriott. *Unification Revisited,* chapter 15, pages 587–625. Foundations of Deductive Databases and Logic Programming. Morgan Kaufmann Publishers, 1987.
8. C. X. Ling. Learning and invention of horn clause theories. *Methodologies for Intelligent Systems,* 4:323–331, 1989.
9. C. X. Ling and L. Ungar. Inventing theoretical terms in inductive learning of functions. *Methodologies for Intelligent Systems,* 4:332–341, 1989.
10. R. Milner. A theory of type polymorphism in programming. *Journal of Computer and System Sciences,* 17:348–375, 1978.
11. R. Milner and M. Tofte. *Commentary on Standard ML.* The MIT Press, 1991.
12. R. Milner, M. Tofte, and R. Harper. *The Deffinition of Standard ML.* The MIT Press, 1990.
13. S. Muggleton, editor. *Inductive Logic Programming.* Academic Press Inc., 1992.
14. M. J. O'Donnell. *Computing in Systems Described by Equations.* Lecture Notes in Computer Science 58. Springer-Verlag, 1977.
15. G. D. Plotkin. *A Note on Inductive Generalization,* chapter 8, pages 153–163. Machine Intelligence 5. December 1969.
16. E. Y. Shapiro. *Algorithmic Program Debugging.* MIT Press, 1983.
17. P. D. Summers. Program construction from examples. Technical Report RC-5637, IBM Res., 1975.
18. P. D. Summers. A methodology for lisp program construction from examples. *JACM,* 24:161–175, 1977.
19. A. Togashi. Inductive inference of term rewriting systems realizing algebras. In *In Proc. ALT '90,* pages 411–424. JSAI, 1990.

Finding Tree Patterns Consistent with Positive and Negative Examples Using Queries

Hiroki Ishizaka   Hiroki Arimura   Takeshi Shinohara
{ishizaka, arim, shino}@ai.kyutech.ac.jp

Department of Artificial Intelligence Kyushu Institute of Technology
680-4, Kawazu, Iizuka 820, Japan
TEL: +81-948-29-7600, FAX: +81-948-29-7601

Abstract. This paper is concerned with the problem of finding a hypothesis in $\mathcal{TP}^2$ consistent with given positive and negative examples. The hypothesis class $\mathcal{TP}^2$ consists of all the sets of at most two tree patterns and represents the class of unions of at most two tree pattern languages. Especially, we consider the problem from the point of view of the consistency problem for $\mathcal{TP}^2$. The consistency problem is a problem to decide whether there exists a consistent hypothesis with given positive and negative data within some fixed hypothesis space. Efficient solvability of that problem is closely related to the possibility of efficient machine learning or machine discovery. Unfortunately, however, the consistency problem is known to be NP-complete for many hypothesis spaces, including the class $\mathcal{TP}^2$. In order to overcome this computational hardness, in this paper, we try to use additional information obtained by making queries. First, we give an algorithm that, using restricted subset queries, solves the consistency problem for $\mathcal{TP}^2$ in time polynomial in the total size of given positive and negative examples. Next, we show that each subset query made by the algorithm can be replaced by several membership queries under some condition on a set of function symbols. As a result, we have that the consistency problem for $\mathcal{TP}^2$ is solved in polynomial time using membership queries.

1 Introduction

The consistency problem is a problem to decide whether there exists a consistent hypothesis with given positive and negative data within some fixed hypothesis space. A related search problem, called a fitting, to find such a consistent hypothesis is very essential in machine learning. For example, in the context of PAC learning [11], polynomial time computability of a fitting for a class of polynomial Vapnik-Chervonenkis dimension is sufficient for the class to be polynomial time learnable [7].

Unfortunately, the consistency problem is shown to be NP-complete for many hypothesis spaces such as k-term DNF [8] and regular patterns [5]. To realize efficient learning algorithms, we have to overcome this computational hardness. In most studies on practical machine learning, a target hypothesis space is restricted so that the consistency problem becomes efficiently solvable. Another approach is to use information in addition to initially given positive and negative examples. In this paper, we adopt the latter approach, that is, we investigate an efficient algorithm for solving a consistency problem *using queries*.

A tree pattern is a first order term. The language of a tree pattern p is the set of all the ground instances of p. The tree pattern p is consistent with given positive and negative examples if and only if the language of p includes all the positive examples and no negative example. The consistency problem for the class $\mathcal{TP}$ of tree patterns is solvable in polynomial time, because the least general generalization [10, 9] of positive examples is always consistent with both positive and negative examples whenever there exists a tree pattern consistent with the both examples.

In this paper, we focus on the consistency problem for the hypothesis space $\mathcal{TP}^2$, where $\mathcal{TP}^k$ consists of all the sets of at most k tree patterns and represents the class of unions of at most k tree pattern languages. The consistency problem for $\mathcal{TP}^k$ is also known to be NP-complete even if $k = 2$. We consider two kinds of queries which the given algorithm is allowed to use. The one is a restricted subset query and the other is a membership query. It is well-known that the inclusion and the membership are undecidable and NP-complete respectively for standard string pattern languages, while both of them are solvable in polynomial time for tree pattern languages. We assume a teacher, called a minimally consistent oracle, that answers queries from the algorithm. A minimally consistent oracle answers each query according to some fixed hypothesis H in $\mathcal{TP}^k$ such that H is consistent with given positive and negative examples and the number of elements of H is less than or equal to that of any consistent hypotheses. First, we give an algorithm that, using restricted subset queries, solves the consistency problem for $\mathcal{TP}^2$ in time polynomial in the total size of given positive and negative examples. Next, we show that each subset query made by the algorithm can be replaced by several membership queries under some condition on a set of function symbols. As a result, we prove that the consistency problem for $\mathcal{TP}^2$ is solved in polynomial time using membership queries.

2 Preliminaries

Let Σ be a finite alphabet. Each element of Σ is called a *function symbol* and associated with a non-negative integer called an *arity*. A function symbol with arity 0 is also called a *constant*. We assume that Σ contains at least one constant. Let V be a countable set of symbols disjoint from Σ. Each element of V is called a *variable*. We adopt some informal notational conventions for the symbols. Variable symbols will normally be denoted by X, Y, and Z, possibly subscripted. Constant symbols will normally be denoted by a, b, and c. Other function symbols will normally be denoted by f, g, and h.

A *tree pattern* over Σ and V is a first order term defined recursively as follows:

1. A function with arity 0 or a variable is a tree pattern.
2. For a function f with arity n $(n \geq 1)$ and tree patterns $t_1, \ldots, t_n$, $f(t_1, \ldots, t_n)$ is a tree pattern.

For a non-variable tree pattern t, the outer-most function symbol of t is called the *principal functor* of t.

For a set S, $|S|$ denotes the number of elements in S. The *size* of a tree pattern p, denoted by $size(p)$, is the number of symbol occurrences in p minus the number of distinct variables occurring in p. For example, $size(f(g(X,Y), h(X,Z), Y)) = 8 - 3 = 5$. For a set S of tree patterns, $size(S)$ is defined as $\sum_{p \in S} size(p)$. Note that if a tree pattern p contains no variable then $size(p)$ is the total number of symbol occurrences in p.

A tree pattern is said to be *ground* if it contains no variable. The set of all the tree patterns is denoted by $\mathcal{TP}$ and the set of all the ground tree patterns is denoted by $\mathcal{TP}(\Sigma)$. For some non-negative integer k, the class of all the sets consisting of at most k tree patterns is denoted by $\mathcal{TP}^k$ and called a *hypothesis space*. Each element in $\mathcal{TP}^k$ is called a *hypothesis*. As a convention, we define $\mathcal{TP}^0 = \emptyset$ (empty set).

A *substitution* θ is a finite set of the form $\{X_1/t_1, \ldots, X_n/t_n\}$, where X_i is a variable, each t_i is a tree pattern different from X_i, and the variables $X_1, \ldots, X_n$ are mutually distinct. An *instance* of a tree pattern p by a substitution $\theta = \{X_1/t_1, \ldots, X_n/t_n\}$, denoted by $p\theta$, is the tree pattern obtained from p by simultaneously replacing each occurrence of the variable X_i by the term t_i $(1 \leq i \leq n)$.

For a tree pattern p, the *language of p*, denoted by $L(p)$, is the set of all the ground instances of p. For a set S of tree patterns, the *language of S* is also denoted by $L(S)$ and defined as $L(S) = \bigcup_{p \in S} L(p)$. For a set T of ground tree patterns, a set S of tree patterns is said to be *reduced* with respect to T if $T \subseteq L(S)$ and $T \not\subseteq L(S - \{p\})$ for any $p \in S$.

If a tree pattern q is an instance of p, that is, there exists a substitution θ such that $p\theta = q$, then p is said to be a *generalization* of q and denoted by $p \succeq q$. If $p \succeq q$ but $q \not\succeq p$, then p is said to be a *proper generalization* of q (or q is said to be a *proper instance* of p) and denoted by $p \succ q$. If both $p \succeq q$ and $q \succeq p$ hold, then p and q are said to be *variants* and denoted by $p \equiv q$. In what follows, we do not distinguish any tree patterns which are variants. The following property is called the *compactness* of tree pattern languages [2].

Proposition 1. *Suppose that* $|\Sigma| \geq k+1$. *Then, for any tree patterns* $p, p_1, \ldots, p_k$, $L(p) \subseteq L(p_1) \cup \cdots \cup L(p_k)$ *if and only if* $p \preceq p_i$ *for some* $i \in \{1, \ldots, k\}$.

For a nonempty set S of tree patterns, a tree pattern p is said to be a *generalization* of S if $p \succeq q$ for any q in S. A *least generalization* of S, denoted by $lg(S)$, is a generalization p of S such that $p \preceq q$ for every generalization q of S. Here, we introduce a special tree pattern, *null tree pattern*, denoted by $\bot$. As a convention, we define that $\bot \prec p$ for any non-null tree pattern p, $\bot \equiv \bot$, $size(\bot) = \infty$, $lg(\emptyset) = \bot$, and $L(\bot) = \emptyset$. For any set S of tree patterns, $lg(S)$ always exists and is unique modulo $\equiv$. Furthermore, the following properties hold (see e.g. [10, 4]).

Proposition 2. *Let* p, q *be tree patterns and* S_1, S_2 *be finite sets of tree patterns. Then the following propositions hold.*

1. *If* $p \succeq q$ *then* $size(q) \geq size(p)$.
2. *If* $p \succeq lg(S_1)$ *then* $L(p) \supseteq S_1$.
3. *If* $S_1 \supseteq S_2$ *then* $lg(S_1) \succeq lg(S_2)$.
4. *If* $p \succeq q$ *then* $L(p) \supseteq L(q)$.
5. *If* $|\Sigma| \geq 2$ *then* $lg(L(p)) \equiv p$.

3 Consistency problem

First, we show that the consistency problem for the hypothesis space $\mathcal{TP}^k$ ($k \geq 2$) is NP-complete. To show the NP-completeness, we use a transformation from the consistency problem for k-term DNF to that for $\mathcal{TP}^k$.

Let T and F be mutually disjoint nonempty finite sets of ground tree patterns. A set H of tree patterns is *consistent with* $\langle T, F \rangle$ if $T \subseteq L(H)$ and $F \cap L(H) = \emptyset$. The *consistency problem for* $\mathcal{TP}^k$ is a problem to decide whether there exists a hypothesis $H \in \mathcal{TP}^k$ consistent with given positive and negative examples $\langle T, F \rangle$.

Let $U = \{u_1, \ldots, u_n\}$ ($n \geq 1$) be a set of boolean variables. We call a variable u_j or its negation $\bar{u}_j$ a *literal*. A k-term DNF is a disjunction $C_1 + \cdots + C_l$ of at most k terms, where each term C_i is a conjunction of literals. We denote by a vector $b = (b_1, \ldots, b_n) \in \{0,1\}^n$ the assignment that assigns b_j to u_j for every $1 \leq j \leq n$. A k-term DNF is *consistent with* a pair $\langle T, F \rangle$ of sets of assignments if it is true under all the assignments in T and false under all the assignments in F. The *consistency problem for k-term DNF* is a problem to decide whether there exists a k-term DNF H consistent with given a pair $\langle T, F \rangle$ of mutually disjoint sets of assignments.

In what follows, we use a special form of tree patterns. Let f, g be function symbols of arity n and a be a constant. For any $1 \leq i \leq n$, we define tree patterns $\mathbf{1}_1, \ldots, \mathbf{1}_n$ recursively as $\mathbf{1}_i = f(a, \ldots, a, \mathbf{1}_{i-1})$, where $\mathbf{1}_0 = a$. Similarly, we define $\mathbf{0}_1, \ldots, \mathbf{0}_n$ as $\mathbf{0}_i = g(a, \ldots, a, \mathbf{1}_{i-1})$. Note that $\mathbf{1}_i$ and $\mathbf{0}_i$ are the same tree patterns except their principal functors. We associate an assignment $b = (b_1, \ldots, b_n)$ with a ground tree pattern $\mathbf{b} = f(\mathbf{b}_1, \ldots, \mathbf{b}_n)$, where $\mathbf{b}_i$ is either $\mathbf{0}_i$ or $\mathbf{1}_i$ according to $b_i \in \{0, 1\}$. We will use this informal notation without notice.

For tree patterns p and q, an *occurrence* of p in q is represented by a string α of positive integers defined as follows: if $p = q$ then p occurs at the empty string ε in p; if $q = f(q_1, \ldots, q_m)$ and p occurs at α in q_i ($1 \leq i \leq m$) then p occurs at $i\alpha$ in q. A tree pattern p is said to be *regular* if any variable occurs at most once in p.

Lemma 3. *Let T and F be mutually disjoint sets of assignments, and $T' = \{\mathbf{b} \mid b \in T\}$ and $F' = \{\mathbf{b} \mid b \in F\}$ be the sets of ground tree patterns. Then, there is a k-term DNF consistent with $\langle T, F \rangle$ if and only if there is a set of at most k regular tree patterns consistent with $\langle T', F' \rangle$.*

Lemma 4. *Let S be any set of ground tree patterns of the form $f(\mathbf{b}_1, \ldots, \mathbf{b}_n)$ for some $(b_1, \ldots, b_n) \in \{0, 1\}^n$. Then, for any tree pattern p there is a regular tree pattern $\hat{p}$ such that $L(p) \cap S = L(\hat{p}) \cap S$.*

Theorem 5. *The consistency problem for $\mathcal{TP}^k$ is NP-complete for any $k \geq 2$.*

Proof. By Proposition 2, if a tree pattern language $L(p)$ has a nonempty intersection with a set $T \subseteq \mathcal{TP}(\Sigma)$ then $size(p) \leq size(t)$ for some $t \in T$. Thus, it is easy to see that the consistency problem for $\mathcal{TP}^k$ is in NP because there exists a nondeterministic algorithm that simply guesses at most k tree patterns $p_1, \ldots, p_l$ of size at most $\max\{size(t) \mid t \in T\}$ and checks in polynomial time whether $T \subseteq L(H)$ and $F \cap L(H) = \emptyset$, where $H = \{p_1, \ldots, p_l\}$.

We transform the consistency problem for k-term DNF to the consistency problem for $\mathcal{TP}^k$. Let T and F be mutually disjoint sets of assignments over $U = \{u_1, \ldots, u_n\}$ in an arbitrary instance of the consistency problem for k-term DNF. We associate T and F with sets of ground tree patterns $T' = \{\mathbf{b} \mid b \in T\}$ and $F' = \{\mathbf{b} \mid b \in F\}$.

By restricting the hypothesis space to the class of sets of at most k regular tree patterns, we obtain Lemma 3. From Lemma 4, we can remove the restriction that all the tree patterns in a consistent hypothesis should be regular. Hence, it immediately follows from Lemma 3 that there exists a k-term DNF consistent with $\langle T, F \rangle$ if and only if there exists a set $H' \in TP^k$ consistent with $\langle T', F' \rangle$.

It is not difficult to see that the transformation can be computed in deterministic log space. By Pitt and Valiant [8], the consistency problem for k-term DNF is NP-complete for any $k \geq 2$. This completes the proof. $\qquad \square$

Proof of Lemma 1. Suppose that there exists a k-term DNF $H = C_1 + \cdots + C_l$ consistent with $\langle T, F \rangle$ and C_i $(1 \leq i \leq l)$ does not contain both a variable and its negation. We may assume $T \neq \emptyset$ and $F \neq \emptyset$ without loss of generality. We associate each term C_i $(1 \leq i \leq l)$ with a regular tree pattern $p_i = f(q_1, \ldots, q_n)$, where for every $1 \leq j \leq n$,

$$q_j = \begin{cases} 1_j, & \text{if } C_i \text{ contains } u_j, \\ 0_j, & \text{if } C_i \text{ contains } \bar{u}_j, \\ X_j, & \text{otherwise,} \end{cases}$$

and $X_1, \ldots, X_n$ are mutually distinct variables. We then set $H' = \{p_1, \ldots, p_l\}$. For any assignment $b = (b_1, \ldots, b_n) \in T \cup F$ and the corresponding ground tree pattern $\mathbf{b} = f(\mathbf{b}_1, \ldots, \mathbf{b}_n)$, we can easily see that C_i is true under b if and only if $\mathbf{b} \in L(p_i)$. Thus, if H is consistent with $\langle T, F \rangle$ then $H' = \{p_1, \ldots, p_l\}$ is consistent with $\langle T', F' \rangle$.

We show the converse. Let $H' = \{p_1, \ldots, p_l\}$ be a set of at most k regular tree patterns reduced with respect to T' and consistent with $\langle T', F' \rangle$. We construct a k-term DNF H as follows: For each $1 \leq i \leq l$, p_i is a generalization of some member in T' because H' is reduced with respect to T'. Since $F' \neq \emptyset$, p_i is not a variable. Moreover, it follows from $T' \neq \emptyset$ that p_i must be a tree pattern of the form $f(q_1, \ldots, q_n)$ satisfying either $0_j \prec q_j$ or $1_j \prec q_j$ for every $1 \leq j \leq n$. Then, we associate p_i with a term $C_i = L_1 \cdots L_n$ such that for every $1 \leq j \leq n$,

$$L_j = \begin{cases} u_j, & \text{if } 0_j \npreceq q_j \text{ and } 1_j \preceq q_j, \\ \bar{u}_j, & \text{if } 0_j \preceq q_j \text{ and } 1_j \npreceq q_j, \\ 1, & \text{if } 0_j \preceq q_j \text{ and } 1_j \preceq q_j. \end{cases}$$

By construction, if C_i is true under $b = (b_1, \ldots, b_n)$ then $\mathbf{b}_1 = q_1\theta_1, \ldots, \mathbf{b}_n = q_n\theta_n$ for some substitutions $\theta_1, \ldots, \theta_n$. Since p_i is regular, the domains of $\theta_1, \ldots, \theta_n$ are mutually disjoint. We can take a substitution $\theta = \theta_1 \cup \cdots \cup \theta_n$ so that $\mathbf{b} = p_i\theta$ holds. Thus, $\mathbf{b} \in L(p_i)$. It is easy to verify that C_i is true under $b \in \{0,1\}^n$ if and only if $\mathbf{b} \in L(p_i)$. We then set $H = C_1 + \cdots + C_l$. It is clear that if H' is consistent with $\langle T', F' \rangle$ then H is also consistent with $\langle T, F \rangle$. Consequently, the claim is proved. $\qquad \square$

Proof of Lemma 2. Assume $L(p) \cap S \neq \emptyset$ without loss of generality. Let $p = f(p_1, \ldots, p_n)$ and $\mathbf{b} = f(\mathbf{b}_1, \ldots, \mathbf{b}_n) \in L(p) \cap S$. Suppose that some variable X

occurs at least twice in p, say, X occurs at α in p_i and at β in p_j, where i and j are possibly the same. If α and β are both ε, then X must match both $\mathbf{b}_i$ and $\mathbf{b}_j$. However, it is impossible since $\mathbf{b}_i \neq \mathbf{b}_j$ if $i \neq j$. Therefore, at least one of α and β, say α, is not ε, that is, α is a properly internal occurrence in both $\mathbf{b}_i$ and p_i. Let s be the subexpression of $\mathbf{b}$ occurring at α in $\mathbf{b}_i$. Let $\mathbf{b}' = f(\mathbf{b}'_1, \ldots, \mathbf{b}'_n)$ be an arbitrary member in $L(p) \cap S$. Then, the subexpression of $\mathbf{b}'_i$ occurring at α is also s because $\mathbf{b}_i$ and $\mathbf{b}'_i$ are either $\mathbf{0}_i$ or $\mathbf{1}_i$, and exactly the same at any internal position. For this reason, we can obtain a tree pattern $p\sigma$ that does not contain the variable X by applying the substitution $\sigma = \{X/s\}$ to p. Since $\mathbf{b}' \in L(p\sigma)$ whenever $\mathbf{b}' \in L(p)$, we have $L(p\sigma) \cap S = L(p) \cap S$. In the same way, we can obtain a regular tree pattern $\hat{p}$ with $L(p) \cap S = L(\hat{p}) \cap S$ from the given tree pattern p by removing all the variables occurring more than once.   □

Theorem 5 states that there is no algorithm for solving the consistency problem for $\mathcal{TP}^k$ $(k \geq 2)$ in polynomial time unless P = NP. Note that the problem remains NP-complete even in the case where the class $\mathcal{TP}^k$ has the compactness, that is, $|\Sigma| \geq k + 1$.

4 A polynomial time algorithm using queries

In this section, we give an algorithm for solving the consistency problem for $\mathcal{TP}^2$ using queries. We also show that the algorithm runs in time polynomial in the size of given examples. The algorithm starts with the least generalization of given positive examples T then gradually refines it to approximate a fellow, a tree pattern p, of a hypothesis in $\mathcal{TP}^2$. The other fellow of the hypothesis is approximated as $lg(T - L(p))$. The search process is one-way, that is, without backtracking. This one-way search is accomplished by additional information obtained from making queries.

4.1 Queries and minimally consistent oracles

The types of queries we use in this paper are subset queries and membership queries. A *subset query* is to propose a tree pattern p and query whether $L(p)$ is a subset of a target language. A *membership query* is to propose a ground tree pattern α and query whether α is in a target language. A minimally consistent oracle is a device which answers each query as defined bellow.

Let T and F be mutually disjoint nonempty finite sets of ground tree patterns. A hypothesis space $\mathcal{TP}^k$ $(k \geq 1)$ is said to be *least* with respect to $\langle T, F \rangle$ if there exists a hypothesis in $\mathcal{TP}^k$ which is consistent with $\langle T, F \rangle$ but no hypothesis in $\mathcal{TP}^{k-1}$ is consistent with $\langle T, F \rangle$. Note that, for any disjoint nonempty finite sets T and F, T itself is in $\mathcal{TP}^{|T|}$ and consistent with $\langle T, F \rangle$. Thus there always exists the least hypothesis space with respect to $\langle T, F \rangle$, since $k < k'$ implies $\mathcal{TP}^k \subset \mathcal{TP}^{k'}$.

A *subset oracle* is a device which receives a tree pattern as its input then returns "Yes" or "No" as its output according to some mapping from tree patterns to {"Yes", "No"}. A subset oracle is said to be *consistent* with a hypothesis H in $\mathcal{TP}^k$ if it returns "Yes" whenever it receives a tree pattern p such that $L(p) \subseteq L(H)$ and "No" otherwise. Let T and F be mutually disjoint nonempty finite sets of ground tree patterns. A subset oracle is said to be *minimally consistent* with $\langle T, F \rangle$ if it is consistent with some hypothesis H in the least hypothesis space with respect to $\langle T, F \rangle$ such that H is consistent with $\langle T, F \rangle$. Note that the subset oracle is not required to return a *counter example* [1]. That is , the subset query we consider in this paper corresponds to a *restricted subset query* in Angluin's framework.

A minimally consistent membership oracle is also defined similarly. A *membership oracle* is a device which receives a ground tree pattern as its input then returns "Yes" or "No" as its output according to some mapping from ground tree patterns to {"Yes", "No"}. A membership oracle is said to be *consistent* with a hypothesis H in $\mathcal{TP}^k$ if it returns "Yes" for any element in $L(H)$ and "No" for any element in $\mathcal{TP}(\Sigma) - L(H)$. Let T and F be mutually disjoint nonempty finite sets of ground tree patterns. A membership oracle is said to be *minimally consistent* with $\langle T, F \rangle$ if it is consistent with some hypothesis H in the least hypothesis space with respect to $\langle T, F \rangle$ such that H is consistent with $\langle T, F \rangle$.

4.2 Refinements of a tree pattern

For a tree pattern p, an instance $p\theta$ is said to be a *refinement* of p if one of the following holds:

1. $\theta = \{X/Y\}$, where X and Y are distinct variables occurring in p.
2. $\theta = \{X/f(X_1, X_2, \ldots, X_n)\}$ for some function symbol f with arity n in Σ, $n \geq 0$, where X is a variable that occurs in p and $X_1, \ldots, X_n$ are mutually distinct variables not occurring in p.

A *refinement operator* ρ over $\mathcal{TP}$ is a mapping from tree patterns to their refinements, that is, for a tree pattern p,

$$\rho(p) = \{p\theta \mid \theta \text{ satisfies one of the above two conditions }\}.$$

The refinement operator defined above is *complete* in the sense of [3], that is, the following proposition holds.

Proposition 6. *For any tree patterns p and q, if $p \succ q$ then there exists a finite sequence $r_0, r_1, \ldots, r_m$ ($m \geq 1$) of tree patterns such that $p = r_0$, $q = r_m$, and $r_i \in \rho(r_{i-1})$ for any $1 \leq i \leq m$.*

In other words, for any tree pattern p, any proper instance of p can be obtained by finitely many applications of ρ to p. Furthermore, from the definition of ρ, it is clear that the following propositions hold.

Proposition 7. *For any tree pattern p and its refinement $q \in \rho(p)$, $size(q) \geq size(p) + 1$.*

Proposition 8. *Let n be the number of different variables appearing in a tree pattern p. Then it holds that $|\rho(p)| \leq n|\Sigma| + n(n-1)/2$.*

4.3   The algorithm and its correctness and complexity

The discussion developed in this section fully uses the compactness of tree pattern languages and Proposition 2 and our target is to search $\mathcal{TP}^2$ for a consistent hypothesis. Thus, in what follows, we assume that $|\Sigma| \geq 3$.

Figure 1 is the main procedure of the algorithm. The sub-procedure RS appears in Figure 2. In what follows, we assume that T and F are mutually disjoint nonempty finite sets of ground tree patterns.

Procedure: $FCH(T, F)$
Input: T, F: Mutually disjoint nonempty finite sets of ground tree patterns.
Given: A subset oracle which is minimally consistent with $\langle T, F \rangle$.
Output: A consistent hypothesis in $\mathcal{TP}^2$ or "Fail"
begin
    if $\{lg(T)\}$ is consistent with $\langle T, F \rangle$ **then**
        return $\{lg(T)\}$;
    else
        return $RS(T, F, lg(T))$;
end

Fig. 1. A procedure for finding a consistent hypothesis

If $\{lg(T)\}$ is consistent with $\langle T, F \rangle$, the algorithm outputs $\{lg(T)\}$ which is in $\mathcal{TP}^1 \subseteq \mathcal{TP}^2$. Thus, for the present, we focus on the case where a consistent hypothesis is in $\mathcal{TP}^2$ but not in $\mathcal{TP}^1$.

Let $\{p_1, p_2\}$ be a set of tree patterns which is reduced with respect to T. A tree pattern r is said to be *general enough* with respect to T and $\{p_1, p_2\}$ if and

Procedure: $RS(T, F, P)$
Input: T, F: Mutually disjoint nonempty finite sets of ground tree patterns.
            P: A tree pattern. ($lg(T)$ at the initial call)
Given: A subset oracle which is minimally consistent with $\langle T, F \rangle$.
Output: A consistent hypothesis in $T\mathcal{P}^2$ or "Fail"
begin
   if the pair $\{P, lg(T - L(P))\}$ is consistent with $\langle T, F \rangle$ **then**
      return the pair $\{P, lg(T - L(P))\}$;
   for each $R \in \rho(P)$ **do**
      Make a subset query with $lg(T - L(R))$;
      if the answer is "Yes" **then**
         return $RS(T, F, R)$;
   return "Fail";
end

Fig. 2. A recursive search procedure for a consistent hypothesis in $T\mathcal{P}^2 - T\mathcal{P}^1$

only if $r \succeq lg(T - L(p_i))$ for some $i \in \{1, 2\}$. From the definition, $lg(T - L(p_i))$ itself is general enough. Furthermore, since $lg(T) \succeq lg(T - L(p_i))$ follows from Proposition 2, the next proposition holds.

Proposition 9. *Let $\{p_1, p_2\}$ be a set of tree patterns reduced with respect to T. Then, $lg(T)$ is general enough with respect to T and $\{p_1, p_2\}$.*

The role of subset queries made by the algorithm is characterized by the next lemma and corollary. That is, the subset queries are used for testing whether the current refinement is general enough.

Lemma 10. *Let $\{p_1, p_2\}$ be a set of tree patterns reduced with respect to T. Then, a tree pattern r is general enough with respect to T and $\{p_1, p_2\}$ if and only if $lg(T - L(r))) \preceq p_i$ for some $i \in \{1, 2\}$.*

Proof. Suppose that r is general enough with respect to T and $\{p_1, p_2\}$, that is, $r \succeq lg(T - L(p_i))$ for some $i \in \{1, 2\}$. Since $L(r) \supseteq T - L(p_i)$ follows from Proposition 2, it holds that $L(p_i) \supseteq T - L(r)$. Hence, it holds that $p_i \equiv lg(L(p_i)) \succeq lg(T - L(r))$ for some $i \in \{1, 2\}$.
   Conversely, suppose that $lg(T - L(r)) \preceq p_i$ for some $i \in \{1, 2\}$. Since $T - L(r) \subseteq L(p_i)$ follows from Proposition 2, it holds that $T - L(p_i) \subseteq L(r)$. Hence, it holds that $lg(T - L(p_i)) \preceq lg(L(r)) \equiv r$ for some $i \in \{1, 2\}$. $\qquad\square$

From Proposition 1, the next corollary follows.

Corollary 11. *Let $\{p_1, p_2\}$ be a set of tree patterns reduced with respect to T. Then, a tree pattern r is general enough with respect to T and $\{p_1, p_2\}$ if and only if $L(lg(T - L(r))) \subseteq L(p_1) \cup L(p_2)$.*

The next lemma ensures the termination of the algorithm with a correct output when the least hypothesis space with respect to $\langle T, F \rangle$ is $\mathcal{TP}^2$.

Lemma 12. *Let $\{p_1, p_2\}$ be a set of tree patterns reduced with respect to T and consistent with $\langle T, F \rangle$. If $r \equiv lg(T - L(p_i))$ for some $i \in \{1, 2\}$, then the pair $\{r, lg(T - L(r))\}$ of tree patterns is consistent with $\langle T, F \rangle$.*

Proof. Without loss of generality, we may assume that $i = 1$. Furthermore, since it is clear that $T \subseteq L(r) \cup L(lg(T - L(r)))$, it is sufficient to show that

$$F \cap (L(r) \cup L(lg(T - L(r)))) = \emptyset.$$

Since $\{p_1, p_2\}$ is reduced with respect to T, it holds that $T - L(p_1) \subseteq L(p_2)$. Hence, it follows from Proposition 2 that $r \equiv lg(T - L(p_1)) \preceq lg(L(p_2)) \equiv p_2$ and $L(r) \subseteq L(p_2)$.

On the other hand, applying Proposition 2 to the reflexive relation $lg(T - L(p_1)) \succeq lg(T - L(p_1))$, we get $L(lg(T - L(p_1))) \supseteq T - L(p_1)$. This implies that $L(p_1) \supseteq T - L(lg(T - L(p_1))) = T - L(r)$. Hence, it follows from Proposition 2 that $p_1 \equiv lg(L(p_1)) \succeq lg(T - L(r))$ and $L(p_1) \supseteq L(lg(T - L(r)))$.

As a consequence, it holds that $L(r) \cup L(lg(T - L(r))) \subseteq L(p_1) \cup L(p_2)$. This completes the proof of the lemma, since it holds that $F \cap (L(p_1) \cup L(p_2)) = \emptyset$ by the assumption ($\{p_1, p_2\}$ is consistent with $\langle T, F \rangle$). $\square$

Theorem 13. *Let T and F be mutually disjoint nonempty finite sets of ground tree patterns. For any minimally consistent subset oracle with $\langle T, F \rangle$, the procedure FCH returns a hypothesis in $\mathcal{TP}^2$ which is consistent with $\langle T, F \rangle$ if such a hypothesis exists in $\mathcal{TP}^2$ and returns "Fail" otherwise.*

Proof. First, we consider the case where the least hypothesis space with respect to $\langle T, F \rangle$ is $\mathcal{TP}^1$. If there exists a consistent hypothesis $\{p\} \in \mathcal{TP}^1$, then both $L(p) \supseteq T$ and $L(p) \cap F = \emptyset$ hold. From Proposition 2, it holds that $p \succeq lg(T)$ and $L(p) \supseteq L(lg(T))$. This implies that $L(lg(T)) \cap F$ is also empty. From the definition of the least generalization, it holds that $L(lg(T)) \supseteq T$. Thus, $\{lg(T)\}$ is consistent with $\langle T, F \rangle$. Conversely, if $\{lg(T)\}$ is consistent with $\langle T, F \rangle$, then there exists the hypothesis $\{lg(T)\}$ in $\mathcal{TP}^1$. Hence, $\mathcal{TP}^1$ is the least hypothesis space with $\langle T, F \rangle$ if and only if $\{lg(T)\}$ is consistent with respect to $\langle T, F \rangle$. Thus, the procedure FCH works correctly if the least hypothesis space with respect to $\langle T, F \rangle$ is $\mathcal{TP}^1$.

Next, assume that the least hypothesis space with respect to $\langle T, F \rangle$ is $\mathcal{TP}^2$. Then, any subset oracle which is consistent with some $H \in \mathcal{TP}^2$ is given to the algorithm where $H = \{p_1, p_2\}$ is consistent with $\langle T, F \rangle$. If H is not reduced with respect to T, then either $\{p_1\}$ or $\{p_2\}$ is consistent with $\langle T, F \rangle$. Since both of them are in $\mathcal{TP}^1$, this contradicts the current assumption. Thus, we may assume that H is reduced with respect to T.

In this case, the procedure FCH calls the sub-procedure RS with inputs T, F, and $lg(T)$. From Proposition 9, the input $lg(T)$ is general enough with respect to T and $\{p_1, p_2\}$. Furthermore, every recursive call of RS, $RS(T, F, R)$, is made with the input R such that $L(lg(T - L(R))) \subseteq L(p_1) \cup L(p_2)$. Thus, from Corollary 11, R is also general enough with respect to T and $\{p_1, p_2\}$. Thus, every call $RS(T, F, P)$ of RS is made with the input P that is general enough with respect to T and $\{p_1, p_2\}$. Hence, it holds that $P \succeq lg(T - L(p_i))$ for some $i \in \{1, 2\}$. From Lemma 12, if $P \equiv lg(T - L(p_i))$ then $\{P, lg(T - L(P))\}$ is consistent with $\langle T, F \rangle$. Thus, the hypothesis $\{P, lg(T - L(P))\}$ in $\mathcal{TP}^2$ is outputted. On the other hand, from Proposition 6, if $P \succ lg(T - L(p_i))$ then there exists a finite sequence $r_0, r_1, \ldots, r_m$ such that $r_0 \equiv P$, $r_m \equiv lg(T - L(p_i))$, and $r_i \in \rho(r_{i-1})$ for any $1 \geq i \geq m$. Thus, even in the worst case, P is refined up to $lg(T - L(p_i))$ for some $i \in \{1, 2\}$. This ensures that the both procedure RS and FCH terminate with the output, $\{lg(T - L(p_i)), lg(T - L(lg(T - L(p_i))))\}$, which is consistent with $\langle T, F \rangle$ and in $\mathcal{TP}^2$ even in the worst case. This completes the proof for the case where the least hypothesis space with respect to $\langle T, F \rangle$ is $\mathcal{TP}^2$.

Finally, we consider the case where the least hypothesis space is $\mathcal{TP}^k$ for some $k \geq 3$. In this case, there is no hypothesis in $\mathcal{TP}^2$ which is consistent with $\langle T, F \rangle$. On the other hand, by the structure of the procedures, it is obvious that if FCH outputs a hypothesis in $\mathcal{TP}^2$ then the hypothesis is consistent with $\langle T, F \rangle$. Thus, if the procedure terminates finitely and makes some output, then the output must be "Fail". The termination of the procedure is ensured by the next theorem. $\qquad\square$

Theorem 14. *The procedure FCH terminates in time polynomial in size($T \cup F$).*

Proof. From the discussion in the proof of the previous theorem, the least hypothesis space with respect to $\langle T, F \rangle$ is $\mathcal{TP}^1$ if and only if $lg(T)$ is consistent with $\langle T, F \rangle$. The least generalization $lg(T)$ can be calculated in time polynomial in $size(T)$ and also tests of the consistency of $lg(T)$ on $\langle T, F \rangle$ terminates in time polynomial in $size(T \cup F)$. Thus, if the least hypothesis space is $\mathcal{TP}^1$, then the statement of the theorem is correct.

Suppose that the least hypothesis space is $\mathcal{TP}^k$ for some $k \geq 2$ and H is a hypothesis in $\mathcal{TP}^k$ which is consistent with $\langle T, F \rangle$. Since H is in the least hypothesis space, H is reduced with respect to T. On the other hand, in this case, the procedure RS is called and recursively searches $\mathcal{TP}^2$ for a hypothesis. For each recursive call $RS(T, F, R)$ made in the procedure call $RS(T, F, P)$, since R is a refinement of P, it follows from Proposition 7 that $size(R) > size(P)$. Thus, at some stage of the recursive search, the size of the input tree pattern exceeds the maximum size, say ℓ, of elements in T. Let P be such an input tree pattern. Then, for any $R \in \rho(P)$ and $\alpha \in T$, it follows from Proposition 2 and Proposition 7 that $R \not\preceq \alpha$. Thus, it holds that $lg(T - L(R)) \equiv lg(T)$ for every $R \in \rho(P)$. If the answer from the oracle for the subset query with $lg(T - L(R))$ is "Yes", that is, $L(lg(T)) \subseteq L(H)$ holds, then it follows from Proposition 1 that $lg(T) \preceq p$ for some $p \in H$. This contradicts that H is reduced with respect to T, since it follows from Proposition 2 that $T \subseteq L(p)$. Thus, the answer from the oracle for the subset query with $lg(T - L(R))$ is "No" for every $R \in \rho(P)$. Hence, RS is called recursively at most $\ell - size(lg(T))$ times, since P is set to $lg(T)$ initially.

For any tree pattern p and a ground tree pattern α, it is clear that if the number of different variables appearing in p is larger than the size of α, then $p \not\preceq \alpha$. Thus, from the above discussion, the number of different variables appearing in any input tree pattern P does not exceeds ℓ. Thus, from Proposition 8, the number of possible refinements of P is bounded by a polynomial in ℓ. Furthermore, it is also clear that the calculation of $lg(T - L(P))$ terminates in time polynomial in $size(T)$ and the test if $\{P, lg(T - L(P))\}$ terminates in time polynomial in $size(T \cup F)$. This completes the proof of the theorem. $\qquad \square$

4.4 Replacing a subset query with membership queries

In this section, we show that the procedure which uses several membership queries instead of a subset query also works well under some condition for Σ.

Lemma 15. *Suppose that Σ $(|\Sigma| \geq 3)$ contains at least one function with nonzero arity. Then, for any tree patterns r, p_1, p_2, there exists a set $G(r)$ of $n + 1$ ground instances of r such that $G(r) \subseteq L(p_1) \cup L(p_2)$ if and only if $r \preceq p_i$ for some $i \in \{1, 2\}$, where n is the number of different variables occurring in r.*

Proof. The *if* direction of the statement is trivial. Thus, we show the *only if* direction. Without loss of generality, we may assume that Σ contains one function with arity 1, say $f(\_)$, and two constants a, b. If r is ground then the proof is trivial. Thus, we assume that r contains n variables, say $x_1, \ldots, x_n$.

Consider the substitutions $\theta_0, \theta_1, \ldots, \theta_n$ which replace each variable by some ground tree pattern as defined in the following table and define $G(r)$ as the set $\{r\theta_0, r\theta_1, \ldots, r\theta_n\}$.

	x_1	x_2	$\cdots$	x_n
θ_0	$f(a)$	$f(f(a))$	$\cdots$	$\overbrace{f(f(\cdots f(a)\cdots)}^{n}$
θ_1	a	b	$\cdots$	b
θ_2	b	a	$\cdots$	b
$\vdots$	$\vdots$	$\vdots$	$\ddots$	$\vdots$
θ_n	b	b	$\cdots$	a

Note that, θ_0 replaces every variables with the mutually distinct ground tree patterns whose principal functors are different from a and b, θ_i ($i \neq 0$) replaces x_j by a if $i = j$, b otherwise. Such a substitution can be constructed even if the arity of f is greater than 1. Then, $lg(\{r\theta_0, r\theta_j\}) \equiv r$ for any $1 \leq j \leq n$. Thus, if $L(p_1)$ contains $r\theta_0$ and at least one $r\theta_j$ for some $1 \leq j \leq n$, then from Proposition 2 $p_1 \succeq r$. On the other hand, if $L(p_1)$ contains no $r\theta_j$ for any $1 \leq j \leq n$, then $L(p_2) \supseteq \{r\theta_1, \ldots, r\theta_n\}$. Since it is clear that $lg(\{r\theta_1, \ldots, r\theta_n\}) \equiv r$, we have $p_2 \succeq r$. The dual discussion holds when $L(p_2)$ contains $r\theta_0$ or no $r\theta_j$ for any $1 \leq j \leq n$. As a consequence, if $S \subseteq L(p_1) \cup L(p_2)$ then it holds that $r \preceq p_i$ for some $i \in \{1, 2\}$. $\qquad\square$

By the above lemma, the following holds as another corollary of Lemma 10.

Corollary 16. *Let $\{p_1, p_2\}$ be a set of tree patterns reduced with respect to T. Suppose that Σ ($|\Sigma| \geq 3$) contains at least one function with non-zero arity. Then, a tree pattern r is general enough with respect to T and $\{p_1, p_2\}$ if and only if $G(lg(T - L(r))) \subseteq L(p_1) \cup L(p_2)$.*

As a consequence, we can replace each subset query made in the procedure RS with $n + 1$ membership queries, where n is the number of different variables occurring in $lg(T - L(r))$ for some tree pattern r. Since n is bounded by the maximal size of elements in T, the following theorem follows from Theorem 13 and Theorem 14.

Theorem 17. *Let T and F be mutually disjoint nonempty finite sets of ground tree patterns. There exists an algorithm $\mathcal{A}$ that, for any given minimally consistent membership oracle with $\langle T, F \rangle$, satisfies the following conditions:*

1. *$\mathcal{A}$ terminates in time polynomial in $size(T \cup F)$.*
2. *$\mathcal{A}$ outputs a hypothesis in $\mathcal{TP}^2$ which is consistent with $\langle T, F \rangle$ if such a hypothesis exists, and outputs "Fail" otherwise.*

5 Concluding remarks

In this paper, we presented an algorithm for solving the consistency problem for TP^2 using queries. There may be a lot of opinions for the use of queries to solve the consistency problem. In some application domains such as motif-discovering in Molecular Biology, it is reasonable to use queries, since making a (membership) query can be regarded as making an experiment. However, there is controversy as to whether the *minimal* consistency of the oracle is reasonable. In this paper, we assume the minimality in order to avoid giving an oracle consistent with a hypothesis in TP^k for $k \geq 3$, while there exists a hypothesis in TP^2 which is consistent with given $\langle T, F \rangle$. An algorithm which works well, for any oracle which is simply consistent with the given sets, might be ideal. However, it seems impossible to find a consistent hypothesis in TP^2 via an oracle which answers according to a trivial consistent hypothesis T such that $|T| \geq 3$. It is our future work to consider more natural settings for solving consistency problem using queries.

Another interesting problem related to this work is the inductive inference with *refutation* [6]. A consistency problem is closely related to the refutability of a hypothesis space. Our work might be understood as an approach to construct an efficient inductive inference algorithm with refutation. We would like to clear the relation between the consistency problem and space refutable inference.

References

1. D. Angluin. Queries and concept learning. *Machine Learning*, 2(4):319–342, 1988.
2. H. Arimura, T. Shinohara, and S. Otsuki. A polynomial time algorithm for finding finite unions of tree pattern languages. In *Proc. of the 2nd International Workshop on Nonmonotonic and Inductive Logics*, 1991. LNAI 659.
3. H. Arimura, T. Shinohara, and S. Otsuki. Finding minimal generalizations for unions of pattern languages and its application to inductive inference from positive data. In P. Enjalbert, E. Mayr, and K. W. Wagner, editors, *Proceedings of the 11th Annual Symposium on Theoretical Aspects of Computer Science*, pp. 649–660. Springer-Verlag, 1994. LNCS 775.
4. J-L.Lassez, M. J. Maher, and K. Marriott. Unification revisited. In J. Minker, editor, *Foundations of Deductive Databases and Logic Programming*, pp. 587–625. Morgan Kaufmann, 1988.
5. S. Miyano, A. Shinohara, and T. Shinohara. Which classes of elementary formal systems are polynomial-time learnable? In S. Arikawa, A. Maruoka, and T. Sato, editors, *Proc. ALT '91*, pp. 139–150. JSAI, 1991.
6. Y. Mukouchi and S. Arikawa. Inductive inference machines that can refute hypothesis spaces. In K. P. Jantke, S. Kobayashi, E. Tomita, and T. Yokomori, editors, *Proc. ALT '93*, pp. 123–136. Springer-Verlag, 1993. LNAI 744.

7. B. K. Natarajan. *Machine Learning, A Theoretical Approach*. Morgan Kaufmann, 1991.

8. L. Pitt and L. G. Valiant. Computational limitations on learning from examples. *JACM*, 35(4):965–984, 1988.

9. G. D. Plotkin. A note on inductive generalization. In B. Meltzer and D. Michie, editors, *Machine Intelligence 5*, pp. 153–163. Edinburgh University Press, 1970.

10. J. C. Reynolds. Transformational systems and the algebraic structure of atomic formulas. In B. Meltzer and D. Michie, editors, *Machine Intelligence 5*, pp. 135–152. Edinburgh University Press, 1970.

11. L. G. Valiant. A theory of the learnable. *Comm. ACM*, 27:1134–1142, 1984.

Program Synthesis in the Presence of Infinite Number of Inaccuracies

Sanjay Jain[1]

Department of Information Systems and Computer Science
Lower Kent Ridge Road
National University of Singapore
Singapore 0511, Republic of Singapore
Email: sanjay@iscs.nus.sg

Abstract. Most studies modeling inaccurate data in Gold style learning consider cases in which the number of inaccuracies is finite. The present paper argues that this approach is not reasonable for modeling inaccuracies in concepts that are infinite in nature (for example, graphs of computable functions).

The effect of infinite number of inaccuracies in the input data in Gold's model of learning is considered in the context of identification in the limit of computer programs from graphs of computable functions. Three kinds of inaccuracies, namely, noisy data, incomplete data, and imperfect data, are considered. The amount of each of these inaccuracies in the input is measured using certain density notions. A number of interesting hierarchy results are shown based on the densities of inaccuracies present in the input data. Several results establishing tradeoffs between the density and type of inaccuracies are also derived.

1 Introduction

Consider the scenario in which a subject is attempting to learn its environment. At any given time, the subject receives a finite piece of data about its environment, and based on this finite information, conjectures an explanation about the environment. The subject is said to *learn* its environment just in case the explanations conjectured by the subject become fixed over time, and this fixed explanation is a correct representation of the subject's environment. Computational learning theory provides a framework for the study of the above scenario when the subject is an algorithmic device. The above model of learning is based on the work initiated by Gold [Gol67] and has been used in inductive inference of both functions and languages. We refer the reader to [AS83, BB75, CS83, OSW86, KW80] for background material in this field.

Most learning situations involve the presence of inaccuracies in the data presented to a learner. In the context of linguistic development, children are likely to face both ungrammatical intrusions and omission of some grammatical sentences from the ambient language; it is to be expected that minor perturbations of this kind would not influence the outcome of linguistic development. Similarly, in the context of scientific discovery, the business of science progresses despite experimental errors and unfeasibility of performing certain experiments. Several attempts have been made to model inaccuracies in Gold's paradigm [FJ89, OSW86, SR86]. Each of these studies, however, only consider cases in which the number of inaccuracies is finite. Now, this may be a suitable approach if the data available about the concepts to be learned is finite in nature, but not when the nature of data is infinite.

A problem of interest is identifying in the limit computer programs from graphs of computable functions. Now, the graph of a computable function is an infinite set of ordered pairs. Considering only finite number of errors in the graph is not a very realistic model of inaccuracies because this may imply that all the inaccuracies are, in some sense, restricted to some small region of the graph. A more suitable model would allow for the inaccuracies to be spread throughout the graph of the function such that "density" of these errors is bounded.

The present paper investigates precisely such models of identification from inaccurate data. To measure the amount of inaccuracy present in the input data when they might be infinite in number we use notions of density from [Roy86] (see also [SV90]).

We discuss three forms of inaccuracies that may be present in the input. For each of these we give a hierarchy of inference criteria based on the density of inaccuracy present in the input. We also give results comparing the three types of inaccuracies with each other. Even though some of our results and arguments also apply to language identification we will mainly be concerned with function inference in this paper.

In section 2 we discuss notation and fundamental inference paradigms. In section 3 we discuss inaccurate information sequences and inference paradigms based on them. In sections 4 and 5 we give our results.

2 Preliminaries

2.1 Notation

Recursion-theoretic concepts not explained below are treated in [Rog67]. N denotes the set of natural numbers, $\{0, 1, 2, 3, \ldots\}$, and N^+ denotes the set of positive integers, $\{1, 2, 3, \ldots\}$. $\in$, $\subseteq$, and $\subset$ denote, respectively, membership, containment, and proper containment for sets (including sets of ordered pairs). e, i, j, k, l, m, n, r, s, x, y, z, with or without decorations[1], range over N. $*$ is a non-member of N satisfying $(\forall n \in N)[n < * < \infty]$. a, b, c, with or without decorations, range over $N \cup \{*\}$. d, with or without decorations, ranges over the real interval $[0, 1]$. We let A, B, R, S, W, X, Y, Z, with or without decorations, range over subsets of N. $\mathrm{card}(S)$ denotes the cardinality of S. So then, '$\mathrm{card}(S) \leq *$' means that $\mathrm{card}(S)$ is finite. $\min(S)$ and $\max(S)$ respectively denote the minimum and maximum element in S. We take $\min(\emptyset)$ to be ∞ and $\max(\emptyset)$ to be 0. $S_1 \triangle S_2$ denotes $(S_1 - S_2) \cup (S_2 - S_1)$, the symmetric difference of S_1 and S_2.

---

[1] Decorations are subscripts, superscripts, primes and the like.

Let $\lambda x, y.\langle x, y \rangle$ denote a fixed pairing function (a recursive, bijective mapping: $N \times N \to N$) [Rog67]. $\langle \cdot, \cdot \rangle$ can be extended to pairing function for multiple arguments in a natural way.

f, g, h, p, F, with or without decorations, range over total functions. $\mathcal{C}$ and $\mathcal{S}$, with or without decorations, range over sets of total functions. $\text{graph}(f)$ denotes the set $\{(x, f(x)) \mid x \in N\}$. η and ξ range over partial functions. For $a \in N \cup \{*\}$, $\eta_1 =^a \eta_2$ means that $\text{card}(\{x \mid \eta_1(x) \neq \eta_2(x)\}) \leq a$. $\text{domain}(\eta)$ and $\text{range}(\eta)$ respectively denote the domain and range of partial function η. $f(A) = y$ is used as a shorthand for $(\forall x \in A)[f(x) = y]$. $\downarrow$ denotes defined and $\uparrow$ denotes undefined.

We fix φ to be an *acceptable programming system* [Rog58, Rog67, MY78] for the partial recursive functions: $N \to N$. φ_i denotes the partial recursive function computed by φ-program i. $\mathcal{R}$ denotes the class of all total recursive functions. Let Φ be an arbitrary Blum complexity measure [Blu67] associated with acceptable programming system φ; such measures exist for any acceptable programming system [Blu67]. $\text{MinProg}(f)$ denotes $\min(\{i \mid \varphi_i = f\})$

The quantifiers '$\overset{\infty}{\forall}$' and '$\overset{\infty}{\exists}$' mean 'for all but finitely many' and 'there exist infinitely many,' respectively.

2.2 Information Sequences and Learning Machines

An *information sequence* is a mapping from N or an initial segment of N, into $\{(x, y) \mid x, y \in N\}$. We let G and T, with or without decorations, range over infinite information sequences. We let σ, τ range over finite information sequences. By $\sigma \subseteq \tau$ we mean that σ is an initial sequence of τ. $G[n]$, denotes the initial sequence of G of length n. $|\sigma|$ denotes the length of σ. $f[n]$, denotes the finite information sequence σ such that

$$\sigma(x) = \begin{cases} (x, f(x)), & \text{if } x < n; \\ \uparrow, & \text{otherwise.} \end{cases}$$

The content of an information sequence G, denoted $\text{content}(G)$ is $\text{range}(G)$. $\text{content}(\sigma)$ is defined similarly. An information sequence, G, is for a function f if $\text{content}(G) = \text{graph}(f)$.

An *inductive inference machine* (IIM) is an algorithmic mapping from finite information sequences into N. We let $\mathbf{M}$, with or without decorations, range over IIMs. $\sigma_1 \diamond (x, y)$ denotes the *concatenation* of (x, y) at the end of the information sequence σ_1; i.e. $\sigma = \sigma_1 \diamond (x, y)$ is defined as follows:

$$\sigma(i) = \begin{cases} \sigma_1(i), & \text{if } i < |\sigma_1|; \\ (x, y), & \text{if } i = |\sigma_1|; \\ \uparrow, & \text{otherwise.} \end{cases}$$

2.3 Fundamental Function Identification Paradigms

In Definition 1 below we spell out what it means for an IIM to converge (in the limit) on an information sequence.

Definition 1. Suppose M is an IIM and G is an information sequence. $M(G)\downarrow$ (read: $M(G)$ *converges*; M converges on G) $\iff (\exists i)(\overset{\infty}{\forall} n)\,[M(G[n]) = i]$. If $M(G)\downarrow$, then $M(G)$ is defined = the unique i such that $(\overset{\infty}{\forall} n)[M(G[n]) = i]$, otherwise we say that $M(G)$ diverges (written: $M(G)\uparrow$).

We now introduce two different criteria for an IIM to successfully infer a function.

Definition 2. [Gol67, BB75, CS83] Let $a \in N \cup \{*\}$.
(a) **M** **Ex^a-identifies** f (written: $f \in \mathbf{Ex}^a(\mathbf{M})$) $\iff$
($\forall$ information sequences G for f)($\exists i \mid \varphi_i =^a f$)$[M(G)\downarrow = i]$.
(b) $\mathbf{Ex}^a = \{\mathcal{C} \mid (\exists M)[\mathcal{C} \subseteq \mathbf{Ex}^a(\mathbf{M})]\}$.

Ex in the above definition stands for *explanatory*.

Case and Smith [CS83] introduced another infinite hierarchy of identification criteria which we describe below. "**Bc**" stands for *behaviorally correct*. Barzdin [Bar74] essentially introduced $\mathbf{Bc}^0$.

Definition 3. [CS83] Let $a \in N \cup \{*\}$.
(a) **M** **Bc^a-identifies** f (written: $f \in \mathbf{Bc}^a(\mathbf{M})$) $\iff$
($\forall$ information sequences G for f)($\overset{\infty}{\forall} n$)$[\varphi_{M(G[n])} =^a f]$.
(b) $\mathbf{Bc}^a = \{\mathcal{C} \mid (\exists M)[\mathcal{C} \subseteq \mathbf{Bc}^a(\mathbf{M})]\}$.

We usually write **Ex** for $\mathbf{Ex}^0$ and **Bc** for $\mathbf{Bc}^0$. For function identification with accurate data, identification (for criteria of inference discussed in this paper) from arbitrary information sequences is equivalent to identification from the canonical information sequence. Theorem 4 below describes some of the basic results about the two kinds of function identification criteria described above.

Theorem 4. *For all* $a \in N$, *(a)* $\mathbf{Ex}^a \subset \mathbf{Ex}^{a+1}$. *(b)* $\bigcup_{a\in N} \mathbf{Ex}^a \subset \mathbf{Ex}^*$. *(c)* $\mathbf{Ex}^* \subset \mathbf{Bc}$. *(d)* $\mathbf{Bc}^a \subset \mathbf{Bc}^{a+1}$. *(e)* $\bigcup_{a\in N} \mathbf{Bc}^a \subset \mathbf{Bc}^*$. *(f)* $\mathcal{R} \in \mathbf{Bc}^*$.

Parts (a), (b), (d), and (e) are due to Case and Smith [CS83]. John Steel first observed that $\mathbf{Ex}^* \subseteq \mathbf{Bc}$ and diagonalization in part (c) is due to Harrington and Case [CS83]. Part (f) is due to Harrington [CS83]. Blum and Blum [BB75] first showed that $\mathbf{Ex} \subset \mathbf{Ex}^*$. Barzdin [Bar74] independently showed $\mathbf{Ex} \subset \mathbf{Bc}$.

3 Inaccurate Data

We consider three kinds of inaccuracies that could creep into natural environments of learners.

- **Noisy data:** Ungrammatical intrusions into the language presented to the child is a very reasonable assumption about a child's environment. Similarly, experimental error caused by a faulty equipment could result in spurious data that is not representative of the reality under investigation.

- **Incomplete data:** Natural linguistic environments may omit sentences from the ambient language, and it is possible that the child's learning function can identify a natural language despite the systematic omission of sentences from its environment. Similarly, some experiments cannot be performed either due to technological limitations or due to ethical considerations.
- **Imperfect data:** Most natural linguistic environments are likely to be victims of both ungrammatical intrusions and omission of sentences from the ambient language. Such environments that contain a mixture of noisy and incomplete inaccuracies are referred to as environments with *imperfect* data. Similarly, in most experimental investigations, the inaccuracies are a mixture of both noisy and incomplete data.

The three kinds of inaccuracies discussed above yield three kinds of information sequences—noisy, incomplete, and imperfect. However, a further distinction is made based on whether the number of inaccuracies in an information sequence is finite or infinite. In [FJ89, OSW86, SR86] the case of finite number of inaccuracies was discussed. In this paper we examine the case when inaccuracies are infinite in number. We first introduce the definitions related with inference from finitely inaccurate information sequence.

It should be noted that the inaccuracies discussed here model spurious data and unavailability of data; they don't say anything about situations like "data is correct within 10% of actual value."

3.1   Information Sequences with Finite Number of Inaccuracies

Pursuant to the classification of inaccuracies, we define three kinds of inaccurate information sequences for functions.

Definition 5. [FJ89, OSW86] Let $a \in N \cup \{*\}$.
(a) An information sequence G is *a-noisy* for f $\iff$ $\text{graph}(f) \subseteq \text{content}(G)$ and $\text{card}(\text{content}(G) - \text{graph}(f)) \leq a$.
(b) An information sequence G is *a-incomplete* for f $\iff$ $\text{content}(G) \subseteq \text{graph}(f)$ and $\text{card}(\text{graph}(f) - \text{content}(G)) \leq a$.
(c) An information sequence G is *a-imperfect* for f $\iff$ $\text{card}(\text{graph}(f)\Delta\text{content}(G)) \leq a$.

An a-noisy information sequence for f can be viewed as an information sequence for f into which up to a "extra" pairs have been inserted. Note that any single such intrusion may occur infinitely often in G. Similarly, a-incomplete information sequences, have at most a pairs removed from them and a-imperfect information sequences have at most a pairs inserted/deleted from them.

In the above definitions, $a = *$ case implies that the number of inaccuracies is any finite number. The other $a \in N$ cases model situations when a scientist may be aware, apriori, of an upper bound on the number of inaccuracies infesting its environment; possible sources of such information could be previous experience and nature of instruments used.

Note that in the case of noisy information sequences for functions, two incorrect values for $f(n)$ count as two distinct noise points, i.e., if the correct value of $f(n) = x$ and both (n, y) and (n, z), where x, y and z are distinct, are present in an inaccurate information sequence for f, then the data points (n, y) and (n, z) contribute separately to noise count. Also, if the actual value of $f(n) = y$, but (n, y) doesn't appear in an information sequence and instead (n, z), $y \neq z$, appears, then these contribute two to imperfection count.

We now introduce the learning criteria based on finite number of inaccuracies in the input.

Definition 6. [FJ89, OSW86] Let $a, b \in N \cup \{*\}$.
(a.1) **M** $\mathbf{N}^a\mathbf{Ex}^b$-*identifies* f (written: $f \in \mathbf{N}^a\mathbf{Ex}^b(\mathbf{M})$) $\Longleftrightarrow$
($\forall$ a-noisy information sequences G for f)$[\mathbf{M}(G)\!\!\downarrow \wedge \varphi_{\mathbf{M}(G)} =^b f]$.
(a.2) $\mathbf{N}^a\mathbf{Ex}^b = \{\mathcal{C} \mid (\exists \mathbf{M})[\mathcal{C} \subseteq \mathbf{N}^a\mathbf{Ex}^b(\mathbf{M})]\}$.
(b.1) **M** $\mathbf{In}^a\mathbf{Ex}^b$-*identifies* f (written: $f \in \mathbf{In}^a\mathbf{Ex}^b(\mathbf{M})$) $\Longleftrightarrow$
($\forall$ a-incomplete information sequences G for f)$[\mathbf{M}(G)\!\!\downarrow \wedge \varphi_{\mathbf{M}(G)} =^b f]$.
(b.2) $\mathbf{In}^a\mathbf{Ex}^b = \{\mathcal{C} \mid (\exists \mathbf{M})[\mathcal{C} \subseteq \mathbf{In}^a\mathbf{Ex}^b(\mathbf{M})]\}$.
(c.1) **M** $\mathbf{Im}^a\mathbf{Ex}^b$-*identifies* f (written: $f \in \mathbf{Im}^a\mathbf{Ex}^b(\mathbf{M})$) $\Longleftrightarrow$
($\forall$ a-imperfect information sequences G for f)$[\mathbf{M}(G)\!\!\downarrow \wedge \varphi_{\mathbf{M}(G)} =^b f]$.
(c.2) $\mathbf{Im}^a\mathbf{Ex}^b = \{\mathcal{C} \mid (\exists \mathbf{M})[\mathcal{C} \subseteq \mathbf{Im}^a\mathbf{Ex}^b(\mathbf{M})]\}$.

Similar to the above definitions one can define the function identification paradigms: $\mathbf{N}^a\mathbf{Bc}^b$, $\mathbf{In}^a\mathbf{Bc}^b$, $\mathbf{Im}^a\mathbf{Bc}^b$.

We now turn our attention to infinite number of inaccuracies.

3.2 Information Sequences with Infinite Number of Inaccuracies

We first define density notions needed to measure the amount of inaccuracy in the input. These notions of "density" are from [Roy86]. Similar notions were also used by Smith and Velauthapillai [SV90] in the context of inductive inference.

Definition 7. (S. Tennenbaum: see page 156 in [Rog67], [Roy86])
(a) Suppose that $A \subseteq N$ and that B is a finite, nonempty subset of N. We define the *density of A in B* (denoted: $\mathbf{den}(A; B)$) as $\mathrm{card}(A \cap B)/\mathrm{card}(B)$.
(b) The *density* of a set A (denoted: $\mathbf{den}(A)$) is $\lim_{n \to \infty} \inf(\{\mathbf{den}(A; \{z \mid z \leq x\}) \mid x \geq n\})$.

Intuitively, $\mathbf{den}(A; B)$ can be thought of as the probability of selecting an element of A when choosing an arbitrary element from B.

Note that, even if $\mathbf{den}(A)$ is 1, A may have "large holes". To overcome this situation, we consider the notion of "uniform density" from [Roy86].

Definition 8. [Roy86] The *uniform density* of a set A in intervals of length $\geq n$ (denoted: $\mathbf{uden}_n(A)$) is $\inf(\{\mathbf{den}(A; \{z \mid x \leq z \leq y\}) \mid x, y \in N \text{ and } y - x \geq n\})$. *Uniform density* of A (denoted: $\mathbf{uden}(A)$) is $\lim_{n \to \infty} \mathbf{uden}_n(A)$.

We now define the inaccurate information sequences with certain density.

Definition 9. Suppose $0 \leq d \leq 1$. An information sequence G is d-Dnoisy for a total function f if

(a) $\text{graph}(f) \subseteq \text{content}(G)$,

(b) $\text{den}(N - \{x \mid (\exists y)[(x,y) \in \text{content}(G) - \text{graph}(f)]\}) \geq 1 - d$ and

(c) $(\forall x)[\text{card}(\{(x,y) \mid (x,y) \in \text{content}(G) - \text{graph}(f)\}) < \infty]$.

Note the difference in the way the inaccuracies in the information sequence are counted for finite inaccuracies and infinite inaccuracies. Instead of the definition used in clause (b) above we may want to define the density of the noise in an information sequence as the limiting value of the ratio:

$$\frac{\text{number of erroneous elements in the information sequence for inputs} \leq x}{x}.$$

We feel that this is not a natural definition for infinite inaccuracies since the density of noise can be infinite. Clause (c) has been added since we believe that the number of possible outcomes, even allowing for errors, in any particular experiment is bounded.

The following definitions give the corresponding notions for incomplete and imperfect information sequences.

Definition 10. Suppose $0 \leq d \leq 1$. An information sequence G is d-Dincomplete for a total function f if

(a) $\text{content}(G) \subseteq \text{graph}(f)$ and

(b) $\text{den}(N - \{x \mid (\exists y)[(x,y) \in \text{graph}(f) - \text{content}(G)]\}) \geq 1 - d$.

Definition 11. Suppose $0 \leq d \leq 1$. An information sequence G is d-Dimperfect for a total function f if $\text{den}(N - \{x \mid (\exists y)[(x,y) \in \text{content}(G)\triangle\text{graph}(f)]\}) \geq 1 - d$.

Note that the equivalent of clause (c) in the definition of Dnoisy information sequence is not necessary for the definition of Dincomplete and Dimperfect information sequences and thus has been dropped.

Similarly by considering uniform density one can define d-UDnoisy, d-UDincomplete, and d-UDimperfect information sequences.

3.3 Identification Criteria on Infinitely Inaccurate Information Sequences

We now define the corresponding notions of function identification.

Definition 12. Suppose $0 \leq d \leq 1$ and $a \in N \cup \{*\}$.

(a.1) $\textbf{M } \textbf{DN}^d\textbf{Ex}^a$ identifies f (written: $f \in \textbf{DN}^d\textbf{Ex}^a(\textbf{M})$) iff $(\forall\ d$-Dnoisy information sequences G for $f)[\textbf{M}(G)\!\downarrow\ \wedge\ \varphi_{\textbf{M}(G)} =^a f]$.

(a.2) $\textbf{DN}^d\textbf{Ex}^a = \{\mathcal{C} \mid (\exists \textbf{M})[\mathcal{C} \subseteq \textbf{DN}^d\textbf{Ex}^a(\textbf{M})]\}$.

(b.1) $\textbf{M } \textbf{DIn}^d\textbf{Ex}^a$ identifies f (written: $f \in \textbf{DIn}^d\textbf{Ex}^a(\textbf{M})$) iff $(\forall\ d$-Dincomplete information sequences G for $f)[\textbf{M}(G)\!\downarrow\ \wedge\ \varphi_{\textbf{M}(G)} =^a f]$.

(b.2) $\textbf{DIn}^d\textbf{Ex}^a = \{\mathcal{C} \mid (\exists \textbf{M})[\mathcal{C} \subseteq \textbf{DIn}^d\textbf{Ex}^a(\textbf{M})]\}$.

(c.1) $\textbf{M } \textbf{DIm}^d\textbf{Ex}^a$ identifies f (written: $f \in \textbf{DIm}^d\textbf{Ex}^a(\textbf{M})$) iff

$(\forall\, d$-Dimperfect information sequences G for $f)[\mathbf{M}(G)\!\downarrow \,\wedge\, \varphi_{\mathbf{M}(G)} =^{a} f]$.

(c.2) $\mathbf{DIm}^{d}\mathbf{Ex}^{a} = \{\mathcal{C} \mid (\exists \mathbf{M})[\mathcal{C} \subseteq \mathbf{DIm}^{d}\mathbf{Ex}^{a}(\mathbf{M})]\}$.

We can similarly define $\mathbf{UDN}^{d}\mathbf{Ex}^{a}, \mathbf{UDIn}^{d}\mathbf{Ex}^{a}, \mathbf{UDIm}^{d}\mathbf{Ex}^{a}$, $\mathbf{DN}^{d}\mathbf{Bc}^{a}$, $\mathbf{DIn}^{d}\mathbf{Bc}^{a}, \mathbf{DIm}^{d}\mathbf{Bc}^{a}, \mathbf{UDN}^{d}\mathbf{Bc}^{a}, \mathbf{UDIn}^{d}\mathbf{Bc}^{a}$, and $\mathbf{UDIm}^{d}\mathbf{Bc}^{a}$.

4 Hierarchy Results

The following theorem demonstrates the disadvantages of increasing the density of noise. It establishes that there are collections of functions that can be **Ex**-identified with noise of a particular density, but cannot be identified if the density of noise is increased, even if the noise is of uniform type and a more liberal criterion of success is used.

Theorem 13. *Suppose* $0 \leq d_1 < d_2 \leq 1$. $\mathbf{DN}^{d_1}\mathbf{Ex} - [\mathbf{UDN}^{d_2}\mathbf{Ex}^{*} \cup \bigcup_{l\in N} \mathbf{UDN}^{d_2}\mathbf{Bc}^{l}] \neq \emptyset$.

Corollary 14. *Suppose* $0 \leq d_1 < d_2 \leq 1$. $\mathbf{DN}^{d_1}\mathbf{Ex} - \mathbf{UDN}^{d_2}\mathbf{Ex}^{*} \neq \emptyset$.

PROOF OF THEOREM 13. Without loss of generality assume $d_1 = j/n$, $d_2 = (j+4)/n$, where $n > j+4$ and $j, n \in N$. Consider the following classes of functions

$$\mathcal{C}_0 = \{f \mid \varphi_{f(0)} = f \,\wedge\, (\overset{\infty}{\exists}\, x)[f(x) \neq 0]\}, \text{ and } \mathcal{C}_1 = \{f \mid (\overset{\infty}{\forall}\, x)[f(x) = 0]\}.$$

It was shown in [CS83] that $\mathcal{C}_0 \cup \mathcal{C}_1 \notin \mathbf{Ex}^{*} \cup \bigcup_{l\in N} \mathbf{Bc}^{l}$. We will use a modification of $\mathcal{C}_0 \cup \mathcal{C}_1$ as our diagonalizing class.
Let $N_0 = 0$ and, for $i > 0$, $N_i = n^{i}$.
Let $X = \{x \mid (\exists r)[N_{2r} \leq x < N_{2r+1}]\}$, $X_0 = X \cap \{x \mid x < (j+4) \bmod n\}$, and $X_1 = X - X_0$.
Let $R_{k,j} = \{x \mid [N_{2\cdot\langle k,j\rangle+1} \leq x < N_{2\cdot\langle k,j\rangle+2}]\}$, and $S_k = \bigcup_{j\in N} R_{k,j}$.
Now for $f \in \mathcal{C}_0 \cup \mathcal{C}_1$ define a function F_f as follows.
$F_f(S_k) = f(k)$.
$F_f(X_1) = 0$.
$F_f(X_0) = 0$, if $f \in \mathcal{C}_0$; $F_f(X_0) = 1$, otherwise.
Let $\mathcal{C} = \{F_f \mid f \in \mathcal{C}_0 \cup \mathcal{C}_1\}$.

Claim 15. $\mathcal{C} \in \mathbf{DN}^{d_1}\mathbf{Ex}$.

Proof. Suppose G is a d_1-Dnoisy information sequence for $F_f \in \mathcal{C}$.

Thus we have:
1. $(\forall x \in N)[(x, F_f(x)) \in \text{content}(G)]$
2. $(\forall y)[\, [(\forall x \in X_0)[(x, y) \in \text{content}(G)]] \Rightarrow F_f(X_0) = y\,]$
    (This holds because: for large enough r, the fraction of noisy points less than N_{2r+1}, is bounded by $(j+1)/n$. Now since $X_0 \cap \{x \mid x < N_{2r+1}\}$, consists of at least $(j+4)/n$ fraction of points less than N_{2r+1}, there exists a point in X_0 which is noise free.)

3. $(\overset{\infty}{\forall} \langle j, k \rangle)(\forall y)[\, [(\forall x \in R_{j,k})[(x, y) \in \text{content}(G)]] \Rightarrow F_f(S_j) = y \,]$.

(Let $\langle j, k \rangle$ be large enough, such that the fraction of noisy points below $\max(R_{j,k})$ is bounded by $(j+1)/n$. Now since $R_{j,k}$ consists of $(n-1)/n$ fraction of points below $\max(R_{j,k})$, there exists a point in $R_{j,k}$ which is noise free.)

Since (1, 2) hold, it is easy to determine $F_f(X_0)$ in the limit from G. Also, since (1, 3) hold, it is easy to determine $F(S_0)$ in the limit. Now if $F_f(X_0) = 0$, then i defined as follows is a program for F_f,

$$\varphi_i(x) = \begin{cases} 0, & \text{if } x \in X_0; \\ 0, & \text{if } x \in X_1; \\ \varphi_{F_f(S_0)}(k), & \text{if } x \in S_k. \end{cases}$$

If $F_f(X_0) = 1$, then $W = \{k \mid F_f(S_k) \neq 0\}$ can be determined in the limit (since (1, 3) hold). A program for F_f can then easily be constructed from W. Thus $\mathcal{C} \in \mathbf{DN}^{d_1}\mathbf{Ex}$. $\square$

Claim 16. $\mathcal{C} \notin [\mathbf{UDN}^{d_2}\mathbf{Ex}^* \cup \bigcup_{l \in N} \mathbf{UDN}^{d_2}\mathbf{Bc}^l]$.

Proof. For $f \in \mathcal{C}_0 \cup \mathcal{C}_1$, we will show (i) how to convert an information sequence for f to an d_2-UDnoisy information sequence for F_f and (ii) (for $a \in N \cup \{*\}$) how to convert an a-error program for F_f into an a-error program for f.

Assuming this we have $[\mathcal{C} \in \mathbf{UDN}^{d_2}\mathbf{Ex}^* \cup \bigcup_{l \in N} \mathbf{UDN}^{d_2}\mathbf{Bc}^l] \Rightarrow [\mathcal{C}_0 \cup \mathcal{C}_1 \in \mathbf{Ex}^* \cup \bigcup_{l \in N} \mathbf{Bc}^l]$. Since, $[\mathcal{C}_0 \cup \mathcal{C}_1 \notin \mathbf{Ex}^* \cup \bigcup_{l \in N} \mathbf{Bc}^l]$ we conclude that $\mathcal{C} \notin \mathbf{UDN}^{d_2}\mathbf{Ex}^* \cup \bigcup_{l \in N} \mathbf{UDN}^{d_2}\mathbf{Bc}^l$.

From an information sequence, G, for f a d_2-UDnoisy information sequence can be constructed for F_f, by forming an information sequence G_{F_f} such that $\text{content}(G_{F_f}) = \{(x, 0) \mid x \in X\} \cup \{(x, 1) \mid x \in X_0\} \cup \{(x, f(k)) \mid x \in S_k\}$. Note, that this construction can be done effectively.

Also, since $f(k) = F_f(S_k) = F_f(N_{2 \cdot \langle k, j \rangle + 1})$, it is easy to convert an a-error program for F_f into an a-error program for f. This completes the proof of the claim $\square$ ∎

It can be similarly shown that $\mathcal{C}$ defined in the above proof is in $\mathbf{DIn}^{d_1}\mathbf{Ex} - [\mathbf{UDIn}^{d_2}\mathbf{Ex}^* \cup \bigcup_{l \in N} \mathbf{UDIn}^{d_2}\mathbf{Bc}^l]$ and $\mathbf{DIm}^{d_1/2}\mathbf{Ex} - [\mathbf{UDIm}^{d_2/2}\mathbf{Ex}^* \cup \mathbf{UDIm}^{d_2/2}\mathbf{Bc}^l]$. Thus we have,

Theorem 17. *Suppose* $0 \le d_1 < d_2 \le 1$.
$$[\mathbf{DN}^{d_1}\mathbf{Ex} \cap \mathbf{DIn}^{d_1}\mathbf{Ex} \cap \mathbf{DIm}^{d_1/2}\mathbf{Ex}] -$$
$$[(\mathbf{UDN}^{d_2}\mathbf{Ex}^* \cup \mathbf{UDIn}^{d_2}\mathbf{Ex}^* \cup \mathbf{UDIm}^{d_2/2}\mathbf{Ex}^*) \cup \bigcup_{l \in N}(\mathbf{UDN}^{d_2}\mathbf{Bc}^l \cup \mathbf{UDIn}^{d_2}\mathbf{Bc}^l \cup \mathbf{UDIm}^{d_2/2}\mathbf{Bc}^l)] \neq \emptyset.$$

Corollary 18. *Suppose* $0 \le d_1 < d_2 \le 1$. $\mathbf{DIn}^{d_1}\mathbf{Ex} - \mathbf{UDIn}^{d_2}\mathbf{Ex}^* \neq \emptyset$.

Corollary 19. *Suppose* $0 \le d_1 < d_2 \le 1/2$. $\mathbf{DIm}^{d_1}\mathbf{Ex} - \mathbf{UDIm}^{d_2}\mathbf{Ex}^* \neq \emptyset$.

Thus identification criteria based on inaccurate information form a strict hierarchy based on the density of inaccuracy.

Let C be a class of functions such that there exist functions f_1, f_2, such that $f_1 \neq^{2a} f_2$. Then it is easy to see that $C \notin \mathbf{UDIm}^{1/2}\mathbf{Bc}^a$ (since the input information sequence may be 1/2-UDimperfect for both f_1 and f_2). For $d < 1/2$ we do not know if $\mathbf{DIm}^d\mathbf{Ex} - \mathbf{DN}^{2d}\mathbf{Ex}$ is empty or not.

We now consider the advantages of a uniformity restriction on the density of inaccuracies over the situation where such a restriction is not there. The next result demonstrates this advantage in the context of noise by showing that there are collections of functions that can be $\mathbf{Ex}$-identified on information sequences with a uniform noise density < 1, but cannot be $\mathbf{Ex}^*$-identified even with 0-density noise if the uniformity constraint on the density of noise is removed.

Theorem 20. *Suppose* $0 \leq d < 1$. $\mathbf{UDN}^d\mathbf{Ex} - \mathbf{DN}^0\mathbf{Ex}^* \neq \emptyset$.

Proof. Without loss of generality let $d = (n-2)/n$, where $n > 2$. Let C_0 and C_1 be as defined in the proof of Theorem 13.

Let $N_0 = 0$, $N_{2i+1} = N_{2i} + (i+1) * n$, and $N_{2i+2} = N_{2i+1} * n$.

Let $X = \{x \mid (\exists j)[N_{2j} \leq x < N_{2j+1}]\}$, $R_{j,k} = \{x \mid N_{2 \cdot \langle j,k \rangle + 1} \leq x < N_{2 \cdot \langle j,k \rangle + 2}\}$, and $S_j = \bigcup_{k \in N} R_{j,k}$.

Now for $f \in C_0 \cup C_1$, define F_f as follows. $F_f(S_j) = f(j)$. $F_f(X) = 0$, if $f \in C_0$; $F_f(X) = 1$ otherwise.

Now proceeding in a way similar to that of Theorem 13 it can be shown that $C \in \mathbf{UDN}^d\mathbf{Ex} - \mathbf{DN}^0\mathbf{Ex}^*$. ∎

We can similarly show that

Theorem 21. *Suppose* $0 \leq d < 1$.
$$[\mathbf{UDN}^d\mathbf{Ex} \cap \mathbf{UDIn}^d\mathbf{Ex} \cap \mathbf{UDIm}^{d/2}\mathbf{Ex}] -$$
$$[(\mathbf{DN}^0\mathbf{Ex}^* \cup \mathbf{DIn}^0\mathbf{Ex}^*) \cup \bigcup_{l \in N}(\mathbf{DN}^0\mathbf{Bc}^l \cup \mathbf{DIn}^0\mathbf{Bc}^l)] \neq \emptyset.$$

Corollary 22. *Suppose* $0 \leq d < 1$. $\mathbf{UDIn}^d\mathbf{Ex} - \mathbf{DIn}^0\mathbf{Ex}^* \neq \emptyset$.

Corollary 23. *Suppose* $0 \leq d < 1/2$. $\mathbf{UDIm}^d\mathbf{Ex} - \mathbf{DIm}^0\mathbf{Ex}^* \neq \emptyset$.

The next result compares the case of finite number of errors with infinite number of errors. It demonstrates that there are collections of functions that can be $\mathbf{Ex}$-identified from information sequences that contain a finite number of imperfections, but cannot be learned from uniform 0-density noise even if a more liberal criterion of identification is used.

Theorem 24. $\mathbf{Im}^*\mathbf{Ex} - [\mathbf{UDN}^0\mathbf{Ex} \cup \bigcup_{l \in N} \mathbf{UDN}^0\mathbf{Bc}^l]$.

Proof. Consider the following classes of functions
$$C_0 = \{f \mid \varphi_{f(0)} = f \wedge (\overset{\infty}{\exists} x)[f(x) \neq 0]\}, \text{ and } C_1 = \{f \mid (\overset{\infty}{\forall} x)[f(x) = 0]\}.$$

It was shown in [CS83] that $C_0 \cup C_1 \notin \mathbf{Ex}^* \cup \bigcup_{l \in N} \mathbf{Bc}^l$. We will use a modification of $C_0 \cup C_1$ as our diagonalizing class.

Let $X = \{2^n + 1 \mid n \geq 1\}$. Let $S_k = \{2 \cdot \langle k, z \rangle \mid z \in N\}$. Let $Z = N - (X \cup \bigcup_k S_k)$.

For $f \in C_0 \cup C_1$, define a function F_f as follows.

$F_f(S_k) = f(k)$,

$F_f(Z) = 0$,

$F_f(X) = 0$, if $f \in C_0$; $F_f(X) = 1$, otherwise.

Let $C = \{F_f \mid f \in C_0 \cup C_1\}$.

Claim 25. $C \in \mathbf{Im^*Ex}$.

Proof. Suppose G is a $*$-imperfect information sequence for $F_f \in C$. Thus, it is easy to determine $F_f(X)$ and $F_f(S_0)$, in the limit from G. Now if $F_f(X) = 0$, then i defined as follows is a program for F_f,

$$\varphi_i(x) = \begin{cases} 0, & \text{if } x \in X; \\ 0, & \text{if } x \in Z; \\ \varphi_{F_f(S_0)}(k), & \text{if } x \in S_k. \end{cases}$$

If $F_f(X) = 1$, then $W = \{k \mid F_f(S_k) \neq 0\}$ can be determined in the limit (since G is $*$-imperfect text for F_f). A program for F_f can then easily be constructed from W. Thus $C \in \mathbf{Im^*Ex}$. $\square$

Claim 26. $C \notin [\mathbf{UDN^0Ex} \cup \bigcup_{l \in N} \mathbf{UDN^0Bc^l}]$.

Proof. For $f \in C_0 \cup C_1$, we will show (i) how to convert an information sequence for f to an 0-UDnoisy information sequence for F_f and (ii) (for $a \in N \cup \{*\}$) how to convert an a-error program for F_f into an a-error program for f.

Assuming this we have $[C \in \mathbf{UDN^0Ex^*} \cup \bigcup_{l \in N} \mathbf{UDN^0Bc^l}] \Rightarrow [C_0 \cup C_1 \in \mathbf{Ex^*} \cup \bigcup_{l \in N} \mathbf{Bc^l}]$. Since, $[C_0 \cup C_1 \notin \mathbf{Ex^*} \cup \bigcup_{l \in N} \mathbf{Bc^l}]$ we conclude that $C \notin \mathbf{UDN^0Ex^*} \cup \bigcup_{l \in N} \mathbf{UDN^0Bc^l}$.

From an information sequence, G, for f a 0-UDnoisy information sequence can be constructed for F_f, by forming an information sequence G_{F_f} such that content$(G_{F_f}) = \{(x, 0) \mid x \in X \cup Z\} \cup \{(x, 1) \mid x \in X\} \cup \{(x, f(k)) \mid x \in S_k\}$. Note, that this construction can be done effectively.

Also, since $f(k) = F_f(S_k) = F_f(2 \cdot \langle k, 0 \rangle)$, it is easy to convert an a-error program for F_f into an a-error program for f. This completes the proof of the claim $\square$ ∎

The next result parallels the above theorem for incomplete data.

Theorem 27. $\mathbf{Im^*Ex} - [\mathbf{UDIn^0Ex} \cup \bigcup_{l \in N} \mathbf{UDIn^0Bc^l}]$.

As a corollary to results in this section and results from [FJ89] we have,

Corollary 28. *Suppose* $0 < d < d' \leq 1$, $a \in N \cup \{*\}$. *Then,* $\mathbf{Ex^a} \supset \mathbf{N^1Ex^a} \supset \cdots \supset \mathbf{N^*Ex^a} \supset \mathbf{DN^0Ex^a} \supset \mathbf{DN^dEx^a} \supset \mathbf{DN^{d'}Ex^a}$.

Similar corollaries can be obtained for incomplete information, imperfect information and for uniform inaccuracies.

5 Comparison Between Different Types of Inaccuracies

We now compare the effects of different kinds of inaccuracies. The following theorem demonstrates the advantages of noise over missing data by establishing that there are collections of functions that can be **Ex**-identified with high noise density but cannot be identified from information sequences in which a single data is missing even if the final program is allowed to make a finite number of errors.

Theorem 29. *Suppose* $0 \leq d < 1$. $\mathbf{DN}^d\mathbf{Ex} - \mathbf{In}^1\mathbf{Ex}^* \neq \emptyset$.

Proof. Without loss of generality let $d = (n - 2)/n$.
Let $N_0 = 1$, $N_{i+1} = n * N_i$.
Let $R_{j,k} = \{x \mid N_{(j,k)} \leq x < N_{(j,k)+1}\}$, and $S_j = \bigcup_{k \in N} R_{j,k}$.
   Now for $f \in \mathcal{R}$, define F_f as follows. $F_f(S_j) = f(j)$. $F_f(0) = \langle i, \langle \mathrm{err}_0, \mathrm{err}_1, \mathrm{err}_2, \ldots, \mathrm{err}_{i-1} \rangle \rangle$, where $i = \mathrm{MinProg}(f)$, and for $j < i$, $\mathrm{err}_j = \min(\{x \mid \varphi_j(x) \neq f(x)\})$.
   Let $\mathcal{C} = \{F_f \mid f \in \mathcal{R}\}$.

Claim 30. $\mathcal{C} \notin \mathbf{In}^1\mathbf{Ex}^*$.

Proof. For $f \in \mathcal{R}$, we will show below (i) how to convert an information sequence for f to an 1-incomplete information sequence for F_f, and (ii) how to convert a *-error program for F_f to a *-error program for f. From this it follows that, $\mathcal{C} \in \mathbf{In}^1\mathbf{Ex}^* \Rightarrow \mathcal{R} \in \mathbf{Ex}^*$. Since $\mathcal{R} \notin \mathbf{Ex}^*$, we conclude that $\mathcal{C} \notin \mathbf{In}^1\mathbf{Ex}^*$.

   Given an information sequence G for $f \in \mathcal{R}$, let G' be an information sequence such that $\mathrm{content}(G') = \{(x, f(k)) \mid x \in S_k\}$. Note that such a G' can be effectively computed from G. Also since $f(k) = F_f(S_k) = F_f(N_{(k,0)})$, a *-error program for F_f can be easily converted to a *-error program for f. $\square$

Claim 31. $\mathcal{C} \in \mathbf{DN}^d\mathbf{Ex}$.

Proof. We describe a IIM **M** which $\mathbf{DN}^d\mathbf{Ex}$-identifies $\mathcal{C}$. Let h be a recursive function such that, for all e, z, j, $\varphi_{h(e,z)}(0) = z$, and $\varphi_{h(e,z)}(S_j) = \varphi_e(j)$.
   Suppose $f \in \mathcal{R}$ and G is an d-Dnoisy information sequence for F_f ($\in \mathcal{C}$). We describe how **M** computes its output on $G[n]$. For this we first describe, $X_n, Y_n^j, Z_n, e_n, z_n$ (which depend on G, n). Let
   $X_n = \{x \mid (0, x) \in \mathrm{content}(G[n])\}$,
   $Y_n^j = \{\langle k, y \rangle \mid (\forall x \in R_{j,k})[(x, y) \in \mathrm{content}(G[n])]\}$,
   $Z_n = \{(j, y) \mid (\exists k)[\langle k, y \rangle = \max(Y_n^j)]\}$.
   Note that, for large enough n, $Z_n \subseteq \mathrm{graph}(f)$. Let
   $e_n = \max(\{i \mid (\exists \mathrm{err}_0, \mathrm{err}_1, \ldots, \mathrm{err}_{i-1} \mid \langle i, \langle \mathrm{err}_0, \mathrm{err}_1, \mathrm{err}_2, \ldots, \mathrm{err}_{i-1} \rangle \rangle \in X_n)[(\forall j < i)[\Phi_j(\mathrm{err}_j) > n \vee (\mathrm{err}_j, \varphi_j(\mathrm{err}_j)) \notin Z_n]]\})$.
   It is easy to see that, for large enough n, $e_n = \mathrm{MinProg}(f)$.
Let $z_n = \langle e_n, \langle \mathrm{err}_0^n, \ldots, \mathrm{err}_{e_n-1}^n \rangle \rangle$,
   where, for $j < e_n$, $\mathrm{err}_j^n = \min(\{n\} \cup \{x < n \mid \Phi_j(x) > n \vee \Phi_{e_n}(x) > n \vee \varphi_j(x) \neq \varphi_{e_n}(x)\})$. From the definition of F_f, it follows that for large enough n, $z_n = F_f(0)$.

Let $\mathbf{M}(G[n]) = h(e_n, z_n)$. It is easy to see that, $F_f \in \mathbf{DN}^d\mathbf{Ex}(\mathbf{M})$. Since F_f was an arbitrary member of $\mathcal{C}$, we have $\mathcal{C} \subseteq \mathbf{DN}^d\mathbf{Ex}(\mathbf{M})$. □ ∎ (Theorem 29)

Similarly we can establish the following result.

Theorem 32. *Suppose* $0 \le d < 1$. $\mathbf{DN}^d\mathbf{Ex} - \bigcup_{j \in N} \mathbf{In}^1\mathbf{Bc}^j \ne \emptyset$.

The following theorem shows the advantages of incomplete information sequences over imperfect information sequences.

Theorem 33. *Suppose* $0 \le d < 1$. $\mathbf{DIn}^d\mathbf{Ex}^* - (\mathbf{Im}^*\mathbf{Ex}^* \cup \bigcup_{j \in N} \mathbf{Im}^*\mathbf{Bc}^j) \ne \emptyset$.

Proof. Consider the following class of functions:
$$\mathcal{C} = \{f \mid (\forall y \in range(f))[\varphi_y =^* f]\}.$$
Clearly $\mathcal{C} \in \mathbf{DIn}^d\mathbf{Ex}^*$. Suppose by way of contradiction that $\mathbf{M}\ \mathbf{Im}^*\mathbf{Ex}^*$ identifies $\mathcal{C}$ (proof for $\mathbf{M}\ \mathbf{Im}^*\mathbf{Bc}^j$-identifying $\mathcal{C}$ is similar; we omit the details). Then by Operator Recursion Theorem [Cas74] there exists a 1-1 recursive p such that the functions $\varphi_{p(\cdot)}$ may be described as follows. Let x_s denote the least x such that $\varphi_{p(0)}(x)$ is not defined before stage s. Let $\varphi_{p(0)}(0) = p(0)$. Let $\sigma_1 = ((0, p(0)))$. Go to stage 1.

Stage s

1. For all $x < x_s$, let $\varphi_{p(2s)}(x) = p(2s)$.
   Dovetail steps $2, 3, 4$ until step 3 or 4 succeeds. If step 3 succeeds before step 4 does, if ever, then go to step 5. If step 4 succeeds before step 3 does, if ever, then go to step 6.

2. Let $z = x_s$. Go to substage 0.
   Substage s'
       Let $\varphi_{p(2s)}(z) = p(2s)$.
       Let $z = z + 1$.
       Go to substage $s' + 1$.
   End substage s'.

3. Search for $y > x_s$ such that $\varphi_{\mathbf{M}(\sigma_s)}(y)\!\downarrow\, = p(2s)$.

4. Search for $y > x_s$ such that $\mathbf{M}(\sigma_s) \ne \mathbf{M}(\sigma_s \diamond (x_s, p(2s)) \diamond \ldots \diamond (y, p(2s)))$.

5. Let y be as found in step 3.
   For $x_s \le x \le y$, let $\varphi_{p(0)}(x) = p(2s + 1)$.
   For $x \le y$, let $\varphi_{p(2s+1)} = \varphi_{p(0)}(x)$. Let $\varphi_{p(2s+1)}$ follow $\varphi_{p(0)}$ from now on (i.e. whenever $\varphi_{p(0)}(x)$ gets defined for $x > y$, let $\varphi_{p(2s+1)}(x) = \varphi_{p(0)}(x)$).
   Let $\sigma_{s+1} = \sigma_s \diamond (x_s, p(2s + 1)) \diamond \ldots \diamond (y, p(2s + 1))$.
   Go to stage $s + 1$.
   (Note that if $p(i)$ is in the range of $\varphi_{p(0)}$, then $\varphi_{p(i)} =^* \varphi_{p(0)}$).

6. Let y be the maximum of y found in step 4 and the y in the last substage executed in step 2. For $x_s \le x \le y$, let $\varphi_{p(0)}(x) = \varphi_{p(2s)}(x) = p(2s)$.
   Let $\varphi_{p(2s)}$ follow $\varphi_{p(0)}$ from now on.
   Let $\sigma_{s+1} = \sigma_s \diamond (x_s, p(2s)) \diamond \ldots \diamond (y, p(2s))$.
   Go to stage $s + 1$.
   (Note that if $p(i)$ is in the range of $\varphi_{p(0)}$, then $\varphi_{p(i)} =^* \varphi_{p(0)}$).
End Stage s

Now consider the following cases:

Case 1: All stages halt.

In this case let $f = \varphi_{p(0)}$. Clearly, $f \in \mathcal{C}$.

Case 1a: **M** does not converge on $G = \bigcup_{s \in N} \sigma_s$, which is an information sequence for f.

In this case **M** does not $\mathbf{Im^*Ex^*}$ identify f.

Case 1b: **M** on $G = \bigcup_{s \in N} \sigma_s$ converges.

In this case only way infinitely many stages can exist is by execution of step 5 infinitely often. But then $\varphi_{\mathbf{M}(G)}$ is infinitely different from f.

Case 2: Stage s starts but never halts.

In this case let $f = \varphi_{p(2s)}$. Let $G = \sigma_s \diamond (x_s, p(2s)) \diamond (x_s + 1, p(2s)) \ldots$. Thus G is a *-imperfect information sequence for f. But **M** on G converges to $\mathbf{M}(\sigma_s)$, and, for all but finitely many x, $\varphi_{\mathbf{M}(\sigma_s)}(x) \neq p(2s)$. Thus **M** does not $\mathbf{Im^*Ex^*}$-identify f.

From the above cases we have that **M** does not $\mathbf{Im^*Ex^*}$ identify $\mathcal{C}$. ∎

Now we consider the possibility of whether noisy data can hurt more than incomplete data. The following theorem almost answers the question negatively. It shows that if a class of functions can be identified from incomplete information sequences then it can also be identified from noisy information sequences as long as the density of inaccuracies is slightly reduced.

Theorem 34. *Suppose* $0 \leq d_1 < d_2 \leq 1$. $(\forall a \in N \cup \{*\})[\mathbf{DIn}^{d_2}\mathbf{Ex}^a \subseteq \mathbf{DN}^{d_1}\mathbf{Ex}^a]$.

Proof. This proof is a complex modification of the proof of Theorem 12 in [FJ89]. In this case we cannot just try to remove the multiple valued points from the input information sequence (as done in the proof of Theorem 12 in [FJ89]), since the number of such points may be infinite. However we know that if we wait long enough all initial segments can be made noise free. Moreover the density of noise beyond a certain point is always smaller than d_2. We use these facts to simulate a IIM **M**, which $\mathbf{DIn}^{d_2}\mathbf{Ex}^a$ identifies $\mathcal{C}$.

Let G be a d_1-Dnoisy information sequence for $f \in \mathcal{C}$. Without loss of generality we can assume that, for all n, content$(G[2n]) \subseteq \{(x, y) \mid x \leq n\}$ and $(\forall x \leq n)(\exists y)[(x, y) \in \text{content}(G[2n])]$ (otherwise such a G can be effectively constructed from the input information sequence). Let $S = \{(x, z) \mid \text{card}(\{(x, y) \in \text{content}(G) \mid y \in N\}) = 1 \wedge (x, z) \in \text{content}(G)\}$. Let G' be the subsequence of G formed by deleting from G all elements not in S. Now if both (x_1, y_1) and (x_2, y_2) are in content(G'), where $x_1 < x_2$, then (x_1, y_1) appears before (x_2, y_2) in G'. Let σ_n denote the smallest initial segment of G' such that, for all $x \leq n$, $(x, y) \in \text{content}(G') \Rightarrow (x, y) \in \text{content}(\sigma_n)$.

Let Good(n) be true iff, for all $n' > n$, there exists a subsequence τ (extending σ_n) of $\sigma_{n'}$ such that,

(A) card$(\{x \mid (\exists y)[(x, y) \in \text{content}(\sigma_n)]\})/(n+1) > (1 - (d_1 + d_2)/2)$

(B) For $n \leq n'' \leq n'$, card$(\{x \leq n'' \mid (\exists y)[(x, y) \in \text{content}(\tau)]\})/(n''+1) > (1 - (d_1 + d_2)/2)$ and

(C) $\mathbf{M}(\sigma_n) = \mathbf{M}(\tau')$ for $\sigma_n \subseteq \tau' \subseteq \tau$.

Clearly, there exists an n such that $\text{Good}(n)$. Also n such that $\neg\text{Good}(n)$, can be enumerated using $\mathbf{M}$ and the information sequence G. Let n_0 be the least n such that $\text{Good}(n)$. An IIM $\mathbf{M}'$ can determine n_0, and thus $\mathbf{M}(\sigma_{n_0})$, in the limit. We now claim that $\mathbf{M}(\sigma_{n_0})$ is a program for an a-variant of f. To see this consider the tree formed by considering all subsequences τ of G' (with a corresponding n') extending σ_{n_0} such that (B) and (C) are satisfied. Clearly this tree is infinite. Moreover the branching factor, in this tree, at any particular node is finite (due to density constraint in (B)). Thus there exists an infinite branch in this tree. Let G'' be the information sequence formed using this infinite branch. Clearly G'' is d_2-Dincomplete for f. Also $\mathbf{M}(G'') = \mathbf{M}(\sigma_{n_0})$. Thus $\mathbf{M}(\sigma_{n_0})$ is a program for an a-variant of f. ∎

Similarly we also have

Theorem 35. *Suppose* $0 \leq d_1 < d_2 \leq 1$. $(\forall a \in N \cup \{*\})[\mathbf{UDIn}^{d_2}\mathbf{Ex}^a \subseteq \mathbf{UDN}^{d_1}\mathbf{Ex}^a]$.

We leave it as an open question whether, for $a \in N \cup \{*\}$ and $d \in [0,1)$, $[\mathbf{DIn}^d\mathbf{Ex}^a \subseteq \mathbf{DN}^d\mathbf{Ex}^a]$ and $[\mathbf{UDIn}^d\mathbf{Ex}^a \subseteq \mathbf{UDN}^d\mathbf{Ex}^a]$.

6   Conclusions

In this paper we considered the effects of infinite number of inaccuracies in the input data on the learning power of IIMs. For $d < 1/2$ it is open whether $\mathbf{DIm}^d\mathbf{Ex} - \mathbf{DN}^{2d}\mathbf{Ex}$ (or $\mathbf{DIn}^{2d}\mathbf{Ex}$) is empty or not. It is also open whether, for $a \in N \cup \{*\}$ and $d \in [0,1)$, $[\mathbf{DIn}^d\mathbf{Ex}^a \subseteq \mathbf{DN}^d\mathbf{Ex}^a]$ or $[\mathbf{UDIn}^d\mathbf{Ex}^a \subseteq \mathbf{UDN}^d\mathbf{Ex}^a]$.

7   Acknowledgements

I would like to thank the referees for several helpful comments. I would also like to thank Arun Sharma for several helpful comments and discussions.

References

[AS83]   D. Angluin and C. Smith. A survey of inductive inference: Theory and methods. *Computing Surveys*, 15:237–289, 1983.

[Bar74] J. M. Barzdin. Two theorems on the limiting synthesis of functions. *In Theory of Algorithms and Programs, Latvian State University, Riga*, 210:82–88, 1974. In Russian.

[BB75]   L. Blum and M. Blum. Toward a mathematical theory of inductive inference. *Information and Control*, 28:125–155, 1975.

[Blu67] M. Blum. A machine independent theory of the complexity of recursive functions. *Journal of the ACM*, 14:322–336, 1967.

[Cas74]   J. Case. Periodicity in generations of automata. *Mathematical Systems Theory*, 8:15–32, 1974.

[CS83]   J. Case and C. Smith. Comparison of identification criteria for machine inductive inference. *Theoretical Computer Science*, 25:193–220, 1983.

[FJ89]   M. A. Fulk and S. Jain. Learning in the presence of inaccurate information. In R. Rivest, D. Haussler, and M. K. Warmuth, editors, *Proceedings of the Second Annual Workshop on Computational Learning Theory, Santa Cruz, California*, pages 175–188. Morgan Kaufmann Publishers, Inc., August 1989.

[Gol67]   E. M. Gold. Language identification in the limit. *Information and Control*, 10:447–474, 1967.

[KW80]   R. Klette and R. Wiehagen. Research in the theory of inductive inference by GDR mathematicians – A survey. *Information Sciences*, 22:149–169, 1980.

[MY78]   M. Machtey and P. Young. *An Introduction to the General Theory of Algorithms*. North Holland, New York, 1978.

[OSW86]   D. Osherson, M. Stob, and S. Weinstein. *Systems that Learn, An Introduction to Learning Theory for Cognitive and Computer Scientists*. MIT Press, Cambridge, Mass., 1986.

[Rog58]   H. Rogers. Gödel numberings of partial recursive functions. *Journal of Symbolic Logic*, 23:331–341, 1958.

[Rog67]   H. Rogers. *Theory of Recursive Functions and Effective Computability*. McGraw Hill, New York, 1967. Reprinted by MIT Press, Cambridge, Massachusetts in 1987.

[Roy86]   J. Royer. Inductive inference of approximations. *Information and Control*, 70:156–178, 1986.

[SR86]   G. Schäfer-Richter. Some results in the theory of effective program synthesis - learning by defective information. *Lecture Notes in Computer Science*, 215:219–225, 1986.

[SV90]   C. Smith and M. Velauthapillai. On the inference of approximate programs. *Theoretical Computer Science*, 77:249–266, 1990.

On monotonic strategies for learning r.e. languages

Sanjay Jain[1] and Arun Sharma[2]

[1] Department of Information Systems and Computer Science
Lower Kent Ridge Road
National University of Singapore
Singapore 0511, Republic of Singapore
Email: sanjay@iscs.nus.sg
[2] School of Computer Science and Engineering
The University of New South Wales
Sydney, NSW 2052, Australia
Email: arun@cse.unsw.edu.au

Abstract. Overgeneralization is a major issue in identification of grammars for formal languages from positive data. Different formulations of monotonic strategies have been proposed to address this problem and recently there has been a flurry of activity investigating such strategies in the context of indexed families of recursive languages.

The present paper studies the power of these strategies to learn recursively enumerable languages from positive data. In particular, the power of strong monotonic, monotonic, and weak monotonic (together with their dual notions modeling specialization) strategies are investigated for identification of r.e. languages. These investigations turn out to be different from the previous investigations on learning indexed families of recursive languages and at times require new proof techniques.

A complete picture is provided for the relative power of each of the strategies considered. An interesting consequence is that the power of weak monotonic strategies is equivalent to that of conservative strategies. This result parallels the scenario for indexed classes of recursive languages. It is also shown that any identifiable collection of r.e. languages can also be identified by a strategy that exhibits the dual of weak monotonic property.

1 Introduction

Consider the identification of formal languages from positive data. A machine is fed all the strings and no nonstrings of a language L, in any order, one string at a time. The machine, as it is receiving strings of L, outputs a sequence of grammars. The machine is said to identify L just in case the sequence of grammars converges to a grammar for L. This is essentially the paradigm of identification in the limit introduced by Gold [Gol67].

Since only strings belonging to the language are available, if a learning machine conjectures a grammar for some superset of the target language, it may not be "rational" for the machine to revise this conjecture as data about the complement of the language is not available. This is the problem of overgeneralization in learning formal languages from positive data.

The notion of monotonic strategies has been proposed to model learning heuristics that gradually refine their hypotheses. Learning machines following these strategies behave in such a way that their successive conjectures are an "improvement" on their previous conjectures. Recently there has been a flurry of results describing the power of these strategies for identifying indexed families of recursive languages (see Lange and Zeugmann [LZ92b, LZ93b, LZ93a, LZ93c, LZ92a], Lange, Zeugmann, and Kapur [LZK92], and Kapur[Kap92, Kap93], Kapur and Bilardi [KB92], Kinber [Kin94], Mukouchi [Muk92a, Muk92b], and Mukouchi and Arikawa [MA93]).

The present paper studies and presents a complete picture of the power of these strategies to identify r.e. languages. To facilitate the discussion of these notions and results, we introduce some notation next.

The symbol φ denotes an acceptable programming system, and φ_i denotes the partial computable function computed by the ith program in the φ system. The language accepted by the φ-program i is denoted W_i. Hence, $W_0, W_1, W_2, \ldots$ is an enumeration of all the recursively enumerable languages, and program i is a grammar (acceptor) for the r.e. language W_i. A text for an r.e. language L is an infinite sequence of numbers such that each element of L appears at least once in the sequence and no nonelement of L ever appears in the sequence.

The three monotonic strategies investigated in the literature are discussed next.

Jantke [Jan91] proposed the notion of *strong monotonic* strategies that upon being fed a text for the language output a chain of hypotheses such that if grammar j is output after grammar i, then $W_i \subseteq W_j$. The consequence of this requirement is that if a learner incorrectly assumes a string to belong to the language being learned then it cannot revise this assumption by emitting a hypothesis that does not include the string.

Wiehagen [Wie90] suggested that the requirement of strong monotonicity is too stringent and proposed the notion of *monotonic* strategies to be those learners that produce more general hypotheses only with respect to the language being identified. More precisely, if grammar j is conjectured after grammar i, then $L \cap W_i \subseteq L \cap W_j$. In other words, a monotonic strategy is allowed to correct its mistaken assumption that certain nonstrings of L belong to L but once it has correctly concluded that a string of L belongs to L it is not allowed to output a hypothesis that contradicts such a conclusion.

Lange and Zeugmann [LZ93b], motivated by the work on non-monotonic logics, introduced the notion of *weak-monotonic* strategies to be such that if grammar j is conjectured after grammar i and the set of strings seen by the machine when grammar j is conjectured is a subset of W_i, then $W_i \subseteq W_j$. In other words, a weak monotonic learner can expel strings from its hypothesis only if it encounters strings that cannot be accounted for by its current hypothesis.

Kapur [Kap92], with a view to model specialization strategies, considered the dual of the above three strategies. The above mentioned papers by Kapur, Lange, and Zeugmann have completely derived the relationship between these strategies in the context of identification of indexed families of recursive languages. The present paper does the same for recursively enumerable languages.

Work on monotonic strategies can be traced back to the notion of *conservative* strategies introduced by Angluin [Ang80]. Conservative strategies are such that they do not change their hypotheses unless they encounter a string that cannot be explained by the current hypothesis. Lange and Zeugmann have shown that for learning indexed families of recursive languages, weak monotonic and conservative strategies have equivalent power. Using new techniques we are able to show that this equivalence also holds for learning recursively enumerable languages.

We compare the power of strong monotonic, monotonic, weak-monotonic, dual-strong monotonic, dual-monotonic, dual-weak-monotonic, and conservative strategies to identify r.e. languages.

2 Preliminaries

2.1 Notation

Any unexplained recursion theoretic notation is from [Rog67]. The symbol N denotes the set of natural numbers, $\{0, 1, 2, 3, \ldots\}$. Unless otherwise specified, $i, j, k, l, m, n, q, r, s, t, x, y$, with or without decorations[3], range over N. Symbols $\emptyset$, $\subseteq$, $\subset$, $\supseteq$, and $\supset$ denote empty set, subset, proper subset, superset, and proper superset, respectively. Symbols A and S, with or without decorations, range over sets. $\overline{A}$ denotes the complement of set A. D, P, Q, with or without decorations, range over finite sets. Cardinality of a set S is denoted by $\text{card}(S)$. The maximum and minimum of a set are denoted by $\max(\cdot), \min(\cdot)$, respectively, where $\max(\emptyset) = 0$ and $\min(\emptyset) = \uparrow$.

A pair $\langle \cdot, \cdot \rangle$ stands for an arbitrary, computable, one-to-one encoding of all pairs of natural numbers onto N [Rog67].

By φ we denote a fixed *acceptable* programming system for the partial computable functions: $N \to N$ [Rog58, Rog67, MY78]. By φ_i we denote the partial computable function computed by program i in the φ-system. Symbol $\mathcal{R}$ denotes the set of all total computable functions. By Φ we denote an arbitrary fixed Blum complexity measure [Blu67, HU79] for the φ-system. By W_i we denote domain(φ_i). W_i is, then, the r.e. set/language ($\subseteq N$) accepted (or equivalently, generated) by the φ-program i. L, with or without decorations, ranges over languages, that is, subsets of N. $\mathcal{L}$, with or without decorations, ranges over sets of languages. $\mathcal{E}$ denotes the set of all r.e. languages. We denote by $W_{i,s}$ the set $\{x \leq s \mid \Phi_i(x) < s\}$.

---

[3] Decorations are subscripts, superscripts and the like.

2.2 Language Learning Theory

A *sequence* σ is a mapping from an initial segment of N into $(N \cup \{\#\})$. The *content* of a sequence σ, denoted content(σ), is the set of natural numbers in the range of σ. The *length* of σ is denoted by $|\sigma|$; the length of the empty sequence is 0. For $n \leq |\sigma|$, the initial sequence of σ of length n is denoted by $\sigma[n]$. Intuitively, $\#$'s represent pauses in the presentation of data. We let σ, τ, and γ, with or without decorations, range over finite sequences. SEQ denotes the set of all finite sequences.

Definition 1. A *language learning machine*, **M**, is an algorithmic device which computes a mapping from SEQ into $N \cup \{\bot\}$ such that if $\sigma \subseteq \tau$ and $\mathbf{M}(\sigma) \neq \bot$ then $\mathbf{M}(\tau) \neq \bot$.

The symbol $\bot$ denotes a nonnumeric element. The output of machine **M** on evidential state σ is denoted by $\mathbf{M}(\sigma)$, where "$\mathbf{M}(\sigma) = \bot$" means that **M** does not issue any hypothesis on σ. The reader should note the further requirement that once a machine **M** on evidential state σ outputs a program (that is, $\mathbf{M}(\sigma) \neq \bot$), **M** continues to do so on all extensions of σ.

A *text* T for a language L is a mapping from N into $(N \cup \{\#\})$ such that L is the set of natural numbers in the range of T. The *content* of a text T, denoted content(T), is the set of natural numbers in the range of T. $T[n]$ denotes the finite initial sequence of T with length n. We next introduce Gold's seminal notion of identification in the limit of r.e. languages.

Definition 2. [Gol67] **M** **TxtEx**-*identifies* L (read: $L \in$ **TxtEx(M)**) $\iff$ ($\forall$ texts T for L) ($\exists i \mid W_i = L$) ($\overset{\infty}{\forall} n)[\mathbf{M}(T[n]) = i]$. We define the class **TxtEx** $= \{\mathcal{L} \subseteq \mathcal{E} \mid (\exists \mathbf{M})[\mathcal{L} \subseteq \mathbf{TxtEx(M)}]\}$.

Some of our proofs depend on the notion of locking sequences which we describe next.

Definition 3. [BB75, Ful90] Let **M** be a learning machine and $L \subseteq N$.

(a) A sequence σ is said to be a *stabilizing sequence* for **M** on L just in case content$(\sigma) \subseteq L$ and $(\forall \tau \mid \sigma \subseteq \tau \wedge$ content$(\tau) \subseteq L)[\mathbf{M}(\tau) = \mathbf{M}(\sigma)]$.
(b) A sequence σ is said to be a *locking sequence* for **M** on L just in case σ is a stabilizing sequence for **M** on L and $W_{\mathbf{M}(\sigma)} = L$.

Following two lemmas are also used in some of our proofs.

Lemma 4. [BB75, OSW82] *If* **M** **TxtEx**-*identifies* L, *then there exists a locking sequence for* **M** *on* L.

Lemma 5. [Ful90] *From any learning machine* **M** *one may effectively construct* **M'** *such that the following hold:*

(a) **TxtEx(M)** $\subseteq$ **TxtEx(M')**.

(b) If $L \in \mathbf{TxtEx(M')}$, then all texts for L contain a locking sequence for $\mathbf{M'}$ on L.

We also compare the power of strategies discussed in the present paper with a restricted version of identification in the limit in which a learning machine is allowed to make only one conjecture which is required to be correct. This criterion of success is referred to as finite identification and was first considered by Trakhtenbrot and Barzdin [TB70].

Definition 6. M TxtFin-*identifies* L (read: $L \in \mathbf{TxtFin(M)}$) $\Longleftrightarrow$ ($\forall$ texts T for L) $(\exists i \mid W_i = L)\ (\exists n_0)[(\forall n \geq n_0)[M(T[n]) = i] \land (\forall n < n_0)[M(T[n]) = \bot]]$. We define the class $\mathbf{TxtFin} = \{\mathcal{L} \subseteq \mathcal{E} \mid (\exists M)[\mathcal{L} \subseteq \mathbf{TxtFin(M)}]\}$.

3 Monotonic Strategies

The three strategies introduced by Jantke [Jan91], Wiehagen [Wie90], and Lange and Zeugmann [LZ93b] are defined next. We consider two versions for each of these strategies: global and class. The global version requires the monotonicity properties to hold on all languages whereas the class version requires the monotonicity properties to hold only on the languages identified by the machines.

Definition 7. [Jan91]

(a) **M** is said to be *strong-monotonic* on L just in case $(\forall \sigma \subseteq \tau \mid \text{content}(\tau) \subseteq L)[M(\sigma) = \bot \lor W_{\mathbf{M}(\sigma)} \subseteq W_{\mathbf{M}(\tau)}]$.

(b) **M** is said to be *strong monotonic* on $\mathcal{L}$ just in case **M** is strong-monotonic on each $L \in \mathcal{L}$.

(c) **M** is *strong-monotonic* just in case **M** is strong-monotonic on each $L \subseteq N$.

We now define the collections of languages identifiable by the global (referred to as **SMON**) and class (referred to as **CLASS-SMON**) versions of strong-monotonicity.

Definition 8. (a) **SMON** = $\{\mathcal{L} \mid (\exists M)[M$ is strong-monotonic and $\mathcal{L} \subseteq \mathbf{TxtEx(M)}]\}$.

(b) **CLASS-SMON** = $\{\mathcal{L} \mid (\exists M)[M$ is strong-monotonic on $\mathcal{L}$ and $\mathcal{L} \subseteq \mathbf{TxtEx(M)}]\}$.

It is easy to show that **SMON = CLASS-SMON**. Hence, we only consider the global version in the sequel.

Definition 9. [Wie90]

(a) **M** is said to be *monotonic* on L just in case $(\forall \sigma \subseteq \tau \mid \text{content}(\tau) \subseteq L)[M(\sigma) = \bot \lor W_{\mathbf{M}(\sigma)} \cap L \subseteq W_{\mathbf{M}(\tau)} \cap L]$.

(b) **M** is said to be *monotonic* on $\mathcal{L}$ just in case **M** is monotonic on each $L \in \mathcal{L}$.

We do not consider global monotonicity constraint on machines since it is easy to observe that the global monotonicity requirement is the same as strong monotonicity requirement. As such in the next definition, we only introduce the class version of monotonicity, and, in keeping with the usage in the literature, refer to the collections of languages identifiable by the class version of monotonic machines as **MON** instead of **CLASS-MON**.

Definition 10. **MON** $= \{\mathcal{L} \mid (\exists M)[M$ is monotonic on $\mathcal{L}$ and $\mathcal{L} \subseteq$ **TxtEx(M)**$]\}$.

Definition 11. [LZ93b]

(a) **M** is said to be *weak-monotonic* on L just in case $(\forall \sigma \subseteq \tau \mid \mathrm{content}(\tau) \subseteq L)[M(\sigma) = \bot \vee [\mathrm{content}(\tau) \subseteq W_{M(\sigma)} \Rightarrow W_{M(\sigma)} \subseteq W_{M(\tau)}]]$.
(b) **M** is said to be *weak-monotonic* on $\mathcal{L}$ just in case **M** is weak-monotonic on each $L \in \mathcal{L}$.
(c) **M** is *weak-monotonic* just in case **M** is weak-monotonic on each $L \subseteq N$.
(d) **WMON** $= \{\mathcal{L} \mid (\exists M)[M$ is weak-monotonic and $\mathcal{L} \subseteq$ **TxtEx(M)**$]\}$.
(e) **CLASS-WMON** $= \{\mathcal{L} \mid (\exists M)[M$ is weak-monotonic on $\mathcal{L}$ and $\mathcal{L} \subseteq$ **TxtEx(M)**$]\}$.

Clearly, **WMON** $\subseteq$ **CLASS-WMON**. Now, using Theorem 17 and proof of Theorem 26, it follows that **WMON** = **CLASS-WMON**. Hence we do not consider **CLASS-WMON** from now on.

Kapur [Kap92] considered the dual of the above requirements to introduce the following three specialization strategies. Again as is the case with generalization strategies, the global and class versions for dual-strong-monotonic and dual-weak-monotonic render the same collections of languages identifiable. We do not consider the global version of dual-monotonicity, as it is essentially the same as dual-strong-monotonicity except that one allows the output grammar to also contain the elements which have already appeared in the input.

Definition 12. [Kap92]

(a) **M** is *dual-strong-monotonic* on L just in case $(\forall \sigma \subseteq \tau \mid \mathrm{content}(\tau) \subseteq L)[M(\sigma) = \bot \vee W_{M(\sigma)} \supseteq W_{M(\tau)}]$.
(b) **M** is *dual-strong-monotonic* on $\mathcal{L}$ just in case **M** is dual-strong-monotonic on each $L \in \mathcal{L}$.
(c) **M** is *dual-strong-monotonic* just in case it is dual-strong-monotonic on each $L \subseteq N$.
(d) **DSMON** $= \{\mathcal{L} \mid (\exists M)[M$ is dual-strong-monotonic and $\mathcal{L} \subseteq$ **TxtEx(M)**$]\}$.

Definition 13. [Kap92]

(a) **M** is *dual-monotonic* on L just in case $(\forall \sigma \subseteq \tau \mid \mathrm{content}(\tau) \subseteq L)[M(\sigma) = \bot \vee \overline{W_{M(\sigma)}} \cap \overline{L} \subseteq \overline{W_{M(\tau)}} \cap \overline{L}]$.
(b) **M** is *dual-monotonic* on $\mathcal{L}$ just in case **M** is dual-monotonic on each $L \in \mathcal{L}$.

(c) **DMON** $= \{\mathcal{L} \subseteq \mathcal{E} \mid (\exists M)[M \text{ is dual-monotonic on } \mathcal{L} \text{ and } \mathcal{L} \subseteq \mathbf{TxtEx}(M)]\}$.

Definition 14. [Kap92]

(a) M is *dual-weak-monotonic* on L just in case $(\forall \sigma \subseteq \tau \mid \text{content}(\tau) \subseteq L)[M(\sigma) = \perp \vee \text{content}(\tau) \subseteq W_{M(\sigma)} \Rightarrow W_{M(\sigma)} \supseteq W_{M(\tau)}]$.

(b) M is *dual-weak-monotonic* on $\mathcal{L}$ just in case M is dual-weak-monotonic on each $L \in \mathcal{L}$.

(c) M is *dual-weak-monotonic* just in case it is dual-weak-monotonic on each $L \subseteq N$.

(d) **DWMON** $= \{\mathcal{L} \mid (\exists M)[M \text{ is dual-weak-monotonic and } \mathcal{L} \subseteq \mathbf{TxtEx}(M)]\}$.

Requiring both the normal and dual conditions yields three additional strategies. We give the definition for strong monotonicity; the other two can be defined similarly.

Definition 15. [LZK92]

(a) M is *both strong and dual-strong-monotonic* on L just in case $(\forall \sigma \subseteq \tau \mid \text{content}(\tau) \subseteq L)[M(\sigma) = \perp \vee W_{M(\sigma)} = W_{M(\tau)}]$.

(b) M is *both strong and dual-strong-monotonic* on $\mathcal{L}$ just in case M is both strong and dual-strong-monotonic on each $L \in \mathcal{L}$.

(c) M is *both strong and dual-strong-monotonic* just in case M is both strong and dual-strong-monotonic on each $L \subseteq N$.

(d) **BSMON** $= \{\mathcal{L} \mid (\exists M)[M \text{ is both strong and dual-strong-monotonic and } \mathcal{L} \subseteq \mathbf{TxtEx}(M)]\}$.

Classes **BMON** and **BWMON** can be defined similarly.

Remark: It should be noted that except for the classes **BMON** and **BSMON** we do not need the machines to output $\perp$. This is because for **SMON, MON, WMON, BWMON** a machine can just output a grammar for $\emptyset$ instead of $\perp$ and for **DSMON, DMON, DWMON**, the machine can output a grammar for N instead of $\perp$. We do not know at this point whether not allowing $\perp$ will make a difference in the class **BMON**. For the class **BSMON**, not allowing $\perp$ essentially means that machine has to output its conjecture on any input (even null input) and which should be a grammar for the input language. This means that a machine following such a strategy can identify at most one language (thus leading to a result such as **BSMON** $\subset$ **TxtFin**).

Finally, we define Angluin's [Ang80] notion of conservative strategies.

Definition 16. (a) M is *conservative* on L just in case $(\forall \sigma \subseteq \tau \mid \text{content}(\tau) \subseteq L)[\text{content}(\tau) \subseteq W_{M(\sigma)} \Rightarrow M(\sigma) = M(\tau)]$.

(b) M is *conservative* on $\mathcal{L}$ just in case M is conservative on each $L \in \mathcal{L}$.

(c) M is *conservative* just in case M is conservative on each $L \subseteq N$.

(d) **CONS** $= \{\mathcal{L} \mid (\exists M)[M \text{ is conservative and } \mathcal{L} \subseteq \mathbf{TxtEx}(M)]\}$.

(e) **CLASS-CONS** $= \{\mathcal{L} \mid (\exists M)[M \text{ is conservative on } \mathcal{L} \text{ and } \mathcal{L} \subseteq \mathbf{TxtEx}(M)]\}$.

As a consequence of Theorem 17 and Theorem 26 we have **CLASS-CONS** = **CONS**.

4 Results

We now present results comparing the power of strategies introduced in the previous section. The reader may wish to see the pictorial summary of the results at the end of this paper. We only present results that are required to complete the picture.

The following theorem follows from the definition of various strategies.

Theorem 17. *(a)* **TxtFin = BSMON.**
(b) **BSMON ⊆ CONS.**
(c) **BSMON ⊆ SMON ∩ DSMON.**
(d) **BMON ⊆ MON ∩ DMON.**
(e) **BWMON ⊆ WMON ∩ DWMON.**
(f) **CONS ⊆ BWMON.**
(g) **SMON ⊆ MON ∩ WMON.**
(h) **DSMON ⊆ DMON ∩ DWMON.**
(i) **BSMON ⊆ BMON ∩ BWMON.**

The next two results can also be proved easily.

Theorem 18. *(a)* **SMON ⊆ BMON.**
(b) **DSMON ⊆ BMON.**

Theorem 19. **SMON − DSMON ≠ ∅.**

Theorem 20. **(DSMON ∩ MON) − WMON ≠ ∅.**

Proof. Consider the following definitions.

$L_j = \{\langle j, x\rangle \mid x \in N\}.$
$L_j^m = \{\langle j, x\rangle \mid x < m\}.$
Let T_j be a text for L_j such that $content(T_j[m]) = L_j^m$.
$S_j = \{(m,n) \mid m > 0 \wedge \{\langle j,x\rangle \mid x \leq m\} \subseteq W_{\mathbf{M}_j(T_j[m]),n}\}.$
$\mathcal{L} = \{L_j \mid S_j = \emptyset\} \cup \{L_j^m \mid S_j \neq \emptyset \wedge (\exists n)[(m,n) = \min(S_j)]\}.$

We claim that $\mathcal{L} \in (\mathbf{DSMON} \cap \mathbf{MON}) - \mathbf{WMON}$.

Let G_N be a grammar for N. Let $G_\emptyset$ be a grammar for $\emptyset$. Let G_j denote a grammar for L_j which can be effectively obtained from j. Let G_j^m denote a grammar for L_j^m, which can be obtained effectively from j, m. Note that S_j is recursive. Let $S_j^s = S_j \cap \{x \mid x \leq s\}$.

$$\mathbf{M}(T[s]) = \begin{cases} G_N, & \text{if } content(T[s]) = \emptyset; \\ G_j, & \text{if } content(T[s]) \neq \emptyset \wedge \\ & \quad content(T[s]) \subseteq L_j \wedge \\ & \quad S_j^s = \emptyset; \\ G_j^m, & \text{if } content(T[s]) \neq \emptyset \wedge \\ & \quad content(T[s]) \subseteq L_j \wedge \\ & \quad S_j^s \neq \emptyset \wedge \\ & \quad (\exists n)[(m,n) = \min(S_j^s)]; \\ G_\emptyset, & \text{otherwise.} \end{cases}$$

It is easy to verify that **M** is monotonic (dual strong monotonic) and **TxtEx**-identifies $\mathcal{L}$.

We now show that $\mathcal{L} \notin \textbf{WMON}$. Suppose $\mathbf{M}_j$ **TxtEx**-identifies $\mathcal{L}$. Now consider L_j. Clearly, $S_j \neq \emptyset$ (otherwise $L_j \in \mathcal{L}$ and $\mathbf{M}_j$ does not **TxtEx**-identifies L_j). Suppose $\langle m, n \rangle = \min(S_j)$. Now $L_j^m \in \mathcal{L}_j$. Suppose σ is an extension of $T_j[m]$, such that content$(\sigma) = L_j^m$ and $W_{\mathbf{M}_j(\sigma)} = L_j^m$ (note that there exists such a σ since $L_j^m \in \mathcal{L}$ and $\mathbf{M}_j$ **TxtEx**-identifies $\mathcal{L}$). Now $W_{\mathbf{M}_j(\sigma)} = L_j^m \not\supseteq W_{\mathbf{M}_j(T_j[m])}$. This contradicts the weak monotonicity property for identification of L_j^m by $\mathbf{M}_j$. Thus $\mathbf{M}_j$ is not weak monotonic in **TxtEx** identifying $\mathcal{L}$. ∎

Theorem 21. CONS − (MON ∪ DMON) ≠ ∅.

Proof. The proof of this theorem adopts a technique used by Lange and Zeugmann. Consider the following languages.

$L_1 = \{\langle 0, x \rangle \mid x \in N\}$;
$L_2^m = \{\langle 0, x \rangle \mid x \le m\} \cup \{\langle 1, x \rangle \mid x > m\}$;
$L_3^{m,n} = \{\langle 0, x \rangle \mid x \le m \ \lor \ x > n\} \cup \{\langle 1, x \rangle \mid m < x \le n\}$.

Let $\mathcal{L} = \{L_1\} \cup \{L_2^m \mid m \in N\} \cup \{L_3^{m,n} \mid m < n\}$.

It can easily be shown that $\mathcal{L} \in \textbf{CONS} - (\textbf{MON} \cup \textbf{DMON})$; we omit the details. ∎

Theorem 22. (DWMON ∩ DMON) − (DSMON ∪ MON) ≠ ∅.

Proof. Consider the following languages.

$L_j = \{\langle j, x \rangle \mid x \in N\}$.
$L_j^m = \{\langle j, x \rangle \mid x < m\}$.
Let T_j be a text for L_j such that content$(T_j[m]) = L_j^m$.
$S_j = \{\langle m, n \rangle \mid m > 0 \ \land \ \{\langle j, x \rangle \mid x \le m\} \subseteq W_{\mathbf{M}_j(T_j[m]),n}\}$.
$\mathcal{L} = \{L_j \mid j \in N\} \cup \{L_j^m \mid S_j \neq \emptyset \ \land \ (\exists n)[\langle m, n \rangle = \min(S_j)]\}$.

Note that this $\mathcal{L}$ is slightly different from that used in the proof of Theorem 20. In this we have included all L_js! In a way similar to the proof of Theorem 20, it can be shown that $\mathcal{L} \in (\textbf{DWMON} \cap \textbf{DMON}) - (\textbf{DSMON} \cup \textbf{MON})$; we omit the details. ∎

Theorem 23. (MON ∩ WMON) − DMON ≠ ∅.

Proof. Consider the following languages.

$L_1 = \{\langle 0, x \rangle \mid x \in N\}$.
$L_2^m = \{\langle 0, x \rangle \mid x \le m\} \cup \{\langle 1, x \rangle \mid x > m\}$.
$L_3^{m,n} = \{\langle 0, x \rangle \mid x \le m\} \cup \{\langle 1, x \rangle \mid m < x < n\} \cup \{\langle 2, n \rangle\}$.
Let $\mathcal{L} = \{L_1\} \cup \{L_2^n \mid n \in N\} \cup \{L_3^{m,n} \mid m < n\}$.

It is easy to show that $\mathcal{L} \in ((\mathbf{MON} \cap \mathbf{WMON}) - \mathbf{DMON})$. ∎

We now introduce a procedure, Proc, that is used in the proof of the next two theorems. $W_{\mathrm{Proc}(M,\sigma)}$ is defined as follows.

Begin $\{W_{\mathrm{Proc}(M,\sigma)}\}$
    Let $j = M(\sigma)$.
    Go to stage 0.
    Stage s
        Let $S = W_{j,s}$.
        if there exists a τ such that
            $|\tau| \le s$,
            $\sigma \subseteq \tau$,
            content$(\tau) \subseteq S$, and
            $M(\sigma) \ne M(\tau)$
        then HALT (*i.e.*, $W_{\mathrm{Proc}(M,\sigma)}$ does not enumerate anything else.)
        else enumerate S and go to stage $s + 1$.
        endif
    End stage s
End $\{W_{\mathrm{Proc}(M,\sigma)}\}$

The following lemma summarizes the properties of Proc.

Lemma 24. *(a) For all* M, σ, *and* s, $L_s = W_{\mathrm{Proc}(M,\sigma)}$ *enumerated before stage* s *can be effectively (in* M, σ, *and* s) *determined.*

(b) For all M, σ, *and* s *it can be effectively determined whether* $\mathrm{Proc}(M,\sigma)$ *halts before stage* s.

(c) $W_{\mathrm{Proc}(M,\sigma)} \subseteq W_{M(\sigma)}$.

(d) Either $\mathrm{Proc}(M,\sigma)$ *halts or* content$(\sigma) \not\subseteq W_{M(\sigma)}$ *or* σ *is a locking sequence for* M *on* $W_{M(\sigma)}$.

(e) If content$(\sigma) \not\subseteq W_{M(\sigma)}$, *then* $W_{\mathrm{Proc}(M,\sigma)} = W_{M(\sigma)}$ *and* $\mathrm{Proc}(M,\sigma)$ *does not halt.*

(f) If content$(\sigma) \subseteq W_{M(\sigma)}$ *and* σ *is a locking sequence for* M *on* $W_{M(\sigma)}$, *then* $W_{\mathrm{Proc}(\sigma)} = W_{M(\sigma)}$.

(g) If content$(\sigma) \subseteq W_{M(\sigma)}$ *and* σ *is a not a locking sequence for* M *on* $W_{M(\sigma)}$, *then* $\mathrm{Proc}(M,\sigma)$ *halts (and thus* $W_{\mathrm{Proc}(M,\sigma)}$ *is finite).*

(h) $W_{\mathrm{Proc}(M,\sigma)}$ *enumerated before stage* s, *is contained in* $W_{M(\sigma),s-1}$. *Thus, if* $\mathrm{Proc}(M,\sigma)$ *halts in stage* s, *then* $W_{\mathrm{Proc}(M,\sigma)} \subseteq W_{M(\sigma),s-1}$.

(i) Suppose $\sigma \subseteq \tau$, content$(\tau) \subseteq W_{M(\sigma),s}$ *and* $M(\sigma) \ne M(\tau)$. *Then* $\mathrm{Proc}(M,\sigma)$ *halts at or before stage* $\max(\{|\tau|,s\})$. *Moreover, either* content(τ) *is contained in* $W_{\mathrm{Proc}(M,\sigma)}$ *enumerated by stage* $|\tau|$ *or* content$(\tau) \not\subseteq W_{\mathrm{Proc}(M,\sigma)}$.

(j) For all σ, τ, *and* M *such that* $\sigma \subseteq \tau$ *and* $M(\sigma) \ne M(\tau)$, *either* content$(\tau) \not\subseteq W_{\mathrm{Proc}(M,\sigma)}$ *or* content$(\tau) \subseteq W_{\mathrm{Proc}(M,\sigma)}$ *enumerated before stage* $|\tau| + 1$.

Proof. (a) to (h) are easy to see from the definition of Proc. For (i) suppose the hypothesis. Clearly, at stage $\max(\{s, |\tau|\})$, the procedure for $\text{Proc}(M, \sigma)$ would detect this mind change and halt. The second clause in the conclusion now follows using part (h). Part (j) follows using parts (c) and (i). ∎

We now consider the following two important simulation results that use Proc and the above properties of Proc (Lemma 24).

Theorem 25. TxtEx $\subseteq$ DWMON.

Proof. Suppose M is given. We assume without loss of generality that M is such that for every $L \in \textbf{TxtEx}(M)$, each text T for L has a locking sequence for M on L as a prefix (Lemma 5).

We define a machine M' on initial sequences of a text T as follows. Together with M' we also define a function X. Intuitively, X just keeps track of the last point n' in the text T, where $\text{Proc}(M, T[n'])$ was output by M'.

Begin $\{M'(T[n]), X(T[n])\}$
0. **if** $n = 0$, **then**
    1.   Let $X(T[n]) = 0$.
    2.   Output $\text{Proc}(M, T[n])$.
    else
    3.   Let $n' = X(T[n - 1])$ (note that n' is such that the last $\text{Proc}(M, T[s])$ considered by M' on initial segments of $T[n]$ was for $s = n'$.)
    4.   **if** $\text{Proc}(M, T[n'])$ halts in $\leq n$ stages
         then
         5.   **if** $\text{content}(T[n]) \not\subseteq W_{\text{Proc}(M, T[n'])}$,
              then
              6.   Let $X(T[n]) = n$.
              7.   Output $\text{Proc}(M, T[n])$.
              else
              8.   Let $X(T[n]) = n'$.
              9.   Output fixed grammar for $\text{content}(T[n])$.
              endif
    10. **elseif** $M(T[n']) \neq M(T[n])$
         then
         11. **if** $\text{content}(T[n]) \not\subseteq W_{\text{Proc}(M, T[n'])}$ enumerated by stage $n + 1$
              then
              12. Let $X(T[n]) = n$.
              13. output $\text{Proc}(M, T[n])$.
              else
              14. Let $X(T[n]) = n'$.
              15. output $\text{Proc}(M, T[n'])$.
              endif
    else
    16. Let $X(T[n]) = n'$.

17.   Output Proc$(M, T[n'])$.
     endif
   endif
End $\{M'(T[n]), X(T[n])\}$

We claim that M' is dual-weak-monotonic and **TxtEx**-identifies each L in **TxtEx**(M). First note that $X(T[n]) \leq n$ and $X(T[n+1]) \geq X(T[n])$. Also note that $X(T[n]) = n \Leftrightarrow [n = 0 \vee X(T[n]) \neq X(T[n-1])]$. Furthermore, if $X(T[n+1]) \neq X(T[n])$, then for all $n' \leq n$, content$(T[n+1]) \not\subseteq W_{\text{Proc}(M,T[X(T[n'])])}$. To see this, note that if $X(T[n+1]) \neq X(T[n])$, then this is because of the execution of step 6 or 12 above for $M'(T[n+1])$, which can happen only if content$(T[n+1]) \not\subseteq W_{\text{Proc}(M,T[n'])}$, where $n' = X(T[n])$ (using Lemma 24 and the success of the corresponding If conditions). Also, if $X(T[n]) = n'$, then $M'(T[n]) = \text{Proc}(M, T[n'])$ or $W_{M'(T[n])} = \text{content}(T[n]) \subseteq W_{\text{Proc}(M,T[n'])}$.

Thus, it only remains to prove that M' **TxtEx**-identifies every language **TxtEx**-identified by M. For this suppose T is a text for $L \in$ **TxtEx**(M). Note that since M satisfies the condition in Lemma 5, T contains a locking sequence for L. Thus, $\lim_{n \to \infty} X(T[n])$ converges. Let $t = \lim_{n \to \infty} X(T[n])$. Now consider the following two cases.

Case 1: Proc$(M, T[t])$ does not halt.

In this case, consider $M'(T[n'])$ for $n' > t$. Clearly, if clause at step 4 does not hold. We claim that if clause at step 10 also cannot hold. To see this suppose otherwise. Thus, using Lemma 24 (i), if clause at step 11 must also hold (since Proc$(M, T[t])$ does not halt). But then $X(T[n']) \neq X(T[t])$. It follows that for all $n' > t$, $M(T[n']) = M(T[t])$ and $M'(T[n']) = \text{Proc}(M, T[t])$. Also, by Lemma 24(parts (d), (e), (f)) $W_{\text{Proc}(M,T[t])} = W_{M(T[t])} = L$. Thus M' **TxtEx**-identifies L.

Case 2: Proc$(M, T[t])$ halts.

In this case for all $n' > t$, in $M'(T[n'])$, if clause at step 4 succeeds and the if clause at step 5 fails. It follows that L is finite and M' outputs, in the limit on T, a grammar for content(T). Thus M' **TxtEx**-identifies L. ∎

Remark: A careful analysis of the above proof reveals that it *almost* shows that **TxtEx** $\subseteq$ **CONS**; the only place the dual-weak-monotonicity (instead of conservativeness) is used is at Step 9. Hence if we modified Step 9 in the above proof to simply output Proc$(M, T[n'])$ then M' becomes a conservative machine that identifies every infinite language identified by M (but is unsuccessful on finite languages). Hence, this shows that if attention is restricted to infinite languages, conservative machines are as powerful as general machines.

Theorem 26. WMON ⊆ CONS.

Proof. Proof of this theorem is similar to that of Theorem 25. There are two issues one needs to address in the simulation as done by M' in Theorem 25. First in step 9, one cannot output a grammar for content($T[n]$), because that could violate conservativeness; hence, one outputs Proc($M, T[n']$) (this is fine since if M is weak monotonic then it cannot identify any proper subset of $W_{\text{Proc}(M,T[n'])}$.) The second difference arises due to the fact that for identification by a weak-monotonic machine one may not be able to assume that every text contains a locking sequence. Thus in steps 6,7 one needs to do some rearrangement of the input text (this is because one needs to argue that if X does not converge on (rearranged) text T, then so does M.) Rest of the proof is similar to the proof of Theorem 25. We now proceed to give the details. For simplicity of presentation we give a somewhat different description of machine M' as compared to that corresponding description in the proof of Theorem 25.

We define M' as follows. Along with M' we define a function X and a function rearrange. Intuitively, X just keeps track of the "last $Proc(M, T[n'])$" output by M' and rearrange is used for the rearrangement of the input text as hinted above. We define rearrange only for the cases when $X(T[n]) = n$ (note that $X(T[n]) = n \Leftrightarrow n = 0 \lor X(T[n]) \neq X(T[n-1])$). Also note that rearrange($T[n]$), if defined, is a rearrangement of $T[n]$.

Begin $M'(T[n])$, $X(T[n])$, rearrange($T[n]$).

0.   **if** $n = 0$, **then**

       Let $X(T[n]) = 0$.

       Let rearrange($T[n]$) = $T[n]$.

       Output Proc($M, T[n]$).

   else

1.   Let $n' = X(T[n - 1])$ (note that n' is such that the last Proc(M, rearrange($T[s]$)) considered by M' on initial segments of $T[n]$ was for $s = n'$.)

2.   **if** there exists a $\sigma \supseteq$ rearrange($T[n']$) such that

         content(σ) $\subseteq$ content($T[n]$) $\land$

         $|\sigma| \leq 2n +$ |rearrange($T[n']$)| $\land$

         $M(\sigma) \neq M$(rearrange($T[n']$)) $\land$

         content(σ) $\not\subseteq W_{\text{Proc}(M, \text{rearrange}(T[n']))}$ enumerated till stage $|\sigma| + $

         1.

     then

2.1.   Let τ denote one such σ. Let τ' be an extension of τ such that content(τ') = content($T[n]$).

2.2.   Let $X(T[n]) = n$.

2.3.   Let rearrange($T[n]$) = τ'.

2.4.   Output Proc(M, τ').

3.   **else**

3.1.   Let $X(T[n]) = n'$.

3.2.   Output Proc(M, rearrange($T[n']$)).

     endif

   endif

Suppose M is weak-monotonic on L and $L \in \mathbf{TxtEx(M)}$. We claim that M' is conservative and $L \in \mathbf{TxtEx(M')}$. First note that $X(T[n]) \leq n$ and $X(T[n+1]) \geq X(T[n])$. Also note that $X(T[n]) = n \Leftrightarrow [n = 0 \vee X(T[n]) \neq X(T[n-1])]$. Also note that, for n such that $X(T[n]) = n$, rearrange($T[n]$) is defined and is a rearrangement of $T[n]$. Also, the only conjectures output by M' are of the form Proc(M, rearrange($T[n]$)), such that $X(T[n]) = n$. Also $M'(T[n+1]) \neq M'(T[n]) \Leftrightarrow X(T[n+1]) = n + 1$.

Furthermore, $M'(T[n+1]) \neq M'(T[n])$ (equivalently, $X(T[n+1]) \neq X(T[n])$) implies that, $T[n+1] \not\subseteq W_{\text{Proc}(M,\text{rearrange}(T[n']))}$, where $n' = X(T[n])$. To see this note that if $X(T[n+1]) \neq X(T[n])$, then this is because of the execution of step 2.2. But then due to the success of the If condition at step 2, we have that $T[n+1] \not\subseteq W_{\text{Proc}(M,\text{rearrange}(T[n']))}$, where $n' = X(T[n])$ (using Lemma 24, and the requirement for if condition to succeed). Thus M' behaves conservatively.

Thus it only remains to prove that M' $\mathbf{TxtEx}$-identifies every language identified by the weak-monotonic machine M. For this suppose T is a text for $L \in \mathbf{WMON(M)}$. We first claim that $\lim_{n \to \infty} X(T[n])$ converges. To see this suppose otherwise. Let T' be the text $\bigcup_{X(T[t+1]) \neq X(T[t])} \text{rearrange}(T[t+1])$. Note that content($T'$) = content($T$), and that M on the text T' changes its mind infinitely often (since $X(T[n+1]) \neq X(T[n])$ implies that, there exists a σ, such that for $n' = X(T[n])$, rearrange($T[n']$) $\subseteq \sigma \subseteq$ rearrange($T[n+1]$) such that $M(\sigma) \neq M(\text{rearrange}(T[n']))$). A contradiction. Thus $\lim_{n \to \infty} X(T[n])$ converges. Let $t = \lim_{n \to \infty} X(T[n])$. Note that $M'(T)\downarrow = \text{Proc}(M, \text{rearrange}(T[t]))$.

Now since the if at step 2 for $M'(T[n])$, does not succeed for any $n > t$, we have that rearrange($T[t]$) is a locking sequence for M on L, or $L \subseteq W_{\text{Proc}(M,\text{rearrange}(T[t]))}$. In the former case clearly, $L = W_{\text{Proc}(M,\text{rearrange}(T[t]))}$. In the later case, since $W_{\text{Proc}(M,\text{rearrange}(T[t]))} \subseteq W_{M(\text{rearrange}(T[t]))}$, it follows that $L \subseteq W_{M(\text{rearrange}(T[t]))}$, and thus by the weak-monotonicity condition we have that $L = W_{M(\text{rearrange}(T[t]))}$. Thus $L = W_{\text{Proc}(M,\text{rearrange}(T[t]))}$.

It follows that M' $\mathbf{TxtEx}$-identifies L. ∎

The results presented in this paper are pictorially presented in Figure 1.

5 Acknowledgements

We are pleased to acknowledge the influence of the work of Angluin, Arikawa, Jantke, Kapur, Kinber, Lange, Mukouchi, Wiehagen, and Zeugmann on the present investigation. Recently Kinber and Stephan [KS] have independently obtained some of the results in this paper.

References

[Ang80] D. Angluin. Inductive inference of formal languages from positive data. *Information and Control*, 45:117–135, 1980.

[BB75] L. Blum and M. Blum. Toward a mathematical theory of inductive inference. *Information and Control*, 28:125–155, 1975.

[Blu67]   M. Blum. A machine independent theory of the complexity of recursive functions. *Journal of the ACM*, 14:322–336, 1967.

[Ful90]   M. Fulk. Prudence and other conditions on formal language learning. *Information and Computation*, 85:1–11, 1990.

[Gol67]   E. M. Gold. Language identification in the limit. *Information and Control*, 10:447–474, 1967.

[HU79]   J. Hopcroft and J. Ullman. *Introduction to Automata Theory Languages and Computation*. Addison-Wesley Publishing Company, 1979.

[Jan91]   K. P. Jantke. Monotonic and non-monotonic inductive inference. *New Generation Computing*, 8:349–360, 1991.

[JS89]   S. Jain and A. Sharma. Recursion theoretic characterizations of language learning. Technical Report 281, University of Rochester, 1989.

[JS94]   S. Jain and A. Sharma. Characterizing language learning by standardizing operations. *Journal of Computer and System Sciences*, 1994. To Appear.

[Kap92]   S. Kapur. Monotonic language learning. In *Proceedings of the Third Workshop on Algorithmic Learning Theory*. JSAI Press, 1992. Proceedings reprinted as Lecture Notes in Artificial Intelligence, Springer-Verlag.

[Kap93]   S. Kapur. Uniform characterizations of various kinds of language learning. In *Proceedings of the Fourth International Workshop on Algorithmic Learning Theory, Lecture Notes in Artificial Intelligence 744*. Springer, 1993.

[KB92]   S. Kapur and G. Bilardi. Language learning without overgeneralization. In *Proceedings of the Ninth Annual Symposium on Theoretical Aspects of Computer Science, Lecture Notes in Computer Science 577*. Springer-Verlag, Berlin, 1992.

[Kin94]   E. Kinber. Monotonicity versus efficiency for learning languages from texts. Technical Report 94-22, Department of Computer and Information Sciences, University of Delaware, 1994.

[KS]   E. Kinber and F. Stephan. Language learning from texts: Mind changes, limited memory and monotonicity. Private Communication. Manuscript.

[LZ92a]   S. Lange and T. Zeugmann. Monotonic language learning on informant. Technical Report 11/92, GOSLER-Report, FB Mathematik und Informatik, TH Lepzig, 1992.

[LZ92b]   S. Lange and T. Zeugmann. Types of monotonic language learning and their characterization. In *Proceedings of the Fifth Annual Workshop on Computational Learning Theory, Pittsburgh, Pennsylvania*, pages 377–390. ACM Press, 1992.

[LZ93a]   S. Lange and T. Zeugmann. Language learning with bounded number of mind changes. In *Proceedings of the Tenth Annual Symposium on Theoretical Aspects of Computer Science, Lecture Notes Computer Science 665*, pages 682–691. Springer-Verlag, Berlin, 1993.

[LZ93b]   S. Lange and T. Zeugmann. Monotonic versus non-monotonic language learning. In *Proceedings of the Second International Workshop on Nonmonotonic and Inductive Logic, Lecture Notes in Artificial Intelligence 659*, pages 254–269. Springer-Verlag, Berlin, 1993.

[LZ93c]   S. Lange and T. Zeugmann. On the impact of order independence to the learnability of recursive languages. Technical Report ISIS-RR-93-17E, Institute for Social Information Science Research Report, Fujitsu Laboratories Ltd., 1993.

[LZK92]   S. Lange, T. Zeugmann, and S. Kapur. Class preserving monotonic language learning. Technical Report 14/92, GOSLER-Report, FB Mathematik und Informatik, TH Lepzig, 1992.

[MA93]   Y. Mukouchi and S. Arikawa. Inductive inference machines that can refute hypothesis spaces. In *Proceedings of the Fourth International Workshop on Algorithmic Learning Theory, Lecture Notes in Artficial Intelligence 744*, pages 123–136. Springer-Verlag, Berlin, 1993.

[Muk92a] Y. Mukouchi. Characterization of finite identification. In *Proceedings of the Third International Workshop on Analogical and Inductive Inference, Dagstuhl Castle, Germany*, pages 260–267, October 1992.

[Muk92b]   Y. Mukouchi. Inductive inference with bounded mind changes. In *Proceedings of the Third Workshop on Algorithmic Learning Theory*, pages 125–134. JSAI Press, 1992. Proceedings reprinted as Lecture Notes in Artificial Intelligence, Springer-Verlag.

[MY78]   M. Machtey and P. Young. *An Introduction to the General Theory of Algorithms*. North Holland, New York, 1978.

[OSW82]   D. Osherson, M. Stob, and S. Weinstein. Learning strategies. *Information and Control*, 53:32–51, 1982.

[Rog58]   H. Rogers. Gödel numberings of partial recursive functions. *Journal of Symbolic Logic*, 23:331–341, 1958.

[Rog67]   H. Rogers. *Theory of Recursive Functions and Effective Computability*. McGraw Hill, New York, 1967. Reprinted, MIT Press 1987.

[TB70]   B. Trakhtenbrot and J. M. Barzdin. *Konetschnyje Awtomaty (Powedenie i Sintez) (in Russian)*. Nauka, Moskwa, 1970. English Translation: Finite Automata–Behavior and Synthesis, Fundamental Studies in Computer Science 1, North Holland, Amsterdam, 1975.

[Wie90]   R. Wiehagen. A thesis in inductive inference. In *Nonmonotonic and Inductive Logic, 1st International Workshop, Karlsruhe, Germany*, pages 184–207. Springer Verlag, 1990. Lecture Notes in Computer Science 543.

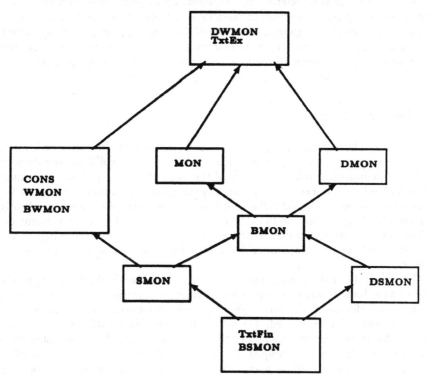

Fig. 1: Relationship between various strategies (classes appearing in the same box are equivalent; → denotes strict inclusion; absence of a directed path between two classes means that the two classes are incomparable)

Language Learning under Various Types of Constraint Combinations

Shyam Kapur*

Department of Computer Science, James Cook University of North Queensland
Townsville, QLD 4811 (Australia)

Abstract. Learnability of families of recursive languages from positive data is studied in the Gold paradigm of inductive inference. A large amount of work has focused on trying to understand how language learning ability of a learner is affected when it is constrained in various ways. For example, motivated by work in inductive logic, different notions of monotonicity have been studied which variously reflect the requirement that the learner's guess must monotonically 'improve' with regard to the target language. Various types of combinations of constraints such as monotonicity are defined and their relationships explored. Under one version of a disjunctive combination of a set of constraints, learning is considered successful as long as on any presentation of a language at least one of the constraints in the set is satisfied. It is also shown that a conjunctive combination of certain monotonicity constraints is less powerful than the set-theoretic intersection of the classes corresponding to the individual constraints.

1 Introduction

The process of hypothesizing a general rule from eventually incomplete data is called inductive inference. Many philosophers of science have focused their attention on problems in inductive inference. Some of the principles developed are very much alive in *algorithmic learning theory*, a rapidly emerging science that started with the seminal papers of Solomonoff [26] and of Gold [8]. The state of the art is excellently surveyed by Angluin and Smith [3, 4]. For more information concerning recent developments in inductive inference, the reader is referred to the proceedings of the annual workshops on computational learning theory and on algorithmic learning theory.

The general situation investigated in *language learning in the limit* can be described as follows: Given more and more information concerning the language to be learned, the inference device has to produce, from time to time, a hypothesis about the phenomenon to be inferred. The set of all admissible hypotheses is called the *space of hypotheses*, or, synonymously, the *hypothesis space*. The information given may contain only *positive examples*, that is, eventually all the strings contained in the language to be learned, or both *positive and negative examples*, i.e., eventually all the strings over the underlying alphabet classified with respect to their containment in the unknown language. The sequence of hypotheses has to converge to a hypothesis correctly describing the object to be learned.

---

* The author would like to thank the anonymous reviewers for some useful suggestions.

A variety of requirements can be postulated on the sequence of hypotheses actually created. In fact, one of the central questions studied so far is whether or not various restrictions on the behavior of an inference machine limit their learning capability. For example, the question whether it is possible to infer a language in such a way that the intermediate hypotheses are all monotonically better generalizations and/or specializations has been extensively investigated [19, 28]. This question was motivated both by work in inductive logic and nonmonotonic reasoning [24, 10, 27] and in natural language acquisition. It has sometimes been claimed that children are *non-overgeneralizing (conservative)* learners, that is, they never guess a subset language of a previous guess. (See [5, 20, 11, 13, 15] for relevant discussion.)

The learner is said to be successful if it eventually (*in the limit*) converges to the target language even though, in general, it is not possible to determine when the learner has converged. On the other hand, conservativeness, monotonicity, and all similar constraints have an absolute nature, i.e., it is mandated that the learner always meets the same constraints. Further, combinations of constraints considered (such as the one that define the class $MON^{\&}-TXT$ [12, 19]) are also strict combinations, i.e., the learner is required to observe each of the constraints all the time. In keeping with the limiting nature of the learning process, we suggest that there is a need to allow other combinations of constraints. For this purpose, we define various disjunctive combinations of a (possibly infinite) set of constraints. Under one version, a learner is said to obey a disjunction of constraints if, on any text for any language in the family, it obeys one or more constraints from the set. We show that this extension of the notion of possible constraints is interesting and insightful. There are real situations where it may be sufficient that, while one or the other constraint must be satisfied, it does not matter exactly which one is satisfied. We also consider a stronger notion of disjunctive combination of constraints in which for each language in the family there is a particular constraint that needs to be satisfied given any text presentation for this language. We relate the various versions of constrained learning. Eventually we hope an entire calculus of constraints can be built in which the various combining operations would form the primitives. In the direction in which we have set out, it would become plausible to ask following kinds of questions:

1. What families can be learned such that the conservativeness constraint can be satisfied on at least measure 1/2 of texts for each language in the family?
2. What families can be learned such that at least two out of the three constraints in a particular set of constraints is always satisfied?

In Section 2, we define the model and provide the necessary background. In Section 3, we investigate the conjunctive combination of constraints in some detail and show one case where the conjunctive combination is weaker than the set-theoretic intersection of the individual constraints. In Section 4, we define and interrelate various kinds of disjunctive combinations of constraints.

Even though language learning from positive and negative examples is a very rich and exciting area of research, in this paper we restrict ourselves to language learning from positive examples. Studying learning from only positive data models the situation of child language acquisition better since children do not appear to use negative evidence to learn.

2 Background

Let $\mathbb{N} = \{0, 1, 2, ...\}$ be the set of all natural numbers. We assume familiarity with formal language theory. (See, for example, [9].) By Σ, we denote any fixed finite alphabet of symbols. Let Σ^* be the free monoid over Σ. Any subset $L \subseteq \Sigma^*$ is called a language. By $co-L$ we denote the complement of L (i.e., $co-L = \Sigma^* \setminus L$). Let L be a language and $t = s_0, s_1, s_2, ...$ an infinite sequence of strings from Σ^* such that $range(t) = \{s_k \,|\, k \in \mathbb{N}\} = L$. Then t is said to be a *text* for L or, synonymously, a *positive presentation*. Suppose t is a text and x a number. Then, t_x denotes the initial segment of t and $t_x^+ = \{s_k \,|\, k \le x\}$.

We deal exclusively with indexed families of recursive languages defined as follows [2]: A sequence $L_0, L_1, L_2, ...$ of languages is said to be an *indexed family $\mathcal{L}$ of recursive languages* (henceforth, indexed family) provided each L_j is non-empty and there is a recursive function f such that, for all numbers j and all strings $s \in \Sigma^*$, we have

$$f(j, s) = \begin{cases} 1 & \text{if } \quad s \in L_j, \\ 0 & \text{otherwise.} \end{cases}$$

For example, all context-sensitive languages over Σ can be represented as an indexed family. Recently, a large amount of research has focussed on studying learning in this scenario. The restriction to an indexed family ensures that a hypothesis is refutable by a string observed in the text and that the set of possible hypotheses can be generated automatically. This is quite natural in view of potential applications to natural language acquisition and other artificial intelligence problems. We sometimes denote both an indexed family and its range by the same symbol $\mathcal{L}$. The meaning will be clear from the context.

Gold [8] defined an *inductive inference machine* (abbr. IIM) to be an algorithmic device which works as follows: The IIM takes as its input larger and larger initial segments of a text t and it either requests the next input string, or it first outputs a hypothesis, that is, a number encoding a certain computer program, and then it requests the next input string.

We next clarify what the space of hypotheses can be and what the goal of the learning process is. We require the IIMs to output grammars. Furthermore, since we exclusively deal with the learnability of indexed families $\mathcal{L} = (L_j)_{j \in \mathbb{N}}$, we always take as hypothesis space an enumerable family of grammars $G_0, G_1, G_2, ...$ over the terminal alphabet Σ satisfying $\mathcal{L} = \{L(G_j) \,|\, j \in \mathbb{N}\}$. (This has been termed in [19] as *class-preserving learning*.) Moreover, we require that membership in $L(G_j)$ is uniformly decidable for all $j \in \mathbb{N}$ and all strings $s \in \Sigma^*$. When an IIM outputs a number j, we interpret it to mean that the machine is hypothesizing the grammar G_j. As it turns out, it is sometimes very important to choose the space of hypotheses appropriately in order to achieve the desired learning goal. (For example, see [17].)

Let σ be a text and $x \in \mathbb{N}$. Then we use $M(\sigma_x)$ to denote the last hypothesis produced by M when successively fed the strings in the sequence σ_x. The sequence $(M(\sigma_x))_{x \in \mathbb{N}}$ is said to *converge in the limit* to the number j if and only if either $(M(\sigma_x))_{x \in \mathbb{N}}$ is infinite and all but finitely many terms of it are equal to j, or $(M(\sigma_x))_{x \in \mathbb{N}}$ is non-empty and finite, and its last term is j. Now we are ready to define learning in the limit.

Definition 1. (Gold, 1967) Let $\mathcal{L}$ be an indexed family, $L \in \mathcal{L}$, and let $\mathcal{G} = (G_j)_{j \in \mathbb{N}}$ be a hypothesis space. An IIM M LIM–TXT–identifies L from text with respect to $\mathcal{G}$ iff for every text t for L, there exists a $j \in \mathbb{N}$ such that the sequence $(M(t_x))_{x \in \mathbb{N}}$ converges in the limit to j and $L = L(G_j)$. Furthermore, M $LIM-TXT$–identifies $\mathcal{L}$ with respect to $\mathcal{G}$ if and only if, for each $L \in \mathcal{L}$, M $LIM-TXT$–identifies L with respect to $\mathcal{G}$. Finally, let $LIM-TXT$ denote the collection of all indexed families $\mathcal{L}$ for which there is an IIM M and a hypothesis space $\mathcal{G}$ such that M $LIM-TXT$–identifies $\mathcal{L}$ with respect to $\mathcal{G}$.

If a target indexed family $\mathcal{L}$ has to be inferred with respect to the hypothesis space $\mathcal{L}$ itself, then we add the prefix E. For example, $ELIM-TXT$ is the collection of indexed families that can be *exactly* learned in the limit.

Next, we define strong-monotonic, monotonic and weak-monotonic inference.

Definition 2. [10, 27] Let $\mathcal{L}$ be an indexed family, $L \in \mathcal{L}$, and let $\mathcal{G} = (G_j)_{j \in \mathbb{N}}$ be a hypothesis space. An IIM M is said to identify a language L from text with respect to $\mathcal{G}$

(A) strong-monotonically
(B) monotonically
(C) weak-monotonically

if and only if M $LIM-TXT$–identifies L with respect to $\mathcal{G}$ and for every text t of L as well as for any two consecutive hypotheses j_x, j_{x+k} which M has produced when fed t_x and t_{x+k}, where $k \geq 1, k \in \mathbb{N}$, the corresponding condition is satisfied:

(A) $L(G_{j_x}) \subseteq L(G_{j_{x+k}})$
(B) $L(G_{j_x}) \cap L \subseteq L(G_{j_{x+k}}) \cap L$
(C) if $t_{x+k}^+ \subseteq L(G_{j_x})$, then $L(G_{j_x}) \subseteq L(G_{j_{x+k}})$.

In particular, Requirement (C) means that M has to work strong-monotonically as long as its guess j_x is consistent with *all* the data fed to M both before and after M has output j_x.

We denote by $SMON-TXT$, $MON-TXT$, and $WMON-TXT$, the collection of all those indexed families for which there is an IIM inferring them strong-monotonically, monotonically, and weak-monotonically from text, respectively. Given any collections of families $\mathcal{L}_1$ and $\mathcal{L}_2$, $\mathcal{L}_1 \# \mathcal{L}_2$ denotes that they are incomparable. Note that even $SMON-TXT$ contains interesting 'natural' families of formal languages. For example, let $\Sigma = \{a, b, ..\}$ be any non-empty finite alphabet. Furthermore, let $X = \{x_0, x_1, x_2, ...\}$ be an infinite set of variables such that $\Sigma \cap X = 0$. *Patterns* are non-empty strings from $\Sigma \cup X$, e.g., ab, ax_1ccc, $bx_1x_1cx_2x_2$ are patterns. If p is a pattern, then $L(p)$, the language generated by pattern p, is the set of strings which can be obtained by substituting non-null strings $s_i \in \Sigma^*$ for each occurrence of the variable x_i in the pattern p [1]. Thus $aabbb$ is generable from pattern ax_1x_2b, while $aabba$ is not. Let $DPAT$ be the family of all languages L for which there are finitely many patterns $p_{i_1}, ..., p_{i_k}$ such that $L = \bigcap_{j=1}^{k} L(p_{i_j})$. Then, there exists a class preserving hypothesis space $\mathcal{G}$ and an IIM M such that M $SMON-TXT$—identifies $DPAT$ with respect to $\mathcal{G}$ (cf. [16, 17]).

We next define three types of dual monotonic language learning.

Definition 3. [12] Let $\mathcal{L}$ be an indexed family, $L \in \mathcal{L}$, and let $\mathcal{G} = (G_j)_{j \in \mathbb{N}}$ be a hypothesis space. An IIM M is said to identify a language L from text with respect to $\mathcal{G}$

(A) dual strong-monotonically
(B) dual monotonically
(C) dual weak-monotonically

if and only if $M\ LIM - TXT$-identifies L with respect to $\mathcal{G}$ and for any text t of L as well as for any two consecutive hypotheses j_x, j_{x+k} which M has produced when fed t_x and t_{x+k}, where $k \geq 1, k \in \mathbb{N}$, the corresponding condition is satisfied:

(A) $co-L(G_{j_x}) \subseteq co-L(G_{j_{x+k}})$
(B) $co-L(G_{j_x}) \cap co-L \subseteq co-L(G_{j_{x+k}}) \cap co-L$
(C) if $t_{x+k}^+ \subseteq L(G_{j_x})$, then $co-L(G_{j_x}) \subseteq co-L(G_{j_{x+k}})$.

By $SMON^d - TXT$, $MON^d - TXT$, and $WMON^d - TXT$, we denote the collection of all those indexed families $\mathcal{L}$ for which there is an IIM identifying them dual strong-monotonically, dual monotonically and dual weak-monotonically from text, respectively. Note that the notions of monotonicity and of dual monotonicity are truly duals of *each other*. Next, we combine the monotonicity constraints from Definition 2 and Definition 3. This helps us gain a better understanding of the relationships between monotonic inference of languages and other well-known types of language learning.

Definition 4. [12] Let $SMON^{\&} - TXT$ denote the class of indexed families learnable from text by an IIM that works strong-monotonically as well as dual strong-monotonically. The learning types $MON^{\&} - TXT$ and $WMON^{\&} - TXT$ are defined analogously.

Figure 1 (reproduced below from [19]) relates various types of class preserving monotonic and dual monotonic inference of indexed families of languages. A directed edge from vertex A to vertex B indicates that A is a proper subset of B. Note that missing edges between learning types not connected by a path in the directed graph are incomparable. $FIN - TXT$ is the class of indexed families learnable by IIMs that on any text for any language in the family produce only a single guess. $CONSERVATIVE - TXT$ is the class of families learnable by IIMs that behave conservatively.

Additional results which give further insights into the relationships among the defined learning types can be found in [19, 17]. We next report some initial work towards building a calculus of constraints. In the next section, we consider conjunctive constraints such as $MON^{\&} - TXT$. Subsequently, we introduce a variety of definitions of disjunctive constraints.

3 Conjunctive Combination of Constraints

So far the only combination of constraints that has been considered is of a conjunctive nature, that is, given two constraints, the combined constraint requires that the

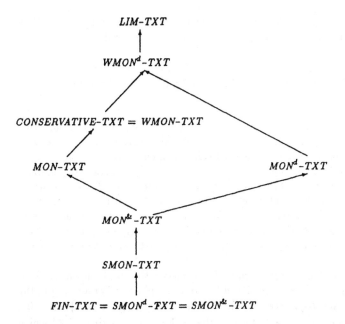

Fig. 1. Relationships among the classes generated under monotonicity constraints

learner always behaves in a manner consistent with both the constraints. While this seems to be the unique way to define conjunctive combinations of constraints, we shall see in the next section that there are quite a few different ways of combining constraints disjunctively.

Suppose we denote by $C - TXT$ the family of languages learnable under the constraint C and by $C_1 \& C_2 - TXT$ the families learnable under the conjunctive combination of the constraints C_1 and C_2. It is clearly the case that $C_1 \& C_2 - TXT \subseteq (C_1 - TXT \cap C_2 - TXT)$. Depending on the relationship between the constraints C_1 and C_2, a few different cases arise.

Suppose for any $\mathcal{L} \in C_1 - TXT$ there is a M such that M learns $\mathcal{L}$ while satisfying both the constraints C_1 and C_2, then clearly $C_1 - TXT = C_1 \& C_2 - TXT$. Thus, for example, the class $SMON^d - TXT = SMON^\& - TXT$. If, on the other hand, $C_1 - TXT$ and $C_2 - TXT$ are incomparable, then the situation can be vastly more interesting. One such case, which arises when one considers the constraints $MON - TXT$ and $MON^d - TXT$, is resolved by the following theorem. ($MON^\& - TXT$ is same as $MON \& MON^d - TXT$.)

Theorem 5. $MON^\& - TXT \subset (MON - TXT \cap MON^d - TXT)$.

Proof. We show that there is an indexed family $\mathcal{L}$ that is in fact in $EMON - TXT \cap EMON^d - TXT$ but not in $MON^\& - TXT$. We will first specify the family. Then, we will show that it is not learnable by any machine that does not violate either monotonicity or dual monotonicity at some point. Finally, we display two machines M and M' which learn $\mathcal{L}$ using $\mathcal{L}$ as the hypothesis space monotonically and dual monotonically, respectively. The following definition helps us specify an enumeration of functions so that all the potential hypothesis spaces are covered.

Definition 6. [25] A sequence of recursive sets $\{V_n\}_{n \in N}$ is *uniformly recursive* if there is a recursive function $g(x, n)$ such that $\lambda x[g(x, n)]$ is the characteristic function, for all n.

Since a uniformly recursive sequence of recursive sets is equivalent to our original formulation of hypothesis spaces, by enumerating all recursive functions $g(x, n)$ (interpreted as functions of two variables), we can get an enumeration of all possible hypothesis spaces. So, for example, let $(M_j)_{j \in N}$ be Gold's (1967) standard enumeration of all inference machines. Also, let there be an enumeration of $g(x, n)$s, which can be viewed as the hypothesis interpretation functions. We can pair each machine with all possible hypothesis interpretation functions $g(x, n)$ to get an indexing of machine-hypothesis interpretation function pairs. We form triples by pairing these pairs with each natural number. Let $(< M_j, g_j, k_j >)_{j \in N}$ be some enumeration of all such triples.

We next give the construction for each of the languages that make up the indexed family $\mathcal{L} = L_0, L_1, L_2, \ldots$. Two letters a and b form the alphabet. For any $j \geq 0$, the languages L_{3j}, L_{3j+1}, and L_{3j+2} are non-empty subsets of $\bigcup_{k=0}^{2} \{a^m b^{3j'+k}\} \mid m \geq 0\}$, where j' is an abbreviation for $j + 1$. Each of them contains the string $b^{3j'+2}$ which we use to distinguish these three languages from all other languages in $\mathcal{L}$. We call the sequence of strings $b^{3j'+2}$, $ab^{3j'}$, $a^2 b^{3j'}$, $a^3 b^{3j'}$, ... text t.

We next specify how given an index $i \geq 1$ and a string $x = a^n b^t$ for $n, t \geq 0$, it can be recursively determined whether or not x is in L_i. First, determine the j such that $i \in \{3j, 3j + 1, 3j + 2\}$. If the following computation terminates without the string x having been specified to be in L_i, then and only then $x \notin L_i$: If $x = b^{3j'+2}$, then x is in L_i. Otherwise, simulate M_j's computation on t_m for exactly m steps where $x = a^m b^{3j'+k}$, for $k = 0$, 1, or 2. (If x is not of this form, then clearly x is not in the language L_i.) We are interested in checking whether the machine M_j guesses one of the languages L_{3j}, L_{3j+1}, or L_{3j+2} during this simulation. For this reason, we can ignore those guesses of M_j which we cannot verify to be one of those three languages within a fixed amount of time. Note that although we have to diagonalize over all hypothesis-interpretation functions, the only ones of real interest are those which in fact satisfy the class preserving property. For a given m, if the machine's guess is r, verification involves determining if $g_j(y, r)$, for the y in question, is 0 or 1, as the case maybe, in m steps. Naturally such a verification by necessity is incomplete. There are two cases to consider.

Case 1 M_j does not guess any of these three languages. (This is checked by verifying if any of the guesses rs the machine made in m steps is such that it can be verified that $g_j(b^{3j'+2}, r)$ is 1 in m steps.) $a^m b^{3j'}$ is in each of the three languages.

Case 2 M_j guessed one of the three languages. Let $m' \leq m$ be the least number of steps after which both M_j guessed one of these three languages and this was verified to be the case within m' steps as above. Suppose r is the first such guess. If $m = m'$, $a^m b^{3j'}$ is in each of the three languages. If $m = m' + 1$ then $a^m b^{3j'}$ is in L_{3j+1} and L_{3j+2}. If $m > m' + 1$, we consider three subcases.

Case 2(A) M_j's guess r is the language L_{3j}. In order to verify this, we check if $g(a^{m'+1}b^{3j'}, r)$ is 0 within $m \leq k_j$ steps. Let $m'' \leq m$ be the maximum of the least number of steps after which M_j presumably guessed $3j$ and $m' + 2$. If $m = m''$, then $a^m b^{3j'}$ is in the languages L_{3j+1} and L_{3j+2} and $a^m b^{3j'+1}$ is in L_{3j}. If $m = m'' + 1$ then $a^m b^{3j'}$ is in L_{3j+2}. If $m > m'' + 1$, simulate M_j's computation on a presentation of $t_{m''}$ followed by infinite repetitions of the string $a^{m''} b^{3j'}$ for exactly m steps. We are interested in checking whether the machine M_j guesses the language L_{3j+1} during this simulation. Accordingly there are two cases to consider.

Case 2(A)(i) M_j guesses the index $3j + 1$ during this simulation. This is verified by checking as above if there is a r' guessed after r had been guessed for which $g(a^{m''+1}b^{3j'}, r')$ is 0, $g(a^{m''}b^{3j'+1}, r')$ is 0 and $g_j(b^{3j'+2}, r')$ is 1 within m steps. Let $m''' \leq m$ be the maximum of the least number of steps after which M_j presumably guessed $3j + 1$ and $m'' + 2$. Then, if $m = m'''$ or $m = m''' + 1$, $a^m b^{3j'}$ is in L_{3j+2}. If $m = m''' + 2$, then $a^m b^{3j'}$ is in the language L_{3j+1}.

Case 2(A)(ii) M_j does not guess $3j + 1$. Then $a^m b^{3j'}$ is in L_{3j+2}.

Case 2(B) M_j's guess r is one of the languages L_{3j+1} or L_{3j+2}. In order to verify the former, we check if $g(a^{m'+1}b^{3j'}, r)$ is 1 within $m \leq k_j$ steps. $a^m b^{3j'}$ is in the languages L_{3j+1} and L_{3j+2}.

Case 2(C) If $m > k_j$, then $a^m b^{3j'}$ is in the languages L_{3j+1} and L_{3j+2}.

Next we show that the family $\mathcal{L}$ is not in $MON^k - TXT$. Suppose there is an IIM M inferring $\mathcal{L}$ monotonically as well as dual monotonically. There must be an index j such that $M = M_j$, the interpretation function is g_j and some suitable k_j such that Case 2(C) does not arise can be found. We can assume that the function g_j indeed defines a uniform recursive sequence such that the class preserving character of learning is satisfied. Clearly, if M_j on the text t never guesses any of the three languages L_{3j}, L_{3j+1}, or L_{3j+2}, then it fails to identify these languages from positive data. Since j can be appropriately chosen, it is ensured that Case 2(C) does not apply. Suppose on text t, it was perceived that M_j guessed L_{3j+1} or L_{3j+2} first (Case 2(B)). Then, it is easy to check that M_j can be forced to violate the monotonicity constraint by forcing it to guess L_{3j} and then one of the other languages. (Note that L_{3j} is a proper subset of the other two languages in this situation.) Consider the only other case, i.e., M_j on text t was perceived to first guess L_{3j} (Case 2(A)). On further simulation, suppose it fails to guess L_{3j+1} (Case 2(A)(ii)). Then, M_j fails to identify L_{3j+1} on positive data. If M_j does guess L_{3j+1} (Case 2(A)(i)), then, since M_j has produced the guess L_{3j} and then L_{3j+1} up to now, it is easy to verify that in order to learn L_{3j+2} the machine may be forced to violate dual monotonicity. Since we have exhaustively covered all the possibilities, it is verified that $\mathcal{L} \notin MON^k - TXT$.

To complete our demonstration, we now show that there is a machine M that identifies $\mathcal{L}$ monotonically and another machine M' that identifies $\mathcal{L}$ dual monotonically. The machine M is conservative, that is, it only changes its guess if the input evidence is inconsistent with its current guess. On the basis of the first string in the input, say $a^m b^{3j'+k}$, for $k = 0, 1, 2$, M determines $3j$. It guesses the language indices $3j$, $3j + 1$, and $3j + 2$ in that order, if necessary.

We argue that M identifies $\mathcal{L}$ in the limit in a monotonic fashion. To see this we exhaustively consider the possibilities as to what the languages L_{3j}, L_{3j+1}, and L_{3j+2} could be like. Suppose M_j did not guess any of the three indices during the simulation (Case 1). Then, the three languages are equal and M learns them in a monotonic fashion. Suppose Case 2(B) or Case 2(C) applies. Then, the languages L_{3j+1} and L_{3j+2} are the same and L_{3j} is a proper subset of them. The machine M will learn the family in a monotonic fashion. Suppose the machine M_j guessed the index $3j$ first (Case 2(A)). Then there are two subcases to consider. If the machine M_j on further simulation did not guess $3j+1$ (Case 2(A)(ii)), then the language L_{3j+1} is a proper subset of the language L_{3j+2}. Further, neither of these two languages are subsets of L_{3j} and there is nothing that L_{3j} and L_{3j+2} share that is not in L_{3j+1}. Clearly, the machine M learns in this case as well in a monotonic fashion. Finally, suppose the situation is the one in Case 2(A)(i), then none of the languages are in a subset-superset relationship. Once again, it is easy to see that the machine M learns in a monotonic fashion. Since we have exhausted all the possibilities, we reach the desired conclusion.

The construction of the machine M' is somewhat more involved. It is important to note that it stores all the evidence it has seen. On the basis of the first string in the input, say $a^m b^{3j'+k}$, for $k = 0, 1, 2$, M determines $3j$. It then guesses the language index $3j+1$ first. It then begins to simulate the machine M_j on the text t (not on the input text). As long as M_j is not perceived to guess any of the three languages L_{3j}, L_{3j+1}, or L_{3j+2}, M' maintains its guess, i.e., $3j+1$. If M_j is perceived to guess L_{3j+1} or L_{3j+2} first or Case 2(C) arises, M' switches its guess to $3j$. Thereafter, only in case of inconsistency, it switches back to $3j+1$ and maintains this guess forever. Finally, if M_j is perceived to guess L_{3j} first during the simulation, then, only in case there is an inconsistency on the basis of the evidence seen so far, it switches to guessing $3j$ or $3j+2$ depending on whichever one contains all the evidence seen. It is easy to see that whatever the situation this decision will be uniquely made. We can easily argue that M' identifies $\mathcal{L}$ in the limit in a dual monotonic fashion.

We argue that M' identifies $\mathcal{L}$ in the limit in a dual monotonic fashion. To see this we exhaustively consider all the possibilities as to what the languages L_{3j}, L_{3j+1}, and L_{3j+2} could be like. If the situation is as in Case 1, i.e., M_j does not guess any of the three indices $3j$, $3j+1$, or $3j+2$, then the three languages are identical and M' learns them in a dual monotonic fashion. Suppose Case 2(B) or Case 2(C) apply. Then, the languages L_{3j+1} and L_{3j+2} are the same and L_{3j} is a proper subset of them. The machine M' will learn the family in dual monotonic fashion. Suppose the machine M_j guessed the index $3j$ first (Case 2(A)). Then there are two subcases to consider. Note though that in these two subcases we only have to show that the machine M' learns the resulting families; since M' is postulated to guess at most two different indices in all, dual monotonicity is automatically guaranteed. If the machine M_j on further simulation did not guess $3j+1$ (Case 2(A)(i)), then the language L_{3j+1} is a proper subset of the language L_{3j+2}. The language L_{3j} is disjoint from both these languages. Clearly, the machine M' learns in this case as well. Finally, suppose the situation is the one in Case 2(A)(ii). Then, none of the languages are in a subset-superset relationship. It is easy to check that the machine M' learns in this case as well. Since we have considered all the possibilities, we have verified that M' learns $\mathcal{F}$ in a dual monotonic fashion.

□

As regards the characterization of families learnable under the conjunctive combination of constraints, we note that the uniform characterization theorem in [14] is adequate.

4 Disjunctive Combinations of Constraints

The most straightforward approach to defining the disjunctive combination of constraints is to require the learner to obey one or the other constraint between every pair of consecutive hypotheses. Thus, for example, the disjunctive combination of strong monotonicity and dual strong monotonicity would require that given any two consecutive hypothesis j_x and j_{x+k}, $L(G_{j_x}) \subseteq L(G_{j_{x+k}})$ or $co-L(G_{j_x}) \subseteq co-L(G_{j_{x+k}})$. Suppose we call the class of families learnable under this combination as $SMON^\vee-TXT$. That such a disjunctive combination is quite powerful is revealed by the next two propositions. While the first one is not surprising, the second one is. Other propositions of a similar nature can be derived for $MON^\vee-TXT$ and $WMON^\vee-TXT$.

Proposition 7. $SMON-TXT \subset SMON^\vee-TXT$.

Proof. Suppose $\Sigma = \{a, b\}$. We define a family $\mathcal{L}$ in $SMON^\vee-TXT \setminus SMON-TXT$. Let $L_0 = \{a\}^* \cup \{b\}$ and, for all $i \geq 1$, $L_i = \{a\}^* \setminus \{a^i\}$.   □

Proposition 8. $SMON^\vee-TXT \# MON-TXT$.

Proof. The family in Proposition 7 cannot be learned monotonically. The following family taken from [16] completes the proof. Let $\Sigma = \{a, b\}$. For any $m \geq 1$ and $k_1, k_2, \ldots, k_m \geq 1$, let

$$L_{<k_1,k_2,\ldots,k_m>} = (\{a\}^* \setminus \{a^{k_1}, a^{k_2}, \ldots, a^{k_m}\}) \cup \{b^{k_1}, b^{k_2}, \ldots b^{k_m}\},$$

where $< ., ., \ldots, . >$ is a pairing function. It can easily be shown that this family is in $MON^\&-TXT$.   □

One of the less appealing aspects of this notion of disjunctive combinations is that the basic transitive nature of constraints is lost. Consider the simple family consisting of just the following three languages: $L_0 = \{a\}$, $L_1 = \{a, a^2\}$, and $L_2 = \{a, a^3\}$. It is in the class $SMON^\vee-TXT$. Even though a move between the languages L_1 and L_2 is prohibited by each of the constraints separately, the learner could move freely between these languages via L_0. We propose alternative notions of disjunctive combinations of constraints which do not have this problem.

Given constraints C_1 and C_2, we consider the requirement that the learner must learn according to one or the other constraint but it need not be the same one for each of the languages in $\mathcal{L}$. The class of learnable families is denoted as $C_1 \vee_L C_2$. This is distinguished from yet another possibility in which the learner is required to obey one or the other constraint on each individual text for a language in the family but it need not obey the same constraint for different texts of the same language. The corresponding class of learnable families is denoted as $C_1 \vee_t C_2$. Clearly, both these definitions are transitive. They are also consistent with the limiting nature of the learning process. Furthermore, just as on any particular text it may not be effectively determinable whether the machine has converged, likewise it may not be effectively determinable which of the constraints the machine obeyed in the limit.

To give an example, consider the constraint obtained by putting an upper bound on the number of *mind changes* (changes in hypothesis) that the learner is permitted to make [6, 7, 21, 18]. An IIM M is said to learn a family with k mind changes if on any text for any language in the family, M makes at most k mind changes. The class of families learnable by IIMs that meet this constraint is denoted as EX_k-TXT. (See [21, 18] for characterizations of this class.) It can be shown that $EX_0-TXT = FIN-TXT \subset EX_1-TXT \subset EX_2-TXT \dots$. Furthermore, $\bigcup_i EX_i-TXT \subset LIM-TXT$; for example, the family of pattern languages [1] is in $LIM-TXT \setminus \bigcup_i EX_i-TXT$.

For any $k \geq 0$, let constraint C_k be the one that permits at most k mind changes. An IIM learns a family under the disjunction of constraints $\bigvee_k C_k$ if, on any text for any language in the family, the machine makes at most a finite number of mind changes. Interestingly, any learnable family is learnable under this combination of constraints.

There are situations where the nature of the problem is such that as long as one of a set of constraints is met, the behavior of the algorithm is adequate for some purpose. For example, in some situations, it may be sufficient if the machine is guaranteed to satisfy at least one of the two constraints of monotonicity and dual monotonicity, especially if during the execution of the learner it can be determined which of the constraints is satisfied. Note that, in practice, as soon as it can be determined that one of those constraints has been violated, it is clear that the only other constraint has to be satisfied.

If the combined constraint is a disjunction of a finite set of constraints and there is some one constraint in the set which is weaker than all the rest, there is no extra power learning under these combined constraints can have over learning where the weakest constraint is always satisfied. This is not the case for an infinite disjunction as we have seen above. If there is no weakest constraint, then, even in the finite case, families which were not learnable under any one of the constraints in the set can be learnable under the combined constraints. This is true for the stronger type of disjunction as well where on each text for a language at least one common constraint has to be satisfied.

We next evaluate the relative power of these two kinds of disjunctive combinations.

Proposition 9. *Consider the complete set of constraints corresponding to bounded mind changes. There is a family $\mathcal{L}$ that is learnable under the $\vee_t$-disjunction of this set of constraints but it is not learnable under the $\vee_L$-disjunction of the same constraints.*

The following theorem shows a similar relationship among the monotonicity constraints as well.

Theorem 10. $(MON\text{-}TXT \vee_L MON^d\text{-}TXT) \subset (MON\text{-}TXT \vee_t MON^d\text{-}TXT)$

Proof. Let $\mathbb{N} \cup \{a\}$ be the universe. Consider the following family $\mathcal{L}$: $L_0 = \{0\}$, $L_1 = \{1, 2, 3, \ldots\}$, $L_2 = \{0, 1, 2, 3, \ldots\}$, and, for each $k \geq 1$, $L_{2k+1} = \{1, 2, \ldots, k\} \cup \{a^k\}$ and $L_{2k+2} = \{0, 1, 2, \ldots, k, k+1, a^k, a^{k+1}\}$.

Suppose a machine M is claimed to $\vee_t$-disjunctively learn the family under the two monotonicity constraints. We establish the *existence* of two presentations t and t' that force a contradiction to emerge. The presentation t starts off with the string 1, then the string 2 and so on. Clearly, after seeing some string m, the language L_1 must be guessed.

The presentation t' starts with repetitions of the string 0 so that at some point the language L_0 must be guessed. Then, strings 1, 2, 3, 4, up to some $n > m$ are presented at which point the guess of the machine must be an index for the language L_2. Now present the strings $n + 1$, a^n, a^{n+1}, and then the string 0 repeatedly. The resulting text t' is a text for the language L_{2n+2} and M must guess it. Notice that, on text t', M only violated dual monotonicity. Consider next extending the presentation corresponding to t with the strings $m + 1, m + 2, \ldots, n$ and then repetitions of the string a^n. At some point, the language L_{2n+1} must be guessed. Now extend the presentation with the strings $n + 1$, a^{n+1}, and then 0 repeatedly. The resulting presentation t is also a text for the language L_{2n+2} and M must guess it at some point. Notice, however, that this time M only violated monotonicity. Thus, we have two texts t and t' for the same language L_{2n+2} on which the machine is forced to obey different constraints.

It can be argued that $\mathcal{L} \in (MON\text{-}TXT \vee_t MON^d\text{-}TXT)$. □

As regards the characterization of families learnable under disjunctive combination of constraints, we note that the $\vee_L$-disjunction can be handled by the uniform characterization theorem in [14].

5 Conclusion

Motivated by studies in natural language acquisition and potential artificial intelligence applications, we only considered the relatively simple setting of *uniformly recursive sequence of recursive sets* [25]. Further, we restricted ourselves to the case of class-preserving learning. Clearly, the various types of combinations of constraints can studied within a wide array of frameworks. For example, we could consider recursively enumerable languages or families that are not indexed or *class-comprising learning* [17]. It is hoped that future work will investigate these issues adequately.

Parallel to some interesting recent work on refutability of hypothesis spaces[23, 22], one could investigate a different kind of refutability of hypothesis spaces in which the machine at some point declares that it can no longer learn the present hypothesis space without violating one of the constraints it was supposed to obey.

References

1. Dana Angluin. Finding patterns common to a set of strings. *Journal of Computer System Sciences*, 21:46–62, 1980.

2. Dana Angluin. Inductive inference of formal languages from positive data. *Information and Control*, 45:117–135, 1980.

3. Dana Angluin and Carl H. Smith. Inductive inference: theory and methods. *Computing Surveys*, 15(3):237–269, September 1983.

4. Dana Angluin and Carl H. Smith. Inductive inference. In S. C. Shapiro, editor, *Encyclopedia of Artificial Intelligence*, volume 1. Wiley-Interscience Publication, New York, 1987.

5. Robert Berwick. *The Acquisition of Syntactic Knowledge*. MIT press, Cambridge, MA, 1985.

6. John Case and C. Lynes. Machine inductive inference and language identification. In *Proceedings of the International Colloquium on Automata, Languages and Programming (ICALP)*, pages 107–115, 1982.

7. John Case and Carl H. Smith. Comparison of identification criteria for machine inductive inference. *Theoretical Computer Science*, 25:193–220, 1983.

8. E. M. Gold. Language identification in the limit. *Information and Control*, 10:447–474, 1967.

9. J. Hopcroft and J. Ullman. *Introduction to Automata Theory, Languages, and Computation*. Addison-Wesley, N. Reading, MA, 1979.

10. Klaus P. Jantke. Monotonic and non-monotonic inductive inference. *New Generation Computing*, 8:349–360, 1991.

11. Shyam Kapur. *Computational Learning of Languages*. PhD thesis, Cornell University, September 1991. Computer Science Department Technical Report 91-1234.

12. Shyam Kapur. Monotonic language learning. In S. Doshita, K. Furukawa, K. P. Jantke and T. Nishida, editors, *Proceedings of the 3rd Workshop on Algorithmic Learning Theory*, volume 743, pages 147–158, Berlin, October 1992. Springer-Verlag. Lecture Notes in Artificial Intelligence.

13. Shyam Kapur. How much of what? Is this what underlies parameter setting? In Eve V. Clark, editor, *Proceedings of the 25th Annual Child Language Research Forum*, pages 50–59, 1993. Also in Cognition. (To appear.).

14. Shyam Kapur. Uniform characterizations of various kinds of language learning. In K. P. Jantke, S. Kobayashi, E. Tomita, and T. Yokomori, editors, *Proceedings of the fourth Workshop on Algorithmic Learning Theory*, volume 744, pages 197–208. Springer-Verlag, November 1993. Lecture Notes in Artificial Intelligence.

15. Shyam Kapur, Barbara Lust, Wayne Harbert, and Gita Martohardjono. Universal grammar and learnability theory: the case of binding domains and the subset principle. In *Knowledge and Language: Issues in Representation and Acquisition*. Kluwer Academic Publishers, 1993.

16. Steffen Lange and Thomas Zeugmann. Monotonic versus non-monotonic language learning. In G. Brewka, K. P. Jantke, and P. H. Schmitt, editors, *Proceedings of the 2nd International Workshop on Nonmonotonic and Inductive Logic (Lecture Notes in Artificial Intelligence Volume 659)*, pages 254–269. Springer-Verlag, 1991.

17. Steffen Lange and Thomas Zeugmann. Language learning in dependence on the space of hypotheses. In *Proceedings of the 6th Annual ACM Conference on Computational Learning Theory*, pages 127–136. Morgan-Kaufman, 1993.

18. Steffen Lange and Thomas Zeugmann. Learning recursive languages with bounded mind changes. *International Journal of Foundations of Computer Science*, 4:157–178, 1994.

19. Steffen Lange, Thomas Zeugmann, and Shyam Kapur. Class preserving monotonic and dual monotonic language learning. Technical Report GOSLER-14/92, FB Mathematik und Informatik, TH Leipzig, August 1992. Also to appear in Theoretical Computer Science.

20. M. Rita Manzini and Kenneth Wexler. Parameters, binding theory and learnability. *Linguistic Inquiry*, 18:413–444, 1987.

21. Yasuhito Mukouchi. Inductive inference with bounded mind changes. In S. Doshita, K. Furukawa, K. P. Jantke and T. Nishida, editors, *Proceedings of the 3rd Workshop on Algorithmic Learning Theory*, volume 743, pages 125–134, Berlin, 1992. Springer-Verlag. Lecture Notes in Artificial Intelligence.

22. Yasuhito Mukouchi. *Inductive Inference of Recursive Concepts*. PhD thesis, Research Institute of Fundamental Information Science, Kyushu University, March 1994. RIFIS-TR-CS-82.

23. Yasuhito Mukouchi and Setsuo Arikawa. Inductive inference machines that can refute hypothesis spaces. In K. P. Jantke, S. Kobayashi, E. Tomita, and T. Yokomori, editors, *Proceedings of the Fourth Workshop on Algorithmic Learning Theory (Springer-Verlag Lecture Notes in Artificial Intelligence Series)*, 1993.

24. E. Y. Shapiro. Inductive inference of theories from facts. Technical Report 192, Department of Computer Science, Yale University, 1981.

25. Robert Irving Soare. *Recursively enumerable sets and degrees : a study of computable functions and computably generated sets*. Springer-Verlag, Berlin; New York, 1987.

26. R. Solomonoff. A formal theory of inductive inference. *Information and Control*, 7:1–22 and 234–254, 1964.

27. Rolf Wiehagen. A thesis in inductive inference. In J. Dix, K. P. Jantke, and P. H. Schmitt, editors, *Proceedings of the 1st International Workshop on Nonmonotonic and Inductive Logic*, pages 184–207. Springer-Verlag, 1991. Lecture Notes in Artificial Intelligence Vol. 543.

28. Thomas Zeugmann, Steffen Lange, and Shyam Kapur. Characterizations of class preserving monotonic and dual monotonic language learning. Technical Report IRCS-92-24, Institute for Research in Cognitive Science, University of Pennsylvania, September 1992. Also to appear in Information and Computation.

Synthesis Algorithm for Recursive Processes by μ-calculus (Extended Abstract) *

Shigetomo Kimura, Atsushi Togashi and Norio Shiratori

Research Institute of Electrical Communication, Tohoku University.
2-1-1 Katahira, Aoba-ku, Sendai, 980-77, Japan.
e-mail : {kimura,togashi,norio}@shiratori.riec.tohoku.ac.jp

Abstract. This paper proposes an inductive synthesis algorithm for a recursive process from the enumeration of facts, which must be satisfied by the target process. We adopt a subcalculus of μ-calculus to represent facts of a process. First, a new preorder $\leq_d$ on recursive processes is introduced in such a way that $p \leq_d q$ means that $p \models f$ implies $q \models f$, for all formulae f in the subcalculus. Then, we present the synthesis algorithm. The correctness of the algorithm consists in that it only produces processes that satisfy the given facts. By adding more and more facts, the algorithm will eventually produce the target process. It will be shown that the algorithm is complete for the subcalculus.

1 Introduction

The studies of process algebras started from the latter half of 1970's to give mathematical semantics for concurrent systems. Typical systems are CSP by Hoare[2, 9] and CCS by Milner[14]. In Feb. 1990, ISO adopted LOTOS[4] as the international standard for OSI specification description language. Those algebraic formalization techniques are utilized as the descriptive languages for communicating processes and concurrent programs. They are also applied to the verification problem, by virtue of the mathematical formality. The processes, however, have the features of such as non-determinacy and concurrency, so their operational semantics are completely different from those of the traditional automata and formal languages.

Temporal logic has been used to describe the required properties of processes, e.g. safety, liveness and deadlock, freeness[16]. Here, formullae are verification conditions to be satisfied by the processes. From this point of view, the inductive inference of the processes forms a basis for automatic synthesis of highly reliable communicating protocols and concurrent programs from the examples, the required properties. However, little has been investigated for inductive inference of concurrent processes, due to the difficulties arising from the situations which were mentioned in the beginning.

---

* A part of this study is supported by Grants from the Asahi Glass Foundation and Research Funds from Japanese Ministry of Education

We have already presented the algorithm that inductively synthesizes a basic process in a subclass of CCS, from concrete examples, modal formulae describing the properties of the process[10]. The validity and improvement of the approach have been demonstrated. However the expressive power of basic processes is too weak, they cannot express recursive behavior of a system. It remains to propose a synthesis algorithm for recursive processes from the modal formulae within finite steps. This paper presents a synthesis algorithm for recursive processes by subcalculus of μ-calculus[5, 12, 21]. The correctness of the algorithm consists in that it only produces processes that satisfy the given facts. By adding more and more facts, the algorithm will eventually produce the target process. It will be shown that the algorithm is complete for the subcalculas.

The outline of this paper is as follows: Section 2 presents the algebraic formulation of processes, together with μ-calculus. Section 3 discusses the discriminative power to distinguish one process from others in the subcalculus of μ-calculus. Section 4 gives an algorithm that synthesizes a process satisfying a given enumeration of formulae. The paper is concluded at Section 5, where a prototype of synthesis system is introduced and related works and future problems are briefly discussed.

2 Preliminaries

In this section we briefly review the preliminary notions such as algebraic processes and μ-calculus. See [5, 7, 9, 12, 14, 21], for more detailed discussions.

2.1 Algebraic Processes

Let $\mathcal{A}$ be an *alphabet*, a finite set of symbols. Its element is called an *action*. This corresponds to a primitive event of a process and this is assumed to be externally observable and controllable from the environment. Throughout this paper, it is assumed that we have a denumerable set $\mathcal{C}$ of *process constants*. In the following BNF, we define *recursive terms* inductively:

$$p ::= 0 \mid c \mid a.p \mid p+p$$

where $c \in \mathcal{C}$ and $a \in \mathcal{A}$. 0 is an *inaction*, which cannot perform any action. $a.p$ is called *action prefix*, which performs an action a first, then behaves as the process p. $p_1 + p_2$ is called a *summation*, whose behavior is same as p_1 or p_2. The selection is by the environment, which sometimes introduces nondeterminacy. A process constant c is defined by a *defining equation* $c \overset{\text{def}}{=} p$, denoted as rec $c.p$. In a recursive term rec $c.p$, every occurrence of c in p is called *bound*. We say p is a scope of rec c. in rec $c.p$. An occurrence of process constant which is not within any scope of rec c. is called *free*. When every free occurrence of c is within some subterm $a.q$ of p, we call c *guarded* in p. When every constant in p is guarded, p is also called *guarded*. If every occurrence of any process constant in p is bound, p is called *closed*. Otherwise it is called *open*. Closed terms are called *processes*.

By renaming process constants, every term p is converted to a term p' such that if rec $c_1.p_1$ and rec $c_2.p_2$ are subterms in p' then $c_1 \neq c_2$. This conversion is the same as α-conversion in λ-calculus[8]. Thus, a term p can be represented as p with a set $\{c_1 \stackrel{\text{def}}{=} p_1, \ldots, c_n \stackrel{\text{def}}{=} p_n\}$ of defining equations, where every subterm of the form rec $c.q$ in p is replaced by c.

Semantics of processes is given by *a labeled transition system* with actions as labels. A labeled transition system is a triple $< S, A, \rightarrow >$, where S is a set of *states* and $\rightarrow$ is a *transition relation* defined as $\rightarrow \subset S \times A \times S$. For $(s, a, s') \in \rightarrow$, we normally write $s \xrightarrow{a} s'$. Thus, the transition relation can be written as $\rightarrow = \{\xrightarrow{a} \mid a \in A\}$. $s \xrightarrow{a} s'$ may be interpreted as "in the state s an action a can be performed and after the action the state moves to s'". s' is called an *a-successor* of s. We use the usual abbreviations as e.g. $s \xrightarrow{a}$ for $\exists s' \in S$ s.t. $s \xrightarrow{a} s'$ and $s \xrightarrow{a}\!\!\!\!/\,$ for $\neg \exists s' \in S$ s.t. $s \xrightarrow{a} s'$. A transition relation on processes is given by the following transition rules:

$$\frac{}{a.p \xrightarrow{a} p} \qquad \frac{p \xrightarrow{a} p'}{p + q \xrightarrow{a} p'} \qquad \frac{q \xrightarrow{a} q'}{p + q \xrightarrow{a} q'} \qquad \frac{\text{rec}\, c.p \xrightarrow{a} p'}{p \xrightarrow{a} p'}$$

Based on the operational semantics given by the transition system, several equivalences and preorders have been proposed in order to capture various aspects of the observational behavior of processes. One of those is the equivalence induced by the notion of a bisimulation [14, 15].

A relation R over processes is a *strong bisimulation* if $(p, q) \in R$ implies, for all $a \in A$:

1. whenever $p \xrightarrow{a} p'$, then there exists q' such that $q \xrightarrow{a} q'$ and $(p', q') \in R$,
2. whenever $q \xrightarrow{a} q'$, then there exists p' such that $p \xrightarrow{a} p'$ and $(p', q') \in R$.

Processes p and q are *strongly equivalent* iff $(p, q) \in R$ for some strong bisimulation R. $p \sim q$ denotes that p and q are strongly equivalent. Clearly, $\sim$ is the largest strong bisimulation and an equivalence relation.

2.2 μ-calculus

The alternative characterization of equivalence on processes depends on the identification of a process with the properties it enjoys. Then we can say that two processes are equivalent if and only if they enjoy exactly same properties. In other words, two processes are inequivalent if one enjoys a property that the other does not enjoy. For this purpose, in this paper we adopt the μ-calculus [5, 12, 21], which includes a modality concerning actions, in order to describe properties of processes. In the following BNF, we define *formulae* in μ-calculus inductively:

$$f ::= \mathbf{tt} \mid x \mid f \vee f \mid \neg f \mid \langle a \rangle f \mid \mu x.f$$

where $x \in \mathcal{X}$, $\mathcal{X}$ is a denumerable set of *logical variables*, and $a \in A$.

In the definition $\mu x.f$, x must occur in f within scopes of positive number of negations.

The notion of freeness, boundness and scope for formulae in μ-calculus defined similarly to the one for recursive terms or λ-calculus. A formula f is sometime written as $f(x)$ to express the free occurrence of x in f, expressly. $f(g)$ denotes the resulting $f(x)$, where every free occurrence of x is replaced by g. In the replacement $f(g)$, every free occurrence of a variable in g is not bound in $f(g)$ by means of renaming bound variables.

The set of all formulae is written as $\mathcal{L}$. In the following, we regard formulae as properties of processes. When a process p satisfies formula f, it is written as $p \models f$. The satisfaction relation $\models$ is defined as follows, where the symbol $\equiv$ is used to denote logical equivalence:

1. For any process p, $p \models$ tt.
2. $p \models f_1 \vee f_2$, if $p \models f_1$ or $p \models f_2$.
3. $p \models \neg f$, if $p \not\models f$, where $p \not\models f$ means that p does not satisfy f.
4. $p \models \langle a \rangle f$, if there exists some q such that $p \xrightarrow{a} q$ and $q \models f$.
5. $p \models \mu x.f(x)$, if for any g such that $\models f(g) \supset g (\equiv \neg f(g) \vee g)$, $p \models g$.

And we define the following logical notations for convenience:

1. ff $\stackrel{\text{def}}{=} \neg$tt.
2. $f_1 \wedge f_2 \stackrel{\text{def}}{=} \neg(\neg f_1 \vee \neg f_2)$.
3. $[a]f \stackrel{\text{def}}{=} \neg\langle a \rangle \neg f$.
4. $\nu x.f(x) \stackrel{\text{def}}{=} \neg \mu x.\neg f(\neg x)$.

Note that $\mu x.f(x)$ and $\nu x.f(x)$ are the minimum and maximum fix point of $f(x)$ respectively. See Proposition 1 for each intuitive meaning under some certain conditions.

For a set of formulae $L(L \subseteq \mathcal{L})$ and a process p, $L(p)$ is defined as follows:

$$L(p) \stackrel{\text{def}}{=} \{f \in L \mid p \models f\}$$

In the same way for a process, we define the notion of *guarded* for a formula. A variable x in a formula f is *guarded*, if every occurrence of x is within some scope of $\langle a \rangle$. A formula f is *guarded* if every variable in f is guarded.

Our definition of μ-calculus differs from that of $STA(\mathcal{X}, \mathcal{A})$ in [5] — since the logical operators $+$ and $b \subseteq \mathcal{A}$ of $STA(\mathcal{X}, \mathcal{A})$ have similar meaning to the summation and the prefix operator of processes respectively, the system of $STA(\mathcal{X}, \mathcal{A})$ is inappropriate for our purpose. Fortunately, the each system has same expressive power when $\mathcal{A}$ is finite and any formula is guarded[11]. The following two propositions are proved by the above fact and same results in [5].

Proposition 1. [11] *Let $f(x)$ be a guarded formula. Then the following conditions are satisfied:*

1. $\mu x.f(x) \equiv \bigvee_{k>0} f^k(\text{ff})$.
2. $\nu x.f(x) \equiv \bigwedge_{k>0} f^k(\text{tt})$. □

Proposition 2. [11] *Processes p and q are strongly equivalent, i.e. $p \sim q$, iff $\mathcal{L}(p) = \mathcal{L}(q)$.* $\square$

The next proposition shows that negation can be removed from a formula.

Proposition 3. *Any formula can be equivalently converted to a formula without negation, i.e. a formula built up with tt, ff, $\wedge$, $\vee$, (a), $[a]$, μ, and ν.* $\square$

From now on, we will consider closed formulae without negation.

3   A subcalculus of μ-calculus

Now, we focus on the formulae built up from the propositions tt, ff, the modal operators $(a), [a]$ for $a \in \mathcal{A}$ and the logical connective $\wedge$. Let $\mathcal{L}_d$ be the set of formulae defined in the following BNF:

$$f :: = \mathbf{tt} \mid \mathbf{ff} \mid x \mid (a)f \mid [a]f \mid f \wedge f \mid \nu x.f$$

where $x \in \mathcal{X}, a \in \mathcal{A}$. A relation $\leq_d$ on processes is defined by $p \leq_d q$ iff $p \models f$ implies $q \models f$, for all formulae $f \in \mathcal{L}_d$. Obviously $\leq_d$ is a preorder and the resulting relation $\sim_d$, which is defined by $p \sim_d q$ iff $p \leq_d q$ and $q \leq_d p$, is an equivalence relation. So $\leq_d$ turns out to be a partial order on the equivalence classes of processes with respect to $\sim_d$, i.e. $[p] \leq_d [q]$ iff $p \leq_d q$, where $[p] = \{q \mid p \sim_d q\}$.

Lemma 4. $p \sim q$ *implies* $p \sim_d q$. *But not vice versa.*

Proof. The implication is straightforward from Proposition 2. The proper implication can be proved by a counter example. Let $p = a.r + a.s$ and $q = a.r + a.s + a.t$, where $r = b.0 + b.a.0 + b.a.b.0$, $s = b.0$, $t = b.0 + b.a.0$. It is obvious that $p \not\sim q$. We assume there exists a formula f such that $p \models f$ but $q \not\models f$. It is sufficient to consider the case that $f = [a]f'$ such that $f' \models r, s$ but $f' \not\models t$. And f' must be form of such $[b]f''$ where $f'' \models 0, a.0, a.b.0$ but $f'' \not\models 0$ or $f'' \not\models a.0$. However there is no such f'' in $\mathcal{L}_d$. On the other hand, let g be a formula such that $p \not\models g$ but $q \models g$. It is also sufficient to consider the case that $g = (a)g'$ where $g' \models t$ but $g' \not\models r, s$. And also g' must be of the form $[b]g''$ where $g'' \models 0, a.0$, but $g'' \not\models a.a.0$. However this is contradiction. $\square$

To compare the discriminative power of this relation $\leq_d$, we have the following results on comparison with the *simulation preorder* $\leq$ [14], and the *ready simulation preorder* $\leq_{RS}$ [17].

Definition 5. *A relation R on processes is a* simulation *if* $(p,q) \in R$ *implies, for all* $a \in \mathcal{A}$, *if* $p \xrightarrow{a} p'$, *then there exists* q' *such that* $q \xrightarrow{a} q'$ *and* $(p',q') \in R$. $\square$

Definition 6. *A* ready simulation preorder *is a binary relation R on processes such that whenever $(p,q) \in R$ and $a \in \mathcal{A}$ then:*

1. if $p \xrightarrow{a} p'$ then $\exists q'.q \xrightarrow{a} q'$ and $(p', q') \in R$.
2. if $q \xrightarrow{a}$ then $p \xrightarrow{a}$. □

Let $\leq$ be the union of all simulations, and $\leq_{RS}$ be the union of all ready simulation preorders. Then we have the following results.

Proposition 7. [6] *Let $\mathcal{L}_M$ be a set of formulae defined by the following BNF:*

$$f ::= \mathbf{tt} \mid x \mid \langle a \rangle f \mid f \wedge f \mid \nu x.f$$

where $x \in \mathcal{X}, a \in A$. Then $p \leq q$ if and only if $\mathcal{L}_M(p) \subseteq \mathcal{L}_M(q)$. □

Lemma 8. $p \leq_d q$ *implies* $p \leq q$. *But not vice versa.*

Proof. The implication is straightforward from Proposition 7. Properness is justified by the examples $p = a.b.0$, $q = a.0 + a.b.0$. Clearly, we have $p \leq q$. But for a formula $f = [a]\langle b \rangle \mathbf{tt}$, $p \models f$, $q \not\models f$. □

Lemma 9. $p \leq_d q$ *implies* $p \leq_{RS} q$. *But not vice versa.*

Proof. The implication is immediate from the definition of the ready simulation preorder. The reverse direction has the following counter example. Let $p = a.(b.c.0 + b.d.0)$ and $q = a.(b.c.0 + b.d.0) + a.b.c.0$, then $p \leq_{RS} q$ but $p \not\leq_d q$ since $[a]\langle b \rangle \langle d \rangle \mathbf{tt}$ is a counterexample. □

We have also the following relation which is more discriminating power than $\leq_d$.

Definition 10. A binary relation $\sqsubseteq_d$ over processes is a maximum relation which satisfies the following conditions. If $p \sqsubseteq_d q$ then for all $a \in Act$:

1. whenever $p \xrightarrow{a} p'$, then there exists q' such that $q \xrightarrow{a} q'$ and $p' \sqsubseteq_d q'$,
2. whenever $q \xrightarrow{a} q'$, then there exist $p'_1, \ldots, p'_n$ such that $p \xrightarrow{a} p'_i$ and $p'_1 + \cdots + p'_n \sqsubseteq_d q'$, where $n \geq 1$. □

Lemma 11. $p \sqsubseteq_d q$ *implies* $p \leq_d q$. *But not vice versa.*

Proof. Suppose $p \sqsubseteq_d q$ and f is a formula such that $p \models f$. Then we show q satisfies f. At first, we assume f has no ν operaters. In this case, the proof is structural induction on f. General case is derived from the above claim and Proposition 1.

A counter example for the reverse direction is $p_1 = a.(a.0 + b.0) + a.(c.0 + d.0)$ and $q_1 = a.(a.0 + b.0) + a.(c.0 + d.0) + a.(a.0 + c.0)$. It is immediate $p_1 \not\sqsubseteq_d q_1$. $p_1 \leq_d q_1$ is proved same as the above proof. □

After all, we have the following theorem.

Theorem 12. $\leq \supsetneq \leq_{RS} \supsetneq \leq_d \supsetneq \sqsubseteq_d \supsetneq \sim$ □

4 Synthesis algorithm

This section describes an inductive synthesis algorithm for recursive processes. Formulae in μ-calculus are regarded as specific properties of the intended process.

4.1 Enumeration of facts

An algorithm we will propose now is an inductive one. It generates an process which satisfies given facts, the properties of the target process, represented as formulae in μ-calculus. Thus, the input to the algorithm is an enumeration of formulae to be satisfied by the target process. Let p_o be the intended target process to be generated from its concrete properties. It should be noted that p_o is neither known initially nor given in a precise manner.

Definition 13. Let U be a set of pairs of a formula $f \in \mathcal{L}$ and a sign $+$ (or $-$), i.e. $\langle f, + \rangle$(or $\langle f, - \rangle$). $S = \{f \mid \langle f, + \rangle \in U\} \cup \{\neg f \mid \langle f, - \rangle \in U\}$ is an enumeration of facts, if either $\langle f, + \rangle$ or $\langle f, - \rangle$ always belongs to U, and S is consistent in the deductive system $\text{STL}(\mathcal{X}, \mathcal{A})^2$[5]. An element of S is called a fact. □

Using p_o, the enumeration of facts may be defined as follows.

$$U = \{\langle f, + \rangle \mid p_o \models f, f \in \mathcal{L}\} \cup \{\langle f, - \rangle \mid p_o \not\models f, f \in \mathcal{L}\}$$

Since p_o is not known a priori, we must consider U as in Definition 13.

4.2 Synthesis algorithm

The algorithm generates a process which satisfies given facts. A fact of disjunctive form, e.g. $f \vee g$, or $\mu x.f(x)(\equiv \bigvee_{k>0} f^k(\text{ff}))$, has non-determinacy, so we can not avoid reconstruction of processes for such formulae. To remedy the difficulty, we focus on the restricted set $\mathcal{L}_d$ of formulae. Thus we remove formulae which does not belong to $\mathcal{L}_d$, from an enumeration of facts. Note that a formula with ν operator also has non-determinacy regarding the number of times loops of process branches unfold.

Given an enumeration of facts, the algorithm synthesizes a process satisfying those facts. In the algorithm, a process is represented as a set of process definitions. Each process definition $\text{rec}\, c.p$ is associated with a set C of formulae, denoted as $c:C$, which must be satisfied by the corresponding process constant c. C can be omitted when it is not important. To describe the algorithm, we adopt a language like Prolog[3], where I/O predicates can backtrack as well. For brief description, let c_i denote process constants associating with the process definitions $c_i \stackrel{\text{def}}{=} p_i$ or $c_i{:}C_i \stackrel{\text{def}}{=} p_i$ where C_i is a set of formulae. The initial state of a process is always fixed to c_0. Thus, a set $\{c_0 \stackrel{\text{def}}{=} p_0, \ldots, c_n \stackrel{\text{def}}{=} p_n\}$ of process definitions determines the process c_0 with its set of process definition.

---

^{2} $\text{STL}(\mathcal{X}, \mathcal{A})$ is sound but unfortunately not complete. A complete deductive system for μ-calculus is not found yet.

For a fact of the form $\nu x.f(x)$, it is important to take an identification of formulae $\nu x.f(x)$ (or bound variables x) with process constants c. If c_i corresponds to x, i.e. the formula $\nu x.f(x)$, the variable x is renamed by x_i. Since x is a bound variable, the meaning of the formula is not changed. We assume further that we can recall the original formula $\nu x_i.f(x_i)$ from x_i. Also we adopt the following abbreviations:

$\bigwedge\{f_1,\ldots,f_n\} = f_1 \wedge \ldots \wedge f_n$

$S[c_1{:}C_1 \stackrel{\text{def}}{=} p_1,\cdots,c_k{:}C_k \stackrel{\text{def}}{=} p_k]$: The resulting set of process definitions S
 where the process definitions of $c_1,\cdots,c_k$ in S are replaced by $c_1{:}C_1 \stackrel{\text{def}}{=} p_1,\cdots,c_k{:}C_k \stackrel{\text{def}}{=} p_k$, respectively, or $c_i{:}C_i \stackrel{\text{def}}{=} p_i$ is added to S if $c_i \notin S$.

$S\{x/y\}$: The resulting S where a free variable y is substituted for by S.

Now, we are in a position to state the synthesis algorithm. For the help of understanding the algorithm, simple comments are attached directly to the corresponding predicates which begin with the mark "%". The detail explanation of the algorithm will be stated after the completion of the algorithm.

Algorithm 14 Synthesis algorithm.

Input: Enumeration of facts $f_1, f_2, \cdots$. It is an enumeration of formulae to be
 satisfied by an intended process. The order of them is arbitrary.

Output: Sequence of infered processes $p_1, p_2, \cdots$. Each p_k satisfies whole input
 formulae f_1 to f_k.

$mpstart$:- $mp(\{c_0{:}\{\text{tt}\} \stackrel{\text{def}}{=} 0\})$. % The initial process is 0.

$mp(S)$:- % S is a set of process definitions.
  $read\text{-}formula(f)$, % Input a formula.
  $makeproc(c_0, S, f, X)$, % Modify the current process according to the new
fact A, the result is set to X.
  $write\text{-}process(X)$, % Output the result.
  $mp(X)$. % Continue the synthesis process for the next fact.

% program clauses of $makeproc(c, S, f, X)$ [3]

% tt .... (a)
$makeproc(c_i, S, \text{tt}, S)$.

% x_j : a bound variable corresponding to the formula $\nu x_j.f(x_j)$ .... (b)
$makeproc(c_i, S, x_i, S)$.

---

[3] In the following procedures (clauses), we use several meta variables and Prolog-like
 variables whose intended meaning is explained below:
  c: the current process constant (meta variable)
  S: the current set of process definitions (meta variable)
  f: the current formula to be satisfied by c (meta variable)
  X: the infered process — a set of process definitions (Prolog-like variable)

$makeproc(c_i, S, x_j, X)$:- % Where $i \neq j$.
$\quad S' \leftarrow (S[c_j{:}C_j \stackrel{\text{def}}{=} p_i + p_j] - \{c_i{:}C_i \stackrel{\text{def}}{=} p_i\})\{x_j/x_i\}\{c_j/c_i\},$
$\quad makeproc(c_i, S', \wedge\{f \mid f \in C_j\}, X).$ ....(b*)
$makeproc(c_i, S, x_j, X)$:-
$\quad$ is-remake,
$\quad makeproc(c_i, S, f(x_j), X).$ ....(b**)

% $\langle a\rangle f$ ....(c)
$makeproc(c_i, S, \langle a\rangle f, X)$:-
$\quad exists(c_j, c_i, S, f, X).$ % $\exists c_j$ such that $c_i \stackrel{a}{\rightarrow} c_j$ and $makeproc(c_j, S, f, X).$
$makeproc(c_i, S, \langle a\rangle f, X)$:-
$\quad$ get-new-process-constant$(c_j),$
$\quad makeproc(c_j, S[c_i{:}C_i \stackrel{\text{def}}{=} p_i + a.c_j, c_j{:}\{tt\} \stackrel{\text{def}}{=} 0], f \wedge (\wedge\{f_k \mid [a]f_k \in C_i\}), X).$
$\quad$ % where $\wedge\emptyset \stackrel{\text{def}}{=} tt.$ ....(c*)

% $[a]f$ ....(d)
$makeproc(c_i, S, [a]f, S)$:-
$\quad$ is-valid$(\wedge C_i \supset [a]f).$ % $\models \wedge C_i \supset [a]f$
$makeproc(c_i, S, [a]f, S[c_i{:}(C_i \cup \{[a]f\}) \stackrel{\text{def}}{=} p_i])$:-
$\quad$ not-transit$(c_i, a).$ % $c_i \stackrel{a}{\nrightarrow} .$
$makeproc(c_i, S, [a]f, X)$:-
$\quad forall(c_j, c_i, S[c_i{:}C_i \cup \{[a]f\} \stackrel{\text{def}}{=} p_i], f, X).$
$\quad$ % $\forall c_j.c_i \stackrel{a}{\rightarrow} c_j, makeproc(c_j, S[c_i{:}C_i \cup \{[a]f\} \stackrel{\text{def}}{=} p_i], f, X).$

% $f_1 \wedge f_2$ ....(e)
$makeproc(c_i, S, f_1 \wedge f_2, X)$:-
$\quad makeproc(c_i, S, f_1, Y),$
$\quad makeproc(c_i, Y, f_2, X).$

% $\nu x.f(x)$ ....(f)
$makeproc(c_i, S, \nu x.f(x), X)$:-
$\quad makeproc(c_i, S, f(x_i), X).$ $\qquad\qquad\qquad\qquad\square$

Now, we explain the intuitive function of clauses.

(a): If the current formula is **tt**, simply return S since **tt** is satisfied by any processes. Note that there are no clauses for the formula **ff**. Since **ff** indicates that the input formulae are inconsistent, therefore it needs backtracking for this case. By means of backtracking mechanism, the intended process will be eventually generated.

(b): If the current formula is x_i return S since there already exists a recursive loop. If the current formula is x_j (a process variable) which does not correspond to the current process constant c_i, c_i with S needs modifications since c_i must satisfy the formula x_j (i.e. $\nu x_j.f(x_j)$) which must be satisfied by c_j. Therefore, the clause identifies c_i and c_j at first, then modifies c_i again to satisfy every condition in C_j (See Fig.1). The third clause in the case of logical variable will be invoked when identification c_i and c_j makes troubles. The troubles may arise from the direct recursive loop, i.e. wrong connection of c_i and c_j. However, this is not always the cases. Therefore, we need a controlling predicate. The predicate *is-remake* judges whether or not unfolding of $\mu x_j.f(x_j)$ is necessary in such a way that *is-remake* successes iff unfolding of the formula $\nu x_j.f(x_j)$ is necessary. Its intended function (meaning) will be explained after the explanation of the algorithm.

(c): If the current formula is of the form $(a)f$, the clause generally makes a branch labeled with a and constructs a new process satisfying f as an a-successor of c_i. However, if there already exists an a-successor c_j of c_i such that c_j can be modified to satisfy f, then neither new constants nor new processes are created. Otherwise, the clause creates a new branch followed by a new process by getting a fresh process constant c_j.

(d): For the current formula $[a]f$ every a-successor must be checked and modified to satisfy the subformula f. This is done by the last clause of this case. This check can be easily verified if the condition $\models \wedge C_i \supset [a]f$ holds. This is why we attach the condition to each process definition, i.e. a process constant. If c_i can not perform the action a, it suffices only add $[a]f$ to C_i.

(e): If the current formula is a conjunction $f_1 \wedge f_2$, apply f_1 and f_2 in this order.

(f): For the recursive formula $\nu x.f(x)$, rename the bound variable x into x_i to adjust it to c_i.

The predicate *makeproc* tries to make a shorter loop as much as possible for the formula $\nu x.f(x)$. However a shorter loop sometimes conflicts with the facts, the situations are explained by the following illustrative examples. Now, consider the situation depicted in Fig.2. The direct loop created at the first stage by the formula $\nu x_0.(a)\langle b\rangle x_0$ conflicts with the third fact $[a][b][b]$ff. Thus, the direct loop must be unfolded to avoid the confliction. The other situation is illustrated in Fig.3. The process constant c_1 with the condition $[b]x_0$ at the first stage has potential power to make a loop, possibly actuated by some facts, e.g. $[a]\langle b\rangle\langle c\rangle$tt in this example. Then, the created direct loop conflicts with the third fact $[c]$ff.

To avoid unnecessary unfolding loops, the procedure *is-remake* checks whether those situations make troubles whenever invoked, that is the current process does not satisfy the given facts. Then, *is-remake* forces backtracking if the trouble does not arise from those situations. Otherwise, the procedure succeeds, i.e. direct loops are unfolded once stated as above.

In the case of Fig.2, *is-remake* traces the path which is passed by a formula occurring inconsistent. And backtracking is allowed if the path has one or more loops and does not end on these loops. In the case of Fig.3, *is-remake* traces the path same as previous case. And it is allowed if the path enters the beginning of a loop, but does not go to body of the loop, and exits the loop directly. In each case, the information about which formula made each branch is needed.

Theorem 15. *Assume there exists a process p_n satisfying the initial segment $f_1, \cdots, f_n$ of an enumeration of facts, where $n \geq 1$. Assume also Algorithm 14*

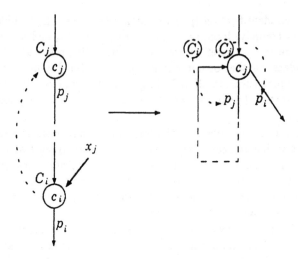

Fig. 1. The function of the clause of (b*).

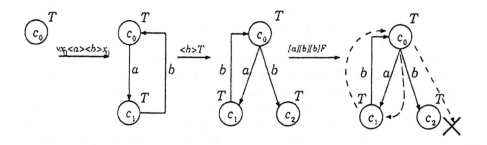

Fig. 2. Some action sequences are possible since a loop is constructed.

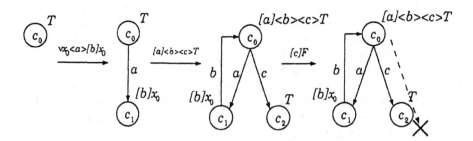

Fig. 3. Some action sequences are possible since a branch is modified to a loop.

outputs a set of process definitions S_{n-1} for the $n-1$ facts $f_1, \cdots, f_{n-1}$. For the n-th fact f_n, we have the followings:

1. Algorithm 14 terminates and returns an output, a set of process definitions S_n with a process constant c_0 (the initial state of S_n).
2. c_0 with S_n satisfies f_n.
3. c_0 satisfies $f_1, \cdots, f_{n-1}$.

Proof. (brief sketch) 1. When the procedure *makeproc* calls itself recursively, let f be a given formula to it, and g be a formula to call itself. Then, the size of g — the number of operators constructing the formula — can be greater than the size of f, only in the clauses (b*), (b**) and (c*) in Algorithm 14. It is sufficient to prove the above case does not occur infinitely many times. For more detail, see [11]. 2 and 3 are immediate from Algorithm 14. □

The algorithm is a non terminating procedure. Therefore, we show its correctness by using the concept of convergence in the limit, which is often used in inductive learning theory[18].

Definition 16. Assume an algorithm inputs an enumeration of facts, and outputs processes sequentially. After some time if the output process is always p, then the infered sequence by this algorithm converges in the limit to p over the enumeration of facts. □

Lemma 17. *Assume p is an intended process, and Algorithm 14 converges in the limit to a process p'. Then $p \leq_d p'$.* □

We define a formula which has sufficient characteristic to synthesize a process. For preliminary, we have the following.

Definition 18. When a set of process definitions S satisfies the following condition, we call S a set of complete process definition of a process p:

1. S has an initial process definition $c_0 \stackrel{\text{def}}{=} q_0$ such that $p \sim c_0$.
2. Each process definition is of the form $c \stackrel{\text{def}}{=} a_1.c_1 + \cdots + a_n.c_n$, where $n \geq 0$ (when $n = 0$, $a_1.c_1 + \cdots + a_n.c_n \stackrel{\text{def}}{=} 0$), each $a_i \in A$ and c_i is a process constant whose process definition belongs in S.
3. For any process definition $c \stackrel{\text{def}}{=} q$ in S, $S - \{c \stackrel{\text{def}}{=} q\}$ cannot define p.

Every guarded process p can be translated to a set of complete process definition of p by the following algorithm. We represent this set $\mathcal{P}(p)$.

Algorithm 19. Let p be a guarded process, and S be a minimum set of process definitions which are needed to define p. Then get a fresh process constant c_0 which is not included in S, and add $c_0 \stackrel{\text{def}}{=} p$ to S. And apply the following algorithm to S until S is not modified any more:

1. If $c \stackrel{\text{def}}{=} a.p \in S$ and p is not a process constant, then get a fresh process constant c', and $S \leftarrow S[c \stackrel{\text{def}}{=} a.c', c' \stackrel{\text{def}}{=} p]$.

2. If $c \stackrel{\text{def}}{=} p + a.q + r \in S$ and q is not a process constant, then get a fresh process constant c', and $S \leftarrow S[c \stackrel{\text{def}}{=} p + a.c' + r, c' \stackrel{\text{def}}{=} q]$.

3. If $c \stackrel{\text{def}}{=} p + c' + q$, $c' \stackrel{\text{def}}{=} r \in S$ and $c \neq c'$, then $S \leftarrow S[c \stackrel{\text{def}}{=} p + r + q]$.

4. If $c \stackrel{\text{def}}{=} c'$ and c' is a process constant, then $S \leftarrow (S - \{c \stackrel{\text{def}}{=} c'\})\{c/c'\}$.

5. If $c \stackrel{\text{def}}{=} q \in S$ where $c \neq c_0$, and c is not used any other process definition, then $S \leftarrow S - \{c \stackrel{\text{def}}{=} q\}$. □

For example, if $S = \{c_0 \stackrel{\text{def}}{=} a.c_1, \ c_1 \stackrel{\text{def}}{=} b.(c_0 + c_1)\}$, then $\mathcal{P}(c_0) = \{c_0 \stackrel{\text{def}}{=} a.c_1, \ c_1 \stackrel{\text{def}}{=} b.c_2, \ c_2 \stackrel{\text{def}}{=} a.c_1 + b.c_2\}$. Observe that c_0 in S and c_0 in $\mathcal{P}(c_0)$ are strongly equivalent.

Lemma 20. *For any guarded process p, Algorithm 19 terminates, and $P(p)$ is a set of complete process definition of p.* □

Definition 21. Let S be a set of complete process definitions and C be a set of process constants whose process definitions belong to S. Then a formula $\mathcal{F}_S(C)$ is defined in the following:

1. $s(c, a) = \{c' \mid c \stackrel{a}{\rightarrow} c'\}$.

2. $comb(\{C_1, \ldots, C_n\}) = \{\{c_1, \ldots, c_n\} \mid c_1 \in C_1, \ldots, c_n \in C_n\}$, where $n \geq 0$.

3. $\mathcal{G}_S(C, a) = \begin{cases} [a]\text{ff}, & \text{if } c \stackrel{a}{\not\rightarrow} \text{ for any } c \in C, \\ [a]\mathcal{F}_S(\bigcup_{c \in C} s(c, a)), & \text{if there exist } c, c' \in C \text{ such that } c \stackrel{a}{\rightarrow} \text{ and } c' \stackrel{a}{\not\rightarrow}, \\ (\bigwedge_{C' \in comb(\{s(c,a) \mid c \in C\})} \langle a \rangle \mathcal{F}_S(C')) \wedge [a]\mathcal{F}_S(\bigcup_{c \in C} s(c, a)), & \text{otherwise.} \end{cases}$

4. $\mathcal{F}_S(C) = \begin{cases} x_C, & \text{if } \mathcal{F}_S(C) \text{ is in the scope of } \nu x_C, \\ \nu x_C \cdot \bigwedge_{a \in \mathcal{A}} \mathcal{G}_S(C, a), & \text{otherwise.} \end{cases}$

When p is a guarded process, $\mathcal{F}(p) \stackrel{\text{def}}{=} \mathcal{F}_{\mathcal{P}(p)}(c_0)$ where c_0 is an initial process constant of $\mathcal{P}(p)$. □

Instinctively, $\mathcal{F}_S(C)$ is a formula which is logically equivalent to $\bigwedge(\bigcap_{c \in C} \mathcal{L}_d(c))$. When $S = \{c_0 \stackrel{\text{def}}{=} a.c_1, \ c_1 \stackrel{\text{def}}{=} a.c_2, \ c_2 \stackrel{\text{def}}{=} a.c_0 + a.c_1 + b.c_1\}$) and $\mathcal{A} = \{a, b\}$, then $\mathcal{F}_S(\{c_0\})$ is in the following:

$$\mathcal{F}_S(\{c_0\}) = \nu x_{\{c_0\}} \cdot \langle a \rangle \mathcal{F}_S(\{c_1\}) \wedge [a]\mathcal{F}_S(\{c_1\}) \wedge [b]\text{ff}$$

$$\mathcal{F}_S(\{c_1\}) = \nu x_{\{c_1\}} \cdot \langle a \rangle \mathcal{F}_S(\{c_2\}) \wedge [a]\mathcal{F}_S(\{c_2\}) \wedge [b]\text{ff}$$

$$\mathcal{F}_S(\{c_2\}) = \nu x_{\{c_2\}} \cdot \langle a \rangle x_{\{c_0\}} \wedge \langle a \rangle x_{\{c_1\}} \wedge [a]\mathcal{F}_S(\{c_0, c_1\}) \wedge \langle b \rangle x_{\{c_1\}} \wedge [b]x_{\{c_1\}}$$

$$\mathcal{F}_S(\{c_0, c_1\}) = \nu x_{\{c_0, c_1\}} \cdot \langle a \rangle \mathcal{F}_S(\{c_1, c_2\}) \wedge [a]\mathcal{F}_S(\{c_1, c_2\}) \wedge [b]\text{ff}$$

$$\mathcal{F}_S(\{c_1, c_2\}) = \nu x_{\{c_1, c_2\}} \cdot \langle a \rangle \mathcal{F}_S(\{c_0, c_2\}) \wedge \langle a \rangle x_{\{c_1, c_2\}} \wedge [a]\mathcal{F}_S(\{c_0, c_1, c_2\})$$

$$\mathcal{F}_S(\{c_0, c_2\}) = \nu x_{\{c_0, c_2\}} \cdot \langle a \rangle x_{\{c_0, c_1\}} \wedge \langle a \rangle x_{\{c_1\}} \wedge [a]x_{\{c_0, c_1\}}$$

$$\mathcal{F}_S(\{c_0, c_1, c_2\}) = \nu x_{\{c_0, c_1, c_2\}} \cdot \langle a \rangle x_{\{c_0, c_1\}} \wedge \langle a \rangle x_{\{c_0, c_1, c_2\}} \wedge [a]x_{\{c_0, c_1, c_2\}}$$

Lemma 22. *Let S be a complete set of process definitions and C is a set of process constants whose process definitions belong to S. Then for any $c \in C$, $c \models \mathcal{F}_S(C)$.*

Proof. Let f be a formula expanded in finite times from $\mathcal{G}_S(C, a)$. We can prove $c \models f$ by structure induction on f. □

Lemma 23. *For two processes p, q such that $q \models \mathcal{F}(p)$, let C_p and C_q be a set of all process constants of $\mathcal{P}(p)$ and $\mathcal{P}(q)$ respectively. For some formula f, suppose there exists $C \subseteq C_p$ such that for any $c_p \in C$, $c_p \models f$. Then there exists $C' \subseteq C_q$ such that for any $c_q \in C'$, $c_q \models f$.*

Proof. First, we can prove for f without ν operator by structural induction on f. For a general formula, the proof is by Proposition 1. □

Proposition 24. *1. $p \models \mathcal{F}(p)$.*
2. $p \leq_d q$ implies $q \models \mathcal{F}(p)$.
3. $q \models \mathcal{F}(p)$ implies $p \leq_d q$.

Proof. 1. From Lemma 22.
2. Immediate from 2.
3. From Lemma 23. □

The validity of Algorithm 14 is also shown by the following theorem.

Theorem 25. *Under the assumption of algorithm 14, if there exists a process p satisfying an enumeration of facts, the infered sequence of processes by Algorithm 14 converges in the limit to a process p' such that $p \leq_d p'$.* □

5 Concluding Remarks and Related Works

This paper presented the synthesis algorithm for a recursive process based on the enumeration of facts, which must be satisfied by the process. Its validity was also discussed. The algorithm has been implemented as a prototype system SORP: Synthesizer of Recursive Processes. This system adopts a graphical user interface to display the synthesized processes, (See Fig.4). This system is implemented using SICStus Prolog and X-window system.

As we mentioned in introduction, little had been investigated for inductive inference of processes. However, some synthesis algorithms by deductive approaches exist. These approaches find a model which satisfies a given formula. [12] provided an algorithm by tableau method to show consistency of a formula in μ-calculus. The algorithm builds a finite tree-like model which a given formula f satisfies. Since the model is a tree, not a graph, the algorithm cannot treat a loop, i.e. a recursive process. Actually, he shows the model of depth exponential in $|f|^3$. Streett and Emerson[22] presented a decision procedure to to build a automaton model which satisfies a given formula f. The constructed automaton is a finite tree with nodes in $O(2^{2|p|})$. Similar approaches for temporal logic is [13]. [13] presented a satisfiability algorithm to create a model satisfied by a given formul in liner time propositional temporal logic using tablaue method, though the logic has no fixed point operators. Stirling's work[19] seems to be

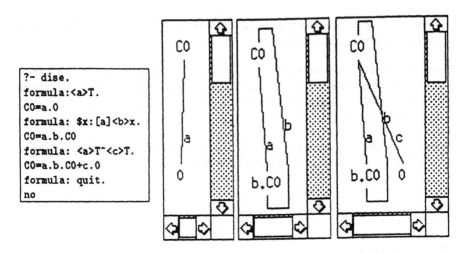

```
?- dise.
formula:<a>T.
CO=a.0
formula: $x:[a]<b>x.
CO=a.b.CO
formula: <a>T^<c>T.
CO=a.b.CO+c.0
formula: quit.
no
```

Fig. 4. Output examples in the prototype system.

related with our work, though he does not mention. In [19], he showed a sound and complete deductive system NL for processes. Using NL, we can deduce that which process does satisfy a certain formula. For example, $p \vdash \langle a \rangle f$ implies $p + q \vdash \langle a \rangle f$, and also $p \vdash [a]f$, $q \vdash [a]f$ imply $p + q \vdash [a]f$. From these rules, a formula $[a]\langle b \rangle T \wedge \langle a \rangle \langle c \rangle T$ can infer, for example, a process $a.b.0 + a.(b.0 + c.0)$. In this sense, we can regard his system as a deductive system for process synthesis. Of course, the NL has no recursive expression we need to extend it for recursive processes.

Let us return to our main subject. There is the restriction on input formulae in our algorithm. In other words, the formulae must be within $\mathcal{L}_d$. Consider the formula with either $\vee$ or μ operator, for example, $\langle a \rangle \mathbf{tt} \vee \langle b \rangle \mathbf{tt}$. It says the target process can execute an action a or b (or both). When it is input to the synthesis algorithm, the algorithm is unsure which formula, i.e. $\langle a \rangle \mathbf{tt}$ or $\langle b \rangle \mathbf{tt}$, is really needed. Suppose that the algorithm trusts $\langle a \rangle \mathbf{tt}$ and output a process p which satisfies it. But after some times, $[a]\mathbf{ff}(\equiv \neg \langle a \rangle \mathbf{tt})$ may be input. In such case, the algorithm must backtrack at the point before p was synthesized, and adopt the other formula (i.e. $\langle b \rangle \mathbf{tt}$). Especially, since a formula with μ operator has infinite many $\vee$ operators (see Proposition1), it may cause to backtrack infinite many times. To solve this problem, the predicate *is-satisfied* will be more complicated. However overcoming the problem leads us a process synthesis algorithm whose output converges in the limit to a process equivalent to a target one.

The time or space complexity of the algorithm is not discussed, which is left for a future study.

References

1. Angluin, D.: "Learning Regular Sets from Queries and Counterexamples", Inf. and Comput, 75, pp.87–106(1987).
2. Brookes, S.D., C.A.R Hoare and A.W. Roscoe: "A Theory of Communicating Sequential Processes", J. ACM., 31, 3, pp.560–599(1984).
3. Clocksin, W.F. and C.S. Mellish: "Programming in Prolog", Springer-Verlag(1981).
4. Fantechi, A., S. Gnesi S. and G. Ristori: "Compositional Logic Semantics and LOTOS", Protocol Specification, Testing and Verification, XL., IFIP, pp.365–378
5. Graf, S. and J. Sifakis: "A Logic for the Description of Non-deterministic Programs and Their Properties", Inf. and contr., 68, pp.254–270(1986)
6. Hennessy, M. and R. Milner: "Algebraic Laws for Nondeterminism and Concurrency", J. ACM., 32, 1, pp.137–161(1985).
7. Hennessy, M.: "Algebraic Theory of Processes", The MIT Press(1988).
8. Hindley, J.R. and J.P. Seldin: "Introduction to Combinators and λ-Calculus", London Mathematical Society Student Texts 1, Cambridge Univ. Press(1986).
9. Hoare, C.A.R.: "Communicating Sequential Process", Prentice Hall(1985).
10. Kimura, S., A. Togashi and S. Noguchi: "A Synthesis Algorithm of Basic Processes by Modal Formulas" (in Japanese), Trans. IEICE, J75-D-I, pp.1048–1061(1992).
11. Kimura, S., A. Togashi and N. Shiratori: "Synthesis Algorithm for Recursive Processes by μ-calculus", preprint.
12. Kozen, D.: "Results on the Propositional μ-calculus", Theoret. Comput. Sci., 27, pp.333–354(1983).
13. Manna, Z. and P. Wolper: "Synthesis of Communicating Processes from Temporal Logic Specifications", ACM Trans. on Programming Languages and Systems, 6-, 1, pp68–93(1984).
14. Milner, R.: "Communication and Concurrency", Prentice-Hall(1989).
15. Park, D.: "Concurrency and automata on infinite sequences", Lecture Notes in Comput. Sci. 104, pp.167–183, Springer-Verlag(1981).
16. Gotzhein, R.: "Specifying Communication Services with Temporal Logic", Protocol Specification, Testing and Verification, XL, pp.295–309(1990).
17. van Glabbeek, R.J.: "The Linear Time – Branching Time Spectrum", Lecture Notes in Comput. Sci. 458, Springer-Verlag(1990).
18. Shapiro, E.Y.: "Inductive Inference of Theories From Facts", Technical Report 192, Yale Univ(1981).
19. Stirling, C.: "A Proof-Theoretic Characterization of Observational Equivalence", Theoretical Computer Science, 39, pp.27–45(1985).
20. Stirling, C.: "Modal Logics For Communicating Systems", Theoretical Computer Science, 49, pp.311–347(1987).
21. Stirling, C.: "An Introduction to Modal and Temporal Logics for CCS", Lecture Notes in Comput. Sci. 491, Springer-Verlag, pp.2–20(1991).
22. Streett, R.S. and E.A. Emerson: "An Automata Theoretic Decision Procedure for the Propositional Mu-Calculus", Info. and Comput. 81, Academic Press, pp249–264(1989).

Monotonicity versus Efficiency for Learning Languages from Texts

Efim Kinber
Department of Computer and Information Sciences
University of Delaware
Newark, DE 19716
kinber@cis.udel.edu

Abstract

One of the central problems of learning languages from texts is: how various restrictions on the behaviour of a learner limit the learning abilities. We consider restrictions of two types. Restrictions of the first type concern monotonicity of learning. Monotonicity means actually that the learner, fed more and more positive examples of the language, produces better and better generalizations. Our second assumption is that of restricted efficiency of the learner. We consider limits on two types of efficiency: number of mind changes and (long-term) memory. Restrictions on monotonicity and efficiency are combined to answer the following question: how much one can gain in the number of mind changes, or memory, by weakening monotonicity constraints ? We show that, weakening monotonicity constraints, a (uniformly bounded) constant number of mind changes can replace indefinitely many. As concerns learning with limited memory, it turns out that, weakening monotonicity requirements from one level to another, we can gain in memory (at least) exponentially. Some open problems are also formulated.

1 Introduction

Learning languages from texts has become a subject of intensive research within recent years. One of the central problems in this area is: how various restrictions on the behaviour of a learner limit the learning abilities. We consider restrictions of two types. Restrictions of the first type concern monotonicity of learning, originally introduced by Jantke [8], as well as its dual version, specialization [9]. Monotonicity (specialization, respectively) means actually that the learner, being fed more and more positive examples of the language, produces better and better generalizations (specializations, respectively). In this strongest interpretation, the learner has to infer a sequence of hypotheses describing growing (descending, respectively) chain of languages, i.e., $L_i \subseteq L_j$ ($L_i \supseteq L_j$, respectively) iff L_j is guessed later than L_i. Several natural approaches to monotonicity are defined and explored in [8, 9, 13, 14].

Our second assumption is that of restricted amount of memory used by a learner. The effects of limiting memory for inductive inference of functions were first studied in [5]. However, an analysis of learning languages with limited memory seems to be even more important. A natural motivation for this approach is human language acquisition. Linguists have elaborated many mechanisms in attempt to explain how children learn languages. For example, Braine [4] suggests that human memory is organized as a cascading sequence of memories. The items to be remembered enter initially the first level of the memory and then later move to succesive levels, finally reaching long term memory. Each of the transitional levels of memory are subjects to degradation: if items to be remembered are not supported by forthcoming inputs, they might be eliminated from transitional level of memory before they become permanently fixed in long term memory. A comprehensive formal study of language learning was initiated in [16] and [17], including some models of learning, where a learning device had access to most recent input data and most recent conjectures.

We also use the number of mind changes the learner makes on a text as a measure of learning complexity. Learning languages with restrictions on the number of mind changes was widely explored in many works, including papers [12] and [15].

We combine restrictions on monotonicity and efficiency in order to answer the following question: how much one can gain in the number of mind changes, or memory, weakening monotonicity requirements ? We show that, weakening monotonicity constraints, just one mind change can replace infinitely many. As concerns learning with limited memory, it turns out that, weakening monotonicity requirements from one level to another, we can gain in memory at least exponentially.

2 Learning Paradigm

We consider the Gold-style formal language learning model, as defined in [1, 2, 3, 6]. A learning algorithmic device, being fed by the sequence of strings s in the target language L and symbols # (representing pauses in the presentation of data), produces a sequence of hypotheses $H_1, H_2, ...$ such that the limit of this sequence is a program for the target language. More formally, Let Σ denote a fixed finite alphabet of symbols. Let Σ^* be the free monoid over Σ. Any subset $L \subseteq \Sigma^*$ is called a language. $co - L$ denotes the complement of L. Let # be not in Σ. An infinite sequence $t = s_1, s_2, ..., s_n, ...$ of strings from $\Sigma^* \bigcup \{\#\}$ such that $\mathbf{range}(t) = \{s_i | s_i \in \Sigma^* \bigcap t\} = L$ for some language L is called a text for L. For any $x \in N$, let t_x denote the initial segment of t of the length x, and $\mathbf{range}(t_x)$ denote $\{s_i | s_i \in \Sigma^* \bigcup t_x\}$ (in the expression $\Sigma^* \bigcup t_x$ we consider t_x as a set of strings, rather than a sequence).

Following Gold, we define an Inductive Inference Machine (IIM, for short) to be an algorithmic device which works as follows: it takes larger and larger initial segments of input text t and either requires the next input string, or it first outputs a hypothesis, i.e. a number encoding a computer program, and then it requires the next input string (cf. e.g. [1]). Since we consider the most general case of learning grammars for recursively enumerable languages, we select an arbitrary acceptable numbering $\{W_e\}_{e=0,1,\ldots}$ as our hypotheses space; thus, a learner produces codes (of grammars) in the given numbering.

Definition 1. Let $\mathcal{L}$ be a family of languages, $L \in \mathcal{L}$, An IIM M $LIM - TXT$ - identifies L on a text t iff either the output sequence of M, denoted by $M(t_x)_{x \in N}$, is finite and the last number in the sequence is a number j such that $L = W_j$, or the sequence converges to such a number j.

Moreover, M $LIM - TXT$-identifies L iff it $LIM - TXT$-identifies L on every text for L. For any $k \in N$, we say that an IIM M $LIM_k - TXT$ (or with at most k mind changes) identifies L, if for any text t for L

$$card\{x | M(t_x) \neq M(t_{x+1})\} \leq k$$

We set $LIM - TXT(M) = \{L \in \mathcal{L} | M LIM - TXT\text{-identifies } L\}$.

Let $LIM - TXT$ denote the collection of all families $\mathcal{L}$ of recursive enumerable languages for which there is an IIM M such that $\mathcal{L} \subseteq LIM - TXT(M)$. Similarly, for any $k \in N$, we define the collections of families $LIM_k - TXT$.

3 Monotonicity Requirements

Informally speaking, an IIM learns monotonically if it produces better and better generalizations. However, monotonicity can be defined mathematically in various ways. Here we follow [8], [9], and [13].

Definition 2. ([13]). An IIM M is said to identify a language L from text

(A) strongly - monotonically
(B) monotonically
(C) weakly - monotonically

iff $M LIM - TXT$ - identifies L, and for any text t of L as well as for any two consequtive hypotheses j_x, j_{x+k} which M has produced when fed t_x and t_{x+k}, for some $k \geq 1, k \in N$, the following conditions are satisfied:

(A) $L(G_{j_x}) \subseteq L(G_{j_{x+k}})$
(B) $L(G_{j_x}) \bigcap L \subseteq L(G_{j_{x+k}}) \bigcap L$
(C) if $t_{x+k} \subseteq L(G_{j_x})$, then $L(G_{j_x}) \subseteq L(G_{j_{x+k}})$.

The requirement (A) is straightforward and very strong. If the learner erroneously adds a word to a hypothesis, he can never remove this word from the target language description. In the case (B) the learner can correct mistakes. However, he cannot change his mind about the words in the target language. In the case (C) the learner may expel words from the current hypothesis only if a new word appears in the input.

By $SMON - TXT, MON - TXT$ and $WMON - TXT$ we denote the set of those families of languages that are learnable strongly-monotonically, monotonically, conservatively, and weakly-monotonically.

The following definition deals with dual counterparts of monotonic learning.

Definition 3. An IIM M is said to identify a language L from text

    (A') dual strongly - monotonically
    (B') dual monotonically
    (C') dual weakly - monotonically

iff $MLIM - TXT$-identifies L and for any text t of L as well as for any two consecutive hypotheses $G_{j_x}, G_{j_{x+k}}$ which M has produced when fed t_x and t_{x+k}, for some $k \geq 1, k \in N$, the following conditions are satisfied:

    (A') $co - L(G_{j_x}) \subseteq co - L(G_{j_{x+k}})$
    (B') $co - L(G_{j_x}) \bigcap co - L \subseteq co - L(G_{j_{x+k}}) \bigcap co - L$
    (C') if $t_{x+k} \subseteq L(G_{j_x})$, then $co - L(G_{j_x}) \subseteq co - L(G_{j_{x+k}})$.

$SMON^d, MON^d - TXT$ and $WMON^d - TXT$ stand for the corresponding collections of families of languages.

Now, $SMON_k$ stands for the collection of families $\mathcal{L}$ in $SMON$ such that for some IIM M, for any text t for a language $L \in \mathcal{L}$

$$card\{t_x | M(t_x) \neq M(t_{x+1})\}$$

is uniformly bounded by k.

Similarly, we define $MON_k, CONS_k, WMON_k, SMON_k^d$, etc.

The full picture of relationships between various types of monotonic and dual-monotonic learning can be found in papers [7] and [10] (the case of learning indexed families of recursive languages was explored in [14]). For example, MON-learnability not necesserily implies $WMON$-learnability, although the latter type of learning seems to be weaker.

4 Limited Memory

Following [5], we assume that every IIM M has two types of memory: long term memory and short term memory. M uses the long term memory to remember any information that can be useful on forthcoming stages of inference (for instance, portions of the input it has seen, prior conjectures, etc.). The short term memory is potentially unlimited and is annihilated every time the IIM either outputs a new conjecture or begins to read the new word in the input. The short term memory clearing is done automatically and takes one time step. Separation of the short term memory is very useful (and proved to be very fruitful in [5]) to insure an accurate accounting of the real long term memory needed for learning the unknown language.

For any text t and any it's initial segment t_x, let $|t_x|$ denote the number $|\alpha_1| + |\alpha_2| + ... + |\alpha_k|$, where $\{\alpha_1, \alpha_2, ..., \alpha_k\}$ =**range**(t_x) (thus, k is the number of pairwise *distinct* words in t_x). We say that $\mathcal{L} \subseteq LIM - TXT : g(M)$ if g is a recursive function such that $\mathcal{L} \subseteq \text{LIM-TXT}(M)$ and for any $L \in \mathcal{L}$ and any text t with $\text{range}(t) = L$ for any x, M uses at most $g(|t_x|)$ bits of long term memory. Similarly, LIM-TXT:$g = \{\mathcal{L}|\exists M(\mathcal{L} \subseteq \text{LIM-TXT}:g(M)\}$.

Similarly, we can define memory limited monotonically inferrable classes: SMON-TXT:g, MON-TXT:g, etc.

Linear long term memory was proved in [5] to be sufficient for learning any inferrable classes of recursive functions. It can be easily shown that linear long term memory is enough for *set-driven* language learning when the behaviour of the learner depends only on the $\text{range}(t_x)$. It is proved in [11] that long term memory can be bounded by no (rapidly increasing) recursive function in the general case.

5 Monotonicity versus Mind Changes

In this section we consider IIMs with no restrictions on the memory. Our results show that weakening monotonicity constraints can result in decreasing indefinitely many mind changes to just one.

Theorem 1 *There exists an indexed family $\mathcal{L}$ of languages that is $MON_1 - TXT$-learnable and $SMON - TXT$ - learnable with no constant bound on the number of mind changes.*

Proof. Let $<,>$ denote a Cantor pairing (one-one computable) function. For any i, we define

$$V_i = \{< i, x > |x, i \in \{0,1\}^*, x \in W_i, \text{ and } x < i\}.$$

Now, for any i and any j, we define

$$U_{i,j} = (V_i \bigcap \{1, 2, ..., j\}) \bigcup \{i * j\},$$

where $*$ is a new symbol not used to represent natural numbers. The family $\mathcal{L}$ consists of all V_i and $U_{i,j}$ for all i and j.

First we show that our family is $MON - TXT$ - learnable with at most one mind change. Being fed words $< i, x >$, the IIM M outputs the conjecture V_i while $i * j$ does not appear in the input. If it happens, it outputs $U_{i,j}$. The $SMON - TXT$ IIM simply outputs the contents of the input tape as its current guess.

Now we will show that there exists no constant bound on the number of mind changes for any IIM $SMON - TXT$ - learning our family. By way of contradiction, suppose there exists such an IIM M and a constant bound c. We will define the process of definition of the language $W_{f(i)}$ for any i. We take an arbitrary i, add 0 to $W_{f(i)}$ and begin to feed M by the input $< i, 0 >, <$ $i, 0 >, ...$ If M never outputs a conjecture, then, applying recursion theorem (and taking sufficiently large fixed-point) we get a contradiction: M does not learn V_i for the fixed point i. If M outputs a guess, say, H_1 for some input (for the sake of simplicity, let it be $< i, 0 >$), we add 1 to $W_{f(i)}$ and begin to feed $M < i, 1 >, < i, 1 >, ...$ Now three events are possible:

1. Running H_1, we get that it contains $< i, 1 >$. Then we stop. M has to drop $< i, 1 >$ from hypotheses on the language $U_{0,1}$, therefore, it cannot be $SMON$.

2. M changes its mind. Then we add 2 to $W_{f(i)}$ and begin to feed it $< i, 2 >, < i, 2 >, ...$

3. Neither 1, nor 2. Then, applying recursion theorem, we see that M does not learn V_i.

We repeat the above stage $c + 1$ times. Since M can change its mind at most c times, it finally will output an "overgeneralizing" hypothesis and will be refuted on some $U_{i,j}$ (for a sufficiently large fixed point i). Q.E.D.

It is proved in [7,10] that MON - learnability does not imply $WMON$ - learnability in the general case. As our next result shows, if a MON - learnable family is $WMON$ - learnable, one might save a considerable number of mind changes.

Theorem 2 *There exists an indexed family of languages $\mathcal{L}$ that is $WMON_2 - TXT$-learnable and $MON.-TXT$-learnable with no constant bound on the number of mind changes.*

Proof. We modify the family $\mathcal{L}$ defined in the above theorem. Namely, we add to the above family the languages

$$S_{i,j} = V_i \bigcup \{i * j, *\}.$$

This family is easily weakly monotonically learnable with at most two mind changes: the IIM first guesses V_i, if $i * j$ appears in the input, it guesses $U_{i,j}$, and, finally, if $*$ appears, it outputs $S_{i,j}$. Since all languages are finite, the family is easily $SMON - TXT$-learnable.

Now, by way of contradiction, assume that the family is $MON - TXT$ - learnable with at most c mind changes. We define the sets $W_{f(i)}$ exactly as in the proof of the above theorem. Thus, applying recursion theorem, we get that, at some stage, being fed some input

$$< i, 0 >, < i, 0 >, ..., < i, 0 >, < i, 1 >, < i, 1 >, ..., < i, 1 >, ... < i, r >, < i, r >$$
$$, ..., < i, r >,$$

the IIM M outputs an "overgeneralizing" hypothesis H that contains $< i, r+1 >$ (where $r < c$). At this moment we stop the definition of $W_{f(i)}$. Now, if from this point on we will feed M the words $i * r, i * r, ...$ then, at some stage M will have to output a hypothesis H' that does not contain $< i, r + 1 >$ (we do not know when it will happen, but it must happen, because otherwise M fails to learn the language $U_{i,j}$ for sufficiently large fixed point i). However, if, after this event, we will feed M the words $*$, M will have to output eventually the language $S_{i,j}$, thus failing to be a MON IIM. Q.E.D.

Our next result trades the general type of learning versus $WMON - TXT$.

Theorem 3 *There exists an indexed family* $\mathcal{L}$ *of languages that is* LIM_2-TXT-*learnable and* $WMON-TXT$ *learnable with no constant bound on the number of mind changes.*

Proof. Let $\{M_i\}_{i=0,1,2,...}$ denote an acceptable numbering of all IIMs. Let c denote Cantor coding function of all pairs of natural numbers. For each $i \in N$ we define a language $L_{c(i,0)}$ and (possibly) $L_{c(i,1)}$. When a language appears in our construction, we add it to the numbering ν (of the class $\mathcal{L}$) we will be defining simultaneously.

CONSTRUCTION

Add to ν the language $L_{c(i,0)}$ defined by the following procedure:

STAGE 0: Add the word $a^i b$ to $L_{c(i,0)}$. Feed M_i the input

$$a^i b, \#, \#, \#, \cdots$$

If M_i outputs a hypothesis, say, H_0 on the fragment t_x, set $inp_1 = t_x$ and go to Stage 1.

STAGE n: If $n = i$, then terminate the procedure. Otherwise, add the word $a^i b^{n+1}$ to $L_{c(i,0)}$. Feed M_i the input

$$inp_n, a^i b^{n+1}, \#, \#, \#, \cdots$$

Simultaneously, enumerate the set $W_{H_{n-1}}$. If M_i changes its mind to a new hypothesis H_n on some initial fragment t_x of the given input, then set $inp_{n+1} = t_x$ and go to Stage $n+1$. If at some moment all words $a^i b^j, 1 \le j \le n+1$ appear in W_{H_1}, then add the language $L_{c(i,1)} = \{a^i b, a^i b^2, ..., a^i b^n\}$ to the numbering ν (thus, $L_{c(i,1)}$ contains one word less than $L_{c(i,0)}$), and terminate the procedure.

END OF CONSTRUCTION

Claim A. $\mathcal{L}$ is $LIM-TXT$-learnable with at most two mind changes.

Proof. An appropriate IIM, recieving any word $a^i b^j$, outputs $L_{c(i,0)}$ as its first guess (using the above procedure for enumerating $L_{c(i,0)}$). If the language $L_{c(i,1)}$ is added to ν at some moment, the IIM changes its mind to this language; note that $L_{c(i,1)}$ is completely defined at the moment of its appearance in ν. If a word $w \notin L_{c(i,1)}$ appears in the input, the IIM changes its mind back to $L_{c(i,0)}$.

Claim B. $\mathcal{L} \in SMON-TXT$.

Proof. Since all languages in $\mathcal{L}$ are finite, one can easily define an appropriate $SMON$ - IIM learning $\mathcal{L}$.

Claim C. There is no constant bound on the number of mind changes for any IIM $WMON-TXT$ - learning the class $\mathcal{L}$.

Proof. By way of contradiction, suppose there exist an IIM M that $WMON-TXT$ -learns the class $\mathcal{L}$ with the uniform bound k on the number of mind changes. Let $i > k$ be a number of such a IIM in the numbering $\{M_i\}_{i=0,1,2,...}$. It follows from our construction, that at some moment, the language $L_{c(i,1)}$ is added to the numbering ν. It happens when M_i outputs a guess H that overgeneralizes $L_{c(i,1)}$. Thus, M_i, being a $WMON-TXT$ - IIM, can never change its mind to $L_{c(i,1)}$, if no word $w \ne \#$ appears in the input any more. Q.E.D.

Similar questions for dual-monotonic types of learning are considered in [10].

6 Monotonicity versus Limited Memory

Theorem 4 *There is a family of languages $\mathcal{L} \in MON - TXT : c$ for a constant c such that $\mathcal{L} \in SMON - TXT : g$, for a function $g \in O(n)$, and $\mathcal{L} \notin SMON - TXT : h$, for any $h \in o(n)$.*

Proof. We define the family of languages as follows. Let $\Sigma = \{0, 1, *\}$. Let "$\prec$" denote "lexicographically less than". For any two nonempty words $\alpha, \beta \in \{0, 1\}^*$ such that $\alpha \prec \beta$, we define three languages:

$$S(\alpha, \beta) = \{\alpha * \beta, \alpha, \beta\}$$
$$R(\alpha, \beta) = \{\alpha * \beta, \alpha * \beta * 0, \alpha\}$$
$$T(\alpha, \beta) = \{\alpha * \beta, \alpha * \beta * 1, \beta\}.$$

One can easily define a (natural) recursive numbering for the given family. A $MON - TXT$ - style IIM M works on any text t as follows. If the word $\alpha * \beta$ appears in the input before any word $\alpha * \beta * 0$ or $\alpha * \beta * 1$, then it outputs the hypothesis $S(\alpha, \beta)$. If then $\alpha * \beta * 0$ or $\alpha * \beta * 1$ appears, M produces $R(\alpha, \beta)$ or $T(\alpha, \beta)$, respectively and terminates. Note that M does not need long term memory at all.

On the other hand, a $SMON - TXT$ - style IIM K has to remember at least one of the words α or β if they appear before any of the words $\alpha*\beta, \alpha*\beta*0, \alpha*\beta*1$. If $\alpha * \beta$ appears in the input first, the IIM K, contrary to the above IIM M, outputs nothing yet. Now if a word $\alpha \in \{0, 1\}^*$ appears in the input, K saves it in long term memory. If a different word β appears in the input, K outputs the language $S(\alpha, \beta)$ as its hypothesis if $\alpha \prec \beta$, and $S(\beta, \alpha)$, otherwise, and terminates (note that neither R, nor T can be the target language now). If any word containing two asterisks, say, $\beta * \alpha * 1$ appears in the input, K outputs the language $T(\beta, \alpha)$ (R in case of $\beta * \alpha * 0$) and terminates. Thus, K infers any language in the given family in $SMON$ sense (since it never changes its mind; note that then our class $\mathcal{L}$ is in FIN-TXT:n, that is, it is learnable with no mind changes).

Now we show that any $SMON$ IIM M for $\mathcal{L}$ needs at least linear memory. By way of contradiction, assume that there is a function $g(n) \in o(n)$ such that for almost all n, the long term memory used by M on inputs t_x of the size $|t_x| = n$ is bounded by $g(n)$. Then there exist long enough distinct words $\alpha, \beta \in \{0, 1\}^*$ and initial fragments of texts t_x and t'_y with ranges $\mathbf{range}(t_x) = \alpha$ and $\mathbf{range}(t'_y) = \beta$ such that the configurations of M just after updating t_x and t'_y, respectively, are equal. Assume that $\alpha \prec \beta$. Now, suppose M has been fed t_x. Feed M by the input

$$\beta, \alpha * \beta, \#, \#, ...$$

until it produces the hypothesis $S(\alpha, \beta)$ (if it does not then it fails to learn the language $S(\alpha, \beta)$). Observe that then M has to produce the hypothesis $S(\alpha, \beta)$ on the input $t'_y, \beta, \alpha * \beta, \#, \#, ...$ as well. When it happens, add to the input the word $\alpha * \beta * 1$. Then M has to output $T(\alpha, \beta)$, therefore, failing to be $SMON$ - IIM. Q.E.D.

A different example witnessing the tradeoff proved in the above theorem is the family consisting of the languages $\{x, x * 1\}, \{x, y\}$, where x is any binary word containing at least one letter 0 and y is the word $111...1$ of the length $|x|$. A $MON - TXT$ - learner, being fed a word x, outputs the hypothesis $\{x, 111...1\}$ with $111...1$ of the length $|x|$. If the word $x * 1$ appears on the input, the learner changes its mind to $\{x, x * 1\}$. A constant long term memory is obviously enough to accomplish this strategy: the idea is that the leaner can retrieve x from $x * 1$ (he cannot do it, given a word $111...1$, because this word corresponds to a large set of possible x-s; this reason forces the learner, fed x, to choose $\{x, 111...1\}$ as the first hypothesis).

Our next result witnesses a bit weaker trade off between $WMON$ and MON.

Theorem 5 *For any slowly monotonically increasing function $g(n) \in O(n)$, there is an indexed family of languages $\mathcal{L} \in WMON - TXT : g$ such that $\mathcal{L} \in MON - TXT : g$, for a function $g \in O(n)$, and $\mathcal{L} \notin MON - TXT : h$, for any $h \in o(n)$.*

Proof. Let $r = g(m)$ for some m and r. For any word $\gamma = \alpha_1 * \alpha_2 * ... * \alpha_r$ where all $\alpha_i \in \{0, 1\}^*$ and $|\alpha_i| \geq m$, and all α_i are pairwise distinct let $S(\gamma)$ denote the set of all words $\alpha_{i_1} * \alpha_{i_2} * ... * \alpha_{i_s}$ such that $i_1, i_2, ..., i_s \in 1, 2, ..., r, i_1 < i_2 < ... < i_s$, and $i_1, i_2, ..., i_s \neq 1, 2, ..., r - 1$. One can easily define a natural recursive numbering $\mathcal{L}$ for all these languages.

The $WMON - TXT$ IIM M for the given family holds in the long term memory the length of the longest input word seen so far. If a longer word $\alpha_1 * \alpha_2 * ... * \alpha_r$ appears, M produces the number for the language $S(\alpha_1 * \alpha_2 * ... * \alpha_r)$.

Any $MON - TXT$ - style IIM M has to hold the longest word (rather than its length) seen so far in the long term memory. Suppose M is holding in the long term memory a word β. If a longer word $\gamma = \alpha_1 * \alpha_2 * ... * \alpha_j$ appears in the input, then there are two cases. If β is an initial fragment of γ and γ contains exactly one more star than β then we ignore this γ. Otherwise, M outputs the hypothesis $S(\gamma)$, and stores γ in the long term memory. The IIM we have described certainly uses a linear long term memory.

Suppose now that there is an IIM M that $MON - TXT$ - learns the given family of languages with long term memory bounded by a recursive function $g(n) \in o(n)$. Note that there exists a constant c such that for any sufficiently large n the number of pairwise different words γ defining languages $S(\gamma)$ is at least 2^{cn}. Then there exist sufficiently long distinct words $\gamma = \alpha_1 * \alpha_2 * ... * \alpha_r$ and $\gamma' = \alpha'_1 * \alpha'_2 * ... * \alpha'_s$, and initial fragments t_x and t'_y with ranges $\text{range}(t_x) = \{\gamma\}$ and $\text{range}(t'_y) = \{\gamma'\}$ such that the configurations of M after reading t_x and t'_y are equal. We actually can assume that γ and γ' differ only on the last subword α_r. Consider the word $\delta = \gamma * \alpha'_r$, where α'_r is the last subword α in γ'. It is quite obvious that $S(\delta)$ contains all words in $(S(\gamma) \setminus \{\gamma\}) \bigcup \{\gamma'\}$, but does not contain γ.

Assume now that M has been fed t_x. Consider the set $T = S(\gamma) \setminus \{\gamma\}$. Feed M from this point on the elements of T. As the $\text{range}(t) = S(\gamma)$ for this text t, there is an extension t_z of t_x such that M outputs $S(\gamma)$ on t_z. Then M outputs

$S(\gamma)$ on some input t'_v with the **range**$(t'_v) = \{\gamma'\} \bigcup (S(\gamma) \setminus \{\gamma\})$. Now, let $S(\delta)$ be a language that contains $\gamma', S(\gamma) \setminus \{\gamma\}$, but not γ. Extend the input t'_v by elements of $S(\delta)$. Then M has to output $S(\delta)$ on some extension t'_u of t'_v. Now take a language $S(\delta')$ that contains $S(\delta)$ and γ. Extend t'_u by the elements in $S(\delta')$. M must output the hypothesis $S(\delta')$ on some extension t'_w of t'_u. However, this violates the MON - condition. Q.E.D.

The question whether one can gain in long term memory weakening $WMON$ requirement to LIM is solved in [10].

7 Dual-Monotonicity versus Limited Memory

Theorem 6 *There is an indexed family of languages $\mathcal{L} \in MON^d - TXT : c$ for some constant c such that $\mathcal{L} \in SMON^d - TXT : f$, for a function $f \in O(n)$, and $\mathcal{L} \notin SMON^d - TXT : g$, for any $g \in o(n)$.*

Proof. We use the family from the theorem 4. Since this family is in $FIN - TXT : n$, it is in $SMON^d - TXT : n$ as well. The IIM in the proof of theorem 4 that $MON - TXT$-learns the languages in this family is also $MON^d - TXT$ IIM. It remains to show that $\mathcal{L} \notin SMON^d - TXT : g$ for any $g \in o(n)$. The proof of this is similar to that of $\mathcal{L} \notin SMON - TXT : g$ in the proof of theorem 4. Q.E.D.

Theorem 7 *There is an indexed family of languages $\mathcal{L} \in WMON^d - TXT : c$ for some constant c such that $\mathcal{L} \in MON^d - TXT : f$ for some $f \in O(n)$, and $\mathcal{L} \notin MON^d - TXT : g$, for any $g \in o(n)$.*

Proof. We slightly modify the family in the proof of theorem 4. Namely, we add to the alphabet the symbol 2. Now, we let $P = \{2\}$ and for any $\alpha, \beta \in \{0, 1\}^*$ such that $\alpha \prec \beta$ in the lexicographic order,

$$S(\alpha, \beta) = \{2, \alpha * \beta, \alpha, \beta\}$$
$$R(\alpha, \beta) = \{2, \alpha * \beta, \alpha * \beta * 0, \alpha\}$$
$$T(\alpha, \beta) = \{2, \alpha * \beta * 1, \alpha\}.$$

The family $\mathcal{L}$ consists of all languagess P, S, R, T.

First we define an IIM M that $WMON^d - TXT$-learns $\mathcal{L}$. If any word different from 2 appears in the input, the IIM M simulates the MON-machine in the proof of theorem 1. If the word 2 appears first, it outputs the hypothesis P. One can easily check that this IIM is $WMON^d$-style and requires at most constant long term memory.

The MON^d IIM K operates as follows. If the word 2 appears in the input first, it outputs the hypothesis P. If a different word appears first, or more words appear in the input, it simulates the $SMON$ IIM in the proof of the theorem 1.

Suppose now that there exists a MON^d IIM F that $MON^d - TXT$-learns $\mathcal{L}$ with less than linear long term memory. Feed this machine the input 2,2,2,... till the moment when it outputs the guess P (if it does not happen then F cannot learn the family). When it happens, simulate the corresponding piece of the proof of theorem 4 and get the contradiction: F cannot be a $MON^d - TXT$-IIM. Q.E.D.

8 Conclusion

In the first part we trade monotonicity versus mind changes. Our approach to learning in this part is most general: we put constraints neither on the families of languages to be learned, nor on hypotheses spaces. In particular, our nonlearnability results imply nonlearnability in any recursively enumerable hypotheses space. Similar results for learning indexed families of recursive languages were obtained in [11]. In the second part, all the families witnessing trade offs for learning with limited memory are indexed families of recursive languages, thus solving the problem in the most strong sense.

Still, it would be interesting to explore similar problems for particular families of languages and for particular hypotheses spaces. For example, changing hypotheses space, one might expect considerable gain in memory and (or) in mind changes, even in conditions of stronger monotonicity requirements.

The technique used for trading monotonicity versus mind changes is general: it is based on either direct diagonalization, or the recursion theorem. The results for limited memory are of a different nature: the ideas of examples witnessing trade offs are based on informal reasoning, rather than on definite techniques. A more general technique for solving problems of this sort is elaborated in [10].

It would be interesting also to explore how, for any of monotonicity and dual-monotonicity types, sublinear bound on the long term memory affects the short memory to be used (a similar problem is still open for learning recursive functions, cf [5]).

9 Acknowledgements

The author is thankful to T. Zeugmann, J. Case, S. Mandayam, R. Wiehagen, J. Foster and F. Stephan for helpful duscussions and remarks.

References

1. ANGLUIN, D. (1980), Inductive inference of formal languages from positive data, *Information and Control* 45, pp. 117 - 135.

2. ANGLUIN, D., AND SMITH, C.H. (1983), Inductive inference: theory and methods, *Computing Surveys* 15, pp. 237 - 269.

3. ANGLUIN, D., AND SMITH, C.H. (1987), Formal inductive inference, *in* "Encyclopedia of Artificial Intelligence" (St.C. Shapiro, Ed.), Vol. 1, pp. 409 - 418, Wiley-Interscience Publication, New York.

4. BRAINE, M.D.S. (1971), On the types of models of the internalization of grammars, *in* "The Ontogenesis of Grammar" (D.I.Slobin, Ed.), pp. 153-186, Academic Press.

5. FREIVALDS, R., KINBER E., AND SMITH, C.H. (1993), On the impact of forgetting on learning machines, *in* "Proceedings 6th Annual ACM Conference on Computational Learning Theory", Santa Cruz, July 1993, pp. 165-174.

6. GOLD, E.M. (1967), Language identification in the limit, *Information and Control* 10, pp. 447 - 474.

7. JAIN, S., AND SHARMA, A. (1994), On monotonic strategies for learning r.e. languages, Proc. of ALT'94.

8. JANTKE, K.P. (1991) Monotonic and non-monotonic inductive inference, *New Generation Computing* 8, pp. 349 - 360.

9. KAPUR, S. (1992), Monotonic language learning, *in* "Proceedings 3rd Workshop on Algorithmic Learning Theory," October 1992, Tokyo, JSAI, pp. 147 - 158.

10. KINBER, E., AND STEPHAN, F. (1994), Learning languages from texts: mind changes, limited memory and monotonicity, submitted for publication.

11. LANGE, S., AND ZEUGMANN, T. (1994), A guided tour across the boundaries of learning recursive languages, to appear in *Lecture Notes in Artificial Intelligence*, Klaus P. Jantke, ed.

12. LANGE, S., AND ZEUGMANN, T. (1993), Learning recursive languages with bounded mind changes, *International Journal of Foundations of Computer Science*, 8, No. 2, pp. 157-178.

13. LANGE, S., AND ZEUGMANN, T. (1993a), Types of monotonic language learning and their characterization, *in* "Proceedings 5th Annual ACM Conference on Computational Learning Theory," Pittsburgh, July 1992, pp. 377-390, ACM Press, New York.

14. LANGE, S., ZEUGMANN, T., AND KAPUR, S. (1994), Class preserving monotonic and dual monotonic learning, *Theoretical Computer Science*, to appear.

15. MUKOUCHI, Y. (1992), Inductive inference with bounded mind changes, *in* "Proceedings 3rd Workshop on Algorithmic Learning Theory", Tokyo, October 1992, JSAI, pp. 125-134.

16. OSHERSON, D., STOB, M., AND WEINSTEIN, S. (1986), "Systems that Learn, An Introduction to Learning Theory for Cognitive and Computer Scientists," MIT-Press, Cambridge, Massachusetts.

17. WEXLER, K., AND CULICOVER, P.W., (1980), Formal principles of language acquisition. The MIT-Press, Cambridge, Massachusets.

Learning Concatenations of Locally Testable Languages from Positive Data

Satoshi Kobayashi   Takashi Yokomori
Department of Computer Science and Information Mathematics
The University of Electro-Communications

1-5-1, Chofugaoka, Chofu, Tokyo 182, Japan
e-mail:{satoshi,yokomori}@cs.uec.ac.jp

Abstract

This paper introduces the class of concatenations of locally testable languages and its subclasses, and presents some results on the learnability of the classes from positive data. We first establish several relationships among the language classes introduced, and give a sufficient condition for a concatenation operation to preserve finite elasticity of a language class C. Then we show that, for each k, the class $CLT^{\leq k}$, a subclass of concatenations of locally testable languages, is identifiable in the limit from positive data. Further, we introduce a notion of *local parsability*, and define a class (k, l)-$CLTS$, which is a subclass of the class of concatenations of strictly locally testable languages. Then, for each $k, l \geq 1$, (k, l)-$CLTS$ is proved to be identifiable in the limit from positive data using reversible automata with the conjectures updated in polynomial time. Some possible applications of this result are also briefly discussed.

1   Introduction

Inductive inference is a process of acquiring a concept from its examples. This process was formulated by Gold as a process of identifying a target concept in the limit, which is called Gold's idetification in the limit [Gol67]. He also showed that *a superfinite class*, i.e., a class which contains all finite concepts and at least one infinite concept, is not identifiable in the limit from positive data only, which was shocking to us because it leads us to the negative result on the learnability of the class of regular languages from positive data.

On the other hand, we have also known some interesting classes of languages, k-reversible languages [Ang82], pattern languages [Ang80], etc., which are identifiable in the limit from positive data. However, as is mentioned in [Ang82], further research on the learnability from positive data for subclasses of regular languages remains open to be studied. In particular, [Ang82] refers to a possibility of close relationships between *noncounting languages* and *reversible languages*, and suggests that a certain synthetic approach to learning these two language classes might give some useful results for analyzing subclasses of regular languages learnable from positive data. Recently, in [Yok90], Yokomori has shown results on the learnability of the class of strictly locally testable languages from positive data and presents an interesting relationship between strictly k-testable languages and $(k+1)$-reversible languages.

This paper introduces some subclasses of noncounting languages, and investigates relationships among those classes and the class of reversible languages. Further, we present some learnability results on the classes. In section 2, we introduce the class of concatenations of locally testable languages $CLTS$ and its subclasses, and then we compare them with the class of reversible languages in section 3. Section 4 presents theoretical results on the learnability of $CLTS$ and its subclasses. Especially we show that the class (k,l)-$CLTS$, which is a subclass of $CLTS$ with *local parsability*, is identifiable in the limit using $(k+2l)$-reversible automata with the conjectures updated in polynomial time. Some possible applications of the results are also briefly discussed.

2 Concatenations of Locally Testable Languages

Let Σ be a finite alphabet and Σ^* be the set of all finite length strings over Σ. Let Σ^k be the set of all strings over Σ of length k. We denote the null string by λ. Σ^+ is defined as $\Sigma^* - \lambda$. The length of a string $w \in \Sigma^*$ is denoted by $|w|$. Please do not confuse it with the notation $|S|$ for a set S, which represents the cardinality of S. A *language* is a subset of Σ^*. In this section, we consider only non-null languages. Therefore, in this section, we assume that a language over Σ is a subset of Σ^+. A concatenation of languages, $L_1 \cdot L_2$, is defined as a set of strings $\{w_1 w_2 \mid w_1 \in L_1, w_2 \in L_2\}$. $L_k(w)$ and $R_k(w)$ are defined as the k-length prefix and k-length suffix of w, respectively. These notations are defined only when w has length k or more. Further, let $I_k(w)$ be the set of all interior substrings of length k. Note that, for any string w with $|w| \leq k+1$, it holds that $I_k(w) = \emptyset$, where $\emptyset$ denotes an empty set.

Then, we define the class of locally testable languages as follows [MP71]. Let k be a positive integer. A language L over Σ is k-*testable* iff for all strings, w_1, w_2, of length k or more, if $L_k(w_1) = L_k(w_2)$, $R_k(w_1) = R_k(w_2)$ and $I_k(w_1) = I_k(w_2)$, then either w_1 and w_2 are in L or neither are. A language L is *locally testable* iff L is k-testable for some positive integer k. The class of k-testable languages and the class of locally testable languages are denoted by $LT^{=k}$ and LT, respectively. We denote $\cup_{i \leq k} LT^{=i}$ by $LT^{\leq k}$.

The definition of k-testable languages says nothing about strings of length less than k. So, a k-testable language may include any subset of strings of length less than k.

For any positive integer k, a language L over Σ is said to be *strictly k-testable* iff there exist finite sets A, B, and C such that $A, B, C \subseteq \Sigma^k$, and for any string w with $|w| \geq k$, $w \in L$ iff $L_k(w) \in A$, $R_k(w) \in B$, and $I_k(w) \subseteq C$. Here,

$< A, B, C >$ is called *a triple for L* and denoted by $triple(L)$. A language L is *strictly locally testable* iff L is strictly k-testable for some positive integer k. We denote the class of strictly k-testable languages and the class of strictly locally testable languages by $LTS^{=k}$ and LTS, respectively. The class $\cup_{i \leq k} LTS^{=i}$ is denoted by $LTS^{\leq k}$.

Theorem 1 [MP71]

(1) The class of locally testable languages (k-testable languages) is closed under the Boolean operations.

(2) The class of strictly locally testable languages (strictly k-testable languages) is closed under intersection.

(3) The class of locally testable languages (k-testable languages) is the closure of that of strictly locally testable languages (strictly k-testable languages) under the Boolean operations.

Example 1 Let us consider a strictly 2-testable language L over $\Sigma = \{a, b\}$, for which $< \{aa\}, \{bb\}, \{aa, ab, bb\} >$ is a triple. This language is also denoted by a regualr exssression aaa^*bbb^*. Here we can easily show that L is a strictly 3-testable language for which $< \{aaa, aab\}, \{bbb, abb\}, \{aaa, aab, abb, bbb\} >$ is a triple. At first thought, it seems to hold that for any positive integer k, $LTS^{=k}$ and $LT^{=k}$ are contained in $LTS^{=k+1}$ and $LT^{=k+1}$, respectively. However, this is not the case. For example, let us consider a strictly k-testable language $L' = \{a^k, a^{k+1}\}$ for which $< \{a^k\}, \{a^k\}, \emptyset >$ is a triple. Then, it holds that L' is not in $LT^{=k+1}$ because for $w_1 = a^{k+1} \in L'$ and $w_2 = a^{k+2} \notin L'$, we have $L_{k+1}(w_1) = L_{k+1}(w_2)$, $R_{k+1}(w_1) = R_{k+1}(w_2)$, and $I_{k+1}(w_1) = I_{k+1}(w_2)(= \emptyset)$. Therefore, in general it holds that $LTS^{=k} \not\subseteq LT^{=k+1}$. Further, by Theorem 1, we have $LT^{=k} \not\subseteq LT^{=k+1}$ and $LTS^{=k} \not\subseteq LTS^{=k+1}$. $\square$

Here, let us consider a slightly different definition of locally testable language as follows. In this setting, we say that a language L is k-testable iff for all strings, w_1, w_2, of length $\underline{k+1}$ or more, if $L_k(w_1) = L_k(w_2)$, $R_k(w_1) = R_k(w_2)$ and $I_k(w_1) = I_k(w_2)$, then either w_1 and w_2 are in L or neither are. The difference between this definition and the original one is underlined. In this definition, we can prove that $LT^{=k}$ is contained in $LT^{=k+1}$ in the following manner.

Let L be a language in $LT^{=k}$ and w_1, w_2 be strings of length $k+2$ or more such that $L_{k+1}(w_1) = L_{k+1}(w_2)$, $R_{k+1}(w_1) = R_{k+1}(w_2)$, and $I_{k+1}(w_1) = I_{k+1}(w_2)$. It suffices to show $w_1 \in L$ iff $w_2 \in L$.

First, we prove $L_k(w_1) = L_k(w_2)$, $R_k(w_1) = R_k(w_2)$ and $I_k(w_1) = \dot{I}_k(w_2)$. It is easy to see $L_k(w_1) = L_k(w_2)$ and $R_k(w_1) = R_k(w_2)$. For proving $I_k(w_1) = I_k(w_2)$, we consider the next two cases.

In case $\mid w_1 \mid \geq k + 3$, $I_{k+1}(w_1) = I_{k+1}(w_2)$ immediately implies $I_k(w_1) = I_k(w_2)$.

In case $\mid w_1 \mid = k + 2$, we have $I_{k+1}(w_2) = I_{k+1}(w_1) = \emptyset$. Therefore, $\mid w_2 \mid = k + 2$ holds. Let aw be $L_{k+1}(w_1)(=L_{k+1}(w_2))$, where $a \in \Sigma$ and $w \in \Sigma^*$. Then we have $I_k(w_1) = \{w\} = I_k(w_2)$.

Hence, in any case, we have $I_k(w_1) = I_k(w_2)$.

Therefore, it holds that $w_1 \in L$ iff $w_2 \in L$, since $L \in LT^{=k}$. This implies that L is a $(k+1)$-testable language.

As disscussed above, if we use the new definition, then we have interesting inclusion properties among the classes of k-testable languages. However, in the rest of the paper, we restrict the attention to the original definition of locally testable languages.

Let us consider the class of concatenations of locally testable languages. For any class of languages $\mathcal{C}$, we denote by $Con(\mathcal{C})$ the class of languages which is the smallest class of languages that includes $\mathcal{C}$ and is closed under concatenation. Then, by CLT, $CLT^{=k}$, $CLT^{\leq k}$, $CLTS$, $CLTS^{=k}$, and $CLTS^{\leq k}$, we denote $Con(LT)$, $Con(LT^{=k})$, $Con(LT^{\leq k})$, $Con(LTS)$, $Con(LTS^{=k})$, and $Con(LTS^{\leq k})$, respectively.

Example 2 Let us consider languages L_1 and L_2 over $\Sigma = \{a, b, c\}$, which are denoted by regular expressions $(a + b)(a + b)^*$ and $(b + c)(b + c)^*$, respectively. It is easy to see that L_1 and L_2 are strictly 1-testable languages such that $triple(L_1) = < \{a,b\}, \{a,b\}, \{a,b\} >$, $triple(L_2) = < \{b,c\}, \{b,c\}, \{b,c\} >$. Let $L_3 = L_1 \cup L_2$. Then, by Theorem 1, we have that L_3 is 1-testable, so $L_3 \in LT$. Please note that L_3 is k-testable for any positive integer k since both L_1 and L_2 are strictly k-testable for any positive integer k.

However, we can prove that $L_3 \notin CLTS$. Let us assume $L_3 \in CLTS$. Then there exist some positive integer n and a sequence of strictly locally testable languages $S_1, S_2, ..., S_n$ such that $L_3 = S_1 \cdot S_2 \cdots S_n$ and S_i is strictly k_i-testable for some positive integer k_i. Here we have $n = 1$ since $a \in L_3$. (Recall we consider only non-null languages.) Let $< A, B, C >$ be a triple for $S_1 = L_3$. Then, since $a^{k_1+1}b^{k_1+1} \in L_3$ and $b^{k_1+1}c^{k_1+1} \in L_3$, it holds that $a^{k_1}, b^{k_1} \in A$, $b^{k_1}, c^{k_1} \in B$, and $0 \leq \forall j \leq k_1 (a^{k_1-j}b^j \in C \wedge b^{k_1-j}c^j \in C)$. Therefore, $a^{k_1}b^{k_1}c^{k_1} \in L_3$, which is a contradiction.

Let $L_4 = L_1 \cdot L_2 \cdot L_1$. Then, L_4 is in $CLTS$ by its definition. Please note that L_4 is in $CLTS^{=k}$ for any positive integer k. However, we can prove $L_4 \notin LT$ as follows.

Let us assume that $L_4 \in LT$. Then there exists some positive integer k such that L_4 is k-testable. Here we have $w_1 = a^{k+1}ca^k \in L_4$, $w_2 = a^k ca^k ca^k \notin L_4$. It is easy to see that $L_k(w_1) = L_k(w_2)$, $R_k(w_1) = R_k(w_2)$, and $I_k(w_1) = I_k(w_2)$ hold. This is a contradiction. $\square$

From the discussion above, we have the next lemma.

Lemma 1 (1) There exists a language L such that, for any positive integer k, $L \in LT^{=k}$ and $L \notin CLTS$.

(2) There exists a language L such that, for any positive integer k, $L \in CLTS^{=k}$ and $L \notin LT$.

Then, we have the followings.

Theorem 2 (1) $CLTS$, $CLTS^{=k}$, and $CLTS^{\leq k}$ are incomparable to LT.

(2) $CLTS(CLTS^{=k}, CLTS^{\leq k})$ properly includes $LTS(LTS^{=k}, LTS^{\leq k}$, respectively).

(3) $LT(LT^{=k}, LT^{\leq k})$ properly includes $LTS(LTS^{=k}, LTS^{\leq k}$, respectively).

(4) $CLT(CLT^{=k}, CLT^{\leq k})$ properly includes $LT(LT^{=k}, LT^{\leq k}$, respectively).

(5) $CLT(CLT^{=k}, CLT^{\leq k})$ properly includes $CLTS(CLTS^{=k}, CLTS^{\leq k}$, respectively).

In this paper, we define noncounting languages by using the notion of **locally testable languages**. The class NC of *noncounting languages* is defined as the smallest class of languages that contains LT and is closed under the Boolean operations and concatenation. Therefore, all of the language classes introduced in this section are subclasses of NC.

3   Comparison with Reversible Languages

In this section, we compare the classes of languages introduced in section 2, with the class of reversible languages which is identifiable in the limit from positive data [Ang82].

Here we give the definition of reversible languages based on the language-theoretic characterization [Ang82]. Let k be a non-negative integer. A language L is *k-reversible* iff whenever u_1vw and u_2vw are in L and $|\ v\ | = k$, it holds that for any $x \in \Sigma^*$, $u_1vx \in L$ iff $u_2vx \in L$. (In case $k = 0$, we say L is *zero-reversible* rather than *0-reversible*.) A language L is said to be *reversible* iff L is k-reversible for some non-negative integer k. The class of k-reversible languages and the class of reversible languages are denoted by $Rev(k)$ and Rev, respectively.

Then we have the following.

Lemma 2 [Ang82] For any non-negative integer k, $Rev(k)$ is properly contained in $Rev(k + 1)$.

Example 3 The language denoted by a regular expression $(bb)^+$ is zero-reversible. However, this language is not contained in NC. (cf. [MP71], p.6)

Let L_1 and L_2 be strictly 1-testable languages such that $triple(L_1) = < \{a\}, \{a\}, \{a\} >$ and $triple(L_2) = < \{c\}, \{c\}, \{a\} >$. Then, by the definition, $L_3 = L_1 \cdot L_2 \in CLTS$ holds. Please note that L_3 is in $CLTS^{=k}$ for any positive integer k. However, we can prove that $L_3 \notin Rev$ as follows.

Let us assume that L_3 is k-reversible for some non-negative integer k. Then, $aa^kc \in L_3$, $aca^kc \in L_3$, and $aa^kcac \in L_3$ hold. Therefore, by the definition of k-reversible language, we have that $aca^kcac \in L_3$, which is a contradiction.

Let L_4 and L_5 be strictly 1-testable languages such that $triple(L_4) = < \{a\}, \{a, b\}, \{a\} >$ and $triple(L_5) = < \{c\}, \{a\}, \{a\} >$. Then $L_6 = L_4 \cup L_5$ is in LT. Please note that L_6 is k-testable for any positive integer k. We can prove that L_6 is not in Rev.

Let us assume that L_6 is k-reversible for some non-negative integer k. Then, $a(a)^k a \in L_6$, $c(a)^k a \in L_6$, and $a(a)^k b \in L_6$ hold. Therefore, by the definition of k-reversible language, we have that $c(a)^k b \in L_6$, which is a contradiction. □

Using the discussion above, we have the followings.

Lemma 3 (1) There exists a language L such that, for any positive integer k, $L \in CLTS^{=k}$, and $L \notin Rev$.

(2) There exists a language L such that, for any positive integer k, $L \in LT^{=k}$, and $L \notin Rev$.

Further, the next fact is proved.

Lemma 4 [Yok90] $LTS^{=k}$ is properly contained in $Rev(k+1)$.

Therefore, we have the followings.

Theorem 3 (1) The following classes are incomparable to Rev.
$NC, LT, LT^{=k}, LT^{\leq k}, CLTS, CLTS^{=k}, CLTS^{\leq k}, CLT, CLT^{=k}$, and $CLT^{\leq k}$

(2) LTS is properly contained in Rev.

A part of relationships among the classes of languages introduced in this paper is summarized in Figure 1.

4 Learnability Results

4.1 Definitions

Here we briefly introduce some fundamental definitions. For more details, please refer to [Gol67], [BB75], [Ang80], and [LZ93].

Let C be a class of non-empty languages over a fixed alphabet Σ. Then, we consider *a class of representations* $\mathcal{R}$ for C with the following properties.

1. $\mathcal{R}$ is a recursively enumerable language (over some fixed alphabet).

2. For all $L \in C$, there exists $r \in \mathcal{R}$ such that r represents L (denoted by $L(r) = L$).

3. There exists a recursive function f such that for all $r \in \mathcal{R}$ and $w \in \Sigma^*$,

$$f(r, w) = \begin{cases} 1 & \text{if } w \in L(r) \\ 0 & \text{otherwise} \end{cases}$$

We say that a class of representation $\mathcal{R}$ is *class preserving with respect to* C iff $C = \{L(r) \mid r \in \mathcal{R}\}$ holds. A class of representation $\mathcal{R}$ is said to be *class comprising with respect to* C iff $C \subseteq \{L(r) \mid r \in \mathcal{R}\}$ holds.(cf.[LZ93]))

For a given $L \in C$, *a positive presentation of* L is any infinite sequence $w_1, w_2, w_3, ...$ of strings such that $\forall w \in L \; \exists i (w = w_i)$ and $\forall i (w_i \in L)$. Let L be a given language. We say that an algorithm A *identifies* L *in the limit from positive data using* $\mathcal{R}$ iff for any positive presentation of L, the infinite sequence, $r_1, r_2, r_3, ...$, of representations in $\mathcal{R}$ produced by A converges to a representation r such that $L = L(r)$. A class C of languages is said to be *identifiable in the limit from positive data using* $\mathcal{R}$ iff there exists an algorithm A such that A identifies every language in C in the limit from positive data using $\mathcal{R}$.

A learning algorithm A is said to be *responsive on* C iff for any $L \in C$ and any positive presentation of L, A always outputs some conjecture between any consecutive input requests from A. An algorithm A *consistently identifies* C *in the limit from positive data using* $\mathcal{R}$ iff A identifies C in the limit from positive data using $\mathcal{R}$ and for any representation r_i produced by A, the given set of strings $\{w_1, w_2, ..., w_i\}$ is contained in $L(r_i)$. An algorithm A *conservatively identifies* C *in the limit from positive data using* $\mathcal{R}$ iff A identifies C in the limit from positive data using $\mathcal{R}$ and for any output r_i ($i \geq 2$) of A, it holds that, if $L(r_{i-1})$ contains the set of given strings $\{w_1, ..., w_i\}$, then $r_i = r_{i-1}$. A class C of languages is said to be *identifiable in the limit from positive data using* $\mathcal{R}$ *with the conjectures updated in polynomial time* iff there exists some algorithm A which is *responsive* on C and *consistently* and *conservatively* identifies C in the limit from positive data using $\mathcal{R}$ with the property that the time used by A for updating conjectures is bounded by some polynomial with respect to the size of given examples up to that point, i.e. $|w_1| + \cdots + |w_i|$.

It is often the case that a class of representations $\mathcal{R}$ with class preserving property may be encoded by the set of positive integers so that each integer i corresponds to the ith representation in $\mathcal{R}$. In this case, by L_i, we denote the language which is represented by an integer i, and an infinite sequence $L_1, L_2, L_3, ...$ is called *an indexed family of recursive languages*, or *an indexed family* for short.[Ang80]

Note : *In the sequel, if a representation class* $\mathcal{R}$ *is not specified, we always assume that some appropriate enumerable class of representations with class preserving property is attached to a target concept class.*

4.2 Learnability of $CLT^{\leq k}$ from Positive Data

Let C be an indexed family. We say C has *finite thickness* iff for any string $w \in \Sigma^*$, the number of languages in C which contain w is finite. Angluin showed that finite thickness is a sufficient condition for learnability from positive data [Ang80]. Wright introduced another sufficient condition, called *finite elasticity*, for learnability from positive data, originaly in [Wri89], and correctly in [MSW90].

An indexed family C of languages has *infinite elasticity* iff there exist an infinite sequence $w_0, w_1, w_2, ...$ of strings and an infinite sequence $L_1, L_2, ...$ of languages in C such that, for any $k \geq 1$, $\{w_0, w_1, ..., w_{k-1}\} \subseteq L_k$ and $w_k \notin L_k$ hold. A class C has *finite elasticity* iff C does not have infinite elasticity.

As proved in [Wri89], it holds that, if a class C has finite thickness, then C has finite elasticity.

Theorem 4 [Wri89] An indexed family C is identifiable in the limit from positive data if C has finite elasticity.

Since the number of k-testable languages on a *fixed* finite alphabet is finite, we immediately obtain the following.

Lemma 5 $LT^{\leq k}$ has finite thickness, and therefore, finite elasticity.

By Theorem 4 and Lemma 5, we have the following.

Theorem 5 $LT^{\leq k}$ is identifiable in the limit from positive data.

Now, for an indexed family C, let us consider the learnability of $Con(C)$ from positive data. The next result is useful for proving the learnability of $Con(C)$ from positive data, when C has finite elasticity.

Lemma 6 Let us consider an indexed family C with the following properties.

(C1) For any language L in the class, if $\lambda \in L$, then $L = \{\lambda\}$.

(C2) The class has finite elasticity.

Then, $Con(C)$ also satisfies the conditions (C1) and (C2).

Proof
Let us consider a language $L_1 \cdots L_n$ in $Con(C)$ which contains a null-string. Then, each L_i must contain a null-string. From the condition (C1) of C, since each $L_i = \{\lambda\}$, we have $L_1 \cdots L_n = \{\lambda\}$. Therefore, $Con(C)$ satisfies the condition (C1).

The proof for the claim that $Con(C)$ satisfies the condition (C2) is as follows.

Let us assume that $Con(C)$ has infinite elasticity. Then there exist infinite sequences, $w_0, w_1, w_2 ...$, of strings and $L_1, L_2, ...$ of languages in $Con(C)$ such that $\{w_0, w_1, ..., w_{k-1}\} \subseteq L_k$ and $w_k \notin L_k$ for any positive integer k. For any L_k ($k \geq 1$), there is a sequence $L_{k,1}, L_{k,2}, ..., L_{k,l(k)}$ of languages in C such that $L_k = L_{k,1} \cdot L_{k,2} \cdots L_{k,l(k)}$. Here we may assume that $\forall k \geq 1$, $1 \leq \forall i \leq l(k)$ ($\lambda \notin L_{k,i}$), since, otherwise, $L_{k,i} = \{\lambda\}$ by the condition (C1) of C, and therefore, $L_{k,i}$ can be removed from the sequence.

Then we construct the following three infinite sequences: $k_0, k_1, k_2, ...$ of non-negative integers, $N_0, N_1, N_2, ...$ of sets of non-negative integers, and $t_{k_0}, t_{k_1}, t_{k_2}, ...$ of tuples of strings, where by l_i we denote the length of t_{k_i}. The construction is based on the recursive procedure bellow.

Initialization : $i = 0, k_0 = 0, N_{-1} =$ the set of all positive integers.

Stage i :

> For each tuple of strings $t = (s_1, s_2, ..., s_p)$ such that $w_{k_i} = s_1 s_2 ... s_p$ and $1 \leq \forall j \leq p$ $(s_j \in \Sigma^+)$,
> let $A_t = \{k \in N_{i-1} \mid l(k) = p \wedge 1 \leq \forall j \leq p \ (s_j \in L_{k,j})\}$.
>
> Find $t_{k_i} = (w_{k_i,1}, w_{k_i,2}, ..., w_{k_i,l_i})$ such that $\mid A_{t_{k_i}} \mid = \infty$.
>
> Let $N_i = A_{t_{k_i}}$ and $k_{i+1} = min\{j \in N_i\}$.
>
> Initiallize each A_t to $\emptyset$.
>
> Goto stage $i + 1$.

For each tuple $t = (s_1, s_2, ..., s_p)$ of strings, A_t represents the set of all indices i of languages L_i $(= L_{i,1} \cdot L_{i,2} \cdots L_{i,p})$ such that $s_1 \in L_{i,1}, s_2 \in L_{i,2}, ..., s_p \in L_{i,p}$.

Here we can prove, for each stage, that there exists some $A_{t_{k_i}}$ such that $\mid A_{t_{k_i}} \mid = \infty$, and it holds that $k_{i+1} > k_i$, $N_i \subseteq N_{i-1}$ and $\mid N_i \mid = \infty$.

The claim is proved by the induction on i.

Let us consider the case $i = 0$. In this case, we have for all positive integers k, $w_{k_0} = w_0 \in L_k$. Therefore, for any $k \geq 1$, there exists a tuple of strings $t_k = (s_{k,1}, s_{k,2}, ..., s_{k,l(k)})$ such that $w_{k_0} = w_0 = s_{k,1} s_{k,2} \cdots s_{k,l(k)}$ and $1 \leq \forall j \leq l(k)$ $(s_{k,j} \in L_{k,j})$. Here we have $1 \leq \forall j \leq l(k)$ $(s_{k,j} \neq \lambda)$, since $\lambda \notin L_{k,j}$. Therefore, for each k (≥ 1), there exists a tuple t such that $k \in A_t$. The number of tuples $t = (s_1, s_2, ..., s_p)$ such that $w_0 = s_1 s_2 ... s_p$ and $1 \leq \forall j \leq p$ $(s_j \in \Sigma^+)$, is finite. Hence, there exists a tuple t_{k_0} such that $\mid A_{t_{k_0}} \mid = \infty$. Therefore, we have $\mid N_0 \mid = \infty$. It is easy to see $N_0 \subseteq N_{-1}$ by the definition of N_0 and $A_{t_{k_0}}$. From $\forall j \in N_{-1}$ $(j \geq 1)$, we have $k_1 \geq 1 > 0 = k_0$. Therefore, the claim holds in case $i = 0$.

Let us assume the claim holds in case $i = n - 1$ and consider the case $i = n$. In a similar manner as in the case $i = 0$, we can prove that there exists a tuple of strings $t_{k_n} = (w_{k_n,1}, ..., w_{k_n,l_n})$ such that $\mid A_{t_{k_n}} \mid = \infty$. Therefore, we have $\mid N_n \mid = \infty$. It is sufficient to show $k_{n+1} > k_n$ and $N_n \subseteq N_{n-1}$. It is easy to see $N_n \subseteq N_{n-1}$ by the definition of N_n and $A_{t_{k_n}}$.

From $w_{k_n} \notin L_{k_n}$, we have that there is no tuples $t = (s_1, ..., s_p)$ such that $w_{k_n} = s_1 s_2 \cdots s_p, l(k_n) = p$ and $1 \leq \forall j \leq l(k_n)$ $(s_j \in L_{k_n,j})$. Therefore, for any $t = (s_1, ..., s_p)$ such that $w_{k_n} = s_1 \cdots s_p$ and $1 \leq \forall j \leq p$ $(s_j \in \Sigma^+)$, $k_n \notin A_t$ holds. Hence, we have $k_n \notin A_{t_{k_n}} = N_n$. This implies that $k_{n+1} > k_n$. Therefore the claim holds.

Next, for some infinitely many integers $k_i \geq 0$, we select a string $w_{k_i,j}.$ and a language $L_{k_i,j}.$ from $t_{k_i} = (w_{k_i,1}, w_{k_i,2}, ..., w_{k_i,l_i})$ and $L_{k_i,1}, ..., L_{k_i,l(k_i)}$, respectively, and construct an infinite sequence of strings and languages satisfying the condition of infinite elasticity. The construction is as follows.

For $1 \leq \forall j \leq \mid w_0 \mid$, let $P_j = \{k_n \mid j \leq l(k_n) \wedge w_{k_n,j} \notin L_{k_n,j}\}$.

Here, we have that $\forall k_n, 1 \leq \exists j \leq l(k_n)$ $(w_{k_n,j} \notin L_{k_n,j})$, since $w_{k_n} \notin L_{k_n}$. It also holds that, for any positive integer k, $l(k) \leq \mid w_0 \mid$, since $\forall k \geq 1$ $(w_0 \in L_k)$.

These facts imply that, for each k_n, there exists some integer j such that $1 \leq j \leq\mid w_0 \mid$ and $k_n \in P_j$. Therefore, there exists some j^* such that $\mid P_{j^*} \mid = \infty$.

By k_{p_i}, we denote the ith smallest element in P_{j^*}. Let us consider an infinite sequene of strings, $w_{k_{p_1},j^*}, w_{k_{p_2},j^*}, ...$ and an infinite sequence of languages, $L_{k_{p_1},j^*}, L_{k_{p_2},j^*}, ...$ By the relation $N_{p_1} \supseteq N_{p_2} \supseteq N_{p_3} \supseteq \cdots \supseteq N_{p_{i-1}}$, it is easy to see that $k_{p_i} \in N_{p_m}$ holds for $m = 1, 2, ..., i-1$. Therefore, we have $w_{k_{p_m},j^*} \in L_{k_{p_i},j^*}$ for $m = 1, 2, ..., i-1$ by the definition of N_{p_m} and $A_{t_{k_{p_m}}}$. Hence, $\{w_{k_{p_1},j^*}, w_{k_{p_2},j^*}, ..., w_{k_{p_{i-1}},j^*}\} \subseteq L_{k_{p_i},j^*}$ holds. On the other hand, by the definition of P_{j^*}, we have $w_{k_{p_i},j^*} \notin L_{k_{p_i},j^*}$ for any $k_{p_i} \in P_{j^*}$. These facts imply that the class C has infinite elasticity, which is a contradiction. This completes the proof. □

Example 4 Let us consider language classes $C_0 = \{\{a\}, a^*\}$ and $C_1 = \{(\lambda + a), a^*\}$ over $\Sigma = \{a\}$, both of which have finite thickness. $Con(C_0)$ has finite elasticity. However, $Con(C_1)$ does not have finite elasticity, which is because C_1 does not satisfy the condition (C1). Therefore, the condition (C1) is necessary in this sense. Please note that C_1 is identifiable in the limit from positive data but that $Con(C_1)$ is not identifiable in the limit from positive data, since there exists no *finite tell-tale*(cf. [Ang80]) for a^*. □

It was shown in [MS93] that a *fixed* finite number of language concatenations preserves finite elasticity. Here, we have proved that under a condition (C1), $Con(C)$, i.e., *arbitrary* number of language concatenations preserves finite elasticity. Note, however, that without a condition (C1), $Con(C)$ does not preserve finite elasticity of C, as shown in the example above.

Theorem 6 $CLT^{\leq k}$ and $CLTS^{\leq k}$ are identifiable in the limit from positive data.

Proof
By Lemma 5 and Lemma 6, $CLT^{\leq k}$ has finite elasticity. By Therem 2, $CLTS^{\leq k}$ has finite elasticity, too. By Theorem 4, we have the results. □

4.3 Local Parsability

We showed in the previous subsection that the class $CLT^{\leq k}$ and $CLTS^{\leq k}$ are identifiable in the limit from positive data, which does not mean the existence of efficient learning algorithms for $CLT^{\leq k}$ or $CLTS^{\leq k}$. In this subsection, we consider the problem of learning a subclass of $CLTS^{\leq k}$ from positive data with the conjectures updated in polynomial time.

The dificulties of efficient learning of $CLTS^{\leq k}$ seem to lie in the intractability of finding concatenation points of given training examples. Therefore, it would be better to impose some reasonably restrictive conditions on concatinating strictly locally testable languages for obtaining some efficiently learnable subclass of $CLTS^{\leq k}$.

In this paper, we introduce a notion called *local parsability*. This notion has some close relationships to the notion of local parsability originally defined in

[MP71], which is proposed for analyzing *code events*. Intuitively, a language L in $Con(C)$ is said to be locally parsable if we can determine concatenation points of any given string w in L by scanning w with a fixed finite length window. More formally, the notion is defined as follows.

Let k be a positive integer. A parse set of length k is a finite set of pairs of strings (p, q) such that $| p | \leq k, | q | \leq k$. Let PS be a parse set of length k. Then, for any string w in Σ^*, $N(w, PS)$ is defined as the set consisting of 0 and $| w |$, and integers i such that $\exists (p, q) \in PS \exists x, y \in \Sigma^* (w = xpqy \wedge i =| x | + | p |)$. Here, we denote the i-th smallest element of $N(w, PS)$ by j_i.

Let C be a class of languages, PS be a parse set of length k, $L_1, \cdots, L_n$ be a finite sequnce of languages in C and w be a string in $L = L_1 \cdots L_n$. Then, w is *parsable to $L_1, \cdots, L_n$ based on PS*, iff $| N(w, PS) | = n + 1$ and $\forall j_i, j_{i+1} \in N(w, PS) (sub(w, j_i + 1, j_{i+1}) \in L_i)$, where, by $sub(w, i, j)$, we denote the substring of w which starts at the ith and ends at the jth character of w. In case of $i > j$, $sub(w, i, j)$ represents λ. A language $L \in Con(C)$ is said to be *k-parsable* iff there exists a finite sequence $L_1, \cdots, L_n$ of languages in C and a parse set PS of length k such that $L = L_1 \cdots L_n$ and, for any string $w \in L_1 \cdots L_n$, w is parsable to $L_1, \cdots, L_n$ based on PS. A language $L \in Con(C)$ is said to be *locally parsable* iff L is k-parsable for some positive integer k.

The class of languages (k, l)-$CLTS$ is defined as the smallest class of languages that contains all languages $L \in CLTS^{\leq k}$ such that L is l-parsable. The class of languages $PCLTS$ is defined as the smallest class of languages that contains all languages $L \in CLTS$ such that L is locally parsable.

Example 5 Let L_1 and L_2 be strictly 1-testable languages such that $triple(L_1) = < \{a\}, \{a\}, \{a\} >$ and $triple(L_2) = < \{b\}, \{b\}, \{b\} >$. Let $L_3 = L_1 \cdot L_2 \cdot L_1$. Then we can easily prove $L_3 \in (1, 1)$-$CLTS$, since $PS = \{(a, b), (b, a)\}$ is a parse set of length 1 such that for any string $w \in L_3$, w is parsable to L_1, L_2, L_1 based on PS. Please note here that L_3 is in (k, l)-$CLTS$ for any positive integers k and l.

We can prove $L_3 \notin LT$ as follows. Let us assume $L_3 \in LT$. Then there exists some positive integer k such that L_3 is k-testable. We have $w_1 = a^{k+1} b a^k \in L_3$ and $w_2 = a^k b a^k b a^k \notin L_3$. It is easy to see that $L_k(w_1) = L_k(w_2)$, $R_k(w_1) = R_k(w_2)$ and $I_k(w_1) = I_k(w_2)$ hold, which is a contradiction. □

Therefore, we have the following.

Lemma 7 For any positive integers k and l, there exists a language L in (k, l)-$CLTS$ such that $L \notin LT$.

Please note that any language L in $LTS^{\leq k}$ is in (k, l)-$CLTS$, for any positive integer l, since any string in L is l-parsable to L based on $PS = \emptyset$.

Theorem 7 (1) $PCLTS$ and (k, l)-$CLTS$ are incomparable to LT.

(2) $PCLTS((k, l)$-$CLTS)$ properly includes $LTS(LTS^{\leq k}$, respectively).

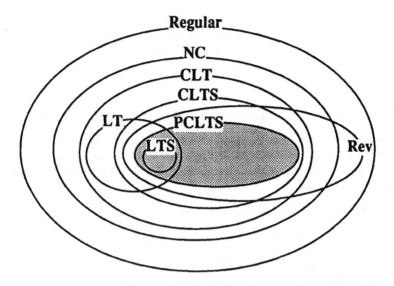

Figure 1: Relationships between subclasses of regular languages

4.4 Efficient Learning of (k,l)-$CLTS$ from Positive Data

In this subsection, we will show that (k,l)-$CLTS$ is identifiable in the limit from positive data using reversible automata with the conjectures updated in polynomial time. This proof is based on a relationship between (k,l)-$CLTS$ and $Rev(k+2l)$.

Lemma 8 Let L be any language in $LTS^{\leq k}$ and u_1, u_2, v, x, and y be any strings over Σ such that $u_1vx, u_2vx, u_1vy \in L$, and $\mid v \mid = k + 1$. Then $u_2vy \in L$ holds.

Proof

There exists some positive integer j ($\leq k$) such that L is strictly j-testable by the definition of $LTS^{\leq k}$. By Lemma 4, L is $(j + 1)$-reversible. Then we have that L is $(k + 1)$-reversible by Lemma 2. Therefore, we have $u_2vy \in L$ by the definition of k-reversible language. □

We then can prove an interesting relationship between (k,l)-$CLTS$ and $Rev(k+2l)$.

Theorem 8 For any positive integers k and l, (k,l)-$CLTS$ is contained in $Rev(k+2l)$.

Proof

Let L be a language in (k,l)-$CLTS$. Then there exist a positive integer n, a sequence of languages $L_1, ..., L_n$ in $LTS^{\leq k}$, and a parse set PS of length l such that $L = L_1 \cdots L_n$, and, for all $w \in L$, w is parsable to $L_1, ..., L_n$ based on PS. Let us consider any strings $u_1, u_2, v, x, y \in \Sigma^*$ such that $w_1 = u_1vx \in L, w_2 = u_2vx \in L, w_3 = u_1vy \in L$ and $\mid v \mid = k+2l$. It is sufficient for us to show $w_4 = u_2vy \in L$.

Here, we denote the i-th smallest element in $N(w_p, PS)$ by j_i^p, for $p = 1, 2, 3, 4$. For proving $w_4 = u_2vy \in L$, it suffices to show $| N(w_4, PS) | = n + 1$ and $\forall j_i^4, j_{i+1}^4 \in N(w_4, PS) \ sub(w_4, j_i^4 + 1, j_{i+1}^4) \in L_i$.

From the assumption above, we have,

(1) $| N(w_p, PS) | = n + 1$ (for $p = 1, 2, 3$)

(2) $\forall j_i^p, j_{i+1}^p \in N(w_p, PS) \ sub(w_p, j_i^p + 1, j_{i+1}^p) \in L_i$ (for $p = 1, 2, 3$)

Further, for a finite set of integers N and an integer m, by $N_{\leq m}(N_{>m})$, we denote the set of all elements in N which are less than or equal to m (grater than m), and, by N/m, we denote the set $\{e - m \mid e \in N\}$. Then we have the followings.(cf. Figure 2)

(3) $N(w_3, PS)_{\leq |u_1|+l} = N(w_1, PS)_{\leq |u_1|+l}$

(4) $N(w_2, PS)_{>|u_2|+l} / | u_2 | = N(w_1, PS)_{>|u_1|+l} / | u_1 |$

(5) $N(w_2, PS)_{\leq |u_2|+l} = N(w_4, PS)_{\leq |u_2|+l}$

(6) $N(w_3, PS)_{>|u_1|+l} / | u_1 | = N(w_4, PS)_{>|u_2|+l} / | u_2 |$

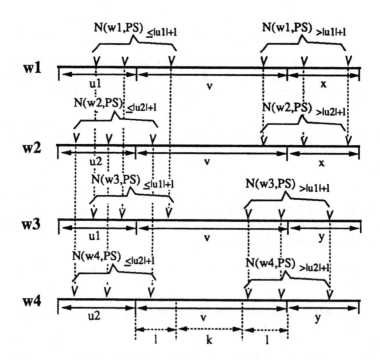

Figure 2: Concatenation points of each string (in case $j_{i+1}^4 \geq | u_2 | + k + l + 1$)

By summing up $(3), (4), (5), (6)$ after taking cardinalities of both sides of the equations, and then using (1), we obtain the equation $| N(w_4, PS) | = n + 1$.

Let $i^* =| N(w_4, PS)_{\leq|u_2|+l}|$. Then, by $(1),(3),(4),(5)$,and (6), we have the following relations.

(7) $i^* =| N(w_1, PS)_{\leq|u_1|+l} |=| N(w_2, PS)_{\leq|u_2|+l} |=| N(w_3, PS)_{\leq|u_1|+l} |.$

(8) $\forall i \leq i^* (j_i^1 = j_i^3 \leq| u_1 | +l \wedge j_i^2 = j_i^4 \leq| u_2 | +l)$

(9) $\forall i > i^* (j_i^1-| u_1 |= j_i^2-| u_2 |> l \wedge j_i^3-| u_1 |= j_i^4-| u_2 |> l).$

By $(2),(8),(9)$, we have

$\forall j_i^4, j_{i+1}^4 \in N(w_4, PS) \ s.t. \ i+1 \leq i^* \ sub(w_4, j_i^4 + 1, j_{i+1}^4) =$
$sub(u_2v, j_i^4 + 1, j_{i+1}^4) = sub(u_2v, j_i^2 + 1, j_{i+1}^2) = sub(w_2, j_i^2 + 1, j_{i+1}^2) \in L_i$

$\forall j_i^4, j_{i+1}^4 \in N(w_4, PS) \ s.t. \ i > i^* \ sub(w_4, j_i^4 + 1, j_{i+1}^4) =$
$sub(vy, j_i^4 +1-| u_2 |, j_{i+1}^4-| u_2 |) = sub(vy, j_i^3 +1-| u_1 |, j_{i+1}^3-| u_1 |) =$
$sub(w_3, j_i^3 + 1, j_{i+1}^3) \in L_i$

Therefore, it is only left for us to show $sub(w_4, j_{i^*}^4 + 1, j_{i^*+1}^4) \in L_{i^*}$,
We consider the two cases of $j_{i^*+1}^4 \leq| u_2 | +k+l$ and $j_{i^*+1}^4 \geq| u_2 | +k+l+1$.
In case $j_{i^*+1}^4 \leq| u_2 | +k+ l$, we have $j_{i^*+1}^2 = j_{i^*+1}^4 \leq| u_2 | +k+ l$, since $N(w_2, PS)_{\leq|u_2|+k+l} = N(w_4, PS)_{\leq|u_2|+k+l}$ holds. Therefore, by (2) and (8), it holds that $sub(w_4, j_{i^*}^4 + 1, j_{i^*+1}^4) = sub(u_2v, j_{i^*}^4 + 1, j_{i^*+1}^4) = sub(u_2v, j_{i^*}^2 + 1, j_{i^*+1}^2) = sub(w_2, j_{i^*}^2 + 1, j_{i^*+1}^2) \in L_{i^*}$.
Let us consider the case $j_{i^*+1}^4 \geq| u_2 | +k + l + 1$. In this case, $j_{i^*+1}^2 \geq| u_2 | +k + l + 1$ holds since otherwise $j_{i^*+1}^4 = j_{i^*+1}^2 \leq| u_2 | +k + l$ holds by the the relation $N(w_2, PS)_{\leq|u_2|+k+l} = N(w_4, PS)_{\leq|u_2|+k+l}$. Therefore, we have $j_{i^*+1}^1, j_{i^*+1}^3 \geq| u_1 | +k + l + 1$ by (9).
Let $q_1 = sub(u_1v, j_{i^*}^1 + 1,| u_1 | +l)$, $q_2 = sub(u_2v, j_{i^*}^2 + 1,| u_2 | +l)$, $z_1 = sub(vx, k + l + 2, j_{i^*+1}^1-| u_1 |)$, $z_2 = sub(vy, k + l + 2, j_{i^*+1}^3-| u_1 |)$, and $r = sub(v, l+1, k+l+1)$. Then, by $(2),(8),(9)$, we have $sub(w_1, j_{i^*}^1 + 1, j_{i^*+1}^1) = q_1rz_1 \in L_{i^*}$, $sub(w_2, j_{i^*}^2+1, j_{i^*+1}^2) = q_2rz_1 \in L_{i^*}$, $sub(w_3, j_{i^*}^3+1, j_{i^*+1}^3) = q_1rz_2 \in L_{i^*}$, and $sub(w_4, j_{i^*}^4 + 1, j_{i^*+1}^4) = q_2rz_2$. Here note that $| r |= k + 1$. Therefore, by Lemma 8 and $L_{i^*} \in LTS^{\leq k}$, we have $sub(w_4, j_{i^*}^4 + 1, j_{i^*+1}^4) = q_2rz_2 \in L_{i^*}$. This completes the proof. $\square$

Theorem 9 [Ang82] The class of k-reversible languages is identifiable in the limit from positive data using k-reversible automata with the conjectures updated in polynomial time.

The learning algorithm for $Rev(k)$ is called k-RI in [Ang82].

Theorem 10 (k,l)-$CLTS$ is identifiable in the limit from positive data using $(k+2l)$-reversible automata with the conjectures updated in polynomial time.
Proof
By Theorem 8 and Theorem 9, we have only to apply the learning algorithm $(k+2l)$-RI for learning (k,l)-$CLTS$. $\square$

Note here that the $(k+2l)$-RI algorithm does not always output a conjecture g_i such that $L(g_i) \in (k,l)$-$CLTS$. Therefore, Theorem 10 does not imply the existence of a *class preserving* efficent learning algorithm, but the *class comprising* efficient learnability of the class (k,l)-$CLTS$. It is an open question whether the class preserving efficient learnability holds for (k,l)-$CLTS$.

5 Concluding Remarks

In [Yok90], Yokomori presented a learning algorithm for the class $LTS^{=k}$ from positive data. In the current paper, we have introduced some extended classes, $CLTS^{\leq k}$, $CLTS^{\leq k}$, (k,l)-$CLTS$, etc., by concatenating locally testable languages, and established their relationships. These classes, $CLTS^{\leq k}$, $CLTS^{\leq k}$, (k,l)-$CLTS$ are proved to properly include $LTS^{=k}$ and to be identifiable in the limit from positive data. Especially, we have shown that the class (k,l)-$CLTS$ is identifiable in the limit from positive data using reversible automata with the conjectures updated in polynomial time, which is based on a close relationship between the class (k,l)-$CLTS$ and the class of $(k+2l)$-reversible languages.

On the other hand, in [YIK94], we applied the learning algorithm for $LTS^{=k}$ to the problem of identifying the α-chain region of amino acid sequences of hemoglobin and obtained the overall success rate of more than 90% correct prediction for unknown α-chain region of amino acid sequences. This work, motivated by the theoretical result by [Hea87], is interesting in that it bridges the gap between the mathematical analysis of splicing process of DNA sequences and formal language theory.

This paper presents some theoretical results on the learnability of some subclasses of concatenations of locally testable languages from positive data. It is strongly suggested by the experimental work [YIK94], that the class of concatenations of locally testable languages may effectively model some classes of amino acid or DNA sequences where sequencial locality changes exist. In fact, the notion of local parsability is strongly motivated from a biological observation that exon-intron boundaries are characterized by a finite set of pairs of base sequences. Therefore, Theorem 10 suggests that Angluin's k-RI algorithm has some potential abilities to find sequentially changing common localities in given samples of amino acid or DNA sequences, provided that local feature changes of biological data are locally parsable. These application issues to amino acid or DNA sequence analysis are left for future works.

It is also left as a theoretical interest to find an efficient learning algorithm for (k,l)-$CLTS$ in which a representation class $\mathcal{R}$ is class preserving with respect to the target class (k,l)-$CLTS$.

Acknowledgement

We would like to thank anonymous referees for their valuable comments. This work was supported in part by Grants-in-Aid for Scientific Research No.06780302 and No.06249202 from the Ministry of Education, Science and Culture, Japan.

References

[Ang80] D. Angluin. Inductive inference of formal languages from positive data. *Information and Control*, vol.45, pp.117-135, 1980

[Ang82] D. Angluin. Inference of reversible languages. *Journal of the ACM*, vol.29, pp.741-765, 1982

[BB75] L. Blum and M. Blum. Toward a Mathematical Theory of Inductive Inference. *Information and Control*, vol.28, pp.125-155, 1975

[Gol67] E. Mark Gold. Language identification in the limit. *Information and Control*, vol.10, pp.447-474, 1967

[Hea87] T. Head. Formal language theory and DNA : An analysis of the generative capacity of specific recombinant behaviors. *Bulletin of Mathematical Biology*, vol.49, pp.737-759, 1987

[LZ93] S. Lange and T. Zeugmann. Language Learning in Dependence on the Space of Hypotheses. *Proc. of 6th Annual ACM Workshop on Computational Learning Theory*, pp.127-136, 1993

[MS93] T. Moriyama and M. Sato. Properties of Language Classes with Finite Elasticity. *Proc. 4th Workshop on Algorithmic Learning Theory*, Lecture Notes in Artificial Intelligence 744, pp.187-196, 1993

[MSW90] T. Motoki, T. Shinohara and K. Wright. The correct definition of finite elasticity: corrigendum to identification of unions. *Proc. of 4th Workshop on Computational Learning Theory*, pp.375-375, 1991

[MP71] R. McNaughton and S. Papert. Counter-Free Automata. *MIT Press*, Cambridge, MA, 1971

[Yok90] T. Yokomori. A note on the polynomial-time identification of strictly local languages in the limit. Report CSIM90-03, Dept. of Comput. Sci. and Inf. Math., Univ. of Elect.-Communi., 1990

[YIK94] T. Yokomori, N. Ishida and S. Kobayashi. Learning Local Languages and Its Application to Protein α-chain Identification. *Proc. of 27th Hawaii International Conference on System Sciences*, Hawaii, pp.113-122, 1994, Janualy

[Wri89] K. Wright. Identification of unions of languages drawn from an identifiable class. *Proc. of 2nd Workshop on Computational Learning Theory*, pp.328-333, 1989

Language Learning from Good Examples

Steffen Lange[*]

HTWK Leipzig

FB Informatik

PF 66

04251 Leipzig

steffen@informatik.th-leipzig.de

Jochen Nessel and Rolf Wiehagen[*]

Universität Kaiserslautern

FB Informatik

PF 3049

67653 Kaiserslautern

{nessel, wiehagen}@informatik.uni-kl.de

Abstract

We study learning of indexable families of recursive languages from *good* examples. We show that this approach is considerably more powerful than learning from *all* examples and point out reasons for this additional power. We present several characterizations of types of learning from good examples. We derive similarities as well as differences to learning of recursive functions from good examples.

1 Introduction

Learning from good examples was introduced in Freivalds, Kinber and Wiehagen (1989, 1993). In contrast to the standard approach of learning from *all* examples, *good* examples

- are intended to be considerably less examples, but they are "important" ones,

- are required to be effectively computable from the objects to be learnt,

- are intended to be sufficient for learning rich classes of objects.

In general, only *finitely many* examples are allowed as good examples. Hence, if there are infinitely many examples then one has to give up almost all examples.

Whereas Freivalds, Kinber and Wiehagen (1989, 1993) are dealing with learning of recursive functions from good examples, we will study this approach for language learning. Thereby we confine ourselves to learning of indexable families of languages, i.e., language families possessing a numbering where membership is uniformly decidable. We exhibit similarities as well as differences to learning of recursive functions from good examples.

In detail we obtain the following results:

[*]This work has been partially supported by the German Ministry for Research and Technology (BMFT) under contract no. 413-4001-01 IW 101 A and E.

(1) Finite language learning from positive good examples is both more powerful than finite learning from all positive examples and less powerful than learning in the limit from all positive examples. Furthermore, finite learning from good examples is exactly of the same power as conservative learning in the limit from all examples. Then we give a numbering-theoretic characterization of finite learning from good examples.

(2) From positive and negative good examples *all* indexable families are finitely learnable. Hence finite learning from positive and negative good examples is of the same power as learning in the limit from all positive and negative examples. In order to achieve this result it is necessary and sufficient to choose the space of hypotheses such that the equivalence of hypotheses is decidable.

(3) We then consider the case that besides finitely many positive good examples there is allowed no more than one negative good example. It turns out that already this type of finite language learning from good examples is of remarkable power. It does contain "rich" superfinite classes, whereas no superfinite class can be learnt from all positive examples even in the limit, cf. Gold (1967). Moreover, it also contains the class of all co-finite languages.

Thus any type of language learning from good examples investigated below is considerably more powerful than its corresponding counterpart of learning from all examples. As it will be clear from the proofs, this additional power mainly comes from the following sources: the knowledge of the language to be learnt when computing the good examples to it and, in a sense simultaneously, the careful choice of an appropriate space of hypotheses. Note that the additional power does not come from any direct encoding of a correct hypothesis into the good examples.

The paper is organized as follows. In Section 2 we give the necessary definitions of learning from all and from good examples, respectively, and refer to approaches by other authors being similar to our approach. Section 3 deals with learning from positive good examples. In Section 4 we consider learning from positive and negative good examples as well as from positive and a uniformly bounded number of negative good examples.

2 Preliminaries

In the sequel we assume familiarity with formal language theory, cf. Hopcroft and Ullman (1969). By Σ we denote any fixed finite alphabet of symbols. Let Σ^* be the free monoid over Σ. Any subset $L \subseteq \Sigma^*$ is called a language. We set $\overline{L} = \Sigma^* \setminus L$. For any sets $L, \hat{L}$, we indicate by $L \subseteq_{fin} \hat{L}$ that L is a finite subset of $\hat{L}$. Furthermore, $L \otimes \hat{L}$ denotes the symmetrical difference of L and $\hat{L}$, i.e., $L \otimes \hat{L} = (L \setminus \hat{L}) \cup (\hat{L} \setminus L)$. By $card(L)$ we denote the cardinality of a set L.

In all what follows, we assume any fixed finite alphabet $\Sigma \supseteq \{a, b\}$. $\prec$ denotes any fixed lexicographical ordering over strings in Σ^*. For any non-empty $L \subseteq \Sigma^*$, let $min(L)$ denote the lexicographically first string of L; if L is finite then $max(L)$ denotes its lexicographically last string.

Let L be a language and $t = s_0, s_1, \ldots$ an infinite sequence of strings from Σ^* such that $L = \{s_k \mid k \in \mathbb{N}\}$. Then t is said to be a *text* for L or, synonymously, a *positive presentation.* Furthermore, let $i = (s_0, b_0), (s_1, b_1), \ldots$ be an infinite sequence of elements of $\Sigma^* \times \{+, -\}$ such that $range(i) = \{s_k \mid k \in \mathbb{N}\} = \Sigma^*$, $i^+ = \{s_k \mid k \in \mathbb{N}, b_k = +\} = L$ and $i^- = \{s_k \mid k \in \mathbb{N}, b_k = -\} = \overline{L}$. Then we refer to i as an *informant.* If L is classified via an informant, then we also say that L is represented by *positive and negative data.* Moreover, let t be a text and let x be a number. Then, t_x denotes the initial segment of t of length $x + 1$, and $t_x^+ = \{s_k \mid k \leq x\}$. Finally, for any informant i and any $x \in \mathbb{N}$, i_x denotes the initial segment of i of length $x + 1$. We set $i_x^+ = \{s_k \mid k \leq x, b_k = +\}$ and $i_x^- = \{s_k \mid k \leq x, b_k = -\}$.

Within the present paper we exclusively deal with indexable families of uniformly recursive languages defined as follows.

Definition 1. *Let C denote a class of non-empty languages over Σ. $\mathcal{L} = (L_j)_{j \in \mathbb{N}}$ is called an indexing of C iff $C = \{L_j \mid j \in \mathbb{N}\}$ and there is a total recursive predicate p over $\mathbb{N} \times \Sigma^*$ such that, for all $j \in \mathbb{N}$ and $s \in \Sigma^*$, $p(j, s) = 1$ if and only if $s \in L_j$.*

Definition 2. *A class C of non-empty languages is called an indexable family iff there is an indexing of C.*

By $\mathcal{IF}$ we denote the class of all indexable families.

As in Gold (1967) we define an *inductive inference machine* (abbr. IIM) to be an algorithmic device which works as follows: The IIM takes as its input larger and larger initial segments of a text t (an informant i) and it either requests the next input, or it first outputs a hypothesis, i.e., a natural number, and then it requests the next input. The numbers outputted by M will be interpreted with respect to some underlying indexing $\mathcal{L}$ of the target family C.

A sequence $(j_x)_{x \in \mathbb{N}}$ of numbers is called *convergent* iff there is a number j such that $j_x = j$ for almost all $x \in \mathbb{N}$.

Now we define some concepts of language learning, cf. Osherson, Stob and Weinstein (1986). We start with learning in the limit, cf. Gold (1967).

Definition 3. *Let $C \in \mathcal{IF}$, $\mathcal{L} = (L_j)_{j \in \mathbb{N}}$ be an indexing of C, and $L \in C$. An IIM M TxtLim(InfLim)-identifies L w.r.t. $\mathcal{L}$ iff on every text t (informant i) for L the IIM M almost always outputs a hypothesis and the sequence $(M(t_x))_{x \in \mathbb{N}} ((M(i_x))_{x \in \mathbb{N}})$ converges to a number j such that $L = L_j$. An IIM M TxtLim(InfLim)-identifies C w.r.t. $\mathcal{L}$ iff M TxtLim(InfLim)-identifies every $L \in C$ w.r.t. $\mathcal{L}$.*
Let TxtLim (InfLim) denote the collection of all $C \in \mathcal{IF}$ such that there is an indexing $\mathcal{L}$ of C and an IIM M TxtLim(InfLim)-identifying C w.r.t. $\mathcal{L}$.

Definition 4. *Let $C \in \mathcal{IF}$ and $m \in \mathbb{N}$. C is called TxtLim-identifiable with at most m mind changes iff there is an IIM M and an indexing $\mathcal{L}$ of C such that M TxtLim identifies C w.r.t. $\mathcal{L}$, and for any $L \in C$ and any text t for L, card $\{n \mid M(t_n) \neq M(t_{n+1})\} \leq m$.*

Let $TxtLim_m = \{C \mid C \in \mathcal{IF}$ and C is $TxtLim$-identifiable with at most m mind changes$\}$.

Suppose, an IIM identifies some language L. Then, after having seen only finitely many data of L the IIM has reached its point of convergence and it has computed a *correct* and *finite* description for the target language. Hence, some form of learning must have taken place. Therefore, we use the terms *infer* and *learn* as synonyms for *identify.*

Note that, in general, it is undecidable whether or not an IIM has already success-fully finished its learning task. If this is decidable, then we obtain finite learning, cf. Gold (1967).

Definition 5. *Let* $C \in \mathcal{IF}$, $\mathcal{L} = (L_j)_{j \in \mathbb{N}}$ *be an indexing of* C, *and* $L \in C$. *An IIM M TxtFin(InfFin)-identifies L w.r.t.* $\mathcal{L}$ *iff on every text t (informant i) for L the IIM M outputs only a single and correct hypothesis j, i.e.* $L = L_j$, *and stops. An IIM M TxtFin(InfFin)-identifies* C *w.r.t.* $\mathcal{L}$ *iff M TxtFin(InfFin)-identifies every* $L \in C$ *w.r.t.* $\mathcal{L}$.

Consequently, every hypothesis produced by a finitely working IIM has to be a correct guess. Let *TxtFin* (*InfFin*) denote the resulting collection of indexable families.

Next to, we sharpen Definition 3 in additionally requiring that any mind change has to be caused by a "provable misclassification" of the hypothesis to be rejected. The notion of conservative learning was introduced in Angluin (1980).

Definition 6. *Let* $C \in \mathcal{IF}$ *and* $\mathcal{L} = (L_j)_{j \in \mathbb{N}}$ *be an indexing of* C. *An IIM M TxtCov(InfCov)-identifies* C *w.r.t.* $\mathcal{L}$ *iff for every* $L \in C$,

(1) *M TxtLim (InfLim)-identifies L w.r.t.* $\mathcal{L}$,

(2) *for every text t (informant i) for L, if M on input* t_x *(input* i_x*) makes the guess* j_x *and then makes the guess* $j_{x+k} \neq j_x$ *at some subsequent step, then* L_{j_x} *must fail to contain some string from* t_{x+k}^+ *(*L_{j_x} *must fail to contain some string* $s \in i_{x+k}^+$ *or it contains some string* $s \in i_{x+k}^-$*).*

The collections of sets *TxtCov* (*InfCov*) are defined in an analogous manner as above.

We now introduce different notions of learning from good examples. Thereby, we adopt the corresponding concepts from Freivalds, Kinber and Wiehagen (1989, 1993).

The intuition is that for any object to be learnt, a supervisor effectively computes a finite set of examples (the "good" examples). Then the learning device receives this finite set, i.e., all of these examples in a lump. After processing this set the device produces its one and only hypothesis (*finite* learning from good examples).

Two remarks seem to us necessary here:

(1) Of course, the requirement that the good examples be effectively computable is in a sense the strongest one (compared with alternatives such as requiring that they be computable in the limit or that they do only exist). However, as our results show this strong requirement can often be fulfilled, and then it yields a remarkable learning power.

(2) Our learning devices are so-called learning strategies. A learning strategy is a partial recursive function mapping finite sets of examples into the set of hypotheses. The reason for using learning strategies rather than inductive inference machines is that just in *finite* learning from good examples it is essential for the learning device to know that the examples seen so far are all it will ever receive.

A family of finite sets $(A_j)_{j \in \mathbb{N}}$ is called recursively generable iff there is a total effective procedure g which, on input j, generates exactly the elements of A_j and stops. If the computation of $g(j)$ stops and there is no output, then A_j is considered to be empty.

Let $\mathcal{F} = (F_j)_{j \in \mathbb{N}}$ denote a fixed canonical enumeration of all finite subsets of Σ^*, i.e., $(F_j)_{j \in \mathbb{N}}$ is recursively generable, $\{F_j \mid j \in \mathbb{N}\}$ is the set of all finite subsets of Σ^*, and $F_i \neq F_j$ for any $i \neq j$. Let $\mathcal{P}$ and $\mathcal{P}^n$ the set of all partial recursive functions of one and $n \geq 2$ arguments, respectively.

Definition 7. *Let $\mathcal{C} \in \mathcal{IF}$. $\mathcal{C}$ is called finitely learnable from good text-examples (abbr. $\mathcal{C} \in TxtGexFin$) iff there is an indexing $(L_j)_{j \in \mathbb{N}}$ of $\mathcal{C}$, a recursively generable family $(ex_j)_{j \in \mathbb{N}}$ of finite sets and a strategy $S \in \mathcal{P}$ such that for any $j \in \mathbb{N}$,*

(1) $ex_j \subseteq L_j$,
(2) *for every $\varepsilon \subseteq_{fin} L_j$, there is a $k \in \mathbb{N}$ such that $L_k = L_j$ and $S(ex_j \cup \varepsilon) = k$.*

Let us neglect the set ε for a moment, i.e., take the special case $\varepsilon = \emptyset$. Then it follows from condition (2) above that for any $L_j \in \mathcal{C}$, the strategy S produces a correct index k of L_j solely from ex_j, the finite set of good examples for L_j. Note that k may be different from j. Furthermore, since the family $(ex_j)_{j \in \mathbb{N}}$ is recursively generable, it follows that any ex_j is effectively computable from j. The finite sets ε from condition (2) are needed in order to avoid "direct encodings" of correct indices into the set of good examples such as $card(ex_j) = j$ and similar "unfair coding tricks" which would make the learning task trivial.

The following definition formalizes learning *in the limit* from good examples. The question immediately arises whether it is reasonable to consider this type of learning, since the information processed will be the same during the whole limiting process. Surprisingly, in Freivalds, Kinber and Wiehagen (1993) it is proved that for learning recursive functions from good examples, learning in the limit is considerably more powerful than finite learning. An intuitive reason for this result is the following. Given any set of good examples, it may be necessary to find the minimal index (with respect to a given numbering of partial recursive functions) of a function being consistent with these examples. In general, such a minimal index can be found only in the limit.

Definition 8. *Let $\mathcal{C} \in \mathcal{IF}$. $\mathcal{C}$ is called learnable in the limit from good text-examples (abbr. $\mathcal{C} \in TxtGexLim$) iff there is an indexing $(L_j)_{j \in \mathbb{N}}$ of $\mathcal{C}$, a recursively generable family $(ex_j)_{j \in \mathbb{N}}$ of finite sets and a strategy $S \in \mathcal{P}^2$ such that for any $j \in \mathbb{N}$,*

(1) $ex_j \subseteq L_j$,
(2) *for every $\varepsilon \subseteq_{fin} L_j$, there is a $k \in \mathbb{N}$ such that $L_k = L_j$ and, for almost all $n \in \mathbb{N}$, $S(ex_j \cup \varepsilon, n) = k$.*

In the sequel, we consider the case that good examples can be both from the language to be learnt and from its complement. Note that the distinction between positive and negative examples is in a sense typical for learning just languages, since for learning functions f, any positive example $(x, f(x))$ automatically yields the set $\{(x, y) \mid y \neq f(x)\}$ of negative examples.

Definition 9. *Let $\mathcal{C} \in \mathcal{IF}$. $\mathcal{C}$ is called finitely learnable from good informant-examples (abbr. $\mathcal{C} \in InfGexFin$) iff there is an indexing $(L_j)_{j \in \mathbb{N}}$ of $\mathcal{C}$, recursively generable families $(ex_j^+)_{j \in \mathbb{N}}$ and $(ex_j^-)_{j \in \mathbb{N}}$ of finite sets and a strategy $S \in \mathcal{P}^2$ such that for any $j \in \mathbb{N}$,*

(1) $ex_j^+ \subseteq L_j$ and $ex_j^- \subseteq \overline{L}_j$,

(2) for every $\varepsilon^+ \subseteq_{fin} L_j$ and $\varepsilon^- \subseteq_{fin} \overline{L}_j$, there is a $k \in \mathbb{N}$ such that $L_k = L_j$ and $S(ex_j^+ \cup \varepsilon^+, ex_j^- \cup \varepsilon^-) = k$.

Definition 10. Let $\mathcal{C} \in \mathcal{IF}$. $\mathcal{C}$ is called learnable in the limit from good informant-examples (abbr. $\mathcal{C} \in InfGexLim$) iff there is an indexing $(L_j)_{j\in\mathbb{N}}$ of $\mathcal{C}$, recursively generable families $(ex_j^+)_{j\in\mathbb{N}}$ and $(ex_j^-)_{j\in\mathbb{N}}$ of finite sets and a strategy $S \in \mathcal{P}^3$ such that for any $j \in \mathbb{N}$,

(1) $ex_j^+ \subseteq L_j$ and $ex_j^- \subseteq \overline{L}_j$,

(2) for every $\varepsilon^+ \subseteq_{fin} L_j$ and $\varepsilon^- \subseteq_{fin} \overline{L}_j$, there is a $k \in \mathbb{N}$ such that $L_k = L_j$ and, for almost all $n \in \mathbb{N}$, $S(ex_j^+ \cup \varepsilon^+, ex_j^- \cup \varepsilon^-, n) = k$.

A possible scenario of learning from good examples is the relationship between teacher and pupil. As a rule the teacher will not tell the pupil the correct answer, nor all about the phenomenon to be learnt (say, a complete text or a complete informant of the unknown language). Actually, the teacher will offer some typical information, just "good examples", in order to enable the pupil to learn the unknown phenomenon by processing the good examples.

Other authors have also dealt with variations of the approach above. Shinohara and Miyano (1991) consider the problem of teaching from a finite number of examples. In contrast to our approach they do not require that these examples be effectively computable and that the learner be successful for any finite superset of these examples. Motoki (1991) and Baliga, Case and Jain (1993) study language learning from positive data and some finite number of negative data. The negative data are not required to be computable and, additionally, the learning strategy is provided with all positive data. On the other hand, our Theorems 6 and 15 were inspired by Theorem 31 in Baliga, Case and Jain (1993).

The approach in Goldman and Mathias (1993) is essentially the same as ours. For some formal definition of "unfair coding tricks", there called collusion, they formally prove that this approach avoids collusion. Finally, note that in Lange and Wiehagen (1991) we proved the learnability of a special indexable family, namely the family of all pattern languages, from polynomially many positive good examples in polynomial time.

3 Learning from Good Text-Examples

First of all, we present one of the main results pointing out the relation between finite learning from good examples and Gold-style formal language learning, namely

$$TxtFin \subset TxtGexFin \subset TxtLim.$$

In order to elaborate the above separations, we show that $TxtGexFin = TxtCov$, cf. Theorem 2. Since $TxtFin \subset TxtCov \subset TxtLim$, cf. Lange and Zeugmann (1992), the result follows immediately.

The following characterization of $TxtCov$ will be used to prove $TxtGexFin = TxtCov$.

Theorem 1. *Let $C \in \mathcal{IF}$. $C \in TxtCov$ iff there is an indexing $(L_j)_{j\in\mathbb{N}}$ of C and a recursively generable family $(T_j)_{j\in\mathbb{N}}$ of finite sets such that*

(1) *for all $j \in \mathbb{N}$, $T_j \subseteq L_j$,*
(2) *for all $j, k \in \mathbb{N}$, if $T_j \subseteq L_k$ and $T_k \subseteq L_j$, then $L_j = L_k$.*

Proof. The main ingredient of this proof is the following lemma.

Lemma A. *Let $C \in TxtCov$. Then there is an indexing $(L_j)_{j\in\mathbb{N}}$ of C, a recursively generable family $(S_j)_{j\in\mathbb{N}}$ of finite sets, and a total recursive predicate p such that*

(1') *for all $j \in \mathbb{N}$, $S_j \subseteq L_j$,*
(2') *for all $j, z \in \mathbb{N}$, $S_j \subseteq L_z$ implies $L_z \not\subseteq L_j$,*
(3') *for all $j, z \in \mathbb{N}$, $p(j, z) = 1$ if and only if $L_j = L_z$.*

Lemma A can be proved in the same way as the characterization of $TxtCov$ in Lange and Zeugmann (1992). We omit the details.

Applying Lemma A we show the desired characterization of $TxtCov$.

Necessity: Let $C \in TxtCov$. Because of Lemma A, there is an indexing $\mathcal{L} = (L_j)_{j\in\mathbb{N}}$ of C, a recursively generable family $(S_j)_{j\in\mathbb{N}}$ of finite sets, and a total recursive predicate p satisfying (1'), (2') and (3'). The definition of the wanted family $(T_j)_{j\in\mathbb{N}}$ is based on $(S_j)_{j\in\mathbb{N}}$ and p.

Algorithm $\mathcal{A}$: "On input j execute (A1).

(A1) Generate S_j and set $T_j^{(0)} = S_j$. For $k = 0, 1, \ldots, j - 1$ execute (α1).

(α1) If $p(j, k) = 1$, then set $T_j^{(k+1)} = T_j^{(k)}$. If $p(j, k) = 0$, then execute (α2).

(α2) Test whether or not $T_j^{(k)} \subseteq L_j$. In case it is not, set $T_j^{(k+1)} = T_j^{(k)}$. Otherwise, set $T_j^{(k+1)} = T_j^{(k)} \cup \{min(L_j \setminus L_k)\}$.

Set $T_j = T_j^{(j)}$ and return T_j."

Since p is a total recursive predicate and $(S_j)_{j\in\mathbb{N}}$ is a recursively generable family of finite sets, instructions (A1) and (α1) can be effectively accomplished. Furthermore, $p(j, k) = 0$ implies $L_j \neq L_k$ by (3'). Together with property (2'), $T_k \subseteq L_j$ yields $L_j \setminus L_k \neq \emptyset$. Consequently, instruction (α2) is effectively executable, since membership is uniformly decidable for $\mathcal{L}$. Hence $(T_j)_{j\in\mathbb{N}}$ is a recursively generable family of finite sets.

Due to the construction above we obtain for all $j \in \mathbb{N}$, $T_j \subseteq L_j$. We continue in showing condition (2). Suppose the converse, i.e., $T_j \subseteq L_k$, $T_k \subseteq L_j$, and $L_k \neq L_j$. Without loss of generality, let $k < j$. Since $L_k \neq L_j$, it holds $p(j, k) = 0$. Furthermore, $T_k \subseteq L_j$ implies the existence of a string $s \in T_j$ with $s \in L_j \setminus L_k$, cf. instruction(α2). This is a contradiction to $T_j \subseteq L_k$.

Sufficiency: It is easy to verify that for all $k, j \in \mathbb{N}$, $T_j \subseteq L_k$ implies $L_k \not\subseteq L_j$. Thus, $C \in TxtCov$ follows immediately from the characterization of $TxtCov$ in Lange and Zeugmann (1992). □

Theorem 2. $TxtGexFin = TxtCov$

Proof. Let $C \in TxtGexFin$. Hence, there is an indexing $\mathcal{L} = (L_j)_{j\in\mathbb{N}}$ of C, a recursively generable family $(ex_j)_{j\in\mathbb{N}}$ of finite sets and a strategy $S \in \mathcal{P}$ satisfying the requirements of Definition 7.

In order to apply Theorem 1 we choose the same indexing $\mathcal{L}$ of C. For all $j \in \mathbb{N}$, we set $T_j = ex_j$. It remains to show that for all $j, k \in \mathbb{N}$, $T_j \subseteq L_k$ and $T_k \subseteq L_j$ implies $L_j = L_k$. Let $k, j \in \mathbb{N}$. Since $ex_j = T_j$ and $ex_k = T_k$, we obtain $ex_j \cup ex_k \subseteq L_j \cap L_k$. Since $C \in TxtGexFin$ by S w.r.t. $\mathcal{L}$, there is a $z \in \mathbb{N}$ such that $S(ex_j \cup ex_k) = S(ex_k \cup ex_j) = z$, $L_z = L_j$, and $L_z = L_k$. Thus, $L_j = L_k$. Hence, $C \in TxtCov$.

Now let $C \in TxtCov$. Because of Theorem 1, there is an indexing $\mathcal{L} = (L_j)_{j\in\mathbb{N}}$ of C and a recursively generable family $(T_j)_{j\in\mathbb{N}}$ of finite sets satisfying (1) and (2).

In order to show $C \in TxtGexFin$, we choose the same indexing $\mathcal{L}$ of C. For all $j \in \mathbb{N}$, we set $ex_j = T_j$. The desired strategy $S \in \mathcal{P}$ will be defined as follows. Let $A \subseteq_{fin} \Sigma^*$.

$$S(A) = \mu z[ex_z \subseteq A \subseteq L_z]$$

Since $(ex_j)_{j\in\mathbb{N}}$ is a recursively generable family of finite sets and membership is uniformly decidable for $\mathcal{L}$, we may conclude that $S \in \mathcal{P}$. Let $j \in \mathbb{N}$ and $ex_j \subseteq A \subseteq_{fin} L_j$. Due to the definition above, there is a $k \in \mathbb{N}$ such that $S(A) = k$. Obviously, $ex_k \subseteq A \subseteq L_j$. On the other hand, $ex_j \subseteq A \subseteq L_k$. Since $ex_j = T_j$ and $ex_k = T_k$, we immediately obtain $L_k = L_j$ by condition (2) of Theorem 1. Hence, $C \in TxtGexFin$. $\square$

Theorem 3. $TxtFin \subset TxtGexFin \subset TxtLim$.

Proof. Immediately from Theorem 2 and $TxtFin \subset TxtCov \subset TxtLim$, cf. Lange and Zeugmann (1992). $\square$

Our next result points out a difference to learning of recursive functions from good examples. We show that for learning of indexable families there is *no* further increase in power when we allow the strategy to process the good examples in the limit. However, we conjecture that for learning not necessarily indexable language families from good examples, Theorem 4 (as well as Corollary 8 below) will not remain valid.

Theorem 4. $TxtGexFin = TxtGexLim$

Proof. Obviously, $TxtGexFin \subseteq TxtGexLim$. Since $TxtGexFin = TxtCov$, it suffices to show that $TxtGexLim \subseteq TxtCov$. Let $C \in TxtGexLim$. Consequently , there is an indexing $\mathcal{L} = (L_j)_{j\in\mathbb{N}}$ of C, a recursively generable family $(ex_j)_{j\in\mathbb{N}}$ of finite sets and a strategy $S \in \mathcal{P}^2$ satisfying the requirements of Definition 8.

In order to apply Theorem 1, we choose the same indexing $\mathcal{L}$ of C. For all $j \in \mathbb{N}$, we set $T_j = ex_j$. It suffices to show that for all $j, k \in \mathbb{N}$, $T_j \subseteq L_k$ and $T_k \subseteq L_j$ implies $L_j = L_k$. Let $k, j \in \mathbb{N}$. Since $ex_j = T_k$ and $ex_k = T_j$, we obtain $ex_j \cup ex_k \subseteq L_j \cap L_k$. Due to condition (2) of Definition 8, $S(ex_j \cup ex_k, n) = S(ex_k \cup ex_j, n) = z$ for almost all $n \in \mathbb{N}$ and some $z \in \mathbb{N}$. Moreover, $L_z = L_j = L_k$, since $C \in TxtGexLim$ by S w.r.t. $\mathcal{L}$. $\square$

As an immediate consequence of the above theorems the following characterization of language learning from good text-examples can be achieved.

Corollary 5. *Let $C \in \mathcal{IF}$ and $Id \in \{Fin, Lim\}$. $C \in TxtGexId$ iff there is an* *indexing* $(L_j)_{j\in\mathbb{N}}$ *of* C *and a recursively generable family* $(ex_j)_{j\in\mathbb{N}}$ *of finite sets such that*

(1) *for all* $j \in \mathbb{N}$, $ex_j \subseteq L_j$,
(2) *for all* $j, k \in \mathbb{N}$, *if* $ex_j \subseteq L_k$ *and* $ex_k \subseteq L_j$, *then* $L_j = L_k$.

The following result exhibits an indexable family finitely learnable from good examples, but not learnable in the limit from text with any uniform bound on the number of mind changes. Consequently, learning from good examples does not only turn out to be "space efficient" in that finitely many examples are sufficient for learning successfully rather than the infinite sequence of examples given by any text. Moreover, learning from good examples can also yield a considerable reduction of the number of mind changes, namely from an arbitrary unbounded number just to zero.

Theorem 6. *There is* $C \in \mathcal{IF}$ *such that*
(1) $C \in TxtGexFin$,
(2) $C \notin \bigcup_{m\in\mathbb{N}} TxtLim_m$.

Proof. The target class C will be defined via its indexing $(L_j)_{j\in\mathbb{N}}$. For all $j \in \mathbb{N}$, let $L_j = \{a\}^+ \setminus \{a^{j+1}\}$.

Now, let $ex_0 = \emptyset$ and for any $j > 0$, let $ex_j = \{a^z | 1 \leq z \leq j\}$. Obviously, $(ex_j)_{j\in\mathbb{N}}$ is recursively generable and, for any $j \in \mathbb{N}, ex_j \subseteq L_j$. Finally, for any $A \subseteq_{fin} \{a\}^+$, let $S(A) = min\{z | z \geq 1, a^z \notin A\} - 1$. Clearly, $C \in TxtGexFin$ by S with respect to $(L_j)_{j\in\mathbb{N}}$. This completes the proof of (1).

In order to prove (2) suppose by way of contradiction that there is an IIM M, an indexing $(\hat{L}_j)_{j\in\mathbb{N}}$ of C and $m \in \mathbb{N}$ such that $C \in TxtLim_m$ by M with respect to $(\hat{L}_j)_{j\in\mathbb{N}}$. Then we define a text t of some $L \in C$ such that the machine M fails on t. The idea of constructing t is the following. Start with $t = a^2, a^3, a^4, \ldots$, thus temporarily (!) keeping a away from t. As soon as M produces a hypothesis j on t such that $a \notin \hat{L}_j$ (note that M has to output such a hypothesis eventually, since t is a text for $L = \{a\}^+ \setminus \{a\}$), a will be added to t (causing M to change its mind!). Then, temporarily, another a^y will be kept away from t. It suffices to play this game $m + 1$ times in order to fool M.

We now define the text t formally.

Definition of t:

Initially, let $s_0 = a$ and simulate M when fed $\hat{t} = a^2, a^3, \ldots$ until the least index x is found such that $M(\hat{t}_x) = j$ with $s_0 \notin \hat{L}_j$. Set $t^{(0)} = \hat{t}_x, s_0$. Go to stage 1.

Stage n $(1 \leq n \leq m)$
  Let $y = max\{k | a^k \in range(t^{(n-1)})\}$ and $s_n = a^{y+1}$.
  Let $\hat{t} = t^{(n-1)}, a^{y+2}, a^{y+3}, \ldots$ Simulate M when fed $\hat{t}$ until the least $x > y$ is found such that $M(\hat{t}_x) = j$ and $s_n \notin \hat{L}_j$. (Comment: Hence $s_{n-1} \in \hat{L}_j$ guaranteeing at least one mind change from stage $n - 1$ to stage n.) Let $t^{(n)} = \hat{t}_x, s_n$.

Let $y = max\{k | a^k \in range(t^{(m)})\}$. Finally, let t be any text for $L = \{a\}^+ \setminus \{a^{y+1}\}$ such that t is an extension of $t^{(m)}$.

Clearly, since the IIM M has already performed m mind changes on $t^{(m)}$, M cannot learn L from text t with at most m mind changes. This contradiction completes the proof of (2). □

4 Learning from Good Informant-Examples

Our next theorem is witnessing that already finite learning from good informant-examples is of the same power as learning in the limit from informant.

In order to prove this result note that for any $C \in \mathcal{IF}$, there is an indexing $\mathcal{L} = (L_j)_{j \in \mathbb{N}}$ of C such that $L_i = L_k$ is decidable for any $i, k \in \mathbb{N}$, cf. Eršov (1977). One can even choose $\mathcal{L}$ in such a way that any language from C possesses exactly one index within $\mathcal{L}$. Observe the analogue between any Gödel numbering of $\mathcal{P}$ where functional equivalence is always undecidable, cf. Rogers (1987), and any Friedberg numbering of the same class $\mathcal{P}$ where any partial recursive function possesses exactly one index and, consequently, functional equivalence is trivially decidable, cf. Friedberg (1958).

Theorem 7. $InfGexFin = InfLim = \mathcal{IF}$

Proof. In Gold (1967), the equivalence $InfLim = \mathcal{IF}$ was proved. Obviously, $InfGexFin \subseteq \mathcal{IF}$. It remains to show that $\mathcal{IF} \subseteq InfGexFin$.

Let $C \in \mathcal{IF}$. Assume any indexing $\mathcal{L} = (L_j)_{j \in \mathbb{N}}$ of C such that $L_j = L_k$ is decidable for all $j, k \in \mathbb{N}$. In order to define the recursively generable families $(ex_j^+)_{j \in \mathbb{N}}$ and $(ex_j^-)_{j \in \mathbb{N}}$, we set $ex_0^+ = ex_0^- \stackrel{.}{=} \emptyset$. We proceed inductively. For all $j \geq 1$, we distinguish the following cases.

Case 1. $L_z = L_j$ for some $z < j$.

We set $ex_j^+ = ex_k^+$ and $ex_j^- = ex_k^-$ where $k < j$ is the least index such that $L_k = L_j$.

Case 2. $L_z \neq L_j$ for all $z < j$.

For $z < j$, let $s_{z,j} = min(L_j \otimes L_z)$. We set $ex_j^+ = \{s_{z,j} | z < j, \ s_{z,j} \in L_j\}$ and $ex_j^- = \{s_{z,j} | z < j, \ s_{z,j} \notin L_j\}$.

Since $L_j = L_k$ is decidable for all $j, k \in \mathbb{N}$, all sets of good informant-examples built according to Case 1 are recursively generable. Since membership is uniformly decidable for $\mathcal{L}$, the sets of good informant-examples built according to Case 2 are recursively generable, too. Due to the construction, $ex_j^+ \subseteq_{fin} L_j$ and $ex_j^- \subseteq_{fin} \overline{L}_j$ for all $j \in \mathbb{N}$.

Let $A \subseteq_{fin} \Sigma^*$ and $B \subseteq_{fin} \Sigma^*$. We define:

$$S(A, B) = \mu z[ex_z^+ \subseteq A \subseteq L_z, \ ex_z^- \subseteq B \subseteq \overline{L}_z]$$

Clearly, $S \in \mathcal{P}^2$. Furthermore, for any $j \in \mathbb{N}$, for any A, B such that $ex_j^+ \subseteq A \subseteq_{fin} L_j$ and $ex_j^- \subseteq B \subseteq_{fin} \overline{L}_j$, $S(A, B)$ is equal to the least index $k \in \mathbb{N}$ such that $L_k = L_j$. □

Theorem 7 immediately yields the following Corollary.

Corollary 8. $InfGexFin = InfGexLim$

As mentioned above, we conjecture that Corollary 8 does not remain valid for learning language families which are not necessarily indexable.

The next result shows that the decidability of $L_j = L_k$ is not only sufficient to prove Theorem 7 but also necessary. Thus we get a characterization that an indexable family C is $InfGexFin$-identifiable with respect to a given indexing of C.

Theorem 9. *Let $C \in \mathcal{IF}$ and $\mathcal{L} = (L_j)_{j \in \mathbb{N}}$ be an indexing of C. Then $C \in InfGexFin$ w.r.t. $\mathcal{L}$ iff $L_j = L_k$ is uniformly decidable for all $j, k \in \mathbb{N}$.*

Proof. Necessity: Let $C \in InfGexFin$ w.r.t. an indexing $(L_j)_{j \in \mathbb{N}}$ of C. Consequently, there are recursively generable families $(ex_j^+)_{j \in \mathbb{N}}$ and $(ex_j^-)_{j \in \mathbb{N}}$ of finite sets and a strategy $S \in \mathcal{P}^2$ satisfying the requirements of Definition 9.

For all $j, k \in \mathbb{N}$, let:

$$p(j, k) = \begin{cases} 1 & , \quad \text{if } ex_j^+ \subseteq L_k, \ ex_k^+ \subseteq L_j, \ ex_j^- \subseteq \overline{L}_k, \ ex_k^- \subseteq \overline{L}_j, \\ 0 & , \quad \text{otherwise.} \end{cases}$$

Obviously, p is a total recursive predicate. Let $j, k \in \mathbb{N}$. It remains to show that $p(j, k) = 1$ iff $L_j = L_k$. Clearly, $p(j, k) = 0$ implies $L_j \neq L_k$. Now let $p(j, k) = 1$. Because of $ex_k^+ \subseteq L_j$ and $ex_k^- \subseteq \overline{L}_j$, there is a $z \in N$ such that $L_z = L_j$ and $S(ex_j^+ \cup ex_k^+, ex_j^- \cup ex_k^-) = z$, since $C \in InfGexFin$ by S w.r.t. $\mathcal{L}$. On the other hand, since $S(ex_k^+ \cup ex_j^+, ex_k^- \cup ex_j^-) = S(ex_j^+ \cup ex_k^+, ex_j^- \cup ex_k^-) = z$, $ex_j^+ \subseteq L_k$, and $ex_j^- \subseteq \overline{L}_k$, we obtain $L_z = L_k$. Hence $L_j = L_k$.

Sufficiency: This part follows immediately from the proof of Theorem 7. $\square$

It is a direct consequence from Theorem 9 that several well-known indexable families such as the context-free languages are *not* finitely learnable from good informant-examples *if* we choose as space of hypotheses all of their grammars. Actually, though membership is uniformly decidable with respect to, say, arbitrary context-free grammars, equivalence of them is not decidable. This emphasizes the need of choosing carefully the space of hypotheses for powerful learning from good examples.

Now, since finite learning from good informant-examples is already of maximal power as it follows from Theorem 7, we find it reasonable to study the effects of bounding the number of the negative good examples.

Definition 11. *Let $C \in \mathcal{IF}$ and $k \in \mathbb{N}$. $C \in Inf_kGexFin$ iff there is an indexing $(L_j)_{j \in \mathbb{N}}$ of C, recursively generable families $(ex_j^+)_{j \in \mathbb{N}}$ and $(ex_j^-)_{j \in \mathbb{N}}$ of finite sets and a strategy $S \in \mathcal{P}^2$ such that for any $j \in \mathbb{N}$,*

(1) *$ex_j \subseteq L_j$, $ex_j^- \subseteq \overline{L}_j$, and $card(ex_j^-) \leq k$,*
(2) *for every $\varepsilon^+ \subseteq_{fin} L_j$ and $\varepsilon^- \subseteq_{fin} \overline{L}_j$, there is a $z \in \mathbb{N}$ such that $L_z = L_j$ and $S(ex_j^+ \cup \varepsilon^+, ex_j^- \cup \varepsilon^-) = z$.*

Obviously, $Inf_0GexFin = TxtGexFin$.

In the following we will show that already $Inf_1GexFin$, i.e., allowing at most *one* negative good example, is of surprising richness. In order to make this explicit we use the following notion. A language class C is called *superfinite* iff C contains all finite languages and at least one infinite language. Using a well-known result from Gold (1967) we obtain Proposition 10, which shows that $Inf_0GexFin$ does not contain any superfinite class. On the other hand, Theorem 11 and Theorem 14 exhibit that $Inf_1GexFin$ does contain even "rich" superfinite classes.

Proposition 10. *Let C be any superfinite class. Then $C \notin TxtGexLim$.*

Proof. $C \notin TxtLim$ is proved in Gold (1967). Since $TxtGexLim \subset TxtLim$ by Theorems 3 and 4, the result follows. $\square$

Since $TxtGexLim = TxtGexFin = Inf_0GexFin$, Proposition 10 yields, in particular, $C \notin Inf_0GexFin$ for any superfinite class C.

Theorem 11. *Let $C \in \mathcal{IF}$ be any superfinite class which contains any finite number of arbitrary infinite languages. Then $C \in Inf_1GexFin$.*

Proof. Let $k \in \mathbb{N}$ and $C \in \mathcal{IF}$ be any superfinite class which contains exactly $k + 1$ arbitrary infinite languages. Recall that $\mathcal{F} = (F_i)_{i \in \mathbb{N}}$ denotes a canonical enumeration of all finite languages over the alphabet Σ. Suppose any repetition-free indexing $\mathcal{L} = (L_j)_{j \in \mathbb{N}}$ of C such that, for all $j \leq k$, L_j is infinite and, furthermore, for all $n \geq 1$, $L_{k+n} = F_{n-1}$.

In order to define the recursive generable families of good examples, we distinguish the following cases. Let $j \in \mathbb{N}$.

Case 1. $j \leq k$.

We set $ex_j^+ = \{min(L_j \otimes L_z) | j \neq z \leq k,\ min(L_j \otimes L_z) \in L_j\}$ and $ex_j^- = \emptyset$.

Case 2. $j > k$.

We set $ex_j^+ = L_j$. Furthermore, $ex_j^- = \{min(L_z \setminus L_j)\}$, if $ex_z^+ \subseteq L_j \subseteq L_z$ for some $z \leq k$. Otherwise, set $ex_j^- = \emptyset$.

The following claim will be used to show that the families $(ex_j^+)_{j \in \mathbb{N}}$ and $(ex_j^-)_{j \in \mathbb{N}}$ do fulfill the desired requirements.

Claim. For any $A \subseteq_{fin} \Sigma^*$, $card(\{z | z \leq k,\ ex_z^+ \subseteq A \subseteq L_z\}) \leq 1$.

Let $A \subseteq_{fin} \Sigma^*$. Suppose to the contrary that the set $\{z | z \leq k,\ ex_z^+ \subseteq A \subseteq L_z\}$ contains different indices m, n. Since $\mathcal{L}$ is repetition-free, $L_m \neq L_n$. Without loss of generality, we may assume that $s = min(L_m \otimes L_n) \in L_m$. Hence, $s \in ex_m^+$, but $s \notin L_n$. Since $ex_m^+ \subseteq A \subseteq L_n$, it follows $s \in L_n$, a contradiction.

Obviously, the above claim yields, in particular, that for all $j > k$, $card\{z | z \leq k,\ ex_z^+ \subseteq L_j \subseteq L_z\} \leq 1$. Hence, for all $j > k$, $card(ex_j^-) \leq 1$.

Due to our construction, $ex_j^+ \subseteq L_j$ and $ex_j^- \subseteq \overline{L}_j$ for any $j \in \mathbb{N}$. Furthermore, $(ex_j^+)_{j \in \mathbb{N}}$ is recursively generable. Since for any $j > k$ and any $z \leq k$, it is uniformly decidable whether or not $ex_z^+ \subseteq L_j \subseteq L_z$, $(ex_j^-)_{j \in \mathbb{N}}$ is recursively generable, too.

We proceed in defining the desired strategy $S \in \mathcal{P}^2$. Let $A \subseteq_{fin} \Sigma^*$ and $B \subseteq_{fin} \Sigma^*$.

$$S(A, B) = \begin{cases} m, & \text{if } \{z | z \leq k,\ ex_z^+ \subseteq A \subseteq L_z\} = \emptyset, \text{ where } L_m = A \\ m, & \text{if } \{z | z \leq k,\ ex_z^+ \subseteq A \subseteq L_z\} = \{n\},\ B \cap L_n \neq \emptyset, \\ & \text{where } L_m = A \\ n, & \text{if } \{z | z \leq k,\ ex_z^+ \subseteq A \subseteq L_z\} = \{n\},\ B \cap L_n = \emptyset \end{cases}$$

Since $(ex_j^+)_{j \in \mathbb{N}}$ is a recursively generable family of finite sets and membership is uniformly decidable in $\mathcal{L}$, the set $\{z | z \leq k,\ ex_z^+ \subseteq A \subseteq L_z\}$ is computable for all finite sets A. Furthermore, according to the claim above all possible cases are considered within the definition of S. Hence, $S \in \mathcal{P}^2$.

Let $j \in \mathbb{N}$, $ex_j^+ \subseteq A \subseteq_{fin} L_j$, and $ex_j^- \subseteq B \subseteq \overline{L}_j$.

Case 1. $\{z | z \leq k,\ ex_z^+ \subseteq A \subseteq L_z\} = \emptyset$.

Hence, $j > k$ and $A = ex_j^+ = L_j$. Consequently, $S(A, B) = m$ with $L_m = A = L_j$. Thus, $L_j = L_m$.

Case 2. $\{z|z \le k,\ ex_z^+ \subseteq A \subseteq L_z\} = \{n\}$.

Because of the claim above, $j \le k$ implies $j = n$. Thus, $S(A, B) = n$ is a correct hypothesis. Otherwise, let $j > k$. Therefore, $A = ex_j^+ = L_j$. Since $ex_n^+ \subseteq A \subseteq L_n$, we obtain $L_j \subseteq L_n$. Due to the definition, $ex_j^- = min(L_n \setminus L_j)$. Thus, $B \cap L_n \ne \emptyset$ and $S(A, B) = m$ with $L_m = A = L_j$.

Consequently, $C \in Inf_1 GexFin$ by S w.r.t. $\mathcal{L}$. $\qquad\qquad\qquad\qquad\qquad$ □

Corollary 12. $\quad TxtGexFin \subset Inf_1 GexFin$

Proof. Immediately from Proposition 10 and Theorem 11. $\qquad\qquad\qquad$ □

Our next result points out another strength of the $Inf_1 GexFin$-approach. Therefore let *COFINITE* denote the class of all co-finite languages. Note that *COFINITE* $\notin TxtLim$, cf. Gold (1967).

Theorem 13. $\quad COFINITE \in Inf_1 GexFin$.

Proof. Assume any repetition-free indexing $\mathcal{L} = (L_j)_{j \in \mathbb{N}}$ of all co-finite languages such that $(\overline{L}_j)_{j \in \mathbb{N}}$ is recursively generable. Without loss of generality, let $L_0 = \Sigma^*$.

In order to define the families $(ex_j^+)_{j \in \mathbb{N}}$ and $(ex_j^-)_{j \in \mathbb{N}}$ of good examples, we set $ex_0^+ = ex_0^- = \emptyset$. If $j > 0$, then we set $ex_j^- = \{max(\overline{L}_j)\}$ and, furthermore, $ex_j^+ = \{s|s \in L_j,\ s \prec max(\overline{L}_j)\}$. Obviously, for all $j \in \mathbb{N}$, ex_j^+ is finite. Since membership is uniformly decidable in $\mathcal{L}$, both families of good examples are recursively generable.

Let $A, B \subseteq_{fin} \Sigma^*$. Let:

$$S(A, B) = \begin{cases} k & ,\ \text{if } B \ne \emptyset, \text{where } k \text{ is the least index such that} \\ & \quad max(B) \in ex_k^-,\ ex_k^+ = \{s|s \in A,\ s \prec max(B)\}, \\ 0 & ,\ \text{if } B = \emptyset. \end{cases}$$

Obviously, $S \in \mathcal{P}^2$. Let $j \in \mathbb{N}$, $ex_j^+ \subseteq A \subseteq_{fin} L_j$ and $ex_j^- \subseteq B \subseteq_{fin} \overline{L}_j$. Since $max(\overline{L}_j) = max(B)$, it follows $COFINITE \in Inf_1 GexFin$ by S w.r.t. $\mathcal{L}$. $\qquad$ □

Using a similar idea we can prove that the class containing all finite as well as all co-finite languages also can be learnt in the sense of $Inf_1 GexFin$. This also yields the following result which we will prove directly.

Theorem 14. $\quad$ There is a $C \in \mathcal{IF}$ such that

(1) C is superfinite,
(2) C contains infinitely many infinite languages,
(3) $C \in Inf_1 GexFin$.

Proof. The desired family C will be defined via the following indexing $\mathcal{L} = (L_j)_{j \in \mathbb{N}}$ of C. For any $j \in \mathbb{N}$, we set:

$$L_j = \begin{cases} \{a^k b^m | m \in \mathbb{N}^+\} & ,\ \text{if } j = 2k, \\ F_k & ,\ \text{if } j = 2k + 1. \end{cases}$$

Obviously, membership is uniformly decidable in $\mathcal{L}$. Furthermore, (1) and (2) hold. The following claims are obviously true.

Claim 1. For any $A \subseteq_{fin} \Sigma^*$, it is decidable whether or not $A \subseteq L_{2j}$ for some $j \in \mathbb{N}$.

Claim 2. For any $A \subseteq_{fin} \Sigma^*$, there is at most one $j \in \mathbb{N}$ such that $A \subseteq L_{2j}$.

For any $j \in \mathbb{N}$, we distinguish the following cases.

Case 1. $j = 2k$.

We set $ex_j^+ = \{a^k b\}$ and $ex_j^- = \emptyset$.

Case 2. $j = 2k + 1$.

We set $ex_j^+ = L_j$. Furthermore, $ex_j^- = \emptyset$, if $L_j \not\subseteq L_{2z}$ for any $z \in \mathbb{N}$, and $ex_j^- = \{min(L_{2z} \setminus L_j)\}$, if $L_j \subseteq L_{2z}$ for some $z \in \mathbb{N}$.

Due to the above claims and the properties of $\mathcal{F}$ and $\mathcal{L}$, it is easy to verify that $(ex_j^+)_{j \in \mathbb{N}}$ and $(ex_j^-)_{j \in \mathbb{N}}$ are recursively generable families of finite sets satisfying condition (1) of Definition 9. Moreover, for any $j \in \mathbb{N}$, $card(ex_j^-) \leq 1$.

Finally, let $A \subseteq_{fin} \Sigma^*$ and $B \subseteq_{fin} \Sigma^*$. Let:

$$S(A, B) = \begin{cases} 2z + 1 & , \text{ if } A = L_{2z+1}, A \not\subseteq L_{2k} \text{ for any } k \in \mathbb{N}, \\ 2z + 1 & , \text{ if } A = L_{2z+1}, A \subseteq L_{2k} \text{ for some } k \in \mathbb{N}, B \cap L_{2k} \neq \emptyset, \\ 2k & , \text{ if } A \subseteq L_{2k} \text{ for some } k \in \mathbb{N}, B \cap L_{2k} = \emptyset. \end{cases}$$

Clearly, $S \in \mathcal{P}^2$. Let $j \in \mathbb{N}$, $ex_j^+ \subseteq A \subseteq_{fin} L_j$ and $ex_j^- \subseteq B \subseteq_{fin} \overline{L_j}$. Now, if there does not exist any $k \in \mathbb{N}$ such that $A \subseteq L_{2k}$, then L_j has to be finite. Hence, $A = ex_j^+ = L_j$ and $S(A, B) = 2z + 1$ with $L_{2z+1} = A$. Consequently, $2z + 1$ is a correct index for L_j. Otherwise, let $A \subseteq L_{2k}$ for some $k \in \mathbb{N}$ and $B \cap L_{2k} \neq \emptyset$. Then L_j is finite, again. Consequently, $S(A, B) = 2z + 1$ is correct. Finally, if $A \subseteq L_{2k}$ for some $k \in \mathbb{N}$ and $B \cap L_{2k} = \emptyset$, then $L_j = L_{2k}$. This proves the correctness of the strategy S. $\square$

The following result strengthens in a sense Theorem 6 above. As it follows from its proof, there is an indexable family $\mathcal{C}$ such that $\mathcal{C}$ is $Inf_1GexFin$-learnable *without* any text-examples, and for any $m \in \mathbb{N}$, $\mathcal{C}$ is not $TxtLim_m$-identifiable.

Theorem 15. *There is $\mathcal{C} \in \mathcal{IF}$ such that*

(1) $\mathcal{C} \in Inf_1GexFin$,
(2) $\mathcal{C} \notin \bigcup_{m \in \mathbb{N}} TxtLim_m$.

Proof. The target class $\mathcal{C}$ will be defined via its indexing $(L_j)_{j \in \mathbb{N}}$. For all $j \in \mathbb{N}$, let $L_j = \{a\}^+ \setminus \{a^{j+1}\}$. Note that $\mathcal{C}$ is the same class as in the proof of Theorem 6.

Now, for any $j \in \mathbb{N}$, let $ex_j^+ = \emptyset$ and $ex_j^- = \{a^{j+1}\}$. Obviously, $(ex_j^+)_{j \in \mathbb{N}}$ and $(ex_j^-)_{j \in \mathbb{N}}$ are recursively generable and fulfill the requirements of Definition 11 (1), even with $card(ex_j^+) = 0$ for any $j \in \mathbb{N}$.

For any $A, B \subseteq_{fin} \mathbb{N}$, let $S(A, B) = min\{z | a^z \in B\} - 1$. Clearly, $\mathcal{C} \in Inf_1GexFin$ by S with respect to $(L_j)_{j \in \mathbb{N}}$. This completes the proof of (1).

Assertion (2) follows immediately from the proof of Theorem 6, (2). $\square$

We are convinced that learning from positive and a bounded number of negative good examples as well as learning from good examples in general deserves further investigation.

References

ANGLUIN, D. (1980), Inductive inference of formal languages from positive data, *Information and Control* 45, 117 - 135.

BALIGA, G., CASE, J. AND JAIN, S. (1993), Language learning with some negative information, *in* "Proc. 10th Annual Symposium on Theoretical Aspects of Computer Science", Lecture Notes in Computer Science 665, pp. 672-681, Springer-Verlag.

ERŠOV, YU.L. (1977), "Theory of Numberings", Nauka, Moscow (Russian).

FREIVALDS, R., KINBER, E.B. AND WIEHAGEN, R. (1989), Inductive inference from good examples, *in* "Proc. Intern. Workshop on Analogical and Inductive Inference", Lecture Notes in Artificial Intelligence 397, pp. 1 - 17, Springer-Verlag.

FREIVALDS, R., KINBER, E.B. AND WIEHAGEN, R. (1993), On the power of inductive inference from good examples, *Theoretical Computer Science* 110, 131 - 144.

FRIEDBERG, R. (1958), Three theorems on recursive enumeration. Journal of Symbolic Logic 23, 309 - 316.

GOLD, E.M. (1967), Language identification in the limit, *Information and Control* 10, 447 - 474.

GOLDMAN, S.A. AND MATHIAS, H.D. (1993), Teaching a smarter learner, *in* "Proc. 6th Annual ACM Conference on Computational Learning Theory", pp. 67 - 76, ACM Press.

HOPCROFT, J.E. AND ULLMAN, J.D. (1969), "Formal Languages and their Relation to Automata", Addison-Wesley, Reading, Massachusetts.

LANGE, S. AND WIEHAGEN, R. (1991), Polynomial–time inference of arbitrary pattern languages, *New Generation Computing* 8, 361 - 370.

LANGE, S. AND ZEUGMANN, T. (1992), Types of monotonic language learning and their characterization, *in* "Proc. 5th Annual ACM Workshop on Computational Learning Theory", pp. 377 - 390, ACM Press.

MOTOKI, T. (1991), Inductive inference from all positive and some negative data, *Information Processing Letters* 39, 177-182.

OSHERSON, D., STOB, M. AND WEINSTEIN, S. (1986), Systems that Learn, An Introduction to Learning Theory for Cognitive and Computer Scientists, MIT Press, Cambridge, Massachusetts.

ROGERS, H. (1987), "Theory of Recursive Functions and Effective Computability", MIT Press, Cambridge, Massachusetts.

SHINOHARA, A. AND MIYANO, S. (1991), Teachability in computational learning, *New Generation Computing* 8, 337 - 347.

Machine Discovery in the Presence of Incomplete or Ambiguous Data *

Steffen Lange and Phil Watson [†]

HTWK Leipzig

FB Informatik

PF 66

04251 Leipzig, Germany

{steffen, phil}@informatik.th-leipzig.de

Abstract

We define a logic for machine discovery, which we call learning with justified refutation, in the style of Mukouchi and Arikawa's learning with refutation. By comparison, our model is more tolerant of the learning agent's behaviour in two particular cases, which we call the cases of incomplete and ambiguous data, respectively. Consequently our formalism correctly learns or refutes a wider spectrum of language classes than its forerunner.

We compare the class of language classes learnable with justified refutation with those learnable under other identification criteria. Comparison of learning with justified refutation from text and from informant shows that these two identification types are mutually incomparable in strength.

Finally we consider whether either of the two formalisms for machine discovery are truly in the tradition of Popper's logic of scientific discovery, the original inspiration for Mukouchi and Arikawa's work.

---

*Work supported by the German Ministry for Research and Technology (BMFT) under contract no. 413-4001-01 IW 101 A.

[†]Now at Department of Computing, University of Bradford, Bradford, West Yorkshire BD7 1DP, United Kingdom (e-mail P.Watson@comp.bradford.ac.uk).

1   Introduction and Motivation

The philosopher Karl R. Popper proposed (Popper (1965)) a logical framework, which he called the logic of scientific discovery, with which to govern and examine the explicable, 'non-creative' part of the process of (empirical) science, and the work of a scientist. This work has been so influential that it is hard today to treat it as a humanly invented model of science. Popper's logic rests on a few very simple assertions: that a scientific hypothesis has the character of a strictly universally quantified statement about the universe; that a hypothesis may *never* be truly proved; that any hypothesis must be capable at any time of refutation; that it is not the business of science to prop up discredited hypotheses, but always to be prepared to abandon such a hypothesis and propose a new one.

In a ground-breaking paper, Mukouchi and Arikawa (1993) defined a computational logic of scientific discovery, closely based on the methods of inductive inference, which in its consistent (a new hypothesis must agree with all known data) and conservative (an existing hypothesis is not abandoned until it conflicts with known data) version already has a strongly Popperian character. They depart from standard inductive inference at one point only, though it is a crucial one: the question of whether the given hypothesis space (the choice of which mirrors the 'creative' part of Popper's model of science) must necessarily include a correct description of the data being fed to the learning agent (machine); they allow the possibility that it may not, and in this case correct behaviour of the machine is to output a special refutation symbol (refuting the entire hypothesis space) and to halt.

Clearly this is an important and natural model of a form of learning or discovery, although we postpone our discussion of whether it is truly Popperian in character until Section 5. We will propose an alternative formulation, which we call machine discovery with justified refutation, to that of Mukouchi and Arikawa (1993). We differ from the earlier paper in that we are more tolerant of a machine's behaviour in two cases, which we may characterize as the cases of incomplete and ambiguous data. Consequently our formalism permits a far wider collection of language classes to be correctly learned or refuted.

2   Notation and Definitions

By $\mathbb{N} = \{0, 1, 2, ...\}$ we denote the set of all natural numbers. By $\langle .,. \rangle : \mathbb{N} \times \mathbb{N} \to \mathbb{N}$ we denote Cantor's pairing function. Let φ_0, φ_1, φ_2, ... denote any fixed acceptable programming system of all partial recursive functions over $\mathbb{N}$, and let Φ_0, Φ_1, Φ_2, ... be any associated Blum-complexity measure (cf. Machtey and Young, 1978). Then φ_k is the partial recursive function computed by program k in the programming system. Furthermore, let $k, x \in \mathbb{N}$. If $\varphi_k(x)$ is defined (abbr. $\varphi_k(x) \downarrow$) then we also say that $\varphi_k(x)$ converges; otherwise, $\varphi_k(x)$ diverges (abbr. $\varphi_k(x) \uparrow$). We will use $\cup$ exclusively to mean class union, i.e. $\mathcal{C}_1 \cup \mathcal{C}_2 = \{A | A \in \mathcal{C}_1 \vee A \in \mathcal{C}_2\}$.

By Σ we denote any fixed finite alphabet of symbols. Let Σ^* be the free monoid over Σ. Any subset $L \subseteq \Sigma^*$ is called a language. We set $\overline{L} = \Sigma^* \setminus L$. For any two sets $L, \hat{L}$, we indicate by $L \subseteq_{fin} \hat{L}$ that L is a finite subset of $\hat{L}$. Let L be a language and $t =$

$s_0, s_1, s_2, \ldots$ an infinite sequence of strings from Σ^* such that $L = \{s_k | k \in \mathbb{N}\}$. Then t is said to be a *text* for L or, synonymously, a *positive presentation*. Furthermore, let $i = (s_0, b_0), (s_1, b_1), (s_2, b_2), \ldots$ be an infinite sequence of elements of $\Sigma^* \times \{+, -\}$ such that $range(i) = \{s_k | k \in \mathbb{N}\} = \Sigma^*$, $i^+ = \{s_k | (s_k, b_k) = (s_k, +), k \in \mathbb{N}\} = L$ and $i^- = \{s_k | (s_k, b_k) = (s_k, -), k \in \mathbb{N}\} = \overline{L}$. Then we refer to i as an *informant*. If L is classified via an informant, then we also say that L is presented by *positive and negative data*. Moreover, let t be a text and let x be a number. Then, t_x denotes the initial segment of t of length $x + 1$, and $t_x^+ =_{df} \{s_k | k \leq x\}$. Finally, for any informant i and any $x \in \mathbb{N}$, i_x denotes the initial segment of i of length $x + 1$. We set $i_x^+ =_{df} \{s_k | (s_k, b_k) = (s_k, +), k \leq x\}$ and $i_x^- =_{df} \{s_k | (s_k, b_k) = (s_k, -), k \leq x\}$.

In all that follows, we assume any fixed underlying alphabet Σ.

Within the present paper we exclusively deal with the learnability of indexable families of uniformly recursive languages defined as follows.

Definition 1. *Let C denote a class of non-empty languages. $\mathcal{L} = (L_j)_{j \in \mathbb{N}}$ is said to be an indexing of C iff $C = \{L_j | j \in \mathbb{N}\}$ and there is a total recursive function p over $\mathbb{N} \times \Sigma^*$ such that, for all $j \in \mathbb{N}$ and $s \in \Sigma^*$, $p(j, s) = 1$ if and only if $s \in L_j$.*

Definition 2. *A class C of non-empty languages is said to be an indexable family iff there exists an indexing of C.*

By $\mathcal{IF}$ we denote the class of all indexable families. For any $C \in \mathcal{IF}$, let $Index(C)$ denote the class of all indexings of C.

Definition 3. *Let $C \in \mathcal{IF}$. Then $C \in ECONS_p$ iff there is a total recursive function p such that for all $F \subseteq_{fin} \Sigma^*$*

$$p(F) = \begin{cases} 1 & , \quad \text{if there exists a } L \in C : \quad F \subseteq L, \\ 0 & , \quad \text{otherwise.} \end{cases}$$

Definition 4. *Let $C \in \mathcal{IF}$. Then $C \in ECONS_c$ iff there is a total recursive function c such that for all $F, \hat{F} \subseteq_{fin} \Sigma^*$*

$$c(F, \hat{F}) = \begin{cases} 1 & , \quad \text{if there exists a } L \in C : \quad F \subseteq L \wedge \hat{F} \subseteq \overline{L} \\ 0 & , \quad \text{otherwise.} \end{cases}$$

It is easy to verify that $ECONS_c \subset ECONS_p \subset \mathcal{IF}$.

As in Gold (1967) we define an *inductive inference machine* (abbr. IIM) to be an algorithmic device which works as follows. The IIM takes as its input larger and larger initial segments of a text t and it either requests the next input string, or it first outputs a hypothesis, i.e. a number encoding a certain computer program, and then it requests the next input string. The numbers output by M will be interpreted with respect to some underlying indexing $\mathcal{L}$ of the target family C.

A sequence $(j_x)_{x \in \mathbb{N}}$ of numbers is said to be convergent in the limit iff there is a number j such that $j_x = j$ for almost all numbers x.

Now we define some concepts of learning. We start with learning in the limit (cf. Gold (1967)).

Definition 5. *Let $C \in \mathcal{IF}$, $\mathcal{L} = (L_j)_{j \in \mathbb{N}} \in Index(C)$, and $L \in C$. An IIM M LIM−TXT(LIM−INF)-identifies L w.r.t. $\mathcal{L}$ iff on every text t (informant i) for L the IIM M almost always outputs a hypothesis and the sequence $(M(t_x))_{x \in \mathbb{N}}$ (resp.*

$(M(i_x))_{x\in\mathbb{N}})$ *converges in the limit to a number j such that* $L = L_j$.
An IIM M LIM−TXT(LIM−INF)-identifies C w.r.t. $\mathcal{L}$ *iff M LIM−TXT(LIM−INF)-identifies every* $L \in C$ *w.r.t.* $\mathcal{L}$.
Let LIM−TXT(LIM−INF) denote the collection of all $C \in \mathcal{IF}$ *such that there is a* $\mathcal{L} \in Index(C)$ *and an IIM M LIM−TXT(LIM−INF)-identifying C w.r.t.* $\mathcal{L}$.

Suppose an IIM identifies some language L. That means, after having seen only finitely many data of L the IIM has reached its point of convergence and it has computed a *correct* and *finite* description for the target language. Hence, some form of learning must have taken place. Therefore, we use the terms *infer* and *learn* as synonyms for identify.

Note that, in general, it is undecidable whether or not an IIM has already successfully finished its learning task. If this is decidable, then we obtain finite learning (cf. Gold (1967)).

Definition 6. *Let* $C \in \mathcal{IF}$, $\mathcal{L} = (L_j)_{j\in\mathbb{N}} \in Index(C)$, *and* $L \in C$. *An IIM M FIN−TXT(FIN−INF)-identifies L w.r.t.* $\mathcal{L}$ *iff on every text t (informant i) for L the IIM M outputs only a single and correct hypothesis j, i.e.* $L = L_j$, *and stops. An IIM M FIN−TXT(FIN−INF)-identifies C w.r.t.* $\mathcal{L}$ *iff M FIN−TXT(FIN−INF)-identifies every* $L \in C$ *w.r.t.* $\mathcal{L}$.

Reliable learning is the oldest identification type in the literature to specify a IIM's behaviour on a text (informant) for arbitrary $\hat{L} \notin C$.

Definition 7. *Let* $C \in \mathcal{IF}$ *and* $\mathcal{L} = (L_j)_{j\in\mathbb{N}} \in Index(C)$. *An IIM M REL−TXT-(REL−INF)-identifies C w.r.t.* $\mathcal{L}$ *iff M LIM−TXT(LIM−INF)-identifies C w.r.t.* $\mathcal{L}$ *and, additionally, on every text (informant) for every language* $\hat{L} \notin C$, *M does not converge.*

Finally, we adopt the notion of refuting inductive inference machines ($RIIM$, for short) as introduced in Mukouchi and Arikawa (1993). A RIIM M is an algorithmic device which either behaves like an IIM or which may produce a special refutation sign $\bot$ and stop after being fed an initial segment of a text (or informant).

Definition 8. *Let* $C \in \mathcal{IF}$ *and* $\mathcal{L} = (L_j)_{j\in\mathbb{N}} \in Index(C)$. *A RIIM M REF−TXT-(REF−INF)-identifies C w.r.t.* $\mathcal{L}$ *iff M LIM−TXT(LIM−INF)-identifies C w.r.t.* $\mathcal{L}$ *and, additionally, M outputs the refutation sign* $\bot$ *and stops on every text t (informant i) for every language* $\hat{L} \notin C$.

3 Language Learning with Justified Refutation

The refuting inductive inference defined by Mukouchi and Arikawa (1993) and above in Definition 8 is a relatively weak identification type, i.e. it permits correct learning or refutation of very few language classes. In particular this is because it requires a RIIM to refute in two cases where this outcome is not justified by any finite initial segment of the data. In this sense refuting inductive inference has a strongly 'total recursive' (yes or no) aspect, while our justified refuting inductive inference has a more 'partial recursive' appearance.

Suppose a text or informant for some non-empty language L is fed to a RIIM, M.

We will define the two cases in which the behaviour of M under justified refuting inductive inference differs from its behaviour under refuting inductive inference. The names we have chosen for the two cases reflect what an observer who expected to see data describing a language in hypothesis space C might say, and apply equally to the language and to any of its presentations (data).

- *incomplete* data (w.r.t. C): L is not in C, but L is a subset of some $L' \in C$.

- *ambiguous* data (w.r.t. C): there is no $L' \in C$ such that $L \subseteq L'$, but for any $D \subseteq_{fin} L$ and $D' \subseteq_{fin} \overline{L}$ there exists $L' \in C$ such that $D \subseteq L'$ and $D' \subseteq \overline{L'}$.

By Theorems 8 and 9 of Mukouchi and Arikawa (1993), a RIIM learning in the refuting inductive inference manner cannot learn from text any hypothesis space C in whose complement lies a language L which is incomplete w.r.t C, and cannot learn from text or informant any C in whose complement lies some L which is ambiguous w.r.t. C.

Our formulation of learning with justified refutation permits any form of behaviour *except* refutation when the data presented is (text case) incomplete or (both cases) ambiguous with respect to the hypothesis space. Due to our less strict requirements in these two cases, the family of language classes learned by justified refuting inductive inference is considerably larger than that learned by refuting inductive inference.

We need two technical definitions relating data to hypothesis spaces. Note that our language learning is *class preserving*, i.e. our hypothesis space indexes exactly our language class.

Definition 9. *Let $C \in \mathcal{IF}$ and t be an infinite sequence of strings. Then t is said to be an unrepresentative text for C iff there is a $x \in \mathbb{N}$ such that for all $L \in C$ it holds $t_x^+ \not\subseteq L$.*
For an unrepresentative text t for C, let x be the least index which satisfies $t_x^+ \not\subseteq L$ for all $L \in C$. We set $wit(t) = t_x$.

Definition 10. *Let $C \in \mathcal{IF}$ and i be an infinite sequence of elements from $\Sigma^* \times \{+,-\}$. Then i is said to be an unrepresentative informant for C iff there is a $x \in \mathbb{N}$ such that for all $L \in C$ it holds either $i_x^+ \not\subseteq L$ or $i_x^- \not\subseteq \overline{L}$.*
For an unrepresentative informant i for C, let x be the least index which satisfies the condition $i_x^+ \not\subseteq L \vee i_x^- \not\subseteq \overline{L}$ for all $L \in C$. We set $wit(i) = i_x$.

We now define our main concept in this paper, inductive learning with justified refutation.

Definition 11. *Let $C \in \mathcal{IF}$, $\mathcal{L} = (L_j)_{j \in \mathbb{N}} \in Index(C)$, and $L \in C$. A RIIM M $JREF–TXT(JREF–INF)$-identifies C w.r.t. $\mathcal{L}$ iff M $LIM–TXT(LIM–INF)$-identifies C w.r.t. $\mathcal{L}$ and, additionally, M outputs the refutation sign $\perp$ and stops on every unrepresentative text t (informant i) for C at some time after having been fed $wit(t)$ $(wit(i))$.*

Definition 12. *Let $C \in \mathcal{IF}$, $\mathcal{L} = (L_j)_{j \in \mathbb{N}} \in Index(C)$, and $L \in C$. A RIIM M $JREF'–TXT(JREF'–INF)$-identifies C w.r.t. $\mathcal{L}$ iff M $LIM–TXT(LIM–INF)$-identifies C w.r.t. $\mathcal{L}$ and, additionally, M outputs the refutation sign $\perp$ and stops on every unrepresentative text t (informant i) for C exactly when fed $wit(t)$ $(wit(i))$.*

Our first theorem is quite surprising; to the best of the authors' knowledge there is no other identification type X in the literature for which $X-TXT \subseteq X-INF$ fails to hold.

Theorem 1. $JREF-TXT \# JREF-INF$

Proof. First, we show $JREF-INF \setminus JREF-TXT \neq \emptyset$. Consider the class C which contains the language $L = \{a\}^+$ as well as all finite languages over the alphabet $\{a\}$. Obviously, C is an indexable family which belongs to $JREF-INF$. Since $C \notin LIM-TXT$ (cf. Gold (1967)), we obtain the desired separation.

On the other hand, consider the class $C = \{L_j | j \in \mathbb{N}\}$ which is defined as follows. For every $k \in \mathbb{N}$, let $L_{2k} = \{a^kb, a^kc\}$. Furthermore, we set $L_{2k+1} = L_{2k}$, if $\varphi_k(k)$ is defined. Otherwise, i.e., $\varphi_k(k)$ is undefined, let $L_{2k+1} = \{a^kb\}$.

Claim 1. C is an indexable family.

We define an indexing $\mathcal{L} = (L_{\langle k,j \rangle})_{k,j \in \mathbb{N}}$ of C such that membership is uniformly decidable according to this indexing. Let $k, j \in \mathbb{N}$. We set $L_{\langle k,0 \rangle} = \{a^kb, a^kc\}$. We distinguish the following cases, if $j > 0$,

Case 1: $\neg \Phi_k(k) \leq j$

Then, let $L_{\langle k,j \rangle} = \{a^kb, a^kc\}$.

Case 2: $\Phi_k(k) \leq j$

Now, let $L_{\langle k,j \rangle} = \{a^kb\}$.

Due to the properties of a Blum complexity measure "$\Phi_k(x) \leq y$" is uniformly decidable in k, x, y. Therefore, membership is uniformly decidable in $\mathcal{L}$. By construction $C = \{L_{\langle k,j \rangle} | k, j \in \mathbb{N}\}$. This completes the proof of Claim 1.

Claim 2. $C \in JREF-TXT$.

We show that there exists a RIIM M which $JREF-TXT$-identifies C w.r.t. the indexing $\mathcal{L}$ defined above. Let t denote any infinite sequence of strings over the underlying alphabet Σ. Furthermore, let $x \in \mathbb{N}$.

$M(t_x) = $ "If $t_x^+ \subseteq L_{\langle k,0 \rangle}$ for some $k \in \mathbb{N}$, then execute Instruction (A). Otherwise, output $\perp$ and stop.

    (A) Let $t_x^+ \subseteq L_{\langle k,0 \rangle}$. Test whether or not $\Phi_k(k) \leq x$. If not, output $\langle k,0 \rangle$ and request the next input. Otherwise, let $\Phi_k(k) = y$. Distinguish the following cases.

        ($\alpha 1$) If $a^kc \in t_x^+$, then output $\langle k,0 \rangle$ and request the next input.
        ($\alpha 2$) If $a^kc \notin t_x^+$, output $\langle k,y \rangle$ and request the next input."

Now, it is not hard to verify that M behaves as required. Obviously, M infers every $L \in C$ from any of its texts. Furthermore, if t defines an unrepresentative text for C, a string $w \notin \bigcup_{k \in \mathbb{N}} L_{\langle k,0 \rangle}$ appears at some time. Due to our definition M eventually refutes t. This proves the claim.

Claim 3. $C \notin JREF-INF$.

Suppose to the contrary that there is a RIIM M which $JREF-INF$-identifies C w.r.t. any indexing $\mathcal{L}$ of C. We show that, given M and $\mathcal{L}$, we can define an algorithm $\mathcal{A}$ which decides for every $k \in \mathbb{N}$ whether or not $\varphi_k(k)$ is defined. Since the Halting Problem is undecidable, this would contradict our assumption.

On input $k \in \mathbb{N}$ algorithm $\mathcal{A}$ executes the following instructions.

(A1) For $x = 0, 1, \ldots$ run M when fed the initial segment i_x of the lexicographically ordered informant for $L = \{a^k b\}$ until $(\alpha 1)$ or $(\alpha 2)$ happens.

   $(\alpha 1)$ $\Phi_k(k) \leq x$.

   $(\alpha 2)$ $M(i_x) = \perp$.

(A2) If $(\alpha 1)$ happens, then output "$\varphi_k(k)$ is defined." Otherwise, output "$\varphi_k(k)$ is undefined."

Let $k \in \mathbb{N}$. First, we show that $\mathcal{A}$ terminates on input k. We distinguish two cases. If $\varphi_k(k)$ is defined, then $(\alpha 1)$ happens. Otherwise, consider the case that $\varphi_k(k)$ is undefined. Now, by definition of C we may conclude that $L \notin C$. Taking the definition of C again into consideration one can easily verify that i defines an unrepresentative informant for C. Hence, M eventually refutes i. Consequently, $(\alpha 2)$ happens.

It remains to show that $\mathcal{A}$ works as desired. Obviously, if $\mathcal{A}$ outputs "$\varphi_k(k)$ is defined", $\Phi_k(k) \leq x$ has been verified for some $x \in \mathbb{N}$. By the definition of a Blum complexity measure then $\varphi_k(k)$ is indeed defined. Finally, assume that $\mathcal{A}$ outputs "$\varphi_k(k)$ is undefined", but $\varphi_k(k)$ is defined. By definition of C it follows $L \in C$. Hence, M has generated the refutation sign when fed an informant of a language L belonging to C. Therefore, M fails to infer L on its lexicographically ordered informant, a contradiction.

Thus, the proof of Claim 3 is finished. $\square$

3.1 The Case of Learning from Positive Data

The following 'timing theorem' greatly simplifies some of our later proofs in the case of learning from text.

Theorem 2. $JREF'-TXT = JREF-TXT$

Proof. Obviously, it suffices to show that $JREF-TXT \subseteq JREF'-TXT$. Therefore, let $C \in JREF-TXT$ and $\hat{M}$ be a RIIM which $JREF-TXT$-identifies C w.r.t. an indexing $\mathcal{L}$ of C.

The desired RIIM M will be defined as follows. Let t denote any infinite sequence of strings and $x \in \mathbb{N}$.

$M(t_x) = $ " Simulate $\hat{M}$'s computation when fed t_x. If $j = \hat{M}(t_x)$ and $t_x^+ \subseteq L_j$, then output j and request the next input. If $\perp = \hat{M}(t_x)$, then output $\perp$ and stop. Otherwise, check for all $z = 0, 1, \ldots$ in parallel whether $(\alpha 1)$ or $(\alpha 2)$ happens.

(α1) $t_x^+ \subseteq L_z$,

(α2) $\hat{M}$ outputs $\bot$ when successively fed the initial segment $\underbrace{t_x, \ldots, t_x}_{z+1-times}$.

If (α1) happens, then output z and request the next input. Otherwise, output $\bot$ and stop."

Now, it is not hard to verify that M $LIM-TXT$-identifies $\mathcal{C}$ w.r.t. $\mathcal{L}$. Obviously, if t is a text for any language $L \in \mathcal{C}$, then M outputs at every step a consistent hypothesis. Otherwise, let t be any unrepresentative text for $\mathcal{C}$. Let $t_x = wit(t)$. If $\hat{M}(t_x) = \bot$, then $M(t_x) = \bot$. On the other hand, since $t_x^+ \not\subseteq L$ for all $L \in \mathcal{C}$, $\hat{M}$ has to refute the text $\hat{t} = t_x, t_x, \ldots$, too. Hence, $\hat{M}(\hat{t}_y) = \bot$ for some $y > x$. Consequently, $M(t_x) = \bot$.

$\square$

Corollary 3. $JREF-TXT = LIM-TXT \cap ECONS_p$

Proof. We show that $LIM-TXT \cap ECONS_p = JREF'-TXT$. Then the Corollary follows directly from Theorem 2.

The direction $JREF'-TXT \subseteq LIM-TXT \cap ECONS_p$ is immediate from Definitions 3, 5 and 11.

Given an IIM M which $LIM-TXT$-identifies $\mathcal{C}$ and the function $p(F)$ for $\mathcal{C}$ from Definition 3, we give a procedure M' to $JREF'-TXT$-identify $\mathcal{C}$.

$M'(t_x) =$ "If $p(t_x^+) = 0$, output $\bot$. Otherwise simulate the computation of M on input t_x."

It is clear that M' defines the behaviour of a RIIM if and only if $p(t_x^+)$ is a recursive function, so we are done.

$\square$

From Corollary 3 it follows that every class belonging to $JREF-TXT$ can be learned by a consistently working RIIM. As a matter of fact, notice that there are language classes in $JREF-TXT$ which cannot be identified by any conservative learning device.

The following result contrasts $JREF-TXT$ with $REF-TXT$ and $REL-TXT$, both of which are known to be closed under class union (but see also Theorem 5).

Theorem 4. There are $\mathcal{C}_1, \mathcal{C}_2 \in JREF-TXT$ such that $\mathcal{C}_1 \cup \mathcal{C}_2 \notin JREF-TXT$.

Proof. Consider the class $\mathcal{C}_1$ of all finite languages and any class $\mathcal{C}_2$ which consists of exactly one infinite recursive language. Obviously, $\mathcal{C}_1 \in JREF-TXT$ and $\mathcal{C}_2 \in JREF-TXT$, respectively. On the other hand, it is well known that $\mathcal{C}_1 \cup \mathcal{C}_2 \notin LIM-TXT$ (cf. Gold (1967)), and $JREF-TXT \subseteq LIM-TXT$, so we are done.

$\square$

Theorem 5. Let $\mathcal{C}_1, \mathcal{C}_2 \in JREF-TXT$ as well as $\mathcal{C}_1 \cup \mathcal{C}_2 \in LIM-TXT$. Then, $\mathcal{C}_1 \cup \mathcal{C}_2 \in JREF-TXT$.

Proof. Let $\hat{M}$ be an IIM which $LIM-TXT$-identifies $\mathcal{C}_1 \cup \mathcal{C}_2$ w.r.t. an indexing $\mathcal{L}$ of $\mathcal{C}_1 \cup \mathcal{C}_2$. Furthermore, let M_1 and M_2 denote any RIIMs which $JREF-TXT$-identify $\mathcal{C}_1$ and $\mathcal{C}_2$, respectively.

An RIIM M which $JREF-TXT$-identifies $C_1 \cup C_2$ w.r.t. $\mathcal{L}$ may be easily defined as follows. Let t denote any infinite sequence of strings and $x \in \mathbb{N}$.

$M(t_x) = $ " If $M_1(t_x) = M_2(t_x) = \perp$, then output $\perp$ and stop. Otherwise, execute (A1).

    (A1) If $\hat{M}$ generates the hypothesis j when fed t_x, then output j and request the next input. Otherwise, output nothing and request the next input."

Now, it is not hard to verify that M behaves as required.

□

3.2 The Case of Learning from Positive and Negative Data

We start with the following result. The proof uses an idea of Kinber which was applied in Mukouchi (1994) to show $REF-INF \subseteq ECONS_c$.

Theorem 6. $JREF-INF \subseteq ECONS_c$

Proof. Assume that a RIIM M $JREF-INF$-identifies a class C. We give a procedure to effectively compute the function $c(T, F)$ of Definition 4, where $T = \{w_1, ..., w_n\} \subseteq \Sigma^*$ and $F = \{w_{n+1}, ..., w_m\} \subseteq \Sigma^*$ are finite sets.

Let σ_0 be any fixed permutation of $(w_1, +), ..., (w_n, +), (w_{n+1}, -), ..., (w_m, -)$, and let $u_1, u_2, ...,$ be any effective enumeration of $\Sigma^* \setminus (T \cup F)$. Then let $\mathcal{T}$ be the binary tree whose nodes are labelled $(u_1, b_1), ..., (u_k, b_k), ..., k \geq 0$, where $(\forall i : 1 \leq i \leq k) b_i \in \{+, -\}$. The binary precedence relation $\sqsubseteq$ over $\mathcal{T}$ is defined as follows: $\sigma_1 \sqsubseteq \sigma_2$ if and only if σ_1 is an initial subsequence of σ_2. We extend $\sqsubseteq$ to informants i in the obvious way: $\sigma_1 \sqsubseteq i$ if and only if σ_1 is an initial subsequence of i. We write . for list concatenation.

Define a subtree S of $\mathcal{T}$ as follows:

$$S = \{\sigma \in \mathcal{T} \mid M(\sigma_0.\sigma) \neq \perp\}$$

Note that because by definition M halts after outputting $\perp$, we can say that $\sigma_1 \sqsubseteq \sigma_2$ and $M(\sigma_1) = \perp$ together imply $M(\sigma_2) = \perp$.

Claim 1.: S has no infinite branch if and only if every i with $\sigma_0 \sqsubseteq i$ is unrepresentative for C.

(i) 'If' part. Assume every i with $\sigma_0 \sqsubseteq i$ is unrepresentative for C. Suppose for a contradiction that S has an infinite branch $\sigma_1, \sigma_2, ...$ where $\sigma_1 = (u_1, b_1)$ and $(\forall j : 1 < j) \sigma_j = \sigma_{j-1}.(u_j, b_j)$, and $(\forall j : 1 \leq j) b_j \in \{+, -\}$. Now define $L = \{u \mid (\exists j \geq 0)(u, +) \in \sigma_j\}$, so that $i = \sigma_0, \sigma_1, ...$ is an informant for L. i is unrepresentative for C, so $L \notin C$, so by assumption there exists n such that $M(\sigma_n) = \perp$. This contradicts our assumption $\sigma_n \in S$ and we are done.

(ii) 'Only if' part. Assume i with $\sigma_0 \sqsubseteq i$ is not unrepresentative for C. Then for all $n \geq 0$, there exists $L \in C$ for which $i_n^+ \subseteq L$ and $i_n^- \subseteq \overline{L}$. Thus i_n is an initial subsequence of some informant i' for L. Then we have $M(i_n) = M(i'_n) \neq \perp$, as by assumption M learns L without refuting. So S has an infinite branch $i_1, i_2, ...$

447

Claim 2.: S is finite if and only if S has no infinite branch.

This is a case of the Finiteness Lemma for finitely branching trees (Rogers(1967)).

Now we can give our procedure to compute $c(T,F)$. Let $T_1, T_2, \ldots$ be the list of all subtrees of T such that T_i contains all nodes labelled by a string of length i or less, and no node labelled by a string of length greater than i.

$c(T,F) = $ " If $T \cap F \neq \emptyset$, output 0. Otherwise simultaneously search $C = L_1, L_2, \ldots$ and $T_1, T_2, \ldots$ until one of $(\alpha 1)$, $(\alpha 2)$ happens.

($\alpha 1$) $L \in C$ is found such that $T \subseteq L$ and $F \subseteq \overline{L}$,

($\alpha 2$) A finite subtree T_i of T is found such that for all σ, if σ labels a leaf of T_i then $M(\sigma) = \bot$.

If ($\alpha 1$) happens then output 1. If ($\alpha 2$) happens output 0."

It is clear that the whole procedure is effective. If $T \cap F \neq \emptyset$ then σ_0 is an initial segment of no language, so $c(T,F) = 0$. Otherwise exactly one of case ($\alpha 1$) and ($\alpha 2$) must eventually happen. In case ($\alpha 1$) happens, L witnesses $c(T,F) = 1$. If there is no such L then $c(T,F) = 0$ and by Claims A and B above S is finite, say with longest node label length i. Then T_{i+1} will be found satisfying the condition of ($\alpha 2$). □

Corollary 7. $JREF'{-}INF = JREF{-}INF = ECONS_c$

Proof. It is obvious from the definitions that $ECONS_c = JREF'{-}INF \subseteq JREF{-}INF$. Then the result follows immediately from Theorem 6. □

The next result contrasts the case of learning from informant with Theorem 4.

Theorem 8. Let $C_1, C_2 \in JREF{-}INF$. Then, $C_1 \cup C_2 \in JREF{-}INF$.

Proof. Since by Corollary 7 $JREF{-}INF = ECONS_c$ and, furthermore, $C_1, C_2 \in ECONS_c$ immediately implies $C_1 \cup C_2 \in ECONS_c$, we may conclude that $C_1 \cup C_2 \in JREF{-}INF$. □

Another difference between learning from informant and learning from text is that any language class in $JREF{-}INF$ can be learned by a consistently as well as conservatively working RIIM.

4 Comparison with other Learning Models

We will compare our identification types $JREF{-}TXT$ and $JREF{-}INF$ with some identification types from the literature. Obviously we wish to make a comparison with $REF{-}TXT$ and $REF{-}INF$ of Mukouchi and Arikawa (1993), but reliable learning is also an obvious case for comparison, as it defines a machine's behaviour on data describing languages from outside the hypothesis space.

Theorem 9.

(a) $FIN-TXT \# JREF-INF$

(b) $FIN-INF \# JREF-TXT$

Proof. Obviously, the class C of all finite languages belongs to $JREF-TXT$ as well as to $JREF-INF$. On the other hand, $C \notin FIN-INF$ and, therefore, $C \notin FIN-TXT$.

To prove the remaining part of the result we use the class $C = \{L_j | j \in \mathbb{N}\}$ defined as follows. For every $k \in \mathbb{N}$ let $L_{2k} = \{a^k b\}$. Let $L_{2k+1} = L_{2k}$, if $\varphi_k(k) \uparrow$. Otherwise, i.e., if $\varphi_k(k) \downarrow$, let $L_{2k+1} = \{a^k c\}$. By applying a similar argument to that used in the proof of Theorem 1 it can be shown that C is an indexable family.

Claim 1. $C \in FIN-TXT$

Consider the indexing $\mathcal{L} = (L_{\langle k,j \rangle})_{k,j \in \mathbb{N}}$ of C. Let k, $j \in \mathbb{N}$. We set $L_{\langle k,0 \rangle} = \{a^k b\}$. In case that $j > 0$, we distinguish the following cases.

Case 1: $\neg \, \Phi_k(k) \leq j$

Then, let $L_{\langle k,j \rangle} = \{a^k b\}$.

Case 2: $\Phi_k(k) \leq j$

Now, let $L_{\langle k,j \rangle} = \{a^k c\}$.

The following IIM M finitely infers every $L \in C$ w.r.t. $\mathcal{L}$. Let t be any text for a language $L \in C$ and $x \in \mathbb{N}$.

$M(t_x) =$ "Determine the unique $k \in \mathbb{N}$ such that either $t_0 = a^k b$ or $t_0 = a^k c$. If $t_0 = a^k b$, then output $\langle k,0 \rangle$ and stop. Otherwise, determine $\Phi_k(k) = y$, output $\langle k,y \rangle$ and stop.

Note that $t_0 = a^k c$ implies that $\varphi_k(k)$ is indeed defined, since t has to be a text for a language belonging to C. This immediately implies that M finitely infers C from text.

Claim 2. $C \notin JREF-TXT \cup JREF-INF$.

Since $JREF-TXT \subseteq ECONS_p$ and $JREF-INF = ECONS_c \subset ECONS_p$ (cf. Corollaries 3 and 7), it remains to show $C \notin ECONS_p$. Suppose to the contrary that $C \in ECONS_p$. Hence, there exists a total recursive predicate p which decides for all $F \subseteq_{fin} \Sigma^*$ whether or not $F \subseteq L$ for any $L \in C$. Now, let $k \in \mathbb{N}$ and $F_k = \{a^k c\}$. Obviously, $F_k \subseteq L$ for some $L \in C$ if and only if $\varphi_k(k)$ is defined. Hence, p can be used to decide the Halting Problem, a contradiction.

This proves the claim and completes the proof of the theorem. $\qquad\square$

Theorem 10.

(a) $JREF-TXT \subset LIM-TXT$

(b) $JREF-INF \subset LIM-INF$

Proof. In both cases the subset property follows immediately from the definitions, and only proper inclusion needs to be proved.

To prove case (a) we use the class $\mathcal{C} = \{L_j \mid j \in \mathbb{N}\}$ from the Proof of Theorem 9. Naturally $\mathcal{C} \subseteq LIM{-}TXT$, but any machine M which $JREF{-}TXT$ identifies $\mathcal{C}$ also solves the Halting Problem.

Finally, since $JREF{-}TXT \subseteq LIM{-}TXT \subset LIM{-}INF$, case (b) follows directly from Theorem 1.

$\square$

Theorem 11.

(a) $REF{-}TXT \subset JREF{-}TXT$

(b) $REF{-}INF \subset JREF{-}INF$

(c) $REF{-}INF \# JREF{-}TXT$

Proof. $REF{-}TXT \subseteq JREF{-}TXT$ as well as $REF{-}INF \subseteq JREF{-}INF$ follow directly from the corresponding definitions. In order to show that both inclusions are proper, recall that the class $\mathcal{C}$ of all finite languages belongs to $JREF{-}TXT$ as well as to $JREF{-}INF$. On the other hand, Mukouchi and Arikawa (1993) have shown that $\mathcal{C} \notin REF{-}INF$. Since $REF{-}TXT \subset REF{-}INF$, propositions (a) and (b) are proven.

$REF{-}INF \setminus JREF{-}TXT \neq \emptyset$ can be shown by using the class $\mathcal{C} = \{L_j \mid j \in \mathbb{N}\}$ where $L_0 = \{a\}^+$ and $L_k = \{a^m \mid 1 \leq m \leq k\}$ for all $k \geq 1$.

$\square$

Theorem 12.

(a) $REL{-}TXT \# JREF{-}TXT$

(b) $JREF{-}INF \subset REL{-}INF$

(c) $REL{-}TXT \# JREF{-}INF$

Proof. Proposition (b) follows directly from $REL{-}INF = LIM{-}INF$ (cf. Osherson, Stob and Weinstein (1986) and Sakurai (1991)) and Theorem 10.

$JREF{-}TXT \cap JREF{-}INF \setminus REL{-}TXT \neq \emptyset$ is an immediate consequence of the fact that any class $\mathcal{C}$ which contains at least one infinite language does not belong to $REL{-}TXT$ (cf. Osherson, Stob and Weinstein (1986)). Obviously, there are classes having this property which belong to $JREF{-}TXT$ and $JREF{-}INF$, respectively.

The remaining part can easily be shown by using the class $\mathcal{C}$ defined in Theorem 9 in order to separate $FIN{-}TXT$ from $JREF{-}TXT$ and $JREF{-}INF$, respectively.

$\square$

5   Some remarks on implementing Popper's logic

It seems appropriate here to make some general remarks about Popper's logic of scientific discovery (Popper (1965) - references throughout this section are to the 1992 Routledge edition of this book) and attempts, both ours and that of Mukouchi and Arikawa (1993), to define a machine version of this logic.

The first obvious remark is that we must beware of anachronistic terminology. When Popper argues, particularly in Chapter 1 of his book, against 'inductive methods' and 'inductive logic', it is a philosophy of science, now outmoded, which he criticises, and not the field of inductive inference, the formulation of which greatly postdates Popper's book (first published, in German, in 1934). In addition, inductive inference, at least when consistent and conservative, proceeds in a truly 'Popperian' manner: hypotheses are tentatively believed until they are refuted, at which point they are abandoned for ever, and a new hypothesis is sought. It's true that our discipline has no counterparts to Popper's ideas on corroboration, degrees of testability/falsifiability, etc. but this is largely because Popper is concerned with the physical sciences while our model dwells in mathematics. In any case we do not rule out some future formulation of inductive inference which more closely mirrors Popper's concerns.

There are some arguments, which deserve to be acknowledged, that both our work and that of Mukouchi and Arikawa (1993) take us no closer to the Popperian ideal.

Certain difficulties arise concerning the role of our hypothesis space if we wish to identify our model closely with Popper's. Popper "distinguish[es] sharply between the process of conceiving a new idea, and the methods and results of examining it logically" (Chapter I Section 2). Clearly the act of choosing the hypothesis space is 'creative' in Popper's sense that the decision is not taken mechanically but rests on the scientist's speculation or belief that it will be the correct one; by contrast, the search for a suitable hypothesis (in the inductive inference sense of the word) within the space is clearly mechanical. Now if we draw Popper's sharp line in the obvious way (so that our hypothesis space corresponds to a Popperian hypothesis) we are led into the problems described below. It is possible to attempt to avoid drawing Popper's line, for example by regarding the hypothesis space as representing the 'mind-set' of the scientist or the scientific community, but there is nothing in Popper's model concerning the refutation or correction of a mind-set.

If the hypothesis space is to play the role of a Popperian hypothesis, we have the following problem. Popper's hypotheses, the raw material of his empirical science, are "all-statements" (Chapter III, Sections 13 and 15), which is to say universally quantified statements. Inductive inference hypotheses clearly have the same form, the simpler case being learning from text: 'all elements in the text are in the given language, and all elements not in the text are in its complement' - the case of informant is similar. Existential statements are regarded by Popper as non-empirical, because they are in general non-falsifiable, but our hypothesis space, if regarded as a Popperian hypothesis, represents a (compound) 'there exists' statement: 'there exists a language L in the given space such that for all elements...'. Thus to attempt to refute a hypothesis space is to attempt to refute a 'there exists' statement, a very un-Popperian goal.

In reply to these objections, we would argue that Popper's model of science, which was developed with the physical sciences in mind, does not fully apply to computer science or mathematics. In particular the creative or 'pseudo-creative' role which can be played by modern computers runs counter to Popper's strict separation of the creative and logical elements. There is a small body of work in the learning theory literature which takes inspiration from Popper without attempting to follow his logic too closely. We mention particularly Case and Smith (1983), Gasarch and Velauthapillai (1992) and Daley, Kalyanasundaram and Velauthapillai (1994). We feel that our own work, and that of Mukouchi and Arikawa (1993) belongs in the same category.

6 Conclusions

We have defined an alternative to Mukouchi and Arikawa's logic for machine discovery. Our formulation, which we call learning with justified refutation, has a more strongly computable 'flavour' than its predecessor, and consequently we can correctly learn and refute a wider spectrum of language classes. We have compared learnability with justified refutation with various other identification types. Of particular interest is the fact that the identification types of learning with justified refutation from informant and from text are of incomparable strength. We have briefly discussed the philosophical aspects of our formalism, and whether it, or the formulation of Mukouchi and Arikawa, can be said to be Popperian in character.

Acknowledgements

The authors wish to thank the anonymous referees, whose comments have improved this paper.

7 References

ANGLUIN, D. (1980), Inductive inference of formal languages from positive data, *Information and Control* 45, pp. 117 - 135.

ANGLUIN, D. AND SMITH, C.H. (1983), Inductive inference: theory and methods, *Computing Surveys* 15, pp. 237 - 269.

CASE, J. AND SMITH, C.H. (1983), Comparison of identification criteria for machine inductive inference, *Theoretical Computer Science* 25, pp. 193 - 220.

DALEY, R., KALYANASUNDARAM, B. AND VELAUTHAPILLAI, M. (1994), The power of probabilism in Popperian FINite learning, *Journal of Experimental and Theoretical Artificial Intelligence* 6(1), pp. 41 - 62.

GASARCH, W.I. AND VELAUTHAPILLAI, M. (1992), Asking questions versus verifiability, *in* "Proceedings 3rd Intern. Workshop on Analogical and Inductive Inference," Lecture Notes in Artificial Intelligence Vol. 642, Springer-Verlag, pp. 197 - 213.

GOLD, E.M. (1967), Language identification in the limit, *Information and Control* 10, pp. 447 - 474.

LANGE, S. AND ZEUGMANN, T. (1992), Types of monotonic language learning and their characterization, *in* "Proceedings 5th Annual ACM Workshop on Computational Learning Theory," ACM Press, pp. 377 - 390.

LANGE, S. AND ZEUGMANN, T. (1993), Learning recursive languages with bounded mind changes, *International Journal of Foundations of Computer Science* 4, pp. 157 - 178.

MACHTEY, M. AND YOUNG, P. (1978) "An Introduction to the General Theory of Algorithms," North-Holland, Amsterdam.

MUKOUCHI, Y. (1994), Inductive inference of Recursive Concepts, Ph.D. Thesis, Technical Report RIFIS-TR-CS-82, Research Institute of Fundamental Information Science, Kyushu University, 1994.

MUKOUCHI, Y. AND ARIKAWA, S. (1993), Inductive inference machines that can refute hypothesis spaces, *in* "Proceedings 4th Intern. Workshop on Algorithmic Learning Theory," Lecture Notes in Artificial Intelligence Vol. 744, Springer-Verlag, pp. 123 - 136.

OSHERSON, D., STOB, M. AND WEINSTEIN, S. (1986), "Systems that Learn, An Introduction to Learning Theory for Cognitive and Computer Scientists," MIT Press, Cambridge, Massachusetts.

POPPER, K.R. (1965) "The Logic of Scientific Discovery," Harper & Row, 1965.

ROGERS, H.JR. (1967) "Theory of Recursive Functions and Effective Computability," McGraw-Hill, 1967.

SAKURAI, A. (1991), Inductive inference of formal languages from positive data enumerated primitive-recursively, *in* "Proceedings 2nd Intern. Workshop on Algorithmic Learning Theory," Ohmsha Ltd., pp. 73 - 83.

Set-Driven and Rearrangement-Independent Learning of Recursive Languages

Steffen Lange*

HTWK Leipzig

FB Mathematik und Informatik

PF 66

04275 Leipzig, Germany

steffen@informatik.th-leipzig.de

Thomas Zeugmann

Research Institute of

Fundamental Information Science

Kyushu University 33

Fukuoka 812, Japan

thomas@rifis.sci.kyushu-u.ac.jp

Abstract

The present paper deals with the learnability of indexed families of uniformly recursive languages from positive data under various postulates of naturalness. In particular, we consider set-driven and rearrangement-independent learners, i.e., learning devices whose output exclusively depends on the range and on the range and length of their input, respectively. The impact of set-drivenness and rearrangement-independence on the behavior of learners to their learning power is studied in dependence on the *hypothesis space* the learners may use. Furthermore, we consider the influence of set-drivenness and rearrangement-independence for learning devices that realize the *subset principle* to different extents. Thereby we distinguish between strong-monotonic, monotonic and weak-monotonic or conservative learning.

The results obtained are twofold. First, rearrangement-independent learning does not constitute a restriction except the case of monotonic learning. Second, we prove that for all but one of the considered learning models set-drivenness is a severe restriction. However, set-driven *conservative* learning is exactly as powerful as unrestricted *conservative* learning provided the *hypothesis space* is appropriately chosen. These results considerably extend previous work done in the field (cf. e.g. Schäfer-Richter (1984) and Fulk (1990)).

---

*Most of this work has been done while the author was visiting ISIS FUJITSU Labs. at Numazu, Japan. It has been partially supported by the German Ministry for Research and Technology (BMFT) under grant no. 01 IW 101.

1. Introduction

Gold-style formal language learning (cf. Gold (1967)) has attracted a lot of attention during the last decades (cf. e.g. Osherson, Stob and Weinstein (1986) and the references therein). The general situation underlying Gold's model can be described as follows: Given more and more eventually incomplete information concerning a language to be learned, an inference device (an IIM, for short) has to produce, from time to time, a hypothesis about the phenomenon to be inferred. The sequence of hypotheses has to converge to a hypothesis correctly describing the language to be learned. Consequently, the inference process is an ongoing one. Within in the present paper we study exclusively language learning from *positive examples* or, synonymously, from *text*, i.e., exactly all strings belonging to the language which should be recognized will be successively presented. The set of all admissible hypotheses is called *space of hypotheses* or *hypothesis space*, for short.

In this paper we investigate the learning capabilities of learners that *simultaneously* fulfill *various combinations* of desirable properties. A central question directly arising when dealing with Gold's-model of learning in the limit is whether or not the *order* of information presentation does really influence the capabilities of IIMs. We distinguish between two degrees of order-independence. An IIM is said to be *set-driven*, if its output does only depend on the *range* of its input. Schäfer-Richter (1984) and Fulk (1990) proved that set-driven IIMs are less powerful than unrestricted ones. A natural weakening of set-drivenness is rearrangement-independence. An IIM is called *rearrangement-independent* if its output does only depend on the *range* and *length* of its input. As it turned out, any collection of languages that can be learned in the limit may also be learned by a rearrangement-independent IIM (cf. Schäfer-Richter (1984), Fulk (1990)). However, the weakness of set-driven IIMs has been proved in a setting allowing self-referential arguments. This might lead to the impression that this result is far beyond any practical relevance, since self-referential arguments are mainly applicable in settings where the *membership problem* for languages is undecidable in general.

Therefore, we study the power of set-driven and rearrangement-independent IIMs in a more realistic setting with respect to potential applications, i.e., we deal exclusively with indexed families of non-empty and uniformly recursive languages. An indexed family is a recursive enumeration of non-empty languages such that membership is uniformly decidable (cf. Angluin (1980)).

A major problem, one has to deal with when learning from text, is to avoid or to detect *overgeneralization*, i.e., hypotheses that describe proper *supersets* of the target language. The impact of this problem results simply from the fact that a text cannot supply counterexamples to such hypotheses. IIMs that strictly avoid overgeneralized hypotheses are called *conservative* (cf. Definition 6). Several authors proposed the so-called *subset principle* to solve the problem of avoiding overgeneralization (cf. e.g. Berwick (1985), Wexler (1992)). Informally, the subset principle requires the learner to hypothesize the "least" language from the hypothesis space with respect to set inclusion that fits with the data the IIM has read so far. In Lange and Zeugmann (1993a) different notions of monotonic language learning has been introduced. All these notions of monotonicity may be considered as formalizations of learning realizing the subset principle to different extents. Moreover, the power of all the monotonic learning models heavily depends on the choice of the hypothesis space (cf. Lange and Zeugmann (1993b)).

In the sequel we study the impact of set-drivenness and rearrangement-independence on all the models of monotonic learning in dependence on the hypothesis space. The results obtained prove that rearrangement-independent learning does not constitute a restriction in most cases. Note that neither Schäfer-Richter's (1984) nor Fulk's (1990) transformation of an arbitrary IIM into a rearrangement-independent one preserves conservativeness or any other constraint implementing the subset principle. Furthermore, we show that set-drivenness cannot be achieved in general. However, conservative learning is exactly as powerful as set-driven conservative inference, if one may carefully choose a hypotheses space that contains a description for every target language, and, additionally, grammars that do not represent languages contained in the target family of languages to be learned. We regard this result as a particular answer to the question how a "natural" learning algorithm may be designed.

2. Preliminaries

By $\mathbb{N} = \{0, 1, 2, ...\}$ we denote the set of all natural numbers. We set $\mathbb{N}^+ = \mathbb{N} \setminus \{0\}$. Let φ_0, φ_1, φ_2, ... denote any fixed *programming system* of all (and only all) partial recursive functions over $\mathbb{N}$, and let Φ_0, Φ_1, Φ_2, ... be any associated *complexity measure* (cf. Machtey and Young (1978)). Then φ_k is the partial recursive function computed by program k in the programming system. Furthermore, let $k, x \in \mathbb{N}$. If $\varphi_k(x)$ is defined (abbr. $\varphi_k(x) \downarrow$) then we also say that $\varphi_k(x)$ converges; otherwise, $\varphi_k(x)$ diverges (abbr. $\varphi_k(x) \uparrow$). By $\langle .,. \rangle : \mathbb{N} \times \mathbb{N} \to \mathbb{N}$ we denote *Cantor's pairing function* i.e., $\langle x, y \rangle = ((x + y)^2 + 3x + y)/2$ for all $x, y \in \mathbb{N}$.

In the sequel we assume familiarity with formal language theory (cf. Hopcroft and Ullman (1969)). By Σ we denote any fixed finite alphabet of symbols. Let Σ^* be the free monoid over Σ. Any subset $L \subseteq \Sigma^*$ is called a language. By $co - L$ we denote the complement of L. Let L be a language and $t = s_0, s_1, s_2, ...$ an infinite sequence of strings from Σ^* such that $range(t) = \{s_k | k \in \mathbb{N}\} = L$. Then t is said to be a *text* for L or, synonymously, a *positive presentation*. Let L be a language. By $text(L)$ we denote the set of all positive presentations of L. Moreover, let t be a text and let x be a number. Then, t_x denotes the initial segment of t of length $x + 1$, and $t_x^+ =_{df} \{s_k | k \leq x\}$.

Next, we introduce the notion of the *canonical text* that turned out to be very helpful in proving several theorems. Let L be any non-empty recursive language, and let $s_0, s_1, s_2, ...$ be the lexicographically ordered text of Σ^*. The canonical text of L is obtained as follows. Test sequentially whether $s_z \in L$ for $z = 0, 1, 2, ...$ until the first z is found such that $s_z \in L$. Since $L \neq \emptyset$ there must be at least one z fulfilling the test. Set $t_0 = s_z$. We proceed inductively. For all $x \in \mathbb{N}$ we define:

$$t_{x+1} = \begin{cases} t_x \cdot s_{z+x+1}, & \text{if } s_{z+x+1} \in L, \\ t_x \cdot s, & \text{otherwise, where } s \text{ is the last string in } t_x. \end{cases}$$

In the sequel we deal with the learnability of indexed families of uniformly recursive languages defined as follows (cf. Angluin (1980)). A sequence $L_0, L_1, L_2, ...$ is said to be an **indexed family** $\mathcal{L}$ of uniformly recursive languages provided all L_j are non-empty and there is a recursive function f such that for all numbers j and all strings $s \in \Sigma^*$ we have

$$f(j,s) = \begin{cases} 1, & \text{if} \quad s \in L_j, \\ 0, & \text{otherwise.} \end{cases}$$

In the following we refer to indexed families of uniformly recursive languages as indexed families for short. Moreover, we often denote an indexed family and its range by the same symbol $\mathcal{L}$. The meaning will be clear from the context.

As in Gold (1967) we define an **inductive inference machine** (abbr. IIM) to be an algorithmic device which works as follows: The IIM takes as its input larger and larger initial segments of a text t and it either requests the next input string, or it first outputs a hypothesis, i.e., a number encoding a certain computer program, and then it requests the next input string.

At this point we specify the semantics of the hypotheses an IIM outputs. For that purpose we have to clarify what hypothesis spaces we choose. We require the inductive inference machines to output indices of grammars, since this learning goal fits well with the intuitive idea of language learning. Furthermore, since we exclusively deal with indexed families $\mathcal{L} = (L_j)_{j \in \mathbb{N}}$ we always take as space of hypotheses an enumerable family of grammars $G_0, G_1, G_2, ...$ over the terminal alphabet Σ satisfying $\mathcal{L} \subseteq \{L(G_j) | j \in \mathbb{N}\}$. Moreover, we require that membership in $L(G_j)$ is uniformly decidable for all $j \in \mathbb{N}$ and all strings $s \in \Sigma^*$. When an IIM outputs a number j, we interpret it to mean that the machine is hypothesizing the grammar G_j. Moreover, for notational convenience we use $\mathcal{L}(\mathcal{G})$ to denote $\{L(G_j) | j \in \mathbb{N}\}$ for every hypothesis space $\mathcal{G} = (G_j)_{j \in \mathbb{N}}$.

Let t be a text, and $x \in \mathbb{N}$. Then we use $M(t_x)$ to denote the last hypothesis produced by M when successively fed t_x. The sequence $(M(t_x))_{x \in \mathbb{N}}$ is said to **converge in the limit** to the number j if and only if either $(M(t_x))_{x \in \mathbb{N}}$ is infinite and all but finitely many terms of it are equal to j, or $(M(t_x))_{x \in \mathbb{N}}$ is non-empty and finite, and its last term is j. Now we define some concepts of learning. We start with learning in the limit.

Definition 1. (Gold (1967)) *Let $\mathcal{L}$ be an indexed family, $L \in \mathcal{L}$, and let $\mathcal{G} = (G_j)_{j \in \mathbb{N}}$ be a hypothesis space. **An IIM M CLIM–identifies L from text with respect to $\mathcal{G}$** iff for every text t for L, there exists a $j \in \mathbb{N}$ such that the sequence $(M(t_x))_{x \in \mathbb{N}}$ converges in the limit to j and $L = L(G_j)$.*

Furthermore, M CLIM–identifies $\mathcal{L}$ with respect to $\mathcal{G}$ if and only if, for each $L \in \mathcal{L}$, M CLIM–identifies L from text with respect to $\mathcal{G}$.

Finally, let CLIM denote the collection of all indexed families $\mathcal{L}$ for which there is an IIM M and a hypothesis space $\mathcal{G}$ such that M CLIM–identifies $\mathcal{L}$ with respect to $\mathcal{G}$.

Suppose, an IIM identifies some language L. That means, after having seen only finitely many data of L the IIM reached its (unknown) point of convergence and it computed a *correct* and *finite* description of a generator for the target language. Hence, some form of learning must have taken place. Therefore, we use the terms *infer* and *learn* as synonyms for identify.

In the above Definition LIM stands for "limit." Furthermore, the prefix C is used to indicate **class comprising** learning, i.e., the fact that $\mathcal{L}$ may be learned with respect to some hypothesis space comprising $range(\mathcal{L})$. The restriction of $CLIM$ to **class preserving** inference is denoted by LIM. That means LIM is the collection of all indexed families $\mathcal{L}$ that can be learned in the limit with respect to a hypothesis space $\mathcal{G} = (G_j)_{j \in \mathbb{N}}$ such that $range(\mathcal{L}) = \{L(G_j) \mid j \in \mathbb{N}\}$. Moreover, if a target indexed family $\mathcal{L}$ has to be inferred with respect to the hypothesis space $\mathcal{L}$ itself, then we replace the prefix C by E, i.e., $ELIM$ is the collection of indexed families that can be **exactly** learned in the limit. Finally, we adopt this convention in defining all the learning types below.

Moreover, an IIM is required to learn the target language from every text for it. This might lead to the impression that an IIM mainly extracts the range of the information fed to it, thereby neglecting the length and order of the data sequence it reads. IIMs really behaving thus are called set-driven. More precisely, we define:

Definition 2. (Wexler and Culicover, Sec. 2.2 (1980)) *An IIM is said to be set-driven iff its output depends only on the range of its input; that is, iff* $M(t_x) = M(\hat{t}_y)$ *for all* $x, y \in \mathbb{N}$, *all texts* t, $\hat{t}$ *provided* $t_x^+ = \hat{t}_y^+$.

Schäfer-Richter (1984) as well as Fulk (1990), later, and independently proved that set-driven IIMs are less powerful than unrestricted ones. Fulk (1990) interpreted the weakening in the learning power of set-driven IIMs by the need of IIMs for time to "reflect" on the input. However, this time cannot be bounded by any a priorily fixed computable function depending exclusively on the size of the range of the input, since otherwise set-drivenness would not restrict the learning power. Indeed, Osherson, Stob and Weinstein (1986) proved that any *non-recursive* IIM M may be replaced by a *non-recursive* set-driven IIM $\hat{M}$ learning at least as much as M does. With the next definition we consider a natural weakening of Definition 2.

Definition 3. (Schäfer-Richter (1984), Osherson et al. (1986)) *An IIM is said to be rearrangement-independent iff its output depends only on the range and on the length of its input; that is, iff* $M(t_x) = M(\hat{t}_x)$ *for all* $x \in \mathbb{N}$, *all texts* t, $\hat{t}$ *provided* $t_x^+ = \hat{t}_x^+$.

We make the following convention. For all the learning models in this paper we use the prefix s-, and r- to denote the learning model restricted to set-driven and rearrangement-independent IIMs, respectively. For example, $s - LIM$ denotes the collection of all indexed families that are LIM–inferable by some set-driven IIM. Next we formalize the other inference models that we have mentioned in the introduction.

Definition 4. (Gold (1967)) *Let* $\mathcal{L}$ *be an indexed family,* $L \in \mathcal{L}$, *and let* $\mathcal{G} = (G_j)_{j \in \mathbb{N}}$ *be a hypothesis space. An IIM M CFIN–identifies L from text iff for every text t for L, there exists a $j \in \mathbb{N}$ such that M, when successively fed t, outputs the single hypothesis j, $L = L(G_j)$, and stops thereafter.*

Furthermore, M CFIN–identifies $\mathcal{L}$ with respect to $\mathcal{G}$ if and only if, for each $L \in \mathcal{L}$, M CFIN–identifies L from text with respect to $\mathcal{G}$.

The resulting learning type is denoted by $CFIN$.

Consequently, every hypothesis produced by a finitely working IIM has to be a correct guess.

The next definition formalizes the different notions of monotonicity.

Definition 5. (Jantke (1991), Wiehagen (1991)) *Let $\mathcal{L}$ be an indexed family of languages, $L \in \mathcal{L}$ and let $\mathcal{G} = (G_j)_{j \in \mathbb{N}}$ be a space of hypotheses.* **An IIM M is said to identify a language L from text with respect to $\mathcal{G}$**

(A) **strong-monotonically**

(B) **monotonically**

(C) **weak-monotonically**

iff

M LIM–identifies L from text with respect to $\mathcal{G}$ and for any text $t \in text(L)$ as well as for any two consecutive hypotheses j_x, j_{x+k} which M has produced when fed t_x and t_{x+k} where $k \in \mathbb{N}^+$ the following conditions are satisfied:

(A) $L(G_{j_x}) \subseteq L(G_{j_{x+k}})$

(B) $L(G_{j_x}) \cap L \subseteq L(G_{j_{x+k}}) \cap L$

(C) *if* $t_{x+k}^+ \subseteq L(G_{j_x})$ *then* $L(G_{j_x}) \subseteq L(G_{j_{x+k}})$.

By *CSMON*, *CMON*, and *CWMON*, we denote the set of all indexed families $\mathcal{L}$ for which there is an IIM M and a hypothesis space $\mathcal{G}$ such that M infers $\mathcal{L}$ strong-monotonically, monotonically, and weak-monotonically, respectively, with respect to the hypothesis space $\mathcal{G}$.

Definition 6. (Angluin (1980)) *Let $\mathcal{L}$ be an indexed family, $L \in \mathcal{L}$, and let $\mathcal{G} = (G_j)_{j \in \mathbb{N}}$ be a space of hypotheses.* **An IIM M CCONSERVATIVE–identifies L from text with respect to $\mathcal{G}$ iff**

(1) *M CLIM–identifies L from text with respect to $\mathcal{G}$,*

(2) *for every text t for L the following condition is satisfied:*
   if M on input t_x makes the guess j_x and then outputs the hypothesis $j_{x+k} \neq j_x$ at some subsequent step, then $t_{x+k}^+ \nsubseteq L(G_{j_x})$.

Finally, M CCONSERVATIVE–identifies $\mathcal{L}$ with respect to $\mathcal{G}$ if and only if, for each $L \in \mathcal{L}$, M CCONSERVATIVE–identifies L from text with respect to $\mathcal{G}$.

The collection of sets *CCONSERVATIVE* is defined in an analogous manner as above. Note that $\lambda WMON = \lambda CONSERVATIVE$ for all $\lambda \in \{C, \epsilon, E\}$, where ϵ denotes the empty string (cf. Lange and Zeugmann (1993b)).

3. Learning with Set-driven IIMs.

In this section we study the question under what circumstances set-drivenness does restrict the power of the learning models defined above. We start with finite learning. The next theorem in particular states that finite learning is invariant with respect to the specific choice of the hypothesis space. Moreover, for every hypothesis space comprising the target indexed family $\mathcal{L}$ there is a *set-driven* IIM that finitely learns $\mathcal{L}$.

Theorem 1. $EFIN = FIN = CFIN = s{-}EFIN$

As we have already mentioned, the examples of Schäfer-Richter (1984) and Fulk (1990) witnessing the restriction of set-driven learners are not indexed families. Hence, we ask whether the uniform recursiveness of all target languages may compensate the impact to learn with set-driven IIMs. The answer is no as the following theorem impressively shows.

Theorem 2. $s{-}CLIM \subset ELIM = LIM = CLIM$

Proof. The part $ELIM = LIM = CLIM$ is due to Lange and Zeugmann (1993b). It remains to show that $s{-}CLIM \subset ELIM$.

The desired indexed family $\mathcal{L}$ is defined as follows. For all $k \in \mathbb{N}$ we set $L_{\langle k,0 \rangle} = \{a^k b^n \mid n \in \mathbb{N}^+\}$. For all $k \in \mathbb{N}$ and all $j \in \mathbb{N}^+$ we distinguish the following cases:

Case 1. $\neg\, \Phi_k(k) \leq j$

Then we set $L_{\langle k,j \rangle} = L_{\langle k,0 \rangle}$.

Case 2. $\Phi_k(k) \leq j$

Let $d = 2 \cdot \Phi_k(k) - j$. Now, we set:

$$L_{\langle k,j \rangle} = \begin{cases} \{a^k b^m \mid 1 \leq m \leq d\}, & \text{if } d \geq 1, \\ \{a^k b\}, & \text{otherwise.} \end{cases}$$

$\mathcal{L} = (L_{\langle k,j \rangle})_{j,k \in \mathbb{N}}$ is an indexed family of recursive languages, since the predicate "$\Phi_i(y) \leq z$" is uniformly decidable in i, y, and z.

Claim A. $\mathcal{L} \notin s{-}CLIM$

Since the halting problem is undecidable, Claim A follows by contraposition of the following Claim B.

Claim B. If there exists an IIM M witnessing $\mathcal{L} \in s{-}CLIM$, then one can effectively construct an algorithm deciding for all $k \in \mathbb{N}$ whether or not $\varphi_k(k)$ converges.

Let M be any IIM that learns $\mathcal{L}$ in the limit with respect to some hypothesis space $\mathcal{G}$ comprising $\mathcal{L}$. We define an algorithm $\mathcal{A}$ that solves the halting problem.

Algorithm $\mathcal{A}$: "On input k execute (A1) and (A2).

(A1) For $z = 0, 1, 2, \ldots$ generate successively the canonical text t of $L_{\langle k,0 \rangle}$ until M on input t_z outputs for the first time a hypothesis j such that $t_z^+ \cup \{a^k b^{z+2}\} \subseteq L(G_j)$.

(A2) Test whether $\Phi_k(k) \leq z + 1$. In case it is, output "$\varphi_k(k)$ converges." Otherwise output "$\varphi_k(k)$ diverges."

Since M has to infer $L_{\langle k,0 \rangle}$ in particular from t, there has to be a least z such that M on input t_z computes a hypothesis j satisfying $t_z^+ \cup \{a^k b^{z+2}\} \subseteq L(G_j)$. More-over, the test whether or not $t_z^+ \cup \{a^k b^{z+2}\} \subseteq L(G_j)$ can be effectively performed, since membership in $L(G_j)$ is uniformly decidable. By the definition of a complexity measure, instruction (A2) is effectively executable. Hence, $\mathcal{A}$ is an algorithm.

It remains to show that $\varphi_k(k)$ diverges, if $\neg \, \Phi_k(k) \leq z+1$. Suppose the converse; then there exists a $y > z+1$ with $\Phi_k(k) = y$. In accordance with the definition of $\mathcal{L}$, we obtain $L = t_z^+ \in \mathcal{L}$. Hence, t_z is also an initial segment of a text $\hat{t}$ for L. Due to the definition of $\mathcal{A}$, we have $L(G_j) \neq L$. Since M is a set-driven IIM, $L = t_z^+$ implies $M(\hat{t}_{z+r}) = j$ for all $r \in \mathbb{N}$. Therefore, M fails to infer L from its text $\hat{t}$. This contradicts our assumption that M is a set-driven IIM which $CLIM$–infers $\mathcal{L}$ with respect to $\mathcal{G}$. Hence, Claim B is proved.

The remaining part $\mathcal{L} \in ELIM$ is omitted. The reader is referred to Lange and Zeugmann (1993d).

q.e.d.

As the latter theorem shows, sometimes there is no way to design a set-driven IIM. However, with the following theorems we mainly intend to show that the careful choice of the hypothesis space deserves special attention whenever set-drivenness is desired.

Theorem 3. *There is an indexed family $\mathcal{L}$ such that*

(1) $\mathcal{L} \in r-ESMON$,

(2) $\mathcal{L} \notin s-LIM$,

(3) *there is a set-driven IIM M and a hypothesis space $\mathcal{G}$ such that M $CSMON$–identifies $\mathcal{L}$ with respect to $\mathcal{G}$.*

As we have seen, set-drivenness constitutes a severe restriction. While this is true in general as long as exact and class preserving learning is considered, the situation looks differently in the class comprising case. On the one hand, learning in the limit cannot always be achieved by set-driven IIMs (cf. Theorem 2). On the other hand, conservative learners may always be designed to be set-driven, if the hypothesis space is appropriately chosen.

Theorem 4. $s-CCONSERVATIVE = CCONSERVATIVE$

Proof. We only sketch the main ideas of the proof, and refer the interested reader to Lange and Zeugmann (1993d) for any detail. The proof is partitioned into two parts. The first part establishes the equality of class comprising conservative and class comprising, rearrangement-independent conservative learning. The main ingredients into this proof are the characterization of $CCONSERVATIVE$ (cf. Lange and Zeugmann (1993b)) as well as a technically simple, but powerful modification of the corresponding tell-tale family.

Let $\mathcal{L} \in CCONSERVATIVE$. Then there exists a space $\mathcal{G} = (G_j)_{j \in \mathbb{N}}$ of hypotheses and a recursively generable tell-tale family $(T_j)_{j \in \mathbb{N}}$ of finite and non-empty sets such that

(1) $range(\mathcal{L}) \subseteq \mathcal{L}(\mathcal{G})$,

(2) for all $j \in N$, $T_j \subseteq L(G_j)$,

(3) for all $j, k \in \mathbb{N}$, if $T_j \subseteq L(G_k)$, then $L(G_k) \not\subseteq L(G_j)$.

Using this tell-tale family, we define a new recursively generable family $(\hat{T}_j)_{j\in\mathbb{N}}$ of finite and non-empty sets that allows the design of a rearrangement-independent IIM inferring $\mathcal{L}$ conservatively with respect to $\mathcal{G}$. But surprisingly enough, we can even do better, namely, we can define an IIM witnessing $\mathcal{L}(\mathcal{G}) \in r-ECONSERVATIVE$. For all $j \in \mathbb{N}$, we set $\hat{T}_j = \bigcup_{n \leq j} T_n \cap L(G_j)$. Note that the new tell-tale family fulfills Properties (1) through (3) above.

Now, the wanted IIM can be defined as follows: Let $L \in \mathcal{L}(\mathcal{G})$, $t \in text(L)$, and $x \in N$.

$M(t_x) =$ "Generate $\hat{T}_k$ for all $k \leq x$ and test whether $\hat{T}_k \subseteq t_x^+ \subseteq L(G_k)$. In case there is one k fulfilling the test, output the minimal one, and request the next input. Otherwise, output nothing and request the next input."

Obviously, M is rearrangement-independent. We omit the proof that the IIM M $ECONSERVATIVE$–identifies $\mathcal{L}(\mathcal{G})$.

The second part of the proof establishes set-drivenness. For that purpose, we define a new hypothesis space $\tilde{\mathcal{G}} = (\tilde{G}_j)_{j\in\mathbb{N}}$ as well as a new IIM $\tilde{M}$. The basis for these definitions are the hypothesis space $\mathcal{G} = (G_j)_{j\in\mathbb{N}}$, and the IIM M described above. The hypothesis space $\tilde{\mathcal{G}}$ is the canonical enumeration of all grammars from $\mathcal{G}$ and all finite languages over the underlying alphabet Σ. Before defining the IIM $\tilde{M}$, we introduce the notion of *repetition free* text $rf(t)$. Let $t = s_0, s_1, ...$ be any text. We set $rf(t_0) = s_0$ and proceed inductively as follows: For all $x \geq 1$, $rf(t_{x+1}) = rf(t_x)$, if $s_{x+1} \in rf(t_x)^+$, and $rf(t_{x+1}) = rf(t_x), s_{x+1}$ otherwise. Obviously, given any initial segment t_x of a text t one can effectively compute $rf(t_x)$. Now we are ready to present the definition of $\tilde{M}$. Let $L \in \mathcal{L}(\mathcal{G})$, $t \in text(L)$, and $x \in \mathbb{N}$.

$\tilde{M}(t_x) =$ "Compute $rf(t_x)$. If M on input $rf(t_x)$ outputs a hypothesis, say j, then output the canonical index of j in $\tilde{\mathcal{G}}$ and request the next input. Otherwise, output the canonical index of t_x^+ in $\tilde{\mathcal{G}}$ and request the next input."

Intuitively, it is clear that $\tilde{M}$ is set-driven. The proof that $\tilde{M}$ conservatively infers $\mathcal{L}(\mathcal{G})$ with respect to $\tilde{\mathcal{G}}$ is omitted.

q.e.d.

The latter theorem allows a nice corollary that we present next.

Corollary 5. *Let $\mathcal{L} \in CCONSERVATIVE$. Then, there is a hypothesis space $\hat{\mathcal{G}} = (\hat{G}_j)_{j\in\mathbb{N}}$ comprising $\mathcal{L}$ such that $\mathcal{L}(\hat{\mathcal{G}}) \in s-ECONSERVATIVE$.*

Proof. Let $\mathcal{L} \in CCONSERVATIVE$. Furthermore, due to the latter theorem, there is a set-driven IIM $\tilde{M}$ and a hypothesis space $\tilde{\mathcal{G}}$ such that $\tilde{M}$ conservatively infers $\mathcal{L}$ with respect to $\tilde{\mathcal{G}}$.

Recall that $\tilde{\mathcal{G}}$ is a canonical enumeration of $\mathcal{G} = (G_j)_{j\in\mathbb{N}}$ satisfying $\mathcal{L} \subseteq \mathcal{L}(\mathcal{G})$ and of all finite languages over the underlying alphabet. Without loss of generality we may assume that $\tilde{\mathcal{G}}$ fulfills the following property. If j is even, then $L(\tilde{G}_j) \in \mathcal{L}(\mathcal{G})$. Hence, $\tilde{M}$ infers $L(\tilde{G}_j)$ from text. Otherwise, $L(\tilde{G}_j)$ is a finite language.

We start with the definition of the desired hypothesis space $\hat{\mathcal{G}} = (\hat{G}_j)_{j\in\mathbb{N}}$ If j is even, then we set $\hat{G}_j = \tilde{G}_j$. Otherwise, we distinguish the following cases. If M

when fed the lexicographically ordered enumeration of all strings in $L(\tilde{G}_j)$ outputs the hypothesis j, then we set $\hat{G}_j = \tilde{G}_j$. In case it does not, we set $\hat{G}_j = \hat{G}_{j-1}$.

Now we are ready to define the desired IIM M which witnesses $\mathcal{L}(\hat{\mathcal{G}}) \in s-ECONSERVATIVE$. Let $L \in \mathcal{L}(\hat{\mathcal{G}})$, $t \in text(L)$, and $x \in \mathbb{N}$.

$M(t_x) = $ "Simulate $\tilde{M}$ on input t_x. If $\tilde{M}$ does not output any hypothesis, then output nothing and request the next input.
Otherwise, let $\tilde{M}(t_x) = j$. Output j and request the next input."

Since $\tilde{M}$ is a conservative and set-driven IIM, M behaves thus. It remains to show that M learns L. Obviously, if $L = L(\hat{G}_{2k})$ for some $k \in \mathbb{N}$, then $\tilde{M}$ infers L. Therefore, since M simulates $\tilde{M}$, we are done.

Now, let us suppose, $L \neq L(\hat{G}_{2k})$ for some $k \in \mathbb{N}$. By definition of $\hat{\mathcal{G}}$, we know that L is finite. Moreover, since t is a text for L, there exists an x such that $t_y^+ = L$ for all $y \geq x$. Recalling the definition of $\hat{\mathcal{G}}$, and by assumption, we obtain the following. There is a number j such that $\tilde{M}(t_x) = j$, $L = t_x^+ = L(\tilde{G}_j) = L(\hat{G}_j)$. Hence, $M(t_x) = j$, too. Finally, since M is set-driven, we directly get $M(t_y) = j$ for all $y \geq j$. Consequently, M learns L.

q.e.d.

The next theorem gives some more evidence that set-drivenness is not that restrictive as it might seem.

Theorem 6.

(1) $s-SMON \setminus EWMON \neq \emptyset$,

(2) $s-CSMON \setminus WMON \neq \emptyset$,

(3) $s-EWMON \setminus MON \neq \emptyset$.

Proof. First of all, we show Assertion (1). Let us consider the following indexed family $\mathcal{L}_{sm} = (L_{\langle k,j \rangle})_{j,k \in \mathbb{N}}$. For all $k \in \mathbb{N}$, we set $L_{\langle k,0 \rangle} = \{a^k b^n | n \in \mathbb{N}^+\}$. For all $k \in \mathbb{N}$ and all $j \in \mathbb{N}^+$, we distinguish the following cases:

Case 1. $\neg \, \Phi_k(k) \leq j$.

We set: $L_{\langle k,j \rangle} = L_{\langle k,0 \rangle}$.

Case 2. $\Phi_k(k) \leq j$.

Then, we set: $L_{\langle k,j \rangle} = \{a^k b^m | 1 \leq m \leq \Phi_k(k)\}$.

In Lange and Zeugmann (1993b) it was already shown that the family $\mathcal{L}_{sm}$ is witnessing $SMON \setminus EWMON \neq \emptyset$. Hence, it remains to show the following claim.

Claim A. $\mathcal{L}_{sm} \in s-SMON$.

We have to show that there is a hypothesis space $\mathcal{G} = (G_j)_{j \in \mathbb{N}}$ which satisfies $range(\mathcal{L}_{sm}) = \mathcal{L}(\mathcal{G})$ and a set-driven IIM M such that M does strong-monotonically infer $\mathcal{L}$ with respect to $\mathcal{G}$.

First of all, we define the hypothesis space $\mathcal{G}$. For all $k \in \mathbb{N}$, we set $L(G_{2k}) = \bigcap_{j \in \mathbb{N}} L_{\langle k,j \rangle}$ and $L(G_{2k-1}) = L_{\langle k,0 \rangle}$.

Since $\mathcal{L}_{sm}$ is an indexed family, it is easy to verify that membership is uniformly decidable for $\mathcal{G}$. Moreover, we have $range(\mathcal{L}_{sm}) = \mathcal{L}(\mathcal{G})$.

Let $L \in \mathcal{L}_{sm}$, let t be any text for L, and let $x \in \mathbb{N}$. The desired IIM M is defined as follows.

$M(t_x) = $ "Determine the unique k such that $t_0 = a^k b^m$ for some $m \in \mathbb{N}$. Test whether or not $t_x^+ \in L(G_{2k})$. In case it is, output $2k$. Otherwise, output $2k - 1$."

Obviously, M changes its mind at most once. Since $L(G_{2k}) \subseteq L(G_{2k-1})$, this mind change satisfies the strong-monotonicity requirement. Furthermore, M converges to a correct hypothesis for L. Accordingly to the definition, it is easy to see that M is indeed a set-driven IIM. This proves Claim A, and therefore (1) follows.

In order to prove Assertion (2), we use the following indexed family $\mathcal{L}_{sm} = (L_{\langle k,j \rangle})_{j,k \in \mathbb{N}}$. For all $k \in \mathbb{N}$ we set $L_{\langle k,0 \rangle} = \{a^k b^n \mid n \in \mathbb{N}^+\}$. For all $k \in \mathbb{N}$ and all $j \in \mathbb{N}^+$ we distinguish the following cases:

Case 1. $\neg \Phi_k(k) > j$

We set: $L_{\langle k,j \rangle} = L_{\langle k,0 \rangle}$

Case 2. $\Phi_k(k) \leq j$

Let $d = j - \Phi_k(k)$. Then, we set:

$$L_{\langle k,j \rangle} = \{a^k b^m \mid 1 \leq m \leq \Phi_k(k)\} \cup \{a^k b^{\Phi_k(k) + 2(d+m)} \mid m \in \mathbb{N}^+\}$$

By reducing the halting problem to $\mathcal{L}_{sm} \in WMON$, one may prove that $\mathcal{L}_{sm} \notin WMON$. An IIM M witnessing $\mathcal{L}_{sm} \in s-CSMON$ can be easily designed, if one choose the following space of hypotheses $\mathcal{G} = (G_{\langle k,j \rangle})_{j,k \in \mathbb{N}}$. For all k, $j \in \mathbb{N}$, we set $L(G_{\langle k,0 \rangle}) = \bigcap_{j \in \mathbb{N}} L_{\langle k,j \rangle}$ and $L(G_{\langle k,j+1 \rangle}) = L_{\langle k,j \rangle}$. We omit further details.

The remaining part can be easily shown. One has simply to choose the same indexed family as used in Lange and Zeugmann (1993a) in order to separate $WMON$ and MON.

q.e.d.

4. Learning with Rearrangement-Independent IIMs.

In this section we deal with rearrangement-independent learning. The first theorem summarizes the known results.

Theorem 7. (Angluin (1980), Schäfer-Richter (1984), Fulk (1990))

$$r - ELIM = ELIM = LIM = CLIM$$

A closer look to the proof of the latter theorem shows that neither Schäfer-Richter's (1984) nor Fulk's (1990) transformation of an arbitrary, unrestricted IIM into a rearrangement-independent one preserves any of the monotonicity constraints defined. And indeed, the situation is much more subtle as the following theorems show.

Theorem 8.

(1) $r-ESMON = ESMON$,

(2) $r-SMON = SMON$.

Proof. First, we prove Assertion (2).

Let $\mathcal{L} \in SMON$. Applying the characterization theorem for $SMON$ (cf. Lange and Zeugmann (1992)), we know that there exists a class preserving space of hypothesis $\mathcal{G} = (G_j)_{j \in \mathbb{N}}$ as well as a recursively generable family $(T_j)_{j \in \mathbb{N}}$ of finite non-empty sets such that

(i) for all $j \in \mathbb{N}$, $T_j \subseteq L(G_j)$,

(ii) for all $j, k \in \mathbb{N}$, if $T_j \subseteq L(G_k)$, then $L(G_j) \subseteq L(G_k)$.

On the basis of this family $(T_j)_{j \in \mathbb{N}}$ we define an IIM M witnessing $\mathcal{L} \in r-SMON$. So let $L \in \mathcal{L}$, $t \in text(L)$, and $x \in \mathbb{N}$.

$M(t_x) =$ "Search for the least $j \leq x$ for which $T_k \subseteq t_x^+ \subseteq L(G_k)$. If it is found, output j and request the next input.
Otherwise, output nothing and request the next input."

Obviously, M is a rearrangement-independent IIM. It remains to show that M $SMON$-infers $\mathcal{L}$ with respect to the hypothesis space $\mathcal{G}$.

Claim 1. M infers L on text t.

Let $j = \mu z[L(G_z) = L]$. Hence, there is a least x such that $T_j \subseteq t_x^+$. Therefore, M will output sometimes a hypothesis. For all $k < j$ with $T_k \subseteq L$ we may conclude that $L(G_k) \subset L$. Otherwise, we obtain $L(G_j) = L(G_k) = L$, because of $T_k \subseteq L(G_k)$ and $T_j \subseteq L(G_j)$ (cf. (ii)). Hence, there exists a y such that $t_y^+ \not\subseteq L(G_k)$ for all $k < j$ with $T_k \subseteq L$. Therefore, $M(t_{y+r}) = j$ for all $r \in \mathbb{N}$. This proves the claim.

Claim 2. M works strong-monotonically.

Let $M(t_x) = j$ and $M(t_{x+r}) = k$ for some $x \in \mathbb{N}$ and $r \in \mathbb{N}^+$. Due to the definition of M, we have $T_j \subseteq t_x^+ \subseteq L(G_k)$. Therefore, $L(G_j) \subseteq L(G_k)$ (cf. (ii)). This proves the claim.

To sum up, M is witnessing $\mathcal{L} \in r-SMON$. Thus, Assertion (2) is shown.

Next, we prove Assertion (1). Let $\mathcal{L} \in ESMON$. Because of $ESMON \subseteq SMON$ as well as of Assertion (2), there exists a rearrangement-independent IIM $\hat{M}$ as well as a class preserving hypothesis space $\mathcal{G}$ such that $\hat{M}$ $SMON$-identifies $\mathcal{L}$ with respect to the hypothesis space $\mathcal{G}$.

Applying Theorem 4 of Lange and Zeugmann (1993b), we know that there exists some total recursive function $f : \mathbb{N} \times \mathbb{N} \to \mathbb{N}$ satisfying

(i) for all $j \in \mathbb{N}$, $lim_{x \to \infty} f(j, x) = k$ exists and satisfies $L(G_j) = L_k$,

(ii) for all $j, x \in \mathbb{N}$, $L_{f(j,x)} \subseteq L_{f(j,x+1)}$.

That means, f is a limiting recursive strong-monotonic compiler from $\mathcal{G}$ into $\mathcal{L}$.

Given the IIM $\hat{M}$, the hypothesis space $\mathcal{G}$ as well as the limiting recursive strong-monotonic compiler f, we define an IIM M witnessing $\mathcal{L} \in r - ESMON$. So, let $L \in \mathcal{L}$, $t \in text(L)$, and $x \in \mathbb{N}$.

$M(t_x) = $ "Simulate $\hat{M}$ on input t_x. If $\hat{M}$ when successively fed t_x does not output any guess, then output nothing and request the next input.

Otherwise, let $j = \hat{M}(t_x)$. If $t_x^+ \subseteq L(G_j)$, then execute (A1). Otherwise, output nothing and request the next input.

(A1) Find the least $y \in \mathbb{N}$ for which $t_x^+ \subseteq L_{f(j,y)}$. Output $f(j,y)$ and request the next input."

Since the membership problem for $\mathcal{G}$ is uniformly decidable, the test "$t_x^+ \subseteq L(G_j)$" can be effectively performed. Additionally, since $\mathcal{L}$ is an indexed family, the test within instruction (A1) can be effectively accomplished, too. Furthermore, by Property (i) of f and since $t_x^+ \subseteq L(G_j)$, instruction (A1) has to terminate for every $j \in \mathbb{N}$. Hence, M is indeed an IIM. Due to its definition, M is a rearrangement-independent IIM, since the IIM $\hat{M}$ simulated by M is rearrangement-independent by assumption.

It remains to show that M strong-monotonically infers L from text t. Since $\hat{M}$ infers L from text t and by Property (i) of f, M converges to a correct hypothesis for L. Finally, we show that M fulfills the strong-monotonicity constraint. Let $f(j,y)$ and $f(k,z)$ denote two successively hypotheses generated by M. Hence, $M(t_x) = f(j,y)$ and $M(t_{x+r}) = f(k,z)$ for some $x \in \mathbb{N}$, $r \in \mathbb{N}^+$. We distinguish the following cases.

Case 1. $j = k$

Due to the definition of M, we may conclude $y \leq z$. Hence, Property (ii) guarantees $L_{f(j,y)} \subseteq L_{f(j,z)}$.

Case 2. $j \neq k$

Since f satisfies (i) and (ii), we obtain $L_{f(j,y)} \subseteq L(G_j)$. Furthermore, M's definition implies $t_{x+r}^+ \subseteq L_{f(k,z)}$. Hence, the given IIM $\hat{M}$ has generated the hypothesis j on an initial segment of a text for $L_{f(k,z)} \in \mathcal{L}$. Since $\hat{M}$ works strong-monotonically on every text for every language $L \in \mathcal{L}$, we may conclude that $L(G_j) \subseteq L_{f(k,z)}$. Together with $L_{f(j,y)} \subseteq L(G_j)$, we get $L_{f(j,y)} \subseteq L_{f(k,z)}$.

Thus, M is rearrangement-independent and it works strong-monotonically. This proves the theorem.

$\hfill$ q.e.d.

Theorem 9.

(1) $s - EMON \subset r - EMON \subset EMON$,

(2) $s - MON \subset r - MON \subset MON$.

Proof. First of all, we show $r-EMON \setminus s-MON \neq \emptyset$. By definition, this yields immediately $s-EMON \subset r-EMON$ as well as $s-MON \subset r-MON$.

Lemma 1. $r-EMON \setminus s-MON \neq \emptyset$

By Theorem 3 we already know that $r-ESMON \setminus s-LIM \neq \emptyset$. It is easy to verify that $r-ESMON \subseteq r-EMON$. By definition, $s-MON \subseteq s-LIM$. Hence, we may conclude $r-EMON \setminus s-MON \neq \emptyset$. This proves the lemma.

It remains to show $EMON \setminus r-MON \neq \emptyset$. This statement directly implies $r-EMON \subset EMON$ and $r-MON \subset MON$, and hence, the theorem will be proved.

Lemma 2. $EMON \setminus r-MON \neq \emptyset$

We only present an indexed family $\mathcal{L} = (L_k)_{k \in \mathbb{N}}$ which witnesses the desired separation. A detailed proof can be found in Lange and Zeugmann (1993d). For all $k \in \mathbb{N}$ and all $z \in \{0, \dots, 3\}$ we define:

$$L_{4k+z} = \begin{cases} \{a^k b\} \cup A_k, & \text{if } z = 0, \\ \{a^k c\} \cup B_k, & \text{if } z = 1, \\ \{a^k b, a^k c\} \cup A_k, & \text{if } z = 2, \\ \{a^k b, a^k c\} \cup B_k, & \text{if } z = 3. \end{cases}$$

The remaining languages A_k and B_k will be defined via their characteristic functions f_{A_k} and f_{B_k}, respectively. For all $k \in \mathbb{N}$ and all strings $s \in \{a, b, c\}^+$ we set:

$$f_{A_k}(s) = \begin{cases} 1, & \text{if } s = b^k a^m \text{ and } \Phi_k(k) = m, \\ 0, & \text{otherwise.} \end{cases}$$

$$f_{B_k}(s) = \begin{cases} 1, & \text{if } s = c^k a^m \text{ and } \Phi_k(k) = m, \\ 0, & \text{otherwise.} \end{cases}$$

It is easy to see that $\mathcal{L}$ is indeed an indexed family.

q.e.d.

Finally, we consider rearrangement-independence in the context of exact and class preserving conservative learning. Since conservative learning is exactly as powerful as weak-monotonic one, by the latter theorem one might expect that rearrangement-independence is a severe restriction under the weak-monotonic constraint, too. On the other hand, looking at Theorem 4 we see that conservative learning has its peculiarities. And indeed, exact and class preserving learning can always be performed by rearrangement-independent IIMs.

Theorem 10.

(1) $r-ECONSERVATIVE = ECONSERVATIVE$,

(2) $r-CONSERVATIVE = CONSERVATIVE$.

The following figure summarizes the results obtained and points to the questions that remain open.

	exact learning	class preserving learning	class comprising learning
FIN	*set drivenness* +	*set drivenness* +	*set drivenness* +
SMON	*rearrangement independence* +	*rearrangement independence* +	?
MON	*rearrangement independence* −	*rearrangement independence* −	?
CONSERVATIVE	*rearrangement independence* +	*rearrangement independence* +	*set drivenness* +
LIM	*rearrangement independence* +	*rearrangement independence* +	*rearrangement independence* +

For every mode of learning ID mentioned "*rearrangement-independence* $+$" indicates $r-ID = ID$ as well as $s-ID \subset ID$. "*Rearrangement-independence* $-$" implies $s-ID \subset r-ID \subset ID$ whereas "*set-drivenness* $+$" should be interpreted as $s-ID = ID$ and, therefore, $r-ID = ID$, too.

5. References

ANGLUIN, D. (1980), Inductive inference of formal languages from positive data, *Information and Control* **45**, 117 - 135.

BERWICK, R. (1985), "The Acquisition of Syntactic Knowledge," Cambridge, Mass.: MIT Press.

FULK, M. (1990), Prudence and other restrictions in formal language learning, *Information and Computation* **85**, 1 - 11.

GOLD, E.M. (1967), Language identification in the limit, *Information and Control* **10**, 447 - 474.

HOPCROFT, J.E., AND ULLMAN, J.D (1969), "Formal Languages and their Relation to Automata," Addison-Wesley, Reading, Massachusetts.

JANTKE, K.P. (1991) Monotonic and non-monotonic inductive inference, *New Generation Computing* **8**, 349 - 360.

LANGE, S., AND ZEUGMANN, T. (1992), Types of monotonic language learning and their characterization, *in* "Proceedings 5th Annual ACM Workshop on Computational Learning Theory," July 27 - 29, Pittsburgh, pp. 377 - 390, ACM Press.

LANGE, S., AND ZEUGMANN, T. (1993a), Monotonic versus non-monotonic language learning, *in* "Proceedings 2nd International Workshop on Nonmonotonic and Inductive Logic," December 1991, Reinhardsbrunn, (G. Brewka, K.P. Jantke and P.H. Schmitt, Eds.), Lecture Notes in Artificial Intelligence 659, pp. 254 - 269, Springer-Verlag, Berlin.

LANGE, S., AND ZEUGMANN, T. (1993b), Language learning in dependence on the space of hypotheses, *in* "Proceedings 6th Annual ACM Conference on Computational Learning Theory," Santa Cruz, July 1993, pp. 127 - 136, ACM Press, New York.

LANGE, S., AND ZEUGMANN, T. (1993c), The learnability of recursive languages in dependence on the hypothesis space, GOSLER–Report 20/93, FB Mathematik, Informatik und Naturwissenschaften, HTWK Leipzig.

LANGE, S., AND ZEUGMANN, T. (1993d), On the impact of order independence to the learnability of recursive languages, ISIS-RR-93-17E, ISIS FUJITSU Labs., Numazu.

MACHTEY, M., AND YOUNG, P. (1978) "An Introduction to the General Theory of Algorithms," North-Holland, New York.

OSHERSON, D., STOB, M., AND WEINSTEIN, S. (1986), "Systems that Learn, An Introduction to Learning Theory for Cognitive and Computer Scientists," MIT-Press, Cambridge, Massachusetts.

SCHÄFER-RICHTER, G. (1984), "Über Eingabeabhängigkeit und Komplexität von Inferenzstrategien." Dissertation, Rheinisch Westfälische Technische Hochschule Aachen.

WEXLER, K. (1992), The subset principle is an intensional principle, in "Knowledge and Language: Issues in Representation and Acquisition," (E. Reuland and W. Abraham, Eds.), Kluwer Academic Publishers.

WEXLER, K., AND CULICOVER, P. (1980), "Formal Principles of Language Acquisition," Cambridge, Mass.: MIT Press.

WIEHAGEN, R. (1991), A thesis in inductive inference, in "Proceedings First International Workshop on Nonmonotonic and Inductive Logic," December 1990, Karlsruhe, (J. Dix, K.P. Jantke and P.H. Schmitt, Eds.), Lecture Notes in Artificial Intelligence Vol. 543, pp. 184 - 207, Springer-Verlag, Berlin.

Refutably Probably Approximately Correct Learning

Satoshi Matsumoto and Ayumi Shinohara

Research Institute of Fundamental Information Science
Kyushu University 33, Fukuoka 812, Japan
e-mails:{matumoto, ayumi}@rifis.kyushu-u.ac.jp

Abstract. We propose a notion of the *refutably PAC learning*, which formalizes the refutability of hypothesis spaces in the PAC learning model. Intuitively, the refutably PAC learning for a concept class $\mathcal{F}$ requires that the learning algorithm should refute $\mathcal{F}$ with high probability if a target concept can not be approximated by any concept in $\mathcal{F}$ with respect to the underlying probability distribution. We give a general upper bound of $O((1/\varepsilon + 1/\varepsilon')\ln(|\mathcal{F}^{[n]}|/\delta))$ on the number of examples required for refutably PAC learning of $\mathcal{F}$. Here, ε and δ are the standard accuracy and confidence parameters, and ε' is the refutation accuracy. Furthermore we also define the *strongly refutably PAC learning* by introducing the refutation threshold. We prove a general upper bound of $O((1/\varepsilon^2 + 1/\varepsilon'^2)\ln(|\mathcal{F}^{[n]}|/\delta))$ for strongly refutably PAC learning of $\mathcal{F}$. These upper bounds reveal that both the refutably learnability and the strongly refutably learnability are equivalent to the standard learnability within the polynomial size restriction. We also define the polynomial-time refutably learnability of a concept class, and characterize it.

1 Introduction

In the standard PAC learning model due to Valiant [12] and most of its variants [4, 10], a target concept is assumed to be in a hypothesis space. In these models, a learning algorithm has only to find a hypothesis which is consistent with given examples. There have been some studies [5, 8, 7, 13] which weakened the assumption. However, their main subjects are to find the best approximation in the hypothesis space, and they have paid little attention to determine whether or not the hypothesis space is suitable to approximate the target concept.

As a practical application of PAC learning, we developed a machine learning system which finds a motif from given positive and negative strings [2, 3, 11], and made some experiments on amino acid sequences. In particular, we applied it to the following two problems. One is the transmembrane domain identification, which is rather an easy problem. The other is the protein secondary structure prediction, which is one of the most challenging problem in Molecular Biology. Our learning system succeeded in discovering some simple and accurate motifs for the transmembrane domain sequences in very short time. On the other hand, it has failed to find a rule to predict the secondary structures of proteins with high accuracy. Thus, we have suspected that the hypothesis space is not suitable for the secondary structure prediction problem. Nevertheless, we have no criterion to terminate the learning algorithm even if there remains no possibility to find any good hypotheses. We need to refute all hypotheses in the current hypothesis space before trying some other space. If the learning algorithm can tell us that there are no target concept in the hypothesis space which explains a given sample, we may give a new other hypothesis space.

The refutability of the hypothesis space was originally introduced by Mukouchi and Arikawa [9] in the framework of inductive inference. It is an essence of a logic of machine discovery.

In this paper, we formalize the refutability of hypothesis spaces in the PAC learning model. We propose a notion of the *refutably PAC learning*. In this model, a learning algorithm tries to find a good approximation for a target concept with respect to the underlying probability distribution, in the same way as the standard PAC learning model. Additionally, the learning algorithm is required to refute the hypothesis space with high probability, if the target concept cannot be approximated by any concept in the hypothesis space. Furthermore we also define the *strongly refutably PAC learning* by introducing the refutation threshold.

We prove general upper bounds of the number of examples which are required for both the refutably PAC learning and the strongly refutably PAC learning. These upper bounds reveal that the polynomial-sample refutably learnability and polynomial-sample strongly refutably learnability are equivalent to the standard polynomial-sample learnability.

We also formalize a notion of the polynomial-time strongly refutably learnability. In order to characterize it, we propose a random polynomial-time refutably hypothesis finder. We show that the polynomial-time strongly refutably learnability of a concept class $\mathcal{F}$ in representation R is equivalent to the existence of a random polynomial-time hypothesis finder for $\mathcal{F}$ in R under some conditions.

2 Preliminaries

This section briefly summarizes the PAC-learnability due to Valiant [12].

Let $X = \Sigma^*$ be the set of all strings over a finite alphabet Σ. We call an element of X a *word* and X a *learning domain*. X_n denotes the set of all strings of length at most n for $n \geq 1$. A *concept* f is a subset of X. A *concept class* is a set $\mathcal{F} \subseteq 2^X$. Let I_f be the indicator function for f, that is, $I_f(x) = 1$ if $x \in f$ and $I_f(x) = 0$, otherwise. An *example* for a concept f on $x \in X$ is a pair $\langle x, I_f(x) \rangle$. If $I_f(x) = 1$, $\langle x, I_f(x) \rangle$ is a *positive* example; otherwise, it is a *negative* example. A *sample* of f is a nonempty sequence of examples for f. The *size* of a sample is the number of examples it contains. The *length* of a sample is the total length of the strings in the sample. We say that a concept g is *consistent* with a sample $\langle x_1, a_1 \rangle, \cdots, \langle x_m, a_m \rangle$ if $I_g(x_i) = a_i$ for all $1 \leq i \leq m$. For a sample S and a concept $g \in \mathcal{F}$, let $d(g, S)$ denote the number of examples in S which are inconsistent with g. For convenience, we assume hereafter that a polynomial

$p(x_1, \ldots, x_n)$ is nondecreasing with respect to each argument x_i, and its value is rounded up to an integer $\lceil p(x_1, \ldots, x_n) \rceil$.

For a *target concept* $f \subseteq X$ and a probability distribution P on X, let EXAMPLE(P, f) be an oracle which randomly returns a single example $\langle x, I_f(x) \rangle$ with probability $P(x)$ at each call.

The following definition is the standard PAC-learnability.

Definition 1. [10] Let $\mathcal{F}$ be a concept class on X. An algorithm $\mathcal{A}$ is a *learning algorithm* for $\mathcal{F}$ if the following conditions hold:

(a) $\mathcal{A}$ takes ε, δ and n ($0 < \varepsilon, \delta < 1$, $n \geq 1$) as inputs.
(b) For any concept $f \in \mathcal{F}$ and any probability distribution P on X_n, by using EXAMPLE(P, f), $\mathcal{A}$ satisfies the following condition:
   $\mathcal{A}$ outputs a concept $h \in \mathcal{F}$ which satisfies $P(f \triangle h) < \varepsilon$ with probability at least $1 - \delta$.

Definition 2. [10] Let $\mathcal{A}$ be a learning algorithm for a concept class $\mathcal{F}$. The *sample complexity* of $\mathcal{A}$ is the function $s : \mathbf{R} \times \mathbf{R} \times \mathbf{N} \to \mathbf{N}$ such that $s(\varepsilon, \delta, n)$ is the maximum number of calls of EXAMPLE(P, f) by $\mathcal{A}$, the maximum being taken over all runs of $\mathcal{A}$ on inputs ε, δ and n, with the target concept f ranging over all $f \in \mathcal{F}$ and the probability distribution P ranging over all distributions on X_n. If no finite maximum exists, $s(\varepsilon, \delta, n) = \infty$.

Definition 3. A concept class $\mathcal{F}$ is said to be *polynomial-sample learnable* if there exists a polynomial $p(\cdot, \cdot, \cdot)$ and a learning algorithm $\mathcal{A}$ for $\mathcal{F}$ with sample complexity $p(1/\varepsilon, 1/\delta, n)$.

Theorem 4. [10] *Let $\mathcal{F}$ be a concept class. Then, there exists a learning algorithm for $\mathcal{F}$ with sample complexity*

$$p\left(\frac{1}{\varepsilon}, \frac{1}{\delta}, n\right) = \left\lceil \frac{1}{\varepsilon} \ln \frac{|\mathcal{F}^{[n]}|}{\delta} \right\rceil .$$

Definition 5. [10] For a concept class $\mathcal{F}$ and an integer $n \geq 1$, we define the *n-th subclass* of $\mathcal{F}$ by $\mathcal{F}^{[n]} = \{f \cap X_n \mid f \in \mathcal{F}\}$. The *dimension* of n-th subclass is defined by $\dim \mathcal{F}^{[n]} = \log_2 |\mathcal{F}^{[n]}|$. We say that $\mathcal{F}$ is of *polynomial dimension* if there is a polynomial $p(\cdot)$ with $\dim \mathcal{F}^{[n]} \leq p(n)$ for any $n \geq 1$.

Theorem 6. [10] *A concept class $\mathcal{F}$ is polynomial-sample learnable if and only if $\mathcal{F}$ is of polynomial dimension.*

3 Refutably PAC Learnability

This section introduces a notion of the refutably PAC learnability, and show a general upper bound on the number of examples required.

For a concept class $\mathcal{F}$ and a probability distribution P, we define $opt_f(P, \mathcal{F}) = \min_{g \in \mathcal{F}} P(f \triangle g)$. For convenience, we treat $opt_f(P, \mathcal{F}) = \infty$ if $\mathcal{F}$ is empty. We remark that if f is in $\mathcal{F}$, then $opt_f(P, \mathcal{F}) = 0$ for any probability distribution P.

Now we formalize the refutably PAC learnability. Intuitively, we intend to capture a refutably learning algorithm by modifying Definition 1 (b) to the following (b');

(b') For any concept $f \subseteq X$ and any probability distribution P on X_n, by using EXAMPLE(P, f), $\mathcal{A}$ satisfies the following conditions.

    (i) If $opt_f(P, \mathcal{F}) = 0$, then $\mathcal{A}$ outputs a concept $h \in \mathcal{F}$ which satisfies $P(f \triangle h) < \varepsilon$ with probability at least $1 - \delta$.

    (ii) If $opt_f(P, \mathcal{F}) > 0$, then $\mathcal{A}$ refutes the concept class $\mathcal{F}$ with probability at least $1 - \delta$.

However, the condition (b')(ii) seems to be too strict. Let us imagine the following situation:

Example 1. $X = \{x_1, x_2, x_3, x_4\}$, $\mathcal{F} = \{\{x_1\}, \{x_1, x_2\}, \{x_1, x_3, x_4\}, \{x_2, x_3, x_4\}\}$, and $f = \{x_1, x_3\}$. For a large integer α, let P be the following probability distribution:

$$P(x_1) = \frac{1}{10}$$

$$P(x_2) = \frac{3}{10}$$

$$P(x_3) = \left(\frac{1}{10}\right)^{\alpha}$$

$$P(x_4) = \frac{6}{10} - \left(\frac{1}{10}\right)^{\alpha}$$

In this case, $opt_f(P, \mathcal{F}) = P(x_3) = \left(\frac{1}{10}\right)^{\alpha} > 0$. Therefore we expect that $\mathcal{A}$ refutes $\mathcal{F}$ with high probability. However, it is hard for $\mathcal{A}$ to predict whether or not $opt_f(P, \mathcal{F}) = 0$ by calling EXAMPLE(P, f) since the probability $P(x_3)$ is quite small. Thus, we relax the requirement by introducing a new parameter $\varepsilon' > 0$ called *refutation accuracy*. That is, $\mathcal{A}$ should refute $\mathcal{F}$ with high probability only when $opt_f(P, \mathcal{F}) \geq \varepsilon'$.

We now give the formal definition.

Definition 7. Let $\mathcal{F}$ be a concept class on X. An algorithm $\mathcal{A}$ is a *refutably learning algorithm* for $\mathcal{F}$ if the following conditions hold:

(a) $\mathcal{A}$ takes ε, ε', δ and n $(0 < \varepsilon, \varepsilon', \delta < 1, n \geq 1)$ as inputs.

(b) For any concept $f \subseteq X$ and any probability distribution P on X_n, by using EXAMPLE(P, f), $\mathcal{A}$ satisfies the following conditions.
  (i) If $opt_f(P, \mathcal{F}) = 0$, then $\mathcal{A}$ outputs a concept $h \in \mathcal{F}$ which satisfies $P(f \triangle h) < \varepsilon$ with probability at least $1 - \delta$.
  (ii) If $opt_f(P, \mathcal{F}) \geq \varepsilon'$, then $\mathcal{A}$ refutes the concept class $\mathcal{F}$ with probability at least $1 - \delta$.

We define the sample complexity of a refutably learning algorithm in the same way as Definition 2, with the target concept f ranging over all $f \subseteq X$ instead of $f \in \mathcal{F}$.

Definition 8. A concept class $\mathcal{F}$ is said to be *polynomial-sample refutably learnable* if there exists a polynomial $p(\cdot, \cdot, \cdot, \cdot)$ and a refutably learning algorithm $\mathcal{A}$ for $\mathcal{F}$ with sample complexity $p(1/\varepsilon, 1/\varepsilon', 1/\delta, n)$.

Now we show a general upper bound of the sample complexity for the refutably learnability. It should be noticed that the upper bound is essentially the same as that for standard PAC learnability in Theorem 4.

Theorem 9. *Let $\mathcal{F}$ be a concept class. Then, there exists a refutably learning algorithm for $\mathcal{F}$ with sample complexity*

$$p\left(\frac{1}{\varepsilon}, \frac{1}{\varepsilon'}, \frac{1}{\delta}, n\right) = \left\lceil \frac{1}{\kappa} \ln \frac{|\mathcal{F}^{[n]}|}{\delta} \right\rceil,$$

where $\kappa = \min\{\varepsilon, \varepsilon'\}$.

Proof. The algorithm $\mathcal{A}_1$ in Figure 1 is a refutably learning algorithm for $\mathcal{F}$. First, we estimate the number of examples from which the algorithm $\mathcal{A}_1$ refutes the concept class $\mathcal{F}$ with probability at least $1 - \delta$.

Let $f \subseteq X$ be a target concept. By the definition, we may consider only a probability distribution P on X_n. Then, without loss of generality, we can assume that a concept class is the n-th subclass $\mathcal{F}^{[n]}$. Suppose that $opt_f(P, \mathcal{F}) \geq \varepsilon'$. If the algorithm $\mathcal{A}_1$ outputs some concept g, all examples produced by EXAMPLE(P, f) are consistent with g. By the supposition, $P(f \triangle g) \geq \varepsilon'$ for any concept $g \in \mathcal{F}^{[n]}$. Then, the probability that any call of EXAMPLE(P, f) will produce an example consistent with g is at most $(1 - \varepsilon')$. Hence, the probability that m calls of EXAMPLE(P, f) will produce examples all consistent with g is at most $(1 - \varepsilon')^m$. Now, there are at most $|\mathcal{F}^{[n]}|$ choices for g. We will make m sufficiently large to bound the probability $|\mathcal{F}^{[n]}|(1 - \varepsilon')^m$ by δ.

Using the approximation $(1 - \varepsilon')^m \leq e^{-m\varepsilon'}$, we get

$$|\mathcal{F}^{[n]}| e^{-m\varepsilon'} \leq \delta.$$

Simplifying, we obtain the following inequality;

$$m \geq \frac{1}{\varepsilon'} \ln \frac{|\mathcal{F}^{[n]}|}{\delta}.$$

Algorithm $\mathcal{A}_1$
input: ε, ε', δ, n;
begin
    let $\kappa = \min\{\varepsilon, \varepsilon'\}$;
    let $m = \left\lceil \dfrac{1}{\kappa} \ln \dfrac{|\mathcal{F}^{[n]}|}{\delta} \right\rceil$;
    make m calls of EXAMPLE(P, f);
    let S be the set of examples seen;
    if there exists a concept $g \in \mathcal{F}$ that is consistent with S **then**
        begin
            pick a concept $h \in \mathcal{F}$ that is consistent with S;
            output h;
        end
    else
        refute the concept class $\mathcal{F}$;
end

Fig. 1. Refutably Learning Algorithm $\mathcal{A}_1$

Next, for the case (ii), we can apply the sample complexity of the standard PAC learnability in Theorem 4:

$$m \geq \frac{1}{\varepsilon} \ln \frac{|\mathcal{F}^{[n]}|}{\delta}.$$

Therefore,

$$\max\left\{ \frac{1}{\varepsilon'} \ln \frac{|\mathcal{F}^{[n]}|}{\delta}, \frac{1}{\varepsilon} \ln \frac{|\mathcal{F}^{[n]}|}{\delta} \right\} = \frac{1}{\kappa} \ln \frac{|\mathcal{F}^{[n]}|}{\delta}.$$

$\square$

It is clear that a concept class $\mathcal{F}$ is of polynomial dimension if $\mathcal{F}$ is polynomial-sample refutably learnable.

Corollary 10. *A concept class $\mathcal{F}$ is of polynomial dimension if and only if $\mathcal{F}$ is polynomial-sample refutably learnable.*

4 Strongly Refutably PAC Learnability

In a practical setting, it is unusual that there exists a concept $g \in \mathcal{F}$ with $P(f \triangle g) = 0$. As long as the minimum error $opt_f(P, \mathcal{F})$ is small enough, it is desirable that a learning algorithm should produce some approximation instead of refuting $\mathcal{F}$. For this purpose, we introduce a new parameter η $(0 \leq \eta < 1)$, which is a *refutation threshold*. Informally, we require a learning algorithm to output a concept $g \in \mathcal{F}$ with $P(f \triangle g) \leq \eta$ if any, and refute $\mathcal{F}$ otherwise. The formal definition is as follows.

Definition 11. Let $\mathcal{F}$ be a concept class on X. An algorithm $\mathcal{A}$ is a *strongly refutably learning algorithm* for $\mathcal{F}$ if the following conditions hold:

(a) $\mathcal{A}$ takes ε, ε', δ, η and n ($0 < \varepsilon, \varepsilon', \delta < 1$, $0 \leq \eta < 1$, $n \geq 1$) as inputs.
(b) For any concept $f \subseteq X$ and any probability distribution P on X_n, by using EXAMPLE(P, f), $\mathcal{A}$ satisfies the following conditions:
  (i) If $opt_f(P, \mathcal{F}) \leq \eta$, then $\mathcal{A}$ outputs a concept $h \in \mathcal{F}$ which satisfies $P(f \triangle h) < \eta + \varepsilon$ with probability at least $1 - \delta$.
  (ii) If $opt_f(P, \mathcal{F}) \geq \eta + \varepsilon'$, then $\mathcal{A}$ refutes the concept class $\mathcal{F}$ with probability at least $1 - \delta$.

Definition 12. The *sample complexity* of a strongly refutably learning algorithm $\mathcal{A}$ is the function $s : \mathbf{R} \times \mathbf{R} \times \mathbf{R} \times \mathbf{N} \to \mathbf{N}$ such that $s(\varepsilon, \varepsilon', \delta, n)$ is the maximum number of calls of EXAMPLE(P, f) by $\mathcal{A}$, the maximum being taken over all runs of $\mathcal{A}$ on inputs ε, ε', δ, η and n, with the target concept f ranging over all $f \subseteq X$ and the probability distribution P ranging over all distributions on X_n.

Remark that we do not permit the sample complexity to depend on the parameter η.

Definition 13. A concept class $\mathcal{F}$ is said to be *polynomial-sample strongly refutably learnable* if there exists a polynomial $p(\cdot, \cdot, \cdot, \cdot)$ and a strongly refutably learning algorithm $\mathcal{A}$ for $\mathcal{F}$ with sample complexity $p(1/\varepsilon, 1/\varepsilon', 1/\delta, n)$.

We prepare some lemmas which will be useful in the Theorem 18 and Theorem 23.

Lemma 14. [1] *If $0 \leq p \leq 1$, $0 \leq r \leq 1$, and m is any positive integer then*

$$\sum_{k=\lceil m(p+r) \rceil}^{m} \binom{m}{k} p^k (1-p)^{m-k} \leq e^{-2r^2 m},$$

and

$$\sum_{k=0}^{\lfloor m(p-r) \rfloor} \binom{m}{k} p^k (1-p)^{m-k} \leq e^{-2r^2 m}.$$

Lemma 15. *Let $\mathcal{F}$ be a concept class, n be an integer $(n \geq 1)$, ε, κ, η, δ be real numbers $(0 < \varepsilon, \delta < 1, 0 \leq \eta < 1, 0 < \kappa \leq \varepsilon)$, f be a target concept $(f \subseteq X)$, and P be a probability distribution on X_n. For*

$$m \geq \left\lceil \frac{2}{\kappa^2} \ln \frac{|\mathcal{F}_n|}{\delta} \right\rceil,$$

let S be a sequence of m examples which are chosen randomly and independently according to P. Then the probability that there exists a concept $g \in \mathcal{F}$ which satisfies $P(f \triangle g) \geq \eta + \varepsilon$ and $d(g, S) \leq \lfloor m(\eta + (1/2)\kappa) \rfloor$ is at most δ.

Proof. By assumption that P is a probability distribution on X_n, we may assume that a concept class is the n-th subclass $\mathcal{F}^{[n]}$. For a concept $g \in \mathcal{F}^{[n]}$ with $P(f \triangle g) > \eta + \varepsilon$, the probability that m calls of EXAMPLE(P, f) will produce a sample S such that $d(g, S) \leq \lfloor m(\eta + (1/2)\kappa) \rfloor$ is at most

$$\sum_{i=0}^{\lfloor m(\eta + \frac{1}{2}\kappa) \rfloor} \binom{m}{i} P(f \triangle g)^i (1 - P(f \triangle g))^{m-i}.$$

We denote $P(f \triangle g)$ by ν_g. Then,

$$\sum_{i=0}^{\lfloor m(\eta + \frac{1}{2}\kappa) \rfloor} \binom{m}{i} \nu_g{}^i (1 - \nu_g)^{m-i} \leq \sum_{i=0}^{\lfloor m(\nu_g - \frac{1}{2}\kappa) \rfloor} \binom{m}{i} \nu_g{}^i (1 - \nu_g)^{m-i}$$

$$\leq e^{-2m\left(\frac{1}{2}\kappa\right)^2}, \qquad \text{(byLemma 14)}.$$

Now, there are at most $|\mathcal{F}^{[n]}|$ choices for g. We will make m sufficiently large to bound this probability $|\mathcal{F}^{[n]}|e^{-2m\left(\frac{1}{2}\kappa\right)^2}$ by δ. Thus we obtain the following inequality;

$$m \geq \frac{2}{\kappa^2} \ln \frac{|\mathcal{F}^{[n]}|}{\delta}.$$

Hence, if m examples are drawn, the probability that there exists a concept $g \in \mathcal{F}^{[n]}$ such that $P(f \triangle g) \geq \eta + \varepsilon$ and $d(g, S) \leq \lfloor m(\eta + (1/2)\kappa) \rfloor$ is at most δ. $\qquad\qquad\square$

The following two lemmas can be proved in the same way as Lemma 15.

Lemma 16. *Let $\mathcal{F}$ be a concept class, n be an integer $(n \geq 1)$, ε, κ, η, δ be real numbers $(0 < \varepsilon, \delta < 1, 0 \leq \eta < 1, 0 < \kappa \leq \varepsilon)$, f be a target concept $(f \subseteq X)$, and P be a probability distribution on X_n. Assume that there exists a concept $g \in \mathcal{F}$ with $P(f \triangle g) \leq \eta$. For*

$$m \geq \left\lceil \frac{2}{\kappa^2} \ln \frac{|\mathcal{F}_n|}{\delta} \right\rceil,$$

let S be a sequence of m examples which are chosen randomly and independently according to P. Then the probability that $d(g, S) \geq \lfloor m(\eta + (1/2)\kappa) \rfloor + 1$ for all $g \in \mathcal{F}$ is at most δ.

Lemma 17. *Let $\mathcal{F}$ be a concept class, n be an integer $(n \geq 1)$, ε, κ, η, δ be real numbers $(0 < \varepsilon', \delta < 1, 0 \leq \eta < 1, 0 < \kappa \leq \varepsilon')$, f be a target concept $(f \subseteq X)$, and P be a probability distribution on X_n. Assume that $P(f \triangle g) \geq \eta + \varepsilon'$ for all concepts $g \in \mathcal{F}$. For*

$$m \geq \left\lceil \frac{2}{\kappa^2} \ln \frac{|\mathcal{F}_n|}{\delta} \right\rceil,$$

let S be a sequence of m examples which are chosen randomly and independently according to P. Then the probability that there exists a concept $g \in \mathcal{F}$ which satisfies $d(g, S) \leq \lfloor m (\eta + (1/2)\kappa) \rfloor$ is at most δ.

Using the above lemmas, we show that a general upper bound of the sample complexity for the strongly refutably learnability.

Theorem 18. *Let $\mathcal{F}$ be a concept class. Then, there exists a strongly refutably learning algorithm for $\mathcal{F}$ with sample complexity*

$$p\left(\frac{1}{\varepsilon}, \frac{1}{\varepsilon'}, \frac{1}{\delta}, n\right) = \left\lceil \frac{2}{\kappa^2} \ln \frac{2|\mathcal{F}^{[n]}|}{\delta} \right\rceil,$$

where $\kappa = \min\{\varepsilon, \varepsilon'\}$.

Proof. The algorithm $\mathcal{A}_2$ in Figure 2 is a strongly refutably learning algorithm for $\mathcal{F}$.

Let f be a target concept. First we assume that $opt_f(P, \mathcal{F}) \leq \eta$. We now calculate the probability that $\mathcal{A}_2$ fails to output a concept h satisfying $P(f \triangle h) < \eta + \varepsilon$. It occurs only when $\mathcal{A}_2$ outputs a concept h satisfying $P(f \triangle h) \geq \eta + \varepsilon$ or $\mathcal{A}_2$ refutes $\mathcal{F}$.

By Lemma 15 and the definition of Algorithm $\mathcal{A}_2$, the probability that $\mathcal{A}_2$ outputs a concept h satisfying $P(f \triangle h) \geq \eta + \varepsilon$ is at most $\delta/2$. Similarly, by Lemma 16, the probability that $\mathcal{A}_2$ refutes $\mathcal{F}$ is at most $\delta/2$. Thus, we see that the probability that $\mathcal{A}_2$ outputs a concept h such that $P(f \triangle h) < \eta + \varepsilon$ is at least $1 - \delta$.

Next we assume that $opt_f(P, \mathcal{F}) \geq \eta + \varepsilon'$. Then, by Lemma 17, we can show that if $m \geq (2/\kappa^2) \ln(2|\mathcal{F}^{[n]}|/\delta)$ then the probability that the algorithm $\mathcal{A}_2$ refutes the concept class $\mathcal{F}$ is at least $1 - \delta$. $\quad\square$

It is clear that a concept class $\mathcal{F}$ is of polynomial dimension if $\mathcal{F}$ is polynomial-sample strongly refutably learnable.

Corollary 19. *A concept class $\mathcal{F}$ is of polynomial dimension if and only if $\mathcal{F}$ is polynomial-sample strongly refutably learnable.*

Corollary 20. *For a concept class $\mathcal{F}$, the following three statements are equivalent.*

(a) F is polynomial-sample learnable.
(b) F is polynomial-sample refutably learnable.
(c) F is polynomial-sample strongly refutably learnable.

Algorithm $\mathcal{A}_2$
input: $\varepsilon, \varepsilon', \delta, \eta, n;$
begin

    let $\kappa = \min\{\varepsilon, \varepsilon'\};$

    let $m = \left\lceil \dfrac{2}{\kappa^2} \ln \dfrac{2|\mathcal{F}^{[n]}|}{\delta} \right\rceil;$

    make m calls of EXAMPLE$(P, f);$
    let S be the sequence of examples seen;
    if there exists a concept $g \in \mathcal{F}$ such that $d(g, S) \leq \left\lfloor m\left(\eta + \dfrac{1}{2}\kappa\right)\right\rfloor$ **then**
        begin

            pick a concept $h \in \mathcal{F}$ such that $d(h, S) \leq \left\lfloor m\left(\eta + \dfrac{1}{2}\kappa\right)\right\rfloor;$
            output $h;$
            halt
        end
    else
        refute the concept class $\mathcal{F};$
end

Fig. 2. Strongly Refutably Learning Algorithm $\mathcal{A}_2$

5   The Problem of Finding Hypothesis

In this section, we define the polynomial-time refutably learnability. Then we characterize it by the dimension and the existence of a hypothesis finder.

Let $\mathcal{F}$ be a concept class. A mapping $R : \mathcal{F} \to 2^{\Sigma^*}$ is called *a representation* for $\mathcal{F}$ in R such that $R(g) \neq \phi$ for all $g \in \mathcal{F}$, and $R(f) \cap R(g) = \phi$ for any two distinct $f, g \in \mathcal{F}$. For any $g \in \mathcal{F}$, a set $R(g)$ is the set of *names* for g. The length of a name $r \in R(f)$ is simply the string length of r. For $s \geq 1$, we define $\mathcal{F}_{s,R} = \{f \in \mathcal{F} \mid l_{\min}(f, R) \leq s\}$, where $l_{\min}(f, R)$ denotes the length of the shortest name for f in R. When R is clear from the context, we omit it.

A representation R for $\mathcal{F}$ is *polynomial-time computable* if there is a polynomial-time algorithm that, given a name $r \in R(f)$ and a string $x \in X$, determines whether or not $x \in f$.

Definition 21. Let $\mathcal{F}$ be a concept class and R be a representation for $\mathcal{F}$. An algorithm $\mathcal{A}$ is a *polynomial-time strongly refutably learning algorithm* for $\mathcal{F}$ in R if the following conditions hold:

(a) $\mathcal{A}$ takes ε, ε', δ, η, n and s $(0 < \varepsilon, \varepsilon', \delta < 1, 0 \leq \eta < 1, n, s \geq 1)$ as inputs. The parameter s is a *complexity measure*.
(b) For any concept $f \subseteq X$ and any probability distribution P on X_n, by using EXAMPLE(P, f), $\mathcal{A}$ satisfies the following conditions:
    (i) If $opt_f(P, \mathcal{F}_{s,R}) \leq \eta$, then $\mathcal{A}$ outputs $r \in R(g)$ for some concept $g \in \mathcal{F}_{s,R}$ such that $P(f \triangle g) < \eta + \varepsilon$ with probability at least $1 - \delta$.

    (ii) If $opt_f(P, \mathcal{F}_{s,R}) \geq \eta + \varepsilon'$, then $\mathcal{A}$ refutes the concept class $\mathcal{F}$ with probability at least $1 - \delta$.

(c) $\mathcal{A}$ runs in time polynomial with respect to $1/\varepsilon$, $1/\varepsilon'$, $1/\delta$, n and s.

We say that $\mathcal{F}$ is *polynomial-time strongly refutably learnable* in R if there exists such a polynomial-time strongly refutably learning algorithm $\mathcal{A}$ for $\mathcal{F}$ in R.

We are interested in identifying the family of pairs $\mathcal{F}$ and R, such that $\mathcal{F}$ is polynomial-time strongly refutably learnable in R.

Recall that Blumer et al [4] characterized the polynomial-time learnability by the existence of a *random polynomial-time hypothesis finder* which finds a hypothesis consistent with a given sample. Here we introduce a notion of the randomized refutably hypothesis finder, which is an extension.

Definition 22. Let $\mathcal{F}$ be a concept class and R be a representation for $\mathcal{F}$. An algorithm Q is said to be a *randomized refutably hypothesis finder* for $\mathcal{F}$ in R if the following conditions hold:

(a) Q takes a sample S and integers $k \geq 0$, $s \geq 1$ as inputs.
(b) There exists a real number γ $(0 < \gamma < 1)$ that satisfies the following conditions:
    (i) If there exists a concept $g \in \mathcal{F}_{s,R}$ with $d(g, S) \leq k$, then Q outputs a name $r \in R(g)$ with probability at least γ.
    (ii) Otherwise, Q refutes the concept class $\mathcal{F}$ with probability at least γ.

We call γ *success rate*. We say that Q is a *random polynomial-time refutably hypothesis finder* for $\mathcal{F}$ in R if Q runs in polynomial time with respect to the length of sample S and s.

Theorem 23. *Let $\mathcal{F}$ be a concept class and R be a polynomial-time computable representation for $\mathcal{F}$. If $\mathcal{F}$ is of polynomial dimension and there exists a random polynomial-time refutably hypothesis finder for $\mathcal{F}$ in R, then $\mathcal{F}$ is strongly refutably learnable in R.*

Proof. The basic idea is also due to [4, 6]. Assume that we have a random polynomial-time refutably hypothesis finder Q for $\mathcal{F}$ in R with success rate γ. By using Q, we construct a strongly refutably learning algorithm $\mathcal{A}_3$ for $\mathcal{F}$ in R (Figure 3).

First note that the size of a sample used by $\mathcal{A}_3$ is bounded by a polynomial in $1/\varepsilon$, $1/\varepsilon'$, $1/\delta$ and n, since $\mathcal{F}$ is of polynomial dimension. In addition, since Q is a random polynomial-time refutably hypothesis finder, the time required for a single execution of the simulation $Q(S, k, s)$ is bounded by a polynomial in the length of the sample and s. Since R is polynomial-time computable, the computation of $d(g, S)$ can be executed in time polynomial in the length of the sample and the length of the name produced during the simulation. Finally, since

Algorithm $\mathcal{A}_3$
input:ε, ε', δ, η, n, s;
begin

    let $\kappa = \min\{\varepsilon, \varepsilon'\}$;

    let $m = \left\lceil \dfrac{2}{\kappa^2} \ln \dfrac{4|\mathcal{F}^{[n]}|}{\delta} \right\rceil$;

    let $k = \left\lfloor m\left(\eta + \dfrac{1}{2}\kappa\right) \right\rfloor$;

    make m calls of EXAMPLE(P, f);

    let S be the sequence of examples seen;

    let $i = 1$;

    while $(i \leq \dfrac{1}{\gamma} \ln \dfrac{2}{\delta})$;

    begin

        simulate $Q(S,k,s)$;

        if Q outputs a name $r \in R(g)$ for some $g \in \mathcal{F}_{s,R}$ then

            begin

                compute $d(g, S)$;

                if $d(g, S) \leq k$ then

                    output r;

                    halt

            end

        $i = i + 1$;

    end

    refute the concept class $\mathcal{F}$;

end

Fig. 3. Polynomial-time Strongly Refutably Learning Algorithm $\mathcal{A}_3$

the maximum number of repetitions in $O(\log(1/\delta))$, which implies that the total run time of $\mathcal{A}_3$ is bounded by a polynomial in $1/\varepsilon$, $1/\varepsilon'$, $1/\delta$, n and s.

We have the following two cases:

(1) In case of $opt_f(P, \mathcal{F}_s) \leq \eta$; We now calculate the probability that $\mathcal{A}_3$ fails to produce a name of a concept $h \in \mathcal{F}_s$ with $P(f \triangle h) \leq \eta + \varepsilon$. It occurs only when the number of repetitions exceeds $(1/\gamma)\ln(2/\delta)$, or $\mathcal{A}_3$ finds a concept $h \in \mathcal{F}_s$ such that $P(f \triangle h) \geq \eta + \varepsilon$ and $d(g, S) \leq k$, or $\mathcal{A}_3$ refutes $\mathcal{F}$. By the definition, the probability that Q fails to produce a name of a concept h such that $d(h, S) \leq k$ on any single iteration of the simulation $Q(S, k, s)$ is at most $1 - \gamma$. Hence the probability that the number of iterations exceeds $(1/\gamma)\ln(2/\delta)$ is at most

$$(1 - \gamma)^{\frac{1}{\gamma}\ln\frac{2}{\delta}} \leq e^{-\ln\frac{2}{\delta}} = \frac{\delta}{2}.$$

By Lemma 15, the probability that there is any concept h in $\mathcal{F}_s$ such that $P(f \triangle h) \geq \eta + \varepsilon$ and $d(h, S) \leq k$ is at most $\delta/4$. Hence the probability that $\mathcal{A}$ finds a concept $h \in \mathcal{F}_s$ such that $P(f \triangle h) \geq \eta + \varepsilon$ and $d(h, S) \leq k$ is at most

$\delta/4$. By Lemma 16, the probability that A_3 refutes $\mathcal{F}$ is at most $\delta/4$. Therefore the probability that $\mathcal{A}$ fails to output a name of a concept h with $P(f \triangle h) \le \eta + \varepsilon$ is at most δ.

(2) In case of $opt_f(P, \mathcal{F}_s) \ge \eta + \varepsilon'$; $P(f \triangle g) \ge \eta + \varepsilon'$ for all $g \in \mathcal{F}_s$. By Lemma 17, the probability that there is any concept h in $\mathcal{F}_s$ such that $d(h, S) \le k$ is at most $\delta/4$ Hence the probability that $\mathcal{A}$ finds a concept $h \in \mathcal{F}_s$ such that $d(h, S) \le k$ is at most $\delta/4$. So the probability that $\mathcal{A}$ does not refute $\mathcal{F}$ is at most δ. $\qquad\qquad\square$

Theorem 24. *Let $\mathcal{F}$ be a concept class and R be a representation for $\mathcal{F}$. If $\mathcal{F}$ is polynomial-time strongly refutably learnable in R then there exists a random polynomial-time refutably hypothesis finder for $\mathcal{F}$ in R.*

Proof. The basic idea is due to [4, 6]. Assume that $\mathcal{F}$ is polynomial-time strongly refutably learnable in R. Let $\mathcal{A}$ be a polynomial-time strongly refutably learning algorithm for $\mathcal{F}$ in R. Using $\mathcal{A}$, we construct a random polynomial-time refutably hypothesis finder Q for $\mathcal{F}$ in R with success rate $1/2$ as follows. Suppose that Q is given a sample S of some concept $f \subseteq X$ and integers $k \ge 0$, $s \ge 1$. Let m be the size of the sample S, and n be the length of the longest word in S. We define a distribution P over X_n by $P(x) = o(x, S)/m$ for each $x \in X_n$, where $o(x, S)$ is the number of occurrences of x in S. Algorithm Q simulates $\mathcal{A}$ on inputs $\varepsilon = 1/(m + 1)$, $\eta = k/m$, $\varepsilon' = 1/m$, $\delta = 1/2$, n and s. Each time $\mathcal{A}$ calls EXAMPLE(P, f), Q chooses an integer i uniformly at random from $\{1, \ldots, m\}$ and gives the i-th example in S to $\mathcal{A}$. Thus examples given to $\mathcal{A}$ are drawn independently from the distribution P defined above. If $\mathcal{A}$ outputs a name r then Q outputs r, and if $\mathcal{A}$ refutes $\mathcal{F}$ then Q refutes $\mathcal{F}$.

We have the following two cases.

(1) In case that there exists a concept $g \in \mathcal{F}_s$ with $d(g, S) \le k$; Since $P(f \triangle g) = d(g, S)/m \le k/m = \eta$, we see $opt_f(P, \mathcal{F}_s) \le \eta$. Thus, with probability at least $1 - \delta = 1/2$, $\mathcal{A}$ outputs a name of a concept $h \in \mathcal{F}_s$ such that $P(f \triangle h) < \eta + \varepsilon = k/m + 1/(m + 1) < (k + 1)/m$. It implies $d(h, S) < k + 1$, since $P(f \triangle h) = d(h, S)/m$. Therefore Q outputs $h \in \mathcal{F}_s$ such that $d(h, S) \le k$ with probability at least $1/2$.

(2) In case that there is no concept $g \in \mathcal{F}_s$ with $d(g, S) \le k$; Since $opt_f(P, \mathcal{F}_s) \ge \eta + \varepsilon'$, $\mathcal{A}$ refutes $\mathcal{F}$ with probability at least $1 - \delta = 1/2$. That is, Q refutes $\mathcal{F}$ with probability at least $1/2$.

Finally, we estimate the running time of Q. For the length l of the given sample S, we see $m \le l$ and $n \le l$. Since $\mathcal{A}$ runs in polynomial time with respect to $1/\varepsilon = m + 1$, $1/\varepsilon' = m$, $1/\delta = 2$, n, and s, the running time of Q is bounded by a polynomial with respect to l and s. $\qquad\qquad\square$

Theorem 23 and Theorem 24 yield the following theorem.

Theorem 25. *Let $\mathcal{F}$ be a concept class and R be a polynomial-time computable representation for $\mathcal{F}$. If $\mathcal{F}$ is of polynomial dimension, then $\mathcal{F}$ is polynomial-time* *strongly refutably learnable in R if and only if there exists a random polynomial-time refutably hypothesis finder for $\mathcal{F}$ in R.*

6 Conclusion

We have formalized the refutability of hypothesis space in the PAC-learning model, and proved general upper bounds of the sample complexity both for the refutably PAC learnability and for the strongly refutable PAC learnability. We will give a general lower bound for the strongly refutable learnability in future works.

Acknowledgment

The authors would like to thank Prof. Setsuo Arikawa for helpful discussions.

References

1. Angluin, D. and Laird, P.: Learning from noisy examples. Machine Learning **2** (1988) 343–370.
2. Arikawa, S., Kuhara, S., Miyano, S., Shinohara, A. and Shinohara, T.: A learning algorithm for elementary formal systems and its experiments on identification of transmembrane domains. In Proc. 25th Hawaii International Conference on System Sciences (1992) 675–684.
3. Arikawa, S., Miyano, S., Shinohara, A., Kuhara, S., Mukouchi, Y. and Shinohara, T.: A machine discovery from amino acid sequences by decision trees over regular patterns. New Generation Computing **11** (1993) 361–375.
4. Blumer, A., Ehrenfeucht, A., Haussler, D. and Warmuth, M.: Learnability and the Vapnik-Chervonenkis dimension. Journal of the ACM **36** (1989) 929–965.
5. Haussler, D.: Generalizing the PAC model: Sample size bounds from metric dimension-based uniform convergence results. In Proceedings of the 2nd Annual Workshop on Computational Learning Theory (1989) 385.
6. Haussler, D., Kearns, M., Littlestone, N. and Warmuth, M.: Equivalence of models for polynomial learnability. Information and Computation **95** (1991) 129–161.
7. Kearns, M. and Schapire, R.: Efficient distribution-free learning of probabilistic concepts. In Proceedings of the 31st Annual Symposium on Foundations of Computer Science (1990) 382–391.
8. Kearns, M., Schapire, R. and Sellie, L.: Toward efficient agnostic learning. In Proceedings of the 5th Annual ACM Workshop on Computational Learning Theory (1992) 341–352.
9. Mukouchi, Y. and Arikawa, S.: Inductive inference machines that can refute hypothesis spaces. In Proceedings of 4th International Workshop on Algorithmic Learning Theory (1993) 123–136.
10. Natarajan, B.: MACHINE LEARNING A Theoretical Approach. Morgan Kaufmann 1991.

11. Shimozono, S., Shinohara, A., Shinohara, T., Miyano, S., Kuhara, S. and Arikawa, S.: Finding alphabet indexing for decision trees over regular patterns: an approach to bioinformatical knowledge acquisition. In Proc. 26th Annual Hawaii International Conference on System Sciences (1993) 763–772.
12. Valiant, L.: A theory of the learnable. Communications of the ACM **27** (1984) 1134–1142.
13. Yamanishi, K.: A learning criterion for stochastic rules. Machine Learning **9** (1992) 165–203.

Inductive Inference of an Approximate Concept from Positive Data

Yasuhito Mukouchi*

Research Institute of Fundamental Information Science
Kyushu University 33, Fukuoka 812, Japan

Abstract. In ordinary learning paradigm, a target concept, whose examples are fed to an inference machine, is assumed to belong to a hypothesis space which is given in advance. However this assumption is not appropriate, if we want an inference machine to infer or to discover an unknown rule which explains examples or data obtained from scientific experiments.

In their previous paper, Mukouchi and Arikawa discussed both refutability and inferability of a hypothesis space from examples. In this paper, we take a minimal concept as an approximate concept within a hypothesis space, and discuss inferability of a minimal concept of the target concept which may not belong to the hypothesis space. That is, we force an inference machine to converge to a minimal concept of the target concept, if there is a minimal concept of the target concept within the hypothesis space. We also show that there are some rich hypothesis spaces that are minimally inferable from positive data.

1 Introduction

Inductive inference is a process of hypothesizing a general rule from examples. As a correct inference criterion for inductive inference of formal languages and models of logic programming, we have mainly used Gold's identification in the limit[7]. An inference machine M is said to identify a concept L in the limit, if the sequence of guesses from M, which is successively fed a sequence of examples of L, converges to a correct expression of L. Under this criterion, many productive results concerning inductive inference from positive data have been reported by Angluin[2], Wright[23], Shinohara[20, 21] and Moriyama&Sato[10].

In this criterion, a target concept, whose examples are fed to an inference machine, is assumed to belong to a hypothesis space which is given in advance. However this assumption is not appropriate, if we want an inference machine to infer or to discover an unknown rule which explains examples or data obtained from scientific experiments. In their previous paper, Mukouchi and Arikawa[12, 13] discussed both refutability and inferability of a hypothesis space from examples. If a target concept is a member of the hypothesis space, then an inference machine should identify the target concept in the limit, otherwise it should refute the hypothesis space itself in a finite time. They showed that there are some rich hypothesis spaces that are refutable and inferable from complete data (i.e. positive and negative data), but refutable and inferable classes from only positive data (i.e. text) are very small.

---

* Present address: Department of Mathematical Sciences and Information Sciences, College of Integrated Arts and Sciences, University of Osaka Prefecture, Sakai, Osaka 593, Japan

In practical applications of inductive inference, there are many cases where we want an inference machine to infer an approximate concept within the hypothesis space concerned, even when there is no concept which exactly coincides with the target concept. In this paper we take a minimal concept as an approximate concept within the hypothesis space, and discuss inferability of a minimal concept of the target concept which may not belong to the hypothesis space. That is, we force an inference machine to converge to a minimal concept of the target concept, if there is a minimal concept of the target concept within the hypothesis space.

In 1989, Wright[23] showed that if a class has so-called finite elasticity, then the class is inferable in the limit from positive data. Using this result, Shinohara[20, 21] showed that the classes definable by length-bounded EFS's with at most n axioms are inferable in the limit from positive data. On the other hand, Sato&Moriyama[16] introduced the notion of M-finite thickness to show another condition for inferability from positive data. Here we show that the classes with both finite elasticity and M-finite thickness are minimally inferable from positive data. Using the result, we show that the classes that were introduced by Shinohara[20] are also minimally inferable from positive data. This means that there are some rich hypothesis spaces that are minimally inferable from positive data.

This paper is organized as follows: In Section 2 we prepare some necessary concepts for our discussions and introduce our definitions of inferability. In Section 3 we discuss some sufficient conditions for a class to be minimally inferable from positive data. In Section 4 we also show the differences between the powers of inference machines whose behaviors differs from each other when there is no minimal concept of the target concept in the class concerned. In Section 5 we discuss minimal inferability of length-bounded EFS definable classes from positive data, and show that there are some rich hypothesis spaces that are minimally inferable from positive data.

2 Preliminaries

We start with basic definitions and notions on inductive inference of indexed families of recursive concepts.

Let U be a recursively enumerable set to which we refer as a *universal set*. Then we call $L \subseteq U$ a *concept*. In case the universal set U is the set Σ^+ of all nonnull finite strings over a finite alphabet Σ, we also call $L \subseteq U$ a *language*.

Definition 1. Let $N = \{1, 2, \cdots\}$ be the set of all natural numbers. A class $\mathcal{C} = \{L_i\}_{i \in N}$ of concepts is said to be an *indexed family of recursive concepts*, if there is a recursive function $f : N \times U \to \{0, 1\}$ such that

$$f(i, w) = \begin{cases} 1, & \text{if } w \in L_i, \\ 0, & \text{otherwise.} \end{cases}$$

In what follows, we assume that a class of concepts is an indexed family of recursive concepts without any notice, and identify a class with a hypothesis space.

Definition 2. A *positive presentation*, or a *text*, of a *nonempty* concept L is an infinite sequence $w_1, w_2, \cdots$ of elements in L such that $\{w_1, w_2, \cdots\} = L$.

In what follows, σ denotes a positive presentation, $\sigma[n]$ denotes the σ's initial segment of length $n \geq 1$, and $\sigma[n]^+$ denotes the set of all facts in $\sigma[n]$. For a positive presentation σ, each element in σ is called a *fact*.

An *inductive inference machine* (*IIM*, for short) is an effective procedure, or a certain type of Turing machine, which requests inputs from time to time and produces positive integers from time to time.

An *inductive inference machine that can refute hypothesis spaces* (*RIIM*, for short) is an effective procedure which requests inputs from time to time and either (i) produces positive integers from time to time or (ii) refutes the class and stops after producing some positive integers. The outputs produced by the machine are called *guesses*.

For an IIM M or an RIIM M and a finite sequence $\sigma[n] = w_1, w_2, \cdots, w_n$, by $M(\sigma[n])$, we denote the last guess or the 'refutation' sign produced by M which is successively presented $w_1, w_2, \cdots, w_n$ on its input requests.

For more details about an IIM and an RIIM, please refer to Mukouchi&Arikawa[13].

An IIM M or an RIIM M is said to *converge to an index i for a positive presentation σ*, if there is an $n \geq 1$ such that for any $m \geq n$, $M(\sigma[m])$ is defined and equal to i. An RIIM M is said to *refute a class C from a positive presentation σ*, if there is an $n \geq 1$ such that $M(\sigma[n])$ is defined as the 'refutation' sign. In this case we also say that M refutes the class C from $\sigma[n]$.

Definition 3 (Gold[7]). An IIM M is said to *infer a class C in the limit from positive data*, if for any $L_i \in C$ and any positive presentation σ of L_i, M converges to an index j for σ such that $L_j = L_i$.

A class C is said to be *inferable in the limit from positive data*, if there is an IIM which infers C from positive data.

In the above definition, the behavior of an inference machine is not specified, when we feed a positive presentation of a concept which is not in the class concerned. In the following Definition 4 and 6, we consider arbitrary target concepts that may *not* be recursively enumerable.

Let $L \subseteq U$ be a concept and let C be a class. Then a concept $L_n \in C$ is said to be a *minimal concept of L within C*, if (i) $L \subseteq L_n$ and (ii) for any $L_i \in C$, $L \subseteq L_i$ implies $L_i \nsubseteq L_n$.

Hereafter, for a concept $L \subseteq U$, we write $L \in C$, if there is an $L_i \in C$ such that $L_i = L$.

Definition 4 (Sakurai[14]). An IIM M is said to *semi-reliably infer a class C from positive data*, if it satisfies the following condition: For any nonempty concept L and any positive presentation σ of L, (i) if $L \in C$, then M converges to an index i for σ such that $L_i = L$, (ii) otherwise if M converges to an index i for σ, then L_i is a minimal concept of L within C.

A class C is said to be *semi-reliably inferable from positive data*, if there is an IIM which semi-reliably infers C from positive data.

Theorem 5 (Sakurai[14]). *A class C is semi-reliably inferable from positive data, if and only if C is inferable in the limit from positive data.*

Now we introduce our definitions of minimal inferability.

Definition 6. An IIM M is said to *minimally infer a class C from positive data*, if it satisfies the following condition: For any nonempty concept L and any positive presentation σ of L, if there exists a minimal concept of L within C, then M converges to an index of a minimal concept of L within C for σ.

An RIIM M is said to *refutably minimally infer a class C from positive data*, if it satisfies the following condition: For any nonempty concept L and any positive presentation σ of L, (i) if there exists a minimal concept of L within C, then M converges to an index of a minimal concept of L within C for σ, (ii) otherwise M refutes the class C from σ.

An IIM M is said to *reliably minimally infer a class C from positive data*, if it satisfies the following condition: For any nonempty concept L and any positive presentation σ of L, (i) if there exists a minimal concept of L within C, then M converges to an index of a minimal concept of L within C for σ, (ii) otherwise M does not converge to any index for σ.

An IIM M is said to *strong-minimally infer a class C from positive data*, if for any nonempty concept L and any positive presentation σ of L, M converges to an index of a minimal concept of L within C for σ.

A class C is said to be *minimally* (resp., *strong-minimally, refutably minimally* or *reliably minimally*) *inferable from positive data*, if there is an IIM or an RIIM which minimally (resp., strong-minimally, refutably minimally or reliably minimally) infers C from positive data.

We note that a strong-minimally inferable class C has the strong property that for any nonempty concept L, there always exists a minimal concept of L within C. To the contrary, by definition, for a class with this property, (refutably or reliably) minimal inferability is equivalent to strong-minimal inferability. In Section 5 we show that there are some rich hypothesis spaces that are strong-minimally inferable from positive data.

Let M be an IIM or an RIIM which (refutably, reliably or strong-) minimally infers a class C from positive data. If we feed a positive presentation σ of a concept $L_i \in C$ to M, then M converges to an index j with $L_j = L_i$ for σ, because L_i itself is the unique minimal concept, i.e. the least concept, of L_i within C. Therefore M also infers C in the limit from positive data. Thus minimal inferability can be regarded as a natural extension of ordinary inferability.

The ordinary inferability from positive data was characterized by Angluin[2] as follows:

Definition 7 (Angluin[2]). Let $C = \{L_i\}_{i \in N}$ be a class. A set $T_i \subseteq U$ is said to be a *finite tell-tale of a concept $L_i \in C$ within C*, if (i) T_i is a finite subset of L_i and (ii) for any $L_j \in C$, $T_i \subseteq L_j$ implies $L_j \not\subseteq L_i$.

Theorem 8 (Angluin[2]). *A class $C = \{L_i\}_{i \in N}$ is inferable in the limit from positive data, if and only if there is an effective procedure which on input i enumerates a finite tell-tale T_i of $L_i \in C$ within C.*

Furthermore some practical sufficient conditions for inferability from positive data are presented.

Definition 9 (Wright[23], Motoki et al.[11]). A class C is said to *have infinite elasticity*, if there are two infinite sequences $w_0, w_1, w_2, \cdots \in U$ and $L_{j_1}, L_{j_2}, \cdots \in C$ such that for any $i \geq 1$,

$$\{w_0, w_1, \cdots, w_{i-1}\} \subseteq L_{j_i} \quad \text{but} \quad w_i \notin L_{j_i}.$$

A class C is said to *have finite elasticity*, if C does not have infinite elasticity.

Theorem 10 (Wright[23]). *If a class $C = \{L_i\}_{i \in N}$ has finite elasticity, then there is an effective procedure which on input i enumerates a finite tell-tale T_i of L_i within C.*

Definition 11 (Angluin[2]). A class C is said to *have finite thickness*, if for any nonempty finite set $T \subseteq U$, the cardinality of $\{L_i \in C \mid T \subseteq L_i\}$ is finite.

Proposition 12 (Wright[23]). *If a class C has finite thickness, then C has finite elasticity.*

By Theorem 8, 10 and Proposition 12, we see that a class with finite elasticity or finite thickness is inferable in the limit from positive data. Hence many studies on inferability from positive data concentrate on uniform and recursive enumerability of finite tell-tales (cf. Angluin[2], Wright[23], Sato&Umayahara[15], Sato&Moriyama[16] and Kapur[8]).

However, by investigating the algorithm used in showing Theorem 8 and by the following Proposition 13, we see that if we force an inference machine to converge to an index of a minimal concept of a target concept not in the class concerned, finite tell-tales turn to be of no use.

Proposition 13. *Let $C = \{L_i\}_{i \in N}$ be a class of concepts each of which has a finite tell-tale within C, let $L \notin C$ be a concept, and let $L_{j_1}, L_{j_2}, \cdots \in C$ be minimal concepts of L within C. Then for any $i \geq 1$, there is a finite tell-tale T_i of L_{j_i} within C such that $T_i \nsubseteq L$.*

Proof. For $i \geq 1$, let T_i' be a finite tell-tale of L_{j_i} within C. Since L_{j_i} is a minimal concept of L within C and $L \neq L_{j_i}$ holds, it follows that $L \subsetneq L_{j_i}$. Thus there is a $w_i \in L_{j_i} \setminus L$. Put $T_i = T_i' \cup \{w_i\}$. Then it is easy to see that T_i is a finite tell-tale of L_{j_i} within C which satisfies the proposition. $\qquad\square$

3 Some Sufficient Conditions for Minimal Inferability

We start with some basic definitions and lemmas necessary for showing some sufficient conditions for minimal inferability.

Definition 14 (Sato&Moriyama[16]). A class C is said to *satisfy MEF-condition*, if for any nonempty finite set $T \subseteq U$ and any $L_i \in C$ with $T \subseteq L_i$, there is a minimal concept L_j of T within C such that $L_j \subseteq L_i$.

A class C is said to *satisfy MFF-condition*, if for any nonempty finite set $T \subseteq U$, the cardinality of $\{L_i \in C \mid L_i$ is a minimal concept of T within $C\}$ is finite.

A class C is said to *have M-finite thickness*, if C satisfies both MEF-condition and MFF-condition.

We note that if a class C contains all nonempty finite concepts, then C has M-finite thickness. For a class with M-finite thickness, the existence of a finite tell-tale of each concept in the class leads to the enumerability of it.

Theorem 15 (Sato&Moriyama[16]). *If a class $C = \{L_i\}_{i \in N}$ has M-finite thickness and each concept in C has a finite tell-tale within C, then there is an effective procedure which on input i enumerates a finite tell-tale T_i of L_i within C, and thus it is inferable in the limit from positive data.*

Here we note that the condition of M-finite thickness alone is not sufficient for inferability from positive data.

Example 1. Let SFC be a so-called superfinite class, that is, it contains all finite concepts and at least one infinite concept.

It is easy to see that this class has M-finite thickness. However as shown in Gold[7], this class is not inferable in the limit from positive data.

Therefore this class is also not (refutably, reliably or strong-) minimally inferable from positive data.

Lemma 16. *Let $C = \{L_i\}_{i \in N}$ be a class which satisfies MEF-condition and has finite elasticity, let $L \subseteq U$ be a nonempty concept, and let $L_n \in C$ be a concept.*

(a) If $L \subseteq L_n$, then there is a minimal concept L_j of L within C such that $L_j \subseteq L_n$.

(b) If L_n is a minimal concept of L within C, then there is a finite subset T of L such that L_n is a minimal concept of T within C.

Proof. (a) Assume $L \subseteq L_n$, and suppose that there does not exist a minimal concept L_j of L within C such that $L_j \subseteq L_n$.

Let $w_0 \in L$, and define w_i's and j_i's ($i \geq 1$) inductively by the following stages:

Stage i (≥ 1):

Since $\{w_0, \cdots, w_{i-1}\}$ is a finite subset of L_n, it follows by MEF-condition that there is a minimal concept L_j of $\{w_0, \cdots, w_{i-1}\}$ within C such that $L_j \subseteq L_n$. Put $j_i = j$.

Here we see that $L \not\subseteq L_{j_i}$ holds. In fact, $L \subseteq L_{j_i}$ means that L_{j_i} is a minimal concept of L within C, because $\{w_0, \cdots, w_{i-1}\} \subseteq L$. This contradicts the assumption.

Thus there is a $w \in U$ such that $w \in L \setminus L_{j_i}$. Put $w_i = w$. We note that $\{w_0, \cdots, w_i\} \subseteq L \subseteq L_n$ holds. Go to Stage $i + 1$.

Then by the construction, two infinite sequences $w_0, w_1, w_2, \cdots$ and $L_{j_1}, L_{j_2}, \cdots$ satisfy the following condition: For $i \geq 1$,

$$\{w_0, w_1, \cdots, w_{i-1}\} \subseteq L_{j_i} \quad \text{but} \quad w_i \notin L_{j_i}.$$

That is, C has infinite elasticity. This contradicts the assumption.

(b) Assume that L_n is a minimal concept of L within C, and suppose that for any finite subset T of L, L_n is not a minimal concept of T within C.

Let $w_0 \in L$, and define w_i's and j_i's ($i \geq 1$) inductively by the following stages:

Stage i (≥ 1):

Since $\{w_0, \cdots, w_{i-1}\}$ is a finite subset of L_n, it follows by MEF-condition that there is a minimal concept L_j of $\{w_0, \cdots, w_{i-1}\}$ within C such that $L_j \subseteq L_n$. Put $j_i = j$.

Here we see that $L_{j_i} \subsetneq L_n$ holds. In fact, $L_{j_i} = L_n$ means that L_n is a minimal concept of $\{w_i, \cdots, w_{i-1}\}$ within C. This contradicts the assumption.

Hence $L \not\subseteq L_{j_i}$ holds, because L_n is a minimal concept of L within C. Thus there is a $w \in U$ such that $w \in L \backslash L_{j_i}$. Put $w_i = w$. We note that $\{w_0, \cdots, w_i\} \subseteq L \subseteq L_n$ holds. Go to Stage $i + 1$.

Then by the construction, two infinite sequences $w_0, w_1, w_2, \cdots$ and $L_{j_1}, L_{j_2}, \cdots$ satisfy the following condition: For $i \geq 1$,

$$\{w_0, w_1, \cdots, w_{i-1}\} \subseteq L_{j_i}, \quad \text{but} \quad w_i \notin L_{j_i}.$$

That is, C has infinite elasticity. This contradicts the assumption. □

In the above Lemma 16 (a) and (b), we see by considering the class $\mathcal{SFC}$ (cf. Example 1) that the condition of finite elasticity is necessary. We only show the case of (b). It is easy to see that $\mathcal{SFC}$ has infinite elasticity. Let L be an infinite concept in $\mathcal{SFC}$. Then the unique minimal concept, i.e. the least concept, of L within $\mathcal{SFC}$ is L itself and that for any nonempty finite set $T \subseteq U$, the unique minimal concept of T within $\mathcal{SFC}$ is T itself. Thus for any finite set $T \subseteq U$, L is not a minimal concept of T within $\mathcal{SFC}$.

Definition 17. Let $w_1, w_2, \cdots$ be an effective enumeration of the universal set U, and let $L \subseteq U$ be a concept. Then the finite subset of L masked by $\{w_1, w_2, \cdots, w_n\}$ is denoted by $L^{(n)}$, that is, $L^{(n)} = L \cap \{w_1, w_2, \cdots, w_n\}$.

Lemma 18. *Let $L_1, L_2 \subseteq U$ be concepts.*

(a) If $L_1 \subsetneq L_2$, then there is a $j \geq 1$ such that for any $n \geq j$, $L_1^{(n)} \subsetneq L_2^{(n)}$.

(b) If $L_1 \not\subseteq L_2$, then there is a $j \geq 1$ such that for any $n \geq j$, $L_1^{(n)} \not\subseteq L_2^{(n)}$.

We note that for any indexed family $C = \{L_i\}_{i \in N}$ of recursive concepts and any $i, j, n \geq 1$, whether or not $L_i^{(n)} \subsetneq L_j^{(n)}$ is recursively decidable.

Here we have the main theorem.

Theorem 19. *If a class C has both finite elasticity and M-finite thickness, then C is reliably minimally inferable from positive data.*

Proof. Let us consider the procedure in Figure 1.

Assume that we feed a positive presentation σ of a nonempty concept L to the procedure.

(I) In case there is no minimal concept of L within C. Suppose that the procedure converges to an index i for σ. Then we see by Lemma 16 (a) that $L \not\subseteq L_i$. Therefore there is an $n \geq 1$ such that $\sigma[n]^+ \not\subseteq L_i$, and it follows that the index i does not satisfy the condition (1) in the procedure after reading the n-th fact. This is a contradiction.

```
Procedure IIM M;
begin
    T = φ;   n = 0;
    repeat
        read the next fact and store it in T;
        n = n + 1;
        search for the least index i ≤ n such that
            (1) T ⊆ Lᵢ, and
            (2) ∀j ≤ n, [T ⊆ Lⱼ ⇒ Lⱼ⁽ⁿ⁾ ⊄ Lᵢ⁽ⁿ⁾];
        if such an index i is found then output i else output n;
    forever;
end.
```

Fig. 1. An IIM which reliably minimally infers a class from positive data

(II) In case there is a minimal concept of L within C. Let i_0 be the least index i such that L_i is a minimal concept of L within C, that is,

$$i_0 = \min\{i \mid L \subseteq L_i \in C \text{ and } \forall j, [L \subseteq L_j \Rightarrow L_j \not\subseteq L_i]\}.$$

Claim A: There is an $n \geq 1$ such that any index $i < i_0$ does not satisfy the condition (1) or (2), after reading the n-th fact.

Proof of the claim. We define m_i's $(1 \leq i < i_0)$ as follows:

(i) In case $L \not\subseteq L_i$. It is easy to see that there is an $m \geq 1$ such that for any $j \geq m$, $\sigma[j]^+ \not\subseteq L_i$. Put $m_i = m$.

(ii) Otherwise. By the definition of i_0 and the fact $i < i_0$, there is a $j \geq 1$ such that $L \subseteq L_j$ and $L_j \subsetneq L_i$. Since $L_j \subsetneq L_i$, we see by Lemma 18 (a) that there is an $m \geq 1$ such that for any $n \geq m$, $L_j^{(n)} \subsetneq L_i^{(n)}$. Put $m_i = \max\{j, m\}$.

Then any index $i < i_0$ does not satisfy the condition (1) or (2), after reading the $\max\{m_i \mid 1 \leq i < i_0\}$-th fact. ∎

It is clear that i_0 satisfies the condition (1) at any point.

Claim B: There is an $n \geq 1$ such that i_0 always satisfies the condition (2), after reading the n-th fact.

Proof of the claim. For $i \geq 1$, put $T_i = \sigma[i]^+$. Since L_{i_0} is a minimal concept of L within C, it follows by Lemma 16 (b) that there is a finite subset T of L such that L_{i_0} is a minimal concept of T within C. Since σ is a positive presentation of L, it follows that there is an $m \geq 1$ such that $T \subseteq T_m$. Since $T \subseteq T_m \subseteq L \subseteq L_{i_0}$, it follows that L_{i_0} is also a minimal concept of T_m within C.

Let $\{L_{j_1}, \cdots, L_{j_k}\}$ be the collection of all minimal concepts of T_m within C, which is of finite cardinality by MFF-condition. Since L_{i_0} is a minimal concept of T_m within C and $T_m \subseteq L_{j_i}$ holds, it follows that $L_{j_i} \not\subseteq L_{i_0}$ for any i with $1 \leq i \leq k$. Therefore, by Lemma 18 (b), we can take n_i's $(1 \leq i \leq k)$ such that for any $n \geq n_i$, $L_{j_i}^{(n)} \not\subseteq L_{i_0}^{(n)}$. Let $n_{\max} = \max\{n_i \mid 1 \leq i \leq k\}$. Then for any i with $1 \leq i \leq k$ and any $n \geq n_{\max}$, $L_{j_i}^{(n)} \not\subseteq L_{i_0}^{(n)}$ holds.

On the other hand, for any $n \geq 1$, if $L_{j_i}^{(n)} \not\subseteq L_{i_0}^{(n)}$, then for any $L_j \supseteq L_{j_i}$, $L_j^{(n)} \not\subseteq L_{i_0}^{(n)}$ holds. By MEF-condition and the definition of $\{L_{j_1}, \cdots, L_{j_k}\}$, for any index j, if $T_m \subseteq L_j$, then there is an i with $1 \leq i \leq k$ such that $T_m \subseteq L_{j_i} \subseteq L_j$. Therefore for any $n \geq n_{\max}$ and any $j \geq 1$, $T_m \subseteq L_j$ implies $L_j^{(n)} \not\subseteq L_{i_0}^{(n)}$. Since $T_m \subseteq T_{m+1} \subseteq \cdots$, it follows that for any $n \geq \max\{m, n_{\max}\}$ and any $j \geq 1$, $T_n \subseteq L_j$ implies $L_j^{(n)} \not\subseteq L_{i_0}^{(n)}$. Therefore i_0 always satisfies the condition (2), after reading the $\max\{m, n_{\max}\}$-th fact. ∎

By Claim A and B, the procedure converges to i_0 for σ. □

Here we note that the procedure in Figure 1 is a sufficiently general one in the following sense: By directly using the procedure, we can show that (i) the classes with finite elasticity or (ii) the classes with M-finite thickness, each of which concept has a finite tell-tale within the class, are inferable in the limit from positive data (cf. Theorem 10 and 15).

For a class C which has finite elasticity but does not have M-finite thickness, the procedure in Figure 1 may not minimally infer C from positive data, even when C is reliably minimally inferable from positive data.

Example 2 (Kapur[9]). Let $w_1, w_2, \cdots$ be the effective enumeration of the universal set U, which we used in defining $L_i^{(n)}$ (cf. Definition 17). Without loss of generality, we assume $w_i \neq w_j$ if $i \neq j$.

We put

$$L = \{w_1\} \quad \text{and} \quad L_i = \{w_1, w_{i+1}\} \quad \text{for } i \geq 1.$$

Then let $C = \{L_i\}_{i \in N}$ be the class of interest. It is easy to see that this class has finite elasticity but does not have M-finite thickness.

On the other hand, any concept in C is a minimal concept of L within C. Let $\sigma = w_1, w_1, w_1, \cdots$ be the positive presentation of L. Since for any $n \geq 1$ and any i with $1 \leq i < n$, $L_n^{(n)} = \{w_1\}$ and $L_i^{(n)} = \{w_1, w_{i+1}\}$ hold, it follows that the procedure does not converge to any index for σ.

That is, the procedure does not minimally infer C from positive data.

However it is easy to see that this class is refutably minimally inferable from positive data. We omit the details.

In Example 1, we have seen that the condition of M-finite thickness is not sufficient for inferability from positive data. Furthermore, by the following Example 3, the condition for a class with M-finite thickness to have finite elasticity is not necessary for minimal inferability.

Example 3. Let $\mathcal{FC}$ be the class of all nonempty finite concepts on the universal set U. It is easy to see that this class has M-finite thickness, but does not have finite elasticity.

We can easily show that $\mathcal{FC}$ is reliably minimally inferable from positive data. We omit the details.

By Lemma 16 and Theorem 19, we have the following Corollary 20.

Corollary 20. *Let $C = \{L_i\}_{i \in N}$ be a class with both finite elasticity and M-finite thickness. Then if C contains the universal set U as its member, then C is strong-minimally inferable from positive data.*

Proof. Assume that C contains the universal set U as its member. Then by Lemma 16 (a), for any concept L, there is a minimal concept of L within C. Thus, by Theorem 19, we have the corollary. □

Lemma 21. *If a class C does not satisfy MEF-condition, then there are a nonempty finite set $T \subseteq U$ and an infinite sequence $L_{j_1}, L_{j_2}, \cdots \in C$ such that $L_{j_1} \supsetneq L_{j_2} \supsetneq \cdots \supsetneq T$.*

Proof. Assume that C does not satisfy MEF-condition. Then by Definition 14, there are a nonempty finite set $T \subseteq U$ and an $L_i \in C$ such that (i) $T \subseteq L_i$ and that (ii) there is no minimal concept L_j of T within C such that $L_j \subseteq L_i$.

Put $j_1 = i$, and define j_i's $(i \geq 2)$ inductively by the following stages:

Stage i (≥ 2):

Since $L_{j_{i-1}} \subseteq L_i$, we see by (ii) that $L_{j_{i-1}}$ is not a minimal concept of T within C. Therefore there is a $j \geq 1$ such that $T \subseteq L_j \subsetneq L_{j_{i-1}}$. Put $j_i = j$. Go to Stage $i + 1$.

Then it is clear that $L_{j_1} \supsetneq L_{j_2} \supsetneq \cdots \supsetneq T$. □

The following Corollary 22 is a weak form of Theorem 19 and Corollary 20.

Corollary 22. *(a) If a class C has finite thickness, then C is reliably minimally inferable from positive data.*

(b) If a class C with finite thickness contains the universal set U as its member, then C is strong-minimally inferable from positive data.

Proof. (a) Assume that a class C has finite thickness. By Theorem 19, it suffices for us to show that C has finite elasticity and satisfies both MEF-condition and MFF-condition. By Proposition 12, C has finite elasticity. It is easy to see that C satisfies MFF-condition.

Suppose that C does not satisfy MEF-condition. Then by Lemma 21, there are a nonempty finite set $T \subseteq U$ and an infinite sequence $L_{j_1}, L_{j_2}, \cdots \in C$ of concepts such that $L_{j_1} \supsetneq L_{j_2} \supsetneq \cdots \supsetneq T$. This means that C has infinitely many distinct concepts that include T. This contradicts the assumption that C has finite thickness.

(b) is clear by the above (a) and Corollary 20. □

Example 4. Let $\mathcal{PAT}$ be the class of pattern languages (cf. Angluin[1, 2]). Angluin[2] showed that $\mathcal{PAT}$ has finite thickness. Furthermore $\mathcal{PAT}$ contains the universal set $U (= \Sigma^+)$ as its member. Thus, by Corollary 22 (b), $\mathcal{PAT}$ is strong-minimally inferable from positive data.

We devote the rest of this section to showing some conditions for a class to be refutably minimally inferable from positive data.

Lemma 23 (Kapur[9],Sato[17]). *Let $C = \{L_i\}_{i \in N}$ be a class with finite elasticity, and let $L \subseteq U$ be a concept. Then if L is not a subset of any $L_i \in C$, then there is a finite subset T of L such that T is not a subset of any $L_i \in C$.*

Proof. Assume that L is not a subset of any $L_i \in C$. Thus wee see that L is nonempty.

Here we suppose that for any finite subset T of L, there is an $L_i \in C$ such that $T \subseteq L_i$. Let w_0 be an arbitrary element in L, and define w_i's and L_{j_i}'s $(i \geq 1)$ inductively by the following stages:

Stage i (≥ 1):

Since $\{w_0, w_1, \cdots, w_{i-1}\} \subseteq L$, it follows by assumption that there is an $L_j \in C$ such that $\{w_0, w_1, \cdots, w_{i-1}\} \subseteq L_j$. Put $j_i = j$. Then by assumption, L is not a subset of L_{j_i}, it follows that there is a $w \in L \setminus L_{j_i}$. Put $w_i = w$. Go to Stage $i+1$.

Then by the construction, two infinite sequences $w_0, w_1, w_2, \cdots$ and $L_{j_1}, L_{j_2}, \cdots$ satisfy the following condition: For $i \geq 1$,

$$\{w_0, w_1, \cdots, w_{i-1}\} \subseteq L_{j_i} \quad \text{but} \quad w_i \notin L_{j_i}.$$

That is, C has infinite elasticity. This contradicts the assumption. □

If a class with both finite elasticity and M-finite thickness has a computable function econs defined below (cf. Mukouchi&Arikawa[12]), then an inference machine can refute the class when there is no minimal concept of the target concept within the class.

Definition 24. For a finite set $T \subseteq U$, let

$$\text{econs}(T) = \begin{cases} 1, & \text{if there exists an } L_i \in C \text{ such that } T \subseteq L_i, \\ 0, & \text{otherwise.} \end{cases}$$

Theorem 25. *(a) Let C be a class with both finite elasticity and M-finite thickness. Then if the function econs for C is recursive, then C is refutably minimally inferable from positive data.*

(b) Let C be a class with finite thickness. Then if the function econs for C is recursive, then C is refutably minimally inferable from positive data.

Proof. (a) Assume that the function econs for C is recursive. Then let us consider the procedure in Figure 2.

Assume that we feed a positive presentation σ of a nonempty concept L to the procedure.

Claim: There is an $n \geq 1$ such that $\text{econs}(\sigma[n]^+) = 0$, if and only if there is no minimal concept of L within C.

Proof of the claim. (I) The 'if' part. Assume that there is no minimal concept of L within C. Then by Lemma 16 (a), for any $L_i \in C$, $L \nsubseteq L_i$ holds. Therefore, by Lemma 23, there is a finite set $T \subseteq L$ such that for any $L_i \in C$, $T \nsubseteq L_i$. Hence for any positive presentation σ of L, there is an $n \geq 1$ such that $T \subseteq \sigma[n]^+$, and it follows that $\text{econs}(\sigma[n]^+) = 0$.

(II) The 'only if' part. Assume that there is a minimal concept of L within C. It is easy to see that for any positive presentation σ of L and any $n \geq 1$, $\text{econs}(\sigma[n]^+) = 1$. ■

By this claim and the proof of Theorem 19, it is easy to see that the procedure is an RIIM which refutably minimally infers C from positive data.

(b) is clear by the above (a) and Corollary 20. □

```
Procedure RIIM M;
begin
    T = φ;   n = 0;
    repeat
        read the next fact and store it in T;
        n = n + 1;
        if econs(T) = 0 then refute the class and stop;
        search for the least index i ≤ n such that
            (1) T ⊆ Li, and
            (2) ∀j ≤ n, [T ⊆ Lj ⇒ Lj^(n) ⊄ Li^(n)];
        if such an index i is found then output i else output n;
    forever;
end.
```

Fig. 2. An RIIM which refutably minimally infers a class from positive data

4   Separations

In this section, we show that there are differences between the powers of strong-minimal inferability, refutably minimal inferability, reliably minimal inferability and inferability in the limit from positive data.

Example 5. Let $\Sigma = \{a\}$ be a finite alphabet, and let $\mathcal{PAT}'$ be the class of pattern languages over Σ each of which does not contain the string 'a'. That is, let $\mathcal{PAT}' = \mathcal{PAT} \setminus \{L(x), L(a)\}$, where $L(x) = \Sigma^+$ is the pattern language of the single variable 'x' and $L(a) = \{a\}$ is that of the single constant symbol 'a'.

Then, by Theorem 25, it is easy to see that this class is refutably minimally inferable from positive data.

However there is no minimal concept of the concept Σ^+ within $\mathcal{PAT}'$, it follows that this class is not strong-minimally inferable from positive data.

Example 6. We consider the class $\mathcal{FC}$ of all nonempty finite concepts on the universal set U. As stated in Example 3, this class is reliably minimally inferable from positive data.

On the other hand, by a similar discussion to that in Mukouchi&Arikawa[13], we can easily show that this class is not refutably minimally inferable from positive data.

Theorem 26 (Kapur[9]). *There is an indexed family C of recursive concepts such that C is inferable in the limit but not minimally inferable from positive data.*

Proof. Let $M_1, M_2, \cdots$ be an enumeration of all inference machines, and let $c : N \times N \to N$ be Cantor's pairing function. For $j \geq 1$, let p_j be the j-th prime number, and put $\sigma_j = p_j, p_j, p_j, \cdots$. For $j, n \geq 1$, let $M_j^{(n)}(\sigma_j)$ be the last guess of M_j executed in n steps on input σ_j.

For $j, k \geq 1$, let

$$L_{c(j,k)} = \begin{cases} \{p_j, p_j^{n+1}\}, & \text{if there is an } m \geq 1 \text{ such that } M_j^{(m)}(\sigma_j) = c(j,k), \\ & \qquad \text{where } n = \min\{m \mid M_j^{(m)}(\sigma_j) = c(j,k)\}, \\ \{p_j\}, & \text{otherwise.} \end{cases}$$

Then let $C = \{L_i\}_{i \in N}$. This class is an indexed family of recursive concepts. In fact, for any $i, q \geq 1$, we can decide whether or not $q \in L_i$ as follows: Let j, k be integers such that $i = c(j,k)$.

(i) In case $q = p_j$. Then q is in L_i.

(ii) In case $q = p_j^{n+1}$ for some $n \geq 1$. Then we execute M_j in n steps on input σ_j. If it outputs $i\, (= c(j,k))$ for the first time at just n-th step, then $q\, (= p_j^{n+1})$ is in L_i. Otherwise q is not in L_i.

(iii) Otherwise q is not in L_i.

Thus this class is an indexed family of recursive concepts.

(I) This class is inferable in the limit from positive data. This is because this class consists of finite concepts, and it follows that we can construct an effective procedure which recursively enumerates a finite tell-tale of any concept in C within C (cf. Theorem 8).

(II) This class is not minimally inferable from positive data. In fact, suppose that there is an IIM M_j which minimally infers C from positive data. It is easy to see that there is a minimal concept of $\{p_j\}$ within C. Therefore M_j should converge to an index i for σ_j such that L_i is a minimal concept of $\{p_j\}$ within C.

Since $p_j \in L_i$, there is a $k \geq 1$ such that $i = c(j,k)$. Furthermore since M_j outputs i, there is an $m \geq 1$ such that $M_j^{(m)}(\sigma_j) = i\,(= c(j,k))$. Let $n = \min\{m \mid M_j^{(m)}(\sigma_j) = c(j,k)\}$. Then by definition, $L_i = L_{c(j,k)} = \{p_j, p_j^{n+1}\}$ holds.

However there should be a $k' \geq 1$ such that $L_{c(j,k')} = \{p_j\}$. In fact, suppose the converse. Then for any $k' \geq 1$, $L_{c(j,k')} \neq \{p_j\}$. By the construction, this means that M_j changes its mind infinitely many times for σ_j, which contradicts the fact that M_j converges to the index i for σ_j.

This means that L_i is not a minimal concept of $\{p_j\}$ within C, which contradicts the assumption. $\square$

By Definition 3, 4, 6, Theorem 5, 26, Example 5 and 6, it is easy to see that the following implications hold:

C is strong-minimally inferable from positive data,

$\downarrow\!\not\uparrow$

C is refutably minimally inferable from positive data,

$\downarrow\!\not\uparrow$

C is reliably minimally inferable from positive data,

$\downarrow\,(\not\uparrow?)$

C is minimally inferable from positive data,

$\downarrow\!\not\uparrow$

C is inferable in the limit from positive data,

$$\downarrow \uparrow$$

C is semi-reliably inferable from positive data.

It is unknown at present whether or not the classes that are minimally inferable from positive data are reliably minimally inferable from positive data.

5 EFS Definable Classes

In this section, we consider so-called model inference (cf. Shapiro[18]) and language learning using *elementary formal systems* (*EFS*'s, for short).

The EFS's were originally introduced by Smullyan[22] to develop his recursion theory. In a word, EFS's are a kind of logic programming language which uses strings instead of terms in first order logic[24], and they are shown to be natural devices to define languages[3].

In this paper, we briefly overview the obtained results on minimal inferability for EFS definable classes. For more details about ordinary inferability of EFS definable classes, please refer to Shinohara[20], Sato&Moriyama[16] and Arikawa et al.[4, 5].

We denote by $\mathcal{LB}^{[\leq n]}$ the class of all length-bounded EFS's with at most n axioms. Then $M(\mathcal{LB}^{[\leq n]})$ denotes the class of the least Herbrand models of EFS's in $\mathcal{LB}^{[\leq n]}$, and $L(\mathcal{LB}^{[\leq n]})$ denotes the class of all languages defined by EFS's in $\mathcal{LB}^{[\leq n]}$ with a fixed unary predicate symbol p.

Theorem 27 (Shinohara[20]). *For any $n \geq 1$, the classes $M(\mathcal{LB}^{[\leq n]})$ and $L(\mathcal{LB}^{[\leq n]})$ have finite elasticity, respectively.*

We see by this Theorem 27 that $M(\mathcal{LB}^{[\leq n]})$ and $L(\mathcal{LB}^{[\leq n]})$ are inferable in the limit from positive data, respectively (cf. Theorem 10).

Lemma 28 (Sato&Moriyama[16]). *For any $n \geq 1$, the classes $M(\mathcal{LB}^{[\leq n]})$ and $L(\mathcal{LB}^{[\leq n]})$ have M-finite thickness, respectively.*

Theorem 29. *(a) For any $n \geq 1$, the class $L(\mathcal{LB}^{[\leq n]})$ is strong-minimally inferable from positive data.*

(b) For any $n \geq 1$, the class $M(\mathcal{LB}^{[\leq n]})$ is refutably minimally inferable from positive data.

Here we note that by the same discussion to prove Lemma 28, we can show that the class of unions of at most n pattern languages has M-finite thickness, and thus this class is strong-minimally inferable from positive data (cf. Wright[23]).

6 Concluding Remarks

We have introduced the notion of minimal inferability for a class of recursive concepts from positive data, and presented some sufficient conditions. Then we showed that there are some rich hypothesis spaces that are (refutably or strong-) minimally inferable from positive data.

Using only positive data, it is natural to consider a minimal concept of a target concept within the class concerned, because a minimal concept explains all obtained facts and, in a sense, it is one of the best concept within the class. Moreover we can regard it as a natural extension of ordinary inferability from positive data, because minimal inferability directly leads to inferability of the class in the ordinary sense.

As stated in Section 2, if we consider an inference of a minimal concept, finite tell-tales turn to be of no use. However various conditions, properties and notions introduced to show uniform and recursive enumerability of a finite tell-tale seem to be valid to some degree. I think this is because these notions, including a finite tell-tale, more or less lead to how to avoid overgeneralization, that is, how to identify a minimal concept. In order to work finite tell-tales intendedly, the target concept should be in the class (cf. Proposition 13).

In Section 5 we have shown that classes definable by length-bounded EFS's with at most n axioms are minimally inferable from positive data. The argument to prove this is also valid for the classes definable by monotonic formal systems with bounded finite-thickness (cf. Shinohara[21]). Thus we can also show various classes are minimally inferable from positive data. For example, the classes definable by weakly reducing EFS's[24] and linear prolog programs[19] (or weakly reducing logic programs in [6]) with at most n axioms, and the class of languages definable by context-sensitive grammars with at most n productions are (refutably or strong-) minimally inferable from positive data for any $n \geq 1$, respectively (cf. Shinohara[21]).

Acknowledgements

The author wishes to thank Prof. Setsuo Arikawa for many suggestions, productive discussions and constant encouragements. He also wishes to thank Prof. Masako Sato and Mr. Takashi Moriyama at University of Osaka Prefecture for their suggestions and encouragements. He also thank Prof. Takeshi Shinohara, Dr. Shyam Kapur and Mr. Takashi Tabe for essential comments, valuable discussions and finding errors in the earlier version of the paper.

References

1. Angluin, D.: *Finding patterns common to a set of strings*, in Proc. 11th Annual Symposium on Theory of Computing (1979) 130–141.

2. Angluin, D.: *Inductive inference of formal languages from positive data*, Information and Control **45** (1980) 117–135.

3. Arikawa, S.: *Elementary formal systems and formal languages - simple formal systems*, Memoirs of Fac. Sci., Kyushu Univ., Ser. A, Math. **24** (1970) 47–75.

4. Arikawa, S., Shinohara, T. and Yamamoto, A.: *Elementary formal systems as a unifying framework for language learning*, in Proc. 2nd Workshop on Computational Learning Theory (1989) 312–327.

5. Arikawa, S., Shinohara, T. and Yamamoto, A.: *Learning elementary formal systems*, Theoretical Computer Science **95** (1992) 97–113.

6. Arimura, H.: *Completeness of depth-bounded resolution for weakly reducing programs*, in Proc. Software Science and Engineering (1991) (World Scientific Series in Computer Science Vol. 31) 227–245.

7. Gold, E.M.: *Language identification in the limit*, Information and Control **10** (1967) 447–474.

8. Kapur, S.: *Computational learning of languages*, PhD thesis, Technical Report 91-1234, Cornell University, 1991.

9. Kapur, S.: Personal communication.

10. Moriyama, T. and Sato. M.: *Properties of language classes with finite elasticity*, in Proc. 4th International Workshop on Algorithmic Learning Theory, Lecture Notes in Artificial Intelligence **744** (1993) 187–196.

11. Motoki, T, Shinohara, T. and Wright, K.: *The correct definition of finite elasticity: corrigendum to identification of unions*, in Proc. 4th Workshop on Computational Learning Theory (1991) 375–375.

12. Mukouchi, Y. and Arikawa, S.: *Inductive inference machines that can refute hypothesis spaces*, in Proc. 4th International Workshop on Algorithmic Learning Theory, Lecture Notes in Artificial Intelligence **744** (1993) 123–137.

13. Mukouchi, Y. and Arikawa, S.: *Towards a mathematical theory of machine discovery from facts*, in preparation.

14. Sakurai, A.: *Inductive inference of formal languages from positive data enumerated primitive-recursively*, in Proc. 2nd Workshop on Algorithmic Learning Theory (1991) 73–83.

15. Sato, M. and Umayahara, K.: *Inductive inferability for formal languages from positive data*, in Proc. 2nd Workshop on Algorithmic Learning Theory (1991) 84–92 (also in IEICE Trans. Inf. &Syst. **E75-D** No. 4 (1992) 415–419).

16. Sato, M. and Moriyama, T.: *Inductive inference of length-bounded EFS's from positive data*, in preparation (1993).

17. Sato, M.: Personal communication.

18. Shapiro, E.Y.: *Inductive inference of theories from facts*, Technical Report 192, Yale University Computer Science Dept., 1981.

19. Shapiro, E.Y.: *Alternation and the computational complexity of logic programs*, J. Logic Programming **1** No. 1 (1984) 19–33.

20. Shinohara, T.: *Inductive inference from positive data is powerful*, Proc. 3rd Workshop on Computational Learning Theory (1990) 97–110 (to appear as *Rich classes inferable from positive data: Length-bounded elementary formal systems*, in Information and Computation).

21. Shinohara, T.: *Inductive inference of monotonic formal systems from positive data*, In Proc. 1st International Workshop on Algorithmic Learning Theory (1990) 339–351 (also in New Generation Computing **8** No. 4 (1991) 371–384).

22. Smullyan, R.M.: "Theory of formal systems," Princeton Univ. Press, 1961.

23. Wright, K.: *Identification of unions of languages drawn from an identifiable class*, in Proc. 2nd Workshop on Computational Learning Theory (1989) 328–333.

24. Yamamoto, A.: *Procedural semantics and negative information of elementary formal system*, J. Logic Programming **13** No. 4 (1992) 89–98.

Efficient Distribution-free Population Learning of Simple Concepts

Atsuyoshi Nakamura   Naoki Abe   Jun-ichi Takeuchi

Theory NEC Laboratory, RWCP[1]
c/o C&C Research Laboratories, NEC Corporation
4-1-1 Miyazaki, Miyamae-ku Kawasaki 216, Japan
E-mail: {atsu,abe,tak}@sbl.cl.nec.co.jp.

Abstract

We consider a variant of the 'population learning model' proposed by Kearns and Seung, in which the learner is required to be 'distribution-free' as well as computationally efficient. A population learner receives as input hypotheses from a large population of agents and produces as output its final hypothesis. Each agent is assumed to independently obtain labeled sample for the target concept and outputs a hypothesis. A polynomial time population learner is said to 'PAC learn' a concept class, if its hypothesis is probably approximately correct whenever the population size exceeds a certain bound which is polynomial, even if the sample size for each agent is fixed at some constant. We exhibit some general population learning strategies, and some simple concept classes that can be learned by them. These strategies include the 'supremum hypothesis finder,' the 'minimum superset finder' (a special case of the 'supremum hypothesis finder'), and various voting schemes. When coupled with appropriate agent algorithms, these strategies can learn a variety of simple concept classes, such as the 'high-low game,' conjunctions, axis-parallel rectangles and others. We give upper bounds on the required population size for each of these cases, and show that these systems can be used to obtain a speed up from the ordinary PAC-learning model, with appropriate choices of sample and population sizes. With the population learner restricted to be a voting scheme, what we have is effectively a model of 'population prediction,' in which the learner is to *predict* the value of the target concept at an arbitrarily drawn point, as a threshold function of the predictions made by its agents on the same point. We show that the population learning model is strictly more powerful than the population prediction model. Finally we consider a variant of this model with classification noise, and exhibit a population learner for the class of conjunctions in this model.

1 Introduction

In their pioneering work, Kearns and Seung [6] proposed a model of learning from a population of hypotheses ('population learning') and gave some general characterization of the sample complexity of population learning, with the assumption that the underlying distribution (for sampling) was known to the population learner. In this paper, we insist that the population learner be 'distribution-free' and computationally efficient as in the original PAC-learning

---

[1]Real World Computing Partnership

model, and investigate conditions on learnability of simpler and more specific concept classes under these stronger requirements.

In the population learning model, the learner (called the 'population learner') receives as input hypotheses from a large population of agents and produces as output its final hypothesis. Each agent is assumed to independently obtain labeled sample for the target concept drawn according to some fixed but unknown distribution over the domain, and output a hypothesis. A polynomial time population learner is said to 'PAC learn' a concept class, if its hypothesis is probably approximately correct whenever the population size exceeds a certain (polynomial) bound even if the sample size for each agent is fixed at some constant. We also require that the agent algorithm itself is a PAC-learning algorithm, and that for some appropriate choices of sample and population sizes, the population learner can be used to speed up the best sequential PAC-learning algorithm for the same class.

Within this model, we obtain a number of learnability results. We first exhibit some general population learning strategies, and establish sufficient conditions on concept classes and agent algorithms for these strategies to be PAC learners. We then exhibit some concrete concept classes and agent algorithms satisfying such conditions: These strategies include the 'supremum hypothesis finder,' the 'minimum superset finder' (a special case of the 'supremum hypothesis finder'), and various voting schemes including the 'majority vote.' When coupled with appropriate agent algorithms, these strategies can be shown to PAC learn a variety of simple concept classes such as the 'high-low game,'[2] conjunctions, axis-parallel rectangles and others, with reasonable population sizes.

A population learner can be said to achieve *ideal parallelization*, if the population size required is the sample complexity of the agent divided by the sample size of each agent. For some concept classes having an appropreate lattice structure, this can be done by a population learner that outputs the 'supremum' consistent hypothesis, coupled with the agent algorithm that picks the smallest consistent hypothesis. We call such a population learner 'supremum hypothesis finder.' Intersection closed concept classes[7, 5] are learnable in this fashion, where the smallest consistent hypothesis is found by a 'closure algorithm' [5], and the supremum by a 'minimum superset finder' which output the minimum hypothesis containing all input hypotheses. Thus, using this strategy, various classes like 'high low game,' conjunctions and axis-parallel rectangles are learnable. '2-dimensional half-spaces' (going through the origin) and 'two disjoint length-1 intervals' (containing $\{1, -1\}$), which are not intersection closed, are also learnable by the 'supremum hypothesis finder.' The population size required for these classes is $O(\frac{1}{m\epsilon} \log \frac{1}{\delta})$, with respect to ϵ and δ. Note that by setting $m = O(\sqrt{\frac{1}{\epsilon} \log \frac{1}{\delta}})$, we can achieve speed-up in overall computation time from $\Omega(\frac{1}{\epsilon} \log \frac{1}{\delta})$ in the ordinary PAC-learning model to $O(\sqrt{\frac{1}{\epsilon} \log \frac{1}{\delta}})$, provided that the computation time is linear in the sample size and the population size.

---

[2] The 'high-low game' is the following concept class considered by Kearns and Seung, $\{[0, b] | b \in [0, 1]\}$.

A population learner is a voting scheme if its hypothesis can be expressed as a threshold function of the input hypotheses, including the majority vote, OR-gate and AND-gate. In a brief remark motivating their distribution specific maximum likelihood approach, Kearns and Seung [6] noted that the simple majority vote, when coupled with the natural agent algorithm that outputs a consistent hypothesis from the uniform distribution, is *not* a PAC-learner for the high-low game. We show, however, that this concept class can be PAC-learned by the majority vote population learner, if the agent algorithm outputs the largest consistent hypothesis and the smallest consistent hypothesis, each with probability a half. This learner is both efficient and distribution-free and the population size required is $\frac{2}{(1-(1-\epsilon)^m)^2} \ln \frac{2}{\delta}$, where m is the sample size of each agent. By setting $m = (\frac{1}{\epsilon})^{\frac{2}{3}}$, we can achieve speed-up in overall computation time from $\Omega(\frac{1}{\epsilon} \log \frac{1}{\delta})$ in the ordinary PAC-learning model to $O((\frac{1}{\epsilon})^{\frac{2}{3}} \log \frac{1}{\delta})$.

When using the OR-gate as the population learner, we can show that the class of axis-parallel rectangles of an arbitrary dimension n can be learned with population size of $O((\frac{2n}{m\epsilon})^{2n} \log \frac{1}{\delta})$. In deriving this result, we needed a tighter bound on the probability of obtaining examples to rule out all non-ϵ-approximations, than what is used in a typical uniform convergence argument. By setting $N = m = (\frac{2n}{\epsilon})^{2n/2n+1} (\log \frac{1}{\delta})^{1/2n+1}$, we can obtain a speed-up from $\Omega(\frac{2n}{\epsilon} \log \frac{1}{\delta})$ to $O((\frac{2n}{\epsilon})^{2n/2n+1} (\log \frac{1}{\delta})^{1/2n+1})$.

When we restrict the population learner to be a voting scheme, what we obtain is effectively a model of 'population prediction,' in which the learner is to *predict* the value of the target concept at an arbitrarily drawn point, as a threshold function of the predictions made by its agents on the same point. We show that the population learning model is strictly more powerful than the population prediction model, by showing that the class of parity functions can be PAC learned in the former model but not in the latter. The population learning of parity functions is possible by a minimum superset finder for the complements, with the agents employing the closure algorithm. For the non-predictability of the parity functions in the population prediction model, we first show that any class that is population predictable by any voting scheme, can be predicted by majority vote. We then show that there is no agent algorithm, in combination with majority vote, that can predict this class, by making use of a super constant lower bound on the sample complexity for weak learning of the same class, due to Goldman, Kearns and Schapire [4].

Finally, we consider a variant of this model in which the samples are affected by classification noise of a (known) constant rate η. In this setting, we exhibit an efficient population learning system for conjunctions requiring population size $2n^2((1 - e^{-\frac{4}{3n}m})^2 \epsilon^2 (1 - 2\eta)^2)^{-1} \ln \frac{2n}{\delta}$. Note that this gives a polynomial upper bound even when the sample size m is constant, although it does not provide any speed-up. One can show a less rigorous asymptotic bound of $O(\frac{1}{m^{1-2\alpha}\epsilon^2} \log \frac{n}{\delta})$, for any $\alpha > 0$ and any constant η, for a slightly modified population learner. The total computation time can be made[3] $O((\frac{n}{\epsilon})^{3/2(1-\alpha)} + (\frac{n}{\epsilon})^{1/1-2\alpha} \log \frac{n}{\delta})$ by

---

[3]Furthermore, it can be shown asymptotically that the agent algorithm is a learning algorithm.

setting $m = (\frac{n}{\epsilon})^{3/2(1-\alpha)} + (\frac{n}{\epsilon})^{1/1-2\alpha} \log \frac{n}{\delta}$, which is a speed-up from the best known computational complexity upper bound of $O((\frac{n}{\epsilon})^2 \log \frac{n}{\delta})$.

2 Preliminaries

The definition of our learning model closely parallels Valiant's PAC learning model for boolean concepts [8]. Concepts are subsets of some fixed set X. We also view them as 0,1-functions : $X \rightarrow \{0, 1\}$, mapping an element $x \in X$ to 1 just in case x is in the concept. A concept (representation) class C is a subset of 2^X with an associated size measure, and so is a hypothesis class H. A population learning system is a pair (A, L) of an agent algorithm A and a population learner L, and (A, L) with sample size m and population size N, written $(A, L)_{m,N}$, proceeds as follows. Each of N copies of A independently obtains a labeled sample of size m drawn according to some fixed but unknown distribution D over X and labeled according to the target concept c, and outputs a hypothesis from some hypothesis class H. L takes these N hypotheses as input and outputs a single hypothesis.

Definition 1 *We say that a population learning system (A, L) is a population PAC-learner for a concept class C if all of the following conditions are satisfied:*

(α) *There exists a polynomial $f(n, s, 1/\epsilon, 1/\delta)$ and a constant m_0 such that for all $m \geq m_0$, for an arbitrary target concept c in C (of size s over domain of size n), for arbitrary $\epsilon, \delta > 0$ and an arbitrary distribution D, whenever the population size N exceeds $f(n, s, 1/\epsilon, 1/\delta)$, the hypothesis h obtained by (A, L) is an ϵ-approximation of c (i.e. $D(h \triangle c) \leq \epsilon$) with probability at least $1 - \delta$.*

(β) *A is a PAC-learning algorithm.*

(γ) *For each target concept c in C, (A, L) PAC-learns c in total running time (the running time of A plus that of L) strictly less than the running time of the best PAC learning algorithm (in the ordinary PAC-learning model), for all small enough ϵ and δ.*

Whenever some subset $\Psi \subseteq \{\alpha, \beta, \gamma\}$ is satisfied by a population learning system (A, L), (A, L) is said to be a Ψ-population PAC-learner.

Note that condition (α) parallels the original definition of population learning due to Kearns and Seung, except the distribution-free requirement. Condition (β) reflects the idea that population learning consists of a large population of *learners*. Condition (γ) provides justification for a population learning system, and in particular excludes trivial population learners in which the agent simply passes on its sample in an encoded form to the population learner.

Definition 2 *The population 'prediction' model is the same as the population learning model defined above, except the following : A population predictor takes as input a test point $x \in X$ and feeds the agents with the same test point, and* *makes its prediction as a threshold function of the input predictions $\vec{y}$ it receives from the agents. That is, the population predictor L can be defined as $L(\vec{y}) = 1$ if and only if $\vec{w} \cdot \vec{y} \geq \theta$ (or $\vec{w} \cdot \vec{y} > \theta$), for some $\vec{w} \in \Re^N$ and $\theta \in [0,1]$. Its population size is to be bounded by some polynomial $f(n, s, 1/\epsilon)$, where ϵ is the prediction accuracy.*

The concept classes considered in this paper are as follows. The 'high-low game' is the concept class $\{[0, b] | b \in [0, 1]\}$ over the domain $[0, 1]$. The class of '2-dimensional half spaces' (going through the origin) is $\{c_\theta : 0 \leq \theta < \pi\}$ over $\Re^2$, where $c_{\theta^*} = \{(r, \theta) : \theta^* < \theta \leq \theta^* + \pi\}$ in the polar coordinates. 'Two disjoint length-1 intervals' (containing $\{-1, 1\}$) is $\{(-2 + a, -1 + a] \cup (b, 1 + b] : 0 \leq a, b < 1\}$ over $\Re$. 'Axis-parallel rectangles' is $\{[a_1, b_1] \times ... \times [a_n, b_n] : a_i, b_i \in \Re, i = 1, ..., n\}$ over $\Re^n$. As usual, 'Conjunctions' is $\{l_1 \wedge ... \wedge l_k : l_1, ...l_k \in \{x_1, \overline{x_1}, ...x_n, \overline{x_n}\}\}$ over $\{0, 1\}^n$, and 'Parity' is $\{v_1 \oplus ... \oplus v_k : v_1, ...v_k \in \{x_1, ...x_n\}\}$ over $\{0, 1\}^n$. Finally k-CNF and k-DNF are as defined in [8].

In the sequel, we usually let S denote a labeled sample, and in this case S_+ and S_- denote the sets of positive examples and negative examples in S, respectively. We sometimes use S to denote an unlabeled sample, i.e. $S \in X^m$, and in this case, we let $c(S)$ denote S labeled by concept c, and similarly for any $\lambda \in \{0, 1\}^m$, $\lambda(S)$ denote S labeled by λ. We write S^N for a population of samples of size N, and $c(S^N)$ for the same, each labeled by c. Also, for simplicity, we will write $E_{x \in D}[f]$ for the 'expectation of $f(x)$ when x is drawn according to D.' Also we define $a =?b$ to be 1 if $a = b$ and 0 otherwise.

3 Various Population Learners and Population Sizes

3.1 Ideal Parallelization in Population Learning

Suppose that the input sample S is partitioned into k sub-samples, $S_i, 1 \leq i \leq k$, and each is fed to a copy of the agent algorithm A to obtain hypothesis h_i, and then the population learner L outputs $h = L(A(S_1), .., A(S_k))$. Suppose that the following equality always holds:

$$L(A(S_1), .., A(S_k)) = A(\cup_{i=1}^{k} S_i). \tag{a}$$

Clearly when this is the case, the partitioning of the sample at the agents' level costs the population learner no additional overall sample size. Hence, the population size required is $\frac{1}{m} f(n, s, 1/\epsilon, 1/\delta)$, giving the optimal population size.

Condition 1 is a sufficient condition for the existence of a population learning system satisfying (a).

Condition 1 *A hypothesis class H is said to satisfy Condition 1, if there exists a lattice structure $(\leq, H)$ satisfying both of the following.*

1. *$\forall h_1, h_2, h \in H$, $\forall S$: sample*
   (h_1, h_2 is consistent with S)
   $\Rightarrow$ (h satisfying $h_1 \leq h \leq h_2$ is consistent with S).

2. *There exists a unique minimum consistent hypothesis for any sample S.*

Proposition 1 *Let C be a target concept class and H a hypothesis class such that $H \supseteq C$ satisfying Condition 1. If*

1. *A outputs the minimum (with respect to $\leq$) consistent hypothesis, and*

2. *L outputs the least upper bound (with respect to $\leq$) hypothesis from those output by the agents,*

then the population learning system (A, L) is a population PAC-learner for C in terms of H with population size $\frac{1}{m} f(n, s, 1/\epsilon, 1/\delta)$, where $f(\cdot, \cdot, \cdot, \cdot)$ denotes the sample complexity of A for learning C in terms of H.

Proof of Proposition 1: We show that (a) holds. Let $c \in C$ be the target concept, and S_i be the sample fed to the ith agent, H_i the subset of H consistent with S_i, and h_i the hypothesis output by the ith agent. Let h be the hypothesis output by L when $\{h_1, ..., h_N\}$ is fed, and h' be the hypothesis output by A when $\bigcup_{i=1}^{N} S_i$ is fed. $h' = \min \bigcap_{i=1}^{N} H_i$ holds trivially. For all i, $h_i \leq c$ holds because c is consistent with S_i. Thus, $h_i \leq h \leq c$. This means $h \in H_i$ for all i, and hence $h \geq h'$. That $h \leq h'$ holds follows from $h_i \leq h'$. □

We call a population learner defined as in Proposition 1 a 'supremum hypothesis finder'.

Intersection closed classes [7, 5], which are well-known to be learnable with one-sided error, satisfy Condtion 1 trivially. In this case, the desired lattice on H is given by the set inclusion relation. The agent algorithm as defined in Proposition 1 in this case is the 'closure algorithm'[5], which outputs the minimum hypothesis containing all the positive examples in the input sample. A 'supremum hypothesis finder' in this case is the 'minimum superset finder,' which outputs the minimum member of H containing $\bigcup_{i=1}^{N} h_i$, given inputs $\{h_1, h_2, ..., h_N\}$. Therefore, for an intersection closed class, the previous proposition can be restated as in the following corollary.

Corollary 1 *Let C be a target concept class and H a hypothesis class satisfying $H \supseteq C$, and assume that H is intersection closed. Then the population learning system (A, L), where A is a closure algorithm and L is a minimum superset finder, is a population PAC-learner for C in terms of H with population size $\frac{1}{m} f(n, s, 1/\epsilon, 1/\delta)$, where $f(\cdot, \cdot, \cdot, \cdot)$ denotes the sample complexity of A for learning C in terms of H.*

Below are some examples of concept classes which can be shown to be population PAC learnable by a 'minimum superset finder,' by an application of Corollary 1.

Example 1 *'Axis-parallel rectangles' is population PAC-learnable by population learning system (A, L): A outputs $[x_1, y_1] \times ... \times [x_n, y_n]$ where x_i and y_i are the minimum and maximum values of the i-th component of any example in S_+, and it outputs $\emptyset$ when there is no positive example. L outputs $\prod_{i=1}^{n} [\min_T x_i, \max_T y_i]$, where T is the set of input hypotheses, and it outputs the empty set if T contains the empty set only. The population size required is at most $\frac{2n}{m\epsilon} \ln \frac{2n}{\delta}$.*

Example 2 *'Conjunctions' is population PAC-learnable by population learning system (A, L): A outputs the conjunction of all literals that are satisfied by all of the positive examples. L outputs the conjunction of all literals that are included in all of the hypotheses. The population size required is $\frac{1}{m\epsilon}(\ln\frac{1}{\delta} + n\ln 3)$.*

The above population learners achieve a speed-up, with respect to ϵ and δ, from $\Omega(\frac{1}{\epsilon}\log\frac{1}{\delta})$ to $O((\frac{1}{\epsilon}\log\frac{1}{\delta})^{\frac{1}{2}})$ by setting $m = O((\frac{1}{\epsilon}\log\frac{1}{\delta})^{\frac{1}{2}})$. Note that k-CNF can be learned by an essentially the same method. Also the *dual* of the above method can be used to learn disjunctions and k-DNF.

The next two examples are concept classes satisfying Condition 1, but are not intersection closed.

Example 3 *'2-dimensional half spaces (going through the origin)' is population PAC-learnable by population learning system (A, L): A outputs the hypothesis with the smallest θ among all consistent hypotheses. L outputs the hypothesis with the largest θ among all input hypotheses. The population size required is at most $\frac{1}{m\epsilon}\ln\frac{1}{\delta}$.*

Example 4 *'Two disjoint length-1 intervals' (containing $\{-1, 1\}$) is population PAC-learnable by population learning system (A, L): A outputs the hypothesis with the smallest (a, b) among all consistent hypotheses, where the order in this class is defined by $(a_1, b_1) \leq (a_2, b_2) \Leftrightarrow a_1 \leq a_2$ and $b_1 \leq b_2$. L outputs $(\max_T a, \max_T b)$, where T is the set of input hypotheses. The population size required is at most $\frac{2}{m\epsilon}\ln\frac{2}{\delta}$.*

Similarly as before, the above population learner achieves a speed-up from $\Omega(\frac{1}{\epsilon}\log\frac{1}{\delta})$ to $O((\frac{1}{\epsilon}\log\frac{1}{\delta})^{\frac{1}{2}})$.

3.2 Voting Schemes

A population learner L is a voting scheme, if its hypothesis can be determined pointwise (on each $x \in X$) by $L(\{h_1, ..., h_N\})(x) \stackrel{\triangle}{=} f(h_1(x), ..., h_N(x))$, for some threshold function f, namely $f(y_1, ..., y_N) = 1$ if and only if $g(y_1, ..., y_N) \geq \theta N$ for some g and θ, where θ is in general a function of N. With $g(y_1, ..., y_N) = \sum_{i=1}^{N} y_i$ and $\theta = \frac{1}{N}$, we obtain the OR-gate (OR), with $\theta = \frac{1}{2}$ the majority vote (MAJ), and with $\theta = 1$ the AND-gate (AND).

3.2.1 The Majority Vote

We show that the majority vote, when coupled with an agent algorithm that randomly outputs a 'super' concept and a 'sub' concept each with probability a half, can be shown to be a population learner for the high-low game and other related concept classes.

Theorem 1 *Let $c \in C$ and let A_+, A_- be agent algorithms that satisfy the following.*

1. $A_-(S) \subseteq c \subseteq A_+(S)$ *for all labeled samples S for c.*

2. $\forall D$ over $X, \forall \epsilon > 0, \exists U_-(\epsilon) \subseteq c \subseteq \exists U_+(\epsilon)$ such that
$D(c - U_-(\epsilon)) \leq \epsilon, D(U_+(\epsilon) - c) \leq \epsilon,$
$p[U_-(\epsilon)] \overset{\triangle}{=} D^m\{S \in X^m : A_-(S) \supseteq U_-(\epsilon)\} > 0,$
$p[U_+(\epsilon)] \overset{\triangle}{=} D^m\{S \in X^m : A_+(S) \subseteq U_+(\epsilon)\} > 0$

Let $0 < \epsilon, \delta < 1$. Then, if the agent A mixes the outputs of A_+ and A_- each with probability a half (we write $A = rmix[A_+, A_-]$), and the population learner L outputs h by the majority vote, then whenever the population size is at least $2 \ln \frac{2}{\delta} \max\{\frac{1}{p^2[U_-(\epsilon)]}, \frac{1}{p^2[U_+(\epsilon)]}\}$, h satisfies[4] $\Pr\{D(h \triangle c) > \epsilon\} \leq \delta$.

Proof of Theorem 1: Let h be the output hypothesis of (A, MAJ). By the properties of $A_-(S)$ and $A_+(S)$, h can have only one-sided error, namely $D(h - c) = 0$ or $D(c - h) = 0$. Assume without loss of generality that $D(c-h) = 0$. Now suppose that $D(h - c) > \epsilon > 0$. Since L employs the majority vote, this implies that more than half of the agents' hypotheses are not contained in $U_+(\epsilon)$. But the probability that A outputs such a hypothesis (i.e. one not contained in $U_+(\epsilon)$) is $\frac{1 - p[U_+(\epsilon)]}{2}$. Hence, the probability of this occurring is $GE(\frac{1 - p[U_+(\epsilon)]}{2}, N, \frac{1}{2}N)$, where we let $GE(p, m, r)$ denote the probability that an event with probability p occurs at least r times in m Bernoulli trials. Now by Hoeffding's inequality, we have $GE(\frac{1 - p[U_+(\epsilon)]}{2}, N, \frac{1}{2}N) \leq e^{-\frac{1}{2}p^2[U_+(\epsilon)]N}$. Hence whenever $N \geq \frac{2}{p^2[U_+(\epsilon)]} \ln \frac{2}{\delta}$ holds, the probability of having $D(h - c) > \epsilon$ is at most $\frac{\delta}{2}$. Similarly, the same bound implies that the probability that $D(c - h) > \epsilon$ is also at most $\frac{\delta}{2}$. $\qquad \square$

Corollary 2 'The high-low game' is population PAC-learnable by population learning system (A, L): $A = rmix[A_+, A_-]$ where $A_+(S) = [0, \min(\{1\} \cup S_-))$ and $A_-(S) = [0, \max(\{0\} \cup S_+)]$. The population size required is $\frac{2}{(1-(1-\epsilon)^m)^2} \ln \frac{2}{\delta}$, and (A, L) achieves a speed-up in overall computation time from $\Omega(\frac{1}{\epsilon} \log \frac{1}{\delta})$ to $O((\frac{1}{\epsilon})^{\frac{2}{3}} \log \frac{1}{\delta})$.

Proof of Corollary 2: It follows easily from Theorem 1 that the population size for this class is at most $\frac{2}{(1-(1-\epsilon)^m)^2} \ln \frac{2}{\delta}$. If we substitute $m = (\frac{1}{\epsilon})^{\frac{1}{3}}$, then this bound becomes $O((\frac{1}{\epsilon})^{\frac{2}{3}} \log \frac{1}{\delta})$ since $(1 - (1 - \epsilon)^m)^2$ is bounded below by $K^2 \epsilon^{\frac{2}{3}}$ for some constant K, for all small enough ϵ, as shown below.

$$(1 - (1 - \epsilon)^m)^2 \geq (1 - e^{-\epsilon m})^2 = (1 - e^{-\epsilon^{1/3}})^2 \geq (1 - (1 - K\epsilon^{1/3}))^2 \geq K^2 \epsilon^{2/3}.$$

Since the computation time of (A, L) is both linear in m and N, it is $O((\frac{1}{\epsilon})^{\frac{2}{3}} \log \frac{1}{\delta})$ when $m = (\frac{1}{\epsilon})^{\frac{1}{3}}$. $\qquad \square$

3.2.2 The AND and OR Gates

Proposition 2 Let $c \in C$ be the target concept. Suppose that the agent A satisfies the following conditions.

---

[4] Note that $U_+(\epsilon), U_-(\epsilon)$ may depend on D.

1. $A(c(S)) \subseteq c$ for all $S \in X^m$

2. $p(\epsilon) \triangleq D^m \{S \in X^m : D(c - A(c(S))) \leq \epsilon)\} > 0$ for all $\epsilon > 0$

Let $0 < \epsilon, \delta < 1$. Then, whenever the population size is at least $\frac{1}{p(\epsilon)} \ln \frac{1}{\delta}$, hypothesis h obtained by the OR gate satisfies[5] $\Pr\{D(h \triangle c) > \epsilon\} \leq \delta$.

Proof of Proposition 2: The proposition follows easily from the fact that the probability that h fails to be an ϵ-approximation is at most $(1 - p(\epsilon))^N$, where N is the population size. □
The dual of the above proposition holds for the AND gate.

Corollary 3 *Let A be the same agent algorithm as in Example 1. Then, (A, OR) is a (β, γ)-population PAC-learner for 'Axis-parallel rectangles' of an arbitrary dimension n, with population size $O((\frac{2n}{\epsilon})^{2n} \log \frac{1}{\delta})$. (A, OR) achieves a speed-up from $\Omega(\frac{2n}{\epsilon} \log \frac{1}{\delta})$ to $O((\frac{2n}{\epsilon})^{2n/2n+1} (\log \frac{1}{\delta})^{1/2n+1})$, by setting $N = m = (\frac{2n}{\epsilon})^{2n/2n+1}(\log \frac{1}{\delta})^{1/2n+1}$.*

Proof of Corollary 3: First, it is easy to see that for each target n-dimensional rectangle, $2n$ disjoint regions each with probability $\frac{\epsilon}{2n}$ can be found such that obtaining an example in each of them guarantees that A outputs an ϵ-approximation (with one-sided error only). Now if we let $P(m, k, \alpha)$ denote the probability that each of k events of probability α occurs at least once in m trials, then we can show[6] that $P(m, k, \alpha) \geq \frac{1}{4} m(m-1) \cdot \ldots \cdot (m-k+1)\alpha^k$, whenever $k\alpha \leq \frac{1}{m}$, since $P(m, k, \alpha)$ is lower bounded by the probability that each of the k events occurs exactly once, which is $k! \binom{m}{k} \alpha^k (1 - k\alpha)^{m-k}$. By Proposition 2, the population size of (A, OR) is at most $\frac{1}{P(m, 2n, \frac{\epsilon}{2n})} \ln \frac{1}{\delta}$, which is seen to be $O((\frac{2n}{m\epsilon})^{2n} \log \frac{1}{\delta})$. □

4 A Separation Result

Theorem 2 *There exists a concept class $C \subseteq 2^{\{0,1\}^n}$ such that C is population PAC learnable, but C is not population PAC predictable.*

Proof Sketch of Theorem 2: The theorem follows from the following three lemmas. □

Lemma 1 *'Parity' is population learnable.*

Lemma 2 *If a concept class $C \subseteq 2^{\{0,1\}^n}$ is (α, β)-population predictable, then C is (α, β)-population predictable by majority vote.*

Lemma 3 *'Parity' is not (α, β)-population predictable by majority vote.*

---

[5] $p(\epsilon)$ can depend on D as well.
[6] Note that if we use a naive bound of $P(m, 2n, \frac{\epsilon}{2n}) \geq 1 - 2n(1 - \frac{\epsilon}{2n})^m$, the bound on the population size we would obtain would be negative when the sample size m is small.

Proof Sketch of Lemma 1: Our proof is an application of a result by Fisher and Simon that the same class is learnable from negative examples only [3]. By Lemma 13 in [3], the complement of a parity function f, namely $f^{-1}(0)$, is a linear sub-space of $\{0,1\}^n$ spanned by some basis. Now define a population learning system (A, L) by $A(S) = MI(S^-)$, where S^- denotes the set of negative examples in S, and $L(B_1, .., B_N) = MI(\cup_{i=1}^N B_i)$, where $MI(T)$ is in general a maximal independent set of T. It is easy to see that A is a closure algorithm and L is a minimum superset finder, and hence by Corollary 1, (A, L) is an (α, β)-population learner with population size $O(\frac{n}{m\epsilon} \log \frac{1}{\delta})$. By setting $N = m = \sqrt{\frac{n}{\epsilon} \log \frac{1}{\delta}}$, the total running time of (A, L) can be made $O(n^{\frac{2}{3}} \sqrt{\frac{1}{\epsilon} \log \frac{1}{\delta}})$, which is a speed-up (with respect to ϵ and δ) from the lower bound in the sequential case, $\Omega(\frac{n}{\epsilon} \log \frac{1}{\delta})$. $\qquad\square$

Proof Sketch of Lemma 2: Suppose that (A, L) is an (α, β)-population predictor for C with population size $f(1/\epsilon, n, s)$ and the minimum required agent sample size m_0. We can assume that L is of the form $L(\vec{y}) = 1$ if and only if $\vec{w} \cdot \vec{y} \geq \theta$ (except when L is a weighted OR-gate) where $\vec{w}$ and $\vec{y}$ are N-dimensional vectors $[w_i]$ and $[y_i]$, respectively. When L is a weighted OR-gate, L can be defined with a strict inequality by $L(\vec{y}) = 1$ if and only if $\vec{w} \cdot \vec{y} > 0$. Here we can assume without loss of generality that the weights w_i sum to unity, and that the threshold θ is a real number belonging to the interval $[0, 1]$. Since the only meaningful information available to the population predictor is the number of 1's among the input y_i, we can also assume that all the weights are equal, namely $w_i = 1/N$ for each i. So we are left to show that any threshold $\theta \in [0, 1]$ can be converted to a half. First, suppose that L is the OR-gate, that is $L(\vec{y}) = 1$ if and only if $\sum y_i/N > 0$. (The argument for the AND-gate is analogous.) Then, convert A to A' defined by $A'(S) = 1$ if $A(S) = 1$, and $A'(S) = 1$ with probability $1/2$ if $A(S) = 0$. Now assume that the population size N exceeds $f(1/\epsilon, n, s)$, for some fixed n, s and $\epsilon < e^{-2}$. Now let α denote the random variable standing for the prediction value output by the agent algorithm having received a sample of size m and a randomly drawn test point x, given that x is a *positive* example, and γ the random variable standing for the prediction output by the population learner under the same condition, with population size N. (Also define β as the analogue of α for *negative* examples.) Then we must have $\Pr\{\alpha = 1\} \geq 1/N$, since otherwise we would have $\Pr\{\alpha = 1\} < 1/N$ which can be shown to imply $\Pr\{\gamma = 0\} > (1 - 1/N)^N \geq e^{-2} > \epsilon$ for all $N \geq 2$, which contradicts the fact that $f(1/\epsilon, n, s)$ is an upper bound on the population size of (A, L). So if we let α' denote the random variable for A', analogously defined as α with A, then we must have $\Pr\{\alpha' = 1\} \geq 1/2 + 1/2N$. (We can show the analogous statement for β', which is defined for A' as β was defined for A.) It is straightforward to show, using Hoeffding's inequality, that (A', OR) will be a population PAC learner for the same class with population size bounded above by $O(N^{2+\Delta})$ for any $\Delta > 0$. Next, we assume that $\theta \in (0, 1)$. Then the population learner (A_θ, MAJ), where A_θ is as defined below, will be a population PAC-learner for C.

(If $\theta > \frac{1}{2}$) $A_\theta(S) = 1$ with probability $\frac{1}{2\theta}$ if $A(S) = 1$

$$= 0 \text{ with probability } 1 - \frac{1}{2\theta} \text{ if } A(S) = 1$$
$$= 0 \text{ if } A(S) = 0$$
$$(\text{If } \theta \leq \tfrac{1}{2}) \ A_\theta(S) = 1 \text{ if } A(S) = 1$$
$$= 0 \text{ with probability } \frac{1}{2(1-\theta)} \text{ if } A(S) = 0$$
$$= 1 \text{ with probability } 1 - \frac{1}{2(1-\theta)} \text{ if } A(S) = 0$$

We can show easily that if $\Pr\{A(S) = 1\} > \theta$, then we must also have $\Pr\{A_\theta(S) = 1\} > \frac{1}{2}$, and if $\Pr\{A(S) = 1\} \leq \theta$, then $\Pr\{A_\theta(S) = 1\} \leq \frac{1}{2}$. Hence, if (A, L) is a population PAC-learner for C, then (A_θ, MAJ) must also be a population PAC-learner for the same class. $\qquad\square$

Proof of Lemma 3: Let (A, MAJ) be a population learner. Consider the experiment in which a target concept c is drawn from the uniform distribution U_C over Parity of size at most s, written C, and a test point x is drawn from the uniform distribution U_X over X of size n, and then (A, MAJ) predicts the value of $c(x)$ by majority vote on the predictions made by the agents $A_i, i = 1, ..., N$, each outputting a prediction for $c(x)$ based on m examples S drawn from D^m for some fixed D over X and labeled by c, written $c(S)$.

Fix one of the agents A and an input labeled sample of size m. As pointed out by Goldman, Kearns and Schapire [4] in their proof of a lower bound on the sample complexity of weakly learning Parity, the sample defines a system of linear equations whose solution space is exactly the version space, namely the set of consistent hypotheses. Furthermore, if $r \ (< n)$ is the rank of this system of equations, then except for 2^r many points which depend on the sample, all the points in X are labeled '1' by exactly half of the functions in the version space and labeled '0' by the other half.

Now suppose, for contradiction, that (A, MAJ) is an (α)-population learner for Parity with population size $f(n, s, 1/\epsilon)$. Then, if we write $(A, MAJ)_{c(S^N)}(x)$ for the prediction value on x of (A, MAJ) given a population of labeled samples $c(S^N)$, we must have for any $N \geq f(n, s, 16)$,

$$E_{x \in D} E_{S^N \in (D^m)^N} E_{c \in U_C}[(A, MAJ)_{c(S^N)}(x) = ?c(x)] \geq 1 - 1/16$$

Then by Markov's inequality, we must have

$$D(\{x | E_{S^N \in (D^m)^N} E_{c \in U_C}[(A, MAJ)_{c(S^N)}(x) = ?c(x)] \geq 1 - \sqrt{1/16}\}) \geq 3/4. \quad \text{(b)}$$

Suppose now for any fixed $x \in X$, we have $E_{S^N \in (D^m)^N} E_{c \in U_C}[(A, MAJ)_{c(S^N)}(x) = ?c(x)] \geq 3/4$. Then since the standard deviation of a binomial distribution is of order $\sqrt{N}$, for this x we must have $P_{A,m}(x) \stackrel{\triangle}{=} E_{S \in D^m} E_{c \in U_C}[A_{c(S)}(x) = ?c(x)] \geq 1/2 + K/\sqrt{N}$, for some constant $K > 0$ independent of x. So if we now define $X_0 \subseteq X$ by

$$X_0 \stackrel{\triangle}{=} \{x \in X | P_{A,m}(x) \geq 1/2 + K/\sqrt{N}\} \quad \text{(c)}$$

then it follows from (b) that $D(X_0) \geq 3/4$. Now define $P_{A,m,X_0}(S) \stackrel{\triangle}{=} E_{x \in D_0} E_{c \in U_C}[A_{c(S)}(x) = ?c(x)]$, where we let D_0 be the distribution obtained by restricting D to X_0. Then, since for every labeled sample $\lambda(S)$, all but 2^r points in X are labeled '1' by exactly half of the hypotheses in the version space for $\lambda(S)$, written $VS(\lambda(S))$, and $|X_0| > 2^{n-1}$, we must have for every $S \in X^m$,

$$P_{A,m,X_0}(S) = \sum_{\lambda \in \{0,1\}^m} \sum_{c \in VS(\lambda(S))} U_C(c)(E_{x \in D_0}[A_{\lambda(S)}(x) = ?c(x)])$$

$$\leq \sum_{\lambda \in \{0,1\}^m} \frac{|VS(\lambda(S))|}{|C|}(\frac{1}{2} + \frac{1}{2^{n-r}}) \leq \frac{1}{2} + \frac{1}{2^{n-r}}. \tag{d}$$

If we now let P_{A,m,X_0} denote the prediction accuracy of A with sample size m on a test example x drawn from X_0 with respect to D_0, then from (c) and (d) we have, respectively,

$$P_{A,m,X_0} \triangleq E_{x \in D_0}[P_{A,m}(x)] \geq \frac{1}{2} + \frac{K}{\sqrt{N}}. \tag{e}$$

$$P_{A,m,X_0} = E_{S \in D^m}[P_{A,m,X_0}(S)] \leq \frac{1}{2} + \frac{1}{2^{n-r}}. \tag{f}$$

Finally from (e) and (f), it follows that $\frac{1}{2} + \frac{1}{2^{n-r}} \geq \frac{1}{2} + \frac{K}{\sqrt{N}}$, and hence $N \geq K^2 2^{2(n-r)}$. Thus if $m \geq r$ is $o(n)$ then N must be exponential in n, contradicting our assumption. □

5 Population Learning with Classification Noise

In this section, we consider a variant of the population learning model in which each example is labeled incorrectly with a known probability η (c.f. [1]), and exhibit an (α)-population PAC learner for the class of conjunctions, whose sample size is independent of ϵ, δ, and η.

Let $GE(p, l, k)$ denote the probability that an event with probability p occurs at least k times in l Bernoulli trials. We extend $GE(p, l, x)$ for non-negative reals x by $GE(p, l, x) = (1 - (\lceil x \rceil - x))GE(p, l, \lceil x \rceil) + (\lceil x \rceil - x)GE(p, l, \lceil x \rceil - 1)$. We then define the function ϕ by $GE(\eta, l, \phi(l)) = \eta$. Let S_L denote the set of examples in S that do not satisfy literal L and θ_L the probability that L is not satisfied. Now define a population learning system (A_0, L_0) as follows.

A_0 : Let $\mathcal{L} = \{x_1, \overline{x_1} ..., x_n, \overline{x_n}\}$ initially. Given a labeled sample S, remove literal L with $|S_L| \geq 1$ from $\mathcal{L}$ with probability 1 if there are at least $\lceil \phi(|S_L|) \rceil$ positive examples in S_L, and with probability $\lceil \phi(|S_L|) \rceil - \phi(|S_L|)$ if there are $\lceil \phi(|S_L|) \rceil - 1$ positive examples in S_L. For literal L with $|S_L| = 0$, remove it with probability η. Output $\bigwedge_{L \in \mathcal{L}} L$.

L_0 : Let $\mathcal{L} = \{x_1, \overline{x_1} ..., x_n, \overline{x_n}\}$ initially. Remove L from $\mathcal{L}$ if more than $(\eta + \frac{1}{2}(1 - e^{-\frac{\epsilon}{2n}m})\frac{\epsilon}{2n}(1 - 2\eta))N$ hypotheses given by the agents do not contain L, where N is the population size and m is the sample size of each agent. Output $\bigwedge_{L \in \mathcal{L}} L$.

Theorem 3 (A_0, L_0) as defined above is an (α)-population learner for conjunctions with population size $\frac{2n^2}{(1 - e^{-\frac{\epsilon}{2n}m})^2 \epsilon^2 (1 - 2\eta)^2} \ln \frac{2n}{\delta}$ when the classification error rate is η, $0 < \eta < \frac{1}{2}$.

Proof of Theorem 3 Let c be the target concept and D be the sampling distribution. Let $f_l(p) = GE(p, l, \phi(l))$. It follows from the fact that for $l \geq 1$, f_l is monotonically increasing, f_l is convex for $p \leq p_0$ and concave for $p \geq p_0$ for some $p_0, 0 \leq p_0 \leq 1$, $f_l(0) = 0$, $f_l(1) = 1$ and $f_l(\eta) = \eta$, that $f_l(p) \geq p$ holds whenever $p \geq \eta$. Now if L is '$\frac{\epsilon}{2n}$-bad,' i.e. $D(c - L) \geq \frac{\epsilon}{2n}$, then the conditional probability that a random example $\vec{x}$ is labeled positive given that $\vec{x} \not\models L$ is at least $\eta + \frac{\epsilon}{2n}(1 - 2\eta)$, and since $|S_L| \geq 1$ holds with probability at least $1 - e^{-\frac{\epsilon}{2n}m}$, A_0 removes L with probability at least $\eta + (1 - e^{-\frac{\epsilon}{2n}m})\frac{\epsilon}{2n}(1 - 2\eta)$. Finally, it can be shown (using Hoeffding's inequality) that with probability at least δ L_0 removes all literals not appearing with probability at least $\eta + (1 - e^{-\frac{\epsilon}{2n}m})\frac{\epsilon}{2n}(1 - 2\eta)$ and removes no literal not appearing with probability η, whenever the population size exceeds $\frac{2n^2}{(1 - e^{-\frac{\epsilon}{2n}m})^2 \epsilon^2 (1 - 2\eta)^2} \ln \frac{2n}{\delta}$. $\square$

Although Theorem 3 shows only that (A_0, L_0) is an (α)-population PAC learner, (A_0, L_0) can be modified so that it asymptotically satisfies conditions (β) and possibly (γ) as well. (We say 'possibly' here, because the population learner we exhibit can be shown asymptotically to give a speed-up with respect to the best known sequential PAC learning algorithm for the same class, but not with respect to the best known lower bound.)

A_1 : Let $\mathcal{L} = \{x_1, \bar{x}_1 ..., x_n, \bar{x}_n\}$ initially. Given a labeled sample S, remove literal L from $\mathcal{L}$, if more than $\phi_m(|S_L|) \overset{\triangle}{=} |S_L|\eta + \sqrt{|S_L|\eta(1 - \eta)}f(m)$ samples belonging to S_L are labeled positive, where $f(m) \overset{\triangle}{=} \sqrt{\log m^\alpha}$.

L_1 : Let $\mathcal{L} = \{x_1, \bar{x}_1, ..., x_n, \bar{x}_n\}$ initially. Remove L from $\mathcal{L}$ if[7] more than

$$t(\epsilon, m)N \overset{\triangle}{=} \left(\Pr\{X_{0,1} \geq f(m)\} + \min\{\frac{\epsilon m^{\frac{1-2\alpha}{2}}}{4e^{\frac{1}{8}}n\sqrt{\pi}}, \frac{1}{4}\} \right)N$$

hypotheses given by the agents do not contain L, where N is the population size and m is the sample size of each agent, where $X_{0,1}$ denotes the random variable that obeys the standard normal distribution (i.e. with zero mean and unit variance). Then output $\wedge_{L \in \mathcal{L}} L$.

Theorem 4 Let $\alpha \in (0, \frac{1}{2})$. For all sufficiently[8] small $\epsilon > 0$, the agent A_1 is a PAC-learns conjunctions with sample size of order $O(\frac{n^2}{\epsilon^2} \log \frac{n}{\delta} + (\frac{n}{\epsilon})^{\frac{2}{\alpha}})$.

Theorem 5 Let $\alpha \in [0, \frac{1}{2})$. For all sufficiently small ϵ and δ, (A_1, L_1) learns conjunctions in time of order $O((\frac{n}{\epsilon})^{\frac{3}{2(1-\alpha)}} + (\frac{n}{\epsilon})^{\frac{1}{1-2\alpha}}(\log \frac{n}{\delta})^{\frac{1}{2(1-2\alpha)}})$, by setting $N = C(\frac{n}{\epsilon})^{\frac{1}{1-2\alpha}}(\log \frac{n}{\delta})^{\frac{1}{2(1-2\alpha)}}$, $m = C((\frac{n}{\epsilon})^{\frac{3}{2(1-\alpha)}} + (\frac{n}{\epsilon})^{\frac{1}{1-2\alpha}}(\log \frac{n}{\delta})^{\frac{1}{2(1-2\alpha)}})$, where C is some constant.

Theorem 4 is proved using the following two lemmas.

---

[7] Note that $\Pr\{X_{0,1} \geq f(m)\}$ can be calculated within precision Δ in time $O(1/\sqrt{\Delta})$.

[8] It should be noted that 'sufficiently small' here depends on the noise rate η, and thus the sample comlexity shown here is an 'asymptotic' result.

Lemma 4 *Let $\alpha \in (0, \frac{1}{2})$ and let L be one of the literals that belong to the target conjunction. When m is sufficiently large compared to $(1/\theta_L)^{\frac{1}{1-\alpha}}$, the probability that A_1 removes L is upper bounded by $2(2\pi\alpha m^\alpha \log m)^{-\frac{1}{2}}$.*

Proof of Lemma 4: The probability that we wish to bound is equal to $GE(\eta, |S_L|, \phi_m(|S_L|))$, which can be approximated using the Edgeworth expansion (see for example [2]) as follows.

$$GE(\eta, |S_L|, \phi_m(|S_L|)) = \Pr\{X_{0,1} \geq f(m)\} + o(|S_L|^{-\frac{1}{2}}), \tag{g}$$

Next some calculations will show the following upper bound on the tail probability of $X_{0,1}$.

$$\Pr\{X_{0,1} \geq f(m)\} \leq \frac{e^{-\frac{f(m)^2}{2}}}{f(m)\sqrt{2\pi}} = \frac{1}{\sqrt{2\pi\alpha m^\alpha \log m}} \tag{h}$$

Now, the probability that $|S_L| \leq \frac{m\theta_L}{2}$ holds can be upper bounded by $e^{-\frac{\theta_L m}{8}}$, using a Chernoff bound. Hence, whenever $m \gg (1/\theta_L)^{\frac{1}{1-\alpha}}$, the first term of (g) becomes dominating with probability at least $1 - e^{-\frac{\theta_L m}{8}}$ and thus twice (h) is an upper bound on (g) plus $e^{-\frac{\theta_L m}{8}}$. $\square$

Lemma 5 *Let L be a literal which is $\frac{\epsilon}{2n}$-bad, and assume $\epsilon\sqrt{m} \geq 2\sqrt{2}nf(m)$. Then the probability that A_1 does not remove L is upper bounded by $2\exp(-\frac{\epsilon^2 m}{16n^2})$.*

Proof of Lemma 5: The probability we wish to bound is the sum of the following two probabilities: $\Pr A$; the probability of event A that A_1 does not remove L under the condition $|S_L| \geq \theta_L m/2$ and $\Pr B$; the probability of event B that $|S_L| < \theta_L m/2$ occurs. $\Pr B$ is upper-bounded by $e^{-\frac{\theta_L m}{8}} \leq e^{-\frac{\epsilon m}{16n}}$. The latter inequality follows from $\theta_L \geq \frac{\epsilon}{2n}$, which follows from the fact that L is $\frac{\epsilon}{2n}$-bad.

Now we evaluate $\Pr A$. Assume $|S_L| \geq \theta_L/m$. $\Pr A$ is less than $LE(\eta + \frac{\epsilon}{2n\theta}, |S_L|, \phi_m(|S_L|))$. From the assumption that $\epsilon\sqrt{m} \geq 2\sqrt{2}nf(m)$, it follows that $\frac{\epsilon}{2n\theta_L} \geq 2 \cdot \frac{\sqrt{\eta(1-\eta)}f(m)}{\sqrt{m\theta_L/2}}$. The right hand side of this inequality bounds from above $2(\frac{\phi_m(|S_L|)}{|S_L|} - \eta)$. Hence, using Hoeffding's inequality, $LE(\eta + \frac{\epsilon}{2n\theta_L}, |S_L|, \phi_m(|S_L|))$ can be upper bounded by $\exp(-\frac{\epsilon^2 m\theta_L}{16n^2\theta_L^2}) \leq \exp(-\frac{\epsilon^2 m}{16n^2})$. Hence, we have the bound claimed in the lemma. $\square$

Given these lemmas, we can prove Theorem 4.

Proof of Theorem 4: Let L_{not} be a literal L such that L belongs to the target and $\theta_L \leq \frac{\epsilon}{2n}$. Even if A_1 removes L_{not}, the error of the hypothesis output by A_1 can increase by at most $\theta_{L_{not}} \leq \frac{\epsilon}{2n}$, so we need not worry about the possibility that A_1 removes L_{not}. Let T denote the set of literals belonging to the target and $\mathcal{L}_b$ the set of $\frac{\epsilon}{2n}$-bad literals. If we now let $\mathcal{L}_c = \{L | L \in T, \theta_L \geq \frac{\epsilon}{2n}\}$, then the probability that the output of A_1 is not ϵ-good is upper bounded by $\sum_{L \in \mathcal{L}_c} \Pr\{A_1 \text{ removes } L\} + \sum_{L \in \mathcal{L}_b} \Pr\{A_1 \text{ does not remove } L\}$. Assuming that

m is sufficiently large compared to $(\frac{n}{\epsilon})^{\frac{1}{1-\alpha}}$, then from Lemma 4 and Lemma 5, it follows that this probability is $O(ne^{(-\frac{\epsilon^2}{n^3}m)} + n(m^\alpha \log m)^{-\frac{1}{2}})$. This can be made smaller than δ, by letting $m = C(\frac{n^2}{\epsilon^3} \log \frac{n}{\delta} + (\frac{n}{\epsilon})^{\frac{2}{\alpha}})$ for some constant C. Noting finally that $m \gg (\frac{n}{\epsilon})^{\frac{1}{1-\alpha}}$ is implied by $m \geq \frac{n^2}{\epsilon^3}$ for all small enough ϵ, we verify the bound given in the theorem. $\qquad\square$

We can prove Theorem 5 in the same manner as the proof of Theorem 4, using Lemma 6 and Lemma 7 shown below.

Lemma 6 *Let L be an $\frac{\epsilon}{2n}$-bad literal. For all sufficiently large m, the probability that the learner L_1 does not remove L is $O(\exp(-\frac{\epsilon^2 m^{1-2\alpha} N}{n^2}) + \exp(-\frac{\epsilon m}{n}))$.*

Proof of Lemma 6: If we define $p(x) \triangleq GE(x, |S_L|, \phi_m(|S_L|))$, then the probability that A_1 removes an $\frac{\epsilon}{2n}$-bad literal L is given by $p(\eta + \frac{\epsilon}{2n\theta})$. The probability that $|S_L| < \theta_L m/2$ is upper bounded by $e^{-\frac{\theta_L m}{4}}$ (using Chernoff bound) and this, is less than $p_1 = e^{-\frac{\epsilon m}{16n}}$. We will assume $|S_L| \geq \frac{\theta_L m}{2}$ in the subsequent argument.

There are two cases: (a): $\eta + \frac{\epsilon}{2n\theta} \leq \frac{\phi_m(|S_L|)-1}{|S_L|-1}$, and (b): otherwise.

First, we consider the case (a). Let $a_0 = \frac{\phi_m(|S_L|)-1}{|S_L|-1}$. Since a_0 is the point of inflection of $p(x)$ and $p(x)$ is convex in $[\eta, a_0]$, $p(\eta + \frac{\epsilon}{2n\theta}) - p(\eta) \geq \frac{\epsilon}{2n\theta} \frac{dp}{dx}(\eta)$. Using the fact that $\phi_m(|S_L|) \geq \eta|S_L|$ and Stirling's formula, we can show

$$
\begin{aligned}
\frac{\epsilon}{2n\theta} \frac{dp}{dx}(\eta) &\geq \frac{\epsilon}{2n\theta_L} |S_L| \sqrt{\frac{2e^{-\frac{1}{3}}}{|S_L|\pi}} \exp\left(-\frac{(k-|S_L|\eta)^2}{|S_L|\eta(1-\eta)}\right) \\
&= \frac{\epsilon}{2n\theta_L} \sqrt{|S_L|} \sqrt{\frac{2e^{-\frac{1}{3}}}{\pi}} m^{-\alpha} \geq \frac{\epsilon m^{\frac{1-2\alpha}{2}}}{2e^{\frac{1}{6}} n\sqrt{\pi}}.
\end{aligned}
$$

Whenever m is sufficiently large, $p(\eta) = \Pr\{X_{0,1} \geq f(m)\} + o(1/\sqrt{m\epsilon})$ holds. Hence, we have

$$
p(\eta + \frac{\epsilon}{\theta}) - t(\epsilon, m) \geq \frac{\epsilon m^{\frac{1-2\alpha}{2}}}{4e^{\frac{1}{6}} n\sqrt{\pi}} (\overset{\triangle}{=} d_a).
$$

Therefore, using Hoeffding's inequality, the probability (written p_a) that the number of agents A_1 that removes L does not exceed $t(\epsilon, m)N$ is upper bounded by $e^{-2d_a^2 N}$. These above arguments give an upper bound on the probability we wished to bound, $p_1 + p_a$.

Now, we consider the case (b). In this case, we have $\frac{\epsilon}{2n\theta_L} \geq \frac{\sqrt{\eta(1-\eta)}f(m)}{\sqrt{|S_L|}}$. Define ϵ_0 so that $\frac{\epsilon_0}{2n\theta_L}$ equals the right hand side of the above inequality. We then have $p(\eta + \frac{\epsilon}{2n\theta_L}) \geq p(\eta + \frac{\epsilon_0}{2n\theta_L}) \sim \Pr\{X_{0,1} \leq 0\} = 0.5$. Noting that $GE(\eta, |S_L|, \phi_m(|S_L|)) = O((m^\alpha \log m)^{-0.5})$, we have $p(\eta + \frac{\epsilon}{\theta}) - t(\epsilon, m) \sim 0.25$. Therefore, the probability (written p_b) that L_1 does not remove L is upper bounded by $O(e^{-N})$. Thus the desired upper bound on the probability $p_1 + p_b$ has been obtained. $\qquad\square$

Lemma 7 *Let L be a literal belonging to the target. When m is sufficiently large, compared to $(1/\theta_L)^{\frac{3}{2(1-\alpha)}}$, the probability that L_1 removes L is $O(\exp(-\frac{t^2 m^{1-2\alpha}}{n^2}N)+\exp(-\theta_L m))$.*

Proof of Lemma 7: Since m is assumed to be sufficiently large, as compared to $(1/\theta_L)^{\frac{3}{2(1-\alpha)}}$, we can use Chernoff bound to show that $|S_L| \geq \frac{\theta_L m}{2}$ holds with probability $1 - e^{-\frac{\theta_L m}{4}}$. Since m is sufficiently large, this probability is close to one and $|S_L|$ is also sufficiently large with high probability. This means that we have $|GE(\eta, |S_L|, \phi_m(|S_L|)) - t(\epsilon, m)| \geq t(\epsilon, m)/2 + o(1/\sqrt{|S_L|})$ with probability $1 - e^{-\frac{\theta_L m}{4}}$. Using Hoeffding's inequality, we have the lemma. $\qquad\square$

6 Concluding Remarks

The particular formulation of 'population learning' considered in this paper is one of many possible models of parallel learning. An interesting open problem is to investigate the relationships between various competing models. For example, what is the relationship between (α, β)-population learnability and (α, β, γ)-population learnability, as given in Definition 1 ?

Acknowledgement

The authors would like to thank Mr. Katsuhiro Nakamura of C&C Research Laboratories, NEC Corp. for his constant encouragement.

References

[1] D. Angluin and P. Laird. Learning from noisy examples. *Machine Learning*, 2:343–370, 1988.

[2] W. Feller. *An Introduction to Probability and its Applications*, volume 2. John Wiley and Sons, second edition, 1971.

[3] P. Fischer and H. U. Simon. On learning ring-sum-expansions. *SIAM J. Comput.*, 21(1):181 – 192, 1992.

[4] S. Goldman, M. Kearns, and R. Schapire. On the sample complexity of weak learning. In *Proceedings of the 1990 Workshop on Computational Learning Theory*. Morgan Kaufmann, San Mateo, California, August 1990.

[5] D. Helmbold, R. Sloan, and M. K. Warmuth. Learning nested differences of intersection closed concept classes. *Machine Learning*, 5(1), June 1990.

[6] M. Kearns and S. Seung. Learning from a population of hypotheses. In *Proceedings of the Sixth Annual ACM Workshop on Computational Learning Theory*. Morgan Kaufmann, San Mateo, California, August 1993.

[7] B. K. Natarajan. On learning boolean functions. In *Proc. 19th ACM Symp. on Theory of Computing*, pages 296–304, 1987.

[8] L. G. Valiant. A theory of the learnable. *Communications of A.C.M.*, 27:1134–1142, 1984.

Constructing Predicate Mappings for Goal–Dependent Abstraction

Yoshiaki OKUBO   Makoto HARAGUCHI

Department of Systems Science
Tokyo Institute of Technology
4259 Nagatsuta, Midori-ku, Yokohama 227, JAPAN
E-mail : yoshiaki@sys.titech.ac.jp   makoto@sys.titech.ac.jp

Abstract. This paper is concerned with an abstraction for SLD-refutation. In most studies on abstraction, any goal is proved with a *fixed* abstraction neglecting differences of goals. On the other hand, we propose a new framework of *Goal-Dependent Abstraction* in which an appropriate abstraction can be selected according to each goal to be proved. Towards Goal-Dependent Abstraction, this paper tries to construct an appropriate abstraction for a given goal. The appropriateness is defined in terms of *Upward-Property* and *Downward-Property*. Our abstraction is based on *predicate mapping*. Given a goal, candidate predicate mappings are generated and tested in their appropriateness. To find appropriate abstractions efficiently, we present a property to reduce the computational cost of candidate generation. The numbers of pruned candidates are evaluated in both of the best and worst cases. Some experimental results show that many useless candidates can be pruned with the property and constructed abstractions fit our intuition.

1 Introduction

Using abstraction is an effective approach to improve theorem-proving and planning efficiencies [1, 2, 3, 4, 5, 6]. This paper is concerned with an abstraction for theorem-proving, especially SLD-refutation. Given a provable goal G and a (concrete) theory T, theorem-proving with abstraction consists of the following three steps:

1. Abstracting the goal.
   G is transformed into an abstract goal G'.
2. Constructing an abstract proof.
   A proof of G' from an abstract theory, called an *abstract proof*, is constructed.
3. Instantiating the abstract proof.
   The abstract proof is instantiated in order to obtain a proof of G from T.

In most studies on abstraction, any goal is proved with a *fixed* abstraction neglecting differences of goals. Moreover the abstraction has been required to satisfy "Upward Property for *any* goal" [5] [1]. That is, for any provable goal, a corresponding abstract proof must be constructed.

---

[1] Abstractions satisfying the property are called TI-Abstractions in [5].

However human beings seem to alter an abstraction according to each goal to be proved. From this viewpoint, we propose a new framework of abstraction in which an *appropriate* abstraction can be selected according to which goal we try to prove. We call such an abstraction *Goal-Dependent Abstraction*. Towards Goal-Dependent Abstraction, this paper tries to construct an appropriate abstraction for a given goal. We define the appropriateness of abstraction as follows:

An abstraction is appropriate for a goal if the abstraction satisfies both of Upward-Property for the goal and Downward-Property.

In contrast with "Upward-property for *any* goal", an abstraction f is said to satisfy "Upward-Property for a goal G" if an abstract proof of G can be constructed by means of f. The abstraction f may fail to build an abstract proof of another goal. On the other hand, we say that *Downward-Property* holds for f if any abstract proof can be instantiated into a concrete proof.

Our notion of abstraction is based on *predicate mapping* [2, 3] which maps predicate symbols into abstract predicate symbols. Therefore, constructing an appropriate abstraction for a given goal corresponds to constructing an appropriate predicate mapping for the goal. We use a *generate-and-test* strategy to construct appropriate predicate mappings. Given a concrete theory T (a set of Horn-clauses) and a goal G (an atom), candidate predicate mappings are generated and tested in their appropriateness for G. A subset T_G of T is used to test candidates. The set T_G consists of clauses which *may be used* to prove G from T. For example, a clause $H \leftarrow B_1 \wedge \cdots \wedge B_n$ is contained in T_G if H is unifiable to G. A clause whose head is unifiable to B_i is contained in T_G as well. We consider a candidate predicate mapping to be appropriate for G if for any clause in T_G, the clause can be mapped into an abstract clause under the predicate mapping. Needless to say, it is not practical to test all candidate predicate mappings. In order to reduce the computational cost of generation, we present a property to prune useless candidates. The property is defined in terms of an ordering $\prec$ on predicate mappings. In a word, the property means that if a predicate mapping f is not appropriate for a goal, any predicate mapping f' such that $f \prec f'$ is not appropriate for the goal. The numbers of pruned candidates are precisely evaluated in both of the best and worst cases. In addition, some experimental results show that many candidates can be pruned with the property.

In general, there are a number of appropriate predicate mappings for a goal. A predicate mapping which can construct the smallest (the least number of clauses) abstract theory is selected as the most appropriate one since we desire an abstract theory to be simple as possible. The experimental results show that the selected predicate mapping fits our intuition.

2 Abstraction Based on Predicate Mapping

In this section, the abstraction framework of Tenenberg [2] ,used as the basis of our abstraction, is presented. The abstraction is based on a predicate mapping.

A predicate mapping corresponds to a concept hierarchy, that is, an abstract view of concepts.

2.1 Predicate Mappings

Given two sets of predicate symbols R and R', a predicate mapping f is defined as an onto mapping $f : R \overset{onto}{\mapsto} R'$. This is clearly extensible to an onto mapping $f : L \overset{onto}{\mapsto} L'$ between two first-order languages L and L', where the sets of predicate symbols in these languages are R and R', respectively, and any non-predicate symbol is mapped into itself. An expression E in L is called an *instance* of an expression E' in L' under f if $f(E) = E'$. Expressions in L are considered to be *analogous* under f if they are instances of the same expression [2] in L' under f. For example, consider a predicate mapping f such that $f(p1) = f(p2) = p'$ [3]. Clauses $C1 : p1(X, b) \leftarrow p1(X, a)$ and $C2 : p2(Y, b) \leftarrow p2(Y, a)$ are mapped into the same clause $C' : p'(X, b) \leftarrow p'(X, a)$ under f. Then, $C1$ and $C2$ are instances of C' and analogous under f. In addition, $f^{-1}(E')$ is interpreted as the set of instances of E' under f.

2.2 Abstracting First-Order Theories

Given a predicate mapping $f : L \overset{onto}{\mapsto} L'$, let L be a first-order language at a concrete level and L' be one at an abstract level. Under f, we can abstract a set of clauses in L (called a *concrete theory*) into one in L' (called an *abstract theory*) according to the following definition. In the definition, for any clause C, $|C|$ denotes the number of literals in C, $neg(C)$ denotes the disjunction of negative literals in C ($\Box$ if there are none) and $pos(C)$ denotes the disjunction of positive literals in C ($\Box$ if there are none).

Definition 1 (*MembAbs* Clause Mapping[2])
Let $f : L \overset{onto}{\mapsto} L'$ be a predicate mapping and T be a set of clauses in L. $MembAbs_f(T)$ defined as follows is the abstract clause set of T under f:

$$MembAbs_f(T) = \{C' \mid \text{for every } N \in f^{-1}(neg(C')) \text{ having } |neg(C')| \\ \text{distinct literals, there exists } P \in f^{-1}(pos(C')) \\ \text{such that } N \vee P \in T\}. \blacksquare$$

Let us consider an equivalence relation $\sim_f$ defined as $C1 \sim_f C2$ iff $f(C1) = f(C2)$ for any clauses $C1$ and $C2$ in L. T can be partitioned into some equivalence classes under $\sim_f$. Abstracting T under *MembAbs* corresponds to selecting some (not necessarily all) of the equivalence classes and combining all clauses in each selected class into a clause in L'. Fig. 1 shows an example of relationship between T and $MembAbs_f(T)$ [4].

---

[2] For any expression, alphabetic variants of the expression are identified.
[3] For each example of predicate mapping in this paper, non-predicate symbols are omitted for simplicity. And some mappings are represented in hierarchical form.
[4] The representation of clauses is Prolog-like and some predicate symbols are simplified.

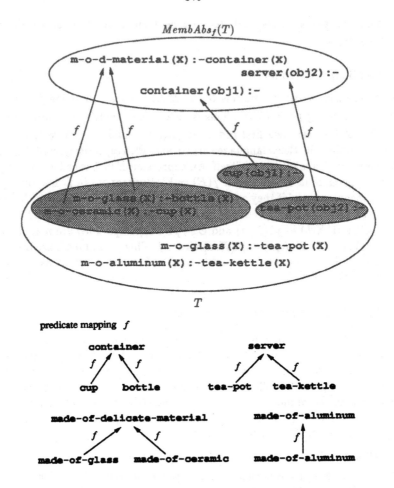

Fig. 1. Relationship between T and $MembAbs_f(T)$

An important theorem can be derived from the definition of *MembAbs* clause mapping.

Theorem 1 (Proof-Theoretic Property [2])

Let $f : L \overset{onto}{\mapsto} L'$ be a predicate mapping, T be a Horn-clause set in L and G' be an atom in L'. If $T'_\mathcal{R}$ is a refutation proof tree of G' from $MembAbs_f(T)$, there exists a refutation proof tree $T_\mathcal{R}$ of G from T such that G is an instance of G' under f, $T_\mathcal{R}$ is isomorphic to $T'_\mathcal{R}$ and for any node in $T_\mathcal{R}$, the clause labeled at the node is an instance of the clause labeled at the corresponding node in $T'_\mathcal{R}$ under f. ∎

Theorem 1 ensures that *Downward-Property* holds. That is, any abstract proof $T'_\mathcal{R}$ can be instantiated into a proof $T_\mathcal{R}$. However there is a case where

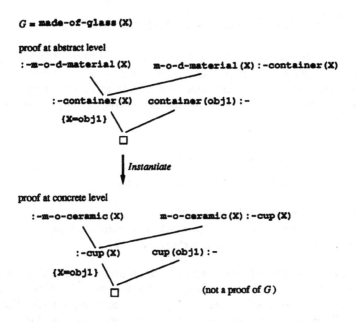

Fig. 2. Proof of Analogous Goal

even if a given goal G is provable at concrete level, any abstract proofs of G can not be instantiated into a proof of G. For example, let us consider to prove a goal G =made-of-glass(X) from T in Fig. 1. The goal is transformed into an abstract goal $f(G)$ =made-of-delicate-material(X). As shown in Fig. 2, *only one* abstract proof of $f(G)$ can be constructed and instantiated into a concrete proof. However it is not a proof of G. Although G is provable at concrete level, we can obtain no proofs of G.

2.3   Features of Abstraction Based on Predicate Mapping

As previously explained, given a predicate mapping $f : L \stackrel{\text{onto}}{\mapsto} L'$ and a theory T in L, abstracting T under *MembAbs* is to combine *some* clauses in T into clauses in L'. In general, Upward-Property for *any* goal is not satisfied since there may exist clauses in T which have no corresponding clause at abstract level. However, Upward-Property for a *certain* goal may be satisfied.

On the other hand, it is ensured that Downward-Property holds. We consider the property very important in theorem-proving with abstraction, since abstract proofs which can not be instantiated into any proofs are useless to obtain a proof of a given goal.

These features are available for our Goal-Dependent Abstraction since given a goal to be proved, our abstraction is required to satisfy both of Upward-Property for the goal (not "*any* goal") and Downward-Property. We use the abstraction based on predicate mapping as the basis of our abstraction.

3   Towards Goal-Dependent Abstraction

Towards Goal-Dependent Abstraction, this paper tries to construct an appropriate abstraction for a given goal. Our abstraction is based on predicate mapping. That is, constructing an abstraction corresponds to constructing a predicate mapping. We describe in this section how to construct an appropriate predicate mapping for a given goal.

3.1   Appropriate Predicate Mappings

An appropriateness of abstraction is defined as follows.

Definition 2 (Appropriate Abstraction)
An abstraction is appropriate for a goal if the abstraction satisfies both of Upward-Property for the goal and Downward-Property.   ■

We consider a predicate mapping to be appropriate for a goal if the abstraction based on the mapping is appropriate for the goal. As stated in the previous section, any abstraction based on predicate mapping satisfies Downward-Property. Therefore, a predicate mapping is appropriate for a goal if the abstraction based on the mapping satisfies Upward-Property for the goal.

Let $f : L \overset{onto}{\mapsto} L'$ be a predicate mapping and T be a theory (a set of Horn-clauses) in L. For an atom G, let us assume that there is a proof of G from T. It is obvious that f is appropriate for G if $f(C) \in MembAbs_f(T)$ for any clause C in T which is used in the proof. However the only way to identify such a clause C is to prove G from T. Then we use a subset T_G of T to know whether f is appropriate or not, where T_G is the set of clauses in T which *may be used* in the proof of G. For example, a clause $H \leftarrow B_1 \wedge \cdots \wedge B_n$ such that H is unifiable to G is contained in T_G. A clause whose head is unifiable to B_i is contained as well. An algorithm for identifying T_G is shown in Fig. 3. The worst case complexity of the algorithm is $O(N)$, where N is the number of clauses in T.

Given a predicate mapping, we can know whether the mapping is appropriate for G or not by the following theorem [5].

Theorem 2 (Appropriate Predicate mapping)
A predicate mapping f is appropriate for G if

   for any clause $C \in T_G$, $f(C) \in MembAbs_f(T)$.   ■

Proof:
Let T_R be a refutation proof tree of G from T. It is obvious that any clause C in T which is used in T_R is contained in T_G. Therefore, if $f(C) \in MembAbs_f(T)$ for any $C \in T_G$, there exists a refutation proof tree $f(T_R)$ [6] of $f(G)$ from

---

[5] Strictly speaking, we can not decide that a mapping is *not* appropriate by the theorem. In this paper, however, we consider any mapping to be not appropriate which does not satisfy the condition of the theorem.

[6] Mapping a refutation tree is to map all clauses in the tree.

```
INPUT(T, G){T is a set of Horn-clauses and G is an atom}
T_G ← φ ; Gs ← {G} ; Res← T ;
Removed ← φ ; Body ← φ;
while Gs ≠ φ do
  begin
    retract g ∈ Gs;
    for C ∈ Res do
      if the head of C is unifiable to g then
        begin
          T_G ← T_G ∪ {C};
          Removed ← Removed ∪{C};
          Body ← the set of atoms in the body of C;
          Gs ← Gs∪ Body;
        end;
      Res ← Res − Removed;
      Removed ← φ;
  end;
OUTPUT(T_G){T_G is the set of clauses in T
                    which may be used to prove G from T}
```

Fig. 3. Algorithm for Identifying T_G

$MembAbs_f(T)$. That is, Upward-Property for G holds. ■

As shown in Fig. 1 and Fig. 2, there exists a case in the framework of Tenenberg where even if a goal G is provable at concrete level, any abstract proofs of G can not be instantiated into a concrete proof of G. However such a case never occur if an appropriate predicate mapping for G is used.

Theorem 3
Let us assume that a goal G is provable from T. If f is an appropriate predicate mapping for G, there exists a proof of $f(G)$ from $MembAbs_f(T)$ which can be instantiated into a proof of G from T. ■

Proof:
Assume that f is appropriate for G and T_R is a refutation proof tree of G from T. Obviously, $f(T_R)$ is a proof tree of $f(G)$ from $MembAbs_f(T)$. It is needless to say that $f(T_R)$ can be instantiated into T_R. Then the theorem holds. ■

Example 1
In Fig. 1 and Fig. 2, although the clause C =made-of-glass(X):-tea-pot(X) may be used to prove the goal made-of-glass(X), $MembAbs_f(T)$ does not contain $f(C)$. Therefore we consider the predicate mapping f to be not appropriate for the goal.
On the other hand, a predicate mapping f' is appropriate for the goal, where

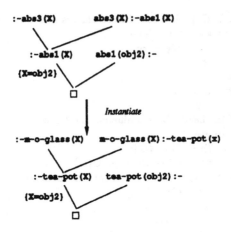

Fig. 4. Proof of Original Goal

$f'(\texttt{cup}) = f'(\texttt{bottle}) = f(\texttt{tea-pot}) =\texttt{abs1}$,
$f'(\texttt{tea-kettle}) =\texttt{abs2}$,
$f'(\texttt{made-of-glass}) = f'(\texttt{made-of-ceramic}) =\texttt{abs3}$ *and*
$f'(\texttt{made-of-aluminum}) =\texttt{abs4}$.

For any clause C which may be used to prove the goal, the abstract theory under f', *MembAbs*$_{f'}(T) = \{$ abs1(obj1):-, abs1(obj2):-, abs3(X):-abs1(X), abs4(X):-abs2(X)$\}$, *contains* $f'(C)$. *As shown in Fig. 4, a proof of* $f'(G)$ *from the abstract theory can be constructed and instantiated into a concrete proof. It is a proof of G. Thus, if an appropriate predicate mapping for the goal is used, we can obtain a proof of the goal.*

3.2 Constructing Appropriate Predicate Mappings

Given a theory T and a goal G to be proved, the set of clauses T_G which may be used to prove G is identified by the algorithm in Fig. 3. Based on T_G, we can construct appropriate predicate mappings for G by the following *generate-and-test* strategy:

Generation-Stage.
   A candidate predicate mapping f is generated and then *MembAbs*$_f(T)$ is computed.

Test-Stage.
   It is tested according to Theorem 2 whether f is appropriate for G or not.

Candidate predicate mappings are generated from the set of predicate symbols in T_G [7]. A candidate mapping can be viewed as a partition of the set. Each

---

[7] We consider other predicate symbols in T to be mapped into the symbol $\perp$ under each candidate mapping.

cell of the partition contains analogous predicate symbols. A new symbol is assigned to each cell as an abstract predicate symbol. For example, a partition $\{\{a_1, a_2\}, \{b_1, b_2\}\}$ of $\{a_1, a_2, b_1, b_2\}$ corresponds to a predicate mapping f such that $f(a_1) = f(a_2) = a'$ and $f(b_1) = f(b_2) = b'$.

In general, there exist a large number of partitions (candidates). Needless to say, it is not practical to test all possible candidates. In order to find appropriate mappings efficiently, a property to prune useless candidates will be presented in Theorem 4. It is needed for the property to introduce an ordering $\prec$ on partitions *i.e.* predicate mappings.

Definition 3 (Refinement of Partition)
For any partitions P and P' of a non-empty set, $P \prec P'$ and P is called a refinement of P' iff for any cell c of P, there exists a cell c' of P' such that $c \subseteq c'$. ■

For example, $\{\{a, b\}, \{c\}, \{d, e\}\}$ is a refinement of $\{\{a, b, c\}, \{d, e\}\}$.

Given a set of predicate symbols R, candidate predicate mappings generated from R constitute a lattice under the ordering.

In addition, it is very important for Theorem 4 to consider a case where a predicate mapping f is not appropriate for G. In such a case, there exists a clause C in T_G such that $f(C) \notin MembAbs_f(T)$. Let $f(C)$ be $H' \leftarrow B_1' \wedge \cdots \wedge B_n'$. From the definition of *MembAbs* clause mapping, $MembAbs_f(T)$ does not contain $f(C)$ if the following condition holds:

> *For an instance $B_1 \wedge \cdots \wedge B_n$ of $B_1' \wedge \cdots \wedge B_n'$ under f, there is no clause in T whose body is the instance.*

In such a case, we say that $f(C)$ is not contained in $MembAbs_f(T)$ due to *Body-Instance-Lack*.

Theorem 4
For a predicate mapping f and a clause $C \in T_G$, let us assume that $f(C)$ is not contained in $MembAbs_f(T)$ due to Body-Instance-Lack. Then, for any predicate mapping f' such that $f \prec f'$, $f'(C)$ is not contained in $MembAbs_{f'}(T)$ due to Body-Instance-Lack. ■

Proof :
Let $f(C)$ be $H' \leftarrow B_1' \wedge \cdots \wedge B_n'$. From the assumption, for an instance $I = B_1 \wedge \cdots \wedge B_n$ of $B_1' \wedge \cdots \wedge B_n'$, there is no clause in T whose body is I. Let f' be a predicate mapping such that $f \prec f'$ and $f'(C)$ be $H'' \leftarrow B_1'' \wedge \cdots \wedge B_n''$. Each instance of $B_1' \wedge \cdots \wedge B_n'$ is an instance of $B_1'' \wedge \cdots \wedge B_n''$ since $f \prec f'$. That is, T must contain a clause whose body is I if $f'(C) \in MembAbs_{f'}(T)$ holds. However such a clause is not in T. Therefore $f'(C)$ is not contained in $MembAbs_{f'}(T)$ due to Body-Instance-Lack.

This property holds for any predicate mapping f' such that $f \prec f'$. Then the theorem holds. ■

The theorem means that if a candidate predicate mapping f is found to be not appropriate for G due to Body-Instance-Lack, we do not have to generate any candidate f' such that $f \prec f'$.

Example 2
Given a theory T such that

> $T = \{$ cup(obj1):-, bottle(obj2):-, knife(obj3):-,
> has-open-concavity(X):-cup(X),
> has-open-concavity(X):-bottle(X),
> has-handle(X):-cup(X), has-handle(X):-knife(X),
> liftable(X):-has-handle(X),
> can-contain(X):-has-open-concavity(X) $\}$,

*let us construct an appropriate predicate mapping for a goal G =*liftable(X). *The set of clauses which may be used to prove the goal is*

> $T_G = \{$ cup(obj1):-, knife(obj3):-,
> has-handle(X):-cup(X), has-handle(X):-knife(X),
> liftable(X):-has-handle(X) $\}$.

*The set of predicate symbols in T_G is $R = \{$*cup, knife, has-handle, liftable$\}$. *Candidate predicate mappings generated from R constitute the following lattice* [8].

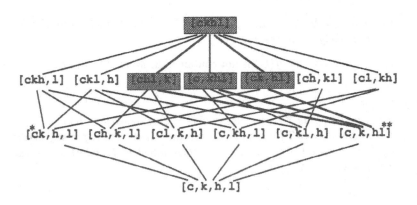

Fig. 5. Candidate Predicate Mappings

Let us consider the candidate with "*" in the lattice. We assign abs1, abs2 *and* abs3 *to the cells, respectively. The candidate corresponds to the predicate*

---

[8] For simplicity, each predicate symbol is denoted by its initial letter and a partition $\{\{c, k\}, \{h\}, \{l\}\}$ is represented by $[ck, h, l]$.

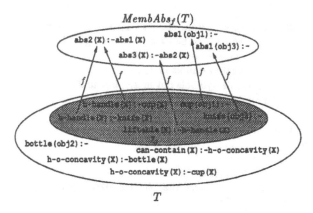

Fig. 6. Abstraction Based on Appropriate Predicate Mapping

mapping f such that $f(\text{cup}) = f(\text{knife}) = \text{abs1}$, $f(\text{has-handle}) = \text{abs2}$ and $f(\text{liftable}) = \text{abs3}$. As shown in Fig. 6, $f(C)$ is contained in $MembAbs_f(T)$ for any clause $C \in T_G$. Therefore f is an appropriate predicate mapping for G.

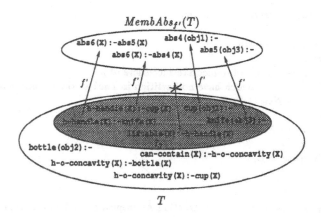

Fig. 7. Abstraction Based on Not Appropriate Predicate Mapping

On the other hand, Fig. 7 shows the abstraction based on the candidate with "∗∗", where symbols abs4, abs5 and abs6 are assigned to the cells, respectively. The mapping is not appropriate for G due to Body-Instance-Lack. The clause liftable(X) : −has − handle(X) *can not be mapped into an abstract clause since there exists no clause in T whose body is* liftable(X). *Therefore, we can know without tests that any candidate darkened in Fig. 5 is not appropriate.* ∎

INPUT(T, T_G) $\{T$ is a set of Horn-clauses , T_G is a set of clauses
which may be used to prove a goal.$\}$
$App \leftarrow \phi$; $Rem \leftarrow \phi$; $Lack \leftarrow \phi$; $New \leftarrow \phi$;
$Pred \leftarrow$ the set of predicate symbols in T_G;
$Bot \leftarrow$ the set of predicate symbols not in T_G, but in T;
$Partitions \leftarrow \{$the minimum partition of $Pred\}$;
repeat
  for $p \in Partitions$ **do**
    begin
      $f \leftarrow p \cup \{Bot\}$;
      compute $MembAbs_f(T)$;
      if there exists $C \in T_G$ such that $f(C) \notin MembAbs_f(T)$
          then begin
              if *Body-Instance-Lack* occurs **then**
                begin
                  $Rem \leftarrow Rem \cup \{p\}$;
                  $Lack \leftarrow Lack \cup \{p\}$;
                end;
              end;
          else begin
              OUTPUT$(f)\{f$ is an appropriate predicate mapping$\}$;
              end;
    end;
  $Partitions \leftarrow Partitions - Rem$;
  $Rem \leftarrow \phi$;
  for $p \in Partitions$ **do**
    begin
      $Next \leftarrow$ the set of immediate successors of p
                which have no partition in $Lack$ as their refinement;
      $New \leftarrow New \cup Next$;
    end;
  $Partitions \leftarrow New$;
  $New \leftarrow \phi$;
until $Partitions = \phi$;
end.

Fig. 8. Algorithm for Constructing Appropriate Predicate Mappings

Fig. 8 shows an algorithm for constructing appropriate predicate mappings. First of all, the algorithm generates the minimum partition (one-to-one mapping). Immediate successors of the partition are generated and tested. Then, for the successors except not appropriate ones due to Body-Instance-Lack, their immediate successors are generated and tested, and so on.

In general, we can obtain a number of appropriate predicate mappings. A predicate mapping which can construct the smallest (the least number of clauses) abstract theory is selected as the most appropriate one since we desire an abstract theory to be simple as possible.

3.3 Evaluating Reduction of Candidate Predicate Mappings

As previously explained, we can prune useless candidate predicate mappings. We evaluate here the numbers of pruned candidates in both of the best and worst cases. The number of partitions of N-element set, B_N, is used in the evaluation. It is defined as

$$B_N = \sum_{k=1}^{N} \binom{N-1}{k-1} B_{N-k} \ , \text{where } B_0 = 1.$$

Let R be a set of predicate symbols. Assume that a candidate (partition) p generated from R is not appropriate for a goal due to Body-Instance-Lack and p consists of n cells. By Theorem 4, we do not have to generate any candidate p' such that $p \prec p'$. The number of such a p' is $B_n - 1$ (minus 1 for p itself).

In general, more than one candidates $p_1, \ldots p_m$ are not appropriate due to Body-Instance-Lack. For each p_i, consider

$$S_{p_i} = \{p'_i \mid p_i \prec p'_i\} \setminus \{p_i\},$$

where the symbol "$\setminus$" denotes set difference. We can obtain the most reduction of generation in the case of

$$\bigcap_{i=1}^{m} S_{p_i} = \{\text{The maximum partition of } R\}.$$

Assume that each p_i consists of n_i cells. As stated above, the number of partitions in S_{p_i} is $B_{n_i} - 1$. Therefore, the number of pruned candidates in the best case is

$$\sum_{i=1}^{m}(B_{n_i} - 1) - (m - 1) = \sum_{i=1}^{m} B_{n_i} - (2m - 1).$$

It is needed to subtract $(m - 1)$ for removing duplicates of the maximum partition.

On the other hand, the least reduction occurs in the case of

$$\bigcap_{i=1}^{m} S_{p_i} = S_{p_1} \ (= S_{p_2} = \cdots = S_{p_m}).$$

Therefore, the number of pruned candidates in the worst case is

$$B_{n_1} - 1 \ (= B_{n_2} - 1 = \cdots = B_{n_m} - 1).$$

```
tea-pot(obj4):-           frypan(obj5):-
made-of-ceramic(X):-cup(X)
made-of-stainless(X):-knife(X)
made-of-heatproof-glass(X):-tea-pot(X)
has-open-concavity(X):-tea-pot(X)
has-handle(X):-frypan(X)
breakable(X):-made-of-ceramic(X)
breakable(X):-made-of-heatproof-glass(X)
can-heat(X):-made-of-heatproof-glass(X)
can-heat(X):-made-of-steel(X)
treat-carefully(X):-breakable(X)
treat-carefully(X):-has-edge(X)
```

Fig. 9. Part of Theory

4 Experimental Results

According to the algorithms in the previous section, we have implemented a system by SICStus Prolog on SparcStation10 model51. Given a theory and a goal, the system automatically constructs appropriate predicate mappings for the goal. We have made some experiments using the system. This section presents our experimental results.

A part of the given theory is shown in Fig. 9. The theory contains also clauses similar to ones in Example 2. The numbers of clauses and predicate symbols are 35 and 20, respectively. The given goals are can-contain(X), can-heat(X), liftable(X) and treat-carefully(X). The results are shown in Fig. 10. For each goal, T_G denotes the set of clauses which may be used to prove the goal and the most appropriate mapping is represented in the form of a partition.

We consider that the obtained predicate mappings fit our intuition. For example, let us consider about the mapping for can-contain(X). The mapping means that viewing mug-cup, beer-bottle, tea-pot and frypan as the same concept is appropriate for proving can-contain(X), that is, differences between these concepts (e.g. having a handle or not) have no effect on proving the goal. Such an abstract view fits our intuition. Although Knoblock has been proposed a framework for constructing an abstraction depending on a given problem in planning[4], the abstraction is constructed by eliminating some literals in the problem domain. Therefore it is difficult to recognize such an abstract view of concepts.

In addition, our experimental results show that many candidates can be pruned with the property in Theorem 4. The ratio of tested candidates to possible candidates is about 0.15 on the average. In the most effective case, the ratio is about 0.006. However, it is expected that the number of candidates to be tested become very large for a more practical theorem-proving. Therefore further pruning of candidates are desired. These are currently under study.

5 Conclusion

Towards Goal-Dependent Abstraction, this paper tried to to construct appropriate predicate mappings (abstractions) for a given goal. These mappings are constructed by a generate-and-test strategy. In order to reduce the computational cost of generation, a property to prune useless candidates was presented. We precisely evaluated the numbers of pruned candidates in both of the best and worst cases. Some experimental results showed that many useless candidates can be pruned with the property. In addition, the results showed that the constructed abstractions fit our intuition.

Acknowledgments

We would like to thank anonymous referees of ALT'94 for their helpful comments.

References

1. David A.Plaisted, "Theorem Proving with Abstraction", Artificial Intelligence, vol.16, 47-108, 1981.
2. Josh D.Tenenberg, "Abstracting First-Order Theories", Change of Representation and Inductive Bias (D.Paul Benjamin ed.), Kluwer Academic Publishers, pp.67-79, 1989.
3. Josh D.Tenenberg, "Abstraction in Planning", Reasoning about Plans (James F.Allen et al.), Morgan Kaufmann Publishers, pp.213-283, 1991.
4. Craig A.Knoblock, "Automatically Generating Abstractions for Problem Solving", Technical Report CMU-CS-91-120, School of Computer Science, Carnegie Mellon University, 1991.
5. Fusto Giunchiglia and Toby Walsh, "A Theory of Abstraction", Artificial Intelligence, vol.57, pp.323-389, 1992.
6. Y.Okubo and M.Haraguchi, "Planning with Abstraction Based on Partial Predicate Mappings", Proc. of the Third Workshop on Algorithmic Learning Theory, pp.183-194, 1992.

Appropriate Predicate Mappings for `can-contain(X)` :
    The number of clauses in $T_G = 9$
    The number of predicate symbols in $T_G = 6$
    The number of possible candidates = 203
    The number of tested candidates = 57
    The number of appropriate predicate mappings = 15
    The most appropriate predicate mapping f :
        {{can-contain},{has-open-concavity},
          {mug-cup,beer-bottle,tea-pot,frypan}}
    The number of clauses in $MembAbs_f(T) = 6$
    The total time of construction = 560 msec.

Appropriate Predicate Mappings for `can-heat(X)` :
    The number of clauses in $T_G = 6$
    The number of predicate symbols in $T_G = 5$
    The number of possible candidates = 52
    The number of tested candidates = 19
    The number of appropriate predicate mappings = 3
    The most appropriate predicate mapping f :
        {{can-heat},{tea-pot,frypan},
          {made-of-heatproof-glass,made-of-steel}}
    The number of clauses in $MembAbs_f(T) = 4$
    The total time of construction = 164 msec.

Appropriate Predicate Mappings for `liftable(X)` :
    The number of clauses in $T_G = 17$
    The number of predicate symbols in $T_G = 9$
    The number of possible candidates = 21147
    The number of tested candidates = 129
    The number of appropriate predicate mappings = 67
    The most appropriate predicate mapping f :
        {{liftable},{light},
         {has-thin-part,has-handle},
         {beer-bottle,mug-cup, kitchen-knife,tea-pot,frypan}}
    The number of clauses in $MembAbs_f(T) = 8$
    The total time of construction = 2470 msec.

Appropriate Predicate Mappings for `treat-carefully(X)` :
    The number of clauses in $T_G = 13$
    The number of predicate symbols in $T_G = 10$
    The number of possible candidates = 115975
    The number of tested candidates = 21156
    The number of appropriate predicate mappings = 44
    The most appropriate predicate mapping f :
        {{treat-carefully},{breakable,has-edge},
         {mug-cup,beer-bottle,tea-pot},
         {made-of-ceramic,made-of-glass,,
             made-of-heatproof-glass,kitchen-knife}}
    The number of clauses in $MembAbs_f(T) = 7$
    The total time of construction = 490747 msec.

Fig. 10. Experimental Results

Learning Languages by Collecting Cases and Tuning Parameters

Yasubumi Sakakibara[1], Klaus P. Jantke[2] and Steffen Lange[2]

[1] Institute for Social Information Science, Fujitsu Laboratories Ltd.,
140, Miyamoto, Numazu, Shizuoka 410-03, Japan
(email: yasu@iias.flab.fujitsu.co.jp)
[2] HTWK Leipzig (FH), Fachbereich IMN, Postfach 66,
04251 Leipzig, Germany
(email: {janos,steffen}@informatik.th-leipzig.de)

Abstract. We investigate the problem of case-based learning of formal languages. Case-based reasoning and learning is a currently booming area of artificial intelligence. The formal framework for case-based learning of languages has recently been developed by [JL93] in an inductive inference manner.

In this paper, we first show that any indexed class of recursive languages in which finiteness is decidable is case-based representable, but many classes of languages including the class of all regular languages are not case-based learnable with a fixed universal similarity measure, even if both positive and negative examples are presented.

Next we consider a framework of case-based learning where the learning algorithm is allowed to learn similarity measures, too. To avoid trivial encoding tricks, we carefully examine to what extent the similarity measure is going to be learned. Then by allowing only to learn a few parameters in the similarity measures, we show that any indexed class of recursive languages whose finiteness problem is decidable is case-based learnable. This implies that all context-free languages are case-based learnable by collecting cases and learning parameters of the similarity measures.

1 Introduction

Case-based reasoning is deemed an important technology to widen the bottleneck of knowledge acquisition in AI. In case-based reasoning, knowledge is represented in the form of particular cases with an appropriate similarity measure rather than any form of rules. Recently, there is an enormous amount of approaches and applications. Within case-based reasoning, case-based learning as investigated in [AKA91] is a natural way of designing learning procedures. The main task of case-based learning is to collect good cases which will be stored in the case base for describing knowledge and classifying unknown examples. Thus, case-based learning algorithms do not construct explicit generalizations from examples which most other supervised learning algorithms derive.

In this paper, we investigate the power and the limitations of such case-based learning algorithms working in a case-based manner as introduced in [Jan92] and, furthermore, applied to certain formal languages in [JL93].

A formal framework for case-based learning has recently been developed by [Jan92] and [JL93] in an inductive inference manner. Inductive inference is the very theory of learning from usually incomplete information (cf. [AS83], e.g.). Learning algorithms which have an architecture and a behavior motivated by artificial intelligence research seem particularly relevant both to the theory of inductive inference and to AI applications. In this paper, we are exclusively dealt with inductive inference from *informant*, i.e. from both examples and counterexamples.

Learning of formal languages is one of the most thoroughly studied areas of inductive inference. In particular, there is a remarkable amount of work on inductive inference of *indexed classes* of formal languages (cf. [A80], e.g.). An indexed class is an effective enumeration of formal languages that admits a uniform procedure for deciding membership. The formal languages acceptable by *containment decision lists* as investigated in [SS92] may be considered an indexed class, for instance. We have chosen these languages as target objects of learning, as they seem particularly tailored to case-based knowledge processing. The key reason is that prototypical cases occur as immediate constituents of containment decision lists they are describing. Thus, the area seems particularly promising for gaining new insights into fundamental phenomena of case-based learning. Our research is especially focussed to the effects of learning similarity concepts by tuning defining parameters.

In Section 2, we show that any indexed class of recursive languages in which finiteness is decidable is case-based representable. We also show that under the assumption that the underlying similarity measure is fixed and not learned during the learning process, many classes of languages including the class of all regular languages are not case-based learnable, even if both positive and negative examples are presented, while [JL93] has shown that some interesting classes of formal languages are case-based learnable under this assumption. In Section 3, we consider a framework of case-based learning where the learning algorithm is allowed to learn similarity measures, too. To avoid trivial encoding tricks, we carefully examine to what extent the similarity measure is going to be learned. An interesting and important method for learning similarity measures is given by adopting weighting scheme for cases like the weighted nearest neighbor algorithm [CS93]. This can be accomplished with the weights in similarity measures: reliable cases are given larger weights, making them appear closer to words in the domain. Then by allowing only to learn parameters for such weights in the similarity measures, we show that any indexed class of recursive languages whose finiteness problem is decidable is case-based learnable. In Section 4, we apply the above theoretical results on case-based learning to containment decision lists.

2 Case-based representation and learning of formal languages

We first give formal definitions of case-based representation and cased-based learning for formal languages introduced by [JL93]. Next we show general results for case-based representability and case-based non-learnability of formal languages in that framework. That is, any indexed class of recursive languages whose finiteness problems are decidable is case-based representable but it is not case-based learnable with a fixed universal similarity measure.

2.1 Definitions of case-based representation and learning

Let Σ be a finite alphabet (i.e. a finite set of symbols). Let Σ^* denote the set of all strings (words) over Σ and Σ^+ denote the set of all non-empty strings over Σ. A *language* over Σ is a set of strings in Σ^*. For a language L over Σ, let $\overline{L}$ denote the complement of L, i.e. $\overline{L} = \Sigma^* \setminus L$. Let ε denote the empty string.

A *similarity measure* σ on Σ^* which defines a similarity between two strings is a computable function from $\Sigma^* \times \Sigma^*$ to real interval $[0, 1]$. A *case base CB* is a finite subset of $\Sigma^* \times \{0, 1\}$. We call a case $(w, 1)$ in CB a *positive case* and $(w, 0)$ a *negative case*. Two semantics, *standard* semantics and *competing* semantics, are considered in [JL93] to resolve conflicts of classifications. In this paper, we adopt the *standard* semantics. Under standard semantics, the language represented by a similarity measure σ and a finite case base CB is defined as follows.

Definition 1.

$$L(CB, \sigma) = \{ w \in \Sigma^* \mid \exists (u, 1) \in CB[\sigma(u, w) > 0 \wedge$$
$$\forall (v, 0) \in CB[\sigma(u, w) > \sigma(v, w)]] \}$$

We restrict all positive cases to be taken from the target language and all negative cases to be taken from the complement of the language. Any case base CB describing some $L = L(CB, \sigma)$ must be a finite subset of $L \times \{1\} \cup \overline{L} \times \{0\}$. This is a very natural requirement in case-based representation.

Next we characterize case-based learning in an inductive inference manner [JL93]. In this section, we consider the definition of case-based learning where a similarity measure is *a priori* fixed for a target class of languages. Thus the problem of case-based learning becomes the problem of just collecting an appropriate case base. Later, we will consider case-based learning where a similarity measure is allowed to be learned.

Let $\mathbb{N}$ denote the set of positive natural numbers. Let L be the target language to be learned. An *informant* i for L is an infinite sequence $(s_1, d_2), (s_2, d_2),$ $(s_3, d_3), \ldots$ of elements of $\Sigma^* \times \{0, 1\}$ such that $range(i) = \{s_k \mid k \in \mathbb{N}\} = \Sigma^*$, $i^+ = \{s_k \mid k \in \mathbb{N} \wedge d_k = 1\} = L$ and $i^- = \{s_k \mid k \in \mathbb{N} \wedge d_k = 0\} = \overline{L}$. An element (example) of the form $(s_k, 1)$ is called *positive* and an element of the form $(s_k, 0)$ is called *negative*. By $Inf(L)$ we denote the set of all informants for L. For an informant i and a natural number n, $i_{\leq n}$ denotes the initial segment of i of length n and $i_{>n}$ denotes the segment of i after the nth element. A language L' is called *consistent* with $i_{\leq n}$ if L' contains all positive examples and no negative examples in $i_{\leq n}$, i.e. $L' \supseteq i_{\leq n}^+$ and $L' \cap i_{\leq n}^- = \emptyset$.

The learning algorithm takes as its input larger and larger initial segments of any informant i and outputs hypotheses, accordingly. A sequence $(j_n)_{n \in \mathbb{N}}$

is said to be *convergent in the limit* if and only if there is some element j and some natural number m such that $j_n = j$ for all natural numbers $n \geq m$. This is abbreviated by $\lim_{n \to \infty} j_n = j$.

Definition 2. Let $\mathcal{C}$ be a class of languages. $\mathcal{C}$ is *case-based learnable (in the limit) from informant* if and only if there are a learning algorithm M and a similarity measure σ such that for all $L \in \mathcal{C}$ and for all $i \in Inf(L)$, there exists some case base CB:

1. $\forall n \in I\!N : M(i_{\leq n}) = CB_n$ is defined,
2. $\forall n \in I\!N : \emptyset \subseteq \tilde{C}B_1 \subseteq \{(s_1, d_1)\}$ and $CB_n \subseteq CB_{n+1} \subseteq CB_n \cup \{(s_{n+1}, d_{n+1})\}$,
3. $\lim_{n \to \infty} M(i_{\leq n}) = CB$,
4. $L = L(CB, \sigma)$.

To indicate that some case base CB is a *finite* subset of some appropriate set of labelled words W, we write $CB \subseteq_{fin} W$.

2.2 Representability and non-learnability of formal languages

We will prove that any indexed class of recursive languages whose finiteness problems are decidable is case-based representable. We first quote the following lemma the proof of which is straightforward from Theorem 4 in [JL93].

Lemma 3. *Let $\mathcal{C}$ be any indexed class of recursive languages which contains all singleton languages and at least one infinite language. There is no universal similarity measure σ which allows to represent every language L in $\mathcal{C}$ by using a case base consisting of only positive cases in L.*

In order to prove the following theorem, we use an encoding technique developed in [JL93] that chooses any effective enumeration of words to represent languages and to relate words and languages in a somehow artificial but effective way.

Let $L_1, L_2, L_3, \ldots$ be an enumeration of languages in an indexed class of languages. Membership is said to be *uniformly decidable w.r.t. this enumeration* if there is a total recursive function f which decides for all $j \in I\!N$ and for all strings w whether or not $w \in L_j$.

Theorem 4. *Let $\mathcal{C}$ be any indexed class of recursive languages whose finiteness problems are decidable. There is a universal similarity measure σ such that every language L in $\mathcal{C}$ can be represented by σ and a finite case base CB of positive and negative cases, i.e. $L = L(CB, \sigma)$ for some $CB \subseteq_{fin} L \times \{1\} \cup \overline{L} \times \{0\}$.*

Proof. We are going to define a similarity measure σ satisfying the desired condition:

$$\forall L \in \mathcal{C} \exists CB \subseteq L \times \{1\} \cup \overline{L} \times \{0\}[L = L(CB, \sigma)].$$

Let $\mathcal{FC}$ denote the set of all finite languages which belong to $\mathcal{C}$ and $\mathcal{PC}$ denote the set of all infinite languages in $\mathcal{C}$, i.e. $\mathcal{C} = \mathcal{FC} \cup \mathcal{PC}$. Since any language in C is recursive and its finiteness problem is decidable, there are an effective enumeration of languages in $\mathcal{FC}$, say $F_1, F_2, \ldots$, and an effective enumeration of languages in $\mathcal{PC}$, say $L_1, L_2, \ldots$ In order to represent the finite languages $\mathcal{FC}$ in a case-based manner, the result of Lemma 3 requires to use *counterexamples*. For any $i \in \mathbb{N}$, let $\overline{F_i}$ denote the complement of F_i.

Now we construct some effective, repetition-free enumeration $u_1, u_2, \ldots$ of all words in Σ^* such that every word u_{3i-2} is a member of L_i and every word u_{3i-1} belongs to $\overline{F_i}$. We assume a repetition-free enumeration $w_1, w_2, w_3, \ldots$ of all words in Σ^*. The construction proceeds in steps as follows, where U is used to collect all words u_i specified so far and μ denotes the minimum operator:

Set $U := \emptyset$;

In the ith step $(i \geq 1)$, there are defined u_{3i-2}, u_{3i-1} and u_{3i} as follows:

$$u_{3i-2} := w_{\mu k[w_k \notin U \wedge w_k \in L_i]}; \quad U := U \cup \{u_{3i-2}\};$$
$$u_{3i-1} := w_{\mu k[w_k \notin U \wedge w_k \in \overline{F_i}]}; \quad U := U \cup \{u_{3i-1}\};$$
$$u_{3i} := w_{\mu k[w_k \notin U]}; \qquad U := U \cup \{u_{3i}\};$$

The similarity measure σ is defined by the standard definition $\sigma(w, w) = 1$, for all $w \in \Sigma^*$, and the following additional requirements: For all $i \geq 1$ and $w \in \Sigma^*$,

$$\sigma(u_{3i-2}, w) = \begin{cases} 1 \text{ if } w \in L_i \\ 0 \text{ otherwise} \end{cases} \qquad \sigma(u_{3i}, w) = \begin{cases} 1 \text{ if } w = u_{3i} \\ 0 \text{ otherwise} \end{cases}$$

$$\sigma(u_{3i-1}, w) = \begin{cases} 1 \text{ if } w \in \overline{F_i} \\ 0 \text{ otherwise} \end{cases}$$

Since the membership problem for all languages in C is uniformly decidable, $\sigma(u, w)$ is effectively defined for all $u, w \in \Sigma^*$ and σ is effectively computable. For every infinite language L_i in $\mathcal{PC}$, the appropriate case base is $\{(u_{3i-2}, 1)\}$. For every finite language, say $F_l = \{w_1, \ldots, w_n\}$, in $\mathcal{FC}$, the appropriate case base w.r.t. σ is $\{(w_1, 1), \ldots, (w_n, 1), (u_{3i-1}, 0)\}$. In the case to represent a finite language F_l, the negative case is taken from the complement of the language, i.e. $\overline{F_l}$ and, hence, it satisfies the requirement that all positive cases should be taken from the target language and all negative cases should be taken from the complement of the language.

Corollary 5. *The class of context-free languages is case-based representable.*

Proof. The finiteness problem for context-free languages is decidable [HU79]. Thus, the result follows from Theorem 4.

The following result gives the general negative answer concerning the case-based learnability of formal languages.

Theorem 6. *Let C be the class of all finite and all co-finite languages. Then C is not case-based learnable from informant.*

Proof. We assume that there is a case-based learning algorithm M for $\mathcal{C}$ which works w.r.t. a universal similarity measure σ for $\mathcal{C}$. ¿From this, we will derive a contradiction.

We start with the following observation. Since M has to learn $L = \Sigma^* \in \mathcal{C}$, there is an informant i for L and an $x \in I\!\!N$ such that $M(i_{\leq x}) = M(i_{\leq x}, (u, 1)) = CB_x$, for all $u \in \Sigma^*$, and $L(CB_x, \sigma) = L$. Otherwise, one can easily define an informant for L on which M changes its actual case base infinitely many times. Consequently, M would fail to infer L on this particular informant. Notice that CB_x contains only positive cases.

Now, consider M's behavior when fed any informant $\hat{i}$ for the finite language $\hat{L} = \{w \mid (w, 1) \in i_{\leq x}\}$ where $\hat{i}$ has the initial segment $i_{\leq x}$. Since M learns $\hat{L}$ from $\hat{i}$, there has to be a $y > x$ such that $M(\hat{i}_{\leq y}) = CB_y$, $CB_x \subseteq CB_y$ and $L(CB_y, \sigma) = \hat{L}$. Let us consider any string u which does not appear in $\hat{i}_{\leq y}$. Obviously, $u \in L$, but $u \notin \hat{L}$. Since $L(CB_x, \sigma) = L$, $L(CB_y, \sigma) = \hat{L}$ and $CB_x \subseteq CB_y$, there must be a counterexample in the case base CB_y causing u not to belong to $L(CB_y, \sigma) = \hat{L}$. Such a counterexample, say $(v, 0)$, must meet $\sigma(w, u) < \sigma(v, u)$ for all $(w, 1) \in CB_x$. Otherwise, we would obtain $u \in L(CB_y, \sigma)$ which contradicts $L(CB_y, \sigma) = \hat{L}$.

In the sequel, assume any two strings u, v satisfying the above requirements. Furthermore, consider the finite sequence $i_{\leq x}, (u, 1), (v, 0)$ which defines an initial segment of an informant of the co-finite language $\tilde{L} = \Sigma^* \setminus \{v\}$. Let $CB_{x+2} = M(i_{\leq x}, (u, 1), (v, 0))$. Due to the choice of $i_{\leq x}$, we may conclude that $(u, 1) \notin CB_{x+2}$, because of $M(i_{\leq x}) = M(i_{\leq x}, (u, 1))$. On the other hand, $(v, 0)$ has to be an element of CB_{x+2}. Otherwise, M, in particular, fails to learn $\tilde{L}$ from any of its informants having the initial segment $i_{\leq x}, (u, 1), (v, 0)$ and containing the example $(v, 0)$ exactly once. When fed such an informant, M may only add further positive cases to its actual case base CB_x. But, this does not help to accumulate a case base which allows to represent $\tilde{L}$, because already $L(CB_x, \sigma) = L \supset \tilde{L}$.

Finally, let us assume any informant for the finite language $\hat{L} \cup \{u\}$ which has the initial segment $i_{\leq x}, (u, 1), (v, 0)$ and which contains only negative examples $(w, 0)$ past this point. Now, we know that $M(i_{\leq x}, (u, 1), (v, 0)) = CB_{x+2} = CB_x \cup \{(v, 0)\}$. Since $\sigma(CB_x, u) < \sigma(v, u)$, we obtain $u \notin L(CB_{x+2}, \sigma)$. Obviously, in every subsequent step, M can only add negative cases to its actual case base CB_{x+2}. Therefore, M will never produce a case base $CB \supset CB_{x+2}$ such that $u \in L(CB, \sigma)$. Hence, M fails to infer the finite language $\hat{L} \cup \{u\}$ from this particular informant, a contradiction. This proves the theorem.

Corollary 7. *The class of regular languages is not case-based learnable from informant.*

Proof. It is clear that the class of regular languages contains all finite languages and all co-finite languages.

3 Learning similarity measures by tuning parameters

Up to now, we have considered the case-based representations where a similarity measure is fixed and universal for the target class of languages and the case-based learning is just developing a case base. However, using universally fixed similarity measures is much too restrictive.

In this section, we consider the case-based representation and learning where the similarity measure is also specified or learned for each target language. That is, we consider the case-based representations where for a class C of languages, there is a class S of similarity measures such that for each $L \in C$, $L = L(CB, \sigma)$ for some $\sigma \in S$ and a finite case base CB. However, if we take into account the class of all computable similarity measures, every problem can be reduced to defining or learning only similarity measures and, hence, there is nothing of interest from the view point of case-based learning [Jan92]. Thus, we need to carefully specify a class of similarity measures to be considered.

3.1 Introducing parameters into similarity measures to be learned

An interesting class of similarity measures is given by adopting weighting scheme for cases like the weighted nearest neighbor algorithm [CS93]. This scheme is based on the idea that some stored cases are more reliable classifiers than others. This can be accomplished with the weights in similarity measures: reliable cases are given larger weights, making them appear closer to words in the domain.

Definition 8. Let C be a class of languages and assume the fixed base measure σ_b for C. A *weighted similarity measure* σ based on σ_b is defined to be

$$\sigma(u, w) = \alpha_u \cdot \sigma_b(u, w) \quad \text{for } u \text{ and } w \text{ in } \Sigma^*,$$

where α_u are computable real values (rational numbers will do).

When we construct a weighted similarity measure σ to define a language L with a finite case base CB such that $L = L(CB, \sigma)$, since $\sigma(u, w)$ would never be used for any $u \in \Sigma^*$ such that $(u, d) \notin CB$, we do not need any such α_u. For our convenience, we simplify the concept of a weighted similarity measure σ based on σ_b as follows:

$$\sigma(u, w) = \begin{cases} \alpha_u \cdot \sigma_b(u, w) & \text{for } u \in \Sigma^* \text{ such that } \exists d : (u, d) \in CB \\ 0 \ (= 0 \cdot \sigma_b(u, w)) & \text{for } u \in \Sigma^* \text{ such that } \exists d : (u, d) \notin CB \end{cases}$$

$S[\sigma_b]$ denotes the class of weighted similarity measures σ based on σ_b. The weighted similarity measure can simulate *forgetting* a case (u, d) simply by setting the weight α_u to zero.

Definition 9. Let C be a class of languages and S be a class of similarity measures. C is *case-based learnable (in the limit) from informant w.r.t.* S if and only if there is a learning algorithm M such that for all $L \in C$ and for all $i \in Inf(L)$, there exists some case base CB and some similarity measure $\sigma \in S$:

1. $\forall n \in I\!N : M(i_{\leq n}) = (CB_n, \sigma_n)$ is defined,
2. $\forall n \in I\!N : \sigma_n \in \mathcal{S}$,
3. $\forall n \in I\!N : \emptyset \subseteq CB_1 \subseteq \{(s_1, d_1)\}$ and $CB_n \subseteq CB_{n+1} \subseteq CB_n \cup \{(s_{n+1}, d_{n+1})\}$,
4. $\lim_{n \to \infty} M(i_{\leq n}) = (CB, \sigma)$,
5. $L = L(CB, \sigma)$.

In $\mathcal{S}[\sigma_b]$, the problem of learning similarity measures becomes the problem of tuning parameters $\alpha_1, \ldots, \alpha_n$.

3.2 Learnability w.r.t. weighted similarity measures

Now, we will show that any indexed class of recursive languages whose finiteness problems are decidable is case-based learnable from informant w.r.t. a class of weighted similarity measures, while non-learnability of formal languages has been shown in Theorem 6 for any fixed universal similarity measure.

Theorem 10. *Any indexed class of recursive languages whose finiteness problems are decidable is case-based learnable from informant w.r.t. some class of weighted similarity measures.*

Proof. Let $\mathcal{C}$ denote the target class of languages to be learned. As we have seen in representability consideration (Theorem 4), in order to represent finite languages in $\mathcal{C}$, we need to use the complements of those finite languages. Let $\mathcal{PC}$ denote the set of all infinite languages in $\mathcal{C}$ and $\mathcal{FC}$ denote the set of all finite languages in $\mathcal{C}$. We dovetail the enumeration $L_1, L_2, \ldots$ of $\mathcal{PC}$ and the enumeration of finite languages in $\mathcal{FC}$. We denote the resulting enumeration by $H_1, H_2, H_3, \ldots$ and assume, for simplicity, that exactly the elements with odd indices are from $\mathcal{PC}$, i.e. $H_{2j-1} = L_j \in \mathcal{PC}$ and $H_{2j} = F_j$ for $F_j \in \mathcal{FC}$ for all natural numbers j.

To achieve case-based learnability, we need an infinite sequence of representing words for every language in $\mathcal{PC}$ and the complement of every finite language in $\mathcal{FC}$. For this purpose, we may construct an effective "two-dimensional" enumeration $v_{1,1}, v_{2,1}, v_{1,2}, v_{3,1}, v_{2,2}, v_{1,3}, v_{4,1}, \ldots$ of Σ^* such that every $v_{2m-1,n}$ is a member of H_{2m-1} and every $v_{2m,n}$ belongs to $\overline{F_{2m}}$ for $n \geq 1$. The construction is completely similar to the "one-dimensional" one above. We skip it, for shortness. Let $m, n \in I\!N$. The base similarity measure σ_b is defined by:

$$\sigma_b(v_{2m-1,n}, w) = \begin{cases} 1 \text{ if } w \in H_{2m-1} \\ 0 \text{ otherwise} \end{cases} \qquad \sigma_b(v_{2m,n}, w) = \begin{cases} 1 \text{ if } w \in \overline{H_{2m}} \\ 0 \text{ otherwise} \end{cases}$$

Note that every infinite sequence $v_{2m-1,1}, v_{2m-1,2}, \ldots$ is representing H_{2m-1} and every infinite sequence $v_{2m,1}, v_{2m,2}, \ldots$ is representing $\overline{H_{2m}}$. Then, a weighted similarity measure σ is defined as $\sigma(u, w) = \alpha_u \cdot \sigma_b(u, w)$ for a case (u, d) and its parameter's value α_u.

To construct a case-based learning algorithm M for $\mathcal{C}$, we assume some consistent inductive inference algorithm M_{base} which identifies $\mathcal{C}$ in the limit and produces as output indices on the above enumeration $H_1, H_2, H_3, \ldots$ For instance, any inductive inference algorithm which realizes the *identification by enumeration principle* w.r.t. the enumeration $H_1, H_2, H_3, \ldots$ (cf. [Gol67]) behaves as required. M constructed below will simulate M_{base}.

Let $i = (s_1, d_1), (s_2, d_2), \ldots$ be any given informant for the target language L_t in $\mathcal{C}$. Let $M_{base}(i_{\leq x})$ denote the index generated by M_{base} when fed $i_{\leq x}$. For the sake of readability, we write $L_{base}(i_{\leq x})$ as a shorthand for the language $H_{M_{base}(i_{\leq x})}$ actually guessed by M_{base}.

The algorithm M for the input $i_{\leq x}$ is described in Figure 1. We assume that, initially, $CB_0 = \emptyset$ and $FLAG_0 = 0$.

Algorithm $M(i_{\leq x})$:

begin
    read (s_x, d_x);
    if $d_x = 1$ and $L_{base}(i_{\leq x})$ is a finite language H_{2m}
      then
        $CB_x := CB_{x-1} \cup \{(s_x, d_x)\}$;
    if $FLAG_{x-1} = 1$ and $M_{base}(i_{\leq x-1}) = M_{base}(i_{\leq x})$
      then
        $CB_x := CB_{x-1}$;
        $FLAG_x := FLAG_{x-1}$;
      else
        $CB_x := CB_{x-1} \cup \{(s_x, d_x)\}$;
        $\alpha_{s_y} := 0$ for all (s_y, d_y) in CB_x;
        $FLAG_x := 0$;
        if $L_{base}(i_{\leq x})$ is an infinite language H_{2m-1}
          then
            if there is some $(s_y, 0) \in CB_x$ such that $s_y = v_{2m-1,n}$
              then
                $\alpha_{s_y} := 1$;
                $FLAG_x := 1$;
        if $L_{base}(i_{\leq x})$ is a finite language H_{2m}
          then
             if there is some $(s_y, 0) \in CB_x$ such that $s_y = v_{2m,n}$
              then
                $\alpha_{s_y} := 1$;
                $\alpha_{s_y} := 1$ for all $(s_y, 1)$ in CB_x;
                $FLAG_x := 1$;
end

Fig. 1. A case-based learning algorithm for formal languages.

First, note that the algorithm M is effectively computable (i.e. it always halts and produces an output) because M_{base} is assumed to output indices on the enumeration $H_1, H_2, H_3, \ldots$ so that it is decidable whether $L_{base}(i_{\leq x})$ is finite or not.

We start with the following observation which immediately follows from both the definition of σ_b and the definition of M:

Observation If $L_{base}(i_{\leq x})$ describes an infinite language H_{2m-1} and, furthermore, $FLAG_x = 1$, then $L_{base}(i_{\leq x}) = L(CB_x, \sigma_x)$ where CB_x denotes the actual case base and σ_x is the actual weighted similarity measure guessed by M.

To see this, take into consideration that CB_x contains a representative example $(v_{2m-1,n}, 1)$ for H_{2m-1}. This guarantees that $\sigma_b(v_{2m-1,n}, w) = 1$ if and only if $w \in H_{2m-1}$. By the definition of σ_x, we obtain $\alpha_{v_{2m-1,n}} = 1$ and for all other examples $(s_y, d_y) \in CB_x \setminus \{(v_{2m-1,n}, 1)\}$, $\alpha_{s_y} = 0$. Consequently, $L_{base}(i_{\leq x}) = L(CB_x, \sigma_x)$.

In order to show that M behaves as required we distinguish the following cases.

Case 1. L_t is an infinite language.

Since M_{base} infers L_t on i, there has to be a least x such that $M_{base}(i_{\leq x}) = M_{base}(i_{\leq x+r})$ for all $r \in \mathbb{N}$. Moreover, $L_{base}(i_{\leq x}) = L_t = H_{2m-1}$ for some $m \in \mathbb{N}$.

If CB_x contains already a representative example $(v_{2m-1,n}, 1)$ for H_{2m-1}, then M converges to the final case base $CB := CB_x$ and the weighted similarity measure $\sigma := \sigma_x$. By construction $FLAG_x = 1$. Thus, we obtain $L(CB, \sigma) = L_t$ from the observation above.

Otherwise, take into consideration that there are infinitely many representative cases for L_t. Thus, there has to be a least $y \geq x$ such that $(s_y, 1) = (v_{2m-1,n}, 1)$. By definition, M converges to the final case base $CB := CB_y$ and the corresponding similarity measure $\sigma := \sigma_y$. Moreover, $FLAG_y = 1$. As above, $L(CB, \sigma) = L_t$ follows.

Case 2. L_t is a finite language.

Since i is an informant for L_t, there is a $y \in \mathbb{N}$ such that $i_y^+ = L_t$. Moreover, since M_{base} infers L_t on i, there is a least $x > y$ such that $M_{base}(i_{\leq x}) = M_{base}(i_{\leq x+r})$ for all $r \in \mathbb{N}$. Applying the same arguments as above we can conclude that M converges to a finte case base CB which contains at least one representative case $(v_{2m,n}, 0)$ for the complement of $L_{base}(i_{\leq x}) = H_{2m} = L_t$. Let σ denote the weighted similarity measure M converges to. By definition of σ, it follows $L(CB, \sigma) \subseteq L_t$. Moreover, $CB^+ := \{w \mid (w, 1) \in CB\} \subseteq L(CB, \sigma)$, since $\sigma(v_{2m,n}, w) = 0$ for all $w \in CB^+$. Obviously, $CB^+ = L_t$ implies $L(CB, \sigma) = L_t$.

Finally, assume $CB^+ \subset L_t$. Let w be any string from $L_t \setminus CB^+$. In order to show $w \in L(CB, \sigma)$ it suffices to show there is an example $(v, 1) \in CB$ such that $\sigma(v, w) = 1$. Due to the definition of σ this requires, in fact, $\sigma_b(v, w) = 1$. By the choice of y, there is a $z \leq y$ such that $(s_z, d_z) = (w, 1)$. Now, take M's definition into account: If M was prevented to store the positive case $(w, 1)$ in its actual case base $CB_z \subseteq CB$, the requirements $M_{base}(i_{\leq z-1}) = M_{base}(i_{\leq z})$ and $FLAG_{z-1} = 1$ were fulfilled. Furthermore, $L_{base}(i_{\leq z-1})$ is an infinite language. Thus, by the observation made above we can conclude that $L_{base}(i_{\leq z-1}) = L(CB_{z-1}, \sigma_{z-1})$. Furthermore, M_{base} is a consistent inductive inference algorithm. Therefore, $w \in L_{base}(i_{\leq z-1})$, Thus, $w \in L_{base}(i_{\leq z})$. This implies $w \in L_{base}(i_{\leq z-1})$, since $L_{base}(i_{\leq z}) = L_{base}(i_{\leq z-1})$. Consequently, $w \in L(CB_{z-1}, \sigma_{z-1})$ and, therefore, there is an example $(v, 1) \in CB_{z-1}$ such that $\sigma_{z-1}(v, w) = 1$. Due to the choice of σ_{z-1} it follows $\sigma_b(v, w) = 1$, too. Since, finally, $CB_{z-1} \subseteq CB$, we have done.

Corollary 11. *The classes of regular languages and context-free languages are case-based learnable from informant w.r.t. a class of weighted similarity measures.*

The general case-based learning algorithm described in Figure 1 is allowed to use a full set of examples presented so far, i.e. $i_{\leq x}$ at any point x while it is required to collect a case base in stepwise starting with the empty case base (this corresponds to the condition (3) in Definition 9 of case-base learning). This type of learning is called *operationally incremental* in [Jan93]. The usual *incremental learning* is defined in inductive inference. That does not allow the inference algorithm to look back at the whole history of informant presented during the learning process. The formal definition of *incremental case-based learning* can be given by changing the condition (1) in Definition 9 to $M(CB_{n-1}, \sigma_{n-1}, (s_n, d_n)) = (CB_n, \sigma_n)$ where CB_0 is the empty case base and σ_0 is assumed to be some initial similarity measure. Since the case-based learning algorithm described in Figure 1 just simulates the base algorithm M_{base}, we have the following.

Corollary 12. *Let C be an indexed class of recursive languages whose finiteness problems are decidable. If there exists an incremental (iterative) consistent inductive inference algorithm for C, then C is incrementally case-based learnable from informant w.r.t. a class of weighted similarity measures.*

The incremental learning is especially important in case-based reasoning because case-based learning which is intended to model human expert's learning behavior considers learning processes over a usually quite long time period. This means that when updating a theory in processing recently recognized cases, the history of the whole theory development is usually not available. Thus, an adequate learning model is essentially incremental.

4 Application - case-based learning of containment decision lists

In this section, we introduce *containment decision lists*, a class of representations for formal languages, and apply the above theoretical results on case-based learning to them.

Containment decision lists have been introduced in [SS92] to study the effect of noise on learning languages in the PAC learning framework. Their case-based learnability has also been studied in [Jan93]. The class of containment decision lists is a simple class of representations to define formal languages based on *decision lists* [Riv87]. The class of languages defined by it is a subclass of regular languages.

The definition of containment decision lists is quite simple. First we define a relation between two strings u and v in Σ^*. We say $u \preceq v$ if v contains u as a substring, i.e. there are $w_1, w_2 \in \Sigma^*$ such that $w_1 u w_2 = v$.

Definition 13. A *containment decision list* over Σ is a list T of pairs

$$\langle (u_1, d_1), (u_2, d_2), \ldots, (u_n, d_n), (\varepsilon, d_{n+1}) \rangle$$

where each u_i is a string in Σ^+ and each d_i is a label in $\{0, 1\}$. A containment decision list T defines a language, denoted $L(T)$, over Σ as follows: for any string $w \in \Sigma^+$, $w \in L(T)$ if and only if the label d_k is equal to 1 where k is the *least* index such that $u_k \preceq w$. (Since the last item is always true, this is well defined.)

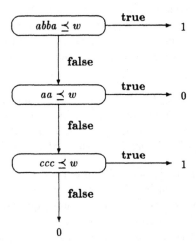

Fig. 2. Diagram of the containment decision list $\langle (abba, 1), (aa, 0), (ccc, 1), (\varepsilon, 0) \rangle$

We may think of a containment decision list as an "**if** − **then** − **elseif** − ... **else**−" rule. For example, the containment decision list $T = \langle (abba, 1), (aa, 0), (ccc, 1), (\varepsilon, 0) \rangle$ may be diagrammed as in Figure 2, where $\Sigma = \{a, b, c\}$. For example, $L(abbcaaccc) = 0$; this value is specified by the second pair in the containment decision list.

From Theorem 4, one may conclude that the class of all languages acceptable by containment decision lists is case-based representable w.r.t. some fixed similarity measure. On the other hand, since the class of all finite and all co-finite languages can be represented by containment decision lists, the following non-learnability result for containment decision lists is derived from Theorem 6.

Theorem 14. *The class of containment decision lists is not case-based learnable from informant.*

To gain learnability, we need an appropriate class of tunable similarity measures. As base measure, we define a simple and natural similarity measure σ_{cont} as follows. For two strings u and w in Σ^*, $\sigma_{cont}(u, w) = 1$ if and only if $u \preceq w$. Containment decision lists are case-based representable using weighted similarity measures based on σ_{cont}.

Theorem 15. *Let $\mathcal{D}$ be the class of containment decision lists. For every containment decision list T in $\mathcal{D}$, $L(T)$ can be represented by a weighted similarity measure σ based on σ_{cont} and a finite case base CB, i.e. for each $(u, d) \in CB$, σ can be defined as $\sigma(u, w) = \alpha_u \sigma_{cont}(u, w)$ for some real value α_u such that $L(CB, \sigma) = L(T)$.*

Proof. Let $T = \langle (u_1, d_1), (u_2, d_2), \ldots, (u_n, d_n), (\varepsilon, d_{n+1}) \rangle$ be a containment decision list in $\mathcal{D}$. To represent $L(T)$, the case base CB and the weighted similarity measure σ based on σ_{cont} are defined as follows:

$$
\begin{aligned}
CB &= \{(u_1, d_1), (u_2, d_2), \ldots, (u_n, d_n), (\varepsilon, d_{n+1})\} \\
\sigma(u_i, w) &= 1/i \cdot \sigma_{cont}(u_i, w) \quad \text{for } 1 \le i \le n \\
\sigma(\varepsilon, w) &= 1/(n+1) \cdot \sigma_{cont}(\varepsilon, w).
\end{aligned}
$$

Since every string in $L(T)$ is of length at least 1, it is clear that $L(CB, \sigma) = L(T)$.

It has been shown in [Jan93] that the class of containment decision lists is not case-based learnable in an incremental way. This applies to the class of similarity measures defined in Theorem 15 which reflect the ordering of representing cases in some case base. By adopting the idea of [Jan93], we obtain the following statement.

Theorem 16. *The class of all containment decision lists is not case-based learnable from informant w.r.t. $\mathcal{S}[\sigma_{cont}]$.*

Proof. For any properly increasing sequence of exponents $k_1, k_2, \ldots, k_n \in \mathbb{N}$, we define a containment decision list

$T_{k_1, k_2, \ldots, k_n} =$
$\langle (ba^{k_1}b, 1), (ab^{k_1}a, 0), (ba^{k_2}b, 1), (ab^{k_2}a, 0), \ldots, (ba^{k_n}b, 1), (ab^{k_n}a, 0), (\varepsilon, 1) \rangle$

Assume any informant i for $L(T_{k_1, k_2, \ldots, k_n})$. Each initial segment $i_{\le l}$ can be continued by a sequence of postive cases of the form $(ba^m b, 1)$, where m exceeds k_n. For simplicity, we take the sequence $(ba^{k_n+1}b, 1), (ba^{k_n+2}b, 1), \ldots$ For any learning algorithm, there must be some sufficiently large m such that $(ba^{k_n+m}b, 1)$ is *not* put into the current case base to get stabilization of the learning process. If the informant under consideration is now completed to provide a repetition-free informant for $L(T_{k_1,k_2,\ldots,k_n,k_{n+m}})$, the case $(ba^{k_n+m}b,1)$ will never occur again. Thus, the learning algorithm investigated must necessarily fail.

The key reason is a normal form result about containment decision lists. Instead of developing the general theory, it is sufficient for our purpose to know that every containment decision list T with $L(T) = L(T_{k_1,k_2,\ldots,k_n})$ must contain the nodes $\{\ (ba^{k_1}b,1),(ab^{k_1}a,0),(ba^{k_2}b,1),(ab^{k_2}a,0),\ldots,(ba^{k_n}b,1),(ab^{k_n}a,0)\ \}$, at least. There is a similar normal form result for representations built upon $S[\sigma_{cont}]$. Thus, any learning algorithm which has dropped the case $(ba^{k_n+m}b,1)$ can only collect an appropriate case base for $L(T_{k_1,k_2,\ldots,k_n})$, if this case is presented again. Otherwise, it would fail.

The natural similarity measure introduced above did not allow learnability. But in contrast, the seemingly unnatural approach invoked to prove Theorem 10 above provides a properly greater learning power. This yields the following result.

Theorem 17. *The class of all containment decision lists is case-based learnable from informant w.r.t. a class of weighted similarity measures.*

Proof. As all languages represented by containment decision lists are regular, one may invoke the decidability of finiteness for regular languages (cf. [HU79]). Thus, the proof is straightforward from Theorem 10.

Beyond our deterministic approach to learning, the containment decision lists have been shown to be polynomial-time learnable in the PAC learning model. The algorithm presented in Theorem 10 naively simulates an identification by enumeration strategy and is not efficient in the sense of polynomial-time learning.

5 Conclusions

Case-based learning is essentially based on collecting cases and tuning similarity measures appropriately. We have attempted a natural formalization in an area which seems particularly tailored to case-based reasoning.

Our results above exhibit the enormous power of learning similarity measures, even if the class of similarity measures taken into account is considerably restricted, opposed to those approaches where any particularly fixed similarity concept is assumed. This coincides with results on case-based learning of recursive functions already known (cf. [Jan92]).

It is of a particular methodological value, in our opinion, to discover the importance of non-standard similarity concepts for learning. Whereas certain seemingly natural classes of similarity measures do not admit learnability of all containment decision lists, certain non-standard concepts do so. This nicely illustrates the limitations of common-sense reasoning in automating learning processes, and it stresses the importance of approaches firmly based on theoretical computer science results. In a sense, it opposes cognitive science ideas to certain formal approaches. The reader may consult [JL93] for a couple of similar results in this respect.

Furthermore, a detailed inspection of the constructions and proofs above exhibits the importance of particularly distinguished cases used to represent target languages to be learned in a case-based fashion. This raises the question for an appropriate formalization of the cognitive science concept of *prototypes*.

Acknowledgement

The work of the second and third author has been partially supported by the DEUTSCHE FORSCHUNGSGEMEINSCHAFT (DFG) within the projekt IND-CBL. It is worth to be mentioned that the origin of the present investigations has been at the FUJITSU Laboratories in Numazu, Japan, where the authors had several opportunities to collaborate.

References

[AKA91] David W. Aha, Dennis Kibler, and Marc K. Albert. Instance-based learning algorithms. *Machine Learning*, 6:37–66, 1991.

[A80] Dana Angluin. Inductive inference of formal languages from positive data. *ACM Computing Surveys*, 15:237–269, 1983.

[AS83] Dana Angluin and Carl H. Smith. Inductive inference : Theory and methods. *Information and Control*, 45:117–135.

[CS93] Scott Cost and Steven Salzberg. A weighted nearest neighbor algorithm for learning with symbolic features. *Machine Learning*, 10:57–78, 1993.

[Gol67] E Mark Gold. Language identification in the limit. *Information and Control*, 10:447–474, 1967.

[HU79] John E. Hopcroft and Jeffrey D. Ullman. *Introduction to Automata Theory, Languages, and Computation*. Addison-Wesley, 1979.

[Jan92] Klaus P. Jantke. Case-based learning in inductive inference. In *Proceedings of 5th Workshop on Computational Learning Theory (COLT'92)*, pages 218–223. ACM Press, 1992.

[Jan93] Klaus P. Jantke. Types of incremental learning. In *Working Notes, AAAI Spring Symposium on Training Issues in Incremental Learning*, pages 26–32, Stanford University, 1993.

[JL93] Klaus P. Jantke and Steffen Lange. Case-based representation and learning of pattern languages. In *Proceedings of 4th Workshop on Algorithmic Learning Theory (ALT'93)*, Lecture Notes in Artificial Intelligence 744, pages 87–100. Springer-Verlag, 1993.

[Riv87] Ronald L. Rivest. Learning decision lists. *Machine Learning*, 2:229–246, 1987.

[SS92] Yasubumi Sakakibara and Rani Siromoney. A noise model on learning sets of strings. In *Proceedings of 5th Workshop on Computational Learning Theory (COLT'92)*, pages 295–302. ACM Press, 1992.

Mutual Information Gaining Algorithm and Its Relation to PAC-Learning Algorithm

Eiji Takimoto, Ichiro Tajika and Akira Maruoka

Graduate School of Information Science, Tohoku University
Sendai, 980-77, Japan

Abstract. In this paper, the mutual information between a target concept and a hypothesis is used to measure the goodness of the hypothesis rather than the accuracy, and a notion of mutual information gaining (MI-gaining) algorithms is introduced. In particular, strong and weak MI-gaining algorithms are defined depending on the amount of information acquired, and their relation to strong and weak PAC-learning algorithms are investigated. It is shown that although a strong MI-gaining algorithm is equivalent to a strong PAC-learning algorithm, a weak MI-gaining algorithm does not necessarily imply a weak PAC-learning algorithm, and vice versa. Moreover, a general boosting scheme for weak MI-gaining algorithms is given. That is, any weak MI-gaining algorithm can be used to build a strong one. Since a strong MI-gaining algorithm is also a strong PAC-learning algorithm, the result can be viewed to give a sufficient condition for a class of algorithms to be boosted into strong learning algorithms.

1 Introduction

An algorithm is a weak learning algorithm if with high probability it outputs a hypothesis with error slightly smaller than 1/2. The hypothesis with error less than 1/2 is considered to be better than random guessing. Is it true? It turns out that, in some cases, we can extract information about the target concept from a hypothesis that approximates the concept with probability just 1/2. In fact, Natarajan showed that any one-sided error learning algorithm that, with high probability, outputs a hypothesis with error slightly below 1 (so, including just 1/2) can be used to build a strong learning algorithm [5]. In particular, this construction (henceforth we call it a boosting scheme) invokes the one-sided error learning algorithm repeatedly with filtered sequence of samples to obtain a hypothesis each time. These hypotheses are then combined to form a master hypothesis that approximates the concept with high probability. Although each hypothesis obtained may have just 1/2 error according to the filtered distribution, the boosting scheme provides the mechanism to extract information about target concept from it. This can be done because the boosting scheme uses the structure of the error (i.e., no negative error exists) rather than the value of the error itself.

So, it is natural to measure the goodness of a hypothesis in terms of the amount of information, concerning a target, in the hypothesis. In this extended abstract, we provide a framework in which we use the mutual information between a target concept and a hypothesis to measure the accuracy of a hypothesis. Informally, the mutual information of a hypothesis means the amount of information, concerning the target concept, which is gained after knowing the hypothesis. In contrast to our approach based on the mutual information, there was another information theoretic approach [3][4] for design of learning algorithms where a prior probability distribution on a concept class is assumed. In this approach information concerning a target is associated with each example and, based on the information, they design efficient learning algorithms that work well under a prior distribution on a concept class. In the a prior distribution approach, the information obtained by observing an example depends on a prior distribution, whereas, in the approach based on mutual information, we take into account neither a concept class nor a prior distribution on it. So the former approach is useful to identify a target concept among a concept class, while the latter one is expected to be useful to investigate how to improve a hypothesis in the process of learning, without paying attention to the concept class in question, e.g., how to construct a general boosting scheme.

In this paper, we introduce a notion of mutual information gaining (MI-gaining) algorithms, and explore relationship between MI-gaining algorithms and PAC-learning algorithms. In particular, we introduce notions of strong and weak MI-gaining algorithms corresponding to strong and weak PAC-learning algorithms, respectively, and show that although strong MI-gaining algorithms are equivalent to strong PAC-learning algorithms, weak MI-gaining algorithms are incomparable with weak PAC-learning algorithms. Also we show a boosting scheme for weak MI-gaining algorithms, namely, a scheme to obtain a strong learning algorithm from arbitrarily given weak MI-gaining algorithm.

In Section 2, the definition of PAC-learning algorithm is presented, and in Section 3 the definition of strong and weak MI-gaining algorithms are given. In Section 4, relationship between MI-gaining algorithms and PAC-learning algorithms is given. Finally, in Section 5, a boosting scheme for weak MI-gaining algorithms is given.

2 Preliminaries

Let X denote a set of instances called the domain, and F denote a set of subsets of X called the concept class. We may sometimes assume the domain to be real-valued. A concept f in F also denotes its corresponding characteristic function, which maps X to $\{0, 1\}$.

An example of f is a labeled instance $(x, f(x))$ for some $x \in X$, and a sample of f is a finite sequence of examples of f. The size of a sample is the number of examples in the sample.

A learning algorithm for a concept class F is a function from samples of f to a set of concepts. More formally, a learning algorithm A for F, when given as input a sample of some $f \in F$, outputs a concept h called a hypothesis. Here, the hypothesis h does not necessarily belong to F. In this paper, we do not require that the mapping realized by a learning algorithm is computable. So we do not need to take care how to represent concepts. Each instance x in the example $(x, f(x))$ which is given to a learning algorithm is assumed to be independently generated according to some probability distribution D over X. Thus, the hypothesis h produced by a learning algorithm can be regarded as a random variable over D^m, where m is the size of the sample.

For a subset c of X, $D(c)$ denotes the probability of c under D, that is, the probability that $x \in c$ holds when x is drawn according to D.

Now we define (strong) PAC-learning algorithms. In the usual definition, PAC-learning algorithms are required to output, with high probability, hypotheses close to target concepts with sufficiently high accuracy. In this paper, allowing the hypotheses to be almost incorrect as well as to be almost correct, we modify somehow the definition of PAC-learning algorithms. It is easy to see the modification does not change the notion of PAC-learnability for concept classes. Later we will see that the modified definition is convenient to show the equivalence between PAC-learning algorithms and MI-gaining algorithms.

Definition 1 (strong PAC-learning algorithm). Algorithm A is a (strong) PAC-learning algorithm for F if for any ε and δ $(0 < \varepsilon, \delta \leq 1)$, there exists an $m \geq 1$ such that for any $f \in F$ and any probability distribution D over X, when algorithm A is given a sample of size at least m, algorithm A, with probability at least $1 - \delta$, outputs h such that either $D(f \bigtriangleup h) \leq \varepsilon$ or $D(f \bigtriangleup h) \geq 1 - \varepsilon$ hold.

Next we define weak PAC-learning algorithms. A weak learning algorithm is a learning algorithm that, with high probability, outputs a hypothesis with error slightly below $1/2$. Again we allow the hypothesis to have error slightly above $1/2$ as well.

Definition 2 (weak PAC-learning algorithm). Algorithm A is a weak PAC-learning algorithm for F if there exists a $\gamma > 0$ such that for any δ $(0 < \delta \leq 1)$, there exists an $m \geq 1$ such that for any $f \in F$ and any probability distribution D over X, when algorithm A is given a sample of size at least m, algorithm A, with probability at least $1 - \delta$, output h such that either $D(f \bigtriangleup h) \leq 1/2 - \gamma$ or $D(f \bigtriangleup h) \geq 1/2 + \gamma$ hold.

3 Mutual Information Gaining

Let f be a target concept and h be a hypothesis that some learning algorithm outputs. As we will see shortly, in order to evaluate how good a hypothesis is, it is more appropriate to employ information that a hypothesis h possesses concerning a target concept f rather than the probability $D(f \bigtriangleup h)$.

Consider the case that the probability distribution D is such that $D(f) < 1/3$ and that h is the empty set. In this case, although the error probability of h is less than $1/2$ (in this case $D(f \bigtriangleup h) < 1/3$), it is hard to say that h has some information about f.

On the other hand, consider the case that $D(f \triangle h) = 1/2$ and $h \subseteq f$. In this case, although the error of h is worst, we can combine many such hypotheses into a good hypothesis that is an ε-approximation to f [5]. This implies that a hypothesis with error around $1/2$ can have information about f.

So, it is natural that the goodness of a hypothesis is measured in terms of the amount of information we can extract from the hypothesis in order to get a good approximation to the target concept. In order to quantify such kind of information, we adopt the mutual information between f and h.

Now let us consider f and h to be random variables over D that take values in $\{0, 1\}$. The relationship between the random variables f and h can be illustrated through the binary channel with input and output terminals as usual. See Figure 1. Here, $p_0 = D(X - f)$, $p_1 = D(f)$ and α_0 and α_1 denote the negative and positive errors of h, respectively. That is,

$$\alpha_0 = \Pr_D(h = 1|f = 0)$$

and

$$\alpha_1 = \Pr_D(h = 0|f = 1).$$

Note that

$$D(f \triangle h) = p_0\alpha_0 + p_1\alpha_1.$$

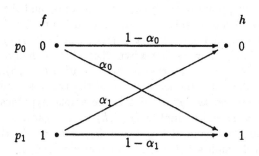

Fig.1. Binary channel between f and h

Then, the mutual information between f and h over D is defined as

$$I_D(f; h) = H(f) - H(f|h),$$

where H denotes the entropy function. $H(f)$ denotes the uncertainty about the value of f, and it is assumed to be known before seeing h. This assumption is natural since the value $D(f)$ (and hence $H(f)$ as well) can be easily estimated by simply observing the fraction of positive examples. On the other hand, the conditional entropy $H(f|h)$, which is defined as

$$\sum_a \Pr(h = a) H(f \text{ on the condition that } h = a)$$

denotes the uncertainty about the value of f remained after seeing the value of h. Therefore, the mutual information $I_D(f;h)$ can be interpreted as the information gain about f obtained throuth h.

In the case of Figure 1, the mutual information between f and h can be written in terms of p_0, p_1, α_0 and α_1. In what follows, H_n denotes the binary entropy function that maps $[0,1]$ to $[0,1]$. That is, for any $p \in [0,1]$,

$$H_n(p) = -p \log p - (1-p) \log(1-p),$$

where the logarithm is to base 2.

Theorem 3. Let f and h be random variables described as Figure 1. Then,

$$I_D(f;h) = H_n(p_0\alpha_0 + p_1(1-\alpha_1)) - \{p_0 H_n(\alpha_0) + p_1 H_n(1-\alpha_1)\}.$$

Proof. It is well known that $I_D(f;h) = H(h) - H(h|f)$, and thus the theorem follows. □

From this theorem, you can see that the mutual information corresponds to the length of a geometric line segment. The first term of $I_D(f;h)$ means the binary entropy of the value corresponding to the internally dividing point of α_0 and $1 - \alpha_1$ with ratio being $p_1 : p_0$. On the other hand, the second term means the internally dividing point of the binary entropy of α_0 and that of $1 - \alpha_1$ with the same ratio. We illustrate this observation as in Figure 2.

It is easily seen from Figure 2 that unless $p_0, p_1 > 0$, $I_D(f;h) = 0$ if and only if $\alpha_0 + \alpha_1 = 1$. This implies that a hypothesis better than random guessing, i.e., $D(f \triangle h) < 1/2$, does not necessarily have positive $I_D(f;h)$, and vice versa. This observation illustrates the learnability of the two cases mentioned at the beginning of this section as follows. If h is the empty hypothesis, then clearly $\alpha_0 = 0$ and $\alpha_1 = 1$, which implies $I_D(f;h) = 0$ regardless of the value of $D(f \triangle h)$. On the other hand, if $h \subseteq f$ and $D(f \triangle h) = 1/2$, then $\alpha_0 = 0$ and $\alpha_1 = 1/(2p_1)$, which implies $I_D(f;h) > 0$ whenever $p_1 > 1/2$.

Now we introduce a notion of mutual information gaining algorithm in terms of the mutual information between f and h. By the definition of the mutual information, it is clear that $I_D(f;h) \leq H_n(p_1)(= H(f))$, where the equality holds only when $\alpha_0 = \alpha_1 = 0$ or $\alpha_0 = \alpha_1 = 1$. The following definition of (strong) MI-gaining algorithm is natural.

Definition 4 (strong MI-gaining algorithm). Algorithm A is a (strong) MI-gaining algorithm for F if for any ε and δ $(0 < \varepsilon, \delta \leq 1)$, there exists an $m \geq 1$ such that for any f in F and any probability distribution D over X, when algorithm A is given a sample of size at least m, algorithm A, with probability at least $1 - \delta$, outputs h such that $I_D(f;h) \geq H_n(D(f)) - \varepsilon$. Moreover, if $H_n(D(f)) \leq \varepsilon$, then $h = \phi$.

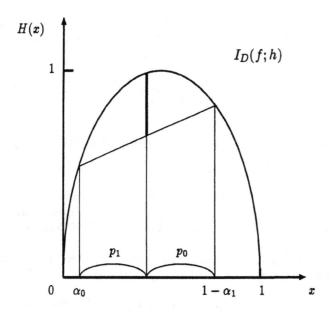

Fig.2. The mutual information between f and h

The last condition of the above definition is inessential. It makes the notion of strong MI-gaining imply that of strong PAC-learning even when the distribution D is near the extremes, i.e., $D(f) = 0$ or $D(f) = 1$.

Similarly, we can define the weak MI-gaining algorithms. It is natural for us to require them to output hypotheses with slightly positive mutual information gain in a distribution-free sense. But it is difficult to establish the mutual information is positive even when the distribution D is near the extremes.

Definition 5 (weak MI-gaining algorithm). Algorithm A is a weak MI-gaining algorithm for F if there exists a $\gamma > 0$ such that for any δ ($0 < \delta \leq 1/2$), there exists an $m \geq 1$ such that for any $f \in F$ and any probability distribution D over X such that $H_n(D(f)) \geq \delta$, when algorithm A is given a sample of size at least m, algorithm A, with probability at least $1 - \delta$, outputs h such that $I_D(f;h) \geq \gamma H_n(D(f))$.

The above definition is so designed that weak MI-gaining algorithms produce hypotheses with non-zero mutual information in a distribution-free sense, and that they are properly weaker notion of information gaining than strong MI-gaining algorithms. The next theorem shows this fact.

Theorem 6. Any strong MI-gaining algorithm for F is also a weak MI-gaining algorithm for F.

Proof. Let A be a strong MI-gaining algorithm for F. Fix δ arbitrarily, and put $\varepsilon = \delta/2$. Then, there exists an $m \geq 1$ such that for any f in F and any probability distribution D over X, when algorithm A is given a sample of size at least m, algorithm A, with probability at least $1 - \delta$, outputs h such that $I_D(f;h) \geq H_n(D(f)) - \delta/2$. Thus, when $H_n(D(f)) \geq \delta$, $I_D(f;h) \geq H_n(D(f)) - \delta/2$ implies $I_D(f;h) \geq H_n(D(f))/2$, completing the theorem. $\square$

4 Relationship between PAC-learning algorithms and MI-gaining algorithms

In this section, we give a relationship between PAC-learning and MI-gaining. In particular, we show that strong PAC-learning and strong MI-gaining are equivalent, but the notion of weak MI-gaining and that of weak PAC-learning are not equivalent.

First we show the key lemma that gives the upper and lower bounds of the mutual information between f and h when $D(f \triangle h)$ is given.

Lemma 7. Let f and h be concepts and D be a probability distribution over X. Suppose that $D(f \triangle h) = \alpha$ for some $0 \leq \alpha \leq 1$. Then,

$$H_n(p) - H_n(a) \leq I_D(f;h) \leq H_n(p) - (p + a)H_n\left(\frac{a}{p + a}\right),$$

where $p = \min\{D(f), 1 - D(f)\}$ and $a = \min\{\alpha, 1 - \alpha\}$.

The proof of this lemma is straightforward but boaring, so we put it away in the appendix of this paper.

Note that since the mutual information is always non-negative, the inequality above says nothing about the lower bound on $I_D(f;h)$ when $H_n(p) < H_n(a)$.

By virtue of this lemma, it is easy to show the equivalence between strong PAC-learning and strong MI-gaining algorithms.

Theorem 8. A is a strong PAC-learning algorithm for F if and only if A is a strong MI-gaining algorithm for F

Proof. Suppose that A is a strong PAC-learning algorithm for F. Fix ε and δ arbitrarily, and put $\varepsilon' = \varepsilon^2/4$. Then, there exists an m such that for any f in F and any probability distribution D over X, when algorithm A is given a sample of size at least m, algorithm A, with probability at least $1 - \delta$, outputs h such that $D(f \triangle h) \leq \varepsilon'$. By Lemma 7, $D(f \triangle h) \leq \varepsilon'$ implies $I_D(f;h) \geq H_n(D(f)) - H_n(\varepsilon')$. Since $H_n(x) < 2\sqrt{x}$ for any x, this implies $I_D(f;h) \geq H_n(D(f)) - 2\sqrt{\varepsilon'} = H_n(D(f)) - \varepsilon$. Hence, A is also a strong MI-gaining algorithm for F.

Conversely, suppose that A is a strong MI-gaining algorithm for F. Fix ε and δ arbitrarily, and put $\varepsilon' = \varepsilon^2/4$. Then, there exists an m such that for any f in F and any probability distribution D over X, when algorithm A is given a sample of size at least m, algorithm A, with probability at least $1 - \delta$, outputs h such that $I(f; h) \geq H_n(D(f)) - \varepsilon'$. By Lemma 7, $I(f; h) \geq H_n(D(f)) - \varepsilon'$ implies $(p + a)H_n\left(\frac{a}{p+a}\right) \leq \varepsilon'$, where $p = \min\{D(f), 1 - D(f)\}$ and $a = \min\{D(f \triangle h), 1 - D(f \triangle h)\}$. Since $H_n(x) \geq x$ or $H_n(x) \geq 1 - x$ for any x, this implies $p \leq \varepsilon'$ or $a \leq \varepsilon'$. If $p \leq \varepsilon'$, then $H_n(D(f)) \leq 2\sqrt{\varepsilon'} = \varepsilon$. In this case, $h = \phi$ and thus $a \leq \varepsilon'$. So, A is also a strong PAC-learning algorithm for F. $\quad\square$

Note that the sample size m that satisfies the $(\varepsilon^2/4, \delta)$-condition for strong PAC-learning also satisfies the (ε, δ)-condition for strong MI-gaining. Since the sample size for strong PAC-learning is a polynomial in $1/\varepsilon$ and $1/\delta$[1], so is for strong MIG-gaining.

On the other hand, weak PAC-learning does not necessarily imply weak MI-gaining, and weak MI-gaining does not necessarily imply weak PAC-learning. We show these results in the following two theorems.

Theorem 9. There exists a weak PAC-learning algorithm A for F that is not a weak MI-gaining algorithm for F.

Proof. Let F be a concept class that is weak PAC-learnable, and let A be a weak PAC-learning algorithm for F. Then, we can construct a learning algorithm A' that behaves as follows. First A' estimates the value of $D(f)$. If $D(f) > 1/3$, then A' simulates A and outputs the hypothesis that A outputs. Otherwise A' outputs the empty set. Clearly A' is still a weak PAC-learning algorithm for F. Now let $D(f) = 1/4$. Then, with high probability, A outputs the empty hypothesis even if δ is smaller than $H_n(1/4)$, i.e., $H_n(D(f)) \geq \delta$ holds. Since the empty hypothesis has zero mutual information with any target concept, the theorem follows. $\quad\square$

Next in Theorem 10, considering a learning algorithm with one-sided error, we give a natural example of weak MI-gaining algorithms which are not weak PAC-learning algorithms. As stated in the previous section, the mutual information between the random variables corresponding to a target concept and a hypothesis can possibly be large even if the error of the hypothesis is around $1/2$.

Theorem 10. There exists a weak MI-gaining algorithm A for F that is not a weak PAC-learning algorithm for F.

Proof. Let F be a concept class that can be strongly PAC-learnable with one-sided error. Then, it is easy to construct an algorithm A that behaves as follows for any target concept f. First A estimates the value of $D(f)$. If $D(f) \leq 4/5$, then A, with high probability, outputs a hypothesis h that is contained in f such that $D(f \triangle h)$ is around $2D(f)/3$. Otherwise, A strongly learns f.

First we show that A is not a weak PAC-learning algorithm for F. Let $D(f) = 3/4$. Then, with high probability, A outputs h with $D(f \triangle h)$ around $1/2$. More precisely, there is no constant that bounds $|D(f \triangle h) - 1/2|$ from below. Thus, A is not a weak PAC-learning algorithm for F.

Next we show that A is a weak MI-gaining algorithm for F. When $D(f) \leq 4/5$, A outputs h with $h \subseteq f$ and $D(f \triangle h) = 2D(f)/3$. This is the case that $p_0 = 1 - D(f)$, $p_1 = D(f)$, $\alpha_0 = 0$ and $\alpha_1 = 2/3$ in Fig. 1. Therefore, Theorem 3 says that $I_D(f;h) = H_n(\frac{p_1}{3}) - p_1 H_n(\frac{1}{3})$. By a standard analysis, we can show that there exists a constant $\gamma > 0$ such that $I_D(f;h) \geq \gamma H_n(p_1)$. When $D(f) > 4/5$, A behaves as a strong PAC-learning algorithm for F. So, by Theorem 8 and Theorem 6, the theorem follows. $\qquad\square$

5   On the sufficiency for boosting

In this section, we discuss about a boosting scheme that transforms a weak learning algorithm to a strong learning algorithm. A boosting scheme combines many hypotheses produced by a weak learning algorithm into a master hypothesis. Here, the process to form a master hypothesis can be viewed as accumulation of small amount of information brought by weak hypothesis. So, it seems that the efficiency of boosting is determined by how much information each hypothesis contains.

As we have seen in the previous section, a hypothesis produced by a weak PAC-learning algorithm may have zero mutual information depending on the probability distribution. Nevertheless, Schapire [6] and Freund [2] gave efficient boosting schemes for weak PAC-learning algorithms. Especially, the boosting scheme of Freund uses only $O(\log 1/\varepsilon)$ weak hypotheses to achieve an ε-approximation.

On the other hand, a weak MI-gaining algorithm outputs a hypothesis with positive mutual information for any distribution except around the extremes. So, the questions that we have to solve are: Is there a boosting scheme for weak MI-gaining algorithms? And, if it exists, how efficient the scheme is? Natarajan gave a boosting scheme for a class of learning algorithms with one-sided error[5], which turns out to be a special case of weak MI-gaining algorithms as stated in the proof of Theorem 10. His scheme is very simple, and uses $O(\log 1/\varepsilon)$ weak hypotheses to achieve an ε-approximation. We show in this section that there exists a general boosting scheme for weak MI-gaining algorithms using also $O(\log 1/\varepsilon)$ hypotheses. But it is left as an open problem to decide whether the number of hypotheses can be reduced.

First we give a definition of boosting schemes formally.

Definition 11. Let A be a weak MI-gaining algorithm and γ and m be the information gain and the sample complexity (a function in δ) associated with A. By $B(\gamma, m, A)$ we mean a learning algorithm with additional inputs γ, m, and A. B is a boosting scheme for a class M of weak MI-gaining algorithms if for any A in M that is a weak MI-gaining algorithm for some concept class F, $B(\gamma, m, A)$ is a strong MI-gaining algorithm for F.

Note in the above definition that the boosting scheme B for M is uniform in the sense that it is independent of $A \in M$.

Now we show a uniform transformation from weak MI-gaining algorithms to weak PAC-learning algorithms. This transformation combined with the boosting scheme of Schapire or Freund gives a boosting scheme for the weak MI-gaining algorithms.

Lemma 12. If A is a weak MI-gaining algorithm for F, then a weak PAC-learning algorithm B can be constructed from A.

Proof. Let A be a weak MI-gaining algorithm for F and γ be the information gain of A. Let γ' be a constant sufficiently small positive constant. Then, the algorithm B works as follows. B first estimates $D(f)$. Then if $|D(f) - 1/2| > \gamma'$ then B outputs the empty set as its hypothesis, and otherwise B simulates A and outputs the hypothesis produced by A. Let h denotes the hypothesis B outputs. Clearly in the case that $|D(f) - 1/2| > \gamma'$, $|D(f \bigtriangleup h) - 1/2| > \gamma'$ holds. So, it suffices to show that if $|D(f) - 1/2| \le \gamma'$, A outputs a hypothesis h such that $|D(f \bigtriangleup h) - 1/2| > \gamma'$. Since A is a weak MI-gaining algorithm, Lemma 7 says that

$$\gamma H_n(p) \le I_D(f; h) \le H_n(p) - (p + a)H_n(\frac{a}{p + a}),$$

where $p = \min\{D(f), 1 - D(f)\} > 1/2 - \gamma'$ and $a = \min\{D(f \bigtriangleup h), 1 - D(f \bigtriangleup h)\}$. This implies that

$$(p + a)H_n(\frac{a}{p + a}) \le (1 - \gamma)H_n(p) < (1 - \gamma)H_n(1/2 - \gamma').$$

Now assume that $a > 1/2 - \gamma'$. Then, we would have

$$(1 - 2\gamma') \le (1 - \gamma)H_n(1/2 - \gamma') \le (1 - \gamma)(1 - 2(\log e)\gamma'^2),$$

which is a contradiction when γ' is a sufficiently small constant. $\square$

Thus, we have the boosting scheme for weak MI-gaining algorithms.

Theorem 13. There exists a boosting scheme for weak MI-gaining algorithms.

Unfortunately, this scheme is constructed by help of the scheme for weak PAC-learning algorithms. So, in order to achieve an ε-approximation to the target concept, It requires weak hypotheses as many as that for weak PAC-learning algorithms. If we could find a boosting scheme directly, the scheme would be more efficient.

Appendix: Proof of Lemma 7

In this appendix, we give the sketch of proof of Lemma 7.

Lemma 7 Let f and h be concepts and D be a probability distribution over X. Suppose that $D(f \triangle h) = \alpha$ for some $0 \leq \alpha \leq 1$. Then,

$$H_n(p) - H_n(a) \leq I_D(f; h) \leq H_n(p) - (p + a)H_n\left(\frac{a}{p + a}\right),$$

where $p = \min\{D(f), 1 - D(f)\}$ and $a = \min\{\alpha, 1 - \alpha\}$.

Proof. Let α_0 and α_1 be negative and positive errors of h, respectively. That is, $\alpha_0 = D(h - f)$ and $\alpha_1 = D(f - h)$. Note that $p_0 \alpha_0 + p_1 \alpha_1 = \alpha$. Then, by Theorem 3,

$$I(f; h) = H_n(\alpha_0 p_0 + (1 - \alpha_1)p_1) - \{p_0 H_n(\alpha_0) + p_1 H_n(\alpha_1)\}.$$

We can regard $I(f; h)$ as a function of α_0 and α_1, and rewrite it as $I(\alpha_0, \alpha_1)$. Thus, the problem we have to solve is to show the minimum and the maximum values of $I(\alpha_0, \alpha_1)$ on the condition that $p_0 \alpha_0 + p_1 \alpha_1 = \alpha$.

Since $\frac{d}{dx} H_n(x) = (\log e) \log \frac{1-x}{x}$,

$$\frac{d}{d\alpha_1} I(\alpha_0, \alpha_1) = -2p_1 (\log e) \log \frac{1 - \alpha_0 p_0 - (1 - \alpha_1)p_1}{\alpha_0 p_0 + (1 - \alpha_1)p_1} + p_1 (\log e) \log \frac{1 - \alpha_0}{\alpha_0}$$

$$- p_1 (\log e) \log \frac{1 - \alpha_1}{\alpha_1}.$$

Note that α_0 is an implicit function of α_1. Using the fact that $(\alpha_0 p_0 + (1 - \alpha_1)p_1) + ((1 - \alpha_0)p_0 + \alpha_1 p_1) = 1$, we have

$$\frac{d}{d\alpha_1} I(\alpha_0, \alpha_1) = (p_1 \log e) \log \left\{ \left(\frac{\alpha_0 p_0 + (1 - \alpha_1)p_1}{(1 - \alpha_0)p_0 + \alpha_1 p_1} \right)^2 \left(\frac{1 - \alpha_0}{\alpha_0} \right) \left(\frac{\alpha_1}{1 - \alpha_1} \right) \right\}.$$

Thus, the sign of the function

$$J(\alpha_1) = \left(\frac{\alpha_0 p_0 + (1 - \alpha_1)p_1}{(1 - \alpha_0)p_0 + \alpha_1 p_1} \right)^2 \left(\frac{1 - \alpha_0}{\alpha_0} \right) \left(\frac{\alpha_1}{1 - \alpha_1} \right) - 1$$

indicates the increase and decrease behavior of $I(\alpha_0, \alpha_1)$. Let

$$A = (\alpha_0 p_0 + (1 - \alpha_1)p_1)^2 (1 - \alpha_0)\alpha_1$$

and

$$B = ((1 - \alpha_0)p_0 + \alpha_1 p_1)^2 \alpha_0 (1 - \alpha_1).$$

Then,

$$J(\alpha_1) = \frac{A - B}{B}$$

$$= \frac{1}{B}(\alpha_0 + \alpha_1 - 1)(p_1^2\alpha_1^2 - p_0^2\alpha_0^2 - p_1^2\alpha_1 + p_0^2\alpha_0).$$

Eliminating α_0 by using $\alpha_0 = \frac{\alpha - p_1\alpha_1}{p_0}$, we have

$$J(\alpha_1) = \frac{1}{p_0 B}\big((1 - 2p_1)\alpha_1 + \alpha + p_1 - 1\big)\big((2\alpha - 1)p_1\alpha_1 + (1 - p_1 - \alpha)\alpha\big).$$

Let J_1 and J_2 be the first and second terms of the above equation, respectively. Since B is non-negative, the sign of J is the product of those of J_1 and J_2.

Now, we estimate the signs of J_1 and J_2 to obtain the increase-decrease behavior of $I(\alpha_0, \alpha_1)$ for various combination of p_1 and α.

Case 1: $0 < p_1 < 1/2$ and $p_1 \leq \alpha \leq 1 - p_1$

α_1	$0 \sim$	$\frac{1-\alpha-p_1}{1-2p_1}$	~ 1
J_1	$-$	0	$+$
J_2		$+$	
J	$-$	0	$+$
I	$\searrow$	0	$\nearrow$

Case 2: $1/2 < \alpha \leq 1$ and $1 - \alpha \leq p_1 \leq \alpha$

α_1	$0 \sim$	$\frac{(1-\alpha-p_1)\alpha}{(1-2\alpha)p_1}$	~ 1
J_1		$+$	
J_2	$-$	0	$+$
J	$-$	0	$+$
I	$\searrow$	$|H(p_1) - H(\alpha)|$	$\nearrow$

Case 3: $1/2 < p_1 < 1$ and $1 - p_1 \leq \alpha \leq p_1$

α_1	$0 \sim$	$\frac{1-\alpha-p_1}{1-2p_1}$	~ 1
J_1	$+$	0	$-$
J_2		$-$	
J	$-$	0	$+$
I	$\searrow$	0	$\nearrow$

Case 4: $0 \leq \alpha < 1/2$ and $\alpha \leq p_1 \leq 1 - \alpha$

α_1	$0 \sim$	$\frac{(1-\alpha-p_1)\alpha}{(1-2\alpha)p_1}$	~ 1
J_1		$-$	
J_2	$+$	0	$-$
J	$-$	0	$+$
I	$\searrow$	$|H(p_1) - H(\alpha)|$	$\nearrow$

Case 5: $p_1 = \alpha = 1/2$

α_1	$0 \sim 1$
J_1	0
J_2	0
J	0
I	0

Thus, in either case, we have $I(\alpha_0, \alpha_1) \geq H_n(p_1) - H(\alpha)$. Moreover, $I(\alpha_0, \alpha_1)$ becomes maximum when $\alpha_0 = 0$ or $\alpha_1 = 0$. Estimating the value at these extreme points carefully, we have the upper bound for $I(\alpha_0, \alpha_1)$. □

In the proof above, we can see that the maximum mutual information gain is achieved by the hypothesis with one-sided error, i.e., $\alpha_0 = 0$ or $\alpha_1 = 0$. More precisely, the hypothesis with one-sided error brings us the maximum mutual information about a target concept among those hypotheses with the same accuracy. This implies that one-sided error learning algorithms are optimal in the sense of MI-gaining.

References

1. A. Blumer, A. Ehrenfeucht, D. Haussler, and M. K. Warmuth. Learnability and the Vapnik-Chervonenkis dimension. *Journal of the Association for Computing Machinery*, 36(4):929–965, Aug. 1989.
2. Y. Freund. Boosting a weak learning algorithm by majority. In *Proceedings of the 3rd Workshop on Computational Learning Theory*, pages 202–216, 1990.
3. D. Haussler, M. Kearns, and R. Schapire. Bounds on the sample complexity of bayesian learning using information theory and the vc dimension. In *Proceedings of the 4th Workshop on Computational Learning Theory*, 1991.
4. D. Helmbold and M. K. Warmuth. Some weak learning results. In *Proceedings of the 5th Workshop on Computational Learning Theory*, 1992.
5. B. K. Natarajan. *Machine Learning: A Theoretical Approach*. Morgan Kaufmann, San Mateo, 1991.
6. R. Schapire. The strength of weak learnability. In *Proceedings of the 30th Annual IEEE Symposium on Foundations of Computer Science*, pages 28–33, 1989.

Inductive Inference of
Monogenic Pure Context-free Languages

Noriyuki TANIDA*and Takashi YOKOMORI[†]

Department of Computer Science and Information Mathematics,
University of Electro-Communications,
1-5-1, Chofugaoka, Chofu, Tokyo, 182 JAPAN

Abstract

This paper concerns a subclass of context-free languages, called *pure context-free languages*, which is generated by context-free grammar with only one type of symbol (i.e., terminals and nonterminals are not distinguished), and investigates the problem of identifying from positive data a restricted class of monogenic pure context-free languages (mono-PCF languages, in short). The class of mono-PCF languages is incomparable to the class of regular languages.

We show that the class of mono-PCF languages is polynomial time identifiable from positive data. That is, there is an algorithm that, given a mono-PCF language L, identifies from positive data, a grammar generating L, called a monogenic pure context-free grammar (mono-PCF grammar) satisfying the property that the time for updating a conjecture is bounded by $O(N^3)$, where N is the sum of lengths of all positive data provided. This is in contrast with another result in this paper that the class of PCF languages is not identifiable in the limit from positive data.

1 Introduction

Inductive inference is a process of hypothesizing a general rule from examples. We adopt Gold's "identification in the limit" as a criterion for inductive inference. In the study of inductive inference of formal languages, Gold ([Gol67]) showed that the class of languages containing all finite sets and one infinite set (this class is called *superfinite*) is not identifiable in the limit from positive data only. This fact was shocking in the sense that even the class of regular languages is not identifiable in the limit from positive data.

Angluin ([Ang80]) has given several conditions for the class of languages to be identifiable in the limit from positive data, and presented some examples of identifiable classes. She has also proposed subclasses of regular languages called k-reversible languages for each $k \geq 0$ and shown these classes are identifiable in the limit from positive data with the polynomial time of updating conjectures ([Ang82]).

---

*E-mail : tanida@eliot.cs.uec.ac.jp
[†]E-mail : yokomori@base.cs.uec.ac.jp

Although a superfinite class is not identifiable in the limit from positive data, when we think of the practical application of inference algorithms, we believe that "efficient" identification is more important than "wide" identification.

Informally, we say that a class of languages $\mathcal{L}$ is *identifiable in the limit in polynomial time* using a class of representations $\mathcal{R}$ if and only if there is an algorithm $\mathcal{A}$ which, given L in $\mathcal{L}$, identifies r in $\mathcal{R}$ representing L in the limit, with the property that there exists a polynomial p such that the time for updating a conjecture is at most $p(N)$, where N is the sum of lengths of data provided.

This paper concerns a special type of grammars, called *pure context-free grammars* (PCF grammars, in short). Pure grammars are thought of as semi-Thue systems without nonterminals.

Conventionally, the distinction between terminals and nonterminals has been widely and reasonablly accepted in formal language theory. There is, however, another type of linguistic research stream where no distinction is made between the two alphabets. The idea of string analysis by Harris ([Har81]) is one of such exceptions. A version of string analysis, called string adjunct grammars, was formalized by Joshi et al. ([JKY72]) to characterize certain aspects of natural language structures. One can find some arguments in relation to the applicability of their grammars to natural languages, which seems to give some justifications to the study of such grammars that operate on only terminal strings.

Another exception of this kind is well known as L-systems where every (terminal) symbol in a string is rewritten in parallel. This idea was originally proposed from biological motivations and, afterwards, has been extensively investigated from formal language theoretic view point as well. In this respect, pure grammars might be taken as a *sequential* counterpart of L-systems.

On the other hand, the study on properties of sentential forms of a Chomsky type grammar is sometimes of great importance in linguistic context, and the class of sets of such forms, in fact, constitutes a class of languages generated by pure grammars.

Thus, pure grammars have a variety of connections to other grammatical tools with the common feature, i.e., monotonicity in alphabet.

In this paper, we mainly restrict ourselves to the class of *monogenic pure context-free languages* (mono-PCF languages, in short), and show that the class is identifiable in the limit in polynomial time using mono-PCF grammars. In fact, the identification of this class is achieved using only positive data.

2 Definitions

2.1 Basic Definitions and Notations

We assume the reader to be familiar with the basics of formal language theory. If not stated here, we follow the conventional and standard notions and notations in formal language theory (e.g., [Har78], [HU79]). An *alphabet* Σ is a finite set of symbols. The set Σ^* consists of all finite length sequences formed by concatenating zero or more elements of Σ. Elements of Σ^* are called *strings*. The unique string of length 0 is denoted by λ. Further, let $\Sigma^+ = \Sigma^* - \{\lambda\}$. By $lg(u)$ we denote the length of a string u. A *language* over Σ is any subset L of Σ^*. The concatenation of strings u and v is denoted by uv. The cardinality of a set S is denoted by $|S|$.

2.2 Pure Languages and Pure Grammars

Now, we introduce the notion of a special type of languages and grammars. The description here, is based on [MSW80], [Mäk86] and [Mäk91].

A pure grammar is defined as a triple $G = (\Sigma, P, S)$, where Σ is a finite alphabet, S is a finite subset of Σ^+, and P is a finite set of *productions* of the form $x \rightarrow y$, where x and y are strings over Σ. An element of S is called *axiom*.

A string w is said to *directly generate* w' by using the production of G, written $w \Rightarrow_G w'$ (or briefly $w \Rightarrow w'$ when G is understood), if and only if there exist w_1 and w_2 and $x \rightarrow y$ in P such that $w = w_1 x w_2$ and $w' = w_1 y w_2$.

We denote the reflexive and transitive closure of $\Rightarrow$ by $\overset{*}{\Rightarrow}$.

The language generated by G is defined as follows :

$$L(G) = \{w \mid s \overset{*}{\Rightarrow} w, \text{ for some } s \in S\}.$$

Languages generated by pure grammars are referred to as *pure languages*.

We say that G is *length-increasing* if and only if each production $x \rightarrow y$ has the property such that $lg(x) \leq lg(y)$, and denote by PLI grammar and PLI language for a pure length-increasing grammar and pure length-increasing language generated by PLI grammars, respectively. We call G a *pure context-free* grammar (abbr. PCF grammar) if and only if for each production $x \rightarrow y$ of P, x is a symbol. A symbol of Σ is said to be *active* if and only if it appears as the lefthand side of some production of P. Languages generated by PCF grammars are called *pure context-free* languages (abbr. PCF languages).

Finally, we define some important notions of pure grammars. A pure grammar G is said to be *monogenic* if and only if, whenever w is in $L(G)$ and $w \Rightarrow w'$, then there exist unique strings w_1 and w_2 such that $w = w_1 x w_2$ and $w' = w_1 y w_2$, and $x \rightarrow y$ is a production and, moreover, there is no string w'' such that $w'' \neq w'$ and $w \Rightarrow w''$. Thus, each string generated by a monogenic grammar is uniquely determined by its predecessor in a derivation, i.e., the production to apply and the position of application in the predecessor. A monogenic PCF grammar (mono-PCF grammar) G is said to be *reduced* if and only if $Alph(L(G)) = \Sigma$, where $Alph(L(G))$ denote the set of all symbols in $L(G)$. A PCF grammar is said to be *deterministic* if and only if for each alphabet symbol there is at most one production.

Remark 1 There are languages defined by sentential forms of context-free grammars (*sentential form languages* (SFL)). An SFL is a language generated by a special type of PCF grammar. In fact, an SFL is generated by a PCF grammar with a single start symbol of length 1.

Remark 2 For a monogenic PCF grammar G, if G is reduced, then G is clearly deterministic. However, in general, deterministic PCF grammars are not always monogenic.

Example 2.1 The language $\{a^n c b^n \mid n \geq 1\}$ is generated by a PCF grammar $G = (\{a, b, c\}, P, S)$, where $S = \{acb\}$, $P = \{c \rightarrow acb\}$. G is reduced and monogenic, and hence, deterministic. On the other hand, a language $\{a^n b^n \mid n \geq 1\}$ is not PCF. $\square$

2.3 Polynomial-time identification in the limit

Let $\mathcal{L}$ be a class of languages over a fixed alphabet Σ. Further, let $\mathcal{G}$ be the class of grammars such that for all $L \in \mathcal{L}$, there exists $G \in \mathcal{G}$ such that $L = L(G)$.

Let G be a grammar in $\mathcal{G}$ representing a given L (i.e., $L = L(G)$). A *positive presentation* of language L is any infinite sequence of strings such that every string $w \in L$ occurs at least once in the sequence, and no other strings not in $L(G)$ occur in the sequence.

An algorithm $\mathcal{A}$ is said to *identify a language L in the limit from positive data using $\mathcal{G}$* if and only if for any positive presentation of L the infinite sequence of G_is in $\mathcal{G}$ produced by $\mathcal{A}$ satisfies the property that there exists G in $\mathcal{G}$ such that for all sufficiently large i, the i-th conjecture G_i is identical to G and $L(G) = L$. A class of languages $\mathcal{L}$ is *identifiable in the limit from positive data using $\mathcal{G}$* if and only if there exists an algorithm $\mathcal{A}$ that, given an L in $\mathcal{L}$, identifies L in the limit from positive data using $\mathcal{G}$. In this paper we omit a phrase "using $\mathcal{G}$, if no confusion arises.

We are interested in the question of whether or not there exists an efficient algorithm (or polynomial time algorithm) that identifies the class of languages in the limit from positive data.

A class $\mathcal{L}$ is *polynomial-time* identifiable in the limit from positive data using $\mathcal{G}$ if and only if (1) $\mathcal{L}$ is identifiable in the limit from positive data using $\mathcal{G}$, and (2) the inference algorithm $\mathcal{A}$ for $\mathcal{L}$ satisfies the property that there exists a polynomial p such that for any L in $\mathcal{L}$ and for any positive presentation of L, the time used by $\mathcal{A}$ between receiving the i-th example w_i and outputting the i-th conjectured grammar G_i is at most $p(l_1 + \cdots + l_i)$, where $l_j = lg(w_j)$.

3 Preliminary Results

We summarize some results from [Gab81] and [MSW80].

Fact 1 ([Gab81], [MSW80])

(i) The family of pure languages over a one-symbol alphabet $\{a\}$ conincides with the family of regular languages over $\{a\}$.

(ii) There are non-recursive pure languages.

(iii) Every regular language is generated by a PLI grammar.   □

Let us consider the differences as follows :

$$\mathcal{L}(\text{RE}) - \mathcal{L}(\text{REC}), \mathcal{L}(\text{REC}) - \mathcal{L}(\text{CS}), \mathcal{L}(\text{CS}) - \mathcal{L}(\text{CF}), \mathcal{L}(\text{CF}) - \mathcal{L}(\text{REG}),$$

where $\mathcal{L}(\text{RE})$, $\mathcal{L}(\text{REC})$, $\mathcal{L}(\text{CS})$, $\mathcal{L}(\text{CF})$, $\mathcal{L}(\text{REG})$ denotes the class of recursively enumerable, recursive, context-sensitive, context-free and regular languages, respectively.

Fact 2 ([MSW80])

(i) Each difference above contains both of pure and non-pure languages.

(ii) All PLI languages are context-sensitive and constitute a proper subclass of pure languages.

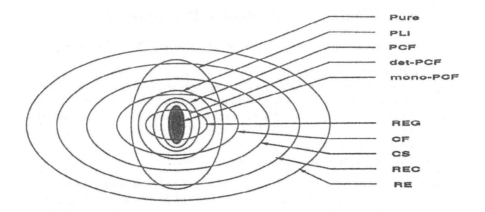

Figure 1: Relations of language classes

(iii) Every reduced mono-PCF grammar is deterministic. But the converse of it does not necessarily true. □

Fact 3 ([MSW80]) Every mono-PCF language L is a finite union of languages of the form $\{xu^n bv^n y | n \geq 1\}$, where x, u, v, y are strings and b is a symbol.

PROOF. Let $G = (\Sigma, P, S)$ be a mono-PCF grammar. From the definition of mono-PCF grammar, we know that no word generated by G can have two or more different active symbols. Thus, we can deduce that an axiom w of G uniquely defines the following derivation :

$$w = xb_0 y \Rightarrow xu_1 b_1 v_1 y \Rightarrow xu_1 u_2 b_2 v_2 v_1 y \Rightarrow \cdots \Rightarrow xu_1 \cdots u_i b_i v_i \cdots v_1 y \Rightarrow \cdots .$$

Let i be the smallest integer such that $b_i = b_j$ for some $j > i$. Then, all the words derived from an axiom w are :

$$(*) \begin{cases} xb_0 y, \ xu_1 b_1 v_1 y, \ \cdots, \ xu_1 \cdots u_i b_i v_i \cdots v_1 y, \ \ldots, \\ xu_1 \cdots u_i \cdots u_{j-1} b_{j-1} v_{j-1} \cdots v_i \cdots v_1 y, \\ \{xu_1 \cdots u_i (u_{i+1} \cdots u_j)^n b_i (v_j \cdots v_{i+1})^n v_i \cdots v_1 y | n \geq 1\}, \\ \cdots \\ \{xu_1 \cdots u_{j-1} (u_j u_{i+1} \cdots u_{j-1})^n b_{j-1} (v_{j-1} \cdots v_{i+1} v_j)^n v_{j-1} \cdots v_1 y | n \geq 1\}. \end{cases}$$

This takes the form of a finite union of languages $\{xu^n bv^n y | n \geq 1\}$. □

The next fact suggests a monogenicity can be obtained in the transition from PCF grammars to PLI grammars.

Fact 4 ([MSW80]) There is a PCF language L which is not mono-PCF but is mono-PLI. □

From above facts, we can obtain the structure of the classes of languages as Figure. 1.

4 Identification of mono-PCF languages

4.1 Negative results for identifiability of PCF languages

We first consider the learnability of the class of PCF languages in the limit from positive data. However, the class of PCF languages is not learnable from positive data because this class is obviously superfinite. (Note that an axiom set S in PCF grammar can be arbitrary finite set.) Furthermore, unfortunately, we can also show a negative result even for the class of restricted PCF languages generated by PCF grammar with a single axiom.

The following theorem is essential for our purpose.

Theorem 4.1 ([Ang80]) *Let* $\Gamma = L_1, L_2, \ldots$ *be an indexed class of nonempty recursive languages. Then, the class* Γ *is identifiable in the limit from positive data if and only if it satisfies the condition : there exists an effective procedure which on any input* $i \geq 1$ *enumerates a set of strings* T_i *such that* (i) T_i *is finite,* (ii) $T_i \subseteq L_i$, *and* (iii) *for* $j \geq 1 \neg (T_i \subseteq L_j \subset L_i)$.

Lemma 4.2 *The class of PCF languages restricted as above is not identifiable from positive data.*

PROOF. Let PCF grammar $G = (\Sigma, R, S)$, where $\Sigma = \{a, b, c, d, e\}$, $R = \{b \rightarrow ae, e \rightarrow ee, e \rightarrow c, e \rightarrow d\}$ and $S = \{b\}$. Then, clearly $L' = L(G) = a(\Sigma - \{a, b\})^+ \cup \{b\}$.

Given any subset $T = \{t_1, t_2, \ldots, t_k\}$ of L', we construct a language : $L_T = (t_1 + t_2 + \cdots + t_k)^+ \cup \{b\}$ (In case when T contains $b(= t_k)$, then $L_T = (t_1 + \cdots + t_{k-1})^+ \cup \{b\}$). This language is generated by a PCF grammar $(\Sigma, R, \{b\})$, where $P = \{b \rightarrow t_i, a \rightarrow t_i a\}$ $(i = 1, \ldots, k)$. Obviously it holds that $T \subseteq L_T \subseteq L'$. Furthermore, take $s = ac^m$ from L', where $m = \max_{i=1,\ldots,k} lg(t_i) + 1$. Then, since $lg(t_i) < m$ $(i = 1, \ldots, k)$, we have $s \notin L_T$. Thus, we can get $L_T \subset L'$. Hence, the class of PCF languages is not identifiable from positive data. □

Thus, in order to obtain a positive result for learning PCF languages, we will make another restriction to PCF grammars in the next subsection.

4.2 The identification algorithm for mono-PCF languages

We now consider the problem of learning the class of mono-PCF languages and show that the class is polynomial-time identifiable in the limit form positive data.

In fact, we describe an identification algorithm $\mathcal{A}$ for mono-PCF language. In this paper, for simplicity, we consider the algorithm which learns a mono-PCF grammar with a single axiom. However, the algorithm can be easily extended to a mono-PCF grammar with k axioms for a given k.

Let L be a mono-PCF language over $\Sigma = \{a_1, \ldots, a_m\}$ and $T_i = \{w_1, \ldots, w_i\}$ be a finite sample set of positive examples of L provided up to the i-th stage of the inference process.

(1) **Updating production set P**
We describe the manner of updating P.

Let w_i be the i-th positive example provided at the i-th stage of the inference process and let $G_i = (\Sigma, P_i, S_0)$ be the conjectured mono-PCF grammar at the i-th stage. (Unless any confusion arises, P_i is denoted by P.)

Now, suppose that w_i is not consistent with G_{i-1}, that is, $w_i \notin L(G_{i-1})$.

In the procedure, we use the following notations :

- $\mathrm{lcp}(u, v)$ denotes the longest common prefix of u and v and

- $\mathrm{lcs}(u, v)$ denotes the longest common suffix of u and v.

When $\mathrm{lcp}(u, v)$ and $\mathrm{lcs}(u, v)$ are well-defined, we can describe : $u = \mathrm{lcp}(u, v)x\mathrm{lcs}(u, v)$ and $v = \mathrm{lcp}(u, v)y\mathrm{lcs}(u, v)$, where $x, y \in \Sigma^*$. Assuming $lg(x) \le lg(y)$, we use the following notations :

- $\mathrm{rem\text{-}short}(u, v)$ denotes x, and

- $\mathrm{rem\text{-}long}(u, v)$ denotes y.

Example 4.1 Let $u = abcdefg$ and $v = abhfg$. Then, we can get the followings : $\mathrm{lcp}(u, v) = ab$, $\mathrm{lcs}(u, v) = fg$, $\mathrm{rem\text{-}short}(u, v) = h$, $\mathrm{rem\text{-}long}(u, v) = cde$. □

Remark 3 If L is a mono-PCF language and u, v are in L, then $\mathrm{lcp}(u, v)$ and $\mathrm{lcp}(u, v)$ are uniquely determined. Furthermore, $\mathrm{rem\text{-}short}(u, v)$ is a symbol.

Now we describe the procedure "UPDATE" that, given u, v and a current production set produces the new production, where each rule is in the form of $\gamma \rightarrow p\delta q$, where γ and δ are active symbols and $p, q \in \Sigma^*$.

Procedure UPDATE(P, u, v) :
let $P = \{a_1 \rightarrow t_{a_1}, \ldots, a_m \rightarrow t_{a_m}\}$;
let $\mathrm{rem\text{-}short}(u, v) = \alpha (\in \Sigma)$;
let $\mathrm{rem\text{-}long}(u, v) = \beta$;
if $lg(u) = lg(v)$ then
   case $(t_\alpha = \alpha \wedge t_\beta = \beta)$
      replace $\alpha \rightarrow \alpha$ with $\alpha \rightarrow \beta$ in P
   case $(t_x = x \wedge t_y \ne y)\,(x, y \in \{\alpha, \beta\})$
      let $t_y = u_1$ (i.e., $y \rightarrow u_1$);
      replace $y \rightarrow u_1$ with $y \rightarrow x$ in P;
      replace $x \rightarrow x$ with $x \rightarrow u_1$ in P
   case $(t_\alpha \ne \alpha \wedge t_\beta \ne \beta)$
      let $t_\alpha = u_2$ and $t_\beta = v_2$;
      replace $\alpha \rightarrow u_2$ with $\alpha \rightarrow \beta$ in P;
      call **UPDATE**(P, u_2, v_2)
else $(lg(u) \ne lg(v))$
   begin
      if $t_\alpha = \alpha$ then replace $\alpha \rightarrow \alpha$ with $\alpha \rightarrow \beta$ in P;
      else call **UPDATE**(P, t_α, β).
   end

(2) Identification algorithm $\mathcal{A}$

The identification algorithm $\mathcal{A}$ is described by using procedure **UPDATE** as follows :

Algorithm $\mathcal{A}$:
Input : a positive presentation of a mono-PCF language L.
Output : a sequence of mono-PCF grammars for mono-PCF languages.
Procedure :

    let $P = \{a_1 \rightarrow a_1, \ldots, a_m \rightarrow a_m\}$;
    read the first positive example w_1;
    let $T_1 = \{w_1\}$;
    output $G_1 = (\Sigma, P, \{w_1\})$;
    let $i = 2$;
    repeat (forever)
    [i-th stage]
        let $G_{i-1} = (\Sigma, P, S_0)$ be the $(i-1)$-th conjectured mono-PCF grammar;
        let s be the unique element in S_0;
        read the next positive example w_i;
        let $T_i = T_{i-1} \cup \{w_i\}$;
        if $lg(w_i) \leq lg(s)$ **then**;
            begin
                call **UPDATE**(P, w_i, s);
                $S_0 = \{w_i\}$;
            end
        if $w_i \in L(G_{i-1})$ **then** output $G_i(= G_{i-1})$ as the i-th conjecture;
        else
            for all $w \in T_{i-1}$ **do** the following;
            begin
                UPDATE(P, w_i, w);
            end
         output $G_1 = (\Sigma, P, S_0)$ as the i-th conjecture;
        $i := i + 1$.

4.3   The Correctness of $\mathcal{A}$

In order to show the correctness of the algorithm $\mathcal{A}$, we need the notion of a characteristic sample for a target mono-PCF language. Let L be a mono-PCF language. A finite set S is called a *characteristic sample* of L if and only if L is the smallest mono-PCF language containing S ([Ang82]). Firstly, we will show there effectively exists a characteristic sample of mono-PCF languages.

[Constructing Characteristic Sample]

From (*) of Fact. 3 (see Section 3), for any given mono-PCF language L, we have a mono-PCF grammar $G = (\Sigma, P, S_0)$ in *standard form*, where $P = \{b_0 \rightarrow u_1 b_1 v_1, \cdots, b_{i-1} \rightarrow u_i b_i v_i, b_i \rightarrow u_{i+1} b_{i+1} v_{i+1}, \ldots, b_{j-1} \rightarrow u_j b_j v_j\}, S_0 = \{x b_0 y\}$. Then, a mono-PCF language L is given as follows :

$$L = \{xb_0y, xu_1b_1v_1y, \ldots, xu_1 \cdots u_ib_iv_i \cdots v_1y, \ldots,$$
$$xu_1 \cdots u_i \cdots u_{j-1}b_{j-1}v_{j-1} \cdots v_i \cdots v_1y\}$$
$$\cup \{xu_1 \cdots u_i(u_{i+1} \cdots u_j)^n b_i(v_j \cdots v_{i+1})^n v_i \cdots v_1y | n \geq 1\}$$
$$\cdots$$
$$\cup \{xu_1 \cdots u_{j-1}(u_ju_{i+1} \cdots u_{j-1})^n b_{j-1}(v_{j-1} \cdots v_{i+1}v_j)^n v_{j-1} \cdots v_1y | n \geq 1\}.$$

Then construct a finite set S_G of L as follows :

$$S_G = \{xb_0y, xu_1b_1v_1y, \ldots, xu_1 \cdots u_ib_iv_i \cdots v_1y, \ldots,$$
$$xu_1 \cdots u_i \cdots u_{j-1}b_{j-1}v_{j-1} \cdots v_i \cdots v_1y,$$
$$xu_1 \cdots u_i(u_{i+1} \cdots u_j)b_i(v_j \cdots v_{i+1})v_i \cdots v_1y, \ldots,$$
$$xu_1 \cdots u_{j-1}(u_ju_{i+1} \cdots u_{j-1})b_{j-1}(v_{j-1} \cdots v_{i+1}v_j)v_{j-1} \cdots v_1y\}.$$

Example 4.2 Consider a mono-PCF grammar $G = (\Sigma, P, \{xb_0y\})$ with the production set

$$P = \{b_0 \rightarrow u_1b_1v_1, \ b_1 \rightarrow u_2b_2v_2, \ b_2 \rightarrow u_3b_3v_3, b_3 \rightarrow u_4b_2v_4\},$$

where $x, y, u_i, v_i \in \Sigma^*$ $(i = 1, 2, 3, 4)$, $b_i \in \Sigma$ $(i = 0, 1, 2, 3)$. Then S_G is as follows :

$$S_G = \{xb_0y, xu_1b_1v_1y, xu_1u_2b_2v_2v_1y, xu_1u_2u_3b_3v_3v_2v_1y, xu_1u_2u_3u_4b_2v_4v_3v_2v_1y\}.$$

We note that no other strings are in S_G. □

The next lemma is obvious from the definition of mono-PCF languages.

Lemma 4.3 *Let* $L = L(G)$ *be a mono-PCF language. Suppose that* $w_1 = \alpha\beta\gamma$ *and* $w_2 = \alpha b\gamma$ *are in* L *(where* $\alpha, \gamma \in \Sigma^*, \beta \in \Sigma^+$ *and* b *is an active symbol in* G*). Then, there uniquely exists a derivation :* $b \Rightarrow_G \beta$ *and* β *contains exactly one active symbol.* □

Then, we show that a finite set S_G constructed avobe·is a characteristic sample of $L(G)$.

Lemma 4.4 *Let* G *be a mono-PCF grammar such that* $L = L(G)$*. Then, a finite set* S_G *constructed above is a characteristic sample of* L*.*

PROOF. Let $G = (\Sigma, P, S)$ be a mono-PCF grammar for L. Let L' be any mono-PCF language containing S_G, where $L' = L(G')$ and $G' = (\Sigma, P', S')$.

Let w be any string in L. We may assume that L is infinite and w is of the form $x\alpha_1\alpha_2^n b\beta_2^n\beta_1y$ $(n \geq 0)$, where $x, y, \alpha_1, \alpha_2, \beta_1, \beta_2 \in \Sigma^*$, b is an active symbol in G. Consider two strings $w_1 = x\alpha_1b\beta_1y$ and $w_2 = x\alpha_1\alpha_2b\beta_2\beta_1y$ in S_G, where b is active. From Lemma 4.3, w_1 and w_2 specify a derivation $b \Rightarrow_G \alpha_2b\beta_2$. Further, since S_G is contained in L', we also have a derivation $b \Rightarrow_{G'} \alpha_2b\beta_2$.

Then, we show by induction on n that w is in L'.

i) $n = 0$:
    $w = x\alpha_1b\beta_1y \in S_G \subseteq L'.$

ii) $n = k+1$:

Assume that a string $w = x\alpha_1\alpha_2^{k+1}b\beta_2^{k+1}\beta_1 y$ is in L. From the inductive hypothesis, $x\alpha_1\alpha_2^k b\beta_2^k\beta_1 y$ is in L' and moreover there is a derivation $b \Rightarrow_{G'} \alpha_2 b\beta_2$. Thus, we have that w is in L'. □

For each i, let $T_i = \{w_1, \cdots, w_i\}$ be a sample set of L and let G_i be a mono-PCF grammar conjectured by the algorithm $\mathcal{A}$, at the i-th stage.

Now, let us consider the sequence of active symbols used in a derivation of a mono-PCF language. Observing the sequence of active symbols of mono-PCF languages, we see that it forms a *ultimately periodic sequence*, which we call UP-sequence of G. Then, all the active symbols which occur in the UP-sequence are distinct.

To show the next lemma, we introduce the ordering $\preceq_G$ on mono-PCF languages. Let $G = (\Sigma, P, S_0)$ be a mono-PCF grammar for a mono-PCF language L. For any strings $w_1 = \alpha b\beta$ and $w_2 = \alpha u b' v\beta$, $w_1 \preceq_G w_2$ if and only if there exists a derivation $b \Rightarrow_G^* u b' v$. Further, if $w_1 \preceq_G w_2$ and $w_2 \preceq_G w_1$, then $lg(w_1) = lg(w_2)$, and we say that w_1 is equivalent to w_2.

Suppose that there is some length-preserved derivation such that $ua_1v \Rightarrow_G ua_2v \Rightarrow_G \cdots \Rightarrow_G ua_kv$. Since strings $ua_1v, ua_2v, \ldots, ua_kv$ are equivalent each other, those strings may be derived in any order, without changing the language $L(G)$. Because, from the observation above, the active symbols $a_1, \ldots, a_k$ uniquely occur in the UP-sequence of G.

Lemma 4.5 *For each $i \geq 1$, it holds that $T_i \subseteq L(G_i) \subseteq L$.*

PROOF. Let $G = (\Sigma, P, S_0)$ be the target grammar such that $L = L(G)$ and $G_i = (\Sigma, P_i, S_i)$ be the i-th conjecture. Note that each of elements from L is linearly ordered by the relation $\preceq_G$.

(1) We have to show that $T_i \subseteq L(G_i)$ (for each $i \geq 1$). This is proven by induction on i. The case when $i = 1$ is trivially holds. Suppose that w_i in T_i is read by the algorithm $\mathcal{A}$. If $lg(w_i)$ is less than the length of any string in T_{i-1}, then w_i takes place the axiom of G_{i-1}, so it trivially holds that w_i is in $L(G_i)$. Otherwise, since there is a string $w \in T_{i-1}$ such that $lg(w) \leq lg(w_i)$. After **UPDATE**(P_{i-1}, w_i, w) is called, we see that there is a derivation such that $w \Rightarrow_{G_i}^* w_i$, so by the inductive hypothesis, we have that w_i is in $L(G_i)$.

(2) We now show that $L(G_i) \subseteq L$ (for each $i \geq 1$). It suffices to show that the closure of P_i is contained in that of P. This is seen from the manner of constructing a procedure **UPDATE**. □

Thus, it is assured that the identification algorithm $\mathcal{A}$ makes no overgeneralization.

Further, we observe that the manner of constructing **UPDATE** assures that the closure of P_i is contained in that of P_j for $i < j$. This leads to the following.

Lemma 4.6 *Let $G_T = (\Sigma, P_T, S), G_{T'} = (\Sigma, P_{T'}, S')$ be mono-PCF grammars constructed from sample sets T, T' by the identification algorithm $\mathcal{A}$, respectively. It holds that*

$$T \subseteq T' \qquad \text{implies} \qquad L(G_T) \subseteq L(G_{T'}).$$

Then the identification algorithm $\mathcal{A}$ is called *strong-monotonic* ([Jan91], [LZ93a] and [LZ93b]).

Lemma 4.7 *Let $R \subseteq T \subseteq L$ and L be a mono-PCF language. Let $G_T = (\Sigma, P_T, S)$, $G_R = (\Sigma, P_R, S)$ be mono-PCF grammars constructed from sample sets T, R by the identification algorithm $\mathcal{A}$, respectively. Then, if R is a characteristic sample of L, then $L = L(G_R) = L(G_T)$ holds.*

PROOF. Obviously, $R \subseteq L(G_R)$. By the definition of a characteristic sample, $L \subseteq L(G_R)$ holds. Therefore, from Lemma 4.5, $L(G_R) \subseteq L$. Thus,

$$L = L(G_R). \tag{1}$$

And since $L(G_T)$ is the smallest mono-PCF language including T,

$$L(G_T) \subseteq L. \tag{2}$$

Furthermore, form Lemma 4.6,

$$R \subseteq T \qquad \text{implies} \qquad L(G_R) \subseteq L(G_T). \tag{3}$$

Therefore, from (1), (2) and (3), $L = L(G_R) = L(G_T)$ holds. □

Thus, when the sample set T_i contains a characteristic sample S_G for G, the algorithm $\mathcal{A}$ converges to a correct mono-PCF grammar G for the target language L. Hence, the next theorem holds :

Theorem 4.8 *The class of mono-PCF languages is identifiable in the limit from positive data.* □

4.4 Time analysis of $\mathcal{A}$

In this section we analyze the time complexity of the identification algorithm $\mathcal{A}$.

Let P_i be the set of productions of the i-th conjecture. The time complexity of $\mathcal{A}$ is at most $\mathcal{O}(N^3)$, where N is the sum of length of all positive examples presented.

(1) The time complexity of $\mathcal{A}$ is dominated by a process of updating conjectures. So, we consider **UPDATE**(P_i, u, v). Each calling of **UPDATE**(P_i, u, v) requires at most a linear time in $lg(u) + lg(v)$. Hence, it eventually terminates at most in time $\mathcal{O}(N^2)$.

(2) In the second "if clause" of **repeat** procedure, **UPDATE**(P_i, u, v) terminates at most in time $\mathcal{O}(N^2) \times N = \mathcal{O}(N^3)$.

Theorem 4.9 *The identification algorithm $\mathcal{A}$ may be implemented to run in time $\mathcal{O}(N^3)$, where N is the sum of length of all positive examples presented.* □

4.5 Properties of Identification Algorithm $\mathcal{A}$

We consider properties of the identification algorithm $\mathcal{A}$ of mono-PCF languages.

Let $L_1, L_2, L_3, \cdots$ be a class of nonempty languages. Let $\mathcal{A}^*$ be an identification algorithm. $\mathcal{A}^*$ is called *consistent* if and only if at the i-th stage of an identification process a currently conjectured grammar G_i satisfies all the input strings provided so far, i.e., $\{w_1, w_2, \ldots, w_{i-1}, w_i\} \subseteq L(G_i)$. $\mathcal{A}^*$ is called *responsive* if and only if $\mathcal{A}^*$

produces at least one conjecture in response to each input string before receiving another input string. And we say A^* is *conservative* if and only if A^* never changes the conjecture G_{i-1} as long as it is consistent with new string w_i, that is, $w_i \in L(G_{i-1})$.

Then, we claim that the identification algorithm A presented in the subsection 4.2 is consistent, responsive and conservative.

Theorem 4.10 *The class of mono-PCF languages is consistently, responsively and conservatively polynomial-time identifiable in the limit.*

Lange and Zeugmann studied the learnability of indexed families $\mathcal{L} = (L_j)_{j \in N}$ of uniformly recursive languages under certain monotonicity constraints ([LZ93b]). In their work, it was proved that for a strong-monotonic and conservative identification algorithm, the choice of the representation class (hypothesis class) of $\mathcal{L}$ is in general very important and might considerably influence the learnability. They proved that, whenever monotonicity requirements are involved, class preserving learning is almost always weaker than class comprising learning. The identification algorithm A of a class of mono-PCF languages is class preserving, and a class of mono-PCF languages is "rare" case that is strong-monotonic and that has a class preserving algorithm in their framework.

5 Concluding Remarks

We have shown that the class of monogenic pure context-free languages is identifiable in the limit from positive data, and presented an algorithm which runs in polynomial time for updating conjectures.

Mäkinen ([Mäk90]) discusses the learning problem of left Szilard languages of linear grammars and gives a linear time algorithm for it. In a previous paper, we showed the identifiability of the class of strictly regular languages, which properly includes the class of the left Szilard languages of linear grammars ([TY92]). Moreover, Mäkinen shows that left Szilard languages of context-free grammars are pure context-free languages ([Mäk91]) and, therefore, left Szilard languages of linear grammars are pure context-free. The class of mono-PCF languages in this paper is neither comparable to the class of left Szilard languages of linear grammars nor to the class of strictly regular languages.

One of the results by Shinohara ([Shi90]) shows that the class of context sensitive grammars having a given fixed number of rules is identifiable in the limit from positive data, which implies the identifiability of the class of deterministic PCF languages with a *fixed* number of axioms, and hence, that of the class of mono-PCF languages in this paper. However, his result does not suggest any efficient (polynomial-time) algorithm for this class.

As previously mentioned, PCF grammars have some connection to L-systems, a mathematical model for describing biological developmental behaviours, and therefore, it seems to have a potential application to molecular biological research. (For example, the iterative structure of mono-PCF languages like $xu^n bv^n y$ $(n \geq 0)$ may be suitable for characterizing "biological palindromes", one of the typical secondary structures that often appears in RNA sequences.)

An interesting open problem is to show the efficient identifiability of deterministic PCF grammars with a fixed number of axioms in the framework of in the limit from positive data.

Acknowledgement

We would like to thank Satoshi Kobayashi for his helpful comments. We would also like to thank the anonymous referees for their valuable suggestions and comments. This work was supported in part by Grants-in-Aid for Scientific Research No. 06249202 from the Ministry of Education, Science and Culture, Japan.

References

[Ang80] D. Angluin. Inductive inference of formal languages from positive data. *Information and Control*, 45:117–135, 1980.

[Ang82] D. Angluin. Inference of reversible languages. *Journal of the ACM*, 29:741–765, 1982.

[Gab81] A. Gabrielian. Pure Grammars and Pure Languages. *International Journal of Computer Mathematics*, 9:3–16, 1981.

[Gol67] E.M. Gold. Language identification in the limit. *Information and Control*, 10:447–474, 1967.

[Har78] M.A. Harrison. *Formal Language Theory*. Addison-Wesley, Reading, Massachusetts, 1978.

[Har81] Z.S. Harris. *String Analysis of Sentence Structure*. The Hague, Mouton, 1981.

[HU79] J.E. Hopcroft and J.D. Ullman. *Introduction to Automata Theory, Languages, and Computation*. Addison-Wesley, Reading, Massachusetts, 1979.

[Jan91] K.P. Jantke. Monotonic and non-monotonic inductive inference. *New Generation Computing*, 8:349–360, 1991.

[JKY72] A.K. Joshi, S.R. Kosaraju, and H.M. Yamada. String Adjunct Grammars: I. Local and Distributed Ajunction. *Information and Control*, 21:93–116, 1972.

[LZ93a] S. Lange and T. Zeugmann. Language Learning in Dependence on the Space of Hypotheses. In *Proceedings of 6th Workshop on Computational Learning Theory*, pages 127–136, 1993.

[LZ93b] S. Lange and T. Zeugmann. The Learnability of Recursive Language in Dependence on the Hypotheses Space. FOSLER-Report 20/93, FB Mathematik und Informatik, TH Leipzig, 1993.

[Mäk86] E. Mäkinen. A Note on Pure Grammars. *Information Processing Letters*, 24:271–274, 1986.

[Mäk90] E. Mäkinen. The grammatical inference problem for the Szilard languages of linear grammars. *Information Processing Letters*, 36:203–206, 1990.

[Mäk91] E. Mäkinen. On Pure Context-free Languages and Left Szilard languages. *Fundament Informaticae XV*, pages 86–89, 1991.

[MSW80] H.A. Maurer, A. Salomaa, and D. Wood. Pure Grammars. *Information and Control*, 44:47–72, 1980.

[Shi90] T. Shinohara. Inductive Inference from Positive Data is Powerful. In *Proceedings of 3rd Workshop on Computational Learning Theory*, pages 97–110, 1990.

[TY92] N. Tanida and T. Yokomori. Polynomial-time Identification of Strictly Regular Languages in the Limit. *IEICE Transactions on Information and Systems*, E75-D(1):125–132, 1992.

Index of Authors

Lecture Notes in Artificial Intelligence (LNAI)

Lecture Notes in Computer Science